Lecture Notes in Computer Science 1827

Edited by G. Goos, J. Hartmanis and J. van Leeuwen

Springer
Berlin
Heidelberg
New York
Barcelona
Hong Kong
London
Milan
Paris
Singapore
Tokyo

Didier Bert Christine Choppy
Peter Mosses (Eds.)

Recent Trends in Algebraic Development Techniques

14th International Workshop, WADT'99
Château de Bonas, September 15-18, 1999
Selected Papers

Springer

Volume Editors

Didier Bert
CNRS, Laboratoire LSR-IMAG
681, rue de la Passerelle, BP 72
38402 Saint-Martin-d'Hères CEDEX, France
E-mail: Didier.Bert@imag.fr

Christine Choppy
LIPN, Institute Galilée - Université Paris XIII
99 Avenue Jean-Baptiste Clément
93430 Villetaneuse, France
E-mail: Christine.Choppy@lipn.univ-paris13.fr

Peter Mosses
University of Aarhus
BRICS Department of Computer Science
Ny Munkegade Building 540, 8000 Aarhus C, Denmark
E-mail: pdmosses@brics.dk

Cataloging-in-Publication Data applied for

Die Deutsche Bibliothek - CIP-Einheitsaufnahme

Recent trends in algebraic development techniques : 14th international workshop ; selected papers / WADT '99, Châteaux de Bonas, France, September 1999. Didier Bert ... (ed.). - Berlin ; Heidelberg ; New York ; Barcelona ; Hong Kong ; London ; Milan ; Paris ; Singapore ; Tokyo : Springer, 2000
(Lecture notes in computer science ; Vol. 1827)
ISBN 3-540-67898-0

CR Subject Classification (1998): D.1.1-2, D.2.4, D.2.m, D.3.1, F.3.1-2

ISSN 0302-9743
ISBN 3-540-67898-0 Springer-Verlag Berlin Heidelberg New York

Springer-Verlag Berlin Heidelberg New York
a member of BertelsmannSpringer Science+Business Media GmbH

Printed in Germany

Typesetting: Camera-ready by author, data conversion by DA-TeX Gerd Blumenstein
Printed on acid-free paper SPIN: 10721161 06/3142 5 4 3 2 1 0

Preface

The algebraic approach to system specification and development, born in the 1970s as a formal method for abstract data types, encompasses today the formal design of integrated hardware and software systems, new specification frameworks and programming paradigms (such as object-oriented, logic, and higher-order functional programming) and a wide range of application areas (including information systems, concurrent and distributed systems). Workshops on Algebraic Development Techniques, initiated in 1982 as Workshops on Abstract Data Types, have become a prominent forum to present and discuss research on this important area.

The 14th International Workshop on Algebraic Development Techniques (WADT'99) took place at the Château de Bonas, near Toulouse, September 15–18, 1999, and was organized by Didier Bert and Christine Choppy. The main topics of the workshop were:

- algebraic specification
- other approaches to formal specification
- specification languages and methods
- term rewriting and proof systems
- specification development systems (concepts, tools, etc.).

The program consisted of invited talks by Michel Bidoit, Manfred Broy, Bart Jacobs, Natarajan Shankar, and 69 presentations describing ongoing research. The parallel sessions were devoted to: algebraic specifications and other specification formalisms, test and validation, concurrent processes, applications, logics and validation, combining formalisms, subsorts and partiality, structuring, rewriting, coalgebras and sketches, refinement, institutions and categories, ASM specifications. There were also sessions reflecting ongoing research achieved in the Common Framework Initiative (CoFI, see http://www.brics.dk/Projects/CoFI/), within its different task groups: CASL (Common Algebraic Specification Language), CASL semantics, CASL tools, methodology, and reactive systems.

The program committee invited submissions of full papers for possible publication in this WADT volume on the basis of the abstracts and the presentations at WADT'99. All the submissions were subject to careful refereeing, and the selection of papers was made following further discussion by the full program committee. The authors of the 26 selected papers were asked to take account of the suggestions of the referees when preparing their final versions for inclusion in the present volume. The selected papers include three which are authored/co-authored by invited speakers at WADT'99.

We are extremely grateful to all the workshop participants, to the invited speakers, to the (other) members of the program committee, and to the external referees for their contribution to the scientific quality of the workshop and of this volume.

The workshop was organized by IFIP WG1.3 (Foundations of System Specification). It was sponsored by CoFI (Common Framework Initiative) ESPRIT Working Group 29432, and received financial support by CNRS (Centre National de la Recherche Scientifique), Ministére des Affaires Etrangéres (French Governement), IMAG Institute (Informatique et Mathématiques Appliquées de Grenoble), INPG (Institut National Polytechnique de Grenoble), UJF (Université Joseph Fourier de Grenoble), and the LSR laboratory (Logiciels, Systémes, Réseaux).

We are grateful to Springer-Verlag for their helpful collaboration and quick publication.

We would like to thank Mme Simon and M. Wozniak at Château de Bonas for hosting the workshop with dedication and care, and for greatly facilitating the innumerable local organization tasks.

Finally, we thank all workshop participants both for lively discussions and for creating a friendly and warm atmosphere!

April 2000 Didier Bert, Christine Choppy, and Peter Mosses

Organization

Program Committee

Didier Bert	(Grenoble, France)
Michel Bidoit	(Cachan, France)
Christine Choppy	(Paris, France)
Hans-Jörg Kreowski	(Bremen, Germany)
Peter Mosses, *chair*	(Aarhus, Denmark)
Fernando Orejas	(Barcelona, Spain)
Francesco Parisi-Presicce	(Rome, Italy)
Donald Sannella	(Edinburgh, Scotland)
Andrzej Tarlecki	(Warsaw, Poland)

External Referees

Stuart Anderson
David Aspinall
Paolo Baldan
Marek Bednarczyk
Saddek Bensalem
Paolo Bottoni
Bettina Buth
Andrea Corradini
Sophie Coudert
Dominique Duval
Hartmut Ehrig
Emanuela Fachini
Marie-Claude Gaudel
Martin Grosse-Rhode
Stefano Guerrini
Kathrin Hoffmann
Shi Hui
Paul Jackson
Peter Knirsch
Manuel Koch
Alexander Kurz
Sabine Kuske
Anna Labella
François Laroussinie
Kazem Lellahi
John Longley
Christoph Lueth
Till Mossakowski
Nikos Mylonakis
Catherine Oriat
Laure Petrucci
Adolfo Piperno
Detlef Plump
Bernhard Reus
Jean-Claude Reynaud
Burkhart Wolff
Elena Zucca

Sponsoring Institutions

CoFI (Common Framework Initiative), ESPRIT Working Group 29432.
Ministére des Affaires Etrangéres, French Governement.
CNRS (Centre National de la Recherche Scientifique).
IMAG Institute (Informatique et Mathématiques Appliquées de Grenoble).
INPG (Institut National Polytechnique de Grenoble).
UJF (Université Joseph Fourier de Grenoble).
Laboratoire LSR (Logiciels, Systémes, Réseaux), de Grenoble.

Table of Contents

Invited Topics

A Type-Theoretic Memory Model for Verification of Sequential Java Programs 1
Joachim van den Berg, Marieke Huisman, Bart Jacobs and Erik Poll

From States to Histories 22
Manfred Broy

Principles and Pragmatics of Subtyping in PVS 37
Natarajan Shankar and Sam Owre

CASL: Language, Methodology and Tools

Extending Casl by Late Binding 53
Davide Ancona, Maura Cerioli and Elena Zucca

Towards an Evolutionary Formal Software-Development Using CASL 73
Serge Autexier, Dieter Hutter, Heiko Mantel and Axel Schairer

Development of Parsing Tools for CASL Using Generic Language Technology 89
Mark G. J. van den Brand and Jeroen Scheerder

Using CASL to Specify the Requirements and the Design: A Problem Specific Approach 106
Christine Choppy and Gianna Reggio

Subsorted Partial Higher-Order Logic as an Extension of CASL 126
Till Mossakowski, Anne Haxthausen and Bernd Krieg-Brückner

Specifying Real Numbers in CASL 146
Markus Roggenbach, Lutz Schröder and Till Mossakowski

Foundations

Specification Refinement with System F – The Higher-Order Case 162
Jo Erskine Hannay

Guarded Algebras: Disguising Partiality so You Won't Know Whether Its There 182
Magne Haveraaen and Eric G. Wagner

A General Completeness Result in Refinement 201
Yoshiki Kinoshita and John Power

An Institution of Hybrid Systems 219
Hugo Lourenço and Amílcar Sernadas

Realization of Probabilistic Automata: Categorical Approach 237
Paulo Mateus, Amílcar Sernadas and Cristina Sernadas

Specifications in an Arbitrary Institution with Symbols 252
Till Mossakowski

A General Algebraic Framework for Studying Modular Systems 271
Fernando Orejas and Elvira Pino

Specification of Processes and Interactions

History Preserving Bisimulation for Contextual Nets 291
Paolo Baldan, Andrea Corradini and Ugo Montanari

A Model for Interaction of Agents and Environments 311
Alexander Letichevsky and David Gilbert

Algebra-Coalgebra Structures and Bialgebras 329
Ataru T. Nakagawa

A Uniform Model Theory for the Specification of Data and Process Types 348
Horst Reichel

Other Topics

Relating Abstract Datatypes and Z-Schemata 366
Hubert Baumeister

Algebraic Specification of Operator-Based Multimedia Scenarios 383
Didier Bert and Stéphane Lo Presti

Higher-Order Logic and Theorem Proving for Structured Specifications ... 401
Tomasz Borzyszkowski

Extraction of Structured Programs from Specification Proofs 419
John N. Crossley, Iman Poernomo and Martin Wirsing

Towards a Verification Logic for Rewriting Logic 438
José Luis Fiadeiro, Tom Maibaum, Narciso Martí-Oliet, Jose Meseguer and Isabel Pita

The Rôle of Normalisation in Testing from Structured Algebraic Specifications 459
Patricia D. L. Machado

Author Index 477

A Type-Theoretic Memory Model for Verification of Sequential Java Programs

Joachim van den Berg, Marieke Huisman, Bart Jacobs, and Erik Poll

Dep. Comp. Sci., Univ. Nijmegen,
P.O. Box 9010, 6500 GL Nijmegen, The Netherlands.
{joachim,marieke,bart,erikpoll}@cs.kun.nl

Abstract. This paper explains the details of the memory model underlying the verification of sequential Java programs in the "LOOP" project ([14,20]). The building blocks of this memory are cells, which are untyped in the sense that they can store the contents of the fields of an arbitrary Java object. The main memory is modeled as three infinite series of such cells, one for storing instance variables on a heap, one for local variables and parameters on a stack, and and one for static (or class) variables. Verification on the basis of this memory model is illustrated both in PVS and in Isabelle/HOL, via several examples of Java programs, involving various subtleties of the language (wrt. memory storage).

1 Introduction

This paper reports on a (part of an) ambitious project to verify sequential Java programs, by making efficient use of modern tools for reasoning and translation. The underlying idea is that the quality of current proof tools (and hardware) should make it possible to change program verification from a purely theoretical discipline, working only for artificial, mathematically civilised programming languages, into a field where actual verification of programs written in a real-life language (namely Java [2,6])—with all its messy semantical details—becomes feasible.

Here we isolate a small part of this larger project (see also [14,20]) dealing with memory organisation and object creation (including initialisation). Therefore, many aspects are necessarily ignored, for example inheritance, casting, exception handling, and basic imperative programming. Some more information can be obtained from [14,9,8,10], but many details are still unpublished. The initialisation procedure that we discuss here follows the Java language specification [6], and the examples we present do not involve certain ambiguities in the language specification about when to start static initialisation procedures, as pointed out in [4].

For our verification work we have developed a special purpose compiler, called LOOP, for *Logic of Object-Oriented Programming*. It is used as a front-end tool to a proof-tool, for which we can use both PVS [16] and Isabelle [17], see Figure 1, so that the tool is of interest for both prover communities. The LOOP tool turns

D. Bert, C. Choppy, and P. Mosses (Eds.): WADT'99, LNCS 1827, pp. 1–21, 2000.

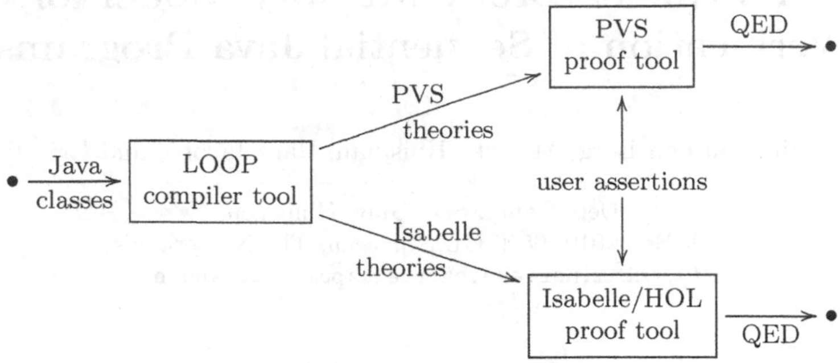

Fig. 1. Use of the LOOP tool, in combination with proof tools PVS or Isabelle/HOL

Java classes[1] into logical theories, embodying the denotational semantics of these classes. A certain semantical prelude contains basic definitions, as explained in Section 5 below. A user can formulate his/her own assertions about the original Java class, and try to prove these on the basis of the logical theories that are produced. Typical are correctness assertions in pre-post-condition style, and class invariants. The semantics that is used is based on so-called coalgebras (see [13,11] for some background information), but that is not really relevant in this paper. Coalgebras arise naturally in this setting since statements and expressions are state transformer functions with structured codomain types, see Section 5.

Of course, getting the semantics of Java right is the first prerequisite for any Java verification project. In this case, there are certain additional constraints.

1. It should be possible to formulate this semantics in the logic of the proof tool that is used. Since we use both PVS and Isabelle/HOL, this means that it should be formulated in typed higher order logic. Especially the typing constraints force us to use a tricky "untyped" definition of memory cells, because they should be capable of storing (the contents of the fields of) arbitrary objects. See Subsection 4.1 for details. In [5] there is also a memory model as basis for program verification in OBJ3. But this model avoids the problems that we are tackling here, because the programming language for which it is used is an imperative one without objects, and only has integer variables.
2. The type theoretic representation should allow efficient proofs, preferably using automatic rewriting. For example, at the lowest level, our translation involves various bureaucratic details about storage positions, but a user need not be concerned with these because appropriate rewriting lemmas take care of memory access.

[1] The LOOP tool is meant to be used only for Java classes which are accepted by a standard (JDK) compiler, and which are in particular type correct.

Thus the translation of Java classes is a fine balancing act. The current version is a result of many proof experiments, aimed at fully automatic memory handling by the back-end proof tool.

What we present is (part of) a *model-based* specification of a significant part of the Java programming language. It is not a *property-based* specification, largely for reasons of efficiency. What we present is a (type theoretic) memory model, and not an abstract property-based specification of a memory (like *e.g.* in [5,18]). The memory locations in our memory model are natural numbers, simply because PVS and Isabelle are very efficient in handling natural numbers. This is relevant when, for instance a write operation at location n is followed by a read operation on location m. When $m \neq n$, this can be simplified to doing the read operation at m directly. The efficiency in the comparison of the locations n and m is lost in an abstract memory representation.

The three Java examples discussed in this paper form part of a larger series of examples [3]. These examples are used in lectures on Java, which do not aim at providing a systematic explanation of the semantics of Java, but of what is called *empirical semantics*: it consists of a large series of well-chosen, small examples of Java programs, each focusing on one specific aspect of the language[2]. This series of examples is a gold mine for the LOOP project: it allows us to test our semantics on a well-conceived set of examples coming from sources outside the LOOP project without knowledge about the particular semantic representation that we have chosen. About 30 of the examples have been translated into PVS and Isabelle with the LOOP tool and proven correct both with PVS and with Isabelle. Section 6 presents three representative (but small) examples from [3]. Correctness proofs are discussed in the subsequent Section 7.

This paper is organised as follows. It starts with a brief description of the higher order logic that will be used to explain our memory model. The primitive types and reference types of Java are translated to types in this logic. Section 4 explains the details of the memory model, and Section 5 describes the representation of Java statements and expressions that we use. Then, Section 6 introduces three short but non-trivial Java programs. The verification of two of these is discussed in Section 7.

2 Type-Theoretic Preliminaries

In this section we shall present the simple type theory and (classical) higher-order logic in which we will be working. It can be seen as a common abstraction from the type theories and logics of both PVS and Isabelle/HOL[3]. Using this general

---

[2] Together with a clear statement about the compiler version and machine that are used for producing certain significant results.

[3] Certain aspects of PVS and Isabelle/HOL are incompatible, like the type parameters in PVS versus type polymorphism in Isabelle/HOL, so that the type theory and logic that we use is not really in the intersection. But with some good will it should be clear how to translate the constructions that we present into the particular languages of these proof tools. See [7] for a detailed comparison.

type theory and logic means that we can stay away from the particulars of the languages of PVS and Isabelle and make this work more accessible to readers unfamiliar with these tools. Due to space restrictions, the explanation will have to be rather sketchy, and some experience in basic type theory is assumed on the reader's side.

Our type theory is a simple type theory with types built up from: type variables $\alpha, \beta, \ldots$, type constants nat, bool, string (and some more), exponent types $\sigma \to \tau$, labeled product (or record) types $[\,\mathsf{lab}_1 \colon \sigma_1, \ldots, \mathsf{lab}_n \colon \sigma_n\,]$ and labeled coproduct (or variant) types $\{\,\mathsf{lab}_1 \colon \sigma_1 \mid \ldots \mid \mathsf{lab}_n \colon \sigma_n\,\}$, for given types $\sigma, \tau, \sigma_1, \ldots, \sigma_n$. New types can be introduced via definitions, as in:

– TYPE THEORY

$$\mathsf{lift}[\alpha] : \mathsf{TYPE} \stackrel{\text{def}}{=} \{\,\mathsf{bot} \colon \mathsf{unit} \mid \mathsf{up} \colon \alpha\,\}$$

where unit is the empty product type $[\,]$. This lift type constructor adds a bottom element to an arbitrary type, given as type variable α. It is frequently used in the sequel.

For exponent types we shall use the standard notation $\lambda x \colon \sigma.\, M$ for lambda abstraction and $N \cdot L$ for application. For terms $M_i \colon \sigma_i$, we have a labeled tuple $(\,\mathsf{lab}_1 = M_1, \ldots, \mathsf{lab}_n = M_n\,)$ inhabiting the corresponding labeled product type $[\,\mathsf{lab}_1 \colon \sigma_1, \ldots, \mathsf{lab}_n \colon \sigma_n\,]$. For a term $N \colon [\,\mathsf{lab}_1 \colon \sigma_1, \ldots, \mathsf{lab}_n \colon \sigma_n\,]$ in this product, we write $N.\mathsf{lab}_i$ for the selection term of type σ_i. Similarly, for a term $M \colon \sigma_i$ there is a labeled or tagged term $\mathsf{lab}_i\, M$ in the labeled coproduct type $\{\,\mathsf{lab}_1 \colon \sigma_1 \mid \ldots \mid \mathsf{lab}_n \colon \sigma_n\,\}$. And for a term $N \colon \{\,\mathsf{lab}_1 \colon \sigma_1 \mid \ldots \mid \mathsf{lab}_n \colon \sigma_n\,\}$ in this coproduct type, together with n terms $L_i(x_i) \colon \tau$ containing a free variable $x_i \colon \sigma_i$ there is a case term $\mathsf{CASES}\ N\ \mathsf{OF}\ \{\,\mathsf{lab}_1\, x_1 \mapsto L_1(x_1) \mid \ldots \mid \mathsf{lab}_n\, x_n \mapsto L_n(x_n)\,\}$ of type τ which binds the x_i. These introduction and elimination terms for labeled products and coproducts are required to satisfy standard (β)- and (η)-conversions.

Formulas in higher-order logic are terms of type bool. We shall use the connectives $\wedge$ (conjunction), $\vee$ (disjunction), $\supset$ (implication), $\neg$ (negation, used with rules of classical logic) and constants true and false, together with the (typed) quantifiers $\forall x \colon \sigma.\, \varphi$ and $\exists x \colon \sigma.\, \varphi$, for a formula φ. There is also a conditional term $\mathsf{IF}\ \varphi\ \mathsf{THEN}\ M\ \mathsf{ELSE}\ N$, for terms M, N of the same type.

All these language constructs are present in both PVS and Isabelle/HOL.

3 Modeling Java's Primitive Types and Reference Types

The primitive types in Java are:

```
byte, short, int, long, char, float, double, boolean
```

The first five of these are the so-called integral types. They have definite ranges in Java (*e.g.* `int` ranges from -2147483648 to 2147483647). For all of these we shall assume corresponding type constants byte, short, int, long, char, float, double and bool in our type theory[4].

Reference types are used in Java for objects and arrays. A reference may be `null`, indicating that it does not refer to anything. In our model, a non-null reference contains a pointer 'objpos' to a memory location (on the heap, see Subsection 4.2), together with a string 'clname' indicating the run-time[5] type of the object, or the run-time elementtype of the array, at this location, and possibly two natural numbers describing the dimension and length of non-null array references. This leads to the following definition.

– TYPE THEORY

$$\begin{aligned}&\mathsf{RefType} : \mathsf{TYPE} \stackrel{\text{def}}{=} \\ &\quad \{\, \mathsf{null} \colon \mathsf{unit} \mid \mathsf{ref} \colon [\, \mathsf{objpos} \colon \mathsf{MemLoc}, \\ &\qquad\qquad\qquad\qquad \mathsf{clname} \colon \mathsf{string}, \\ &\qquad\qquad\qquad\qquad \mathsf{dimlen} \colon \mathsf{lift}[\,[\,\mathsf{dim} \colon \mathsf{nat}, \mathsf{len} \colon \mathsf{nat}\,]\,]\,]\,\}\end{aligned} \tag{1}$$

For reasons of abstraction, we use the type definitions:

– TYPE THEORY

$$\mathsf{MemLoc} : \mathsf{TYPE} \stackrel{\text{def}}{=} \mathsf{nat} \qquad \text{and similarly} \qquad \mathsf{CellLoc} : \mathsf{TYPE} \stackrel{\text{def}}{=} \mathsf{nat} \tag{2}$$

The latter type will be used below for locations in memory cells.

We have included the fields clname and dimlen in references. They could also be included in the memory cells that will be defined next. This does not really change the model.

4 The Memory Model

This section starts by defining memory cells for storing Java objects and arrays. They are used to build up the main memory for storing arbitrarily many such items. This object memory OM comes with various operations for reading and writing.

---

[4] One can take for example the type of integers $\ldots, -2, -1, 0, 1, 2, \ldots$ for the integral types, and the type of real numbers for the floating point types double and float, ignoring ranges and precision.

[5] Recall that a typical feature of object-oriented programming is that the static, declared type of a variable may be different from its dynamic, run-time type. The latter must be a subtype of the former, a property known as type-safety.

4.1 Memory Cells

A single memory cell can store the contents of all the fields from a single object of an arbitrary class. The (translated) types that the fields of objects can have are limited to byte, short, int, long, char, float, double, bool and RefType. Therefore a cell will have entries for all of these. The number of fields for a particular type is not bounded, so we shall simply incorporate infinitely many in a memory cell:

– TYPE THEORY

$$\begin{aligned} \mathsf{ObjectCell} : \mathsf{TYPE} \stackrel{\text{def}}{=} \\ & [\, \mathsf{bytes} \colon \mathsf{CellLoc} \to \mathsf{byte}, \\ & \mathsf{shorts} \colon \mathsf{CellLoc} \to \mathsf{short}, \\ & \mathsf{ints} \colon \mathsf{CellLoc} \to \mathsf{int}, \\ & \mathsf{longs} \colon \mathsf{CellLoc} \to \mathsf{long}, \\ & \mathsf{chars} \colon \mathsf{CellLoc} \to \mathsf{char}, \\ & \mathsf{floats} \colon \mathsf{CellLoc} \to \mathsf{float}, \\ & \mathsf{doubles} \colon \mathsf{CellLoc} \to \mathsf{double}, \\ & \mathsf{booleans} \colon \mathsf{CellLoc} \to \mathsf{bool}, \\ & \mathsf{refs} \colon \mathsf{CellLoc} \to \mathsf{RefType}\,] \end{aligned} \tag{3}$$

Recall that CellLoc is defined as nat in (2). Our memory will be organised in such a way that each memory location points to a memory cell, and each cell location to a position for a label inside the cell.

Storing an object from a class with, for instance, two integer fields and one Boolean field, in a memory cell is done by (only) using the first two values (at 0 and at 1) of the function ints: CellLoc → int and (only) the first value (at 0) of the function booleans: CellLoc → bool. Other values of these and other functions in the object cell are irrelevant, and are not used for objects of this class. Enormous storage capacity is wasted in this manner, but that is unproblematic. The LOOP compiler attributes these cell positions to fields of a class, see Subsection 4.4.

Storing an array of Booleans, say of dimension 1 and length 100, in a memory cell is done by using the first 100 entries of the function booleans: CellLoc → bool, and nothing else. For arrays of objects the refs function is used. Similarly for multi-dimensional arrays.

An empty memory cell is defined with Java's default values (see [6, §§ 4.5.4]) for primitive types and reference types:

– TYPE THEORY

$$\begin{aligned}\mathsf{EmptyObjectCell} : \mathsf{ObjectCell} \stackrel{\text{def}}{=} (\, & \mathsf{bytes} = \lambda n\colon \mathsf{CellLoc}.\, 0, \\ & \mathsf{shorts} = \lambda n\colon \mathsf{CellLoc}.\, 0, \\ & \mathsf{ints} = \lambda n\colon \mathsf{CellLoc}.\, 0, \\ & \mathsf{longs} = \lambda n\colon \mathsf{CellLoc}.\, 0, \\ & \mathsf{chars} = \lambda n\colon \mathsf{CellLoc}.\, 0, \\ & \mathsf{floats} = \lambda n\colon \mathsf{CellLoc}.\, 0, \\ & \mathsf{doubles} = \lambda n\colon \mathsf{CellLoc}.\, 0, \\ & \mathsf{booleans} = \lambda n\colon \mathsf{CellLoc}.\, \mathsf{false}, \\ & \mathsf{refs} = \lambda n\colon \mathsf{CellLoc}.\, \mathsf{null}\,)\end{aligned} \tag{4}$$

Storing an empty object cell at a particular memory position guarantees that all field values stored there get default values.

4.2 Object Memory

Object cells form the main ingredient of a new type OM representing the main memory. It has a heap, stack and static part, for storing the contents of respectively instance variables, local variables and parameters, and static (also called class) variables:

– TYPE THEORY

$$\begin{aligned}\mathsf{OM} : \mathsf{TYPE} \stackrel{\text{def}}{=} & \\ & [\, \mathsf{heapmem}\colon \mathsf{MemLoc} \to \mathsf{ObjectCell}, \\ & \ \ \mathsf{heaptop}\colon \mathsf{MemLoc}, \\ & \ \ \mathsf{stackmem}\colon \mathsf{MemLoc} \to \mathsf{ObjectCell}, \\ & \ \ \mathsf{stacktop}\colon \mathsf{MemLoc}, \\ & \ \ \mathsf{staticmem}\colon \mathsf{MemLoc} \to [\, \mathsf{initialised}\colon \mathsf{bool}, \mathsf{staticcell}\colon \mathsf{ObjectCell}\,]\,]\end{aligned} \tag{5}$$

The entry heaptop (resp. stacktop) indicates the next free (unused) memory location on the heap (resp. stack). These change during program execution. The LOOP compiler assigns locations (in the static memory) to classes with static fields. At such locations a Boolean initialised tells whether static initialisation has taken place for this class. One must keep track of this because static initialisation should not be performed more than once.

So far we have introduced memory cells for storing all the fields of objects and all the entries of arrays. This is actually not the full story, as it applies only to cells on the heap:

- a cell on the stack is used for storing the local variables (and possibly parameters[6]) that are used in a particular Java scope, see Subsection 4.5.

[6] and possibly also a special return variable for temporarily storing the value of an expression `e` in a return statement `return e`.

– a cell in the static part of the memory is used for storing the static fields of a class.

Despite these differences, the general ideas in the three different rôles for memory cells are the same: cell positions are assigned to variables by the LOOP compiler, and the values of these variables can be accessed and changed via get- and put-operations that will be described in the next subsection.

Notice that if we have a local (reference) variable, say `Object obj`, then `obj` will be linked to an entry of the refs function of a cell on the stack. If this entry is a non-null reference, it will point to an object on the heap. So references may be on the stack or in the static part of the memory, but objects are always on the heap.

We should still emphasise that since the heap, stack and static memories in OM are all infinite, a Java `OutOfMemoryError` will never arise in our model. Also, the model does not involve any garbage collection (which should be transparent anyway).

4.3 Reading and Writing in the Object Memory

Accessing a specific value in an object memory $x\colon \mathsf{OM}$, either for reading or for writing, involves the following three ingredients: (1) an indication of which memory (heap, stack, static), (2) a memory location of a cell (in MemLoc), and (3) a cell location (in CellLoc) giving the offset in the cell. These ingredients are combined in the following variant type for memory addressing.

– TYPE THEORY

$$\begin{aligned}\mathsf{MemAdr} : \mathsf{TYPE} \stackrel{\text{def}}{=} \\ &\{\,\mathsf{heap}\colon [\,\mathsf{ml}\colon \mathsf{MemLoc}, \mathsf{cl}\colon \mathsf{CellLoc}\,] \\ &\mid \mathsf{stack}\colon [\,\mathsf{ml}\colon \mathsf{MemLoc}, \mathsf{cl}\colon \mathsf{CellLoc}\,] \\ &\mid \mathsf{static}\colon [\,\mathsf{ml}\colon \mathsf{MemLoc}, \mathsf{cl}\colon \mathsf{CellLoc}\,]\,\}\end{aligned} \tag{6}$$

For each type typ from the collection of types byte, short, int, long, char, float, double, bool and RefType occuring in object cells, as defined in (3), we have two operations:

– TYPE THEORY

$$\begin{array}{rl}\mathsf{gettyp}(x, m)\colon \mathsf{typ} & \text{for } x\colon \mathsf{OM}, m\colon \mathsf{MemAdr} \\ \mathsf{puttyp}(x, m, u)\colon \mathsf{OM} & \text{for } x\colon \mathsf{OM}, m\colon \mathsf{MemAdr}, u\colon \mathsf{typ}\end{array}$$

We shall describe these functions in detail only for typ = byte; the other cases are similar. Reading from the memory is easy: for $x\colon \mathsf{OM}, m\colon \mathsf{MemAdr}$,

– TYPE THEORY

$$\mathsf{getbyte}(x,m) \stackrel{\text{def}}{=} \mathsf{CASES}\ m\ \mathsf{OF}\ \{\ \mid \mathsf{heap}\,\ell \mapsto ((x.\mathsf{heapmem}\cdot(\ell.\mathsf{ml})).\mathsf{bytes})\cdot(\ell.\mathsf{cl})\ \mid \mathsf{stack}\,\ell \mapsto ((x.\mathsf{stackmem}\cdot(\ell.\mathsf{ml})).\mathsf{bytes})\cdot(\ell.\mathsf{cl})\ \mid \mathsf{static}\,\ell \mapsto ((x.\mathsf{staticmem}\cdot(\ell.\mathsf{ml})).\mathsf{staticcell.bytes})\cdot(\ell.\mathsf{cl})\ \}$$

The corresponding write-operation uses updates of records and also updates of functions, for which we write a combined 'WITH', which is hopefully self-explanatory: for x: OM, m: MemAdr and u: byte,

– TYPE THEORY

$$\mathsf{putbyte}(x,m,u) \stackrel{\text{def}}{=} \mathsf{CASES}\ m\ \mathsf{OF}\ \{\ \mid \mathsf{heap}\,\ell \mapsto x\ \mathsf{WITH}\ [\,((x.\mathsf{heapmem}\cdot(\ell.\mathsf{ml})).\mathsf{bytes})\cdot(\ell.\mathsf{cl}) := u\,]\ \mid \mathsf{stack}\,\ell \mapsto x\ \mathsf{WITH}\ [\,((x.\mathsf{stackmem}\cdot(\ell.\mathsf{ml})).\mathsf{bytes})\cdot(\ell.\mathsf{cl}) := u\,]\ \mid \mathsf{static}\,\ell \mapsto x\ \mathsf{WITH}\ [\,((x.\mathsf{staticmem}\cdot(\ell.\mathsf{ml})).\mathsf{staticcell.bytes})\cdot(\ell.\mathsf{cl}) := u\,]\ \}$$

The various get- and put-functions (18 in total) satisfy obvious commutation equations, like:

– TYPE THEORY

$$\mathsf{getbyte}(\mathsf{putbyte}(x,m,u),n) = \mathsf{IF}\ m=n\ \mathsf{THEN}\ u\ \mathsf{ELSE}\ \mathsf{getbyte}(x,n)$$
$$\mathsf{getbyte}(\mathsf{putshort}(x,m,v),n) = \mathsf{getbyte}(x,n)$$

Such equations (81 together) are used for auto-rewriting: the back-end proof-tool simplifies goals automatically whenever these equations can be applied.

4.4 Object Storage

Consider a Java class C with fields as below.

– JAVA

```
class C {
  int j, k;
  static boolean t = true;
  B b;
  float[] f;
  ... }
```

The LOOP compiler will reserve a special static location, say s: MemLoc, for C. Let p: MemLoc be an arbitrary location, intended as location of an object of class C. The LOOP compiler will then, for a given object memory $x\colon \mathsf{OM}$, arrange the instance fields of that object in the memory cell in the heap of x at p, and the static fields in the cell in the static memory of x at s. This is done according to the following table.

field	value in $x\colon \mathsf{OM}$
`j`	$\mathsf{getint}(x, \mathsf{heap}(\mathsf{ml} = p, \mathsf{cl} = 0))$
`k`	$\mathsf{getint}(x, \mathsf{heap}(\mathsf{ml} = p, \mathsf{cl} = 1))$
`t`	$\mathsf{getbool}(x, \mathsf{static}(\mathsf{ml} = s, \mathsf{cl} = 0))$
`b`	$\mathsf{getref}(x, \mathsf{heap}(\mathsf{ml} = p, \mathsf{cl} = 0))$
`f`	$\mathsf{getref}(x, \mathsf{heap}(\mathsf{ml} = p, \mathsf{cl} = 1))$

This involves:

- Storing the integer value of `j` at the first location of the infinite sequence ints of integers in the heap memory cell at p in x, *i.e.* at $((x.\mathsf{heapmem}) \cdot p).\mathsf{ints} \cdot 0$; it can then be read as $\mathsf{getint}(x, \mathsf{heap}(\mathsf{ml} = p, \mathsf{cl} = 0))\colon \mathsf{int}$; and it can be modified, say to value $a\colon \mathsf{int}$, by $\mathsf{putint}(x, \mathsf{heap}(\mathsf{ml} = p, \mathsf{cl} = 0), a)$.
- Storing the integer value of `k` at the second location $((x.\mathsf{heapmem}) \cdot p).\mathsf{ints} \cdot 1$; this value can be read via $\mathsf{getint}(x, \mathsf{heap}(\mathsf{ml} = p, \mathsf{cl} = 1))$ and modified via $\mathsf{putint}(x, \mathsf{heap}(\mathsf{ml} = p, \mathsf{cl} = 1), a)$.
- Storing the value of the *static* Boolean `t` at the first location of the sequence booleans of Booleans in the static memory at s in x, *i.e.* at $((x.\mathsf{staticmem}) \cdot s).\mathsf{staticcell}.\mathsf{booleans} \cdot 0$. It can be read as $\mathsf{getbool}(x, \mathsf{static}(\mathsf{ml} = s, \mathsf{cl} = 0))$, and be modified to value $a\colon \mathsf{bool}$ via $\mathsf{putbool}(x, \mathsf{static}(\mathsf{ml} = s, \mathsf{cl} = 0), a)$. When these get- and put-operations are called, static initialisation of `C` may have to be done. This is indicated by the Boolean $(x.\mathsf{staticmem} \cdot s).\mathsf{initialised}$, which is set to true in static initialisation.
- Storing the object reference of `b` at the first location of the sequence refs of references, *i.e.* at $((x.\mathsf{heapmem}) \cdot p).\mathsf{refs} \cdot 0$, which is of type RefType. Recall from (1) that an element of type RefType may be null or a reference containing a pointer (with label objpos) to another heap memory cell where an object of class `B` is stored. The reference to the `B` object may be read and updated via the getref and putref operations.
- Storing the array reference of `f` at the second location of the sequence refs of references, *i.e.* at $((x.\mathsf{heapmem}) \cdot p).\mathsf{refs} \cdot 1$. If it is not null, it refers to a heap memory cell where the array of floats is actually located. This array reference value may be read and modified via getref and putref. How to access the array at a particular index will be described in the next section (especially in Figure 2).

It should be clear that organising the values of the instance and class variables in such a manner involves a lot of bookkeeping. This may be a problem for humans, but since the translation of Java classes is done by a tool, this bureaucracy is not a burden. Also, since the proof obligations at this memory level can be handled by automatic rewriting, the user does not need to see these details in proofs.

An assignment statement `j = k` for the above fields `j`, `k` from class `C` will ultimately come down to a state transformer function $\mathsf{OM} \to \mathsf{OM}$ sending a state x to putint(x, heap(ml $= p$, cl $= 0$), getint(x, heap(ml $= p$, cl $= 1$))). Thus it will result in a memory update function.

4.5 Local Variables and Parameters

The contents of local variables and parameters are stored at the stack, following the allocation ideas outlined in the previous subsection. That is, if for instance three local variables are declared of type `int` in a method body, then they are stored in the first three integer positions of the ints function of the cell in stackmem at the next free position stacktop. Upon entry of a method body stacktop is incremented by one, allocating one cell for all local variables and parameters (plus return variable) in the body, and upon leaving the body stacktop is decremented by one. For instance, the interpretation of a block statement (inside a method body)

$$[\![\texttt{\{int i = 5; ...\}}]\!]$$

is a function OM → StatResult (see Section 5) given on x: OM by

– TYPE THEORY

```
(LET
    i = λy: OM. getint(y, stack(ml = x.stacktop, cl = 0)),
    i_becomes = λv: int. λy: OM. putint(y, stack(ml = x.stacktop, cl = 0), v),
  IN
    [[i = 5]] ;
    [[...]]) · x
```

The interpretation $[\![$`i = 5`$]\!]$ of the assignment uses the local function i_becomes.

Again, attributing appropriate positions in cells to local variables is done by the LOOP compiler, and is not a concern for the user. Parameters and return variables are treated similarly.

4.6 Object Creation

Creating a new object takes place on the heap of our memory model. Specifically, creating an object of class `C` (via Java's instance creation expression `new C()`) involves the following steps in a memory model x: OM.

1. An EmptyObjectCell is stored in the heap memory x.heapmem at location x.heaptop, providing the default values for the fields of `C` (see [6, §§ 4.5.4]) and x.heaptop is incremented by 1.
2. If `C` has static fields (or static initialiser code), then static initialisation is done next, see [6, §§ 12.4], at the static location s_{C} of `C`—determined by the LOOP compiler. This will make the Boolean (x.staticmem · s_{C}).initialised true—preventing future static initialisation for this class. Static initialisation starts from the top-most superclass of `C`, *i.e.* from `Object`. A subtle matter which is not clearly determined in the Java Language Specification, as

pointed out in [4], is whether static initialisation should also be performed for superinterfaces. In our model it does not happen.

3. Non-static initialisation code of the superclasses of `C` is invoked via appropriate constructors, starting from the top-most superclass `Object`, see [6, §§ 15.8 and 12.5].
4. The relevant constructor plus initialisation code from `C` is executed.
5. A reference to the newly created object at `heaptop` is returned.

5 Statements and Expressions

Statements and expressions in Java may either hang (*i.e.* not terminate at all), terminate normally, or terminate abruptly. Expressions can only terminate abruptly because of an exception (*e.g.* through division by 0), but statements may also terminate abnormally because of a `return`, `break` or `continue` (the latter two with or without label). A `break` statement with a label is used to exit a surrounding (possibly nested) block with the same label. An unlabeled `break` is used to exit the innermost `switch`, `for`, `while` or `do` statement. Within loop statements (`while`, `do` and `for`) a `continue` statement can occur. The effect is that control skips the rest of the loop's body and starts re-evaluating the (update statement, in a `for` loop, and) Boolean expression which controls the loop. A `continue` statement can be labeled, so that the `continue` is applied to the correspondingly labeled loop, and not to the innermost one. More details about the rôle of these abnormalities can be found in [9].

All these options are captured in appropriate datatypes. First, abnormal termination leads to the following types.

– TYPE THEORY

$$\begin{array}{l}\mathsf{StatAbn} : \mathsf{TYPE} \stackrel{\mathrm{def}}{=} \\ \quad \{\, \mathsf{excp} \colon [\, \mathsf{es} \colon \mathsf{OM}, \mathsf{ex} \colon \mathsf{RefType}\,] \\ \quad \mid \mathsf{rtrn} \colon \mathsf{OM} \\ \quad \mid \mathsf{break} \colon [\, \mathsf{bs} \colon \mathsf{OM}, \mathsf{blab} \colon \mathsf{lift}[\mathsf{string}]\,] \\ \quad \mid \mathsf{cont} \colon [\, \mathsf{cs} \colon \mathsf{OM}, \mathsf{clab} \colon \mathsf{lift}[\mathsf{string}]\,]\,\}\end{array} \qquad \begin{array}{l}\mathsf{ExprAbn} : \mathsf{TYPE} \stackrel{\mathrm{def}}{=} \\ \quad [\, \mathsf{es} \colon \mathsf{OM}, \mathsf{ex} \colon \mathsf{RefType}\,]\end{array}$$

These types are used to define the result types of statements and expressions:

– TYPE THEORY

$$\begin{array}{l}\mathsf{StatResult} : \mathsf{TYPE} \stackrel{\mathrm{def}}{=} \\ \quad \{\, \mathsf{hang} \colon \mathsf{unit} \\ \quad \mid \mathsf{norm} \colon \mathsf{OM} \\ \quad \mid \mathsf{abnorm} \colon \mathsf{StatAbn}\,\}\end{array} \qquad \begin{array}{l}\mathsf{ExprResult}[\alpha] : \mathsf{TYPE} \stackrel{\mathrm{def}}{=} \\ \quad \{\, \mathsf{hang} \colon \mathsf{unit} \\ \quad \mid \mathsf{norm} \colon [\, \mathsf{ns} \colon \mathsf{OM}, \mathsf{res} \colon \alpha\,] \\ \quad \mid \mathsf{abnorm} \colon \mathsf{ExprAbn}\,\}\end{array}$$

A Java statement is then translated as a state transformer function $\mathsf{OM} \longrightarrow \mathsf{StatResult}$, and a Java expression of type `Out` as a function $\mathsf{OM} \longrightarrow \mathsf{ExprResult}[\mathsf{Out}]$. Thus both statements and expressions are coalgebras. The result of such functions applied to a memory $x\colon \mathsf{OM}$ yields either hang, norm, or abnorm (with appropriate parameters), indicating the sort of outcome. A slightly more abstract version of this representation of statements and expressions is presented in terms of a computational monad in [12]. It gives rise to compact versions of the explicit definitions below.

On the basis of this representation of statements and expressions all language constructs from (sequential) Java are translated. For instance, the composition $s\,;t\colon \mathsf{OM} \longrightarrow \mathsf{StatResult}$ of two statements $s, t\colon \mathsf{OM} \longrightarrow \mathsf{StatResult}$ is defined as:

– TYPE THEORY

$$
\begin{aligned}
(s\,;t)(x) \stackrel{\text{def}}{=} \mathsf{CASES}\ s \cdot x\ \mathsf{OF}\ \{ & \\
& \mid \mathsf{hang}() \mapsto \mathsf{hang}() \\
& \mid \mathsf{norm}\, y \mapsto t \cdot y \\
& \mid \mathsf{abnorm}\, a \mapsto \mathsf{abnorm}\, a \,\}
\end{aligned}
$$

And Java's two conjunction operations `&` and `&&` are defined type-theoretically on $e, d\colon \mathsf{OM} \longrightarrow \mathsf{ExprResult}[\mathsf{bool}]$ as:

– TYPE THEORY

$$
\begin{aligned}
(e\ \&\ d) \cdot x \stackrel{\text{def}}{=} {} & \mathsf{CASES}\ e \cdot x\ \mathsf{OF}\ \{ \\
& \mid \mathsf{hang}() \mapsto \mathsf{hang}() \\
& \mid \mathsf{norm}\, y \mapsto \mathsf{CASES}\ d \cdot (y.\mathsf{ns})\ \mathsf{OF}\ \{ \\
& \qquad \mid \mathsf{hang}() \mapsto \mathsf{hang}() \\
& \qquad \mid \mathsf{norm}\, z \mapsto \mathsf{norm}(\mathsf{ns} = z.\mathsf{ns}, \mathsf{res} = (y.\mathsf{res} \wedge z.\mathsf{res})) \\
& \qquad \mid \mathsf{abnorm}\, b \mapsto \mathsf{abnorm}\, b \,\} \\
& \mid \mathsf{abnorm}\, a \mapsto \mathsf{abnorm}\, a \,\} \\
(e\ \&\&\ d) \cdot x \stackrel{\text{def}}{=} {} & \mathsf{CASES}\ e \cdot x\ \mathsf{OF}\ \{ \\
& \mid \mathsf{hang}() \mapsto \mathsf{hang}() \\
& \mid \mathsf{norm}\, y \mapsto \mathsf{IF}\ \neg(y.\mathsf{res}) \\
& \qquad \mathsf{THEN}\ \mathsf{norm}\, y \\
& \qquad \mathsf{ELSE}\ d \cdot (y.\mathsf{ns}) \\
& \mid \mathsf{abnorm}\, a \mapsto \mathsf{abnorm}\, a \,\}
\end{aligned}
$$

Notice how the second argument d need not be evaluated for the 'conditional and' operator &&, and also how side-effects are passed on via the states $y.\mathsf{ns}$ and $z.\mathsf{ns}$.

Another example, combining expressions and memory access is the the array_access function used for translation of indexing an array. It is used as:

$$
[\![\, \texttt{a[i]} \,]\!] \stackrel{\text{def}}{=} \mathsf{array\_access}(\mathsf{gettyp}, [\![\, \texttt{a} \,]\!], [\![\, \texttt{i} \,]\!])
$$

assuming that `a[i]` is not the left hand side of an assignment. The function gettyp is determined by the type of `a`. For example, if `a` is an integer array of type `int[]`, then gettyp = getint. And if `a` is a 2-dimensional array of, say Booleans, then gettyp = getref.

The Java evaluation strategy prescribes that first the array expression, and then the index expression must be evaluated. Subsequently it must be checked first if the array reference is non-null, and then if the (evaluated) index is non-negative and below the length of the array. Only then the memory can be accessed. See [6, §§ 15.12.1 and §§ 15.12.2]. Figure 2 describes array indexing in our setting. It omits the details of how exceptions are thrown.

– TYPE THEORY

```
array_access(gettyp, a, i): OM ⟶ ExprResult[typ]
  ≝ λx: OM. CASES a · x OF {
                | hang() ↦ hang()
                | norm y ↦
                    CASES i · (y.ns) OF {
                      | hang() ↦ hang()
                      | norm z ↦
                          CASES y.res OF {
                            | null() ↦ [[new NullPointerException() ]]
                            | ref r ↦
                                CASES r.dimlen OF {
                                  | bot() ↦ hang() // should not happen
                                  | up p ↦
                                      IF z.res < 0 ∨ z.res ≥ p.len
                                      THEN [[new ArrayIndexOutOf-
                                                   BoundsException() ]]
                                      ELSE norm(ns = z.ns, res =
                                        gettyp(z.ns, heap(ml = r.objpos,
                                                     cl = z.res))) } }
                      | abnorm c ↦ abnorm c }
                | abnorm b ↦ abnorm b }
```

Fig. 2. Accessing array a: OM $\rightarrow$ ExprResult[RefType] at index i: OM $\rightarrow$ ExprResult[int]

Notice that arrays, like objects, are stored on the heap. All translated non-null array references have a non-bottom dimlen field by construction, so in the case indicated as "should not happen" we choose to use hang() as output. We could also have thrown some non-standard exception. There is a similar function array_assign which is used for assigning a value at a particular index in an array.

And there is also a function for array creation. It sets up an appropriately linked number of (empty) memory cells, depending on the dimension and lengths of the array that is being created. Space restrictions prevent us from discussing these functions in detail.

6 Examples

We now present three examples of small Java programs from [3], involving aspects that we have discussed above. Hopefully, the reader will appreciate the semantic intricacies.

6.1 Side-Effects and Boolean Logic

Consider the following Java class.

– JAVA

```
class Logic {
  boolean b, r1, r2;        // r1, r2 will store the result
  boolean f() { b = !b; return b; }
  void m() { b = true;
             r1 = f() || !f();
             r2 = !f() && f(); }
}
```

This example shows that side-effects can disrupt the expected behaviour of disjunction ($\varphi \vee \neg\varphi = \mathsf{true}$) and conjunction ($\neg\varphi \wedge \varphi = \mathsf{false}$): after running method `m()`, the field `r1` will be false, and `r2` will be true. This comes out in our model because of the propagation of side-effects as described in Section 5.

6.2 Logically Inconsistent Initialisations

Next we consider two mutually recursive classes:

– JAVA

```
class Yes {
  boolean r1, r2, r3;  // for storing the results
  static boolean y = No.n;
  static void m() { r1 = y;
                    r2 = No.n;
                    r3 = No.m(); }
}
class No {
  static boolean n = !Yes.y;
  static boolean m() { return n; }
}
```

From a logical perspective the initialisation is problematic: `Yes.y = No.n` and `No.n = !Yes.y` leading to `Yes.y = !Yes.y`, using substitution[7]. The right view here is of course the operational one. According to the steps in Subsection 4.6, it is clear what will happen: running `Yes.m()`, when both `Yes` and `No` have not been initialised yet, will start the static initialisation of `Yes` by assigning default values to its fields. The static initialisation code `y = No.n` will then start the static initialisation of `No`. The assignment `n = !Yes.y` will use the default value `false` for `y`, so that `n` becomes `true`. Subsequently `y` will also become `true` through the assignment `y = No.n`. Hence `r1`, `r2` and `r3` will all become `true`.

6.3 Order of Initialisations

Again we consider two simple Java classes:

– JAVA

```
class Master {
  boolean r1, r2, r3, r4;
  void m() { r1 = Slave.a;
             r2 = Slave.b;
             r3 = Slave.s.a;
             r4 = Slave.s.b; }
}
class Slave {
  static Slave s = new Slave();
  static boolean b = !s.a;
  static boolean a = true;
}
```

The first thing to note is that the initialisation `Slave s = new Slave()` in class `Slave` looks like it will lead to an infinite series of initialisations. But since the field `s` is static, this is a static initialisation that will be done only once. Thus, running `m()` in `Master` will lead to an unproblematic initialisation of `Slave`: first all fields are set to their default values; then the initialisation of `s` will start the initialisation of `b` and `a`. When the value for `b` is computed, `a` still has its default value `false`, so that `b` becomes `true`; only then, `a` becomes `true`. Hence, running `m()`, when `Slave` is not initialised yet, will make all the `r`'s `true`.

7 Verification

Having seen the three examples of Java programs in the previous section, we proceed to discuss how we actually verify (with PVS and Isabelle) that the

[7] But from this perspective also an assignment `i = i+1` is problematic!

result variables r have the values as indicated. Of course, we cannot go into all details, and therefore we only try to give the reader an impression of what is going on. We shall present two "user statements" (as in Figure 1), for PVS and Isabelle, and give some further information about the proofs—which in all cases proceed entirely by automatic rewriting[8]. The first example is skipped here because it does not involve significant memory access.

7.1 Verification in PVS

We shall concentrate on the Yes-No example from Subsection 6.2. Running the LOOP tool on these classes will produce several PVS theories, forming the basis of the verification. They are typechecked, together with the semantic prelude containing the definitions for the object memory and for the representations of statements and expressions. Then they are imported into a theory which contains the following user statement.

– PVS

```
IMPORTING ...  % code generated by the LOOP tool is loaded

Yes_lem : LEMMA
  FORALL(p : MemLoc?, x : OM?,
       c : [MemLoc? -> [OM? -> Yes?IFace[OM?]]]) :
    YesAssert?(p)(c(p))
      AND
    p < heap?top(x)
      AND
    NOT Yes_is_Initialized?(x)
      AND
    NOT No_is_Initialized?(x)
        IMPLIES
    norm??(m?(c(p))(x))    % m from Yes terminates normally
      AND
    LET y = ns?(m?(c(p))(x)) IN    % y is 'normal' state after m
      r1(c(p))(y) = TRUE
        AND
      r2(c(p))(y) = TRUE
        AND
      r3(c(p))(y) = TRUE
```

We shall explain some aspects. First of all, there are many question marks '?' in this fragment of PVS code. They are there because they cannot occur in Java identifiers, and so by using them in definitions which are important for

[8] Proofs only by automatic rewriting are not possible for more complicated programs with `for` and `while` loops. To handle these we use a special version of Hoare logic, tailored to Java, see [9].

the translation to PVS, name clashes are prevented. Further, the statement quantifies first over a memory location `p`, which is to be understood as the location of an arbitrary object, which is required to be in the used part of the heap memory, below the heaptop. The quantification also involves an object memory `x`, and a "coalgebra" `c` incorporating all methods from the class `Yes` in a single function. Notice that this coalgebra (or class) is parametrised by memory locations, so it can act on an arbitrary (heap) location. This coalgebra is required to satisfy a predicate `YesAssert?` ensuring that fields of `c` are bound to appropriate memory positions, and methods and constructors of `c` to their bodies.

Under the additional assumptions that classes `Yes` and `No` have not been initialised yet in state `x`, the statement says that method `m` of coalgebra/class `c` at `p` terminates normally, and that in its result state `y`, all the fields `r` of coalgebra/class `c` are `true`.

The proof in PVS of this statement can be done entirely by automatic rewriting. This involves mimicking the computation on the memory model described in Section 4. The actual PVS proof consists of the following sequence of three proof commands.

– PVS

```
(LOAD-CLASSES ("java_lang_Object" "Yes" "No"))
  (LOAD-PRELUDE) (REDUCE)
```

The first one loads the (automatically generated) rewrite rules for the relevant classes `Yes`, `No` and for the root class `Object`. The next command loads the rewrite rules from the semantic prelude (see Figure 1) into the prover. Finally, the `(REDUCE)` command tells PVS to go off and do any simplification it can apply. It will result in a QED, without further user interaction[9].

7.2 Verification in Isabelle/HOL

Here we concentrate on the Master-Slave example from Subsection 6.3. We proceed in a similar way as with the PVS verification. Thus we run the LOOP tool on the Java classes to generate several Isabelle theories, which are typechecked together with the semantic prelude. This semantic prelude contains similar definitions as the semantic prelude in PVS, but of course it is adapted to the specification language of Isabelle.

Subsequently we prove the following user statement.

[9] This QED involves 177 rewrite steps, which, on a reasonably fast machine according to current standards (a 500Mhz Pentium III with 256M RAM) takes about 40 seconds, most of which are needed for loading the rewrite rules.

– ISABELLE
```
(* Code generated by the LOOP tool is loaded *)
Goal "[|MasterAssert p (c p);\
~       p < heap_top x;\
~~ Slave_is_Initialized x |] ==>\
~       let y = PreStatResult.ns(m_ (c p) x)\
~       in r1 (c p) y = True &\
~          r2 (c p) y = True &\
~          r3 (c p) y = True &\
~          r4 (c p) y = True";
```

As in the previous example, `p` denotes the memory location, `c` the coalgebra (or class) and `x` the object memory. Again, we assume that the coalgebra `c` satisfies an assertion `MasterAssert`, ensuring that fields and methods of `c` are appropriately bound. Furthermore, we assume that the class `Slave` is not initialised yet. Under these assumptions we prove that the method `m` terminates normally, resulting in a new (normal) state `y`, in which all the `r`-fields of coalgebra/class `c` are `true`.

The proof in Isabelle is done entirely by automatic rewriting. The actual proof command in Isabelle is the following.

– ISABELLE
```
by (asm_full_simp_tac
      (simpset () addsimps (PreludeRewrites @
                            java_lang_ObjectRewrites @
                            SlaveRewrites @
                            MasterRewrites)) 1);
```

This adds the rewrite rules for the classes `Master`, `Slave` and `Object`, and for the semantic prelude to the simplifier, and subsequently uses these to rewrite the goal to `True`, thus proving the goal[10].

8 Conclusion

We have presented an essential ingredient of the semantics of sequential Java, as used for the tool-assisted verification of Java programs within the LOOP project, namely the object memory used for storing the contents of fields of Java objects in essentially untyped cells. The effectiveness of this formalisation has been demonstrated in the verification of several short, but non-trivial, Java programs. A promising application of this approach, based on the memory model

[10] Isabelle tries to apply over 18,000 rewriting steps, of which only about 800 succeed (including rewrites in conditions of conditional rewrites). This takes approximately 194 seconds on the same 500 Mhz Pentium III with 256M RAM that was used for the PVS verification.

in this paper, is verification of class libraries (like the invariant proof for the `Vector` class in [10]), especially when these libraries are annotated (using the annotation language JML [15] for Java). We are currently developing this approach for the (relatively simple) JavaCard [1] API classes, see [19]. Up-to-date information about the LOOP project is available from the LOOP webpage [20].

References

1. JavaCard API 2.1. http://java.sun.com/products/javacard/htmldoc/. 20
2. K. Arnold and J. Gosling. *The Java Programming Language.* Addison-Wesley, 2nd edition, 1997. 1
3. J. Bergstra and M. Loots. Empirical semantics for object-oriented programs. Artificial Intelligence Preprint Series nr. 007, Dep. Philosophy, Utrecht Univ., 1999. 3, 15
4. E. Borger and W. Schulte. Initialization problems in Java. *Software—Concepts and Tools,* 20(4), 1999. 1, 12
5. J. A. Goguen and G. Malcolm. *Algebraic Semantics of Imperative Programs.* MIT Press, Cambridge, MA, 1996. 2, 3
6. J. Gosling, B. Joy, and G. Steele. *The Java Language Specification.* Addison-Wesley, 1996. 1, 6, 11, 12, 14
7. D. Griifioen and M. Huisman. A comparison of PVS and Isabelle/HOL. In J. Grundy and M. Newey, editors, *Theorem Proving in Higher Order Logics,* number 1479 in Lect. Notes Comp. Sci., pages 123-142. Springer, Berlin, 1998. 3
8. M. Huisman and B. Jacobs. Inheritance in higher order logic: Modeling and reasoning. Techn. Rep. CSI-R0004, Comput. Sci. Inst., Univ. of Nijmegen, 2000. 1
9. M. Huisman and B. Jacobs. Java program verification via a Hoare logic with abrupt termination. In T. Maibaum, editor, *Fundamental Approaches to Software Engineering,* number 1783 in Lect. Notes Comp. Sci., pages 284-303. Springer, Berlin, 2000. 1, 12, 17
10. M. Huisman, B. Jacobs, and J. van den Berg. A case study in class library verification: Java's Vector class. Techn. Rep. CSI-R0007, Comput. Sci. Inst., Univ. of Nijmegen. (An earlier version appeared in: B. Jacobs, G.T. Leavens, P. Miiller, and A. Poetzsch-Heffter (eds.), Formal Techniques for Java Programs. Proceedings of the ECOOP'99 Workshop. Technical Report 251, Fernuniversitat Hagen, 1999, p.37-44), 2000. 1, 20
11. B. Jacobs. Objects and classes, co-algebraically. In B. Freitag, **C.B.** Jones, C. Lengauer, and H.-J. Schek, editors, *Object-Orientation with Parallelism and Persistence,* pages 83-103. Kluwer Acad. Publ., 1996. 2
12. B. Jacobs and E. Poll. A monad for basic Java semantics. In *Algebraic Methodology and Software Technology,* Lect. Notes Comp. Sci. Springer, Berlin, 2000. 13
13. B. Jacobs and J. Rutten. A tutorial on (co)algebras and (co)induction. *EATCS Bulletin,* 62:222-259, 1997. 2
14. B. Jacobs, J. van den Berg, M. Huisman, M. van Berkum, U. Hensel, and H. Tews. Reasoning about classes in Java (preliminary report). In *Object-Oriented Programming, Systems, Languages and Applications,* pages 329-340. ACM Press, 1998. 1
15. G. T. Leavens, A. L. Baker, and C. Ruby. Preliminary design of JML: A behavioral interface specification language for Java. Techn. Rep. 98-06, Dep. of Comp. Sci., Iowa State Univ. (http://www.cs.iastate.edu/ leavens/JML. html), 1999. 20

16. S. Owre, J. M. Rushby, N. Shankar, and F. von Henke. Formal verification for fault-tolerant architectures: Prolegomena to the design of PVS. *IEEE Trans. on Softw. Eng.*, 21(2):107-125, 1995. 1
17. L. C. Paulson. Isabelle: The next 700 theorem provers. In P. Odifreddi, editor, *Logic and computer science*, pages 361-386. Academic Press, London, 1990. The APIC series, vol. 31. 1
18. A. Poetzsch-Heffter and P. Müller. A programming logic for sequential Java. In S. D. Swierstra, editor, *Programming Languages and Systems*, Lect. Notes Comp. Sci., pages 162-176. Springer, Berlin, 1999. 3
19. E. Poll, J. van den Berg, and B. Jacobs. Specification of the JavaCard API in JML. Techn. Rep. CSI-R0005, Comput. Sci. Inst., Univ. of Nijmegen, 2000. 20
20. Loop Project. http://www.cs.kun.nl/~bart/LOOP/. 1, 20

From States to Histories

Manfred Broy

Institut für Informatik, Technische Universität München
D-80290 München, Germany

Abstract. We outline a modular method for specifying and proving safety properties about distributed systems. Data flow networks represent such systems. They are composed of encapsulated units cooperating by asynchronous message passing. The components of such networks are data flow nodes with a black box behavior specified by relations on the communication histories formed by the streams of the input/output channels. State machines described by state transition rules with input and output implement system components. Vice versa, history relations provide an abstraction of state machines. Safety properties are captured by system invariants that help to prove properties about state machines. Our approach provides a bridge from state-based system models defined by state transitions to the more abstract history views on systems and their components.

1. Introduction

Simple and tractable models of interactive distributed systems are crucial for the systematic specification, design, and implementation of highly distributed interactive software in applications typical for reactive control systems, telecommunication, or computer networking. Several mathematical and logical models for such systems have been proposed so far. However, often they are too complex for practical applicability since they are based on sophisticated theories or they do not fulfill essential methodological requirements such as modularity or appropriate techniques for abstraction.

We work with a system model where communication histories are represented by streams. Using stream processing components we model interactive systems by stream processing data flow nodes along the lines of [3]. In this model, a system consists of a network of data flow components connected by channels. This model is *history-*, *action-* or *trace-based* and not explicitly *state-oriented.* Nevertheless, we work with state machines with input and output (see [4], [7], [8], and [9]) for describing the implementation of the stream-processing components. Then the state of a network consists of all the local states of its components and the state of its channels represented by the buffers[1] associated with these channels. To formalize the properties of the global system states we use logical assertions with free variables referring to

[1] For systems communicating asynchronously we need buffers to store messages sent but not yet received.

D. Bert, C. Choppy, and P. Mosses (Eds.): WADT'99, LNCS 1827, pp. 22-36, 2000.

the state attributes of the components and the communication histories associated with the channels.

We work with two classes of system assertions. *State assertions* refer to the states of the attributes and the channels including the content of their buffers. *History assertions* do neither refer to state attributes nor to the buffers of the channels but only to the histories formed by the streams of values sent via the channels.

In [4] we have introduced a graphical notation for defining state machines with input and output. There we showed how to relate history assertions to state machines by a recursive definition of a history relation. In this paper, we introduce a method to prove refinement relations between history assertions and state machines with input and output. We concentrate on safety properties and work with invariants. An invariant is a state assertion that is valid in all reachable states of a system (see [5] for an extensive presentation of state based models working with invariants).

The main advantage of our approach is of methodological nature. We obtain a very solid and general method for a modular system development. By state transition machines we support the development in the small. We relate state machines to state assertions that are invariants speaking about local states of components and channels. From these, we derive history assertions representing abstract system models. These history assertions are used for reasoning in the large.

The paper is structured as follows. Before we start to outline the general approach we introduce the concept of a stream in chapter 2, as well as the notion of a system state in section 3, the concept of a component in section 4, and give a motivating and illustrating example in section 5. Section 6 describes the concept of invariants and their verification. In Section 7 we give a more comprehensive example. Section 8 gives a number of concluding remarks.

2. Streams

A *stream* is a finite or an infinite sequence of messages or actions. In this paper we use streams to represent communication histories for channels.

Let M be a given set; we apply the following notation:

M^* denotes the finite sequences over the set M with the *empty* sequence $\langle\rangle$,

M^∞ denotes the infinite sequences over the set M, which can be represented by mappings $\mathbb{N}\backslash\{0\} \to M$.

A stream is an element of the set M^ω that is defined by the equation

$$M^\omega = M^* \cup M^\infty$$

On the set of streams, we specify the prefix ordering for streams x, y $\in M^\omega$ by the formula

$$x \sqsubseteq y \equiv \exists\, z \in M^\omega: x\hat{\ }z = y$$

Here x^z denotes the concatenation of the stream x to the stream z. For finite streams x it is the well-known operation on sequences. If x is infinite, then we define x^z = x. Throughout this paper we work with some simple notations for streams and operators on streams that are listed in the following. For a stream x we write:

z^x concatenation of a sequence (or stream) z to the stream x,

$\langle\rangle$ empty sequence,
$\langle a \rangle$ one element sequence for $a \in M$,
$\#x$ length of the stream x,
ft.x first element of the stream x,
rt.x rest of the stream or sequence x without its first element,
x.i i-th element of the stream x where $i \in \mathbb{N}$, $1 \le i \le \#x$.

Note. On Notation: Given a set of identifiers $C = \{c_1, ..., c_n\}$ and a set of expressions $E = \{e_1, ..., e_n\}$ of appropriate type where each identifier c_k occurs exactly in the expression e_k then we write for a given formula P

$$P[E/C]$$

for the formula

$$P[e_1/c_1, ..., e_n/c_n]$$

which denotes the simultaneous substitution of the identifiers c_k by the terms e_k in the formula P for all k, $1 \le k \le n$. Given two sets of identifiers $C = \{c_1, ..., c_n\}$ and $C' = \{c_1', ..., c_n'\}$ we write C^C' for the set $\{c_1\hat{\ }c_1', ..., c_n\hat{\ }c_n'\}$ and we write [C^C'/C] for $[c_1\hat{\ }c_1'/c_1, ..., c_n\hat{\ }c_n'/c_n]$. □

Throughout this paper we work with sets X of identifiers. We assume that identifiers are typed. The types are determined by a mapping (called type assignment)

$$\text{type} : X \rightarrow \text{Type}$$

where Type is the set of types. In our case each type is a set of data elements. For instance, the set $\mathbb{N}$ of natural numbers is a type and the set of streams over a type is a type.

Given a set X of typed identifiers we denote by $\vec{X}$ the set of valuations. A valuation $\varphi \in \vec{X}$ is a mapping

$$\varphi : X \rightarrow \{d \in T : T \in \text{Type}\}$$

where $\varphi.x \in \text{type}(x)$ for all $x \in X$. Given a set X of identifiers of type stream we denote by $\vec{X}^*$ the set of valuations of the identifiers in X by finite streams.

Notional conventions: Often we find it useful to work with decorated identifiers. Given a set X of typed identifiers, we write

X' to denote the set of primed identifiers x' for each $x \in X$
X^+ to denote the set of identifiers x^+ for each $x \in X$
X° to denote the set of identifiers x° for each $x \in X$

Given an assertion Q with identifiers from X, and a valuation φ or a term valuation η we write

$Q[\varphi]$ for the predicate, obtained from Q by replacing all identifiers $x \in X$ by $\varphi.x$
$Q[\eta]$ for the predicate, obtained from Q by replacing all identifiers $x \in X$ by $\eta.x$

Given valuations $\varphi_1, \varphi_2 \in \vec{I}$ for a set I of identifiers all being of type stream, we write

$\varphi_1\hat{\ }\varphi_2$ for the term valuation η with $\eta.x = (\varphi_1.x)\hat{\ }(\varphi_2.x)$

This notation will be used when we describe schematically the verification conditions for invariants. □

3. Systems, Histories and States

In this section we introduce the concept of a distributed system. Distributed systems have states. Hence, they can be described by state transitions.

3.1. Interactive Distributed Systems

An interactive system consists of a family of components connected by channels. A component encapsulates a local state and communicates asynchronously via its channels with its environment. A channel is a directed communication link. A component of a system is described by

- a state machine with state attributes and state transitions with input and output,
- a relation on the streams associated with its input and output channels or
- a system of components, called a data flow network.

The component is connected by the input and output streams of the component to its environment.

A data flow network consists of a set of components connected by unidirectional channels. It has the following characteristics:

- Each component has a set of input channels and a set of output channels.
- Each output channel appears at most for one component in its set of input channels,
- Each input channel appears at most for one component in its set of output channels.

Channels are used for unidirectional point-to-point communication. Channels that do not occur as output channels of a component are input channels of the system coming in from the environment. Channels that do not occur as input channels of a component are output channels of the system connecting the system to the environment. The channels and attributes of the components of a system form the set of *system constituents*.

3.2. System States and Histories

The state of a system is given by the states of its channels and its components. A component that is modeled by a state machine has a local state that is characterized by a set A of typed state attributes. Each local state is an element of $\vec{A}$.

Also a channel has a state. A channel has as its state the stream of messages sent over it (its communication history) and the stream of messages sent but not received so far stored in the buffer. To take care of the pending (buffered) messages in state assertions, we associate with each channel c the following three derived variables called the *channel attributes*

c° the sequence of messages sent and received on the channel c, called the *channel past*,

c^+ the sequence of messages sent but not yet received on the channel c, called the *channel buffer*,

c the sequence of messages sent on the channel c, called the *channel history*.

c^+ denotes the content of the buffer. According to the concept of a channel, we assume always the validity of the following equation as an axiom for each channel:

$$c = c^{\circ} \hat{}\, c^+$$

By the identifiers c^+ and c° we may talk about the glass box states of channels. They are called the *channel attributes*. In addition to the channel attributes, we use the attributes of the states of the components to refer to the data and control state of a system.

The identifiers and derived ("decorated") variables for the channels and the attributes form the *alphabet* of a system.

Data flow networks composed of data flow components model communicating systems. Data flow networks communicate via channels.

The history of a channel is the stream of messages communicated over it. The history of a component are the histories of its input and output channels and the history of a system are the histories of its components and thus the histories of its channels. The history of a system consists of the histories of all its channels. Given a system with the set channels C by $\varphi \in \vec{C}$ we denote a system history.

3.3. State and History Assertions

A *state assertion* is a formula of predicate logic that contains the attributes of the components and the channels of a system as free identifiers. Thus it refers to the attributes of the components and/or for the channels c to c°, c^+ and c.

A history assertion is a state assertion that contains as free identifiers only channel names. Each channel identifier denotes the stream of messages sent via that channel so far; for the attributes e of the components we refer at most to their initial values by e_0. This way a history assertion simply defines a mathematical relation between the streams exchanged via the channels of a system.

4. Describing Components

We work with two techniques to describe systems and their components:

- functions or relations on streams, syntactically represented by assertions for the channels,
- state transition relations for the channels and their buffers and the state attributes, syntactically represented by state transition rules with input and output.

The first technique refers to the history view of a component while the second corresponds to the state view. We show how to generate verification conditions for proving the validity of invariants for both description techniques.

4.1. Components as History Assertions

In a *relational specification* we define the behavior of a component by a relation between the streams flowing through its input and output channels. We specify such a relation on its input and output streams by a history assertion H that contains at most the input and output channels of the component as free identifiers.

Example. Relational specification: For a component with two input channels x and y and one output channel z we give the following relational specification

$$\#z = \min(\#x, \#y) \wedge z \sqsubseteq x$$

This formula characterizes a component forwarding its input received on channel x on its output channel z according to triggers on y. □

In the paper we mainly concentrate onto safety properties. A relational specification H with the set of input channels I and the set of output channels O is called a *safety specification* if the following formula is valid:

$$H[\varphi] \equiv \forall \varphi' \in \vec{O}^*: \varphi' \sqsubseteq \varphi \Rightarrow H[\varphi']$$

If this formula holds then H does not refer to any liveness aspects. This definition also indicates how to extract a safety formula H' from a given formula H as it is shown by the following formula (let $\varphi' \in \vec{O}^*$ be a valuation of all the output channels in O by finite streams):

$$H'[\varphi'] \equiv \exists \varphi \in \vec{O}: \varphi' \sqsubseteq \varphi \wedge H[\varphi]$$

Here H' refers exactly to those properties included in the specification H which are safety properties.

Example. Extraction of safety properties: For our example above we extract the safety properties and obtain the specification

$$\#z \leq \#y \wedge z \sqsubseteq x$$ □

While the history specifications, in general, work also with infinite streams, we can restrict safety formulas to finite streams.

4.2. Components as State Transition Relations

A component may be described and implemented by a state. State machines are described by state transition rules together with an assertion describing the initial states of the machine (cf. [4]). In the assertion describing the initial state we refer to the state attributes and to the output channels (that are assumed to be empty, in general). In the transition rules we refer to the states of the components and the channels. In other words, we refer to the buffers associated with the channels. Using the *state-oriented description* of a system we model the state transitions by a relation between the system states and the input and output sequences. A *state transition relation* is a relation on the attributes of a component and their input and output channels.

State transition relations can be described by state transition rules. We represent the transition rules logically by logical formulas that contain the state attributes v in a primed form v' and in an unprimed form v as well. The unprimed identifiers refer to the values of the attributes in the prestate (the state before the state transition) and the primed identifiers refer to the values of the attributes in the poststate (the state after the state transition).

A simple transition rule, with one input message d received over the input channel c, and one output message m send over the output channel e, is of the following syntactic form:

$$\{P\}\ c{:}d\ /\ e{:}m\ \{Q\}$$

where P is a precondition which is a state assertion referring only to the local attributes of the component and Q is an assertion on two states (using primed and unprimed attribute identifiers); primed identifiers denote the attributes of the successor states. The identifier c denotes an input channel and e denotes an output channel and d and m the messages of the respective types of the channels. A rule may contain in addition free identifiers (logical variables or scheme variables) for with arbitrary values may be substituted.

4.3. Invariants, Inductive and Stable Assertions

Given a state space $\Sigma = (\vec{A} \times \vec{I} \times \vec{I}^{+} \times \vec{I}^{o} \times \vec{O} \times \vec{O}^{+} \times \vec{O}^{o})$, which is determined by a set A of typed attributes, a set I of typed input channels, and a set O of typed output channels, a state predicate is a mapping

$$p: \Sigma \to \mathbb{B}$$

which can be represented by a formula that contains the attributes and channel identifiers as free variables. Given a state relation

$$\Delta: \Sigma \to P(\Sigma)$$

and a set of initial states $\Sigma_0 \subseteq \Sigma$ we can talk about properties of computations.

A state machine over the state space Σ is given by a set of initial states described by the set $\Sigma_0 \subseteq \Sigma$ and a state transition relation $\Delta: \Sigma \to \wp(\Sigma)$. For each state machine (Δ, Σ_0) the set of reachable states is fixed. Let R denote the set of reachable states. Assertions represents system state properties. A property $P \subseteq \Sigma$ is called an *invariant of a state machine* (Δ, Σ_0) if $R \subseteq P$. Since we distinguish between history assertions and state assertions we can distinguish between history and state invariants as well. A special case are history safety properties that are state invariants.

A property $Q \subseteq \Sigma$ is called *stable*, if

$$x \in Q \wedge y \in \Delta.x \Rightarrow y \in Q$$

Note that the set of reachable states R is stable.

A property $Q \subseteq \Sigma$ is called an *inductive assertion* of (Δ, Σ_0) if Q is stable and Q holds initially, i.e. $\Sigma_0 \subseteq Q$.

Note that not every stable property is an invariant and not every invariant is stable. To prove particular invariants $P \subseteq \Sigma$ it is therefore often necessary to find an inductive assertion $Q \subseteq \Sigma$ such that $P \subseteq Q$. As experiments have shown, proof support systems such as SteP (see [10]) are useful to find invariants.

5. A Motivating Example

We illustrate our approach by a simple example. We specify a component that calculates the iterated sum of the messages on its input stream and produces it as output. The iterated sum component has one input channel x and one output channel y both of type integer. A history assertion R specifying the behavior of the component computing the iterated sum reads as follows:

$$R: \quad \#x = \#y \wedge \forall\, i \in [1{:}\#y]{:}\ y.i = sum(x, i) \ \textbf{where}\ sum(x, i) = \sum_{j=1}^{i} x.j$$

The assertion R is not a pure safety property. Its safety part T is extracted by a prefix closure for the input channel y as defined in the previous section. It is specified by the following formula:

$$T: \quad \#x \geq \#y \wedge \forall\, i \in [1{:}\#y]{:}\ y.i = sum(x, i)$$

Obviously, we get (as expected) that the safety assertion T is a logical weakening of the assertion R:

$$R \Rightarrow T$$

The state transition specification can be expressed by only one transition rule S and with the only local state attribute s of type integer, initialized by 0.

$$S: \quad \{true\}\ x{:}\ a\ /\ y{:}\ s{+}a\ \{s' = s{+}a\}$$

Note that a is a free variable in this rule that can be instantiated freely. We work with the state invariant W which captures the relationship between the communication streams (identified by the channels x and y) and the state attributes:

$$W: \quad \#y = \#x^{\circ} \wedge y.\#y = s \wedge \forall\, i \in [1{:}\#y]{:}\ y.i = sum(x, i)$$

The formula W can be proven stable for the state transition specification S by proving the following verification condition which will be motivated and explained in more detail in the following section:

$$W \wedge s' = s{+}a \wedge x^{+} = \langle a\rangle\hat{\ }x' \Rightarrow W[s'/s,\ x'/x^{+},\ x^{\circ}\hat{\ }\langle a\rangle/x^{\circ},\ y\hat{\ }\langle s{+}a\rangle/y,\ y^{+}\hat{\ }\langle s{+}a\rangle/y^{+}]$$

The substitutions in the formula reflect the state changes induced by a transition step. This way we express that if the assertion W holds before the transition, it holds after the transition. In addition, to prove that W is an invariant, we have to show that the assertion W holds initially, when we have $s = 0 \wedge x = \langle\rangle \wedge y = \langle\rangle$. This is trivially true.

The verification condition above leads, by unfolding of the assertion W in the verification condition above, to the following explicit form of the proof obligation:

$$\begin{array}{ll}
 & \#y = \#x^{\circ} \\
\wedge & y.\#y = s \\
\wedge & \forall\, i \in [1{:}\#y]{:}\ y.i = sum(x, i) \\
\wedge & x^{+} = \langle a\rangle\hat{\ }x' \\
\Rightarrow & \#(y\hat{\ }\langle s{+}a\rangle) = \#(x^{\circ}\hat{\ }\langle a\rangle) \\
\wedge & (y\hat{\ }\langle s{+}a\rangle).\#(y\hat{\ }\langle s{+}a\rangle) = s{+}a \\
\wedge & \forall\, i \in [1{:}\#(y\hat{\ }\langle s{+}a\rangle)]{:}\ (y\hat{\ }\langle s{+}a\rangle).i = sum(x, i)
\end{array}$$

which simplifies by straightforward logical reasoning to true.

This proves that the assertion W is in fact a state invariant for the state machine with the transition rule S. Moreover, we obviously (using the axiom $x = x°\hat{}x^+$) get

$$W \Rightarrow T$$

Thus, the state invariant W implies the history assertion T. By $W \Rightarrow T$ we conclude that the state machine S is a refinement (the correct implementation) of the history specification T.

6. Verifying Invariants and Safety Properties

In this section, we give methods for proving safety properties from history assertions, for proving invariants for state machines, and for proving safety properties from invariants.

6.1. Verifying Safety Properties Given History Specifications

Let the history assertion H be the specification of a component with the set I of input channels and the set O of output channels. Let W be a safety property.

We prove that W is a safety property of the system described by H by proving directly

$$H[\varphi] \Rightarrow W[\varphi]$$

This shows that in order to prove the history safety formulas, we can work with predicate logic in a straightforward way.

6.2. Verification Conditions for State Transition Rules

For proving that a state assertion P is an invariant of a system, we have to prove the following two propositions that show that P is an inductive assertion:

- P holds in all the initial states of a system,

P is stable:

- P holds in a state then for every state transition that can be carried out in that state, the assertion P holds in its successor states, too.

As it is well known we may restrict the second step of the proof to those states only that are actually reachable by transition from the initial states. Consider a state transition diagram with an arc labeled by the following transition rule (in a more general form than the one shown above)

$$\{P\}\ i_1{:}x_1, ..., i_n{:}x_n\ /\ o_1{:}y_1, ..., o_m{:}y_m\ \{Q\} \qquad (*)$$

Let $i_1, ..., i_n$ be input channels and $o_1, ..., o_m$ be output channels and $x_1, ..., x_n$ and $y_1, ..., y_m$ be sequences of messages of appropriate type. We formalize the verification condition for the rule (*) to prove that a given state assertion V is stable. By I and O we denote the involved sets of input and output channels and by $\alpha \in \vec{I}^*$ and $\beta \in \vec{O}^*$ the channel valuations representing input and output messages consumed or produced in that step. We assume $\alpha.i_k = x_k$ for $1 \le k \le n$ and $\beta.o_k = y_k$ for $1 \le k \le m$.

Let $A = \{a_1, ..., a_k\}$ be the set of attributes of the component and A' the set of primed attributes. We prove the stability of the invariant V for a state transition system by proving stability for each transition rule. For a transition rule of the form (*) above we have to prove then the following verification condition:

$$V \wedge P \wedge Q \wedge \alpha^+ = \alpha''\hat{\ }\alpha' \Rightarrow V[A'/A, \alpha'/\alpha^+, \alpha^\circ\hat{\ }\alpha''/\alpha^\circ, \beta\hat{\ }\beta''/\beta, \beta^+\hat{\ }\beta''/\beta^+]$$

A transition of a component changes for its input channels $x \in I$ the values x° and x^+ but leaves the value of the communication history x unchanged. For output channels $y \in O$ it changes y and the buffer state y^+ but does not change the sequence of consumed messages y° of the output channels.

By this definition every transition rule generates a verification condition.

An assertion V is proved to be an invariant of a system if we show the verification conditions generated by the rule above for each component and each transition and that V holds for the initial states of the system.

In the initial state we have, in general, for all input channels x:

$$x = x^+ \wedge x^\circ = \langle\rangle$$

and for all output channels and all internal channels y:

$$y = y^+ = y^\circ = \langle\rangle$$

We assume in addition an assertion U that characterizes the initial states of a state machine. Then the verification condition is $U \Rightarrow V[\varphi]$ where $\varphi \in \vec{O}^*$ with $\varphi.y = \langle\rangle$ for all $y \in O$. By our formulas we get the proof conditions in a fully schematic way from the state transition diagrams with their state transition rules or from the formulas specifying the input/output relation. Although the formula looks difficult, we can easily implement its generation by a verification condition generator.

In fact, in general, to prove that a state assertion P is an invariant we often have to find an appropriate stronger invariant Q (which in principle characterizes those states for which P holds and that are reachable by transitions from the initial states). Then we prove that Q is an invariant and finally that the implication $Q \Rightarrow P$ holds.

6.3. From State to History Assertions

From the invariants for the state view we prove history assertions. Let V be a state invariant and W be a history assertion. If we have

$$V \Rightarrow W$$

then we have deduced a history assertion from a state invariant. Of course, histories and history assertions are, in general, much less detailed than states, state assertions, and state transition rules. Histories can be seen as an *abstraction* of states.

Note that for the reverse situation, the proposition $W \Rightarrow V$ can hardly be provable, in general, since V contains a number of identifiers not even occurring in the assertion W.

7. A Producer/Consumer Example

We specify and refine the well-known producer/consumer example in the version suggested as an example by the DFKI/VSE (see [6]) using a version of TLA (see [1]). The treatment in Focus given in the following is in contrast to the TLA version shown in [4].

We demonstrate that we can carry out the proof in FOCUS in a more structured manner and that it is considerably simplified that way. We carry out the proof of the correctness of the interaction on more abstract level and then refine the verified system into the DFKI-version. The goal of this exercise is a demonstration and a comparison of two different methods for the specification and verification of interactive systems by looking at a simple but nevertheless illustrative example.

We specify the example of a producer/consumer network according to the data flow diagram given in Fig. 1. The specification of the components and the overall system is given by assertions characterizing the mathematical relation between the input and output streams. These streams model the communication histories of the system and this way show the messages exchanged by the system components.

7.1. Specification of the Components

In the following, we introduce the three components that cooperate in a system. P is the producer, Q is the bounded transmission queue and C is the consumer. The channels x and y carry data messages of a type M while the channels d and e only carry control signals of a type S. The type S contains only one data element *ack* called the *acknowledgment signal*.

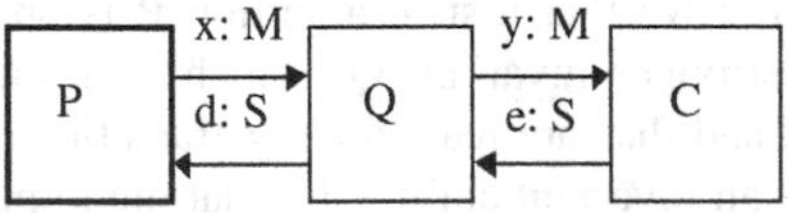

Fig. 1 Data Flow Diagram of the Producer/Consumer Network

We specify the system components by assertions describing mathematical relations between their input and output streams. We only consider safety properties (partial correctness) in the following for the producer and for the consumer. The specifications read as follows:

P: $\#x \le \#d$

C: $\#e \le \#y$

These specifications indicate that the producer P works by the pull principle (it never produces more messages on its data channel x than required by its demand channel d). The consumer C is to be served by the push principle (it never generates more requirements on its requirements channel e than data received on the channel y).

Let lq be the maximal capacity of the buffer in the component Q. This leads to the following specification of the buffer: Q receives data on channel x according to the pull principle and forwards these data elements on its channel y according to the push principle.

$$Q: \#x \le \#d \wedge \#e \le \#y \Rightarrow y \sqsubseteq x \wedge \#y = \min(\#x, 1+\#e) \wedge \#d = \min(lq+\#y, 1+\#x)$$

This specification is written in the assumption/commitment style. The assumption expresses that the channels x and d follow the pull principle while the channels y and e follow the push principle. Strictly speaking, this specification is not a pure safety property. To obtain a pure safety property we have to replace the equalities in the conclusion by "≤". Note that the equation

$$\#d = \min(lq+\#y, 1+\#x)$$

is equivalent to (#d–#y denotes the actual number of messages in the queue Q)

$$\#d-\#y = \min(lq, 1+\#x-\#y)$$

This expresses that the buffer contains exactly the number of messages pulled from the producer but not pushed into the consumer and that this number is bounded by the length lq of the queue. Formally these relations are invariants on the system states described by the histories of communication represented by the streams.

Note that the queue Q is truly concurrent since it can communicate (send and receive messages) on all its channels concurrently.

7.2. Specification of the Composed System

From the components specified by P, C, and Q we may form a composed system as it is shown in Fig. 1. The logical specification of the composed system has the following form (composition is simply conjunction):

$$P \wedge Q \wedge C$$

If we expand this formula according to the specifications given above we get the logical formula

$$\begin{array}{ll} & \#x \le \#d \\ \wedge & \#e \le \#y \\ \wedge & (\#x \le \#d \wedge \#e \le \#y \Rightarrow y \sqsubseteq x \wedge \#y = \min(\#x, 1+\#e) \wedge \#d = \min(lq+\#y, 1+\#x)) \end{array}$$

This formula is logically equivalent to (since the specifications of P and C exactly guarantee the assumption of Q) the formula

$$\begin{array}{ll} & \#x \le \#d \\ \wedge & \#e \le \#y \\ \wedge & y \sqsubseteq x \\ \wedge & \#y = \min(\#x, 1+\#e) \\ \wedge & \#d = \min(lq+\#y, 1+\#x) \end{array}$$

This formula immediately implies, in particular, the relationship

$$y \sqsubseteq x$$

between the communication history on the output channel x of the producer and communication on the input channel y of the consumer, which is the essential safety correctness condition for the correct transmission of messages between the producer and the consumer via the buffer.

7.3. State Machines as Component Descriptions

We may describe the components introduced above also by state machines with input and output. We obtain the following descriptions using state transition rules. The components P and C are simple and do not use any local attributes:

Producer P: d: ack / x: m

Consumer C: y: m / e: ack

The component Q is a bit more complex to specify (c1 and c2 are auxiliary control states here):

Queue Q: **attribute** $q: M^*$, c1, c2: {idle, wait, chaos};

intial: $q = \langle\rangle \wedge c1 = idle \wedge c2 = idle$;

$\{\#q < lq \wedge c1 = idle\}$	-	/ d: ack	$\{c1' = wait\}$
$\{0 \leq \#q \wedge c2 = idle\}$	-	/ y: ft.q	$\{q' = rt.q \wedge c2' = wait\}$
$\{c1 = wait\}$	x: m	/ -	$\{q' = q\hat{\ }\langle m\rangle \wedge c1' = idle\}$
$\{c2 = wait\}$	e: ack	/ -	$\{c2' = idle\}$
$\{c1 = idle\}$	x: m	/ -	{CHAOS}
$\{c2 = idle\}$	e: ack	/ -	{CHAOS}

Here we write CHAOS as an abbreviation for $c1' = chaos \wedge c2' = chaos$.

Based on these state transition descriptions we can prove the validity of the invariants P and Q for the producer and consumer. The proof is straightforward. For the queue described as a state machine we prove the invariant:

$$\#x \leq \#d \wedge \#e \leq \#y \Rightarrow$$
$$((c1 = idle \wedge \#d^\circ = \#x) \vee (c1 = wait \wedge \#q \leq lq \wedge \#d = 1+\#x^\circ))$$
$$\wedge\ ((c2 = idle \wedge \#e^\circ = \#y) \vee (c2 = wait \wedge 0 \leq \#q \wedge \#y = 1+\#e^\circ))$$
$$\wedge\ x^\circ = y\hat{\ }q$$

We have to show that CHAOS cannot be reached. Actually CHAOS can only be reached if input is provided on x (and e resp.) in a state were c1 is idle (or c2 is idle resp.). This happens only in case buffer x^+ (or e^+ resp.) is not empty. However, given that

$$\#x \leq \#d$$

$$\#e \leq \#y$$

(these are preconditions in the invariants and also invariants of the producer and the consumer) we can prove from the invariant

$$c1 = idle \Rightarrow x^+ = \langle\rangle$$

$$c2 = idle \Rightarrow e^+ = \langle\rangle$$

The invariant also shows that the transition leading to CHAOS is never executed.

Clearly the component can only control its received input x° and e° but not its buffers x^+ and e^+. The environment controls these buffers.

However, we know that

$$\#x^\circ \leq \#x$$

$$\#e^{\circ} \leq \#e$$

are axioms. From these axioms and the invariant we can derive the history specification Q.

8. Concluding Remarks

We have shown how to combine history based reasoning with state based reasoning for safety properties. Also, we demonstrated that reasoning with states needs larger, more complex assertions and a much higher number of verification conditions (for a more comprehensive presentation see [2]).

In principle, we have illustrated how to work with two forms of assertions in the specification and verification of communicating systems:

- history assertions only refer to the states of the channels (streams of sent messages) and the initial values of the local attributes.
- state assertions in addition refer to the input buffers associated with components (the streams of messages on a channel not consumed so far) as well as the values of the local attributes.

Of course, history assertions are only a special case of state assertions.

The basic idea of our approach is to do as much as possible of the verifcation by *reasoning in the large* in the history view. This allows us to get rid of all the state details. It can always be done thanks to the modularity of our calculus. State reasoning (*reasoning in the small*) should only be done to derive history assertions (and to do *reasoning in the large*).

This way our method leads to a classical two level modular proof technique. Given a system implementation where each of the data flow nodes is implemented by a state machine we derive a history view for the state machines by selecting state invariants and proving them for the components from the specifications. From these we may abstract history assertions. We may do that in isolation for each state machine and then compose the derived history specifications by logical conjunction. We can also collect a few state machines into a cluster and then derive a relational view for them. In any case we can get rid of a lot of details of local states and continue on a more abstract level with histories.

Acknowledgment. It is a pleasure to thank Max Breitling, Jan Philipps, Bernd Finkbeiner, Zohar Manna, and the colleagues from DFKI for useful discussions.

References

1. M. Abadi, L. Lamport: Composing Specifications. Digital Systems Research Center, SRC Report 66, October 1990
2. M. Breitling, J. Philipps: Black Box View of State Machines. TUM-19916, SFB-Bericht Nr. 34L/07/99A, Institut für Informatik, Technische Universität München, 1999

3. M. Broy: Compositional Refinement of Interactive Systems. DIGITAL Systems Research Center, SRC 89, 1992. Also in: Journal of the ACM, Volume 44, No. 6 (Nov. 1997), 850-891
4. M. Broy: The Specification of System Components by State Transition Diagrams. Technische Universität München, Institut für Informatik, TUM-I9729, Mai 1997
5. K. M. Chandy, J. Misra: Parallel Program Design: A Foundation. Addison Wesley 1988
6. G. Rock, W. Stephan, A. Wolpers: Modular Reasoning about Structured TLA Specifications. In: R. Berghammer, Y. Lakhnech (eds.): Tool Support for System Specification, Development and Verification. Advances in Computing Science, Wien-NewYork: Springer 1999, 217-229
7. Paech, B. Rumpe: A new Concept of Refinement used for Behaviour Modelling with Automata. In: M. Naftalin, T. Denvir, M. Bertran (eds.): FME'94, Formal Methods Europe, Symposium '94, Springer-Verlag: Berlin, LNCS 873, 1994
8. B. Rumpe, C. Klein: Automata Describing Object Behavior. In: H. Kilov, W. Harvey (eds.): Specification of Behavioral Semantics in Object-Oriented Information Modeling. Kluwer Academic Publishers 1996, 265-286
9. P. Scholz, D. Nazareth, F. Regensburger: Mini-Statecharts: A Compositional Way to Model Parallel Systems. In: 9th International Conference on Parallel and Distributed Computing Systems, Dijon, France, 25-27 September 1996
10. N.S. Björner, A. Browne, E. Chang, M. Colon, A. Kapur, Z. Manna, H.B. Sipma, T.E. Uribe: STeP: The Stanford Temporal Prover, User's Manual. Technical Report STAM-CS-TR-95-1562, Computer Science Department. Stanford University, November 1995

Principles and Pragmatics of Subtyping in PVS*

Natarajan Shankar and Sam Owre

Computer Science Laboratory, SRI International
Menlo Park CA 94025 USA
`Phone: +1 (650) 859-5272 Fax: +1 (650) 859-2844`
`{shankar,owre}@csl.sri.com`
`http://www.csl.sri.com/~shankar/`

Abstract. PVS (Prototype Verification System) is a mechanized framework for formal specification and interactive proof development. The PVS specification language is based on higher-order logic enriched with features such as predicate subtypes, dependent types, recursive datatypes, and parametric theories. Subtyping is a central concept in the PVS type system. PVS admits the definition of subtypes corresponding to nonzero integers, prime numbers, injective maps, order-preserving maps, and even empty subtypes. We examine the principles underlying the PVS subtype mechanism and its implementation and use.

The PVS specification language is primarily a medium for communicating formal mathematical descriptions. Formal PVS specifications are meant for both machine and human consumption. The specification language of PVS extends simply typed higher-order logic with features such as predicate subtypes, dependent types, recursive datatypes, and parametric theories. These features are critical for facile mathematical expression as well as symbolic manipulation. Though the language has been designed to be used in conjunction with a theorem prover, it has an existence independent of any specific theorem prover.

The core specification language of PVS is quite small yet poses a number of serious implementation challenges. We outline the difficulties in realizing these features in a usable implementation. Our observations might be useful to designers and implementors of other specification languages with similar features.

There is a long history of formal foundational languages for mathematics. Frege's *Begriffsschrift* [Fre67a] was presented as a system of axioms and rules for logical reasoning in the sciences. Frege's use of function variables was found to be inconsistent by Russell [Rus67,Fre67b]. Poincare attributed the problem to a *vicious circle*, or impredicativity, that allowed an entity to be defined by quantification over a domain that included the entity itself. There were two initial responses to this. Zermelo's solution was to craft an untyped set theory where comprehension was restricted to extracting subsets of existing sets. Russell and Whitehead's system of *Principia Mathematica* [WR27] consisted of a simple theory of types which stratified the universe into the type of individuals, collections

* This work was funded by NSF Grants No. CCR-9712383 and CCR-9509931.

D. Bert, C. Choppy, and P. Mosses (Eds.): WADT'99, LNCS 1827, pp. 37–52, 2000.

of individuals, collections of collections of individuals, etc., and a ramified theory of types that stratified the elements within a type to rule out impredicative definitions.[1]

In computing, specification languages are meant to formalize *what* is being computed rather than *how* it is computed. There are many discernible divisions across these specification languages including

- Set theory (Z [Spi88], VDM [Jon90]) *versus* type theory (HOL [GM93], Nuprl [CAB$^+$86], Coq [DFH$^+$91], PVS [ORSvH95])
- Constructive (Coq, Nuprl) *versus* classical foundations (Z, HOL, PVS)
- First-order (OBJ [FGJM85b], Maude [CDE$^+$99], VDM, CASL [Mos98][2]) *versus* higher-order logic (HOL, Nuprl, Coq, PVS)
- Model-oriented (Z, VDM) *versus* property-oriented (OBJ, Maude, CASL)
- Total function (HOL, PVS) *versus* partial function (OBJ, Maude, VDM, CASL)

The PVS specification language is based on a strongly typed higher-order logic of total functions that builds on Church's simply typed higher-order logic [Chu40,And86]. Higher-order logic captures only a modest fragment of set theory, but it is one that is reasonably expressive and yet effectively mechanizable. Types impose a useful discipline within a specification language. They also lead to the early detection of a large class of syntactic and semantic errors. PVS admits only total functions but this is mitigated by the presence of subtypes since a partial function can be introduced as a total function when its domain of definition can be captured as a subtype. For example, the division operation can be introduced with the domain given as the subtype of numbers consisting of the nonzero numbers. If applied to a term not known to be nonzero, a proof obligation is generated. PVS is based on a classical foundation as opposed to a constructive one since constructive proofs impose a substantial cost in proof construction for a modest gain in the information that can be extracted from a successful proof.

We focus primarily on subtyping and the surrounding issues since this is one of the core features of PVS. We also compare PVS with other specification languages. The paper condenses material from reports: *The Formal Semantics of PVS* [OS97] (URL: `www.csl.sri.com/reports/postscript/csl-97-2.ps.gz`) and *Abstract Datatypes in PVS* [OS93] (URL: `www.csl.sri.com/reports/postscript/csl-93-9.ps.gz`). These reports should be consulted for further details. Rushby, Owre, and Shankar [ROS98] motivate the need for PVS-style subtyping in specification languages.

Following the style of the formal semantics of PVS [OS97], we present an idealized core of the PVS language in small increments by starting from the simple type system, and adding predicate subtypes, dependent types, typing judgements, and abstract datatypes.

[1] Rushby [Rus93] has a lengthy discussion of foundational issues and their impact on specification language features.

[2] CASL also has a higher-order extension.

1 The Simply Typed Fragment

The *base types* in PVS consist of the booleans `bool` and the real number type `real`.[3] From types T_1 and T_2, a *function type* is constructed as $[T_1 \rightarrow T_2]$ and a *product type* is constructed as $[T_1, T_2]$.

The *preterms* t consist of

- constants: c, f
- variables: x
- pairs: $\langle t_1, t_2 \rangle$
- projections: $\mathtt{p}_i\ t$
- abstractions: $\lambda(x : T)\ t$
- applications: $f t$

The typechecking of a preterm a is carried out with respect to a declaration context Γ by an operation $\tau(\Gamma)(a)$ that returns the canonical type. A context is a sequence of bindings of names to types, kinds, and definitions. For an identifier s, $kind(\Gamma(s))$ returns the kind CONSTANT, VARIABLE, or TYPE. Since the contexts and types also need to be typechecked, we have

- $\tau()(\Gamma) = \mathtt{CONTEXT}$ for well-formed context Γ.
- $\tau(\Gamma)(A) = \mathtt{TYPE}$ for well-formed type A.

The definition of $\tau(\Gamma)(a)$ is

$$\begin{aligned}
\tau(\Gamma)(s) &= type(\Gamma(s)), \\
&\quad \text{if } kind(\Gamma(s)) \in \{\mathtt{CONSTANT}, \mathtt{VARIABLE}\} \\
\tau(\Gamma)(f\ a) &= B, \text{ if } \tau(\Gamma)(f) = [A \rightarrow B] \text{ and } \tau(\Gamma)(a) = A \\
\tau(\Gamma)(\lambda(x : T)\ a) &= [T \rightarrow \tau(\Gamma, x : \mathtt{VAR}\ T)(a)], \text{ if } \Gamma(x) \text{ is undefined} \\
&\quad \text{and } \tau(\Gamma)(T) = \mathtt{TYPE} \\
\tau(\Gamma)(\langle a_1, a_2 \rangle) &= [\tau(\Gamma)(a_1), \tau(\Gamma)(a_2))] \\
\tau(\Gamma)(\mathtt{p}_i\ a) &= T_i, \text{ where} \\
&\quad \tau(\Gamma)(a) = [T_1, T_2]
\end{aligned}$$

Type rules [Car97] are conventionally given as inference rules of the form

$$\frac{\Gamma \vdash f : [A \rightarrow B] \qquad \Gamma \vdash a : A}{\Gamma \vdash f\ a : B}$$

We have adopted a functional style of type computation, as opposed to the relational style of type derivation above, since each PVS expression has a canonical type given by the type declarations of its constants and variables.[4] With

---

[3] The actual base number type is an unspecified supertype of the reals called `number` which is there to accommodate possible extensions of the reals such as the extended reals (with $+\infty$ and $-\infty$) or the complex numbers.

[4] This is also the style followed in the PVS Semantics Report [OS97].

subtypes, a single expression, such as 2, can have multiple types such as `real`, `rat` (rational number), `int` (integer), `nat` (natural number), and `even`. The functional computation of a canonical type removes any possibility for nondeterminism without loss of completeness (every typeable term is assigned a canonical type, e.g., the canonical type of 2 is `real`). The soundness argument for the type system follows the definition of the τ operation and is therefore quite straightforward [OS97].

The actual PVS specification language differs from the core PVS presented above. PVS also has record types which can be captured by product types and are therefore omitted from the core language. PVS has n-ary products instead of the binary products used in the core language. In this extended abstract, we are ignoring features of PVS such as type-directed conversions, parametric theories, and recursive and inductive definitions.

If we let **2** represent a two-element set for interpreting the type `bool`, and **R** represent the set of real numbers, the semantics for the simple type system is given with respect to a universe $U = \bigcup_{i<\omega} U_i$, where

$$U_0 = \{\mathbf{2}, \mathbf{R}\}$$
$$U_{i+1} = U_i \bigcup \{X \times Y \mid X, Y \in U_i\} \bigcup \{X^Y \mid X, Y \in U_i\}$$

An *assignment* for a context Γ is a list of bindings of the form $\{x_1 \leftarrow y_1\} \ldots \{x_n \leftarrow y_n\}$ that associates the type, constant, and variable declarations of Γ with subsets and elements of the universe U. A *valid* assignment is one in which the assignment of a constant or variable is an element of the assignment of its declared type. The meaning of a well-formed type A in a context Γ is given as $\mathcal{M}(\Gamma \mid \gamma)(A)$. Correspondingly, the meaning of a well-typed term a with respect to a context Γ and γ is given as $\mathcal{M}(\Gamma \mid \gamma)(a)$. The definitions and proofs of soundness can be found in the PVS semantics report [OS97].

The soundness theorem asserts that for a well-formed context Γ, and valid assignment γ, a well-formed type A, and a type-correct term a,

1. $\mathcal{M}(\Gamma \mid \gamma)(A) \in U$, and
2. $\mathcal{M}(\Gamma \mid \gamma)(a) \in \mathcal{M}(\Gamma \mid \gamma)(\tau(\Gamma)(a))$.

PVS is quite liberal about overloading so that the same symbol can be declared multiply and can also be reused as a constant, variable, type, or theory name. Names declared within parametric theories can also be used without supplying the actual parameters. The type checker uses contextual type information to resolve ambiguities arising from overloading and to determine the precise theory parameters for the resolved names. Other than resolving overloaded names and determining theory parameters, the simple type system does not pose any serious implementation challenges.

2 Predicate Subtyping

Predicate subtypes are perhaps the most important feature of the PVS type system. The subtype of elements of a type T satisfying the predicate p is written as $\{x : T \mid p(x)\}$. Here $p(x)$ can be an arbitrary PVS formula. As examples, the type of nonzero real numbers **nzreal** is given as $\{x : \mathtt{real} \mid x \neq 0\}$, and the type of division is given as [**real**, **nzreal**→**real**]. Subtypes thus allow partial functions to be expressed as total functions over a restricted domain specified as a subtype.[5]

Partial functions do have the advantage of being more expressive. The *subp* example from Cheng and Jones [CJ90] is given by

$$subp(i, j) = \text{ if } i = j \text{ then } 0 \text{ else } subp(i, j+1) + 1 \text{ endif}$$

and is undefined if $i < j$ (when $i \geq j$, $subp(i, j) = i - j$). The formula

$$(subp(i, j) = i - j) \text{ OR } (subp(j, i) = j - i)$$

is perfectly meaningful in most treatments for partial functions, but since it generates unprovable obligations, it is not considered type-correct in PVS. In practice, we have yet to encounter a need for this kind of expressiveness.

Subtypes have many other uses. They can be used to specify intervals and subranges of the integers. Thus arrays can be declared as functions over an index type that is a subrange. If `below(10)` represents the subtype of natural numbers below 10, then a ten-element integer array a can be given the type [`below(10)`→**int**]. Subtypes are also useful for recording properties within the type of an expression. For example, the type of the absolute value function *abs* can be given as [**real**→**nonnegreal**], where **nonnegreal** is the type of nonnegative real numbers.

Predicate subtypes correspond to subsets of the parent type. The equality relation remains the same from a type to a subtype. One might think that predicate subtypes could be translated away since any subtype constraints on quantified variables can be moved into the body of the quantification. However, this is not the case for lambda-expressions since $\lambda(x : A)\ a$ where A is a subtype, is not expressible in the system without subtypes.

Predicate subtyping on higher-order types is especially useful for introducing types corresponding to

- Injective, surjective, bijective, and order-preserving maps
- Reflexive, transitive, symmetric, anti-symmetric, partially ordered, well-ordered relations
- Monotone predicate transformers. This is at least a third-order concept.

Predicate subtyping is orthogonal to structural subtyping used in type systems for object-oriented languages [Car97]. In particular, with predicate subtyping, subtyping on function types is not contravariant on the domain type. The function type $[A \to B]$ is a predicate subtype of $[A' \to B']$ iff B is a predicate subtype of B', and $A \equiv A'$. Since A and A' may contain predicate subtypes, type

[5] Note that in PVS, unlike in Maude or CASL, once division is declared to be of this type, no further declarations may extend its domain. Any use of division whose denominator is not known to be nonzero will generate a proof obligation when type-checked.

equivalence can also generate proof obligations corresponding to the equivalence on predicates.

The proof obligations generated by the PVS typechecker are called type-correctness conditions (TCCs). Subtype TCCs take into account the logical context within which a subtype proof obligation is generated. For example, the expression $x \neq y \supset (x+y)/(x-y)$ generates proof obligation $x \neq y \supset (x-y) \neq 0$ corresponding to the subtype `nonnegreal` for the denominator of the division operation. The logical context of the subtype condition is included as the antecedent to the proof obligation.

The most significant feature of subtyping in PVS is the division of typechecking into

1. Simple type correctness which is established algorithmically by the typechecker, and
2. Proof obligations corresponding to the subtype predicates that are conjectures that have to be proved within a proof system.

As a consequence, typechecking in PVS is undecidable insofar as the generated proof obligations may not always fall within a decidable fragment of the logic. This is the only source of undecidability in the PVS type system. For example, the type $\{x : \texttt{bool} \mid x\}$ is the subtype of booleans that are `TRUE`. Naturally, any theorem has this type and it is easy to see that typechecking with respect to such a subtype is equivalent to theorem proving in general.

Undecidability is not a serious drawback in practice. The typechecker is merely generates proof obligations without actually trying to verify them. Typical proof obligations do fall within an efficiently decidable fragment of the logic and can be discharged by simple proof strategies that rely heavily on the PVS decision procedures. The proliferation of type-correctness proof obligations is a potentially serious drawback, but is mitigated by other features of the PVS type system, particularly,

- Subsumption which ensures that when a stronger proof obligation already exists, a weaker one is never generated. For example, a TCC $x \neq y \supset x-y \neq 0$ would be subsumed by a TCC of the form $x - y \neq 0$ and would therefore be suppressed.
- Typing judgements that can cache subtype information about specific expressions. These are discussed below in greater detail.

There are two basic operations associated with typechecking in the type system with subtypes. One operation $\mu(A)$ returns the maximal supertype of a type A, and the other $\pi(A)$ returns the predicate constraints in the type A with respect to the maximal supertype $\mu(A)$. A variant $\mu_0(A)$ returns the *direct supertype* so that $\mu_0(\{x : T \mid a\}) = \mu_0(T)$, and otherwise, $\mu_0(T) = T$. In contrast to μ_0, $\mu([A \rightarrow B])$ is defined to be $[A \rightarrow \mu(B)]$.

Two types A and B are *compatible* iff $\mu(A)$ and $\mu(B)$ are equivalent. When typechecking an application $f\ a$ where the canonical type of f is $[A \rightarrow B]$ and the canonical type of a is A', we have to ensure that A and A' are compatible (which might generate type equivalence proof obligations) and discharge any proof obligations corresponding to the subtype predicates imposed by A on a. For example, the type of positive integers `posint` and the type of nonzero natural numbers `nznat` are equivalent. The compatibility proof obligations in the context Γ are represented as $(A \sim A')_\Gamma$. The type rules are given by

$$\begin{aligned}
\tau(\Gamma)(\{x : T \mid a\}) &= \texttt{TYPE}, \text{ if } \Gamma(x) \text{ is undefined,}\\
&\quad \tau(\Gamma)(T) = \texttt{TYPE}, \text{ and } \tau(\Gamma, x : \texttt{VAR}\ T)(a) = \texttt{bool}\\
\tau(\Gamma)(f\ a) &= B, \text{ where } \mu_0(\tau(\Gamma)(f)) = [A \rightarrow B],\\
&\quad \tau(\Gamma)(a) = A',\\
&\quad (A \sim A')_\Gamma,\\
&\quad \vdash_\Gamma \pi(A)(a)\\
\tau(\Gamma)(\texttt{p}_i\ a) &= A_i, \text{ where } \mu_0(\tau(\Gamma)(a)) = [A_1, A_2]
\end{aligned}$$

For example, let `g: {f: [nat -> nat] | f(0) = 0}`, and `x: int`. Then

$$\begin{aligned}
\mu_0(\tau(\Gamma)(\texttt{g})) &= \texttt{[nat -> nat]},\\
\tau(\Gamma)(\texttt{x}) &= \texttt{int}, \text{ and}\\
\texttt{int} &\sim \texttt{nat}, \text{ since } \mu(\texttt{int}) = \mu(\texttt{nat}) = \texttt{number}, \text{ hence}\\
\tau(\Gamma)(\texttt{g(x)}) &= \texttt{nat}, \text{ with the proof obligation } \pi(\texttt{nat})(\texttt{x}) = \texttt{(x >= 0)}
\end{aligned}$$

The type rules with subtyping are quite a bit more complicated than those of the simple type system. The implementation of these rules within the PVS typechecker has to cope with the interaction between subtyping and name resolution since there is no longer an exact match between the domain type of a function and its argument type.

For the interpretation of subtyping, the semantic universe has to be expanded to include subsets.

$$\begin{aligned}
U_0 &= \{\mathbf{2}, \mathbf{R}\}\\
U_{i+1} &= U_i \bigcup \{X \times Y \mid X, Y \in U_i\} \bigcup \{X^Y \mid X, Y \in U_i\} \bigcup \bigcup_{X \in U_i} \wp(X)
\end{aligned}$$

The semantics of a predicate subtype is given by the definition

$$\begin{aligned}
&\mathcal{M}(\Gamma \mid \gamma)(\{x : T \mid a\})\\
&= \{y \in \mathcal{M}(\Gamma \mid \gamma)(T) \mid \mathcal{M}(\Gamma, x : \texttt{VAR}\ T \mid \gamma\{x \leftarrow y\})(a) = \mathbf{1}\}.
\end{aligned}$$

Subtyping is one of several sources of proof obligations in PVS. Other sources of proof obligations include

1. Recursive functions, corresponding to termination.
2. Parametric theory instances, corresponding to the *assumptions* in the theory about its parameters.

3. Constant definitions, since the declared type must be shown to be nonempty. This check is not strictly necessary since such a declaration corresponds to an inconsistent axiom. However, the check is there to prevent inconsistencies from being introduced through constant declarations.
4. Inductive relation definitions, since these must be defined as fixed points of *monotone* predicate transformers.

In general, proof obligations are used in PVS to implement complete, or relatively complete, semantic checks instead of incomplete syntactic checks on the well-formedness of PVS specifications.

3 Dependent Typing

The combination of dependent typing with predicate subtyping is extremely powerful and can be used to capture the relationship between the output and the input of a function. This allows the specification of an operation to be captured within the type system. The type $\mathtt{below}(n)$ is actually a dependent type and is declared as

$$\mathtt{below}(n) : \mathtt{TYPE} = \{s : \mathbf{nat} \mid s < n\}.$$

The definition of binomial coefficients $\binom{n}{k}$ serves as a good illustration of dependent typing.

First, the factorial operation is defined recursively. Predicate subtyping is used to note that the result of $\mathtt{factorial}(n)$ is always a positive integer.

```
n: VAR nat

factorial(n):
    RECURSIVE posnat =
    (IF n > 0 THEN n * factorial(n - 1)
              ELSE 1 ENDIF)
    MEASURE n
```

Then $\binom{n}{k}$ given by `chooses0(n, k)` is computed using the `factorial` operation.

```
chooses0(n, (k : upto(n))) : rat =
    factorial(n)/(factorial(k) * factorial(n-k))
```

In the definition of `chooses0`, the domain type of the operation is a dependent tuple type where the type of the second component `upto(n)` depends on the first component `n`, where `upto(n)` is defined as {`s: nat | s <= n`}. The predicate subtyping on the second argument is identical to the informal restriction given in textbook definitions [Lev90].

The type of `chooses0(n, (k : upto(n)))` has been given as `rat` instead of the more accurate `posnat`. This is because it is necessary to establish that the right-hand side of the definition is a positive integral quantity. This nontrivial proof obligation is typically overlooked in textbook presentations. In the PVS development, the definition of chooses0 is used to prove the basic recurrence $\binom{n+1}{k+1} = \binom{n}{k} + \binom{n}{k+1}$, for $0 \leq k < n$. This is stated below as the lemma chooses0_recurrence.

```
chooses0_recurrence: LEMMA
  (FORALL (k:upto(n)):
    chooses0(n, k) =
     (IF (k = 0 OR n = k) THEN 1
      ELSE chooses0(n-1, k) + chooses0(n-1, k-1)
      ENDIF))
```

The above recurrence can be used to show that the definition of $\binom{n}{k}$ always computes a positive integral quantity.

```
chooses(n, (k : upto(n))): posnat =
   chooses0(n, k)
```

The definition of chooses, when typechecked, generates a proof obligation corresponding to the claim that $\binom{n}{k}$ returns a positive integral quantity. This proof obligation is discharged using the recurrence by an interactive inductive proof.[6]

PVS admits only a very restricted form of type dependency. In a dependent type $T(n)$, the parameter n can occur only within subtype predicates in $T(n)$. This means that the structure of $T(n)$ is invariant with respect to n. All possible ways of introducing type dependencies in PVS preserve this invariant. It follows that there is no way of defining a type $T(n)$, where $T(n)$ is A^n, i.e., the n-tuple over the type A. Similarly, the D_∞ model of lambda-calculus [Bar78] is also not definable as a type since its construction involves a dependent type $T(n)$ where $T(n+1) = [T(n) \rightarrow T(n)]$.

Dependent typing adds quite a bit of complexity to the type rules. The substitution operation is needed in the definition of the type rules. The definition of type equivalence and maximal supertype is not straightforward. The PVS formal semantics report [OS97] can be consulted for further details. The implementation of the typechecker for dependent typing is also correspondingly more difficult since it requires more contextual information and quite heavy use of substitution. We intend to investigate whether a representation of types using explicit substitutions might be more efficient for typechecking with dependent types.

---

[6] Note that chooses0 could be defined as a posnat to begin with, but the resulting proof obligation is not trivial to prove. It was in attempting to prove this obligation that the chooses0_recurrence lemma was developed.

4 Judgements

With subtyping, the same term can have more than one type. As we have already seen, the term 2 has the types `real`, `rat`, `int`, `nat`, `posnat`, `even`, and `prime`. An operation can return a result of a more refined subtype than its declared range type, if it is given arguments of a more refined domain type than its declared domain type. The arithmetic operation of multiplication is a good example here. The product of two positive numbers or two negative numbers is positive. Such subtype propagation information can be specified using a `JUDGEMENT` declaration. Typing judgements generate proof obligations corresponding to the validity of the judgement. The judgements are used by the typechecker in a proactive manner to propagate subtype information which minimizes the generation of redundant proof obligations.

There are two kinds of judgements in PVS. Typing judgements assert that a given operation propagates type information in a specific manner. For example, two simple judgements about the propagation of sign information by the addition operation are recorded below.

```
px, py:    VAR posreal
nx, ny:    VAR negreal
nnx, nny: VAR nonneg_real
nnreal_plus_posreal_is_posreal:   JUDGEMENT +(nnx, py) HAS_TYPE posreal
negreal_plus_negreal_is_negreal:  JUDGEMENT +(nx, ny) HAS_TYPE negreal
```

The first judgement asserts that the sum of a nonnegative and a positive real is a positive real. The second judgement asserts that the sum of two negative reals is negative. When the typechecker is applied to a term, say $(-2 + -5)$, it is able to conclude that the term has the type negative real number. Stronger judgements allow the typechecker to conclude that the term $(-2 + -5)$ has the type of negative integers. This, in turn, allows the typechecker to conclude that $(-2 + -5) + -3$ has the type `negreal`.

Judgements thus allow certain classes of proof obligations to be proved once and for all. The typechecker uses judgements to propagate type information from subterms to the terms in a proactive manner. The refined type information computed by the typechecker not only minimizes the number of proof obligations, it is also used by the PVS proof checker in simplification. For example, judgements facilitate the computation of sign information for arithmetic terms. Such sign information is recorded in the data structures of the decision procedures and is employed in arithmetic simplification. The PVS decision procedures are only modestly effective at nonlinear arithmetic so the statically inferred sign information comes in quite handy during simplification.

5 Abstract Datatypes

PVS, like many other specification languages, has a definition mechanism for a certain class of recursive datatypes given by constructors, accessors, and recognizers. The `list` datatype is given in terms of the constructors

- null with recognizer null? and with no accessors, and
- cons with recognizer cons? and accessors car and cdr.

```
list [T: TYPE]: DATATYPE
 BEGIN
  null: null?
  cons (car: T, cdr:list):cons?
 END list
```

The datatype is parametric in the element type T. This definition generates various PVS theories that contain the relevant datatype axioms and a number of useful operators for defining operations over datatype terms.

The predicate subtype of the datatype corresponding to the recognizer cons? is represented by the type expression (cons?). Then the accessor car has the type [(cons?)→T] and the accessor cdr has the type [(cons?)→list].

Whenever an accessor is used in an expression, as in car(cdr(x)), the typechecker generates proof obligations requiring that cons?(x) and cons?(cdr(x)) hold in the context of any conditions given by the context.

Predicate subtypes allow mutually recursive datatypes to be introduced using the same mechanism as recursive datatypes. For a simple example, suppose we wish to construct datatypes consisting of arithmetic expressions constructed from numbers by means of addition and branching, and boolean expressions that are equalities between arithmetic expressions. This could be expressed as

```
expr: DATATYPE
 BEGIN
  eq(t1: term, t2: term): eq?
 END expr

term: DATATYPE
 BEGIN
  num(n:int): num?
  sum(t1:term,t2:term):    sum?
  ift(e: expr, t1: term, t2: term): ift?
 END term
```

But now the induction schema for each of these datatypes relies on the other, making it difficult to work with.[7] We chose a simpler approach that relies on subtypes:

```
arith: DATATYPE WITH SUBTYPES expr, term
 BEGIN
  num(n:int): num?                :term
  sum(t1:term,t2:term):     sum?  :term
  eq(t1: term, t2: term): eq?     :expr
  ift(e: expr, t1: term, t2: term): ift? :term
 END arith
```

[7] This is similar to the problem of describing measures that decrease across mutually recursive function definitions.

In this datatype, `term` is the subtype `{x: arith | num?(x) OR sum?(x) OR ift?(x)}`, and a single induction schema is generated that simultaneously inducts over `terms` and `exprs`.

Ordered binary trees are another demonstration of the interaction of datatypes and predicate subtyping. The type of ordered binary trees can be defined as a subtype of the binary trees datatype that satisfies the ordering condition.

6 Comparisons

Lamport and Paulson [LP99] argue that types are harmful in a specification language. They acknowledge that predicate subtypes remedy some of the expressiveness limitations of type systems, but argue that subtypes are inherently complicated. Indeed, a sizable fraction of the bugs in early implementations of PVS were due to predicate subtyping in particular, and proof obligation generation, in general. However, these bugs stem largely from minor coding errors rather than foundational issues or complexities. The recently released PVS version 2.3 overcomes most of these problems is quite robust and efficient. Much of the popularity of PVS as a specification framework stems from its effective treatment of predicate subtyping. Predicate subtyping is not a trivial addition to a specification language, but the payoff in terms of expressiveness more than justifies the implementation cost.

The specification language VDM [Jon90] has a notion of *data type invariants* where types can be defined with constraints that are similar to those of predicate subtypes. Typechecking expressions with respect to types constrained with invariants generates proof obligations.[8] In VDM, such invariants are part of the type definition mechanism rather than the type system itself. Since VDM is based on a first-order logic, there is nothing corresponding to a higher-order predicate subtype. Dependent types are absent from the VDM type system. VDM treats partiality with a 3-valued logic instead of subtyping.

Systems like HOL [GM93] and Isabelle/HOL [Pau94] are based on Church's simply typed higher-order logic [Chu40]. These have the advantage that the implementations are simple and reliable. PVS extends the simple type system in a number of ways, but these extensions are well supported by means of the proof automation in PVS. PVS has been compared with HOL by Gordon [Gor95] and with Isabelle by Griffioen and Huisman [GH98]. The type systems of PVS and Nuprl [CAB$^+$86] have been compared by Jackson [Jac96].

[8] To quote Jones [Jon90]:

> This [the concept of data type invariants] has a profound consequence for the type mechanism of the notation. In programming languages, it is normal to associate type checking with a simple compiler algorithm. The inclusion of a sub-typing mechanism which allows truth-valued functions forces the type checking here to rely on proofs.

Dependent type theories were introduced as a formalization of constructive logics based on the Curry-Howard isomorphism. Constructive logics like AUTOMATH [dB80], Nuprl [CAB+86], and Coq [DFH+91] feature dependent typing in their type system. The dependencies in these logics are different from those in the PVS type system. In PVS, the dependencies can only affect the predicates in a type but not its structure. For example, the type $[n : nat \rightarrow A^n]$ cannot be defined in PVS. Whereas, the constructive type theories admit dependent types where the structure of the range can depend on the value of the argument. Nuprl also has a form of predicate subtyping but it does not separate typechecking into an algorithmic component and proof obligation generation: all typechecking is carried out within a proof by invoking the type rules. Coq has a fully polymorphic type system whereas PVS features only a limited degree of polymorphism through type parametricity at the theory level. Nuprl also has a hierarchy of type universes where the terms at each level are assigned types at the next level in the hierarchy. PVS on the other hand admits no reasoning at the level of types so that even type equivalence is algorithmically reduced to an ordinary proof obligation.

Algebraic specification languages [FGJM85a,Mos98] typically employ multi-sorted first-order logics. In contrast, PVS is based on a more expressive higher-order logic. In algebraic specification languages, subsorting is analogous to subtyping in PVS. However, the subsorting is not enforced so that, e.g., division by zero is allowed, and in the case of programming languages such as OBJ and Maude simply results in a runtime error. In the case of specification languages such as CASL, proofs involving partial terms tend to require definedness arguments. In principal, this is the same as dealing with PVS proof obligations, but in practice the PVS judgement mechanism greatly reduces the burden on the user.

7 Conclusions

We have argued that predicate subtypes are a fundamental and important extension to a specification language. They allow partial operations such as division to be given as total operations over a subtype. Properties of the result of an operation can be cached in the type. For example, `mod`(a, b) can be defined so that b must be positive, and the result `mod`(a, b) is at most b. In PVS, there are no restrictions on the predicates that can be used to construct predicate subtypes. Typechecking with predicate subtypes is undecidable in general. PVS separates typechecking in the presence of predicate subtypes into simple typechecking and proof obligation generation. An expression is not considered type-correct unless all generated proof obligations have been discharged.

Dependent typing allows the predicates in one component of a compound type to be defined in terms of the other components. With the combination of predicate subtyping and dependent typing, a substantial part of the specification of an operation can be embedded in its type.

With recursive datatypes, several problems associated with the use of multiple-constructor datatypes can be avoided through the use of predicate subtyping. Proof obligations ensure that an accessor is never improperly applied.

A substantial fragment of the PVS language is executable. An execution engine has been implemented for PVS by means of code generation from PVS to Common Lisp [Sha99]. The PVS type system ensures that the execution of every well-typed ground term is safe, i.e., the only possible runtime error occurs when some resource bound has been exhausted. Annotations derived from subtype information also yield an efficiency improvement of about 30%. For example, if the type of a PVS ground term is known to be positive and smaller than the Common Lisp `fixnum` type, a declaration may be added to the generated code that allows the compiler to omit some runtime checks. On some hardware simulation examples, the generated code executes at roughly a fifth of the speed of hand-crafted C.

In summary, PVS is an experimental effort aimed at supporting the development of expressive specifications for both human and machine consumption. Experiments with PVS reveal that subtyping is a crucial language feature that supports expressiveness, clarity, safety, and deductive automation. It merits close consideration for programming languages as well as specification languages.

References

And86. Peter B. Andrews. *An Introduction to Logic and Type Theory: To Truth through Proof.* Academic Press, New York, NY, 1986. 38

Bar78. H. P. Barendregt. *The Lambda Calculus, its Syntax and Semantics.* North-Holland, Amsterdam, 1978. 45

CAB+86. R. L. Constable, S. F. Allen, H. M. Bromley, W. R. Cleaveland, J. F. Cremer, R. W. Harper, D. J. Howe, T. B. Knoblock, N. P. Mendler, P. Panangaden, J. T. Sasaki, and S. F. Smith. *Implementing Mathematics with the Nuprl Proof Development System.* Prentice Hall, Englewood Cliffs, NJ, 1986. 38, 48, 49

Car97. Luca Cardelli. Type systems. In *Handbook of Computer Science and Engineering*, chapter 103, pages 2208–2236. CRC Press, 1997. Available at `http://www.research.digital.com/SRC`. 39, 41

CDE+99. M. Clavel, F. Durán, S. Eker, P. Lincoln, N. Martí-Oliet, J. Meseguer, and J. F. Quesada. Maude: Specification and programming in rewriting logic. Technical Report CDRL A005, Computer Science Laboratory, SRI International, March 1999. 38

Chu40. A. Church. A formulation of the simple theory of types. *Journal of Symbolic Logic*, 5:56–68, 1940. 38, 48

CJ90. J. H. Cheng and C. B. Jones. On the usability of logics which handle partial functions. In Carroll Morgan and J. C. P. Woodcock, editors, *Proceedings of the Third Refinement Workshop*, pages 51–69. Springer-Verlag Workshops in Computing, 1990. 41

dB80. N. G. de Bruijn. A survey of the project Automath. In *To H. B. Curry: Essays on Combinatory Logic, Lambda Calculus and Formalism*, pages 589–606. Academic Press, 1980. 49

DFH+91. Gilles Dowek, Amy Felty, Hugo Herbelin, Gérard Huet, Christine Paulin-Mohring, and Benjamin Werner. The COQ proof assistant user's guide: Version 5.6. Rapports Techniques 134, INRIA, Rocquencourt, France, December 1991. 38, 49

FGJM85a. Kokichi Futatsugi, Joseph Goguen, Jean-Pierre Jouannaud, and José Meseguer. Principles of OBJ2. In Brian K. Reid, editor, *12th ACM Symposium on Principles of Programming Languages*, pages 52–66. Association for Computing Machinery, 1985. 49

FGJM85b. M. Futatsugi, J. Goguen, J-P. Jouanaud, and J. Meseguer. Principles of OBJ2. In *Proceedings of the 12th ACM Symposium on Principles of Programming*, 1985. 38

Fre67a. G. Frege. Begriffsschrift, a formula language, modeled upon that of arithmetic, for pure thought, 1967. First published 1879. 37

Fre67b. G. Frege. Letter to Russell, 1967. Written 1902. 37

GH98. David Griffioen and Marieke Huisman. A comparison of PVS and Isabelle/HOL. In Jim Grundy and Malcolm Newey, editors, *Theorem Proving in Higher Order Logics: 11th International Conference, TPHOLs '98*, volume 1479 of *Lecture Notes in Computer Science*, pages 123–142, Canberra, Australia, September 1998. Springer-Verlag. 48

GM93. M. J. C. Gordon and T. F. Melham, editors. *Introduction to HOL: A Theorem Proving Environment for Higher-Order Logic*. Cambridge University Press, Cambridge, UK, 1993. 38, 48

Gor95. Mike Gordon. Notes on PVS from a HOL perspective. Available at `http://www.cl.cam.ac.uk/users/mjcg/PVS.html`, August 1995. 48

Jac96. Paul Jackson. Undecidable typing, abstract theories and tactics in Nuprl and PVS (tutorial). In Joakim von Wright, Jim Grundy, and John Harrison, editors, *Theorem Proving in Higher Order Logics: 9th International Conference, TPHOLs '96*, volume 1125 of *Lecture Notes in Computer Science*, Turku, Finland, August 1996. Springer-Verlag. 48

Jon90. Cliff B. Jones. *Systematic Software Development Using VDM*. Prentice Hall International Series in Computer Science. Prentice Hall, Hemel Hempstead, UK, second edition, 1990. 38, 48

Lev90. William J. Leveque. *Elementary Theory of Numbers*. Dover, 1990. Originally published by Addison-Wesley, 1962. 44

LP99. Leslie Lamport and Lawrence C. Paulson. Should your specification language be typed? *ACM Transactions on Programming Languages and Systems*, 21(3):133–169, May 1999. 48

Mos98. Peter D. Mosses. CASL: A guided tour of its design. In José Luiz Fiadeiro, editor, *Recent Trends in Algebraic Specification Languages*, number 1589 in Lecture Notes in Computer Science, pages 216–240. Springer Verlag, 1998. 38, 49

ORSvH95. Sam Owre, John Rushby, Natarajan Shankar, and Friedrich von Henke. Formal verification for fault-tolerant architectures: Prolegomena to the design of PVS. *IEEE Transactions on Software Engineering*, 21(2):107–125, February 1995. 38

OS93. Sam Owre and Natarajan Shankar. Abstract datatypes in PVS. Technical Report SRI-CSL-93-9R, Computer Science Laboratory, SRI International, Menlo Park, CA, December 1993. Extensively revised June 1997; Also available as NASA Contractor Report CR-97-206264. 38

OS97. Sam Owre and Natarajan Shankar. The formal semantics of PVS. Technical Report SRI-CSL-97-2, Computer Science Laboratory, SRI International, Menlo Park, CA, August 1997. 38, 39, 40, 45

Pau94. L. C. Paulson. *Isabelle: A Generic Theorem Prover*, volume 828 of *Lecture Notes in Computer Science*. Springer-Verlag, 1994. 48

ROS98. John Rushby, Sam Owre, and N. Shankar. Subtypes for specifications: Predicate subtyping in PVS. *IEEE Transactions on Software Engineering*, 24(9):709–720, September 1998. 38

Rus67. Bertrand Russell. Letter to Frege, 1967. Written 1902. 37

Rus93. John Rushby. Formal methods and the certification of critical systems. Technical Report SRI-CSL-93-7, Computer Science Laboratory, SRI International, Menlo Park, CA, December 1993. Also issued under the title *Formal Methods and Digital Systems Validation for Airborne Systems* as NASA Contractor Report 4551, December 1993. 38

Sha99. N. Shankar. Efficiently executing PVS. Project report, Computer Science Laboratory, SRI International, Menlo Park, CA, November 1999. Available at `http://www.csl.sri.com/shankar/PVSeval.ps.gz`. 50

Spi88. J. M. Spivey. *Understanding Z: A Specification Language and its Formal Semantics*. Cambridge Tracts in Theoretical Computer Science 3. Cambridge University Press, Cambridge, UK, 1988. 38

vH67. Jean van Heijenoort, editor. *From Frege to Gödel*. Harvard University Press, Cambridge, MA, 1967.

WR27. A. N. Whitehead and B. Russell. *Principia Mathematica*. Cambridge University Press, Cambridge, revised edition, 1925–1927. Three volumes. The first edition was published 1910–1913. 37

Extending Casl by Late Binding*

Davide Ancona, Maura Cerioli, and Elena Zucca

DISI - Università di Genova
Via Dodecaneso, 35, 16146 Genova (Italy)
fax: +39-10-3536699
{davide,cerioli,zucca}@disi.unige.it

Abstract. We define an extension of CASL, the standard language for algebraic specification, with a *late binding* mechanism. More precisely, we introduce a special kind of functions called *methods*, for which, differently to what happens for usual functions, overloading resolution is delayed at evaluation time and not required to be conservative. The extension consists, at the semantic level, in the definition of an institution $\mathcal{LB}$ supporting late binding which is defined on top of the standard subsorted institution of CASL and, at the linguistic level, in the enrichment of the CASL language with appropriate constructs for dealing with methods.

In addition to this, we propose a further enrichment of the CASL language which is made possible by introduction of late binding, that is a mechanism for "inheriting" axioms from a supersort with the possibility of overriding them. The aim is to obtain advantages in terms of reuse of specifications similar to those obtained by inheritance in object-oriented programming languages.

1 Introduction

In [ACZ99], we have introduced a specification formalism (formally, an institution) providing a notion of *dynamic type* of a term (a type determined only during evaluation) and *late binding* (that is, the function version to be invoked in a function application depends on the dynamic type of one or more arguments). Differently from subsorted approaches, where overloading is statically solved and required to be *conservative* (that is, functions with the same name must coincide on the common domain), in this formalism overloading resolution is delayed at evaluation time and there are no constraints. Our main motivation was to provide a natural formal framework for modeling object-oriented and other dynamically-typed languages and a basis for developing a specification language especially suited for them.

Though in [ACZ99] we gave a concrete presentation based on partial algebras with Horn clauses, the formalism we have introduced is, actually, partly

* Partially supported by Murst - Tecniche formali per la specifica, l'analisi, la verifica, la sintesi e la trasformazione di sistemi software and by CoFI WG, ESPRIT Working Group 29432

D. Bert, C. Choppy, and P. Mosses (Eds.): WADT'99, LNCS 1827, pp. 53–72, 2000.

"institution-independent", in the sense that the new notions of dynamic type and late binding can be "added" to different formalisms providing some ingredients. Hence, it was quite natural to investigate the possibility of enriching by these notions the Common Algebraic Specification Language CASL [Casl], the standard language for algebraic specification designed within the Common Framework Initiative (see `http://www.brics.dk/Projects/CoFI/`). This is the work we present in this paper, and is very much in the spirit of one of CASL's design principles, which was the possibility of defining extended versions of the specification language particularly suited for specific aims.

The contribution of the paper can be summarized as follows.

In Sect. 3 we define an institution $\mathcal{LB}$ supporting late binding. The definition of $\mathcal{LB}$ is based on the ideas already presented in [ACZ99]; however, in order to obtain a formalism which smoothly fits in the CASL underlying institution of subsorted signatures and models ($\mathcal{SUB}$ in the following) we adopt quite different technical solutions. We introduce a special kind of functions called *methods* (with a distinguished argument, called the *receiver*), and a *most specific membership* test ($t \overset{ms}{\in} s$ means that s is a most specific type of t), in addition to the membership test already present in CASL ($t \in s$ means that s is a type of t). Methods are semantically interpreted by a family of functions, called *method versions*, one for each existing subsort of the receiver's sort plus one more version, called *dynamic*. In method calls, written $t.m(t_1, \ldots, t_n)$, the version of the method which will be selected is determined not by the type of the term t (which is statically known), as it happens in overloaded functions, but by the most specific type of the element obtained evaluating t, that is, the binding is delayed to evaluation time. Technically, this is achieved interpreting m by its dynamic version, which is by definition equal to the version with index r on elements having r as most specific type. We also provide an alternative form of method calls, called *static*, written $t.m[r](t_1, \ldots, t_n)$: in this case the binding is static and the version with index r is always selected.

The framework we have briefly outlined above, while keeping the expressive power of the formalism in [ACZ99], has the great advantage that $\mathcal{LB}$ can be easily defined "on top" of $\mathcal{SUB}$ in the same way as $\mathcal{SUB}$ is defined in [BCH+99] on top of the standard institution $\mathcal{MS}$ of the many-sorted signatures and models; formally, we define a functor $\_^\sharp$ mapping each signature Σ from $\mathcal{SUB}$ into a subsorted theory $\Sigma^\sharp$ where axioms formalize properties related to late binding.

In Sect. 4 we define an extension LBCASL of the CASL language where we introduce new constructs related to late binding: method declarations, the two forms of method calls mentioned above and the most specific membership test.

The semantics for LBCASL can be defined as an "extension" of the semantics of CASL, in the following sense.

- The semantics of a LBCASL specification is defined as a pair consisting of a signature Σ and a set of models for Σ in the institution $\mathcal{LB}$.

- The semantics is inductively defined by a set of clauses following the abstract syntax; in particular, the semantics of "old" constructs (i.e., constructs already present in CASL) is obtained by a canonical extension of "old" clauses.

The situation is summarized in the following (informal) diagram:

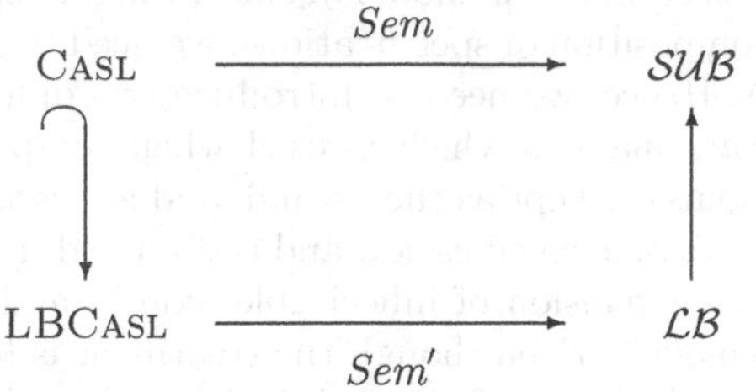

where the left vertical arrow represents the embedding of CASL into LBCASL, *Sem* and *Sem′* represent the "old" and "new" semantics and the right vertical arrow represents the definition of $\mathcal{LB}$ on top of $\mathcal{SUB}$.

Finally, in Sect. 5, we deal with a different problem. In our framework, an axiom, say *ax*, may contain explicit references to a sort, say *s*, in most specific membership test and static method calls, where *s* denotes the version to be invoked. That allows *ax*, from the methodological point of view, to express properties that are required to hold only for elements which have *s* as most specific type, but not for elements of subtypes of *s*, i.e., properties which are, in a sense, non-conservative, but type-specific. However, in many practical situations, it happens that some property is required to hold for *s* and for all the subtypes of *s*, except for a few cases where the property is, in some sense, replaced by another. In these cases the user would be forced to write a "copy" of the axiom *ax* for each subsort s' of *s* for which the property still holds. An alternative possibility, which we investigate in this section, is to provide a syntactic mechanism for "inheriting" axioms, that is, a convention allowing the user to write just one axiom referring to a sort *s* and identified by a name; this axiom is automatically expanded to a set of axioms, one for each subsort s' of *s* for which no axiom with the same name is specified. Axioms of this kind are called *inheritable.*

Note that this mechanism, which mimics inheritance of definitions in object-oriented languages, turns out to be useful especially when composing specifications: indeed, what happens is that inheritable axioms of one specification propagates to new subtypes introduced by the other, unless differently specified, and conversely. Of course it is left to the user the responsability of choosing, for each situation, the suitable kind of axioms: a "traditional" axiom with no use of type-specific ingredients (most specific membership and static method versions) expresses a conservative property, expected to hold for all the - possibly future - subsorts of a sort *s*; using type-specific ingredients in a non inheritable axiom expresses a property expected to hold for *exactly* the sort *s*; if the axiom is inheritable, then the property is expected to hold for s and all the possible future subsorts where no alternative property is explicitly stated.

The introduction of inheritable axioms leads to the necessity of changing the model semantics of LBCASL specifications. Indeed, it is no longer possible to interpret a specification as a set of models (forgetting the set of axioms which has determined the selection of the models), since, roughly speaking, in order to correctly deal with composition of specifications, we need to have the inheritable axioms of arguments. Hence, we need to introduce two different semantics of a specification, an *open* semantics which is used when composing specifications, where inheritable axioms are kept as they stand, and a *closed* semantics which is the end-user's semantics of a specification and is obtained from the open semantics by performing the expansion of inheritable axioms and, finally, taking the corresponding set of models. Even though the treatment is technically different, the underlying idea is the same of the well-known semantics of inheritance in object-oriented languages due to [Coo89,Red88].

Note that deduction, which is performed at the end-user level, naturally uses the closed semantics. A possibility for achieving for proofs the same reusability as we have for specifications is to lift the deduction at the open semantics level, keeping track of the dependency of proofs on the individual inheritable axioms, since any of them could be overridden.

2 Background and Technical Preliminaries

As we are enriching the algebraic language CASLin order to support late binding, let us start with a very short introduction about CASLand its semantics.

The specification language CASLhas been designed within the CoFIinitiative (see `http://www.brics.dk/Projects/CoFI/`), an open group, including some 30 leading researchers in algebraic specification, with representatives from almost all the European groups working in this area recently evolved in a working group (ESPRIT Working Group 29432).

CASLhas been planned from the beginning as a family of languages coherent on the common parts and what we call CASLshould be more precisely called *basic* CASL. The present paper has to be understood as a preliminary investigation on the feasibility of a late binding extension of CASLthat, if successful, would lead to a cooperative formal proposal, accordingly to the procedure established by the *language design* task group.

The main features of CASLthat we will be using in the sequel are the following[1].

[1] This section has no pretension of describing either the syntax or the semantics of CASL(for which we refer to [Casl,BCH+99] or to the web site `http://www.brics.dk/Projects/CoFI/Documents/CASL/Summary/index.html`) and is thought as a reminder for readers already familiar with CASL.

Basic specifications allow the declaration (definition) of sorts, subsorts, functions (both partial and total) and predicates. Terms are built, starting from typed variables, by applying functions to terms of any subsort of the expected argument sort (that is, cohercion to the supersort is implicit) or projecting a term t of some sort onto a subsort s (t *as* s). Terms are used to state axioms, that are first-order formulae built from equations, predicate applications (with the same rules as for function application), definedness assertions, and membership predicates.

Let us consider, as an example, the specification SP_1 of an interpreter for a functional language driven by the rules of its reduction semantics. We expect the signature of SP_1 to contain the sort *term* and *var* corresponding to the expressions and variables of the language, respectively, and some standard functions and predicates over terms:

sorts *term*, *var*, *app*, *abs*
$\quad$ $var < term,\ app, abs < term$
ops $reduce : term \to ?\ term$
$\quad$ $subst : term, var, term \to term$
$\quad$ $fst, snd : app \to term$
$\quad$ $binder : abs \to var$
$\quad$ $body : abs \to term$
pred $normal\_form : term$
$\quad$ $closed : term$

The partial function *reduce* corresponds to term reduction into normal form, whereas $subst(t_1, v, t_2)$ returns the term corresponding to $t_1[t_2/v]$ (capture avoiding substitution). The meaning of the two predicates is straightforward. The sorts *app* and *abs* correspond to application (with selectors *fst* and *snd*) and abstraction (with selectors *binder* and *body*), respectively.

Let us consider now some standard axioms for SP_1:

var $t, t_1, t_2, d : term;\ v : var;\ p : app;\ b : abs;$
axioms

$$normal\_form(t) \Leftrightarrow reduce(t) = t$$
$$closed(t_1) \Rightarrow subst(t_1, v, t_2) = t_1$$
$$(CBN)\ reduce(fst(p)) = t_1 \wedge snd(p) = t_2 \wedge t_1\ as\ abs = b \wedge binder(b) = v \wedge body(b) = d \Rightarrow reduce(p) = reduce(subst(d, v, t_2))$$

The first axiom states that a term is in normal form if and only if the reduction does not affect it, whereas the second states that closed terms are not affected by substitution. These are very general properties that we expect to hold for every implementation and every term.

We call these axioms *conservative axioms* since they state properties that are conserved by all possible subsorts of the sorts involved. Clearly, conservative axioms do not cause problems when trying to extend the specification. In particular, they must hold also for every new kind of term furtherly added to the language by extending SP_1 with new subsorts of *term*.

Finally, note that the policy adopted for application is call by name, as shown by axiom (CBN).

The semantics of a basic specification consists of a signature of the form $(S, TF, PF, P, \leq)$, where $\leq$ is the *subsorting relation*, and a class of many-sorted partial first-order structures, i.e., algebras where the functions are partial (the interpretations of symbols from PF) or total (the interpretations of symbols from TF), and where also predicates (interpretations of symbols from P) are allowed. Subsort inclusions are represented as embeddings, with the natural requirement that any composition of embeddings is an embedding.

An important point to keep in mind about subsorting is the treatment of overloading. In CASLthere are no restrictions on overloaded declaration of functions (and predicates). But, if we have two declarations of the same function symbol f (let us, for simplicity, consider the unary case)

ops $f : s_1 \to s'_1$
$f : s_2 \to s'_2$

with common arguments, that is, there exists a common subsort s for s_1 and s_2, and the result types are "compatible", that is, there exists a supersort s' of s'_1 and s'_2, then the applications of the two versions of f to any element in s when embedded into s' must coincide. Graphically, this property corresponds to the commutativity of the following diagram, where hook arrows represent embeddings.

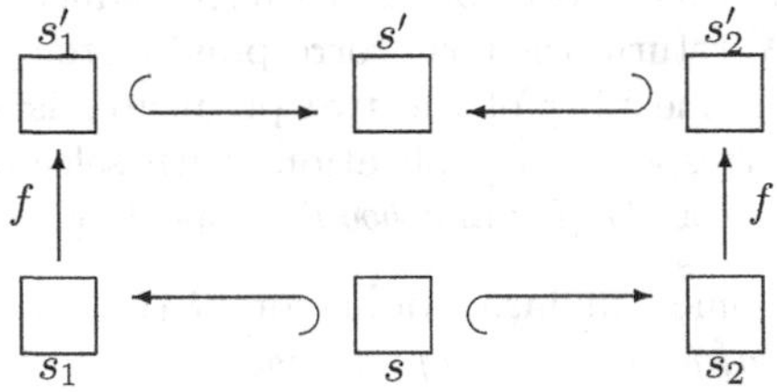

Structured specifications provide constructs for translation, reduction, union, (free) extension[2] of specifications. Generic specifications may also be defined.

The semantics of structured specifications belongs to the same domain as that of basic specifications; more precisely, it is given in a way that extends whichever semantics given for the basic case providing the following ingredients:

- an *institution*, giving the basic ingredients (signatures, models and sentences). In the current CASLsemantics, the underlying institution $\mathcal{SUB}$ is that of partial first-order structures described above.
- a set of *symbols*, representing the names of the parts of signatures interpreting sorts, functions and predicates, together with a functor associating each signature with the set of symbols used in it. This ingredient is required in

[2] Initiality is a special case of this construction.

order to describe symbol maps for parameter fitting and translation of specifications (hiding and revealing as well) and to deal with overloading across signatures, for instance in union.

In the current CASLsemantics, the symbol functor on a signature yields, roughly speaking, the set of fully qualified function and predicate symbols (endowed with the information about totality for the case of functions) united with the set of sorts.

In CASLthere are also *architectural specifications* and *specifications libraries*, but their role is not central to the scope of this paper.

3 Conceptual Tools

In this section we formally define the institution with late binding $\mathcal{LB}$ on top of the subsorted institution $\mathcal{SUB}$. The basic idea behind this construction is to enrich the notion of signature, by adding an extra component of *methods*, which are a special kind of functions with a distinguished argument (the receiver). Then, such signatures are mapped to subsorted theories, and models and sentences for them are defined as subsorted models and sentences for such theories, respectively. This construction is analogous to that used in [BCH+99] to build the subsorted institution on top of the many sorted (partial first order) one.

Definition 1. *A* signature with late binding *(shortly,* LB-signature*)* $\Sigma = (S, TF, PF, P, \leq, M)$ *consists of a subsorted signature* $(S, TF, PF, P, \leq)$ *and a family* $M = \{M_{rws}\}$ *of sets of* method symbols, *one for each* method profile (r, w, s), *consisting of a* receiver sort $r \in S$, *a sequence of* argument sorts $w \in S^*$ *and a* result sort $s \in S$.

Given an LB-signature, for each $m \in M_{rws}$ we will use the *fully qualified* symbol $r.m_{ws}$, in order to avoid ambiguities due to overloading.

Overloading among methods is analogous to that among functions, while, as we will discuss in the following, different method versions can have different interpretation in a model.

Given an LB-signature, for each $m \in M_{r_1 w_1 s_1} \cap M_{r_2 w_2 s_2}$, we say that two fully qualified method symbols $r_1.m_{w_1 s_1}$ and $r_2.m_{w_2 s_2}$ are in the *overloading relation* (written $r_1.m_{w_1 s_1} \sim_M r_2.m_{w_2 s_2}$) iff there exist $w \in S^*$ and $r, s \in S$ such that[3] $w \leq w_1, w_2$, $r \leq r_1, r_2$ and $s_1, s_2 \leq s$.

Definition 2. *Let* $\Sigma = (S, TF, PF, P, \leq, M)$, $\Sigma' = (S', TF', PF', P', \leq', M')$ *be LB-signatures; an* LB-signature morphism $(\sigma^S, \sigma^{TF}, \sigma^{PF}, \sigma^P, \sigma^M)$ *consists of*

[3] Here and in the following, the subsorting relation is extended to sort sequences in the natural way, that is, $w \leq w'$ iff $w = s_1 \ldots s_n$ and $w' = s'_1 \ldots s'_n$ have the same length n and $s_i \leq s'_i$ for each $i = 1, \ldots, n$.

a subsorted signature morphism $(\sigma^S, \sigma^{TF}, \sigma^{PF}, \sigma^P)$ *from* $(S, TF, PF, P, \leq)$ *into* $(S', TF', PF', P', \leq')$ *and, for each method profile* (r, w, s)*, a mapping* σ^M_{rws} *between the corresponding sets of methods* $\sigma^M = \{\sigma^M_{rws} : M_{rws} \rightarrow M'_{\sigma^S(r)\sigma^S(w)\sigma^S(s)}\}$ *preserving the overloading relation, that is, s.t.* $r_1.m_{1\,w_1 s_1} \sim_M r_2.m_{2\,w_2 s_2}$ *implies*

$$\sigma^S(r_1).\sigma^M_{r_1 w_1 s_1}(m_1)_{\sigma^S(w_1)\sigma^S(s_1)} \sim_M \sigma^S(r_2).\sigma^M_{r_2 w_2 s_2}(m_2)_{\sigma^S(w_2)\sigma^S(s_2)}.$$

Notice that the preservation of the overloading relation is equivalent to the requirement that any two qualified method symbols that are in the overloading relation are translated into the same symbol.

Proposition 1. *The composition of LB-signature morphisms does indeed yield an LB-signature morphism.*

Proof. *Straightforward.*

Proposition 2. *LB-signatures and LB-signature morphisms form a finitely cocomplete category,* **LBSig**.

Proof. *It is easy to see that* **LBSig** *is a category. Regarding finite cocompleteness, the proof is a straightforward generalization of that for the category of subsorted signatures (see, e.g., [BCH+ 99]).*

Now we expand LB-signatures into subsorted theories, transforming each method in a family of partial functions, one for each existing subtype of the receiver's type plus the dynamic one, *with different names*, so that the requirement of conservativity for overloading does not apply to different versions of the same method.

Formally, the transformation is performed via two functions *dv* (for *dynamic version*) from method names into partial functions names and *sv* (for *static version*) from pairs (m, s) into partial function names, where m is the method name and s is the sort that we want to statically select, that has also to be (one of) the receiver's sort(s). Moreover, a family of predicate symbols expressing most specific membership is added, via a function *ms_in* from sort into predicate symbols.

Definition 3. *With each LB-signature* $\Sigma = (S, TF, PF, P, \leq, M)$*, a subsorted signature* $\Sigma^{LB} = (S, TF, PF^{LB}, P^{LB}, \leq)$ *is associated, where*

$$PF^{LB}_{ws} = \begin{cases} PF_{ws} \cup \\ \qquad \{dv(m) \mid m \in M_{rw's}\} \cup & \text{if } w = \langle rw' \rangle \\ \qquad\qquad \{sv(m, r) \mid m \in M_{r'w's}, r \leq r'\} & \\ PF_{ws} & \text{otherwise} \end{cases}$$

$$P^{LB}_{w} = \begin{cases} P_w \cup \{ms\_in(s) \mid s \leq s'\} & \text{if } w = \langle s' \rangle \\ P_w & \text{otherwise} \end{cases}$$

All the new symbols ($dv(m)$, $sv(m,r)$ and $ms\_in(s)$) are chosen in a way to be distinct and not already in use in the signature.

Each $sv(m,r)$ is called the static version *of m of type r and $dv(m)$ is called the* dynamic version *of m; moreover, each $ms\_in(s)$ is called the* most specific membership in s predicate *and if $ms\_in(s)$ holds on an element e, we say that e has s as* most specific type.

Notice that an element may have several most specific types or none (the intuition is in the former case that the element belongs to their intersection, in the latter that no most specific type of the element is visible in the signature).

Overloading among static and dynamic versions of methods is equivalent to overloading among the corresponding methods, as shown by the following lemma. This property guarantees that the expansion of LB-signatures to subsorted signatures is functorial.

Lemma 1. *Given an LB-signature Σ, the following facts are equivalent*

1. *$r_1.m_{1w_1s_1}$ and $r_2.m_{2w_2s_2}$ are in the overloading relation in Σ*
2. *$sv(m_1,r)_{\langle rw_1\rangle s_1}$ and $sv(m_2,r)_{\langle rw_2\rangle s_2}$ are in the overloading relation in Σ^{LB} for any $r \le r_1, r_2$;*
3. *$dv(m_1)_{\langle r_1w_1\rangle s_1}$ and $dv(m_2)_{\langle r_2w_2\rangle s_2}$ are in the overloading relation in Σ^{LB};*

Proof. *Let us proof that 1 implies 3. Indeed, $r_1.m_{1w_1s_1} \sim_M r_2.m_{2w_2s_2}$ implies that $m_1 = m_2$ and there exist $w \in S^*$ and $r, s \in S$ such that $w \le w_1, w_2$, $r \le r_1, r_2$ and $s_1, s_2 \le s$. Therefore, $dv(m_1) = dv(m_2)$ and there exist $wr \in S^*$ and $s \in S$ such that $wr \le w_1r_1, w_2r_2$ and $s_1, s_2 \le s$, i.e., $dv(m_1)_{\langle r_1w_1\rangle s_1} \sim_F dv(m_2)_{\langle r_2w_2\rangle s_2}$.*

Analogously it can be proved that 3 implies 1 and that 1 is equivalent to 2.

Definition 4. *Any LB-signature morphism $\sigma : \Sigma_1 \to \Sigma_2$ expands to a subsorted signature morphism $\sigma^{LB} : \Sigma_1^{LB} \to \Sigma_2^{LB}$, preserving the symbols used for most specific membership and mapping static and dynamic versions of methods along the signature morphism component for methods, that is:*

$$\sigma^{LB^S} = \sigma^S$$
$$\sigma^{LB^{TF}} = \sigma^{TF}$$
$$\sigma^{LB^{PF}}_{ws}(f) = \begin{cases} dv(\sigma^M_{rw's}(m)) & \text{if } w = \langle rw'\rangle \text{ and } f = dv(m) \\ sv(\sigma^M_{r'w's}(m), \sigma^S(r)) & \text{if } w = \langle rw'\rangle \text{ and } f = sv(m,r) \\ & \quad \text{for some } m \in M_{r'w's} \\ \sigma^{PF}_{ws}(f) & \text{otherwise} \end{cases}$$
$$\sigma^{LB^P}_w(p) = \begin{cases} ms\_in(\sigma^S(s)) & \text{if } w = \langle s'\rangle, s \le s' \text{ and } p = ms\_in(s) \\ \sigma^P_w(p) & \text{otherwise} \end{cases}$$

Notice that σ^{LB} is indeed a subsorted signature morphism. The only non-trivial cases to be checked are the translations of method versions and most specific membership.

Since any σ^M must preserve types and σ^S the subsorting relation, it is immediate to see that the definition of $\sigma^{LB^{PF}}$ and σ^{LB^P} yields (total) functions[4]. Moreover, by lemma 1, overloading among static and dynamic versions of methods is equivalent to overloading among the corresponding methods. Thus, as σ^M preserves overloading of methods, $\sigma^{LB^{PF}}$ preserves overloading of static and dynamic versions of methods (besides preserving overloading of the original partial functions). Finally, if $ms\_in(s)_{s_1} \sim_P ms\_in(s)_{s_2}$, for some $s \leq s_1, s_2$, then $ms\_in(\sigma^S(s))_{\sigma^S(s_1)} \sim_P ms\_in(\sigma^S(s))_{\sigma^S(s_2)}$, by definition of $\sim_P$, because $\sigma^S(s) \leq \sigma^S(s_1), \sigma^S(s_2)$ as subsorting is preserved.

Proposition 3. *The construction $\_^{LB}$ is a functor from* **LBSig** *into* **SubSig**.

Proof. Straightforward.

The extension of LB-signatures into subsorted signatures provides us with a language (terms and sentences over the extended signatures) to manipulate methods and most specific membership. Now, we want to use as LB-models all the ordinary subsorted models for the extended signature that satisfy properties capturing our intuition of (the semantics of) late binding. In particular, we want to have that:

- embedding preserves most specific types;
- most specific membership in a subsort implies membership in that subsort[5];
- dynamic versions of methods must coincide with static versions of a given sort over elements which have this sort as most specific type.

The first condition is already guaranteed by conservativity of overloading in the subsorted institution. Indeed, for all $s \leq s' \leq s''$, by definition $ms\_in(s)_{s'} \sim_P ms\_in(s)_{s''}$ and hence we have $ms\_in(s)_{s'}\langle x_{s'}\rangle \Leftrightarrow ms\_in(s)_{s''}\langle em_{\langle s'\rangle s''}\langle x_{s'}\rangle\rangle$ for all $x_{s'}$.

Let us axiomatize the other conditions. In the following axioms we will use *strong equality*, denoted by $\stackrel{s}{=}$, holding iff either both sides denote the same value or both are undefined.

Definition 5. *For each LB-signature $\Sigma = (S, TF, PF, P, \leq, M)$ let $LBAx(\Sigma)$ be the set of conditional sentences over the signature Σ^{LB} consisting of:*

4 In particular, for the static case if $m \in M_{r'w's} \cap M_{r''w's}$ with some $r \leq r', r''$, then $r'.m_{w's} \sim_M r''.m_{w's}$ and hence $\sigma^M_{r'w's}(m) = \sigma^M_{r''w's}(m)$, so that the translation of $sv(m, r)$ is unambiguous.

5 Note that, however, the fact that an element e is a member of a sort s and there is no $s' \leq s$ s.t. e is member of s' does not imply that s is a most specific type of e.

- $\forall x_{s'}.ms\_in(s)_{s'}\langle x_{s'}\rangle \Rightarrow in(s)_{s'}\langle x_{s'}\rangle$ *for all* $s \leq s'$
- $\forall \{x_r, y^1_{s_1} \dots y^n_{s_n}\}.ms\_in(r)_r\langle x_r\rangle \Rightarrow$
$$sv(m,r)_{rws}\langle x_r, y^1_{s_1}, \dots, y^n_{s_n}\rangle \stackrel{s}{=} dv(m)_{r'ws}\langle em_{\langle r\rangle r'}\langle x_r\rangle, y^1_{s_1}, \dots, y^n_{s_n}\rangle$$
for all $m \in M_{r'ws}$, *with* $w = s_1 \dots s_n$, *and* $r \leq r'$.

The *LB-models* for Σ are ordinary subsorted models satisfying the axioms in $LBAx(\Sigma)$.

Definition 6. *Let SubTh be the category of subsorted theories*[6].
Let us define the functor $\_^\sharp$: **LBSig** $\rightarrow$ *SubTh as follows:*

- *for each LB-signature* Σ, *the theory* $\Sigma^\sharp$ *is the pair* $(\Sigma^{LB}, LBAx(\Sigma))$ *and*
- *for each LB-signature morphism* σ, *the subsorted signature morphism* $\sigma^\sharp$ *is* σ^{LB}.

It is straightforward (though boring) to verify that the translation of axioms in $LBAx(\Sigma)$ along σ^{LB} belongs to $LBAx(\Sigma')$ for each LB-signature morphism σ from Σ into Σ'.

Definition 7. *The* institution with late binding $\mathcal{LB}$ *has* **LBSig** *as signature category and sentences LBSen, models* **LBMod** *and validity imported from the corresponding component of the subsorted institution, by composition along* $\_^\sharp$.

4 Constructs

Let us now introduce the abstract and concrete syntax of the constructs of basic specifications with late binding, and describe their intended interpretation, extending what was provided for subsorted specifications in CASL summary and semantics [BCH+99,Casl]. We mostly add productions to the part of CASL grammar dealing with *basic items*. In particular we will add constructs for method declaration and application (both static and dynamic) and for testing most specific membership[7].

```
SIG-ITEMS ::=  ...| METH-ITEMS
METH-ITEMS ::=  meth-items METH-ITEM+
METH-ITEM  ::= METH-DECL
```

[6] Objects of *SubTh* are pairs consisting of a subsorted signature and a set of sentences over that signature; morphisms are signature morphisms such that the translation along them of the set of sentences of the source is contained into the set of sentences of the target.

[7] Method definitions (analogous to function definitions) are not described, as their treatment (as in CASLlanguage) reduces to an expansion in terms of declarations and axioms (in this particular case, the most convenient axioms are those described in the next section).

```
METH-DECL ::= meth-decl METH-NAME+ METH-TYPE
METH-NAME ::= ID
METH-TYPE ::= meth-type SORT SORTS SORT
```

A list `METH-ITEMS` of method declarations is written:

meths $MI_1; \ldots\ MI_n;$

each method declaration `METH-DECL` is written:

$m_1, \ldots, m_n : T$

and it declares each method name $m_1, \ldots, m_n$ as a method, with profile as specified by the method type T. Finally each method type `METH-TYPE` is written:

$r, w \rightarrow ?\ s$

Following the definition of semantics for standard CASL, a well-formed basic specification `BASIC-SPEC` of the LBCASL language determines a basic specification of the underlying $\mathcal{LB}$ institution, consisting of an LB-signature and a set of LB-sentences. The models of this signature and set of sentences provide the (model) semantics of the basic specification.

The rules for static and model semantics for LB-constructs are following the style of the definition of semantics for CASL([BCH+99]), slightly modified by adding an extra component, the *method component*, to signatures and signature extensions, that is not modified by the rules.

A LB-extension $\Delta = (S', TF', PF', P', M', \leq')$ relative to an LB-signature $\Sigma = (S, TF, PF, P, \leq, M)$ consists of a (sub-sorted) extension $(S', TF', PF', P', \leq')$ relative to the (sub-sorted) signature $(S, TF, PF, P, \leq)$, and a family M' of sets of method symbols over $S \cup S'$.

The declaration of a list of methods simply adds the methods to the signature.

$$\frac{(S, TF, PF, M, P) = \Sigma \qquad w = \langle s_1, \ldots, s_n \rangle \qquad \{r, s_1, \ldots, s_n, s\} \subseteq S}{\Sigma \vdash \texttt{meth-decl}\ m_1 \ldots m_k\ \texttt{meth-type}\ rws \rhd (\emptyset, \emptyset, \emptyset, \{rws \mapsto \{m_1 \ldots m_k\}\}, \emptyset)}$$

Application of methods is written in a different style[8] w.r.t. total and partial function application: following the tradition of the object-oriented approach, the first argument (receiver) is prefixed to the method name. Moreover, we have two different kinds of application: the *dynamic* one, where the version to be actually called is determined by late binding, and the *static* one, where it is explicitly stated which version has to be used.

```
TERM              ::= ... METH-APPL
METH-APPL         ::= STATIC-METH-APPL | DYNAMIC-METH-APPL
STATIC-METH-APPL  ::= static-meth-appl TERM SORT METH-SYMB TERMS
```

[8] This prevents ambiguity across methods and functions, so that we do not have to deal with this case of overloading.

```
DYNAMIC-METH-APPL ::= dynamic-meth-appl TERM METH-SYMB TERMS
METH-SYMB         ::= METH-NAME | QUAL-METH-NAME
QUAL-METH-NAME    ::= qual-meth-name METH-NAME METH-TYPE
```

A static application of a method symbol m to a receiver t of sort r on some argument terms is written:

$$t.m[r](t_1, \ldots, t_n)$$

while a dynamic application is written

$$t.m(t_1, \ldots, t_n)$$

A dynamic (respectively, static) application is well-sorted for some particular sort s when there is a declaration of m, with the indicated profile if the method name is qualified (and with r subsort of the receiver's sort for that declaration) such that $t_1, \ldots, t_n$ are well-sorted for the respective argument sorts, and the result sort is s. It then expands to an application of the qualified dynamic version (qualified static version of sort r) of m to the fully-qualified expansions of $t_1, \ldots, t_n$ for the argument sorts of m.

Formally, semantic judgments for method application are of the form

$$\boxed{\Sigma, X \vdash \texttt{METH-APPL} \rhd t}$$

where X is required to be a valid set of variables over the sorts of Σ and t is a fully-qualified Σ-term over X; they are defined by the following rules.

$$\frac{\begin{array}{c}\Sigma \vdash \texttt{METH-SYMB} \rhd m, (\langle r, s_1, \ldots, s_n\rangle, s) \\ \Sigma, X \vdash \texttt{TERM} \rhd t \qquad \Sigma, X \vdash \texttt{SORT} \rhd r' \qquad \Sigma, X \vdash \texttt{TERMS} \rhd \langle t_1, \ldots, t_n\rangle \\ sorts(t) = r' \quad r' \leq r \quad sorts(t_1) = s_1 \quad \cdots \quad sorts(t_n) = s_n\end{array}}{\begin{array}{c}\Sigma, X \vdash \texttt{static-meth-appl TERM SORT METH-SYMB TERMS} \rhd \\ sv(m, r')_{\langle r', s_1, \ldots, s_n\rangle, s}\langle t, t_1, \ldots, t_n\rangle\end{array}}$$

$$\frac{\begin{array}{c}\Sigma \vdash \texttt{METH-SYMB} \rhd m, (\langle r, s_1, \ldots, s_n\rangle, s) \\ \Sigma, X \vdash \texttt{TERM} \rhd t \qquad \Sigma, X \vdash \texttt{TERMS} \rhd \langle t_1, \ldots, t_n\rangle \\ sorts(t) = r \quad sorts(t_1) = s_1 \quad \cdots \quad sorts(t_n) = s_n\end{array}}{\Sigma, X \vdash \texttt{dynamic-meth-appl METH-SYMB TERMS} \rhd dv(m)_{\langle r, s_1, \ldots, s_n\rangle, s}\langle t, t_1, \ldots, t_n\rangle}$$

Semantic judgments for method symbols are of the form

$$\boxed{\Sigma \vdash \texttt{METH-SYMB} \rhd f, (rw, s)}$$

(f is a method symbol in Σ with profile (r, w, s)) and are defined by the following rules.

$$\frac{\{r, s_1, \ldots, s_n, s\} \subseteq S \qquad m \in M_{\langle r, s_1, \ldots, s_n\rangle, s}}{(S, TF, PF, M, P, \leq) \vdash m \rhd m, (\langle r, s_1, \ldots, s_n\rangle, s)}$$

$$\frac{\{r, s_1, \ldots, s_n, s\} \subseteq S \qquad m \in M_{\langle r,s_1,\ldots,s_n\rangle,s}}{\begin{array}{l}(S, TF, PF, M, P, \leq) \vdash \\ \quad \texttt{qual-meth-name}\ m\ (\texttt{method-type}\ (\texttt{sort}\ r\ \texttt{sorts}\ s_1 \ldots s_n)\ \texttt{sort}\ s) \rhd \\ \hfill m, (\langle r, s_1, \ldots, s_n\rangle, s))\end{array}}$$

We illustrate now the construct added in formulae, that is, the test for most specific membership.

```
ATOM ::= ... | MOST-SPECIFIC-MEMBERSHIP
MOST-SPECIFIC-MEMBERSHIP ::= most-specific-membership TERM SORT
```

A most specific membership formula is written:

$$t \overset{ms}{\in} s$$

It is well-sorted if the term t is well-sorted for a supersort s' of the specified sort s. It expands to an application of the pre-defined predicate symbol for testing s' values for most specific membership in s.

$$\frac{\Sigma, X \vdash \mathtt{TERM} \rhd t \qquad sorts(t) = s' \qquad s \leq s'}{\Sigma, X \vdash \texttt{most-specific-membership}\ \mathtt{TERM}\ s \rhd ms\_in(s)_{s'}\langle t\rangle}$$

The late binding mechanism turns out to be particularly useful for specifying properties that are non-conservative, that is, are not expected to hold for every possible subsort. Let us illustrate this fact on our running example. Assume that, for instance, we want to extend SP_1 with a sort *app_bv* corresponding to "call by value application". We cannot set *app_bv* < *app* since the previously given axiom corresponding to call by name does not hold for call by value.

Unfortunately, the fact that *app_bv* cannot be a subsort of *app* prevent us to "inherit" all selectors and axioms that hold for both *app* and *app_bv*; everything must be duplicated.

This problem can be avoided, of course, by changing the design from scratch using a supersort of both *app* and *app_bv* where all operations and axioms in common are shared. However, in the framework of late binding it is possible to set *app_bv* < *app* without having the two axioms for call by name and by value in conflict. It is enough to make the call by name axiom applicable only for terms whose most specific sort is *app*. This is shown in the following late binding version of SP_1, where *reduce* is defined as a method (while sorts, other functions and predicates are the same as in SP_1).

meths $reduce : term, \lambda \to ?\ term$

var $p : app;\ b : abs;\ t, t_1, t_2, d : term;\ v : var;$

axioms

$$normal\_form(t) \Leftrightarrow t.reduce() = t$$

$$(cbn)\ fst(p).reduce() = t_1 \wedge snd(p) = t_2 \wedge \\ t_1\ as\ abs = b \wedge binder(b) = v \wedge body(b) = d \wedge p \overset{ms}{\in} app \Rightarrow \\ p.reduce() = subst(d, v, t_2).reduce()$$

The axiom has been changed in order to reflect the new syntax for method invocation. Furthermore, the new condition $p \overset{ms}{\in} app$ has been added in order to specify that this property does hold only for elements whose most specific sort is *app*. Thus, axiom (cbn) does not apply to elements of sort *app_bv* (unless they happen to have *app* as most specific type as well. This can be forbidden, for instance, by an axiom of the form $\forall q : app\_bv . \neg q \overset{ms}{\in} app$).

Structured and Architectural Specification Since the non basic part of CASLis uniformely described in terms of *institutions with symbols* and the institution for LBCASL is very close to the institution of CASL, we need only minor adjustements, in order to be able to use the hierarchical part of CASLon our specifications with late binding.

At the level of basic specifications and their semantics, the only point to be adapted is (as expected) the definition of symbols. Indeed, if we simply define the symbol part for $\mathcal{LB}$ to be inherited from the symbols defined for the institution of CASL, by composition with $\_^{LB}$, we would not have the capability to check that methods are translated into method instead than other partial functions.

Therefore, we have to add a new kind of symbols, that is, the qualified method symbols of the form m^{M}_{rws}.

At the level of structured specifications, symbols are used to define and manage *raw symbols.* A raw symbol may be a symbol, a pair of the form $(implicit, x)$, or for each symbol kind k (where k can be *sort*, *fun*, *pred*) a pair of the form (k, x). Symbols represent uses of fully qualified symbols, (k, x) represent uses of an identifier x that is stated to be of kind k and $(implicit, x)$ represents uses of an identifier x without further information on it. Then, a relation is defined, matching symbols with their possible uses, so that, for instance, any symbol x matches $(implicit, x)$, any sort s matches $(sort, s)$ and so on.

Having introduced a new kind of symbols, we have to add pairs of the form $(meth, m)$ to the raw symbol set, matching, of course, the symbol m^{M}_{rws} if m is a method in the signature with this profile and $(implicit, m)$.

$$\frac{m \in \mathtt{ID}}{meth \vdash m \rhd (meth, m)}$$

$$\frac{m \in \mathtt{ID}}{meth \vdash \mathtt{qual\text{-}id}\, m(\mathtt{meth\text{-}type}\, r\, (\mathtt{sorts}\, s_1, \ldots, s_n)\, s) \rhd m^{M}_{r\, s_1, \ldots, s_n\, s}}$$

At the syntactic level, in order to allow the user to restrict the matching of a symbol only to those occurrences corresponding to a method, we add

```
SYMB-KIND ::= ... | meths
TYPE ::= ...| METH-TYPE
```

5 Inheriting Axioms

As shown by the preceding examples, the framework we have introduced allows one to write axioms expressing type-specific properties, that is, properties which are required to hold *only* for elements having some most specific type s, and not for elements which belong to subtypes. This possibility is new w.r.t. usual algebraic specification formalisms, where expressed properties are conservative, that is, automatically propagated from s to subtypes.

However, in many practical situations it may happen that some property is expected to hold for s and all its subtypes, except for a few cases where the property is, in some sense, replaced by another. In this cases the user would be forced to write "a copy" of the axiom ax for each subsort s' of s for which the property still holds.

For instance, in to our running example, we might find convenient to define a sort *binTerm* of all possible terms having exactly two subterms. In this way, for instance, we can define the two selectors once and for all and use them uniformly, introducing the sorts for all kinds of terms having exactly two subterms as subsorts of *binTerm*.

Since *binTerm* represents a generic kind of terms, it is not easy to find out properties that are guaranteed to hold for *all* elements of possible subsorts. Nevertheless there are properties that we can expect to be satisfied in most cases.

For instance, the predicate *normal_form* will be false for most of the terms having two subterms. Indeed, it is false for all binary arithmetic operators and for application, whereas it may be true for binary constructors. So it seems to be convenient to assert that, by default, *normal_form*(b) does not hold for any element b of sort $s < binTerm$.

In this section, we present a preliminary investigation about the possibility of furtherly enriching the CASL language with a facility for expressing such kind of "default" properties. This proposal is based on the introduction, in addition to usual axioms, of a new kind of axioms, which we call *inheritable*. An inheritable set of axioms differs from a standard CASL set of axioms in three respects: first, it has a distinguishing *name*, say ax; second, it refers to a given sort, say s; third, in the corresponding set of formulae it is allowed to use, at each place where a sort can appear in a CASL formula, a special symbol τ denoting a generic sort. Altogether, a set of inheritable axioms is written:

$$\textbf{inheritable } ax : F_1, \ldots, F_n \textbf{ from } s$$

where $F_1, \ldots, F_n$ are formulae possibly containing τ. The intuitive meaning is that the line above is a shortcut for the following:

axioms

$F_1[s_1/\tau], \ldots, F_n[s_1/\tau]$

$\vdots$

$F_1[s_m/\tau], \ldots, F_n[s_m/\tau]$

where $\_[\_/\_]$ denotes textual replacement and $s_1, \ldots, s_m$ are all the existing subsorts of s for which no set of axioms with the same name has been specified.

We say that the set of axioms *ax* is *inheritable* from *s*; moreover, if there is another set of axioms with the same name inheritable from a subsort s' of s, we say that this set *overrides* the other.

Then, for istance, the sort *binTerm* could be introduced as follows
sorts *binTerm* < *term*
ops *fst*, *snd* : *binTerm* → *term*
inheritable *NF* : $\forall b{:}\tau.\neg normal\_form(b)$ **from** *binTerm*

Assuming that *app* < *binTerm*, we have that axiom (NF) clearly holds also for *app*, therefore there is no need for duplicating it; the special sort symbol τ will be instantiated with *app*.

On the other hand, the axiom has to be overridden in the case of the subsort *pair* of pair constructor (assuming product types in our functional language).
sorts *pair* < *binTerm*
inheritable *NF* : $\forall p{:}\tau.normal\_form(b) \Leftrightarrow$
$normal\_form(fst(b)) \wedge normal\_form(snd(b)))$ **from** *pair*

Formally, the introduction of inheritable axioms corresponds to add the following productions to the CASL abstract syntax.

```
BASIC-ITEMS ::= INH-AXIOMS-ITEMS
INH-AXIOMS-ITEMS ::= inh-axioms-items INH-AXIOMS-ITEM+
INH-AXIOMS-ITEM  ::= inh-axioms-item SORT AXIOMS-NAME INH-FORMULA+
```

where `INH-FORMULA` is defined analogously to `FORMULA`, except that `SORT` is replaced by `SORT-OR-GENERIC` defined by

```
SORT-OR-GENERIC ::= SORT | tau
```

For what concerns model semantics, the introduction of inheritable axioms leads to the necessity of extending the overall interpretation of LBCASL specifications: it is no longer possible to interpret a specification as a set of models. Indeed, as illustrated by the example above, an inheritable axiom actually serves as a "schema" which has to be expanded to a set of usual axioms. However, this expansion can take place only when considering the final (end user's) semantics of a specification, while when applying structuring constructs inheritable axioms must be kept as they stand.

In a different context, the problem is exactly the same of that of giving a formal model of inheritance in programming languages, solved in [Coo89,Red88], and our solution is based on the same idea: the distinction between *open* and *closed* semantics, the former needed in modular composition, the latter as user's semantics.

A further difficulty is caused by the fact that open semantics cannot be correctly defined for some structuring constructs, as reduct and free, since in these cases, roughly speaking, there is no way of safely interpreting the syntactic operator as a transformation of axioms. Hence, we need to distinguish two different kinds of specifications: *virtual* specifications, for which open semantics can be defined, and *frozen* specifications, for which only the closed interpretation is feasible (the terminology comes from the object-oriented approach [Bra92]).

Every virtual specification can be seen (at the stage where it must be effectively used) as frozen via a silent embedding operator which we call *freeze*. Hence, for structuring constructs which do not support an interpretation within open semantics, as reduct and free, we will assume that arguments are implicitly frozen before applying the operator.

We give now an outline of formalization of the ideas described above.

Model semantics for virtual specifications is defined by judgments of the following form:

$$\boxed{\Sigma, \mathcal{M} \vdash \texttt{VIRTUAL-SPEC} \Rightarrow \Phi, \mathcal{M}'}$$

where the $\mathcal{M}'$ component corresponds to the original CASLsemantics (a class of models) and $\Phi \in Sort \times AxiomName \xrightarrow{\text{fin}} FinSet(\texttt{INH-FORMULA})$.

The semantics of basic specifications is obtained by a canonical extension of the rules given in the standard CASL semantics by an empty Φ component which is never modified, except for the new rule related to inheritable axioms.

$$\boxed{\Sigma, X \vdash \texttt{INH-AXIOMS-ITEM} \rhd \Phi}$$

$$\frac{\Sigma \vdash \texttt{INH-FORMULA}_1 \rhd \psi_1, \ldots, \Sigma \vdash \texttt{INH-FORMULA}_n \rhd \psi_n}{\Sigma, X \vdash \texttt{inh-axioms-item}\ s\ \texttt{AXIOMS-NAME}\ \texttt{INH-FORMULA}_1 \ldots \texttt{INH-FORMULA}_n \rhd \{\langle s, \texttt{AXIOMS-NAME}\rangle \mapsto \{\psi_1, \ldots, \psi_n\}\}}$$

In virtual specifications, we consider two example structuring constructs, that is, two different extensions of the original CASLunion of specifications (we consider for simplicity the binary case). The two constructs have the same semantics (that is, that of CASLunion) for what concerns the second component (the class of models), but differ in the way they behave in the case the two arguments have conflicting sets of inheritable axioms (that is, with the same name and from the same sort): the (symmetric) union takes the union of the two sets, while the left preferential union chooses the set of the left argument.

```
VIRTUAL-SPEC ::= BASIC-SPEC |  UNION | LEFT-PREFERENTIAL-UNION ...
```

```
UNION ::= union VIRTUAL-SPEC VIRTUAL-SPEC
LEFT-PREFERENTIAL-UNION ::= left-pref-union VIRTUAL-SPEC VIRTUAL-SPEC
```

Let $\mathcal{M}'$ denote $\{M \in \mathbf{Mod}(\Sigma \cup \Delta) \mid M|_{\Sigma \cup \Delta_i} \in \mathcal{M}_i, i = 1, 2\}$ in both the following rules.

$$\frac{\begin{array}{ccc} \Sigma \vdash SP_1 \rhd \Delta_1 & \Sigma \vdash SP_2 \rhd \Delta_2 & \Delta = \Delta_1 \cup \Delta_2 \\ \Sigma, \mathcal{M} \vdash SP_1 \Rightarrow \Phi_1, \mathcal{M}_1 & \Sigma, \mathcal{M} \vdash SP_2 \Rightarrow \Phi_2, \mathcal{M}_2 & \end{array}}{\Sigma, \mathcal{M} \vdash \texttt{union}\ SP_1\ SP_2 \Rightarrow \{\langle s, ax\rangle \mapsto \Phi_1\langle s, ax\rangle \cup \Phi_2\langle s, ax\rangle\}, \mathcal{M}'}$$

$$\frac{\begin{array}{ccc} \Sigma \vdash SP_1 \rhd \Delta_1 & \Sigma \vdash SP_2 \rhd \Delta_2 & \Delta = \Delta_1 \cup \Delta_2 \\ \Sigma, \mathcal{M} \vdash SP_1 \Rightarrow \Phi_1, \mathcal{M}_1 & \Sigma, \mathcal{M} \vdash SP_2 \Rightarrow \Phi_2, \mathcal{M}_2 & \end{array}}{\Sigma, \mathcal{M} \vdash \texttt{left-pref-union}\ SP_1\ SP_2 \Rightarrow \Phi_2[\Phi_1], \mathcal{M}'}$$

where $\Phi_2[\Phi_1]$ denotes usual substitution on mappings.

Note that in both cases a set of axioms inheritable from a sort s overrides another with the same name inheritable from a supersort s' of s; the only difference is in the way the case $s = s'$ is handled.

We consider now frozen specifications.

```
FROZEN-SPEC ::= FREEZE |  REDUCTION | FREE-SPEC ...
FREEZE ::= freeze VIRTUAL-SPEC
REDUCTION ::= reduction FROZEN-SPEC RESTRICTION
FREE-SPEC ::= free-spec FROZEN-SPEC
```

Model semantics for frozen specifications is defined by judgments of the following form:

$$\boxed{\Sigma, \mathcal{M} \vdash \texttt{FROZEN-SPEC} \Rightarrow \mathcal{M}'}$$

The semantics of all the structuring constructs which require frozen arguments, like reduct and free specifications, is exactly the original CASL semantics.

The semantics of the freeze operator consists in performing expansion of the inheritable axioms, as formalized by the rule below.

$$\frac{\begin{array}{cc} \Sigma \vdash \texttt{VIRTUAL-SPEC} \rhd \Delta : \Sigma \to \Sigma' & \Sigma, \mathcal{M} \vdash \texttt{VIRTUAL-SPEC} \Rightarrow \Phi, \mathcal{M}' \\ \multicolumn{2}{c}{S' = Sort(\Sigma')} \end{array}}{\begin{array}{l} \Sigma, \mathcal{M} \vdash \texttt{freeze VIRTUAL-SPEC} \Rightarrow \\ \{M \in \mathcal{M}' \mid M \models \psi[s/\tau] \text{ for all } \psi \in \Phi^{S'}\langle s, ax\rangle, \text{ for all } \langle s, ax\rangle \in Dom(\Phi^{S'})\} \end{array}}$$

where

- $s \leq^1 s'$ iff $s \leq s'$, $s \neq s'$ and $s \leq s'' \leq s'$ implies $s' \leq s''$
- for each $\Phi \in Sort \times AxiomName \stackrel{\text{fin}}{\to} FinSet(\texttt{INH-FORMULA})$ and each set S of sorts, Φ^S is inductively defined by:

$$\Phi^S\langle s, ax\rangle = \begin{cases} \Phi\langle s, ax\rangle \text{ if } \Phi\langle s, ax\rangle \text{ is defined} \\ \bigcup_{s \leq^1 s'} \Phi^S\langle s', ax\rangle \text{ otherwise} \end{cases}$$

6 Conclusion

In this paper, we have presented an extension of the CASL language which allows the user to use a *most specific membership* predicate and to declare *methods*, that is, special functions for which overloading w.r.t. the first argument is not required to be conservative and is solved at evaluation time. The aim was to make available, together with a style more traditional in algebraic specifications, based on thinking in terms of conservative properties (that is, properties which are preserved by the subtyping relation), a different style based on type-specific properties. This style can be more appealing in the case either the user has a more "object-oriented" way of thinking, or the specification has an object-oriented language as final implementation target.

The proposed extension has the nice property that it smoothly fits in the standard CASL framework, in the sense that it can be completely defined by a canonical expansion into usual CASL specifications.

As already stated, the aim of this paper was to check the feasibility of the extension and to illustrate in a synthetic way all the points which need to be modified in CASL syntax and semantics, in order to be a guide for a possible official extension decided by the language design task group. In particular, we stress again that the mechanism of inheritable axioms proposed in the last section is a further and tentative extension step w.r.t. the contents of preceding sections. However, it has been included since it shows how the late binding framework offers completely new and interesting possibilities in writing and composing specifications.

References

ACZ99. D. Ancona, M. Cerioli, and E. Zucca. A formal framework with late binding. In J.-P. Finance, editor, *Fundamental Approaches to Software Engineering - Second International Conference, FASE'99*, volume 1577 of *Lecture Notes in Computer Science*, pages 30–44. Springer Verlag, 1999. 53, 54

BCH+99. H. Baumeister, M. Cerioli, A. Haxthausen, T. Mossakowski, P. Mosses, D. Sannella, and A. Tarlecki. Formal Methods '99 - CASL, The Common Algebraic Specification Language - Semantics. Available on compact disc published by Springer-Verlag, 1999. 54, 56, 59, 60, 63, 64

Bra92. G. Bracha. *The Programming Language JIGSAW: Mixins, Modularity and Multiple Inheritance.* PhD thesis, Department of Comp. Sci., Univ. of Utah, 1992. 70

Coo89. W. Cook. *A Denotational Semantics of Inheritance.* PhD thesis, Dept. Comp. Sci., Brown University, 1989. 56, 70

Red88. U. S. Reddy. Objects as closures: Abstract semantics of object-oriented languages. In *Proc. ACM Conf. on Lisp and Functional Programming*, pages 289–297, 1988. 56, 70

Casl. The CoFI Task Group on Language Design. Formal Methods '99 - CASL, The Common Algebraic Specification Language - Summary. Available on compact disc published by Springer-Verlag, 1999. 54, 56, 63

Towards an Evolutionary Formal Software-Development Using CASL

Serge Autexier[1], Dieter Hutter[2*], Heiko Mantel[2], and Axel Schairer[3**]

[1] Saarland University
P.O. Box 151150, D-66041 Saarbrücken, Germany
serge@ags.uni-sb.de

[2] German Research Center for Artificial Intelligence
Stuhlsatzenhausweg 3, D-66123 Saarbruecken, Germany
{hutter,mantel}@dfki.de

[3] University of Edinburgh, Division of Informatics
80 South Bridge, Edinburgh EH1 1HN, UK
schairer@dai.ed.ac.uk

Abstract. In practice, the formal development of software is an evolutionary process. Failed proof attempts give rise to changes in the specification and such changes invalidate proofs which have been previously performed. Clearly, it is very desirable to preserve much of the proof effort after such changes. In this paper, we propose development graphs as a general framework for modular specifications and define a structure preserving translation of CASL specifications into these graphs. The feature of development graphs, which is most important for an evolutionary process, is that they simplify the analysis of changes to the specification such that their negative effects can be kept to a minimum.

1 Introduction

It has long been recognized that *specifications in the large* are only manageable if they are built in a structured way. Specification languages, like CASL [CASL98], provide various mechanisms to combine basic specifications to structured specifications. Analogously verification tools have to provide appropriate mechanisms to structure the corresponding logical axiomatizations. In practice, a formal program development is an evolutionary process [VSE96]. Specification and verification are mutually intertwined. Failed proofs give rise to changes of the specification which in turn will render previously found proofs invalid. For practical purposes it is indispensable to restrict the effects of such changes to a minimum in order to preserve as much proof effort as possible after a change of the specification.

Various structuring operations have been proposed (e.g. [DGS91,ST88,ST92]) in order to modularize specifications and proof systems have been described to

* This work was supported by the German Ministry for Education and Technology (BMBF)

** Supported by the German Academic Exchange Service (HSP III)

D. Bert, C. Choppy, and P. Mosses (Eds.): WADT'99, LNCS 1827, pp. 73–88, 2000.

deal with them (e.g. [CM97,HWB97]). Traditionally, the main motivations for modularization have been the sharing of sub-specifications within one specification, the reuse of specifications, and the structuring of proof obligations as well as applicable lemmas. However, the structure of specifications can also be exploited when the effects of changes are analyzed.

In this paper, we substantiate this claim for CASL specifications [CASL98], an emerging standard for algebraic specification languages. We show how the effects of changes can be computed such that much proof effort is preserved. Basically, this is achieved by a two step process. Firstly, any change of the specification is decomposed into smaller changes which each affect only a single module of the specification. Secondly, the effects of these local changes are analyzed based on the structure of the overall specification.

Development graphs (DG) constitute the representational framework on which all of our investigations are based. Each node of a DG corresponds to a specification module and defines a logical theory, i.e. a signature, a consequence relation, and a set of local axioms. The directed links in the graph relate theories to each other via consequence morphisms. Links are classified using two dimensions. In one dimension, the distinction between definition and theorem links allows one to distinguish between properties given by definition and properties to be checked by verification. The other dimension is the basis for a feasible verification process by distinguishing between global and local links which differ in whether they are transitive or not.

DGs provide a general framework which is independent from a specific language. However, for the purposes of this paper we instantiate the framework and define a structure preserving mapping from CASL into DGs. More concretely, the translation is done in two phases using an intermediate representation which is also used to compute the local differences between specifications. These differences are translated into corresponding changes of the development graph and their effects are analyzed. In this process, our management of change for development graphs ensures that the overall development always is in a consistent state.

After this introduction, we present the notion of development graphs in Section 2. In Section 3 the structure preserving mapping from CASL into a representation of DGs is described. The computation of differences between DG representations is defined in Section 4. These differences are then translated into elementary changes to the DG. The main advantage of DGs lies in that they are a suitable basis for an efficient management of change. How this can be achieved is demonstrated in Section 5 and 6. We conclude with some general remarks.

2 Development Graph

A development graph represents the actual state of a formal program development. It is used to encode the structured specifications in various phases of the development. Arising proof obligations are attached to this graph as so-called theorem links. Roughly speaking, each node of the graph represents a theory like for instance NAT, LIST or ELEM in [CASL98]. Leaves in the graph correspond to basic specifications, which do not make use of other theories (e.g. ELEM or PARTIAL_ORDER in [CASL98]). Inner nodes correspond to structured specifications which define theories using other theories (e.g. LIST using ELEM). The links of the graph define how theories can make use of other theories.

Definition 1. *A development graph $\mathcal{S}$ is an acyclic, directed graph $\langle \mathcal{N}, \mathcal{L} \rangle$.*

$\mathcal{N}$ is a finite set of nodes. Each node $N \in \mathcal{N}$ is a tuple $(S^N, \vdash^N, \Phi^N)$ such that $(S^N, \vdash^N)$ is a consequence relation[1] *and $\Phi^N \subseteq S^N$ is the set of* **local axioms** *of N.*

$\mathcal{L}$ is a finite set of directed links, so-called **definition links**, *between elements of $\mathcal{N}$. Each definition link from a node M to a node N is either* **global** *(denoted $M \xrightarrow{\sigma} N$) or* **local** *(denoted $M \overset{\sigma}{\rightharpoonup} N$) and is annotated with a morphism $\sigma : (S^M, \vdash^M) \to (S^N, \vdash^N)$*

To simplify matters, we write $M \xrightarrow{\sigma} N \in \mathcal{S}$ instead of $M \xrightarrow{\sigma} N \in \mathcal{L}$ when $\mathcal{L}$ denotes the links of $\mathcal{S}$.

CASL is based on a fixed institution giving rise to the construction of a sentences S from a given signature Σ and the definition of signature morphisms. To adjust the notion of development graphs to CASL, we make use of this specific CASL institution to specify the sentences S by a signature Σ, restrict possible consequence morphisms to signature morphisms provided by the institution and select appropriate consequence relations.

The proof theoretical semantics of a development graph is given by the following definition:

Definition 2. *Let $\mathcal{S} = \langle \mathcal{N}, \mathcal{L} \rangle$ be a development graph. Let $N \in \mathcal{N}$, then the* **theory** *$Th_{\mathcal{S}}(N)$ of a node N wrt. a development graph $\mathcal{S}$ is defined by*

$$Th_{\mathcal{S}}(N) = \left[\Phi^N \cup \bigcup_{K \xrightarrow{\sigma} N \in \mathcal{S}} \sigma(Th_{\mathcal{S}}(K)) \cup \bigcup_{K \overset{\sigma}{\rightharpoonup} N \in \mathcal{S}} \sigma(\Phi^K) \right]^{\vdash^N}$$

where $[\Psi]^{\vdash^N}$ denotes the closure of Ψ under the consequence relation $\vdash^N$.

Hence, the theory of a node N depends on both, the theories of all nodes which are connected via a global link to N and the local axioms of all nodes which are connected via a local link to N.

Most structuring mechanisms of CASL (like **then** or **and**) relate theories to each other and thus correspond to global definition links.

However, there are mechanisms which involve the proof of non-trivial facts to ensure the soundness of their application. When instantiating a parameterized specification we have to prove that an actual parameter fulfills the requirements of the corresponding formal parameter. In terms of category theory the parameter passing diagram has to be a pushout. Local definition links allow to distinguish between exporting a complete theory (including the axioms of the formal

[1] For definitions of consequence relations and consequence morphisms we refer to [HST94].

parameters) and exporting the local axioms of the parameterized datatype (excluding the axioms of the formal parameters).

Complementary to definition links, which *define* the theories of related nodes, we introduce the notion of a *theorem link* with the help of which we are able to *postulate* relations between different theories. Theorem links are the central datastructure to represent proof obligations arising in formal developments. Again we distinguish between local and global theorem links (denoted by $N \overset{\sigma}{-\!\!\twoheadrightarrow} M$ and $N \overset{\sigma}{-\!\!\to} M$ respectively). The semantics of theorem links are given by the next definition.

Definition 3. *Let $\mathcal{S}$ be a development graph and N, M be nodes in $\mathcal{S}$.*
$\mathcal{S}$ **implies** *a global theorem link $N \overset{\sigma}{-\!\!\twoheadrightarrow} M$ (denoted $\mathcal{S} \vdash N \overset{\sigma}{-\!\!\twoheadrightarrow} M$) iff $Th_{\mathcal{S}}(M) \vdash \sigma(\phi)$ for all $\phi \in Th_{\mathcal{S}}(N)$.*
$\mathcal{S}$ **implies** *a local theorem link $N \overset{\sigma}{-\,-\!\!\to} M$ (denoted $\mathcal{S} \vdash N \overset{\sigma}{-\,-\!\!\to} M$) iff $Th_{\mathcal{S}}(M) \vdash \sigma(\phi)$ for all $\phi \in \Phi^N$.*

Common proof obligations in a formal development can be encoded into properties that specific global theorem links are implied by the actual development graph. A specification **view** *VN:SP* **to** *SP'* = *SM* **end**, for instance, gives rise to a global theorem link between the corresponding nodes of SP and SP' in the development graph. Also the requirement of instantiations that "*each model of an argument FA_i is required to be a model of the corresponding parameter SP_i*" introduces global theorem links between the corresponding formal and actual parameters.

3 Translating CASL into Development Graphs

In order to use development graphs as a basis for structured deduction in CASL (or any other specification language), a translation must be defined. Naturally, such a translation should be *adequate*, i.e. any theorem which can be proven in a node of the development graph does also hold in the corresponding CASL-specification. For the purposes of structured deduction, it is also desirable that the structure of a specification is reflected in the structure of the resulting development graph. In this section, we define a mapping τ from a subset of CASL to development graphs which is both adequate and structure preserving. Furthermore, the translation does not directly map into development graphs, but merely into a syntactical *representation* DGR of development graphs. The representation DGR contains only the structure resulting from the CASL specification, whereas the development graph additionally contains information about the decomposition of global links into local links (cf. Section 5) and proofs of proof obligations arising from local theorem links. The benefit of differentiating between the development graph *representation* of a CASL specification and the actual development graph will become visible in the description of the handling of specification revisions and the merging of concurrent developments (cf. Section 4).

In the rest of the paper we consider the following subset: basic specifications; structured specifications (extensions, unions, translations, closed specifications, generic specifications, instantiations); libraries with definitions of named specification and references to them. We do not consider library downloads, since they can be expanded into equivalent CASL input without downloads and therefore do not need special treatment. Symbol hiding can be handled by renaming the symbols appropriately and free specifications are handled by inserting the generatedness axioms for the appropriate sorts. Architectural specifications are currently not supported because their definition is still under development. However, we intend to handle them by program logics in future work.

The specification definitions in the body of a library are translated in turn, yielding a development graph representation for each of the named, possibly generic, specifications. The body of most of the definitions will refer to other named specifications. In this case the graphs for the specification definitions referred to, are connected to the graph that is currently being built. Our translation τ of CASL input into representations of development graphs is defined on CASL input that is correct wrt. the static semantics. Correct static semantics (as described in [CASL98]) ensure, for instance, that signature items are not used in places in which they are not visible by the CASL scoping rules and that terms as well as formulas are type-correct and well-formed.

The translation itself is defined by a set of rewrite rules which are represented graphically in Figure 1. To translate a CASL construct one starts with a *pre-development graph* consisting of a node which contains the (not-yet translated) CASL construct. In the figures, nodes which are not yet translated are represented as shaded boxes, translated nodes (or *theory representations*) as circles.

Specification Definitions. To translate a non-generic specification definition of the form '**spec** SN = SP' (where SN is a specification name and SP is a structured specification), one starts with the pre-development graph

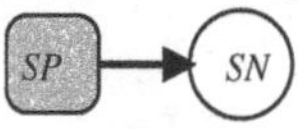

The node SP will subsequently be rewritten to the development graph representation corresponding to the body of the specification definition; SN is an empty node annotated with the name SN of the specification for later references. The only exception to this rule are generic specification definitions

$$\textbf{spec } SN[SP_1]\ldots[SP_n] \textbf{ given } SP'_1,\ldots,SP'_m = SP.$$

In this case we start with the pre-development graph (g) of Fig. 1. For translating instantiations of such a generic specification definition, the theory representations corresponding to each parameter specification SP_i has to be remembered together with the theory representation for the generic specification SN.

The construction of a development graph is an iterated application of rewrite rules from Figure 1 which translate CASL specifications into pre-development graphs (Not yet translated sub-specifications are indicated by grey boxes). These grey boxes are decomposed until one eventually arrives at a graph in which there

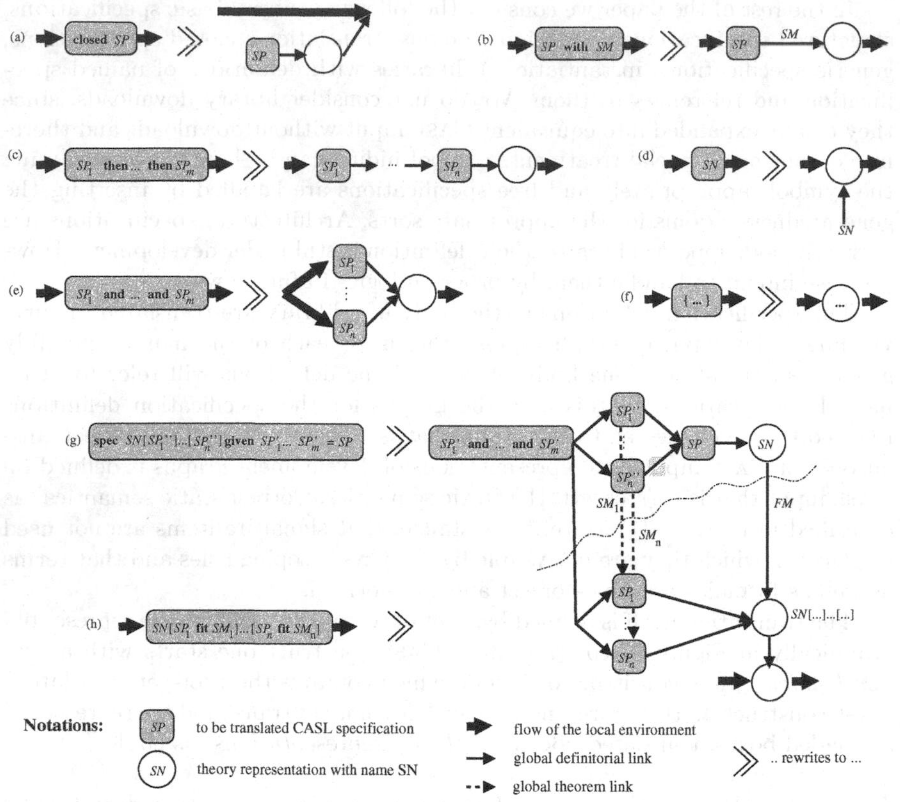

Fig. 1. Translating CASL specifications into development graphs (see text for details)

are no such boxes left, i.e. a development graph. During this process, boxes may be created which have in-going or out-going links. The thick arrows in the Figure indicate how these links are inherited when such a box is rewritten. To be precise, the inheritance of the thick arrows shows only the handling of definition links. The handling of theorem links is not depicted but much simpler. Whenever a box is rewritten, all in-going theorem links are redirected to the empty circle which is created by the rewrite process. This circle also becomes the source of all outgoing theorem links of the original box. In case (h) two empty circles are created, here, the lower circle in the figure is used as source and target for redirected theorem links. Since all definition and all theorem links are treated alike the confluence of the rewrite system is guaranteed.

Basic Specifications. The translation of a basic specification $\{\ldots\}$ results in a theory representation of a single node $N = (\Sigma^N, \vdash^N, \Phi^N)$ in the development graph (cf. Fig. 1, (f)). The declaration of sorts, operations, predicates, and datatypes in the body contribute to the signature Σ^N. The definition of operations and predicates, the attributes of operations and predicates, the declaration of selectors in datatype declarations, and the declaration of free datatypes all result in corresponding local axioms in Φ^N. These axioms, respectively, express the defined equation or equivalence, the attribute, the result of applications of selectors to terms, and the injectivity of constructors. $\vdash^N$ is defined as a consequence relation corresponding to the satisfaction relation of CASL. Each free datatype or sort generation results in the extension of $\vdash^N$ by the corresponding induction scheme. We will not describe this translation in detail, but simply note that it is itself a complicated process involving several steps, including lexical analysis, context free parsing, mix-fix analysis, overloading resolution, type checking, and static semantic analysis (cf. [MKK97]).

Structured Specifications. Note that all rewrite rules for structured specifications insert an empty node (i.e. an empty circle in the diagram) which corresponds to the specification that is being rewritten into the development graph. Hereby, we achieve a close relationship between the structure of a specification and the structure of the resulting development graph. Using this correspondence we can state the adequateness of the translation: every theorem derivable in the theory of an empty node holds also in all models of the corresponding CASL sub-specification. This is the basis for applying the standard technique (e.g. [HW97]) to prove adequateness by structural induction. For each structuring operation, adequateness is proven assuming the adequateness for the component specifications. In the base case, the semantics of basic specifications must be captured by the set of axioms and the consequence relation of the node. This ensures the correctness of the translation. However, it is well-known that any calculus which is feasible for mechanization must be incomplete in the presence of initiality. Therefore, in general, it is impossible to achieve completeness, i.e. that all theorems which hold semantically are also derivable syntactically with the consequence relation.

A reference to a non-generic specification SN (case d) is translated into an empty node and a global definition link from the node annotated with the name SN. This is the node corresponding to the body of the specification definition for SN. A reference to an instance $SN[SP_1$ **fit** $SM_1] \dots [SP_n$ **fit** $SM_n]$ is translated using the fact that it is equivalent to

$$\{SP' \textbf{ with } FM\} \textbf{ and } SP'_1 \textbf{ and } \dots \textbf{ and } SP'_n$$

where SP' is the (implicitly closed) specification which is referenced by the name SN, FM is the morphism which results from $[SP_1$ **fit** $SM_1] \dots [SP_n$ **fit** $SM_n]$, and $SP'_i = SP_i$ **with** SM_i. For further details of these equivalences the reader is referred to Section 6.2 of [CASL98]. In order for the instantiation to be defined, however, the argument specifications SP_i have to satisfy the parameter specifications SP''_i wrt. the morphism SM_i $(1 \leq i \leq n)$ of the generic specification definition for SN. Therefore a global theorem link from SP''_i to SP_i annotated by the morphism SM_i is added to the development graph for each i.

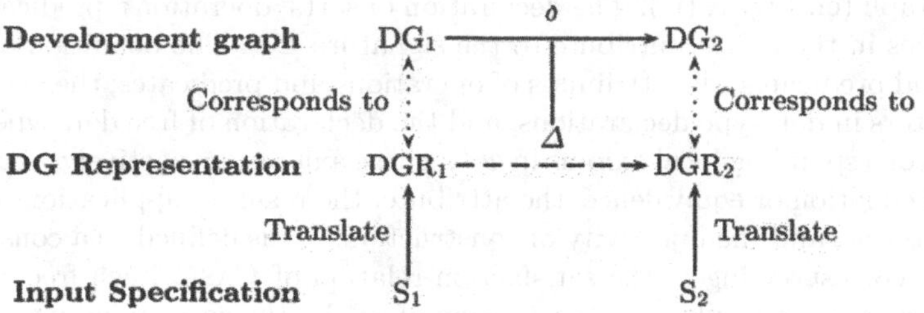

Fig. 2. Evolution of developments

4 Computing Differences of DG-Representations

The evolutionary character of formal software developments involves that the specification is revised several times. Indeed, during a formal development, errors in the specification are detected while trying to prove arising proof obligations. This results in revisions of the specification and the task arises to preserve as much established proofs as possible. Additionally, in practice formal developments are often performed by several developers, each revising independently the original specification because of detected errors. At a certain stage, they merge the various modified specifications to a single specification, representing the new global specification. Again, the task arises to preserve the proofs established by each developer separately by incorporating them into a development graph corresponding to the new global specification.

The first part of this section is devoted to the task of preserving proofs when a single developer revises his specification. The second part of the section addresses the problem of preserving proofs for the case where different developers merge their specifications.

4.1 Differences between Development Graph Representations

In this section we deal with the following scenario (cf. Fig. 2): The development was started with some specification S_1 in some input specification language like CASL. This specification was translated into a development graph representation DGR_1 from which a development graph DG_1 was generated. Within the development graph DG_1 several proofs have been already performed: global theorem links have been decomposed into local theorem links (cf. Section 5) and some of the proof-obligations arising from local theorem links have been proved successfully. Observe that the only differences between the DG representation DGR_1 (resulting directly from S_1) and the actual development graph DG_1 are the decompositions of global links into local links and the proofs of local links. In particular the nodes in DGR_1 and DG_1 are the same. This is a general property which always holds between a development graph *representation* and its development graph.

Now, let us assume that due to an error, the initial specification has to be modified obtaining a specification S_2, which is translated into a new representation DGR_2. We have to determine the modifications Δ, which are used to map DG_1 to DG_2 (δ), where DG_2 corresponds to DGR_2. Of course, as many proofs as possible should be preserved from DG_1. To this end the development graph provides a fixed set of basic operations, e.g. the addition of single nodes, links or axioms into a node. The management of change on the development graph is optimized to preserve as many proofs during the execution of those basic modifications (cf. Section 6). This feature of the development graph implies that the computed modifications Δ must be a sequence of such basic modifications. Thus, the result of the analysis of differences between DGR_1 and DGR_2 is a *workplan* for the update of the development graph.

The problem of how to determine the differences between the old and the new development graph representation consists of finding the differences between two graphs as well as between the contents of nodes and links of identified parts. We identify a node, i.e. a theory in a graph, by its annotated name (if it has one) and a link by the connected theories, its type (local vs. global, definition vs. theorem) and its associated morphism. Let us consider first the case of two theory representations TH and TH' occurring in the old and new specification respectively. If they both are annotated by names and these are equal, we assume that they denote the same "theory", although the content of the old theory TH might differ from the content of the new theory TH'. If TH' is not annotated by a name, we can not a priori decide whether this is a new theory in the development graph or if it corresponds to an unnamed theory in the old development. This problem has no unique solution in general and hence, we need heuristics to identify theories without names. Similarly, we must decide whether links in the new specification are new links or if they correspond to already existing links. This problem is analogous to the identification problem of unnamed theories. Furthermore, the problem to decide whether two unnamed theories correspond to each other depends on the correspondences of the incoming definition links, which themselves depend on the correspondence of their source theories. Therefore, a heuristic to establish the correspondences between two specifications must establish the correspondence of theories and links simultaneously. The result of this mechanism is a correspondence mapping M between theories and links in the old and new specification. The correspondence mapping is a partial function mapping theories (resp. links) of the old specification to theories (resp. links) of the new specification. Although, the mechanism to identify theories and links is a heuristic, the resulting mapping M must fulfill certain properties: M must map a named theory on a named theory which has the same name, if there is one in the new specification. Furthermore, M must map a link to a link which has the same type (local vs. global, definition vs. theorem).

In the following we first present a heuristic to determine a mapping between two specifications. As there can not be in general an optimal mapping, the heuristic is an exemple and other heuristics are possible. Afterwards, we describe how a mapping is used to generate the necessary modifications between an old and a new specification.

Example for the Heuristic Determination of Mappings. Let DGR and DGR' be representations of development graphs obtained by the translation of input specifications. In order to determine a mapping from DGR to DGR', we use the definition parts of the specifications DGR and DGR'. The definition parts of a development graph representation consist of all theories and all definition links and they always represent an acyclic graph. Taking the semantics of development graphs into account, the theory of a node is determined by the local sorts, constants, and axioms together with the theories imported by the morphisms on the incoming definition links. The heuristic to determine the mapping between theories and links is the following: First we consider the *basic* theories of DGR, i.e. those which do not have any incoming definition links. If such a theory T has a name and there is a theory T' in DGR', which has the same name, we define $M(T) = T'$ and remove T' from the list of goal theories in DGR'. If T is unnamed, we compare T to the unnamed basic theories in DGR' and select the theory T', which shares the maximum number of local sorts and local constants. If there is more than one such theory T' the user can be asked to arbitrate. Subsequently we define $M(T) = T'$ and remove T' from the list of goal theories in DGR'. The process is iterated for the outgoing definition links of the basic theories in DGR. An outgoing definition link L of some theory T is compared with all outgoing links of the respective basic theory $M(T)$. From this set the link L' is selected, which shares the maximum number of identical sort and constant mappings and we define $M(L) = L'$. Then the process is iterated for the target theories of those links and we take the incoming definition links into account besides the local sorts and constants.

The whole process is iterated until the top theories are reached, i.e., those theories, which have no outgoing definition links. The next step is to incorporate the theorem links into the mapping. To this end consider a global (resp. local) theorem link L in DGR connecting two theories T_1 and T_2 which are both in the domain of M. L is compared with the global (resp. local) theorem links in DGR' connecting $M(T_1)$ and $M(T_2)$. From those, we select that link L' which shares the maximum number of sort and constant mappings with L and define $M(L) = L'$. Iterating this process for all theorem links which connect theories in the domain of M completes the definition of the mapping M[2].

Computing a Workplan. Suppose the old and new development graph representations DGR and DGR' and a mapping M of theories and links from DGR to DGR' are given. The basic modifications which must be performed on the development graph DG corresponding to DGR in order to obtain a development graph corresponding to DGR' are determined as follows. How these basic modifications are handled by the management of change on the development graph is detailed in Section 6.

[2] Note that the heuristic can be extended to determine a mapping for named theories, which have been renamed in the input specification, but we omit its presentation for sake of readability.

1. Theories and links in DGR, which are not in the domain of M are removed from DG and, analogously, those theories and links in DGR' which are not in the codomain of M are added to DG.
2. Let T be a theory in DGR and T' a theory in DGR', such that $M(T) = T'$. Furthermore, let DT be the theory corresponding to T in the development graph DG. Then each local sort and constant of T which does not occur in T' is removed from DT. Analogously, each local sort and constant in T' not occurring in T is added to DT.
   The axioms are compared as follows: If A is a named axiom in T and there is a named axiom A' in T' which has the same name, we compare the formulas of A and A'. If they are different, we delete the formula of A from DT and add the formula of A'. Otherwise no modifications are necessary.
   If A is unnamed, and we cannot find an unnamed axiom A' in T' with a formula which is equivalent to the formula of A, then the formula in A is deleted from DT. Analogously, if there is an unnamed axiom A' in T', for which there is no unnamed axiom in T, which contains the same formula than A', then the formula of A' is added to DT.
3. Let L be a link in DGR, L' be the link corresponding to L in DGR' (i.e., $M(L) = L'$), and DL be the link corresponding to L in DG. The morphisms μ and μ' resp. of L and L' are compared as follows: Each sort or constant mapping of μ, which is not in μ' is deleted from the morphism on DL. Analogously, any sort and constant mapping of μ', which is not in μ is added to the morphism on DL.

4.2 Merging Concurrent Specifications

We now illustrate how the mechanism to determine necessary modifications can be used to merge concurrent developments. The scenario is that two input specifications S_1 and S_2 are developed concurrently. The actual state of the developments is represented in the respective translations DGR_1 and DGR_2 of S_1 and S_2 (cf. Fig. 3) and respective development graphs DG_1 and DG_2. The developers decide to merge S_1 and S_2 to the new global specification S, which is translated into DGR. The task arises to merge both development graphs DG_1 and DG_2 in order to preserve as many proofs contained in DG_1 and DG_2. Recall that DGR, DGR_1, and DGR_2 never contain any proofs. The merge is achieved by separately computing the modifications to perform on each DGR_i $(i = 1, 2)$ to obtain the representation DGR. These modifications Δ_1 and Δ_2 are determined using the technique presented in the previous section and they are used to transform the respective development graphs DG_1 and DG_2 to the development graphs DG_1' and DG_2' (resp. δ_1 and δ_2). Since DG_1 and DG_2 both correspond to DGR, their structures differ only in the proofs, like the decomposition of some global theorem links, or proofs of proof-obligations on local theorem links. Thus, development graphs are merged into a single development graph DG', which contains the union of the proofs established by both developers.

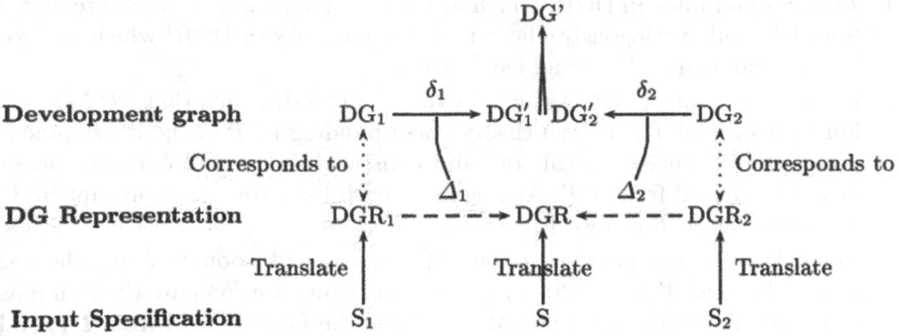

Fig. 3. Merging of specifications and developments

5 Management of Change in a Development Graph

This and the following sections are concerned with the problem of changing a development graph while preserving as much proof information (stored as global or local theorem links) as possible.

The next definition captures the influence of the theory (or the local axioms, respectively) of a node to the theory of any other node.

Definition 4. *Let $\mathcal{S}$ be a development graph. A node M is* **globally reachable** *from a node N via a mapping σ, $N \overset{\sigma}{\Longrightarrow} M \in \mathcal{S}$ for short, iff either $N = M$ and $\sigma = \lambda$, or $N \overset{\sigma'}{\longrightarrow} K \in \mathcal{S}$, $K \overset{\sigma''}{\Longrightarrow} M \in \mathcal{S}$, with $\sigma = \sigma'' \circ \sigma'$.*

A node M is **locally reachable** *from a node N via a mapping σ, $N \overset{\sigma}{\rightarrowtail} M \in \mathcal{S}$ for short, iff $N \overset{\sigma}{\Longrightarrow} M \in \mathcal{S}$ or there is a node K with $N \overset{\sigma'}{\longrightarrow} K \in \mathcal{S}$, $K \overset{\sigma''}{\Longrightarrow} M \in \mathcal{S}$, with $\sigma = \sigma'' \circ \sigma'$.*

Obviously global reachability implies local reachability since the theory of a node is defined with the help of local axioms.

Global theorem links postulate properties between theories. The theory of a node N is a non-local property as it depends on the theories or axioms of other nodes connected with N. Hence, global theorem links describe properties between subgraphs and any change inside of any of these subgraph will affect this property. In order to come up with an efficient management of change we need a more detailed description to localize the effects of a change. Technically speaking, we have to decompose the property between subgraphs into properties between nodes and subgraphs. Local theorem links are used to describe such properties. The next lemma specifies the relation between global and local theorem links.

Lemma 1. *Let $\mathcal{S}$ be a development graph. Then $\mathcal{S} \vdash N \overset{\sigma}{\dashrightarrow} M$ iff $\mathcal{S} \vdash K \overset{\sigma\circ\sigma'}{\dashrightarrow} M$ holds for all K, σ' with $K \overset{\sigma'}{\rightarrowtail} N$.*

Proof. The proof is straight forward.

As global theorem links describe properties about graphs, different global theorem links may share common or related proof obligations. The next lemma gives us a criterion to eliminate subsumed local theorem links. These are theorem links postulating properties which can be deduced from other existing links.

Lemma 2 (Subsumption). *Let $\mathcal{S}$ be a development graph. Then $\mathcal{S} \vdash N \overset{\sigma}{\dashrightarrow} K$ and $K \overset{\sigma'}{\rightarrowtail} M$ implies $\mathcal{S} \vdash N \overset{\sigma \circ \sigma'}{\dashrightarrow} M$.*

Proof. $\sigma(\Phi^N) \subset Th_{\mathcal{S}}(K)$ and $\sigma'(Th_{\mathcal{S}}(K)) \subset Th_{\mathcal{S}}(M)$ implies $\sigma'(\sigma(\Phi^N)) \subset Th_{\mathcal{S}}(M)$.

We are now ready to define a reduction calculus operating on a set of theorem links which reduces the amount of proof obligations as far as possible. Lemma 1 allows us to replace each global theorem link $N \overset{\sigma}{-\!\!\rightarrow} M$ by an appropriate set of local theorem links: each theory K, from which N is reachable via some morphism σ', has to be connected to M by a direct local theorem link attached with a combined morphism $\sigma' \circ \sigma$. Notice that by definition N is reachable from itself via the identity morphism λ. Lemma 2 is used to minimize the set of local theorem links to be proven by removing subsumed ones.

Definition 5. *The* **reduction calculus** *on sets of theorem links is defined by the following rules:*

Glob-Decomposition*:*

$$\frac{\{N \overset{\sigma}{-\!\!\rightarrow} M\} \cup T}{\bigcup_{K \overset{\sigma'}{\rightarrowtail} N} \{K \overset{\sigma \circ \sigma'}{\dashrightarrow} M\} \cup T}$$

Loc-Decomposition I*:*

$$\frac{\{K \overset{\sigma''}{\dashrightarrow} M\} \cup \{K \overset{\sigma}{\dashrightarrow} L\} \cup T}{\{K \overset{\sigma}{\dashrightarrow} L\} \cup T} \textit{ if } L \overset{\sigma'}{\rightarrowtail} M \textit{ and } \sigma''(\Phi(K)) = \sigma'(\sigma(\Phi(K)))$$

Loc-Decomposition II*:*

$$\frac{\{N \overset{\sigma}{\dashrightarrow} M\} \cup T}{T} \textit{ if } N \overset{\sigma'}{\rightarrowtail} M \textit{ and } \sigma(\Phi(N)) = \sigma'(\Phi(N))$$

Using the reduction calculus we obtain a two-step approach for establishing the relations proposed by theorem links. In a first step we make use of the modularity and the dependencies in the formal development to split up global theorem links and to minimize the set of local theorem links. Using the reduction calculus we determine those links which are already consequences of other links. We are left with a set of independent, so-called *elementary* local theorem links. In a second step we have to check the proof obligations arising from an elementary theorem link, i.e. that all mapped local axioms of the source theory are theorems in the target theory.

The reduction calculus as stated in Definition 5 is not confluent as in general applying the reduction rules in different ways may result in different development graphs. However, in the case studies performed, we observed no such alternatives so far in practice.

6 Changing the Development Graph

The application of the reduction calculus depends on the structure of the development graph. Changing the development graph may render such an application invalid. The proof obligations arising from an elementary theorem link depend on the local axioms of the source node and also on the subgraph of the target node. Changing one of these, results again in a change of the corresponding proof obligations. Thus, each change in the development graph may render parts of the verification effort invalid. In this section we present ways to incrementally adjust the proof obligations once we change the development graph by some basic operation.

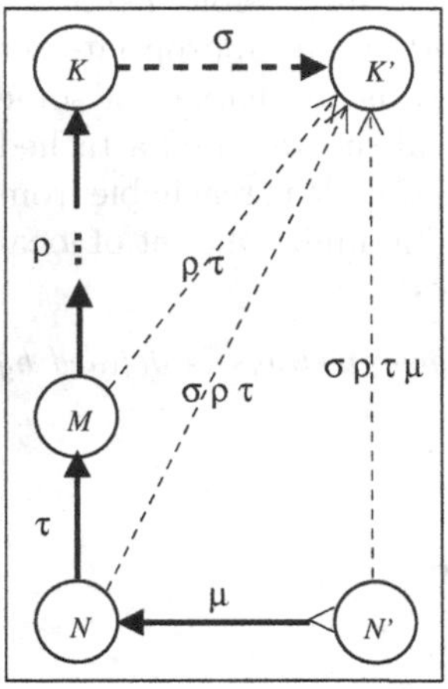

Fig. 4. Changing Definition Links

In the following we always assume that the set of theorem links has been simplified by the reduction calculus. In particular, each global theorem link has been decomposed into a set of local theorem links. In order to come up with a management of change for a development graph, we need an explicit representation of proofs done by the reduction calculus. The management of change will reuse the former proofs to adjust the proof obligations once the development graph has changed. Thus during the first phase, we do not remove global theorem links or subsumed local theorem links, but mark them as redundant by attaching some kind of validation, i.e. the instantiated reduction rule which caused its removal. If we change the development graph then we have to re-inspect the removed theorem links. For each link we have to check or update their validation. For each elementary theorem link we have to update the list of resulting proof obligations and their actual proofs.

In the following we discuss the effects of *basic changes* of the development graph in more detail. Basic changes are the addition or deletion of definition links, the addition or deletion of local axioms of a theory, or the change of the morphism attached to a link. Notice, that adding or deleting an isolated node (i.e. a node without any in-going or out-going link) does not affect the validity of any theorem link.

Adding a Definition Link Adding a new global definition link $N \xrightarrow{\tau} M$ changes the reachability relations inside the graph. Thus, the decomposition of a global theorem link $K \overset{\sigma}{\dashrightarrow} K'$ becomes incomplete if $M \xrightarrow{\rho} K$. For each node N' and morphism μ with $N' \xrightarrow{\mu} N$ we have to add a new local theorem link $N' \overset{\gamma}{\dashrightarrow} K'$ with $\gamma = \sigma \circ \rho \circ \tau \circ \mu$ to the decomposition of the global theorem link. The correctness of the subsumption rule application is not affected by adding new links. Given an elementary local theorem link, the set of theorems to be proven does not change although the set of accessible axioms may increase by adding a definition link. Since the consequence relations have the weakening property, existing proofs are still valid in the enlarged axiomatization. Analogous results hold for adding a local definition link.

Deleting a Definition Link. Deleting an existing global definition link from $N \xrightarrow{\tau} M$ again changes the reachability relations inside the graph. Then, the decomposition of a global theorem link $K \overset{\sigma}{\dashrightarrow} K'$ contains too many local theorem links if $M \xrightarrow{\rho} K$. For each node N' and morphism μ with $N' \overset{\mu}{\rightarrowtail} N$ we have to remove the local theorem link $N' \overset{\gamma}{-\!\!\rightarrow} K'$ with $\gamma = \sigma \circ \rho \circ \tau \circ \mu$ from the decomposition of the global theorem link. Applications of the Loc-decomposition rules have to be checked whether they have used the deleted link and, if they do, their validation has to be deleted and the link becomes an elementary theorem link unless they can be justified by another still existing path. Also the proofs of all elementary theorem links $K \overset{\rho}{-\!\!\rightarrow} K'$ with K' is globally reachable from M are invalidated as they may have imported axioms via the deleted link.

Changing a Morphism. Changing the morphism of a definition link from N to M causes a change of the reachability relation inside the graph. We have to update the morphisms attached to the decomposition of global theorem links $K \overset{\sigma}{\dashrightarrow} K'$ if K is globally reachable from M. Applications of the Loc-decomposition rules have to be checked whether they have used the changed morphism and, if they do, their validation has to be deleted and the link becomes an elementary theorem link. Also the proofs of all elementary theorem links $K \overset{\rho}{-\!\!\rightarrow} K'$ with K' is globally reachable from M are invalidated as they may have imported axioms via the changed link. Essentially this case is handled similarily to the deletion of a definition link.

Adding a New Local Axiom. Adding a new local axiom ψ into a node N does not change the reachability relations of the graph. Thus, all applications of the reduction rules are still valid. For each elementary theorem link $N \overset{\sigma}{-\!\!\rightarrow} M$ we have to add a new proof obligation that $\sigma(\psi)$ holds in $Th_{\mathcal{S}}(M)$. Existing proofs are not affected.

Deleting a Local Axiom. Deleting an existing axiom ψ from a node N does not change the reachability relations of the graph. Thus, all applications of the reduction rules are still valid. For each elementary theorem link $N \overset{\sigma}{-\!\!\rightarrow} M$ we may remove the proof obligation that $\sigma(\psi)$ holds in $Th_{\mathcal{S}}(M)$. But all proofs of elementary theorem links $K \overset{\sigma'}{-\!\!\rightarrow} K'$ are rendered invalid if K' is locally reachable from N.

7 Conclusion

In this paper we presented the notion of a development graph as a basic datastructure for encoding structured CASL-specifications for verification purposes. Constraints on the relation between specifications give rise to theorem links denoting various proof obligations. Such a theorem link can be verified either by reducing it to other existing links or by proving the corresponding theorems explicitly. Changes of the underlying CASL-specification are propagated to (minimal) changes of the development graph in order to preserve as much proof work as possible.

The presented framework has been implemented and successfully tested in various examples in INKA 5.0 [AHMS99]. Its database is organized into deductive units which are linked via morphisms. Proofs are always done within a specific unit where the system has only access to those parts of the database which are accessible from this unit via definition links. The view on these *imported* theories is controlled by the morphisms attached to the links.

References

AHMS99. S. Autexier, D. Hutter, H. Mantel, A. Schairer. System description: INKA 5.0 - a logic voyager. *In H. Ganzinger (Ed.): 16th International Conference on Automated Deduction*, Springer, LNAI 1632, 1999. 88

CASL98. CoFI Language Design Task Group. *The common algebraic specification language (CASL) – summary*, 1998. Version 1.0 and additional Note S-9 on Semantics, available from `http://www.brics.dk/Projects/CoFI`. 73, 74, 75, 77, 79

CM97. M. Cerioli, J. Meseguer. May I borrow your logic? *Theoretical Computer Science*, 173(2):311-347, 1997. 74

DGS91. R. Diaconescu, J. Goguen, P. Stefaneas. Logical support for modularization. *In G. Huet, G. Plotkin (Eds): Workshop on Logical Frameworks*, 1991. 73

HWB97. R. Hennicker, M. Wirsing, M. Bidoit. Proof systems for structured specifications with observability operators. *Theoretical Computer Science*, 173(2):393–443, 1997. 74

HW97. R. Hennicker and M. Wirsing. Proof systems for structured algebraic specifications: An overview. *In Proc. FCT '97, Fundamentals of Computation Theory*, Springer, LNCS 1279, 1997. 79

HST94. R. Harper, D. Sannella, A. Tarlecki. Structured presentations and logic representations. *Annals of Pure and Applied Logic*, 67:113-160, 1994. 75

MKK97. T. Mossakowski, Kolyang, B. Krieg-Brückner. Static semantic analysis and theorem proving for CASL. *In F. Parisi-Presicce (Ed.): Recent Trends in Algebraic Development Techniques*, Tarquinia. Springer, LNCS 1376, 1998. 79

ST88. D. Sannella, A. Tarlecki. Specifications in an arbitrary institution. *Information and Computation*, 76(2/3):165-210, 1988. 73

ST92. D. Sannella, A. Tarlecki. Towards Formal development of programs from algebraic specifications: model-theoretic foundations. *In: 19th nternational Colloquium, ICALP'92*, Springer, LNCS 623, 1992. 73

VSE96. D. Hutter et al.. Verification support environment (VSE), *Journal of High Integrity Systems*, 1(6):523-531, 1996. 73

Development of Parsing Tools for CASL Using Generic Language Technology

Mark G.J. van den Brand and Jeroen Scheerder

CWI, Department of Software Engineering
Kruislaan 413, NL-1098 SJ Amsterdam, The Netherlands
{Mark.van.den.Brand,Jeroen.Scheerder}@cwi.nl

Abstract. An environment for the Common Algebraic Specification Language CASL consists of several independent tools. A number of CASL tools have been built using the algebraic specification formalism ASF+SDF and the ASF+SDF Meta-Environment. CASL supports user-defined syntax which is non-trivial to process: ASF+SDF offers a powerful parsing technology (Generalized LR). Its interactive development environment facilitates rapid prototyping complemented by early detection and correction of errors. A number of core technologies developed for the ASF+SDF Meta-Environment can be reused in the context of CASL. Furthermore, an instantiation of a generic format developed for the representation of ASF+SDF specifications and terms provides a CASL-specific exchange format.

1 Introduction

CASL (Common Algebraic Specification Language) [11] is a new algebraic specification formalism developed as part of the Common Framework Initiative (CoFI). It is a generic algebraic specification formalism incorporating features of most existing algebraic specification languages. To complement the CASL formalism itself, a set of tools to support development of CASL specifications is planned. For this purpose, existing tools and technologies will be reused wherever possible.

The algebraic specification formalism ASF+SDF [13] and the ASF+SDF Meta-Environment [24] have been deployed to prototype CASL's concrete syntax. The user-defined (also known as mixfix) syntax of CASL calls for a two-pass approach. In the first pass, the skeleton of a CASL specification is derived in order to extract user-defined syntax rules. In a second pass these syntax rules are used to parse the expressions using them. ASF+SDF offers the advantages of its underlying powerful parsing technology (Generalized LR parsing) and its interactive development environment that enables early detection of errors, such as lexical and syntactic ambiguities, in the syntax definition of a language. The GLR parsing technology eliminates the need to worry about parse table conflicts, which are especially annoying for languages whose syntax definition is still 'on the move'.

D. Bert, C. Choppy, and P. Mosses (Eds.): WADT'99, LNCS 1827, pp. 89–105, 2000.

At present, two versions of the ASF+SDF Meta-Environment coexist. One is described in [24]; we refer to this environment as the *traditional* one. The other is a next-generation ASF+SDF Meta-Environment [9] under active development; we refer to this enviroment as *current*. The main difference between traditional and current environments is architectural organization: the former is monolithic, the latter consists of a suite of independent components communicating via a software coordination architecture [4]. The ASF+SDF Meta-Environment uses a common exchange format, ASFIX, to represent parse trees for specifications and terms. It contains all relevant information, including applied production rules, layout, and comments. ASFIX stands for ASF+SDF fixed format; it is based on ATERMS [8].

Components from the current ASF+SDF Meta-Environment can be (re)used in the context of other systems – such as a CASL environment – in a flexible way.

This paper discusses the following topics:

- Various techniques involved in implementing a CASL parser using ASF+SDF language technology.
- A mapping, CASFIX, from the concrete syntax of CASL to an abstract syntax in ATERMS.
- Treatment of user-defined annotations.

1.1 Overall Architecture of a CASL Parsing Environment

The overall architecture of a full CASL parser, including user-defined syntax, based on ASF+SDF technology is depicted by Figure 1.

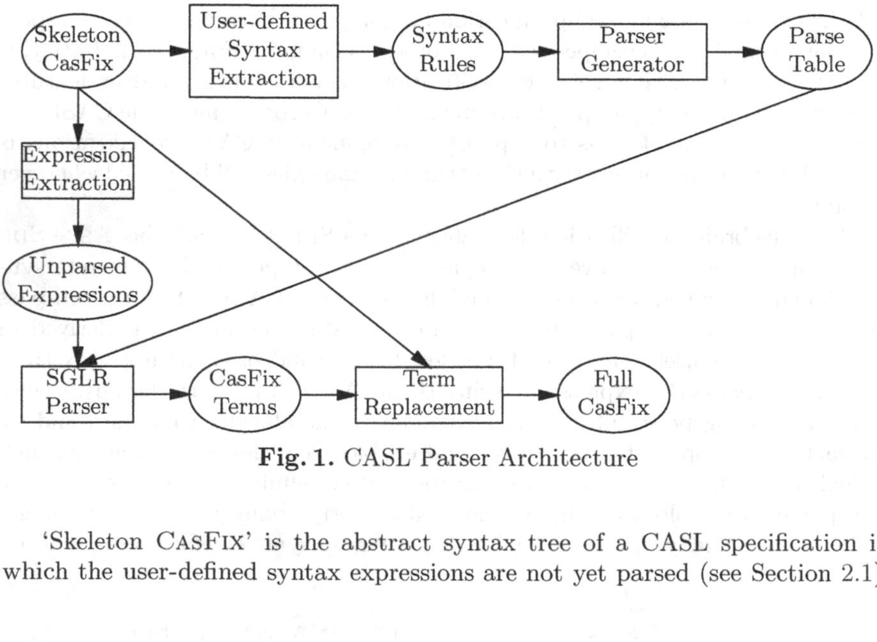

Fig. 1. CASL Parser Architecture

'Skeleton CASFIX' is the abstract syntax tree of a CASL specification in which the user-defined syntax expressions are not yet parsed (see Section 2.1).

The `SyntaxExtraction` tool extracts definitions of user-defined syntax from this abstract syntax tree, flattens parsed CASL specifications and retrieves all visible sorts, operator definitions, and variables. This tool is based on the ATERM library and implemented in C. The syntax information obtained this way is fed to the `ParserGenerator` tool (details in Section 3.1) to generate a parse table.

The expressions that are yet to be parsed, also present in the abstract syntax tree, are extracted by the `ExpressionExtraction` tool and consecutively parsed using the SGLR parser (discussed in Section 3.2), instantiated with the corresponding parse table that was just generated. In case of a successful parse a syntax tree is constructed in a representation (CASFIX, described in Section 4) tailored specifically to the needs of CASL.

Finally, the `TermReplacement` tool, which is the inverse of `ExpressionExtraction`, substitutes the parsed CASL term for its unparsed counterpart. This tool is also based on the ATERM library and implemented in C.

1.2 Related Work

Related work can be divided into two areas. The first is related to tackling user-defined syntax in general and the second is related to parsers developed for CASL.

Other Approaches to Parsing User-Defined Syntax It is impossible to list all systems that deal with formalisms allowing user-defined syntax exhaustively. We restrict ourselves to those systems that arguably relate to the work on CASL.

The first system we mention is the traditional ASF+SDF Meta-Environment. The algebraic specification formalism ASF+SDF [3,17,13] is used, notably for language prototyping. By means of an SDF definition, the lexical and context-free grammar of a language are specified, whereas the ASF definition serves to define the semantics. The SDF part corresponds to signatures in ordinary algebraic specification formalisms. However, syntax is not restricted to plain prefix notation: arbitrary context-free grammars can be defined. The syntax defined in the SDF-part of a module is available for the definition of equations. Therefore, equation syntax is user-defined. In a two-pass approach the SDF definition is parsed, obtaining the definitions necessary for parsing the equations. The parsing technology used to deal with this user-defined syntax is GLR [33,31,34].

The second system, ASD [12], is closely related to ASF+SDF. Again a two-pass approach is used to generate parsers for the user-defined syntax occurring in Action Semantics specifications [29]. In the first pass the user-defined syntax definitions are collected. These are then processed by an ASF+SDF specification and transformed into another SDF definition. The resulting definition is then used to parse the expressions that may contain user-defined syntax.

The third system is CIGALE [35], a parser for ASSPEGIQUE [5]. CIGALE supports incremental grammar definition, and offers a great flexibility in syntax. It is not derived from standard techniques like Earley [15] or LR [1]. At its core lies a restrictive backtracking algorithm.

Finally, we mention the parser used in the ELAN system [6]. ELAN is a specification language based on rewriting logic with additional features, notably strategies. The parser used in the ELAN system is based on the Earley parsing technology. One drawback of ELAN is the way constraints imposed by the Earley parser are visible in the ELAN specification; for example, rewrite rules are grouped according to the 'sort' of the left- and right-hand side in the syntax definition.

Other CASL Parsers Several efforts towards implementing a parser for CASL have been undertaken. The following ones are currently available:

- The parser developed by Frederic Voisin. This parser is based on SYNTAX [7], a LEX/YACC-style parser generator. This CASL parser is comparable to the ASF+SDF-based skeleton parser described in Section 2.1; it also does not parse expressions in user-defined syntax.
- The HOL-CASL parser [28] is a full two-pass CASL parser. It performs skeleton parsing, using a functional implementation of LEX/YACC; user-defined syntax is then parsed using the Isabelle parser, which is based on the Cocke-Younger-Kasami algorithm [19]. The CYK-parser is not very efficient; GLR usually performs better for the most common cases. Except for specifications of very limited size, the difference in performance can on average be expected to be of significant practical relevance.
- The CASL parser by Bastian Kleineidam[1], developed using JAVA[2] and JAVACC[3] at the Max-Planck-Institut für Informatik (Saarbrücken).
- A parser frontend has been developed in order to be able to employ the INKA theorem prover[4] [20] for CASL specifications. This parser is based on LEX/YACC technology. The INKA theorem prover derives proof obligations from CASL specifications, and assists in finding proofs.

2 Developing a CASL Grammar Using ASF+SDF Technology

Generic language technology such as ASF+SDF can be applied at several stages when developing tools for CASL. The first stage, probably the most obvious one, is set at the level of defining the concrete syntax of CASL.

Using the EBNF definition provided by the CASL language summary [11] an SDF definition[5] has been developed. Figure 3 shows a tiny fragment of this SDF definition. It should be noted that EBNF can be mapped to SDF in a straightforward manner, requiring no complex grammar transformations whatsoever.

This SDF definition does not cope with every aspect, particularly not with user-defined syntax; see Section 3.

[1] `http://www.mpi-sb.mpg.de/~calvin/`
[2] `http://www.javasoft.com`
[3] `http://www.suntest.com/javacc/`
[4] `http://www.dfki.de/vse/systems/inka/`
[5] Available at `http://www.cwi.nl/~markvdb/cofi/zcasl-sdf2.html`.

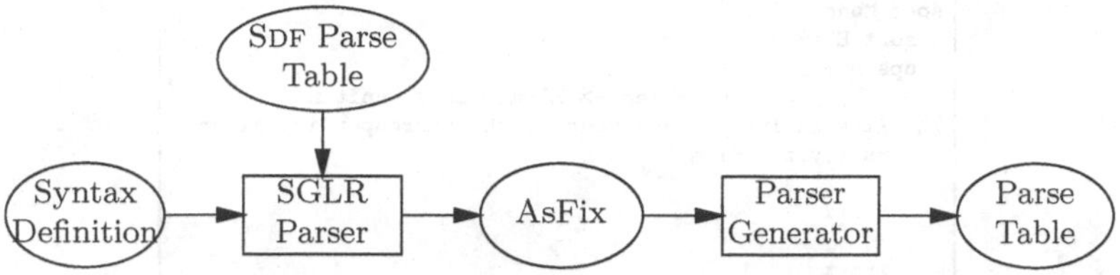

Fig. 2. CASL Parse Table Generation

```
"{" "}"      -> Basic-Spec
Basic-Item+ -> Basic-Spec
Sig-Items                                            -> Basic-Item
"free" Datatype-S { Datatype-Decl ";"}+ Opt-Semi     -> Basic-Item
"generated" Datatype-S {Datatype-Decl ";"}+ Opt-Semi -> Basic-Item
"generated" "{" Sig-Items+ Opt-Semi "}" Opt-Semi     -> Basic-Item
Var-S {Var-Decl ";"}+ Opt-Semi                       -> Basic-Item
Var-S {Var-Decl ";"}+ "."
  {Labelled-Formula "."}+ Opt-Semi                   -> Basic-Item
Axiom-S {Labelled-Formula ";"}+ Opt-Semi             -> Basic-Item
```

Fig. 3. Fragment of the SDF Definition of CASL

2.1 Skeleton Parser

Based on the EBNF definition in [11] the concrete syntax of CASL has been defined. Furthermore, a mapping from concrete syntax to abstract syntax (CASFIX, see Section 4), has been defined in ASF+SDF. Using the parser generator that is part of the ASF+SDF Meta-Environment, a stand-alone parser for CASL has been generated (see Figure 2). At this point it does not yet handle user-defined syntax. This parser, therefore, can be viewed as a skeleton parser that can be invoked as a first-phase parser (shown in Figure 4). By using this parser and applying the CASFIX mapping, the concrete syntax for CASL specifications is obtained. Expressions that may contain user-defined syntax are not parsed,

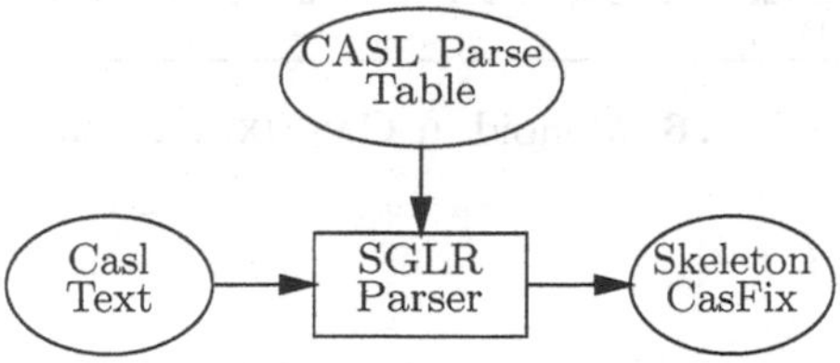

Fig. 4. CASL Skeleton Parser

and are represented as unstructured character sequences, to be analyzed in more detail at some later point, in CASFIX.

```
spec Monoid =
  sort Elem
  ops n : Elem;
      __*__ : Elem *Elem -> Elem, assoc, unit n
%% Alternatively, just specify the corresponding axioms:
  vars x,y,z : Elem
  .
    n*x=x
  .
    x*n=x
  .
    (x*y)*z=x*(y*z)
```

Fig. 5. Monoid, a small CASL Fragment

Figure 5 provides an exemplary CASL specification; Figure 6 reveals its CasFix representation. Note the **unparsed-formulas** in Figure 6 which represent the expressions yet to be parsed later on, as discussed in Section 3.

```
spec-defn(
 SIMPLE-ID(WORDS("Monoid")),
 genericity(params(SPEC*([])),imports(SPEC*([]))),
 BASIC-SPEC(basic-spec(
  BASIC-ITEMS*([
   SIG-ITEMS(sort-items(SORT-ITEM+([
                        sort-decl(SORT+([TOKEN-ID(TOKEN(WORDS("Elem")))]))]))),
   SIG-ITEMS(op-items(OP-ITEM+([
    op-decl(OP-NAME+([ID(TOKEN-ID(TOKEN(WORDS("n"))))]),
            total-op-type(sorts(SORT*([])),
             TOKEN-ID(TOKEN(WORDS("Elem")))),
            OP-ATTR*([])),
    op-decl(OP-NAME+([
             ID(MIXFIX-ID(token-places(TOKEN-OR-PLACE+([
                                  "__",TOKEN(SIGNS(["*"])),"__"]))))]),
            total-op-type(sorts(SORT*([TOKEN-ID(TOKEN(WORDS("Elem"))),
                                  TOKEN-ID(TOKEN(WORDS("Elem")))]))
             TOKEN-ID(TOKEN(WORDS("Elem")))),
            OP-ATTR*([associative,unit-op-attr("n")]))]))),
    local-var-axioms(
     VAR-DECL+([var-decl(VAR+([var(WORDS("x")),var(WORDS("y")),var(WORDS("z"))]),
                        TOKEN-ID(TOKEN(WORDS("Elem"))))]),
     FORMULA+([unparsed-formula(" n * x = x "){label(ID*([])},
              unparsed-formula(" x * n = x "){label(ID*([])},
              unparsed-formula(" ( x * y ) * z = x * ( y * z ) "){label(ID*([])}
             ]))])))))
```

Fig. 6. Monoid in CasFix: Skeletal

3 Parsing Casl Using Asf+Sdf Technology

There are several ways of implementing a CASL parser by means of Asf+Sdf technology. One approach is extensively studied and described in [37]. Asf equations are used to parse expressions in user-defined syntax. This approach has proved feasible, but too slow for most practical purposes. Another approach is described in [12] where ASF+SDF is used to build tools for Action Semantics [14]. A parser for Action Semantics [29] exemplifies this. We propose an alternative approach, based on reusing components of the current ASF+SDF Meta-Environment, most notably the parse table generator and the SGLR parser.

The approach in which CASL specifications are parsed using ASF+SDF technology is directly analogous to the approach taken in the ELAN project [6] for parsing user-defined syntax.

3.1 Parser Generator

The parser generator, part of the current ASF+SDF Meta-Environment, is one of the components that can be (re-)used to generate parse tables for user-defined syntax in CASL.

It generates parse tables, suitable for later perusal by the SGLR parse table interpreter (see Section 3.2) from SDF syntax definitions. Unlike previous ASF+SDF parser generation technology, the current implementation does not use incremental and lazy techniques [18].

The process of generating parse tables consists of two distinct phases. In the first one the SDF definition is normalized to an intermediate, rudimentary, formalism: *Kernel-SDF*. In the second phase this Kernel-SDF is transformed to a parse table.

Grammar Normalization The grammar normalization phase, which derives a Kernel-SDF definition, consists of the following steps:

- A modular SDF specification is transformed into a flat specification.
- Lexical grammar rules are transformed to context-free grammar rules.
- Priority and associativity definitions are transformed to lists of pairs, where each pair consists of two production rules for which a priority or associativity relation holds. The transitive closure of the priority relations between grammar rules is made explicit in these pairs.

Parse Table Generation The actual parse table is derived from the Kernel-SDF definition. To do so, a straightforward SLR(1) approach is taken. However, shift/reduce or reduce/reduce conflicts are not considered problematic, and are simply stored in the table. Some extra calculations are consequently performed to reduce the number of conflicts in the parse table. Based on the list of priority relation pairs the table is filtered; see [25] for more details. The resulting table contains a list of all Kernel-SDF production rules, a list of states with the actions and gotos, and a list of all priority relation pairs. The parse table is represented as an ordinary ATERM.

3.2 Scannerless Generalized LR Parsing

Even though parsing is often considered a solved problem in computer science, every now and then new ideas and combinations of existing techniques pop up.

SGLR (Scannerless Generalized LR) parsing is a striking example of a combination of existing techniques that results in a remarkably powerful parser.

Generalized LR Parsing for Context-Free Grammars The ability to cope with arbitrary context-free grammars is of pivotal importance if one wishes to allow a modular syntax definition formalism. Due to the fact that LR(k)-grammars are not closed under union, a more powerful parsing technique is required. Generalized LR-parsing [33,31] (GLR-parsing) is a natural extension to LR-parsing, from this perspective. The saving grace of GLR-parsing lies in the fact that it does not require the parse table to be conflict-free. Allowing conflicts to occur in parse tables, GLR is equipped to deal with arbitrary context-free grammars. One of the advantages of this approach in the context of CASL is the simple, direct, mapping from the definition of the concrete syntax in EBNF into an SDF definition of same.

The parse result, then, might not be a single parse tree; in principle, a forest consisting of an arbitrary number of parse trees is yielded. Ambiguity produces multiple parse trees, each of which embodies a parse alternative. In case of an LR(1) grammar, the GLR algorithm collapses into LR(1), and exhibits similar performance characteristics. As a rule of thumb, the simpler the grammar, the closer GLR performance will be to LR(1) performance.

Eliminating the Scanner The GLR parser in the traditional ASF+SDF Meta-Environment uses a scanner, just like any conventional LR(k) parser. The use of a scanner in combination with GLR parsing leads to a certain tension between scanning and parsing. The scanner may sometimes have several ways of splitting up the input: a so-called lexical ambiguity occurs. In CASL, compound identifiers like '`s[t[u]]`' exhibited this problem (forcing one to modify the specification to something like '`s[t[u]␣]`'). The CASL syntax was adapted to get rid of this unwanted need to modify valid specifications. In case of lexical ambiguities, a scanner must take some decision; at a later point, when parsing the tokens as offered by the scanner, the selected tokenization might turn out to be not quite what the parser expected, causing the parse to fail.

Scannerless GLR parsing [34] solves this problem by unifying scanner and parser. In other words, the scanner is eliminated by simply considering all elementary input symbols (e.g. octets) as input tokens for the parser. Each character becomes a separate token, and ambiguities on the lexical level are dealt with by the GLR algorithm. This way, in a scannerless parser lexical and context-free syntax are integrated into a single grammar, describing the defined language entirely and exhaustively. Neither knowledge of the (usually complex) interface between scanner and parser nor knowledge of operational details of either is required for an understanding of the defined grammar. In the case of CASL, which is a language of which both the lexical as well as the context-free syntax are rather complex, scannerless parsing technology proved beneficial.

3.3 Parsing User-Defined Syntax

The CASFIX representation (see Section 4) of a CASL specification contains all information necessary for further analysis. Operator definitions, defined sorts, variables and the like can be extracted. Using this additional information a new, enriched, parse table that includes the user-defined syntax can then be constructed.

To be able to make all this happen, the following issues must be addressed:

- CASL is a modular specification formalism with a powerful import mechanism, it allows parameterization of modules and renaming.
- Operator definitions can be global or local, and so can a module import.
- Variables may be defined local to the axioms or globally defined. Globally defined variables are visible for the subsequent axioms of the enclosing specification. Any subsequent declaration (global or local) of a variable with the same name overrides a previous one.
- Axioms, operator definitions and variable definitions can be intermingled, as long as operators and variables are defined before they are used.

The import mechanism necessitates inspecting all imported modules when parsing a module: all global definitions, which may have been affected by an imported module, must be retrieved.

Definitions of sorts, predicates, and operations involve formulae and terms; moreover, variables may be declared by explicit quantifiers within formulae (which can also occur within conditional terms). Because of this fact, each axiom, in principle, might require constructing a new parse table. The speed of parse table generation is therefore of significant practical relevance.

A parse table built to cope with syntax introduced by a particular axiom is constructed from the respective sets of visible sorts, operator definitions, and variables as they pertain to that particular axiom. The generation process consists of two steps. In the first step (the normalization step) the Kernel-SDF grammar is derived. In the second step the parse table is produced from the Kernel-SDF grammar. The first step, the grammar normalization step, is the most interesting from the current perspective, because it is at this point that the appropriate set of extra production rules must be added, in order to recognize layout as well as the overall structure of formulas. The complete set of context-free grammar rules that have to be added can be found in [11].

The Kernel-SDF syntax for the Monoid example is given in Figure 7. Note that this Figure does not reveal all details: for brevity, the Kernel-SDF definition of `LAYOUT` is omitted.

Using this Kernel-SDF specification, it is fairly straightforward to construct a parse table for the unparsed expressions. After a successful parse of such an unparsed expression, the obtained CASFIX representation must be substituted for the unparsed expression in the original abstract syntax tree, yielding a more detailed abstract syntax tree.

```
sorts Elem
syntax
  <START>[\256]                                    -> <Start>
  <LAYOUT?-CF><Elem-CF><LAYOUT?-CF>                -> <START>
  "n"                                              -> <Elem-CF>
  <Elem-CF><LAYOUT?-CF>"*"<LAYOUT?-CF><Elem-CF>    -> <Elem-CF> {assoc}
  "("<LAYOUT?-CF><Elem-CF><LAYOUT?-CF>")"          -> <Elem-CF>
  <<Elem-CF>-VAR>                                  -> <Elem-CF>
  [\110]                                           -> "n"
  [\42]                                            -> "*"
  [\40]                                            -> "("
  [\41]                                            -> ")"
  "x"                                              -> <<Elem-CF>-VAR>
  "y"                                              -> <<Elem-CF>-VAR>
  "z"                                              -> <<Elem-CF>-VAR>
  [\120]                                           -> "x"
  [\121]                                           -> "y"
  [\122]                                           -> "z"
                                                   -> <LAYOUT?-CF>
  <LAYOUT-CF>                                      -> <LAYOUT?-CF>
```

Fig. 7. Monoid in Kernel-SDF

3.4 Drawbacks and Shortcomings

The architecture of the CASL parser presented in Section 1.1 is fairly complex at first glance. The need to translate parse trees, as produced by the SGLR parser, to CASFIX format is mainly responsible for this. One could conceive of a parser implementation with a parameterized output format: such a parser could generate arbitrary representations of syntax trees in a flexible way. In the context of CASL, specifically, it could be instantiated to produce CASFIX directly.

However, the current SGLR implementation cannot (yet) boast of this feature: its output is the rich and versatile ASFIX format. Therefore, an translation from ASFIX to CASFIX must be performed at every stage. In this translation, some of the wealth of the ASFIX representation is lost: it carries only the abstract syntax minus layout. Note that comments are considered layout in the CASL language definition, and are consequently also discarded here.

4 Representing CASL Terms Using ASF+SDF Technology

In order to make CASL a viable formalism for the specification of (complex) systems, a powerful suite of tools to create, manipulate, proof, typeset, and execute CASL specifications is needed. Reuse of existing tools is preferred over reinventing the wheel. However, existing tools are idiosyncratic, typically: they define their own interfaces and representation formats. This observation indicates a need for a common intermediate exchange format, that enables efficient integration of existing tools. Such an intermediate format should allow the storage by a tool of auxiliary information that may be invisible for others. To satisfy these requirements, the CoFI community has decided to use ATERMS [8] as its exchange format.

As an alternative possibility, SGML has also been taken in account while considering exchange format options [30]. If this choice had to be redone at present, some other formats, among which abstract syntax definition language (ASDL) [36,16] and eXtensible Markup Language (XML) [38] deserves explicit mention, would merit consideration.

ATERMS were originally developed to represent parse trees within the ASF+SDF Meta-Environment.

4.1 ATERMS

ATERMS is a generic formalism for the representation of structured information. It is both human-readable and easy to process automatically. A number of libraries that implement the functionality of creating and manipulating terms provide an API for the ATERMS formalism. The primary application area of ATERMS is the exchange of information between components of a programming environment, such as a parser, a (structure) editor, a compiler, and so on. The following data are typically represented as ATERMS: programs, specifications, parse tables, parse trees, abstract syntax trees, proofs, and the like. A generic storage mechanism, called *annotation*, accommodates associating extra information that may be of relevance somehow to specific ATERMS under consideration.

Examples of objects that are typically represented as ATERMS are:

- *constants*: `abc`.
- *numerals*: `123`.
- *literals*: `"abc"` or `"123"`.
- *lists*: `[]`, `[1, "abc", 3]`, or `[1, 2, [3, 2], 1]`.
- *functions*: `f("a")`, `g(1,[])`, or `h("1", f("2"), ["a","b"])`.
- *annotations*: `f("a"){[g,g(2,["a"]])}` or `"1"{[1,[1,2]],[s,"ab"]}`.

ATERMS can be qualified as an *open*, *simple*, *efficient*, *concise*, and *language independent* solution for the exchange of data structures between distributed applications.

ATERMS Libraries In order to employ ATERMS and to provide their associated operations, libraries of predefined functions are available. Currently, implementations in the programming languages C and JAVA exist.

Files that contain ATERMS can either be stored in a compact binary format or in a significantly more space-consuming textual format. In textual format, ATERMS can easily be processed by common off-the-shelf tools, like LEX/YACC. Both the C and JAVA library implementations provide facilities to parse and unparse ATERMS. The C version also provides functions for mapping the textual form into the binary one and vice versa.

Furthermore, both library implementations ensure maximal sharing when creating and manipulating terms – unless this feature is explicitly disabled. Both implementations perform automatic garbage collection, thus freeing storage associated to terms that are no longer in use.

The ATERMS library is documented extensively in its user manual [22].

4.2 CASFIX

By using CASL-specific 'keywords' as ATerm `AFuns`, the abstract syntax as defined in the CASL language summary [11] can be represented in ATerms in a straightforward manner.

It should be noted that there are many ways of defining the abstract syntax of CASL in terms of ATerms. We will restrict ourselves to describing the approach decided upon by the CoFI working group.

The selected approach is based on creating a unique ATerm construct for each abstract syntax rule. This results in a relatively large number of different `AFuns`, but has the benefit of making the representation of abstract syntax trees more compact.

The 'translation' of abstract rules into equivalent ATerm constructs is fairly simple, as the following translation rule illustrates:

```
SORT ::= "rule" MEMBER1 MEMBER2
⇒
rule(<MEMBER1>,<MEMBER2>)
```

There are several design issues to be addressed. The principal ones are how to deal with so-called 'chain rules', and how list structures are to be represented.

AFun Instantiation CASL-specific function names give rise to instantiating an `AFun`:

```
"basic-spec"  -> AFun
"forall"      -> AFun
"op-defn"     -> AFun
...
```

Function names are taken from the abbreviated abstract syntax definition in [11].

Additionally, specific `AFuns` are introduced to represent the anonymous abstract syntax rules (the chain rules), e.g.:

```
BASIC-ITEMS ::= SIG-ITEMS
```

An `AFun` is introduced e.g.:

```
"SIG-ITEMS" -> AFun
```

Finally, `AFuns` to represent lists are introduced, e.g.:

```
"BASIC-ITEMS*" -> AFun
```

Mapping Rules The mapping from the abstract syntax of CASL to an ATerms equivalent is based on the type of the abstract syntax rule.

- Rules with only a terminal in their right-hand side:

  ```
  QUANTIFIER :: "forall"
  ⇒
  forall
  ```

The terminal is mapped onto an ATerm consisting of a single `AFun`: `forall`.
- Rules consisting of a constructor and a list of simple nonterminals:

```
OP-ITEM ::= "op-defn" OP-NEMA OP-HEAD TERM
⇒
op-defn(<OP-NAME>,<OP-HEAD>,<TERM>)
```

The abstract syntax rule is transformed into an ATerm consisting of the `AFun op-defn` with three argument ATerms for `OP-NAME`, `OP-HEAD`, and `TERM`.
- Chain rules:

```
BASIC-ITEMS ::= SIG-ITEMS
⇒
SIG-ITEMS(<SIG-ITEMS>)
```

The sort name on the right hand side is used as the `AFun`.
- Rules with a constructor and one or more lists:

```
BASIC-SPEC ::= "basic-spec" BASIC-ITEMS*
⇒
basic-spec(BASIC-ITEMS*([<BASIC-ITEMS>]))
```

This ATerms expression should be read as follows: `basic-spec` is an `AFun` that indicate that a node of type `basic-spec` is constructed. The `AFun` `BASIC-ITEMS*` indicates a node that contains a (possibly empty) list of `BASIC-ITEM`s. Square brackets delimit the actual list; list elements are separated by commas.

The full mapping can be found on the www[6].

4.3 Annotations

The term 'annotation' is overloaded. First of all, the ATerms support annotations; in that context, it means that nodes in the abstract syntax tree are extended with additional information which is invisible, but can still be accessed by explicit demand. This annotation mechanism can be used by all kinds of tools to store extra information, e.g. a parser can store position information, or pretty printers can store font information.

Secondly, annotations can also occur within a CASL specification, see [11,27,32]. There exist annotations related to labels, displaying, parsing, and semantics.

Examples of syntactical annotations are `%left assoc`, `%right assoc`, and `%prec`; examples of semantical annotations are `%cons` and `%def`. For the exact meaning of these annotations we refer to [32]. The `%cons`, `%def`, `%left assoc`, and `%right assoc` annotations can only occur at a restricted number of positions in a CASL specification.

Some annotations, such as the `%prec`, may occur in arbitrary places in a CASL specification. The CASL language summary [11] is not very specific about

6 `http://www.cwi.nl/~markvdb/cofi/casl.html`

where the various types of annotations may occur. If these locations are fixed, the concrete syntax of CASL can be adapted in order to deal with these annotations, however, it is also possible to consider annotations as a kind of layout. The latter approach would prevent the need to adapt the CASL syntax every time a new annotation is introduced.

Annotations occurring in well-defined locations in CASL specification must also be encoded in the CASFIX representation at the appropriate nodes, with the correct name, as generally approved upon.

In order to prevent excessive use of annotations both at the CASL syntax level as well as at the tool level, annotations have to be approved by the COFI community. Naturally, it is allowed for a tool to add an 'internal' annotation temporarily, but such an annotation may not be exported to the outside world.

5 Conclusions

Generic language technology provided by ASF+SDF proved to be helpful for prototyping the concrete syntax of CASL. The straightforward mapping from EBNF to SDF enabled us to interact directly with the concrete syntax definition of CASL. Serious lexical and syntactical ambiguities were detected at an early stage. This flexibility is based on the SGLR parsing technology which removes the need for (complex) grammar transformations.

Although ASF+SDF proved to be a useful vehicle for prototyping the concrete syntax of CASL, a number of shortcomings can be identified. Firstly, the user-defined syntax of CASL proved to be challenging for ASF+SDF; see [37] for details. The CASL syntax proved to be an interesting test case for the development of both SGLR parser and the parser generator: the complexity of the CASL syntax continuously pushed the envelope, putting a heavy burden on ambiguity-handling mechanisms. As larger parts of the syntax were completed, and more complex examples were held against the current state of technology, it was rapidly adapted, tweaked, corrected, and revised.

Secondly, although the CASL syntax is described entirely in SDF and specifications can be parsed inside the Meta-Environment, the existence of a straightforward translation to other parser generator formalisms like LEX/YACC [26,21], JAVACC, etc., is not guaranteed, mainly because of the limitation of the latter to the class of LALR grammars. Using the powerful and efficient parsers provided by current ASF+SDF technology, the need to migrate from SDF to LEX/YACC-like formalisms becomes less pressing.

The development of parsers for CASL and the definition of an exchange format formed the first steps on the long path that lead to the creation of new tools and the adaptation of existing ones. Although the current ASF+SDF Meta-Environment is entirely based on ATERMS, it is still a question whether ATERMS are indeed powerful enough to contain all information needed by any conceivable CASL-tool – past, present and future. However, previous experience, including experiments carried out in Bremen [28], Nancy [23], and Edinburgh [2], suggest a positive answer; future experiments, with more, and more complex, tools built upon ATERMS foundations, will help gain a firmer grasp on this subject.

Acknowledgements

We thank Jan Heering and Pieter Olivier for reading the draft versions of this paper.

References

1. A. V. Aho, R. Sethi, and J. D. Ullman. *Compilers. Principles, Techniques and Tools.* Addison-Wesley, 1986. 91
2. D. Baillie. Proving Theorems about Algebraic Specifications. Master's thesis, University of Edinburgh, Department of Computer Science, 1999. 102
3. J. A. Bergstra, J. Heering, and P. Klint, editors. *Algebraic Specification.* ACM Press/Addison-Wesley, 1989. 91
4. J. A. Bergstra and P. Klint. The discrete time ToolBus – a software coordination architecture. *Science of Computer Programming*, 31(2-3):205–229, July 1998. 90
5. M. Bidoit and C. Choppy. ASSPEGIQUE: an integrated environment for algebraic specifications. In H. Ehrig, C. Floyd, M. Nivat, and J. Thatcher, editors, *Formal Methods and Software Development - Proceedings of the International Joint Conference on Theory and Practice of Software Development 2*, volume 186 of *LNCS*, pages 246–260. Springer-Verlag, 1985. 91
6. P. Borovanský, C. Kirchner, H. Kirchner, P.-E. Moreau, and M. Vittek. ELAN: A logical framework based on computational systems. In José Meseguer, editor, *Proceedings of the First International Workshop on Rewriting Logic*, volume 4 of *Electronic Notes in Theoretical Computer Science.* Elsevier Science, 1996. 92, 95
7. P. Boullier. Contribution à la construction automatique d'analyseurs lexicographiques et syntaxiques. Thèse d'Etat, Université d'Orléans, 1984. 92
8. M. G. J. van den Brand, H. A. de Jong, P. Klint, and P. Olivier. Efficient Annotated Terms. *Software, Practice & Experience*, 30:259–291, 2000. 90, 98
9. M. G. J. van den Brand, T. Kuipers, L. Moonen, and P. Olivier. Design and implementation of a new asf+sdf meta-environment. In A. Sellink, editor, *Proceedings of the Second International Workshop on the Theory and Practice of Algebraic Specifications (ASF+SDF'97)*, Workshops in Computing, Amsterdam, 1997. Springer/British Computer Society. 90
10. CoFI. The Common Framework Initiative for algebraic specification and development, electronic archives. Notes and Documents accessible by HTTP[7] and FTP[8], 1998. 103, 104
11. CoFI-LD. CASL – The CoFI Algebraic Specification Language – Summary, version 1.0. Documents/CASL/Summary-v1.0, in [10], 1998. 89, 92, 93, 97, 100, 101
12. A. van Deursen. *Executable Language Definitions: Case Studies and Origin Tracking Techniques.* PhD thesis, University of Amsterdam, 1994. 91, 95
13. A. van Deursen, J. Heering, and P. Klint, editors. *Language Prototyping: An Algebraic Specification Approach*, volume 5 of *AMAST Series in Computing.* World Scientific, 1996. 89, 91

[7] http://www.brics.dk/Projects/CoFI/

[8] ftp://ftp.brics.dk/Projects/CoFI/

14. A. van Deursen and P. D. Mosses. Executing Action Semantics descriptions using ASF+SDF. In M. Nivat, C. Rattray, T. Rus, and G. Scollo, editors, *Algebraic Methodology and Software Technology (AMAST'93)*, Workshops in Computing, pages 415–416. Springer-Verlag, 1993. System demonstration. 95
15. J. Earley. An efficient context-free parsing algorithm. *Communications of the ACM*, 13(2):94–102, 1970. 91
16. D. R. Hanson. Early Experience with ASDL in lcc. *Software—Practice and Experience*, 29(3):417–435, 1999. 99
17. J. Heering, P. R. H. Hendriks, P. Klint, and J. Rekers. The syntax definition formalism SDF — Reference manual. *SIGPLAN Notices*, 24(11):43–75, 1989. 91
18. J. Heering, P. Klint, and J. Rekers. Incremental generation of parsers. *IEEE Transactions on Software Engineering*, SE-16:1344–1351, 1990. 95
19. J. Hopcroft and J. D. Ullman. *Introduction to Automata Theory, Language, and Computation*. Addison-Wesley, 1979. 92
20. D. Hutter and C. Sengler. INKA, The Next Generation. In M. A. McRobby and J. K. Slaney, editors, *Automated Deduction - CADE-13*, volume 1104 of *LNAI*, pages 288–292. Springer, 1996. 92
21. S. C. Johnson. *YACC: yet another compiler-compiler*. Bell Laboratories, 1986. UNIX Programmer's Supplementary Documents, Volume 1 (PS1). 102
22. H. A. de Jong and P. Olivier. ATerm Library User Manual, 1999. Available via HTTP[9]. 99
23. H. Kirchner and C. Ringeissen. Executing CASL Equational Specifications with the ELAN Rewrite Engine. Note T-9, in [10], 1999. 102
24. P. Klint. A meta-environment for generating programming environments. *ACM Transactions on Software Engineering and Methodology*, 2:176–201, 1993. 89, 90
25. P. Klint and E. Visser. Using filters for the disambiguation of context-free grammars. In G. Pighizzini and P. San Pietro, editors, *Proceedings ASMICS Workshop on Parsing Theory*, pages 1–20, 1994. Published as Technical Report 126–1994, Computer Science Department, University of Milan. 95
26. M. E. Lesk and E. Schmidt. *LEX - A lexical analyzer generator*. Bell Laboratories, unix programmer's supplementary documents, volume 1 (ps1) edition, 1986. 102
27. T. Mossakowski. Standard annotations for parsers and static semantic checkers — a proposal. Note T-6, in [10], 1998. 101
28. T. Mossakowski. CASL: From Semantics to Tools. In S. Graf and M. Schwartzbach, editors, *TACAS'2000*, volume 1785 of *LNCS*, pages 93–108. Springer-Verlag, 2000. 92, 102
29. P. D. Mosses. *Action Semantics*. Cambridge University Press, 1992. 91, 95
30. P. D. Mosses. Potential use of SGML for the CASL interchange format. Note T-4, in [10], 1997. 98
31. J. Rekers. *Parser Generation for Interactive Environments*. PhD thesis, University of Amsterdam, 1992. 91, 96
32. M. Roggenbach and T. Mossakowski. Proposal of Some Annotations and Literal Syntax in CASL. Note L-11, in [10], 1999. 101
33. M. Tomita. *Efficient Parsing for Natural Languages*. Kluwer Academic Publishers, 1985. 91, 96
34. E. Visser. *Syntax Definition for Language Prototyping*. PhD thesis, University of Amsterdam, 1997. 91, 96
35. F. Voisin. CIGALE: a tool for interactive grammar construction and expression parsing. *Science of Computer Programming*, 7(1):61–86, 1986. 91

[9] `http://www.wins.uva.nl/pub/programming-research/software/aterm/`

36. D. C. Wang, A. W. Appel, J. L. Korn, and C. S. Serra. The Zephyr Abstract Syntax Description Language. In *Proceedings of the Conference on Domain-Specific Languages*, pages 213–227, 1997. 99
37. B. Wedemeijer. Introduction and Basic Tooling for Casl using ASF+SDF. Technical Report P9809, University of Amsterdam, Programming Research Group, 1998. 94, 102
38. Extensible markup language (XML) 1.0. Technical report, World Wide Web Consortium, 1998. Available at: `http:www.w3.org/TR/REC-xml`. 99

Using CASL to Specify the Requirements and the Design: A Problem Specific Approach

Christine Choppy[1] and Gianna Reggio[2]

[1] LIPN, Institut Galilée - Université Paris XIII, France
[2] DISI, Università di Genova, Italy

Abstract. In [11] M. Jackson introduces the concept of *problem frame* to describe specific classes of problems, to help in the specification and design of systems, and also to provide a framework for reusability. He thus identifies some particular frames, such as the translation frame (e.g., a compiler), the information system frame, the control frame (or reactive system frame), ... Each frame is described along three viewpoints that are application domains, requirements, and design.

Our aim is to use CASL (or possibly a sublanguage or an extension of CASL if and when appropriate) to formally specify the requirements and the design of particular classes of problems ("problem frames"). This goal is related to methodology issues for CASL, that are here addressed in a more specific way, having in mind some particular problem frame, i.e., a class of systems.

It is hoped that this will provide both a help in using, in a really effective way, CASL for system specifications, a link with approaches that are currently used in the industry, and a framework for the reusability.

This approach is illustrated with some case studies, e.g., the information system frame is illustrated with the invoice system.

1 Introduction

It is now well established that formal specifications are required for the development of high quality computer systems. However, it is still difficult for a number of practitioners to write these specifications. In this paper we address the general issue of how to bridge the gap between a problem requirements and its specification. We think this issue has various facets. For instance, given a problem, how to guide the specification process? Often people do not know where to start, and then are stopped at various points. Another facet is, given a specification language, how to use it in an appropriate way? We address these facets here through the use of M. Jackson's problem frames (successfully used in industry), which we formalize by providing the corresponding specification skeletons in the CASL language ([12,13]).

A Jackson problem frame [11] is a generalization of a class of problems, thus helping to sort out in which frame/category is the problem under study. The idea here is to provide a help to analyse software development problems and to choose an appropriate method for solving them (with the assumption that there

D. Bert, C. Choppy, and P. Mosses (Eds.): WADT'99, LNCS 1827, pp. 106–126, 2000.

is no "general" method). Then, for each problem frame, M. Jackson provides its expected components together with their characteristics and the way they are connected. The problem frame components always include a domain description, the requirements description, and possibly the design description. The domain description expresses "what already exists", it is an abstraction of a part of the world. The requirements description expresses "what there should be", that is what are the computer system expected concepts and facilities. The design description deals with "how" to achieve the system functions and behaviours. The problem frames identified are the translation (JSP), the information system, the reactive system (or control frame), the workpiece, and the connection frames. While these cover quite a number of applications, it may also be the case that some problems are "multiframe".

While Jackson problem frames may be used to start understanding and analysing the system to be developed, they have no formal underpinning. Our idea here is to still rely on them while providing the corresponding "specification frames". We thus provide a methodological approach to write problem specifications using the problem frames that importantly gives guidelines to *start* and to *do* the problem analysis and specification; combining these two "tools" yields a powerful approach to guide the problem understanding and the specification writing.

The issue of the choice of a formal specification language is non trivial [2]. We think that algebraic specification languages offer an adequate degree of abstraction for our needs, so we chose the latest and more general one, CASL, the Common Algebraic Specification Language ([12,13]) developed within the Common Framework Initiative (CoFI), to express our proposed formal underpinning for problem frames. While CASL was developed to be "a central, reasonably expressive language for specifying conventional software", "the common framework will provide a family of languages" [12]. Thus, restrictions of CASL to simpler languages (for example, in connection with verification tools) will be provided as well as extensions oriented towards particular programming paradigms, e.g., reactive systems. While dealing with the translation frame (Sect. 2 and 3), CASL complies with our needs, but when moving to dynamic systems that may occur within the information system frame (Sect. 4 and 5), we propose an extension of CASL with temporal logic, named CASL-LTL [15], based on the ideas of [3] and [7], that may be more appropriate (and will be shortly presented when used). Since the design of CASL was based on a critical selection of constructs found in existing algebraic frameworks, the reader familiar with these may feel quite "at home", while CASL offers for these convenient syntactic combinations. In this paper, we use some CASL constructs, that we introduce when they appear. While the CASL syntax and semantics are completed, some tools (e.g., parsers, libraries, ...) are being developed. In what follows we shall rely on the available library for basic data types [16].

This paper is organised as follows. In Sect. 2 and 3, we describe the translation problem frame, provide a a method to formalize it using CASL, and illustrate it on a short example that is the Unix grep utility. In Sect. 4 and 5, we work similarly on the information system problem frame and illustrate it with the invoice case study. The information system frame raises various issues, since we are dealing with bigger reactive systems. The size issue leads us to clearly identify sets of properties that need to be expressed and also to search for a legible way to present large specifications of this kind. For lack of room, we cannot report here the complete specifications of the considered case studies, they can be found in [6].

2 Translation Frame

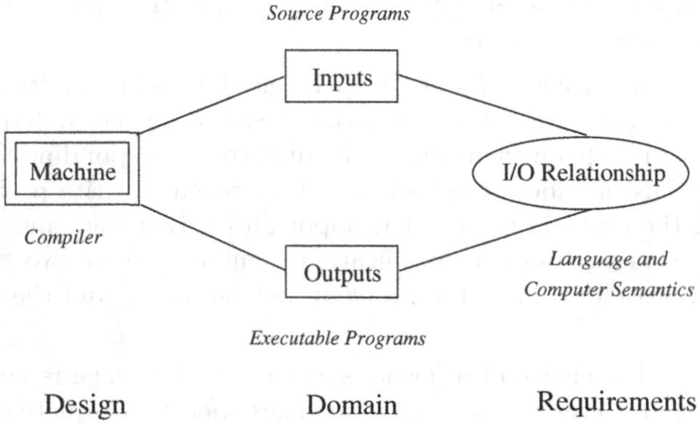

The translation frame we consider here is a simple frame that is quite useful for a number of case studies [5] (it is close to the JSP frame where inputs and outputs are streams). The translation frame domain is given by the Inputs and the Outputs, the requirements are described by the input/output relationship, I/O Relationship, and the design is the Machine. An example of a translation frame problem is a compiler, where the Inputs are the source programs, the Outputs are the executable programs, the I/O Relationship is given by the language and computer semantics, and the Machine is the compiler. In the following, we shall provide the skeletons for the CASL formal specifications of Inputs, Outputs, the I/O Relationship, and the Machine, as well as conditions for correctness of the Machine as regards the I/O Relationship. This will be shortly illustrated on a case study (the Grep utility) in Sect. 3.

2.1 Domain and Requirements

To capture the requirements in this case means:
- to express the relevant properties of the application domain components, i.e., Inputs and Outputs;
- to express the I/O Relationship.

Let us note that this often yields to specify also some basic data that are required by the Inputs, the Outputs and/or by the I/O Relationship.

To use the CASL language to specify the above requirements means to give three CASL specifications of the following form:

spec INPUTS =
  ......

spec OUTPUTS =
  ......

spec IO_RELATIONSHIP =
  INPUTS **and** OUTPUTS **then**
  pred *IO_rel* : *Input* × *Output*
  axioms
  ......

where the IO_RELATIONSHIP specification extends (CASL keyword **then**) the union (**and**) of the INPUTS and OUTPUTS specifications by the *IO_rel* predicate. The axioms in CASL are first-order formulas built from equations and definedness assertions. We can here add some suggestions on the way the axioms of IO_RELATIONSHIP should be written. The *IO_rel* properties could be described along the different cases to be considered and expressed by some conditions on the *Input* and *Output* arguments. This approach has the advantage that the specifier is induced to consider all relevant cases (and not to forget some important ones). Therefore the axioms of IO_RELATIONSHIP have the form

either $IO\_rel(i, o) \Rightarrow cond(i, o)$

or $cond(i, o) \wedge def\ i \wedge def\ o \Rightarrow IO\_rel(i, o)$.

where i and o are terms of appropriate sorts and *cond* is a CASL formula.

2.2 Design

To design a solution of the problem in this case means to define a partial function (or a sequential program or an algorithm) *transl* that associates an element of Outputs with an element of Inputs. To use CASL to specify the above design means to give a CASL specification of the following form:

spec MACHINE =
  INPUTS **and** OUTPUTS **then**
free { %% this CASL "free" construction requires that no additional feature occurs
  op *transl* : *Input* →? *Output* %% the translation function
  axioms
  %% *transl* domain definition
  ......
  %% *transl* definition
  ......}

The axioms for *transl* should exhibit both (i) when is *transl* defined (*transl* domain definition), and (ii) what are *transl* results (*transl* definition).

Again here, we suggest a case analysis approach which yields for the *transl* domain definition axioms of the form

$cond(i) \Rightarrow def\ transl(i)$

and for the *transl* definition axioms of the form

$cond(i, o) \wedge def\ (transl(i)) \wedge def\ o \Rightarrow transl(i) = o$

where i and o are terms of the appropriate sorts, and *cond* is a positive conditional formula. Let us note that, in order to provide a more concise/readable presentation of the axioms, the $def\ (transl(i)) \wedge def\ o$ part may be left implicit.

2.3 Correctness

Here we add some notion of correctness which is not explicited in Jackson's presentation, and which we can deal with thanks to the formalization we provide. It may now be relevant to state under which conditions the MACHINE designed implements the IO_RELATIONSHIP. We propose below three conditions and introduce the following specification, requiring that the predicate *IO_rel* does not belong to the MACHINE signature.

spec TRANSLATION = IO_RELATIONSHIP **and** MACHINE

MACHINE is correct w.r.t. IO_RELATIONSHIP iff

1. MACHINE is sufficiently complete and hierarchically consistent w.r.t. INPUTS and OUTPUTS.
2. TRANSLATION $\models \forall\, i : Input, o : Output, transl(i) = o \;\Rightarrow\; IO\_rel(i, o)$
3. TRANSLATION $\models \forall\, i : Input, o : Output, IO\_rel(i, o) \;\Rightarrow$
   $\exists\, o' : Output \bullet transl(i) = o'$

Condition 1 requires that MACHINE does not introduce some new elements or properties in the specified descriptions of "what already exists" (the application domain), i.e., INPUTS and OUTPUTS. Condition 2 requires that, whenever *transl* is defined for a given i and yields o, then IO_RELATIONSHIP relates i and o, in other words, it ensures that the produced translation is correct. Finally, condition 3 expresses that whenever IO_RELATIONSHIP relates i with some o (recall *IO_rel* is just a relationship not a function), then *transl* applied to i must yield some o', in other words, it requires that the translation produces an output when appropriate given the requirements.

3 Case Study: The Grep Operation

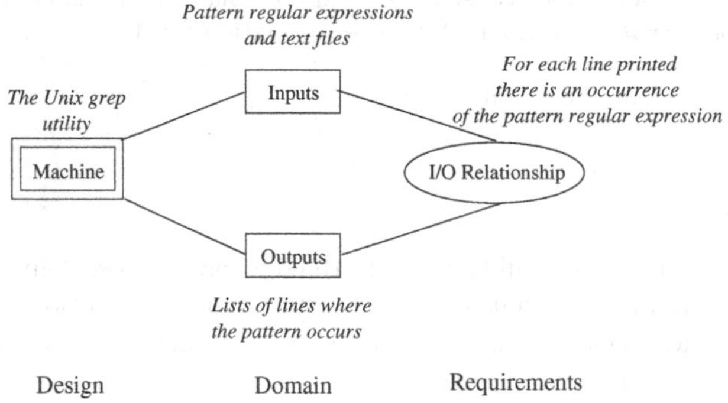

In the previous section, the translation frame was presented with the typical compiler example. Here, we illustrate it with the grep utility that is provided by Unix and we sketch the corresponding specifications (see [6] for the full ones). The grep utility searches files for a pattern and prints all lines that contain that pattern. It uses limited regular expressions to match the patterns.

3.1 Domain and Requirements

In order to provide a specification of the domain, we need to specify the inputs, which are regular expressions and files, the outputs, which are lists of lines, and also the basic data that are required, which are characters, strings and lists.

Basic Data To specify the basic data we use some specifications provided in [16], e.g., CHAR and STRING. For example the specification for strings of [16] is an instantiation of the generic specification LIST[ELEM] together with some symbol mapping ($\mapsto$) for sort names:

spec STRING = LIST[CHAR]
  with sorts *List*[*Char*] $\mapsto$ *String*

Inputs We sketch below the specifications of the Inputs which are regular expressions and files.

spec GREP_INPUTS = REGULAR_EXPRESSION **and** FILE

The CASL construct **free type** allows one to provide for the *Reg_Expr* type constants (*empty* and Λ), operations (__ + __ and __*), and also to state that any character may yield a *Reg_Expr*.

spec REGULAR_EXPRESSION = CHAR **then**
free type *Reg_Expr* ::=
  empty | Λ | __ + __ : (*Reg_Expr Reg_Expr*) | __* : (*Reg_Expr*) | **sort** *Char* ;

spec FILE = STRING **then**
free type *File* ::= *empty* | __ __ : (*Char* ; *File*);
  ops *first_line* : *File* →? *String*;
    drop_line : *File* →? *File*;
%% with the corresponding axioms

Outputs is a list of lines, that is a list of strings.

spec GREP_OUTPUTS = LIST[STRING]
  with sorts *List*[*String*] $\mapsto$ *Grep_Output*

I/O Relationship The I/O Relationship between the Inputs and the Outputs is sketched in the following specification, where the *grep_IO_rel* predicate properties are expressed by means of the predicates *is_gen* (stating when a string matches a regular expression) and *appears_in* (stating when a string is a substring of another one).

spec GREP_IO_REL = GREP_INPUTS **and** GREP_OUTPUTS
then preds *grep_IO_rel* : *Reg_Expr* × *File* × *Grep_Output*;
    __ *is_gen* __ : *String* × *Reg_Expr*;
    __ *appears_in* __ : *String* × *String*;
  vars *reg* : *Reg_Expr*; *ol*, *ol'* : *Grep_Output*; *f* : *File*;

axioms

$grep\_IO\_rel(reg, empty, ol) \Leftrightarrow ol = nil;$
$\neg f = empty \Rightarrow$
$(grep\_IO\_rel(reg, f, ol) \Leftrightarrow$
$((\exists s \bullet is\_gen\ (reg, s) \wedge s\ appears\_in\ first\_line(f) \wedge$
$grep\_IO\_rel(reg, drop\_line(f), ol') \wedge ol = first\_line(f) :: ol')$
$\vee (\neg \exists s \bullet is\_gen\ (reg, s) \wedge s\ appears\_in\ first\_line(f) \wedge$
$grep\_IO\_rel(reg, drop\_line(f), ol)));$

%% axioms defining *appears_in* and *is_gen*

3.2 Design

The MACHINE yields an *Grep_Output* given a *Reg_Expr* and a *File*.

spec GREP_MACHINE = GREP_INPUTS **and** GREP_OUTPUTS
then op $grep\_transl : Reg\_Expr \times File \rightarrow Grep\_Output;$
pred $match : Reg\_Expr \times String;$
vars $reg : Reg\_Expr; f : File;$
axioms

$grep\_transl(reg, empty) = empty;$
$\neg (f = empty) \wedge match(reg, first\_line(f)) \Rightarrow$
$grep\_transl(reg, f) = first\_line(f) :: grep\_transl(reg, drop\_line(f));$
$\neg (f = empty) \wedge \neg match(reg, first\_line(f)) \Rightarrow$
$grep\_transl(reg, f) = grep\_transl(reg, drop\_line(f));$

%% axioms defining *match*

3.3 Correctness

To express correctness we need to introduce the following specification, requiring that the predicate *grep_IO_rel* does not belong to the GREP_MACHINE signature.

spec GREP_TRANSLATION = GREP_IO_REL **and** GREP_MACHINE

GREP_MACHINE is correct w.r.t. GREP_IO_REL iff

1. GREP_MACHINE is sufficiently complete and hierarchically consistent w.r.t. GREP_INPUTS and GREP_OUTPUTS.
2. GREP_TRANSLATION $\models \forall f : File, reg : Reg\_Expr, ol : Grep\_Output,$
$grep\_transl(reg, f) = ol \Rightarrow grep\_IO\_rel(reg, f, ol)$
3. GREP_TRANSLATION $\models \forall f : File, reg : Reg\_Expr, ol : Grep\_Output,$
$grep\_IO\_rel(reg, f, ol) \Rightarrow \exists ol' : Grep\_Output \bullet grep\_transl(reg, f) = ol'$

4 Information System Frame

The information system frame domain description is given by the Real World, the Information Requests and the Information Outputs, the requirements are described by the Information Function, and the design is the System. To quote [11], "In its simplest form, an information system provides information, in response to requests, about some relevant real-world domain of interest." The Real World may be a *static* domain (e.g., if the system provides information on Shakespeare's plays), or a *dynamic* domain (e.g., "the activities of a currently operating business" [11]). Here we consider information system frames with a dynamic domain, so "The Real World is *dynamic* and also *active*." [11].

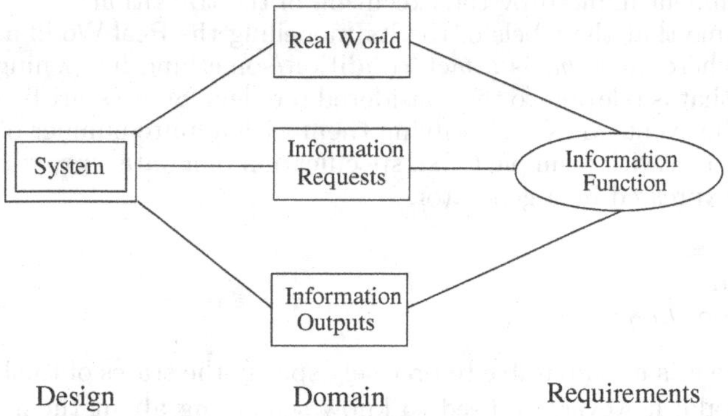

4.1 Domain and Requirements

To capture the requirements in the case of the Simple Information System means:

- to find out the relevant properties of the Real World;
- to determine the Information Requests and the Information Outputs;
- to determine the Information Function.

To use CASL-LTL [15] to specify the above requirements means to give four specifications corresponding to the four parts respectively, as follows.

We consider the case where the Real World is a dynamic system, thus is specified using CASL-LTL by logically specifying an lts (a *labelled transition system*) that models it. A *labelled transition system* (shortly *lts*) is a triple $(S, L, \rightarrow)$, where S and L are two sets, and $\rightarrow \subseteq S \times L \times S$ is the *transition relation*. A triple $(s, l, s') \in \rightarrow$ is said to be a *transition* and is usually written $s \xrightarrow{l} s'$. Using the **dsort** construction introduced in CASL-LTL is a way to declare the lts triple $(S, L, \rightarrow)$ at once and to provide the use of temporal logic combinators in the axioms (as defined in CASL-LTL).

Given an lts we can associate with each $s_0 \in S$ the tree (*transition tree*) whose root is s_0, where the order of the branches is not considered, two identically decorated subtrees with the same root are considered as a unique subtree, and if it has a node n decorated with s and $s \xrightarrow{l} s'$, then it has a node n' decorated with s' and an arc decorated with l from n to n'.

We model a dynamic system D with a transition tree determined by an lts $(S, L, \rightarrow)$ and an initial state $s_0 \in S$; the nodes in the tree represent the intermediate (interesting) situations of the life of S, and the arcs of the tree the possibilities of S of passing from one situation to another. It is important to note here that an arc (a transition) $s \xrightarrow{l} s'$ has the following meaning: D in the situation s has the *capability* of passing into the situation s' by performing a transition, where the label l represents the interaction with the environment during such a move; thus l contains information on the conditions on the environment for the capability to become effective, and on the transformation of such environment induced by the execution of the transition.

We assume that the labels of the lts modelling the Real World are finite sets of events, where an *event* is a fact/condition/something happening during the system life that is relevant to the considered problem. So we start by determining which are the events and by classifying them with a finite number of kinds, then we specify them with a simple CASL specification of a datatype, where any kind of event is expressed by a generator.

spec EVENT =
  ... **then**
  free type *Event* ::= ...

At this stage it is not advisable to precisely specify the states of the lts modelling the Real World; however, we need to know something about them, and we can express that by some CASL operations, called *state observers*, taking the state as an argument and returning the observed value. Finally we express the properties on the behaviour of the Real World along the following schema:

- **Incompatible events:** Express when sets of events are incompatible, i.e., when they cannot happen simultaneously.
- **Relationships between state observers and events** For each state observer *obs* express (i) its initial value, (ii) its value after $E(\ldots)$ happened, for each kind of event E modifying it.
- **Event specific properties** For each kind of event E express the
  - **preconditions** properties on the system state and on the past (behaviour of the system) required for $E(\ldots)$ to take place
  - **postconditions** properties on the state and on the future (behaviour of the system) that should be fulfilled after $E(\ldots)$ took place
  - **liveness** properties on the state under which $E(\ldots)$ will surely happen and when it will happen.

Then the specification of the Real World has the following form (the specification FINITESET has been taken from [16]).

spec REAL_WORLD =
  FINITESET[EVENT **fit** *Elem* ↦ *Event*] ... **then**
  dsort *State* %% **dsort** is a CASL-LTL construction
  free type *Label_State* ::= **sort** *FinSet*[*Event*];
  pred *initial* : *State* %% determines the initial states of the system
  %% State observers
  op *obs* : *State* × ... → ...
  ......
  axioms
  %% Incompatible events
  ...
  %% Relationships between state observers and events

...
%% Event specific properties
...

The postconditions and the liveness properties cannot be expressed using only the first-order logic available for axioms in CASL, thus CASL-LTL extends it with combinators from the temporal logic ([7]) that will be introduced when they will be used in the case study.

The Information Requests and the Information Outputs are two datatypes that are specified using CASL by simply giving their generators.

spec INFORMATION_REQUESTS =
... **then**
free type *Info_Request* ::= ...

spec INFORMATION_OUTPUTS =
... **then**
free type *Info_Output* ::= ...

We assume that the Information Function takes as arguments, not only the information request, but also the history of the system (a sequence of states and labels), because it contains all the pieces of information needed to give an answer.

The Information Function is specified using CASL-LTL by defining it within a specification of the following form.

spec INFORMATION_FUNCTION =
INFORMATION_REQUESTS **and** INFORMATION_OUTPUTS **and** REAL_WORLD **then**
free {
%% histories are partial system lifecycles
type *History* ::= $init(State)$ | $\_\_\_(History; Label\_State; State)?$;
op $last : History \rightarrow State$;
vars $st : State$; $h : History$; $l : Label\_State$;
- $def\ (h\ l\ st) \iff last(h) \xrightarrow{l} st$ %% $\_\_\_$ is partial
- $last(init(st)) = st$
- $def\ (h\ l\ st) \Rightarrow last(h\ l\ st) = st$

op $inf\_fun : History \times Info\_Request \rightarrow Info\_Output$;
axioms
%% properties of *inf_fun* ...

where the properties of *inf_fun* are expressed by axioms having the form
$def\ (h) \wedge def\ (i\_req) \wedge def\ (i\_out) \wedge cond(h, i\_req, i\_out) \Rightarrow$
$inf\_fun(h, i\_req) = i\_out$
and *cond* is a conjunction of positive atoms.

In many cases the above four specifications share some common parts, by using the CASL constructs for the declaration of named specifications, such parts can be specified apart and reused when needed. These specifications are collected together and presented before the others under the title of basic data.

4.2 Design

To design an "Information System" means to design the System, a dynamic system interacting with the Real World (by detecting the happening events), and with the users (by receiving the information requests and sending back the information outputs).

We assume that the System:

– keeps a view of the actual situation of the Real World,
– updates it depending on the detected events,
– decides which information requests from the users to accept in each instant,
– answers to such requests with the appropriate information outputs using its view of the situation of the Real World.

We assume also that the System can immediately detect in a correct way any event happening in the Real World and that the information requests are handled immediately (more precisely the time needed to detect the events and to handle the requests is not relevant).

The design of the System will be specified using CASL-LTL by logically specifying an lts that models it. The labels of this lts are triples consisting of the events detected in the Real World, the received requests and the sent out information output.

spec SYSTEM =
  SITUATION **and** FINITESET[EVENT **fit** *Elem* ↦ *Event*] **and**
  FINITESET[INFORMATION_REQUESTS **fit** *Elem* ↦ *Info_Request*] **and**
  FINITESET[INFORMATION_OUTPUTS **fit** *Elem* ↦ *Info_Output*] **then**
free {
  dtype
    System ::= **sort** *Situation*;
    Label_System ::= __ __ __(*FinSet*[*Event*];
      FinSet[*Info_Request*]; *FinSet*[*Info_Output*]);
  ops *update* : *Situation* × *FinSet*[*Event*] → *Situation*;
    inf_fun : *Situation* × *Info_Request* → *Info_Output*;
  pred *acceptable* : *FinSet*[*Info_Request*];
  axioms
    $i\_reqs = \{i\_req_1\} \cup \ldots \cup \{i\_req_n\} \wedge acceptable(i\_reqs) \wedge$
    $i\_outs = \{inf\_fun(sit, i\_req_1)\} \cup \ldots \cup \{inf\_fun(sit, i\_req_n)\} \Rightarrow$
      $sit \xrightarrow{evs\ i\_reqs\ i\_outs} update(sit, evs)$;
  %% axioms defining *update*, *acceptable* and *inf_fun*
    ......
}

where SITUATION specifies a data structure describing in an appropriate way (i.e., apt to permit to answer to all information requests) the System's views of the possible situations of the Real World.

Thus to specify the design of the System it is sufficient to give:

– the specification SITUATION;
– the axioms defining the operation *update* describing how the System updates its view of the Real World when it detects some events;
– the axioms defining the predicate *acceptable* describing which sets of requests may be accepted simultaneously by the System;
– the axioms defining the operation *inf_fun* describing what is the result of each information request depending on the System's view of the the Real World situation.

4.3 Correctness

We introduce the following specification:

spec INFORMATION_SYSTEM =
  INFORMATION_FUNCTION **and** SYSTEM **then**
  pred *Imp* : *History* × *Situation*
  axioms
  ......

SYSTEM is correct w.r.t. INFORMATION_FUNCTION iff

1. SYSTEM is sufficiently complete and hierarchically consistent w.r.t. EVENT, INFORMATION_REQUESTS and INFORMATION_OUTPUTS.
2. INFORMATION_SYSTEM $\models \forall\ st : Situation, i\_req : Info\_Request,$ $i\_out : Info\_Output, inf\_fun(st, i\_req) = i\_out \Rightarrow$ $\exists\ h : History \bullet Imp(h, st) \wedge inf\_fun(h, i\_req) = i\_out$

Notice that the proof has to be done in the realm of the first-order logic, and not require to consider the temporal extenxion of CASL-LTL, in this frame the temporal combinators are used only to express the properties of the Real World, i.e., of the application domain.

5 Case Study: The Invoice System

5.1 The Invoice System

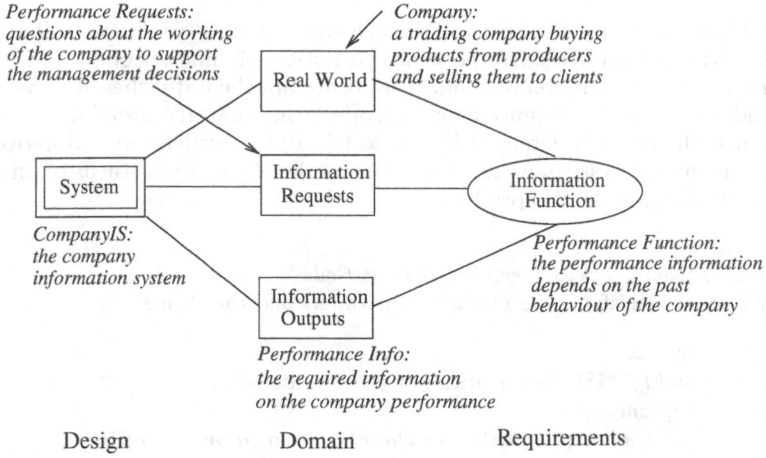

This case study, the invoice system, is inspired from one proposed in [1]. The problem under study is an information system for a company selling products to clients to support the management decisions. The clients send orders to the company, where an order contains one and only one reference to an ordered product in a given quantity. The status of an order will be changed from "pending" to "invoiced" if the ordered quantity is less or equal to the quantity of the corresponding referenced product in stock. New orders may arrive, and there may be some arrivals of products in some quantity in the stock. We also consider that this company may decide to discontinue some products that have not been sold for some given time (e.g., six months). An order may be refused when the product is no more traded, or when the quantity ordered is not available in the stock and a decision was taken to discontinue the product; this refusal should take place within one month after the order was received. We take the hypotheses that the size of the company's warehouse is unlimited and that the traded products are not perishable.

The picture above shows how the invoice system matches the IS frame.

Due to lack of space, the complete specifications of the requirements and the the design part will not be given here but they are available in [6].

5.2 Domain and Requirements

As explained in Sect. 4, to specify the requirements in this case means to provide four specifications corresponding to the four parts of the frame, which are reported in the following subsections. Some specification modules are quite large, thus, for readability sake, we provide some "friendly" abbreviated presentation of them. The domain and requirements specifications share some common data structures, and by using the CASL construct for the declaration of named specifications, we have specified them apart and collected together under the title of basic data.

Basic Data Some obvious basic data are the codes for products, orders, and clients, and the quantities. We need also a notion of time encoded into a date (day/month/year). The components of an order are the date when it is received, the product ordered (referenced by its code), the quantity ordered, the client who issued the order (referenced by its code), and an order code. Moreover, to specify the invoice system, we need also to use the elaboration status of an order and the trading status of a product.

```
spec CODE =
    sorts Product_Code, Order_Code, Client_Code
    %% codes identifying the products, the orders and the clients

spec QUANTITY =
    sort Quantity %% the quantities of the considered products
    ops 0 :→ Quantity;
        __+__ : Quantity × Quantity → Quantity, comm, assoc, unit 0;
        __−__ : Quantity × Quantity →? Quantity, unit 0 ;
    pred __≤__ : Quantity × Quantity;
        ...

spec DATE =
    NAT then
free {
```

type *Date* ::= __/__/__(*Nat*; *Nat*; *Nat*); %% dates as day/month/year
pred __ ≤ __ : *Date* × *Date*;
op *initial_date* :→ *Date*;
...

spec ORDER =
CODE **and** QUANTITY **and** DATE **then**
free type *Order* ::= *mk_order*(*product* : *Product_Code*; *quantity* : *Quantity*; *date* : *Date*; *code* : *Order_Code*; *client* : *Client_Code*)

spec STATUS =
free types
Product_Status ::= *traded* | *not_traded*;
Order_Status ::= *pending* | *invoiced* | *non_existing* | *refused*;
%% elaboration statuses of products and trading statuses of orders

Real World To specify the Real World component of the application domain, we have to express the relevant properties of its behaviour, following the schema introduced in Sect. 4.1; thus, we first determine the "events" and the "state observers", and then we look for the "incompatible events", the "relationships between state observers and events", and for the "event specific properties". We provide below the abbreviated presentation and a sketch of the corresponding CASL-LTL specification (see [6] for the full specification).

Events We present the events by listing the generators (written using capital letters) with their arguments and a short comment.

- *RECEIVE_ORD*(*Order*) to receive an order
- *SEND_INVOICE*(*Order*) to send the invoice for an order
- *REFUSE*(*Order*) to refuse an order
- *RECEIVE_PROD*(*Product_Code*; *Quantity*) to receive some quantity of a product
- *DISCONTINUE*(*Product_Code*) to discontinue a product
- *CHANGE*(*Date*) to change the date

State Observers We simply present the state observers by listing them with the types of their arguments and result, dropping the standard argument of the dynamic sort *State*. We use the notation convention that sort identifiers start with capital letters, whereas operation and predicate identifiers are written using only lower case letters.

- *product_status*(*Product_Code*) : *Product_Status* trading status of a product
- *order_status*(*Order_Code*) : *Order_Status* elaboration status of an order
- *available_quantity*(*Product_Code*) : *Quantity* available quantity of a product in the stock
- *date* : *Date* actual date

With the corresponding formal specification (see [6] for the full specification):

spec STATE_OBSERVERS =
ORDER **and** STATUS **then**
sort *State*
ops $product\_status : State \times Product\_Code \rightarrow Product\_Status$
%% trading status of a product
...

Incompatible Events We simply present the incompatible events by listing the incompatible pairs.

- All events referring to two orders with the same code are pairwise incompatible.
  - $RECEIVE\_ORD(o), SEND\_INVOICE(o')$ **s.t.** $code(o) = code(o')$
  - $RECEIVE\_ORD(o), REFUSE(o')$ **s.t.** $code(o) = code(o')$
  - $SEND\_INVOICE(o), REFUSE(o')$ **s.t.** $code(o) = code(o')$
  - $RECEIVE\_ORD(o), RECEIVE\_ORD(o')$ **s.t.** $code(o) = code(o') \wedge \neg (o = o')$
  - $SEND\_INVOICE(o), SEND\_INVOICE(o')$ **s.t.** $code(o) = code(o') \wedge \neg (o = o')$
  - $REFUSE(o), REFUSE(o')$ **s.t.** $code(o) = code(o') \wedge \neg (o = o')$
- All events referring to the same product are pairwise incompatible.
  - $RECEIVE\_PROD(p, q), SEND\_INVOICE(o)$ **s.t.** $product(o) = p$
  - $RECEIVE\_PROD(p, q), DISCONTINUE(p')$ **s.t.** $p = p'$
  - $SEND\_INVOICE(o), DISCONTINUE(p)$ **s.t.** $product(o) = p$
  - $RECEIVE\_PROD(p, q), RECEIVE\_PROD(p, q')$ **s.t.** $\neg q = q'$
- All change date events are pairwise incompatible.
  - $CHANGE(d), CHANGE(d')$ **s.t.** $\neg d = d'$

In the corresponding CASL specification (see [6]) each pair corresponds to an axiom, e.g., the first two axioms below.

$$st \xrightarrow{l} st' \wedge RECEIVE\_ORD(o) \in l \wedge SEND\_INVOICE(o') \in l \Rightarrow \neg (code(o) = code(o'))$$

$$st \xrightarrow{l} st' \wedge RECEIVE\_ORD(o) \in l \wedge REFUSE(o') \in l \Rightarrow \neg (code(o) = code(o'))$$

Relationships between State Observers and Events We simply present the relationships between state observers and events by listing for each state observer its initial value, which events modify it and how. This last part is given by stating which is the observer value after the happening of the various events. Notice that such value could be expressed by using also the observations on the state before the happening the event. Thus "**after** $RECEIVE\_PROD(p, q)$ **is** $available\_quantity(p) + q$" below means that the new value is the previous one incremented by q.

- $product\_status(p)$
  initially is *traded*
  after $DISCONTINUE(p)$ **is** *not_traded*
  not changed by other events
- $available\_quantity(p)$

initially is 0
after *SEND_INVOICE*(o) **s.t.** $product(o) = p$
is $available\_quantity(p) - quantity(o)$
after *RECEIVE_PROD*(p, q) **is** $available\_quantity(p) + q$
not changed by other events

– $order\_status(oc)$
initially is *non_existing*
after *RECEIVE_ORD*(o) **s.t.** $code(o) = oc$ **is** *pending*
after *SEND_INVOICE*(o) **s.t.** $code(o) = oc$ **is** *invoiced*
after *REFUSE*(o) **s.t.** $code(o) = oc$ **is** *refused*
not changed by other events

– *date*
initially is *initial_date*
after *CHANGE*(d) **is** d
not changed by other events

Below, as an example, we report the complete axioms expressing the relationships between the state observer *product_status* and the events.

$initial(st) \Rightarrow product\_status(st, p) = traded$

$st \xrightarrow{l} st' \wedge DISCONTINUE(p) \in l \Rightarrow product\_status(st', p) = not\_traded$

$st \xrightarrow{l} st' \wedge DISCONTINUE(p) \notin l \Rightarrow$
$product\_status(st', p) = product\_status(st, p)$

Event Specific Properties We present the event specific properties by listing for each event the properties on the system state necessary to its happening (preconditions), the properties on the system state necessary after it took place (postconditions), and under which condition this event will surely happen. The system state before and after the happening of the event are denoted by st and st' respectively. It is recommended to provide as well for each event a comment summarizing its properties in a natural way. We give below the presentation of *RECEIVE_ORD*.

RECEIVE_ORD(o)
Comment: If the order o is received, then the product referred in o was traded, no order with the same code of o existed, the date of o was the actual date, and in any case eventually o will be either refused or invoiced.

before
$product\_status(st, product(o)) = traded$,
$order\_status(st, code(o)) = non\_existing$ **and** $date(o) = date(st)$
after
$order\_status(st', code(o)) = pending$ **and**
$in\_any\_case(st', eventually\ state\_cond(x \bullet$
$order\_status(x, code(o)) = refused \vee order\_status(x, code(o)) = invoiced))$

"$in\_any\_case(st', eventually\ state\_cond(x \bullet \ldots))$" is a formula of CASL-LTL built by using the temporal combinators. "$in\_any\_case(s, \pi)$" can be read "for every path σ starting in the state denoted by s, π holds on σ", where a path is a sequence of transitions having the form either (1) or (2) below:

(1) $s_0\ l_0\ s_1\ l_1\ s_2\ l_2\ \ldots$ (infinite path)

(2) $s_0\ l_0\ s_1\ l_1\ s_2\ l_2\ \ldots\ s_n$ $n \geq 0$

where for all i ($i \geq 0$), $s_i \xrightarrow{l_i} s_{i+1}$ and there does not exist l, s' such that $s_n \xrightarrow{l} s'$.

"*eventually state_cond*($x \bullet F$)" holds on σ if there exists $0 \leq i$ s.t. F holds when x is evaluated by s_i.

Now we can give the formal specification of Real World for the invoice case, i.e., the company.

spec INVOICE_REAL_WORLD =
  ... **then**

  %% *RECEIVE_ORD*(*o*)
    st $\xrightarrow{l}$ *st'* ∧ *RECEIVE_ORD*(*o*) ∈ *l* ⇒
    product_status(*st*, *product*(*o*)) = *traded* ∧
    order_status(*st*, *code*(*o*)) = *non_existing* ∧
    date(*o*) = *date*(*st*) ∧ *order_status*(*st'*, *code*(*o*)) = *pending* ∧
    in_any_case(*st'*, *eventually state_cond*(*x* •
        order_status(*x*, *code*(*o*)) = *refused* ∨
          order_status(*x*, *code*(*o*)) = *invoiced*))
  ......

Information Requests We present the information requests by listing their generators with the types of their arguments; similarly for the information outputs.

- *available_quantity_of?*(*Product_Code*)
  what is the available quantity of a product in the stock?
- *quantity_of Product_Code sold_in Date – Date?*
  what is the quantity of a product sold in the period between two dates?
- *last_time_did Client_Code ordered?*
  what is the last time a client made some order?

Information Outputs

- *the_available_quantity_of Product_Code is Quantity*
- *error* : *prod_not_traded* the product appearing in the request is not traded
- *error* : *wrong_dates* the dates appearing in the request are wrong
- *the_quantity_of Product_Code sold_in Date – Date is Quantity*
- *Client_Code ordered_last_time_at Date*

Information Function Recall that the *inf_fun*, in this case named *invoice_inf_fun*, takes as arguments an information request and a history (a partial system lifecycle), defined as a sequence of transitions, i.e., precisely a sequence of states and labels. We simply present *invoice_inf_fun* by showing its results on all possible arguments case by case; each case is presented by starting with the keyword **on**, followed by the list of the arguments.

on *available_quantity_of?(p), h*
  if *product_status(last(h), p) = traded* **returns**
    the_available_quantity_of p is available_quantity(last(h), p)
  if *product_status(last(h), p) = not_traded* **returns** *error : prod_not_traded*
on *quantity_of p sold_in* $d_1 - d_2$*?, h*
  if $\neg (d_1 \leq d_2$ **and** $d_2 \leq date(last(h)))$ **returns** *error : wrong_dates*
  if $d_1 \leq d_2$ **and** $d_2 \leq date(last(h))$ **returns**
    the_quantity_of p sold_in $d_1 - d_2$ *is sold_aux*(p, d_1, d_2, h)
on *last_time_did cc ordered?, init(st)* **returns** *initial_date*
on *last_time_did cc ordered?, h l st*
  if *RECEIVE_ORD(o)* $\in l$ **and** *client(o) = cc* **returns**
    cc ordered_last_time_at date(st)
  if $\neg (\exists\, o : Order \bullet SEND\_INVOICE(o) \in l$ **and** $client(o) = cc)$ **returns**
    invoice_inf_fun(last_time_did cc ordered?, h)

The auxiliary operation *sold_aux* returns the quantity of a product sold in a certain time interval, for its complete definition see [6].

As an example, we show below the complete CASL axioms corresponding to the definition of *invoice_inf_fun* for the first case.

product_status(last(h), p) = traded ⇒
  invoice_inf_fun(available_quantity_of?(p), h) =
  the_available_quantity_of p is available_quantity(last(h), p)
product_status(last(h), p) = not_traded ⇒
  invoice_inf_fun(available_quantity_of?(p), h) = error : prod_not_traded

6 Conclusions and Future Work

While it is clear that methods are needed to help developing formal specifications, as extensively advocated in [4], this remains a difficult issue. This problem is addressed in [9,10] that define the concept of *agenda* used to provide a list of specification and validation tasks to be achieved, and apply it to develop specifications with Statecharts and Z. [14] also uses agendas addressing "mixed" systems (with both a static and a dynamic part), and provides some means to generate parts of the specification. [5] is the first work we know of that provides a formal characterisation of M. Jackson problem frames. Along this approach, we provide here a formalization of the translation frame and of the information system frame using the CASL language together with worked out case studies. Being in a formal framework lead us to add to the issues addressed by problem frames, the issue of correctness.

Following the approach proposed in this paper to use formal specifications in the development process of real case studies becomes an "engineering" kind of work. Indeed, for each frame we propose an operative method based on "normal" software engineering (shortly SE) concepts (inputs, outputs, events, ...) and not on mathematical/formal ones (existence of initial models, completeness, ...). Moreover, working with large case studies lead us to provide some legible presentations of the various parts of the specifications removing/"abstracting from" some conventional mathematical notations/overhead (while the corresponding complete specifications may be easily recovered from these) as for example, in Sect. 5.2.

We have based our work on some well established SE techniques and concepts (as the clear distinction supported by Jackson among the domain, the requirements and the design) that, for what we know, are not usually very well considered in the formal method community ([5] beeing an exception). Previous algebraic specifications of the case studies considered in this paper made by the authors themselves, without considering the SE aspects, were quite unprecise and perhaps also wrong. In the grep case everything was considered as "requirements" and then realized in the design phase, and so we had implemented also the regular expressions and the files. Instead, for the invoice case the old specifications were confused as regards what should be the responsibilities of system that we have to build (e.g., the information system was responsible to guarantee that an order eventually will be either invoiced or refused instead of simply taking note of when an order is invoiced).

Let us note that, while the selection of the correct frame and the specification of the requirements and the design are essential, specifying the domain part is necessary to produce sensible requirements, and may also be needed to discuss with the clients, or to check about possible misunderstandings with the domain experts (most of the worst errors in developing software systems are due to wrong ideas about the domain).

Another relevant aspect of our work is clearly "reuse": but here we reuse what can be called, by using a current SE terminology, "some best practices", not just some specifications. The ways to handle particular problem frames that we propose encompass the practice on the use of algebraic specifications of the authors; and so our work may be considered in the same line of the use of "patterns" ([8]) for the production of object oriented software. The most relevant difference between [8] and the work presented here is the scale: we consider as a reusable unit a way to solve a class of problem, the patterns of [8] consider, instead, something of much smaller (pieces of the design).

Acknowledgements

We would like to thank the anonymous referees for their careful reading and helpful comments.

References

1. M. Allemand, C. Attiogbe, and H. Habrias, editors. *Proc. of Int. Workshop "Comparing Specification Techniques: What Questions Are Prompted by Ones Particular Method of Specification". March 1998, Nantes (France).* IRIN - Universite de Nantes, 1998. 117
2. E. Astesiano, B. Krieg-Bruckner, and H.-J. Kreowski, editors. *IFIP WG 1.3 Book on Algebraic Foundations of System Specification.* Springer Verlag, 1999. 107
3. E. Astesiano and G. Reggio. Labelled Transition Logic: An Outline. Technical Report DISI–TR–96–20, DISI – Università di Genova, Italy, 1996. 107
4. E. Astesiano and G. Reggio. Formalism and Method. *T.C.S.*, 236, 2000. 123
5. D. Bjørner, S. Kousoube, R. Noussi, and G. Satchok. Michael Jackson's Problem Frames: Towards Methodological Principles of Selecting and Applying Formal Software Development Techniques and Tools. In M.G. Hinchey and Liu ShaoYing, editors, *Proc. Intl.Conf. on Formal Engineering Methods, Hiroshima, Japan, 12-14 Nov.1997.* IEEE CS Press, 1997. 108, 123, 124
6. C. Choppy and G. Reggio. Using CASL to Specify the Requirements and the Design: A Problem Specific Approach – Complete Version. Technical Report DISI-TR-99-33, DISI – Università di Genova, Italy, 1999. `ftp://ftp.disi.unige.it/person/ReggioG/ChoppyReggio99a.ps`. 108, 110, 118, 119, 120, 123
7. G. Costa and G. Reggio. Specification of Abstract Dynamic Data Types: A Temporal Logic Approach. *T.C.S.*, 173(2), 1997. 107, 115
8. E. Gamma, R. Helm, R. Johnson, and J. Vlissides. *Design Patterns: Elements of Reusable Object-Oriented Software.* Addison-Wesley, 1995. 124
9. W. Grieskamp, M. Heisel, and H. Dörr. Specifying Safety-Critical Embedded Systems with Statecharts and Z: An Agenda for Cyclic Software Components. In E. Astesiano, editor, *Proc. FASE'98*, number 1382 in LNCS. Springer Verlag, Berlin, 1998. 123
10. M. Heisel. Agendas – A Concept to Guide Software Development Activities. In R. N. Horspool, editor, *Proceedings Systems Implementation 2000.* Chapman & Hall, 1998. 123
11. M. Jackson. *Software Requirements & Specifications: a Lexicon of Practice, Principles and Prejudices.* Addison-Wesley, 1995. 106, 112, 113
12. P.D. Mosses. CoFI: The Common Framework Initiative for Algebraic Specification and Development. In M. Bidoit and M. Dauchet, editors, *Proc. TAPSOFT '97*, number 1214 in LNCS, Berlin, 1997. Springer Verlag. 106, 107
13. The CoFI Task Group on Language Design. CASL The Common Algebraic Specification Language Summary. Version 1.0. Technical report, 1999. Available on `http://www.brics.dk/Projects/CoFI/Documents/CASL/Summary/`. 106, 107
14. P. Poizat, C.Choppy, and J.-C. Royer. From Informal Requirements to COOP: a Concurrent Automata Approach. In J.M. Wing, J. Woodcock, and J. Davies, editors, *FM'99 - Formal Methods, World Congress on Formal Methods in the Development of Computing Systems*, number 1709 in LNCS. Springer Verlag, Berlin, 1999. 123
15. G. Reggio, E. Astesiano, and C. Choppy. CASL-LTL: A CASL Extension for Dynamic Reactive Systems – Summary. Technical Report DISI-TR-99-34, DISI – Università di Genova, Italy, 1999. `ftp://ftp.disi.unige.it/person/ReggioG/ReggioEtAll99a.ps`. 107, 113

16. M. Roggenbach and T. Mossakovski. Basic Data Types in CASL. CoFI Note L-12. Technical report, 1999. http://www.brics.dk/Projects/CoFI/Notes/L-12/ . 107, 111, 114

Subsorted Partial Higher-Order Logic as an Extension of CASL

Till Mossakowski[2], Anne Haxthausen[1], and Bernd Krieg-Brückner[2]

[1] Dept. of Information Technology, Techn. University of Denmark
DK-2800 Lyngby
[2] Bremen Institute of Safe Systems, TZI, FB3, Universität Bremen
P.O. Box 330440, D-28334 Bremen

Abstract. CASL is a specification language combining first-order logic, partiality and subsorting. This paper generalizes the CASL logic to also include higher-order functions and predicates. The logic is presented in a modular step-by-step reduction: the logic is defined in terms of a generalized subsorted partial logic which in turn is defined in terms of many-sorted partial first-order logic. A new notion of homomorphism is introduced to meet the need to get a faithful embedding of first-order CASL into higher-order CASL. Finally, it is discussed how a proof calculus for the proposed logic can be developed.

1 Introduction

During the past decades, a large number of algebraic specification languages have been developed. The presence of so many similar specification languages with no common framework hinders the dissemination and application of research results in algebraic specification. CoFI [27], the initiative for *a Common Framework for Algebraic Specification and Development* has as goal to get a common agreement in the algebraic specification community about basic concepts, and to provide a family of specification languages at different levels, a development methodology and tool support. The family of specification languages comprises a central, common language, called CASL[1] [21,32], various restrictions of CASL, and various extensions of CASL (e.g. with facilities for particular programming paradigms). Structuring the language family is important to ease the translations to/from other specification languages and thus the incorporation of existing tools, supporting e.g. a logic related to an extended sublanguage of CASL, in a common framework.

CASL provides constructs for writing structured requirement and design specifications as well as architectural specifications. Basic CASL specifications consist of declarations and axioms representing theories of a first-order logic in which predicates, total as well as partial functions, and subsorts are allowed. Predicate and function symbols may be overloaded.

[1] CASL stands for *Common Algebraic Specification Language* and is pronounced like 'castle'.

D. Bert, C. Choppy, and P. Mosses (Eds.): WADT'99, LNCS 1827, pp. 126–145, 2000.

The underlying logic of (first-order) CASL is a subsorted partial first-order logic introduced in [12]. However, in many applications, first-order logic does not suffice. Consider e.g. the specification of functional programs, which often gain their conciseness through the use of higher-order functions, or the specification of predicate transformers, which is inherently higher-order. Thus, the aim of this paper is to extend the first-order CASL logic with higher-order functions and predicates, providing the semantic foundations for a higher-order CASL language in which one can write specifications like

spec TWICE [**sort** *Elem*] =
 ops *twice* : $(Elem \to Elem) \to (Elem \to Elem)$;
 axioms $\forall f : Elem \to Elem; x : Elem \bullet (twice\ f)\ x = f\ (f\ x)$;

In section 5 we give larger motivating examples.

We define the higher-order logic using a modular step-by-step reduction approach: the logic is defined in terms of a generalized subsorted partial first-order logic which in turn is defined in terms of many-sorted partial first-order logic. The purpose of the reduction approach is to carry over well-known notions and results (e.g. proof theories and theorems about the existence of initial models) from a simpler logic to a new, more complex logic. The reduction is made in two steps, each treating a special feature (higher-order entities and subtypes, respectively) such that each feature can be understood separately. This is important, since there are quite a number of non-trivial interactions between the different features.

When defining our logic, we take another major issue into account: (first-order) CASL must be faithfully embeddable into its higher-order extension so that e.g. semantic entailment is preserved and reflected by the embedding.

Higher-order algebra has been studied, among others, in [35,23], subsorted higher-order algebra in [29,22,15], partial higher-order algebra in [4], higher-order logic in [2] and partial higher-order logic in [13]. In our work, we combine subsorting, partiality, higher-order functions and two-valued predicate logic, and this combination is new to our knowledge.

The paper is organized as follows. First, in section 2, we recall many-sorted partial first-order logic and extend it slightly for later needs. Then, in section 3, we generalize the subsorted partial first-order logic used in CASL. In section 4, we define subsorted partial higher-order logic as the underlying logic of higher-order CASL, which, in section 5, is illustrated with examples. Next, in section 6, we discuss how a proof calculus for the proposed logic can be developed. Finally, section 7 contains conclusions.

The reader is assumed to be familiar with algebraic specification. For reading section 5, some familiarity with the CASL syntax would be helpful.

An extended version of this paper including proofs can be found in [26]. The presented proposal has obtained preliminary approval at the CoFI language design meeting in Cachan, November 1998.

2 Extended Many-Sorted Partial First-Order Logic

This section defines the notions of signatures, models, and sentences of *(extended) many-sorted partial first-order logic*. For a full treatment of the topic, see e.g. [11].

2.1 Signatures

Definition 2.1 A *many-sorted signature* $\Sigma = (S, TF, PF, P)$ consists of:

- a set S of *sorts*
- two $S^* \times S$-sorted families $TF = (TF_{w,s})_{w \in S^*, s \in S}$ and $PF = (PF_{w,s})_{w \in S^*, s \in S}$ of *total function symbols* and *partial function symbols*, respectively, such that $TF_{w,s} \cap PF_{w,s} = \{\}$, for each $(w, s) \in S^* \times S$ (constants are treated as functions with no arguments)
- a family $P = (P_w)_{w \in S^*}$ of *predicate symbols*

Signature morphisms are defined as usual, with the specialty that a partial function symbol may be mapped to a total function symbol (but not vice versa).

2.2 Sentences

Let a many-sorted signature $\Sigma = (S, TF, PF, P)$ and an S-sorted family of variables $X = (X_s)_{s \in S}$ be given.

Below, the sets $T_\Sigma(X)_s$ of terms, $AF_\Sigma(X)$ of atomic formulae and $F_\Sigma(X)$ of formulae are defined mutually recursively.

Definition 2.2 The sets $T_\Sigma(X)_s$ of *many-sorted Σ-terms* of sort s, $s \in S$, with variables in X are the least sets satisfying the following rules:

1. $x \in T_\Sigma(X)_s$, if $x \in X_s$
2. $f_{w,s}(u_1, \ldots, u_n) \in T_\Sigma(X)_s$, if $u_i \in T_\Sigma(X)_{s_i}$, $f \in TF_{w,s} \cup PF_{w,s}$, $w = \langle s_1, \ldots, s_n \rangle$
3. $\iota\, x : s \bullet \varphi \in T_\Sigma(X)_s$, if $\varphi \in F_\Sigma(X \cup \{x_s\})$

The set $AF_\Sigma(X)$ of *many-sorted atomic Σ-formulae* with variables in X is the least set satisfying the following rules:

1. $p_w(t_1, \ldots, t_n) \in AF_\Sigma(X)$, if $t_i \in T_\Sigma(X)_{s_i}$, $p \in P_w$, $w = \langle s_1, \ldots, s_n \rangle \in S^*$
2. $t \stackrel{e}{=} t' \in AF_\Sigma(X)$, if $t, t' \in T_\Sigma(X)_s$, $s \in S$
3. $t = t' \in AF_\Sigma(X)$, if $t, t' \in T_\Sigma(X)_s$, $s \in S$
4. *def* $t \in AF_\Sigma(X)$, if $t \in T_\Sigma(X)_s$, $s \in S$

The set $F_\Sigma(X)$ of *many-sorted Σ-formulae* with variables in X are the usual many-sorted first-order logic formulae, built using quantification (over sorted variables), logical connectives and atomic Σ-formulae.

Compared with the many-sorted partial logic presented in [12] terms do not only comprise (1) variables and (2) application of qualified function symbols to terms of appropriate sorts, but also (3) definite description terms $\iota\ x : s \bullet \varphi$ (read as "that $x : s$ with φ"). These are added such that λ-terms of subsorted higher-order logic (in section 4) can be reduced to first-order terms. Atomic formulae still comprise (1) applications of qualified predicate symbols to terms of appropriate sorts, (2) existential equations between terms of the same sort, (3) strong equations between terms of the same sort, and (4) assertions about definedness of terms.

Definition 2.3 *Many-sorted Σ-sentences* are closed many-sorted Σ-formulae.

2.3 Models

Definition 2.4 Given a many-sorted signature $\Sigma = (S, TF, PF, P)$, a *many-sorted Σ-model M* consists of:

- a carrier set s^M for each sort $s \in S$
- a partial function f^M from w^M to s^M for each function symbol $f \in TF_{w,s} \cup PF_{w,s}$, the function being total if $f \in TF_{w,s}$
- a predicate $p^M \subseteq w^M$ for each predicate symbol $p \in P_w$.

We write w^M for the Cartesian product $s_1^M \times ... \times s_n^M$, when $w = \langle s_1, ..., s_n \rangle$.

Definition 2.5 A *many-sorted Σ-homomorphism* $h : M \rightarrow N$ consists of a family of functions $(h_s : s^M \rightarrow s^N)_{s \in S}$ such that for all $f \in TF_{w,s} \cup PF_{w,s}$ and $(a_1, \ldots, a_n) \in w^M$ with $f^M(a_1, \ldots, a_n)$ defined,

$$h_s(f^M(a_1, \ldots, a_n)) = f^N((h_{s_1}(a_1), \ldots, h_{s_n}(a_n))$$

and for all $p \in P_w$ and $(a_1, \ldots, a_n) \in w^M$

$$(a_1, \ldots, a_n) \in p^M \text{ implies } (h_{s_1}(a_1), \ldots, h_{s_n}(a_n)) \in p^N$$

2.4 Satisfaction

The satisfaction of a Σ-sentence by a Σ-model M is defined as usual in terms of the satisfaction of its constituent atomic formulae w.r.t. assignments of values to all the variables that occur in them, the value assigned to variables of sort s being in s^M. Variable assignments are total, but the value of a term w.r.t. a variable assignment may be undefined, due to the application of a partial function during the evaluation of the term. Note, however, that the satisfaction of sentences is two-valued. The value of a definite description term $\iota\ x : s \bullet \varphi$ is defined iff there is a unique assignment of x which makes the formula φ true, and in this case the value of the definite description term is that value.

Fact 2.6 The above definitions give an institution [14], called $EPFOL^{=}$.

2.5 Derived Signature Morphisms

Derived signature morphisms offer more flexibility: constants and functions may be mapped to arbitrary terms [30]. Given a many-sorted signature $\Sigma = (S, TF, PF, P)$, let $d\Sigma = (S, Tot \cup TF, Part \cup PF, P)$, where

$$Part_{\langle s_1,\ldots,s_n\rangle,s} = T_\Sigma(\{x_1 : s_1; \ldots x_n : s_n\})_s$$

and $Tot_{w,s}$ is the restriction of $Part_{w,s}$ to those terms containing neither partial function symbols nor definite description terms. The variables in the terms in $Part_{w,s}$ and $Tot_{w,s}$ can be thought of as formal parameter variables.

Definition 2.7 A *derived signature morphism* $\sigma : \Sigma \rightarrow \Sigma'$ is an ordinary signature morphism $\sigma : \Sigma \rightarrow d\Sigma'$. Derived signature morphisms lead to a translation of terms and sentences, which is obtained by combining ordinary sentence translation with a substitution of formal parameter variables by actual parameters. Composition of derived signature morphisms is done by applying term translation w.r.t. to the second morphism to the terms given by the first morphism. Reducts are defined using interpretation of terms. Altogether, this gives an institution $dEPFOL^=$.

3 Generalised Subsorted Partial First-Order Logic

This section defines the notions of signatures, models, and sentences of *generalized subsorted partial (first-order) logic*. This logic extends the subsorted partial logic [12] used in first-order CASL by using two subsort relations instead of one. The additional subsort relation is interpreted as a family of coercions that, in contrast to the first subsort relation, need not be injective or have inverse projections. We need this in the subsorted partial higher-order logic presented in section 4, in order to cope with a subsort relation between functional sorts that is contravariant w.r.t. argument types. For example, $int \rightarrow nat$ can be seen as a subsort of $nat \rightarrow nat$ by restricting functions to nat, however, the action of restriction is not injective.

3.1 Signatures

Definition 3.1 A *generalized subsorted signature* $\Sigma = (S, TF, PF, P, \leq^1, \leq^2)$ consists of a many-sorted signature (S, TF, PF, P) together with two pre-orders $\leq^1$ and $\leq^2$ of *subsort relations* on S, for which $\leq^1$ is a suborder of $\leq^2$.

Definition 3.2
With each generalized subsorted signature $\Sigma = (S, TF, PF, P, \leq^1, \leq^2)$ we associate a many-sorted signature $\hat{\Sigma}$. $\hat{\Sigma}$ is the extension of (S, TF, PF, P) with a total *coercion* function symbol (from s to s') $\mathtt{inj}_{s,s'}$, for each pair of sorts $s \leq^2 s'$, a partial *projection* function symbol (from s' to s) $\mathtt{pr}_{s',s}$, for each pair of sorts $s \leq^1 s'$, and a unary *membership* predicate symbol (testing whether

terms of sort s' are embeddings of values in s) $\in^s_{s'}$, for each pair of sorts $s \leq^1 s'$. We assume that the symbols used for coercion, projection and membership are not used otherwise in Σ.

For $s \leq^1 s'$ the coercion symbols $\mathtt{inj}_{s,s'}$ are intended to denote injective functions (like embeddings in the underlying logic of first-order CASL) and have the functions denoted by the projection symbols $\mathtt{pr}_{s',s}$ as their inverse (cf. section 3.3). As the coercions $\mathtt{inj}_{s,s'}$ for $s \leq^2 s'$ need not be injective, there are only projection symbols $\mathtt{pr}_{s',s}$ for $s \leq^1 s'$ and not for the more general case $s \leq^2 s'$.

In order to support semantical identifications due to subsorted overloading, we define overloading relations $\sim_F$ and $\sim_P$ on the sets of qualified function symbols and qualified predicate symbols, respectively:

Definition 3.3 Let $f \in (TF_{w_1,s_1} \cup PF_{w_1,s_1}) \cap (TF_{w_2,s_2} \cup PF_{w_2,s_2})$ and $p \in P_{w_1} \cap P_{w_2}$. Then $f_{w_1,s_1} \sim_F f_{w_2,s_2}$ iff there exists a $w \in S^*$ and $s \in S$ such that $w \leq^2 w_1, w_2$ and $s_1, s_2 \leq^2 s$. Similarly, $p_{w_1} \sim_P p_{w_2}$ iff there exists a $w \in S^*$ such that $w \leq^2 w_1, w_2$.

Definition 3.4 Given a signature $\Sigma = (S, TF, PF, P, \leq^1, \leq^2)$, a generalized signature morphism $\sigma : \Sigma \to \Sigma'$ is a many-sorted derived signature morphism from (S, TF, PF, P) to $\hat{\Sigma}'$ preserving the subsort and overloading relations.

We want this generalization, in the subsorted partial higher-order logic defined in section 4 to allow signature morphisms mapping a constant of a partial function type $t1 \to^? t2$ to a constant of the corresponding total function type $t1 \to t2$. These examples can be made into derived signature morphisms by mapping constants to terms with injections.

Signature morphisms $\sigma : \Sigma \to \Sigma'$ can be extended to (derived) signature morphisms $\hat{\sigma} : \hat{\Sigma} \to \hat{\Sigma}'$ by just letting $\hat{\sigma}$ preserve the additional structure.

3.2 Sentences

Definition 3.5 Σ-*sentences* are many-sorted $\hat{\Sigma}$-sentences.

Note that in the sentences, coercions from subsorts to supersorts must be explicit. In the CASL language these are left implicit and must unambiguously be determined by the context.

3.3 Models

Definition 3.6 Σ-*models* are many-sorted $\hat{\Sigma}$-models satisfying the following set of axioms $J(\Sigma)$ (where the variables are all universally quantified): [2]

[2] We write $f_{s',s}(u)$ as a shorthand for $f_{\langle s' \rangle,s}(u)$.

[identity] $\mathtt{inj}_{s,s}(x) \stackrel{e}{=} x$
[coercion-injectivity] $\mathtt{inj}_{s,s'}(x) \stackrel{e}{=} \mathtt{inj}_{s,s'}(y) \Rightarrow x \stackrel{e}{=} y$ for $s \leq^1 s'$
[transitivity] $\mathtt{inj}_{s',s''}(\mathtt{inj}_{s,s'}(x)) \stackrel{e}{=} \mathtt{inj}_{s,s''}(x)$ for $s \leq^2 s' \leq^2 s''$
[projection] $\mathtt{pr}_{s',s}(\mathtt{inj}_{s,s'}(x)) \stackrel{e}{=} x$ for $s \leq^1 s'$
[projection-injectivity] $\mathtt{pr}_{s',s}(x) \stackrel{e}{=} \mathtt{pr}_{s',s}(y) \Rightarrow x \stackrel{e}{=} y$ for $s \leq^1 s'$
[membership] $\in^s_{s'} (x) \Leftrightarrow def\ \mathtt{pr}_{s',s}(x)$ for $s \leq^1 s'$
[function-overloading]
$\mathtt{inj}_{s',s}(f_{w',s'}(\mathtt{inj}_{s_1,s'_1}(x_1), \ldots, \mathtt{inj}_{s_n,s'_n}(x_n))) =$
$\quad \mathtt{inj}_{s'',s}(f_{w'',s''}(\mathtt{inj}_{s_1,s''_1}(x_1), \ldots, \mathtt{inj}_{s_n,s''_n}(x_n)))$
$\quad$ for $w = \langle s_1, \ldots, s_n \rangle$, $w' = \langle s'_1, \ldots, s'_n \rangle$, $w'' = \langle s''_1, \ldots, s''_n \rangle$,
$\quad w \leq^2 w', w'', s', s'' \leq^2 s,\ f \in (TF_{w',s'} \cup PF_{w',s'}) \cap (TF_{w'',s''} \cup PF_{w'',s''})$
[predicate-overloading]
$p_{w'}(\mathtt{inj}_{s_1,s'_1}(x_1), \ldots, \mathtt{inj}_{s_n,s'_n}(x_n)) \Leftrightarrow p_{w''}(\mathtt{inj}_{s_1,s''_1}(x_1), \ldots, \mathtt{inj}_{s_n,s''_n}(x_n))$
$\quad$ for $w = \langle s_1, \ldots, s_n \rangle$, $w' = \langle s'_1, \ldots, s'_n \rangle$, $w'' = \langle s''_1, \ldots, s''_n \rangle$,
$\quad w \leq^2 w', w'', p \in P_{w'} \cap P_{w''}$

Definition 3.7
Reducts along a signature morphism $\sigma : \Sigma \to \Sigma'$ are defined as reducts along $\hat{\sigma}$ in $dEPFOL^=$. This is well-defined because $sen(\hat{\sigma})(J(\Sigma)) \subseteq J(\Sigma')$ ensures that the reduct again satisfies the axioms for being a subsorted model.

Definition 3.8 Σ-homomorphisms are many-sorted $\hat{\Sigma}$-homomorphisms.

3.4 Satisfaction

Since generalized subsorted Σ-models and Σ-sentences are just certain many-sorted $\hat{\Sigma}$-models and $\hat{\Sigma}$-sentences, the notion of satisfaction for the generalized subsorted case follows directly from the notion of satisfaction for the many-sorted case.

Fact 3.9 The above definitions give an institution $GSubPFOL^=$.

Proof. The satisfaction condition for institutions [14] follows from the many-sorted case.

Proposition 3.10 There is a simple institution representation (also called simple map of institutions) in the sense of [24,33] from generalized subsorted partial first-order logic to extended many-sorted partial first-order logic with derived signature morphisms. It sends a signature Σ to the theory $(\hat{\Sigma}, J(\Sigma))$ and is the identity on sentences and models.

4 Subsorted Partial Higher-Order Logic

This section develops a subsorted partial higher-order logic $SubPHOL^=$ that can be used in the semantics of higher-order CASL specifications.

The definitions of this logic are based on the generalized subsorted partial first-order logic ($GSubPFOL^=$) given in section 3. Each higher-order signature is mapped to a $GSubPFOL^=$-signature by enriching it with tupling and apply functions. Note that the apply functions for partial functions are partial, and for predicate application, we need apply predicates. This has the consequence that predicate application is non-strict in both the predicate and the argument: if either of them is undefined, the result is false (it cannot be undefined, since the logic is two-valued). This is more general than the solution in [13], where predicate application is non-strict only in the argument, and the predicate itself is always defined, which is achieved by restricting the type system.

When defining the type system, we make a distinction between total and partial function types. This is motivated by modularity aspects: in this way, it becomes syntactically decidable whether (a part of) a specification belongs to a total sub-logic. We also introduce a type $?t$ [3] being a supertype of t, which is meant to be t plus one ("undefined") element. Normally, within our strict partial logic, undefined is not a value – a deliberate choice, which is useful for the development of requirement specifications. At the design or implementation level, we may need the "undefined" element in $?t'$ to model partial non-strict functions from t to t' (which are not available in the logic) as *total* functions from $?t$ to $?t'$. However, this is only *one* implementation strategy, there also more elaborate ways of error-handling. This is the reason for not including non-strictness as a primitive notion. Note that we cannot replace partial functions from t_1 to t_2 by a total function from t_1 to $?t_2$ in general: at least the projection functions to subsorts must be truly partial. Otherwise, we would not be able to project a term of type $?t$ to a term of type t.[4]

We provide λ-abstraction as terms for anonymous functions and predicates. Since in some types of models introduced in section 4.3, function spaces need not be closed under λ-abstraction, λ-abstraction may be undefined.

Since we have three kinds of λ-abstraction (for total functions, partial functions and predicates), it would be nice to be able to reduce them to some more primitive notion. One idea is to reduce λ-abstraction to combinators, which are purely algebraic [5]. However, λ-abstraction for partial functions is non-strict: if there are enough partial functions in a model, $\lambda x : t \bullet ?\ u$ is defined even if u is undefined.[5] Non-strict λ-abstraction needs a non-strict K-combinator. However, we have chosen our logic to be strict. Therefore, we follow a different idea and reduce λ-abstraction to definite description, which was already introduced in $GSubPFOL^=$.

[3] Note that $?t$ is isomorphic to $unit \rightarrow^? t$. We include it merely for notational convenience.

[4] However, the types $t_1 \rightarrow^? t_2$ and $t_1 \rightarrow (?t_2)$ are in bijective correspondence. In a future version, we will consider to make them subtypes of each other, to obtain their interchangeability. A similar remark holds for the types $pred(t)$ and $t \rightarrow^? unit$.

[5] We use the notation $\lambda x : t \bullet ?\ u$ to indicate that the result may be a partial function, while $\lambda x : t \bullet u$ should yield a total function (and be undefined if this is not possible).

4.1 Signatures

Definition 4.1 A *SubPHOL*$^=$ *signature* $\Sigma = (S, F, \leq_S)$ consists of a set S of (basic) *sorts*, a family $F = (F_t)_{t \in S^{\rightarrow}}$ of $S^{\rightarrow}$ typed *constant symbols* and a preorder $\leq$ on S, the *subsorting relation*. Here, $S^{\rightarrow}$ is the set of *higher-order types*, generated by

$$S^{\rightarrow} = s \mid t_1 \rightarrow t_2 \mid t_1 \rightarrow^? t_2 \mid ?t \mid pred(t) \mid unit \mid t_1 \times \cdots \times t_n$$

where $s \in S$, $t, t_i \in S^{\rightarrow}$, $n > 1$. Here, $t_1 \longrightarrow t_2$ is the type of total functions from t_1 to t_2, $t_1 \rightarrow^? t_2$ that of partial functions from t_1 to t_2, $?t$ is t plus one element, $pred(t)$ is the type of predicates over t, *unit* is the type consisting of the empty tuple, and $t_1 \times \cdots \times t_n$ is the product type. In the sequel, we use $s, s_1, s_2, \ldots$ for elements of S, and $t, t_1, \ldots,$ for elements of $S^{\rightarrow}$.

The subsorting relation $\leq_S$ can be extended from S to $S^{\rightarrow}$ in two different ways - one ($\leq^{\Rightarrow}$) is contravariant with respect to argument types, the other one ($\leq^{\rightarrow}$) requires argument types to be the same.

The need for the contravariant subtype relation is demonstrated by the following toy example (a more realistic example will be given in section 5.2) from the higher-order CASL language: An instantiation of the TWICE specification given in section 1 with natural numbers (*Nat*) gives rise to a *twice* function of type $(Nat \rightarrow Nat) \rightarrow (Nat \rightarrow Nat)$. In order to allow this function to be applied to a square function $sqr : Int \rightarrow Nat$, where $Nat \leq Int$, it must hold that $Int \rightarrow Nat$ is a subtype of $Nat \rightarrow Nat$.

Definition 4.2 Let $\leq^{\rightarrow}$ be the least preorder on $S^{\rightarrow}$ satisfying the rules:

1. $t \leq^{\rightarrow} t'$, if $t \leq t'$
2. $t \rightarrow t_1 \leq^{\rightarrow} t \rightarrow t_2$, if $t_1 \leq^{\rightarrow} t_2$
3. $t \rightarrow^? t_1 \leq^{\rightarrow} t \rightarrow^? t_2$, if $t_1 \leq^{\rightarrow} t_2$
4. $t \rightarrow t' \leq^{\rightarrow} t \rightarrow^? t'$
5. $t \leq^{\rightarrow} ?t$
6. $t_1 \times \cdots \times t_n \leq^{\rightarrow} t'_1 \times \cdots \times t'_n$ if $t_i \leq^{\rightarrow} t'_i$ for $i = 1, \ldots, n$.

The preorder $\leq^{\Rightarrow}$ is defined in the same way, except for the 2. and 3. rules and an additional rule (note that $\leq^{\rightarrow}$ thus becomes a suborder of $\leq^{\Rightarrow}$):

2. $t_1 \rightarrow t_2 \leq^{\Rightarrow} t'_1 \rightarrow t'_2$, if $t'_1 \leq^{\Rightarrow} t_1$ and $t_2 \leq^{\Rightarrow} t'_2$
3. $t_1 \rightarrow^? t_2 \leq^{\Rightarrow} t'_1 \rightarrow^? t'_2$, if $t'_1 \leq^{\Rightarrow} t_1$ and $t_2 \leq^{\Rightarrow} t'_2$
7. $pred(t) \leq^{\Rightarrow} pred(t')$ if $t' \leq^{\Rightarrow} t$

Definition 4.3 With each higher-order signature $\Sigma = (S, F, \leq_S)$ we associate a generalized subsorted *GSubPFOL*$^=$-signature $\Sigma^{\rightarrow} = (S^{\rightarrow}, TF^{\rightarrow}, PF^{\rightarrow}, P^{\rightarrow}, \leq^{\rightarrow}, \leq^{\Rightarrow})$ and a set of $\Sigma^{\rightarrow}$-axioms $K^{\rightarrow}(\Sigma)$ which are the least sets with:

- higher-order constants: $F_t \subseteq TF^{\rightarrow}_{\langle\rangle,t}$ for $t \in S^{\rightarrow}$

- apply functions and predicates:
  $apply_{t\to u} \in TF^{\to}_{\langle(t\to u),t\rangle,u}$ $\quad apply_{t\to ?u} \in PF^{\to}_{\langle(t\to ?u),t\rangle,u}$
  $apply_{pred(t)} \in P^{\to}_{\langle pred(t),t\rangle}$
- tuple constructors and selectors:
  $() \in TF^{\to}_{\langle\rangle,unit}$ $\quad (\_,\dots,\_)_{t_1,\dots,t_n} \in TF^{\to}_{\langle t_1,\dots,t_n\rangle,t_1\times\dots\times t_n}$
  $sel^i_{t_1,\dots,t_n} \in TF^{\to}_{\langle t_1\times\dots\times t_n\rangle,t_i}$, for $i = 1,\dots,n$
- tupling axioms:
  $\forall x : unit.x = () \in K^{\to}(\Sigma)$
  $\forall x_1 : t_1;\dots;x_n : t_n.sel^i_{t_1,\dots,t_n}((x_1,\dots,x_n)_{t_1,\dots,t_n}) = x_i \in K^{\to}(\Sigma)$
  $\forall x : t_1 \times \dots \times t_n.(sel^1_{t_1,\dots,t_n}(x),\dots,sel^n_{t_1,\dots,t_n}(x))_{t_1,\dots,t_n} = x \in K^{\to}(\Sigma)$

Definition 4.4 Given two signatures $\Sigma = (S,F,\leq_S)$ and $\Sigma' = (S',F',\leq'_S)$, then a *signature morphism* $\sigma : \Sigma \to \Sigma'$ is a $GSubPFOL^=$-signature morphism $\sigma : \Sigma^{\to} \to \Sigma'^{\to}$ preserving the apply symbols, tuple constructors and selectors.

4.2 Sentences

Definition 4.5 *Σ-sentences* in $SubPHOL^=$ are $\Sigma^{\to}$-sentences in $GSubPFOL^=$. We can define λ-abstraction for total functions, partial functions and predicates, the "undefined" element and conditional terms as derived notions:

$$\begin{aligned}
\lambda x : t \bullet u &:= \iota f : t \to t' \bullet \forall x : t \bullet apply_{t\to t'}(f,x) = u\\
\lambda x : t \bullet ?\, u &:= \iota f : t \to^{?} t' \bullet \forall x : t \bullet apply_{t\to ?t'}(f,x) = u\\
\lambda x : t \bullet \varphi &:= \iota p : pred(t) \bullet \forall x : t \bullet apply_{pred(t)}(p,x) \Leftrightarrow \varphi
\end{aligned}$$
$$\bot_t := \iota x : ?t \bullet \neg \in^t_{?t}(x)$$
$$\varphi \to u \mid u' := \iota x : s \bullet ((\varphi \Rightarrow x = u) \wedge (\neg\varphi \Rightarrow x = u'))$$

In the higher-order CASL language, application terms are not of the form $apply_{type}(f,x)$, but just abbreviated to $f(x)$ or even just $f\ x$.

4.3 Models

General Σ-models in $SubPHOL^=$ are just $(\Sigma^{\to},K^{\to}(\Sigma))$-models in $GSubPFOL^=$.

In [28], it is advocated to use general models (also called intensional models), because of the following

Proposition 4.6 In $SubPHOL^=$, theories with positive conditional axioms that do not use definite description have initial (and free) models.

A further argument in favour of general models is that in computer science, not only the values of functions for given arguments matter, but also the way they are computed. For example, higher order Petri nets for business process engineering require general models in order to distinguish between different resources which have different performance but the same functional behaviour, cf. [16].

Below, we consider various subclasses of models.

Extensionality Extensionality can be desired in cases where one does not want to distinguish between different ways of computing a function, e.g. when specifying the semantics of a functional language. Therefore we will allow a concise notation for certain axiom schemes restricting the classes of models. The axiom scheme of extensionality consists, for any types t, t', of

$$\forall f, g : t \to^{?} t' \bullet (\forall x : t \bullet apply_{t \to ?t'}(f, x) = apply_{t \to ?t'}(g, x)) \Rightarrow f = g \text{ [6]}$$
$$\forall p, q : pred(t) \bullet (\forall x : t \bullet apply_{pred(t)}(p, x) \Leftrightarrow apply_{pred(t)}(q, x)) \Rightarrow p = q$$

Requiring extensionality destroys the existence of initial models. For the total case, there is a way out by restricting oneself to reachable models [35]. But for the partial case, as shown in [4], even simple first-order signatures do no longer have initial models. This is due to the fact that the extensionality axioms contain a strong equation in the premise and therefore are not positive conditional. However, there is a different way to partially restore the existence of initial models by using a new notion of homomorphism (see Definition 4.8 and Proposition 4.13).

Comprehension (Henkin models) For general models, we have the peculiar phenomenon that a λ-abstraction ($\lambda x : t \bullet u$, $\lambda x : t \bullet ?\, u$, or $\lambda x : t \bullet \varphi$) can be undefined because it describes a functional behaviour possessed by no or more than one value in the model. Function and predicate spaces may even be empty. *Henkin* Σ-models are general Σ-models that satisfy comprehension, that is, for any type t, any term u of type t and any formula φ, where u and ϕ possibly contain free variables,

$$\forall(def(\lambda x : t \bullet ?\, u)), \quad \forall(def(\lambda x : t \bullet \varphi)), \quad \text{and } def(\bot_t)$$

where $\forall(\phi)$ is the universal closure of ϕ (i.e. universal quantification over all free variables). The first two axiom schemes ensure that all λ-definable partial functions and predicates are in the model. This also automatically ensures extensionality, because of the uniqueness condition in the definite description. Still, in Henkin models, a total λ-abstraction $\lambda x : t \bullet u$ can be undefined because the function it denotes may fail to be total. The third axiom scheme ensures that the "undefined" element is really there, i. e. all types $?t$ are interpreted as t plus one ("undefined") element.

Choice Since we do not have a total Hilbert operator as in total higher-order logics, we have to introduce the axiom of choice as an extra axiom scheme:

$$\forall f : t \to t' \bullet (\forall y : t' \bullet \exists x : t \bullet f(x) = y) \Rightarrow$$
$$\exists g : t' \to t \bullet \forall y : t' \bullet apply_{t \to t'}(f, apply_{t' \to t}(g, y)) = y$$

stating that any surjective function has a one-sided right inverse.

[6] The corresponding extensionality property for total functions is derivable from this axiom and the function-overloading axiom given in section 3.3.

Standard Models Standard Σ-models are Henkin Σ-models where each functional sort is interpreted as the full function space, and each predicate sort is interpreted as the full predicate space. We do not allow a restriction to Standard models in higher-order CASL, because there is a (recursively axiomatized) sound and complete calculus for the Henkin model semantics, but due to the Gödel incompleteness theorem, there cannot be one for the Standard model semantics.

Homomorphisms The one and only motivation for homomorphisms in CASL is to interpret the **free** construct, which admits to specify initial models and free extensions.

A candidate for Σ-homomorphisms could be $\Sigma^{\rightarrow}$-homomorphisms (also called *higher-order Σ-homomorphisms*). However, it turns out that with this kind of homomorphisms, there is no faithful embedding of **free** constructs of first-order CASL into higher-order CASL with extensional models. In [4] an example is given illustrating this (here translated into CASL):

spec SP = **free** { **sorts** s **ops** $e : s; f, g : s \rightarrow^{?} s$}
In first-order CASL this specification has an initial model I with s^I being a singleton set $\{v\}$ and $f^I(v)$ and $g^I(v)$ being undefined. However, in higher-order CASL with extensional models, I (lifted in the obvious way to a higher-order model) is not an initial model, if the proposed kind of homomorphism is used (and there are no other initial models). I is not initial, since if it was, there should have been a higher-order homomorphism h from I to the model A with $s^A = s^I$, $apply^A(f^A, v) = v$ and $apply^A(g^A, v)$ undefined. Now, since $apply^I(f^I, x) = apply^I(g^I, x)$ for all x in s^I, extensionality gives $f^I = g^I$, and therefore we would have $h_{s \rightarrow ? s}(f^I) = h_{s \rightarrow ? s}(g^I)$, i.e. $f^A = g^A$, but thist is false.

The problem is due to the fact that higher-order homomorphisms not only map first-order constants, but also higher-order constants, preserving the interpretation of these. In order to overcome this problem, we will use a notion of *first-order homomorphism between higher-order models* (for short: first-order HO-homomorphism) that directly generalizes homomorphisms in the first-order institution. Such homomorphisms only map first-order values and they preserve evaluation of (higher-order) algebraic core terms giving first-order values. The latter requirement is equivalent to the homomorphism condition in the first-order institution, cf. section 9 in [9].

Definition 4.7 An *algebraic core term* is a term containing neither definite description terms, nor notions derived from them such as λ-abstraction and if-then-else. An *algebraic core formula* is an *atomic* formula that only contains algebraic core terms and that does not use strong equality.

Definition 4.8 A *first-order Σ-HO-homomorphism* $h : A \rightarrow B$ is a family of functions $(h_s : s^A \rightarrow s^B)_{s \in S}$ such that if φ is an algebraic core formula with variables in $X = (X_s)_{s \in S}$ (of basic sorts!) and $\nu : X \rightarrow A$ is a valuation, then $A, \nu \models \varphi$ implies $B, h \circ \nu \models \varphi$.

4.4 Satisfaction

Satisfaction is inherited from $GSubPFOL^=$.

Fact 4.9 The above definitions (using general models) give an institution called $SubPHOL^=$. Further institutions can be obtained by restricting the model classes to extensional models, Henkin models, and Henkin models with choice.

Proposition 4.10 There is a simple institution representation in the sense of [24,33] from general, extensional and Henkin subsorted partial higher-order logic to generalized subsorted partial first-order logic. It sends a signature Σ to the theory $(\Sigma^{\rightarrow}, K^{\rightarrow}(\Sigma))$ (augmented by the extensionality axioms, in the extensional model case, and by the comprehension axioms, in the Henkin model case). It is the identity on sentences and models.

4.5 Relation to Subsorted Partial First-Order Logic

While the above institution representation reduces higher-order logic to first-order logic, another question is whether CASL's first-order logic can be faithfully represented in the higher-order logics. The answer is yes:

Proposition 4.11 There are institution representations from $SubPFOL^=$ (the institution underlying CASL) to $SubPHOL^=$ and its restrictions mentioned in 4.9. They are defined as follows: A signature is translated by keeping the sorts and subsort relation, but translating functions and predicates to constants of functional or predicate type. Sentences are translated in the obvious way. Models are translated by just forgetting the interpretations of higher-order types and by using the interpretations of the apply functions and predicates to get functions and predicates from the interpretation of higher-order constants.

Proposition 4.12 The model translation components of these institution representations are surjective on objects.

Regarding the results of [7,34], surjectivity of the model translation is sufficient to get a faithful extension of first-order CASL, except for the free construct, if additionally the institution representation satisfies the condition of weak amalgamation. We conjecture that this condition is actually satisfied.

In order to lift the semantics of initial models and free extensions, we need to impose additional requirements on the institution representations cf. [1]. Indeed, for first-order HO-homomorphisms (but not for higher-order homomorphisms), we have a condition guaranteeing the lifting of initial and free constructions:

Proposition 4.13 For each of the above institution representations the model translation component is a pointwise equivalence of categories.

Since first-order HO-homomorphisms only take into account the definable higher-order functions (or, more precisely, those that are a value of an algebraic core term with first-order variables), and completely ignore the others, we have the very peculiar behaviour that satisfaction is not preserved along isomorphisms.[7] But we do not feel that this is a great loss, since the only purpose of homomorphisms within CASL is to get initial and free models. No better higher-order framework with (extensional) initial models with partial functions has been found so far. The main consideration is how to faithfully embed what we have in first-order CASL, and exactly this can be done with our notion of first-order HO-homomorphism. It is shown in [31] that the expressiveness of second-order logic suffices to simulate free semantics. However, we prefer our way of having free semantics also in higher-order CASL over the use of this simulation with rather complicated results. (Still, we propose that in higher-order CASL, inductive definitions involving true higher-order types should be stated using sort generation constraints or higher-order quantification instead of using free semantics. But this is different from using a complicated general translation scheme.)

The outcome of the above discussion is: We use general models and first-order HO-homomorphisms for the underlying logic of higher-order CASL, mainly because first-order CASL can be embedded faithfully into it. If needed, extensionality, comprehension and choice can be added as axiom schemes. (In the higher-order CASL language, we will provide a special concise notation for these axiom schemes.) In the case of Henkin models, one can derive that each λ-term is defined; this knowledge could be used during the static analysis of totality of terms (e.g. one could allow signature morphisms to map constants to λ-terms).

5 Examples

5.1 Example 1

Below an example of a higher-order CASL specification of finite sets over arbitrary elements together with higher-order image functions (dealing with both total and partial functions) is given.

spec FINSET [**sort** *Elem*] =
free {
  sort *FinSet*[*Elem*]
  ops *empty* : *FinSet*[*Elem*]
    add : *Elem* × *FinSet*[*Elem*] → *FinSet*[*Elem*]
  axioms ... }
then
  ops *image* : (*Elem* → *Elem*) → (*FinSet*[*Elem*] → *FinSet*[*Elem*]);
    image : (*Elem* →? *Elem*) → (*FinSet*[*Elem*] →? *FinSet*[*Elem*]);
  vars x : *Elem*; s : *FinSet*[*Elem*]; f : *Elem* →? *Elem*
  axioms
    image f *empty* = *empty*;
    image f (*add*(x, s)) = *add*($f\ x$, *image* $f\ s$);

[7] Note that the pre-logical relations of [17] show the same behaviour. Also note that they are not useful for obtaining initial models.

Note that in CASL, compound names like *FinSet[Elem]* are renamed during instantiations: if *Elem* is instantiated with *Nat*, *FinSet[Elem]* is automatically renamed to *FinSet[Nat]*. (This avoids unintended identifications when simultaneously using different instantiations of the same generic specification.)

Recall that $t_1 \to t_2$ is a subsort of $t_1 \to^? t_2$. Therefore, due to the semantical identification according to the overloading relation, the axioms suffice to specify the intended behaviour of *both* image functions.

5.2 Example 2

Subsorts propagate properties by static checking and thus decrease the number of proof obligations. A classical example, known from imperative programming languages, are subrange types used as index types for arrays: type checking (or, equivalently, proving adherence to the subrange) need only be done upon assignment to an index variable (of the index type) and need not be done when using this variable in an index expression of an array (with this index type). A similar, but more sophisticated, example can be found below.

spec ORDLISTS [**sort** *Elem*; **op** $\_\_ \leq \_\_$: **pred**$(Elem \times Elem)$] =
  LISTS[**sort** *Elem*] **with op** $map : (Elem \to Elem) \to List[Elem] \to List[Elem]$
then
  ops $isOrdered[\_\_ \leq \_\_] : \mathbf{pred}(List[Elem])$;
    $isOrderPreserving[\_\_ \leq \_\_] : \mathbf{pred}(Elem \to Elem)$
  axioms ...
  sorts $OrdList[Elem, \_\_ \leq \_\_] = \{l : List[Elem] \bullet isOrdered[\_\_ \leq \_\_](l)\}$;
    $OrderPreserving[Elem, \_\_ \leq \_\_] =$
      $\{f : Elem \to Elem \bullet isOrderPreserving[\_\_ \leq \_\_](f)\}$
  op $map : OrderPreserving[Elem, \_\_ \leq \_\_] \to$
      $OrdList[Elem, \_\_ \leq \_\_] \to OrdList[Elem, \_\_ \leq \_\_]$

spec LISTEXAMPLE = INT
then ORDLISTS[INT **fit** $Elem \mapsto Nat$]
then
  ops $sqr : Int \to Nat$;
    $sqrlist(l : List[Nat]) : List[Nat] = map\ sqr\ l$;
    $sqrlist(ol : OrdList[Nat, \_\_ \leq \_\_]) : OrdList[Nat, \_\_ \leq \_\_] =$
      $map\ (sqr\ as\ OrderPreserving[Nat, \_\_ \leq \_\_])\ ol$

In ORDLISTS, lists (with a map function) are extended by concepts of ordering. Thereafter, for any application *map f l*, we only need to prove the order preservation property of its first (functional) argument *f* and (if this is not clear from the subsort) the property of the second (list) parameter *l* that it is in fact ordered; then we get the property that the result is also ordered for free. In LISTEXAMPLE, two profiles are given for the function *sqrlist*, using two different profiles of *map*. Note that both axioms for *sqrlist* rely on the fact that $Int \to Nat$ (the type of *sqr*) is a subtype of $Nat \to Nat$ (assuming that *Nat* is a subtype of *Int*). Since we can prove once and for all that *map* on order-preserving functions preserves orderedness, we know that *sqrlist* on an ordered list always yields an ordered list just by type checking plus the proof that $sqr\ as\ OrderPreserving[Nat, \leq]$ is defined (the latter being equivalent to *sqr* being order-preserving).

6 Proof Theory

Below we propose how a proof calculus can be developed for the presented logics.

The reduction approach in the definition of both generalized subsorted partial first-order logic and subsorted partial higher-order logic presented in this paper makes it possible to use the borrowing technique of Cerioli and Meseguer [10]. Our reductions have the crucial property that the model translation is surjective (cf. Propositions 3.10 and 4.10). With this, we can apply the following theorem of [10]:

Theorem 6.1 Let I and J be two institutions and $\mu = (\Phi, \alpha, \beta) : I \to J$ be an institution representation with surjective model translations β_Σ. Then semantical entailment is preserved: For any signature Σ in I, any set of Σ-sentences Γ in I and any Σ-sentence φ in I, we have

$$\Gamma \models^I_\Sigma \varphi \text{ iff } \alpha_\Sigma(\Gamma) \cup ax(\Phi(\Sigma)) \models^J_{sign(\Phi(\Sigma))} \alpha_\Sigma \varphi$$

That is, we can translate theorem proving goals from subsorted partial higher-order logic to many-sorted partial first-order logic and then use a theorem prover for many-sorted partial first-order logic to prove them. In a similar context, this technique has been practically implemented, resulting in an encoding of first-order CASL in the Isabelle/HOL system [25]. We have also solved the problem of displaying intermediate goals (which live in the target of the translation) using an inverse of the sentence translation. Using the above reductions, it should cause no greater difficulties to extend this encoding to higher-order CASL. The main problem will be the following: Our many-sorted partial first-order logic comes equipped with a definite description operator, while usual first-order theorem provers do not have such a feature.[8] However, if we use Isabelle/HOL as a target and take the encoding of partiality from [25], the description operator can be axiomatized as a combinator (see [13]), since λ-abstraction is available. Because it is desirable to use Isabelle/HOL's higher-order theorem proving directly, our ultimate goal will be to build an institution representation from subsorted partial higher-order logic directly to the HOL logic of Isabelle, without going via first-order logic.

7 Conclusions

The underlying logic of the common algebraic specification language CASL is subsorted partial first-order logic. We have generalized this logic to the higher-order case, using a step-by-step reduction.

[8] Note however that it is possible to translate the sublanguage without λ-abstraction to first-order logic without definite description, if we add if-then-else as a primitive.

First, we have extended many-sorted partial first-order logic with a definite description operator chosing (if existing) the unique element satisfying a given property.

Then, we have defined a generalized subsorted partial first-order logic in terms of many-sorted partial first-order logic. This logic uses two subsorting relations in order to cope with the non-injective subsorting between functional sorts that is contravariant w.r.t. argument types.

In a third step, we have defined subsorted partial higher-order logic in terms of generalized subsorted partial first-order logic. Here, it turns out that λ-abstraction for partial functions cannot be reduced to (strict) combinatory logic. Therefore, we reduce the three different kinds of λ-abstraction (for total functions, partial functions and predicates) to definite description.

This modular way of proceeding has the advantage of a clear conceptual separation between different issues. Moreover, definitions and results carry over from simpler to more complex logics. Another modularity aspect is that we always syntactically distinguish between total functions, partial functions and predicates. This has the advantage that sublanguages of higher-order CASL can be defined very easily; thus relating foreign tools is facilitated.

When defining subsorted partial higher-order logic, there are several design alternatives concerning the choice of model classes and homomorphisms. We chose the most general model classes and provide abbreviations for the usual axiom schemes like extensionality and comprehension. In order to faithfully generalize the notion of homomorphism for first-order CASL, we introduce a notion of first-order HO-homomorphism that differs from the usual notion of higher-order homomorphism studied in the literature. It has the crucial advantage that first-order CASL can be faithfully represented within higher-order CASL. We also give an example specification demonstrating the usefulness of a faithful representation.

It is straightforward (see [26]) to extend the first-order CASL language with higher-order constructs and give semantics to the resulting language using the presented subsorted partial higher-order logic.

It should be easy to extend our framework with a two-valued sort of truth-values (say, *logical*) which can be used as an (almost) normal type in the type system, as in the system of Farmer [13]. We have refrained from doing this here because the reduction semantics gets more complicated. Moreover, our solution to use predicates has almost the same strength: $t \to logical$ is the same as $pred(t)$. We only lose the possibility to define new user-defined logical connectives. But *logical* could be introduced[9] in a future extension.

Related Work The translation of higher-order to first-order logic has been studied in the literature for a long time, see e.g. [35,3,18,15]. In [35], many-sorted higher-order algebra, in [3], partial higher-order algebra and in [15,18],

[9] When introducing *logical*, functions with argument *logical* have to be excluded from algebraic core terms. It is a bit unclear what a homomorphism condition for such functions would be.

subsorted higher-order algebra/logic is translated to first-order algebra/logic. The sort system of [18,19] lacks partial function types and it is not so flexible as ours, since there are certain restrictions on the subsort relation. Moreover, only the covariant subsort relation $\leq^{\rightarrow}$ is considered – there is no contravariant extension of the subsorting relation to higher types. Spectral [20] and Spectrum [8] are languages that combine subsorting, partiality, higher-order functions and predicate logic, as we do. However, for Spectral, this combination has not clearly been worked out, [20] only contains some initial ideas. In Spectrum, the logic is much more complicated than ours, because Spectrum has a cpo-based semantics with a three-valued logic, while we have a set-theoretic semantics with a two-valued logic. We find the latter more natural and simpler, and moreover, first-order logic is directly included as a sublanguage.

Future Work A topic for future work is to include in our framework (free) datatype declarations and sort generation constraints as known from first-order CASL. In [26] we have shown that caution is needed, since some higher-order datatype declarations are inconsistent, and we have some initial thoughts about sort generation constraints.

Future work should also consider the further extension of higher-order CASL with a more flexible type system involving polymorphism and dependent types (cf. Barendregt's λ-cube [6]), in order to come closer to the semantics of functional programming languages. It would also be interesting to embed higher-order CASL into Church's classical higher-order logic, since for the latter logic, many theorem proving systems exist. Work in this direction will be based on the existing embedding of first-order CASL into higher-order logic implemented using the Isabelle/HOL system [25].

Acknowledgements

The authors would like to thank all the participants of CoFI, and in particular (in alphabetical order) Maura Cerioli, Peter Mosses, Olaf Owe, Don Sannella and Andrzej Tarlecki, for their contributions of ideas and discussions.

References

1. J. Adámek, H. Herrlich, and G. Strecker. *Abstract and Concrete Categories.* Wiley, New York, 1990. 138
2. P. B. Andrews. *An Introduction to Mathematical Logic and Type Theory: To Truth Through Proof.* Academic press, 1986. 127
3. E. Astesiano and M. Cerioli. On the existence of initial models for partial (higher-order) conditional specifications. In *Proc. Joint Conf. on Theory and Practice of Software Development*, pages 74–88. Springer LNCS 351, 1989. 142
4. Egidio Astesiano and Maura Cerioli. Partial Higher–Order Specifications. *Fundamenta Informaticae*, 16:101–126, 1992. 127, 136, 137

5. H. P. Barendregt. *The Lambda Calculus.* Number 103 in Studies in Logic and the Foundations of Mathematics. North-Holland, Amsterdam, revised edition, 1991. 133
6. H. P. Barendregt. Lambda calculi with types. In D. M. Gabbai Samson Abramski and T. S. E. Maiboum, editors, *Handbook of Logic in Computer Science.* Oxford University Press, Oxford, 1992. 143
7. T. Borzyszkowski. Moving specification structures between logical systems. Presented at the WADT 98 workshop, Lisbon, 1998. 138
8. Manfred Broy, Christian Facchi, Radu Grosu, Rudi Hettler, Heinrich Hussmann, Dieter Nazareth, Franz Regensburger, and Ketil Stølen. The requirement and design specification language Spectrum, an informal introduction, version 1.0. Technical report, Institut für Informatik, Technische Universität München, March 1993. 143
9. P. Burmeister. *A model theoretic approach to partial algebras.* Akademie Verlag, Berlin, 1986. 137
10. M. Cerioli and J. Meseguer. May I borrow your logic? (transporting logical structures along maps). *Theoretical Computer Science*, 173:311–347, 1997. 141
11. M. Cerioli, T. Mossakowski, and H. Reichel. From total equational to partial first order logic. In E. Astesiano, H.-J. Kreowski, and B. Krieg-Brückner, editors, *Algebraic Foundations of Systems Specifications*, pages 31–104. Springer Verlag, 1999. 128
12. Maura Cerioli, Anne Haxthausen, Bernd Krieg-Brückner, and Till Mossakowski. Permissive subsorted partial logic in CASL. In Michael Johnson, editor, *Algebraic methodology and software technology: 6th international conference, AMAST 97*, volume 1349 of *Lecture Notes in Computer Science*, pages 91–107. Springer-Verlag, 1997. 127, 129, 130
13. W. A. Farmer. A partial functions version of Church's simple type theory. *Journal of Symbolic Logic*, 55:1269–1291, 1991. 127, 133, 141, 142
14. J. A. Goguen and R. M. Burstall. Institutions: Abstract model theory for specification and programming. *Journal of the Association for Computing Machinery*, 39:95–146, 1992. Predecessor in: LNCS 164, 221–256, 1984. 129, 132
15. A. E. Haxthausen. Order-sorted algebraic specifications with higher-order functions. *Theoretical Computer Science*, 183:157–185, 1997. 127, 142
16. K. Hoffmann, H. Ehrig, and U. Wolter. Folding and unfolding construction between algebraic high level nets and contextual higher order nets. Presented at WADT'99, 1999. 135
17. Furio Honsell and Donald Sannella. Pre-logical relations. In *Proc. Computer Science Logic, CSL'99*, volume 1683 of *Lecture Notes in Computer Science*, pages 546–561. Springer, 1999. 139
18. M. Kerber. Sound and complete translations from sorted higher-order logic into sorted first-order logic. In B. W. Wah M. Georgeff, Z. Shi, editor, *Proceedings of PRICAI-94, Third Pacific Rim International Conference on Artificial Intelligence*, pages 149–154, Beijing, China, August 1994. International Academic Publishers, Beijing, China. 142, 143
19. M. Kohlhase. Higher-order automated theorem proving. Unpublished draft, Universität Saarbücken, 1999. 143
20. B. Krieg-Brückner and D. Sannella. Structuring Specifications in-the-large and in-the-small: Higher-Order Functions, Dependent Types and Inheritance in SPECTRAL. In S. Abramsky and T. S. E. Maibaum, editors, *TAPSOFT '91. Proccedings*

of the International Joint Conference on Theory and Practice of Software Development. Volume 1: Colloquium on Trees in Algebra and Programming, pages 103–120. Springer LNCS 493, 1991. 143

21. CoFI Task Group on Language Design. CASL – The CoFI Algebraic Specification Language – Summary, version 1.0. Available at WWW[10], October 1998. 126
22. Narciso Martí-Oliet and José Meseguer. Inclusions and subtypes I: First-order case. *Journal of Logic and Computation*, 6(3):409–438, June 1996. 127
23. K. Meinke. Universal algebra in higher types. *Theoretical Computer Science*, 100(2):385–417, June 1992. 127
24. J. Meseguer. General logics. In *Logic Colloquium 87*, pages 275–329. North Holland, 1989. 132, 138
25. T. Mossakowski, Kolyang, and B. Krieg-Brückner. Static semantic analysis and theorem proving for CASL. In F. Parisi Presicce, editor, *Recent trends in algebraic development techniques. Proc. 12th International Workshop*, volume 1376 of *Lecture Notes in Computer Science*, pages 333–348. Springer, 1998. 141, 143
26. Till Mossakowski, Anne Haxthausen, and Bernd Krieg-Brückner. Subsorted partial higher-order logic as an extension of casl. CoFI Note: L-10. Available at WWW[11], October 1998. 127, 142, 143
27. Peter D. Mosses. CoFI: The Common Framework Initiative for Algebraic Specification and Development. In *TAPSOFT '97: Theory and Practice of Software Development*, volume 1214 of *LNCS*, pages 115–137. Springer-Verlag, 1997. 126
28. Axel Poigné. On specifications, theories, and models with higher types. *Information and Control*, 68(1–3):1–46, January / February / March 1986. 135
29. Z. Qian. An algebraic semantics of higher-order types with subtypes. *Acta Informatica*, 30(6):569–607, 1993. 127
30. D. T. Sannella and R. M. Burstall. Structured theories in LCF. In G. Ausiello and M. Protasi, editors, *Proceedings of the 8th Colloquium on Trees in Algebra and Programming (CAAP'83)*, volume 159 of *LNCS*, pages 377–391, L'Aquila, Italy, March 1983. Springer. 130
31. P. Y. Schobbens. Second-order proof systems for algebraic specification languages. In H. Ehrig and F. Orejas, editors, *Recent Trends in Data Type Specification*, volume 785 of *Lecture Notes in Computer Science*, pages 321–336, 1994. 139
32. CoFI Task Group on Semantics. CASL – The CoFI Algebraic Specification Language (version 1.0) – Semantics. Version 0.95. CoFI Note: S-9. Available at WWW[12], March 1999. 126
33. A. Tarlecki. Moving between logical systems. In M. Haveraaen, O. Owe, and O.-J. Dahl, editors, *Recent Trends in Data Type Specifications. 11th Workshop on Specification of Abstract Data Types*, volume 1130 of *Lecture Notes in Computer Science*, pages 478–502. Springer Verlag, 1996. 132, 138
34. A. Tarlecki. Towards heterogeneous specifications. In D. Gabbay and M. van Rijke, editors, *Frontiers of Combining Systems, 2nd International Workshop*. Kluwer, 1998. To appear. 138
35. A. Tarlecki, B. Möller, and M. Wirsing. Algebraic specifications of reachable higher-order algebras. In D. Sannella; A. Tarlecki, editor, *Proceedings of the 5th Workshop on Recent Trends in Data Type Specification*, volume 332 of *LNCS*, pages 154–169, Berlin, September 1988. Springer. 127, 136, 142

[10] http://www.brics.dk/Projects/CoFI/Documents/CASLSummary/index.html
[11] http://www.brics.dk/Projects/CoFI/Notes/L-10.html
[12] http://www.brics.dk/Projects/CoFI/Notes/S-9.html

Specifying Real Numbers in CASL

Markus Roggenbach, Lutz Schröder, and Till Mossakowski

BISS, Department of Computer Science, University of Bremen
P.O.Box 330440, D-28334 Bremen

Abstract. We present a weak theory BASICREAL of the real numbers in the first order specification language CASL. The aim is to provide a datatype for practical purposes, including the central notions and results of basic analysis. BASICREAL captures for instance e and π, as well as the trigonometric and other standard functions. Concepts such as continuity, differentiation and integration are shown to be definable and tractable in this setting; Newton's Method is presented as an example of a numerical application. Finally, we provide a proper connection between the specified datatype BASICREAL and specifications of the real numbers in higher order logic and various set theories.

There seem to be two obstacles to the specification of the real numbers as a datatype within first order logic: The real numbers form an uncountable set, which may lead to the conclusion that they cannot be specified in first order logic due to the theorem of Löwenheim and Skolem. More importantly, the usual axiomatizations and constructions of the real numbers use higher-order concepts. As a consequence, first order algebraic specification languages up to now either do not provide such a datatype at all or offer only a specification of a floating point system as an approximation. Both solutions are unsatisfactory: The first leaves a great deal of applications out of scope. The second is of course better, but nevertheless problematic: It forces the specifier to deal with implemention details even on the level of a requirement specification, and the development of numerical algorithms cannot be described.

In this paper we present an axiomatization BASICREAL of a weak theory of the real numbers in the first order specification language CASL, the *Common Algebraic Specification Language* [CoF99]. CASL has been designed by COFI, the international *Common Framework Initiative for algebraic specification and development* [CoF]. It is based on a critical selection of concepts and constructs that have already proven successful in various algebraic specification frameworks. Its features include first-order predicate logic, partial functions, and subsorts as well as structured and architectural specifications. The specification presented here can easily be translated into any specification language that supports partial subsorted first order logic with sort generation constraints.

It should be pointed out that our approach is not a constructive one: We use the law of excluded middle as well as non-constructive existential axioms, in particular a weak version of the axiom of choice. Moreover, our main aim is *not* to formalize mathematics within a framework suitable for automated reasoning,

D. Bert, C. Choppy, and P. Mosses (Eds.): WADT'99, LNCS 1827, pp. 146–161, 2000.

but rather to provide a datatype that is usable for practical purposes (although one of the motivations for attempting a first order specification for the real numbers is the fact that first order logic currently has better theorem proving support than higher order logic, in particular regarding the structuring of proofs via structured specifications).

The full specification can be found in "The datatypes REAL and COMPLEX in CASL" [RSM00]. It depends on certain basic datatypes, which are provided in "Basic Datatypes in CASL" [RMS00]. Its style is documented in "Rules of Methodology" [RM00]. The paper is organized as follows: Section 1 discusses the axioms and fundamental concepts of BASICREAL. In Section 2, we describe how notions like continuity, derivability, and integrability can be formalized and which properties of these concepts can be proved within BASICREAL. As an application, we present Banach's Fixed Point Theorem and Newton's Method in Section 3. Finally, in Section 4, we relate the specification BASICREAL with other theories of the real numbers.

1 The Datatype BasicReal

In principle, the first order specification of real numbers is in fact not a problem at all: The usual axiom systems for set theory such as Zermelo-Fraenkel (ZF or ZFC) or, if a finite axiomatization is required (as in CASL), von Neumann-Bernays-Gödel (VNBG) are first order, and the real numbers are of course specifiable in set theory. However, this makes for overly large and complex specifications as well as immense models (supposing that there exist models of set theory) and is hence not practically feasible.

The solution proposed here consists in defining substitutes for some of the required more complex sets (or higher types) in the shape of first order types, together with operators and properties that enforce a behaviour which is similar to that of the intended types. To wit, we define types *Sequence* and *Fun* which are intended to simulate sequences of reals or real-valued unary partial functions on the real numbers, resp.; more ambitious applications may require more complex types of this nature, e.g. binary partial functions in order to deal with families of curves.

These types are equipped with evaluation operators denoted by __@__ (where $f@x$ 'means' $f(x)$), and the obvious extensionality axioms enforce an interpretation by (essentially) subsets of the intended function sets. However, these subsets will in general be proper, and as a consequence, the models of our theory will in general be proper subsets of a set of real numbers in the usual sense. This need not be a drawback as long as the theorems and constructions needed in typical applications can be salvaged; it turns out that this is indeed possible to some extent.

To this end, there will have to be a certain amount of machinery to ensure that the 'higher' types are not interpreted so trivially as to become meaningless; this is achieved on the one hand by suitable constructors such as a constant sequence operator, addition of functions, an iteration operator and the like, and on the other hand by existence axioms. The latter concern certain special cases of the axiom of choice as well as, of course, completeness properties of the real numbers. While a standard theory of real numbers will only have one completeness axiom that comes with a variety of equivalent formulations, the strong limitations of our setting require (for the time being) several explicit completeness axioms, the number of which has been minimized as far as currently possible. It should be noted that all axioms and concepts are chosen in such a way that any model of the classical theory of the real numbers (with choice) will also be a model of our theory (but not vice versa).

1.1 The Type System

As carried out e.g. in the "Basic Datatypes in CASL" [RMS00], the natural, integral and rational numbers, respectively, can be specified monomorphically in CASL using sort generation constraints. Our specification defines a supertype *Real* of the rational numbers which carries the structure of an Archimedian field and is subsequently equipped with choice and completeness axioms. As indicated in the introduction, the specification ceases to be monomorphic at this point.

Moreover, several function types are defined. Polynomials over the real numbers are specified as a monomorphic extension (type *Polynomial*), again using sort generation constraints. The types *Sequence* and *Fun* are designed to simulate sequences of real numbers or real-valued unary partial functions on subsets of the real line, resp.; *Fun* is declared as a supersort of *Polynomial* as well as of *Sequence*. This leads to the type system $Rat < Real < Polynomial < Fun > Sequence$.

The evaluation operators for *Fun* and *Sequence* are denoted $f@x$ and $s@n$ (for $f(x)$ and s_n), respectively. In addition, there are two composition operators $\circ$ and $\diamond$ on *Fun*. $\circ$ is the usual composition of partial maps (i.e. $\circ$ is a total operator, and $(f \circ g)@x$ is defined iff $f@(g@x)$ is defined), and $\diamond$ is a partial composition: $f \diamond g$ is defined (and, in this case, equal to $f \circ g$) iff $f@(g@x)$ is defined whenever $g@x$ is defined.

Both *Sequence* and *Fun* are equipped with further constructor operations; in particular, one has the identity sequence N and identity functions on open and closed intervals, sums, products etc. of sequences and functions, sequences of partial sums, Taylor series (as functions), a faculty operation on sequences, an inverse function operator, and an iteration operator which maps a function f and an initial real value x to the sequence obtained by repeated application of f. This list of operations may have to be extended for future applications. Note that the introduction of these operators does by no means constitute a definitional or even a conservative extension; new operations on sequences or functions will in general require the existence of more sequences and functions.

spec DEFINEBASICREAL =
{ORDEREDFIELDWITHSEQUENCESANDFUNCTIONS
with sorts *Nat*, *Int*, *Rat*, *Elem*, *Sequence*, *Polynomial*, *Fun*
and ARCHIMEDIANFIELD} **with sort** $Elem \mapsto Real$
then LIST[*Sequence*] **and** LIST[*Fun*]
then %% Weak Axiom of Choice
vars $s, t : List[Sequence]; f : List[Fun]$
• %[AC]
$(\sharp s = \sharp t \wedge \sharp t = \sharp f) \Rightarrow$
$((\forall n : Nat \bullet \exists x : Real \bullet \forall i : Nat \bullet (1 \leq i \wedge i \leq \sharp s) \Rightarrow$
$((s!i)@n < (f!i)@x \wedge (f!i)@x < (t!i)@n))$
$\Rightarrow \exists r : Sequence \bullet \forall n : Nat \bullet \forall i : Nat \bullet (1 \leq i \wedge i \leq \sharp s) \Rightarrow$
$((s!i)@n < (f!i)@(r@n) \wedge (f!i)@(r@n) < (t!i)@n)$
)
then **%implies** %% continuity and lim:
var $f : Fun; a : Real$
• %[EpsDelta_equiv_Lim_local] $cont(a, f) \Leftrightarrow contSeq(a, f)$
• %[EpsDelta_equiv_Lim_global] $cont(f) \Leftrightarrow contSeq(f)$
• %[limEpsDelta_equiv_limSeq] $lim(a, f) = limSeq(a, f)$
then %% Completeness
vars $a, b : Real; s : Sequence; f : Fun$
• %[Real_closed_1]
$\forall p : Polynomial \bullet odd(degree(p)) \Rightarrow \exists r : Real \bullet p@r = 0$
• %[Bolzano-Weierstraß]
$isBounded(s) \Rightarrow hasLargestPointOfAcc(s)$
• %[lub_Fun] $hasUpperBound(f, a, b) \Rightarrow \exists l : Real \bullet l = lub(f, a, b)$
then **%implies**
var $a, b : Real; s : Sequence; f : Fun$
• %[Bolzano-Weierstraß_dual]
$hasLowerBound(s) \Rightarrow hasSmallestPointOfAcc(s)$
• %[Cauchy_complete] $isCauchy(s) \Rightarrow converges(s)$
• %[glb_Sequences] $hasLowerBound(s) \Rightarrow \exists g : Real \bullet g = glb(s)$
• %[lub_Sequences] $hasUpperBound(s) \Rightarrow \exists l : Real \bullet l = lub(s)$
• %[glb_Fun] $hasLowerBound(f, a, b) \Rightarrow \exists g : Real \bullet g = glb(f, a, b)$
• %[ex_max] $(\forall c : Real \bullet def\ f@c \Leftrightarrow a \leq c \leq b) \wedge cont(f)$
$\Rightarrow hasMax(f) \wedge hasMin(f)$
• %[Rolle]
$a < b \wedge f@a = f@b \wedge cont(f \diamond idClosed(a, b)) \wedge def\ der(f) \diamond idOpen(a, b)$
$\Rightarrow \exists c : Real \bullet a < c < b \wedge der(c, f) = 0$
• %[Mean_Value] $a < b \wedge cont(f \diamond idClosed(a, b)) \wedge def\ der(f) \diamond idOpen(a, b)$
$\Rightarrow \exists c : Real \bullet a < c < b \wedge der(c, f) = (f@b - f@a)/(b - a)$
end

Fig. 1. Specification DefineBasicReal (cf. Sections 1.2 and 1.3)

1.2 Structure of the Specification

Our specification makes full use of the structuring concepts provided in CASL. The specification is split into several named parts, each describing theories that are of use in their own right.

To begin, the specifications NAT, INT and RAT of natural, integer, and rational numbers, respectively, are used as provided by the CASL standard library of basic datatypes [RMS00]; the same library also contains the specifications COMMUTATIVERING and FIELD (with the expected meaning). The specification POLYNOMIAL then defines the polynomial ring over a given ring R as a free extension of R; at this point, the sort generation constraints offered by CASL are used in a crucial way.

From the specification FIELD, we move on to ordered and archimedian fields (ORDEREDFIELD, ARCHIMEDIANFIELD), adding a new predicate *positive* with the appropriate axioms in the first step and a single new axiom (the Archimedian axiom) in the second. We then define conservative extensions of ORDEREDFIELD by successively adding the substitutes for the higher order types mentioned above: ORDEREDFIELDWITHSEQUENCES defines the additional type *Sequence* and the associated constructors, and ORDEREDFIELDWITHSEQUENCESAND-FUNCTIONS provides the type *Fun*. These specifications also contain the definitions of basic topological concepts such as limits, points of accumulation, and continuity, as well as the definition of the derivative of a function.

The actual specification of the weak real numbers (cf. Figure 1) is formulated as an extension DEFINEBASICREAL of ORDEREDFIELDWITHSEQUENCESAND-FUNCTIONS and ARCHIMEDIANFIELD. The extension consists essentially of additional axioms concerning choice and completeness and a collection of theorems that follow from these axioms (this is expressed in Figure 1 by the annotation %implies). The axiom of choice AC requires lists of sequences and functions, respectively (cf. Figure 1); the datatype LIST is provided by the CASL standard library of basic datatypes [RMS00]. The specification DEFINEBASICREAL is definitionally extended by standard functions such as the exponential and trigonometric functions, constructed via Taylor series, in BASICREAL; cf. Figure 2.

Finally, there are two further extensions aimed at particular applications. Banach's Fixed Point Theorem and Newton's Method can be handled in a definitional extension BASICREALNUMERICS (cf. section 3), while the definition of integration requires, besides definitional extensions concerning partitions of intervals which use the parametrized basic datatype FINSET of finite sets of elements of a given type [RMS00], an additional completeness axiom; hence, we need a non-conservative extension BASICREALINTEGRATION to deal with these matters (cf. subsection 2.3). The overall structure of the specification is visualized in the following diagram; definitional and conservative extensions are

```
spec BasicReal [DefineBasicReal] =
  %def
  ops exp, ln, sqrt,
        sin, cos, sinh, cosh,
        tan, cot, arcsin, arccos,
        arctan, arccot, tanh, coth,
        arsinh, arcosh, artanh, arcoth :   Fun;
  ops exp(x : Real) : Real = e@x;
        e : Real = exp(1);
        ln(x : Real)? : Real = ln@x;
        sqrt(x : Real)? : Real = sqrt@x;
        ... %% further functions
  vars x, y : Real
  •  %[exp_def] exp = TaylorSum(1, 0)
  •  %[ln_def] ln = inv(exp)
  ...  %% further function definitions
end
```

Fig. 2. Specification BasicReal

labelled 'def' and 'cons', respectively.

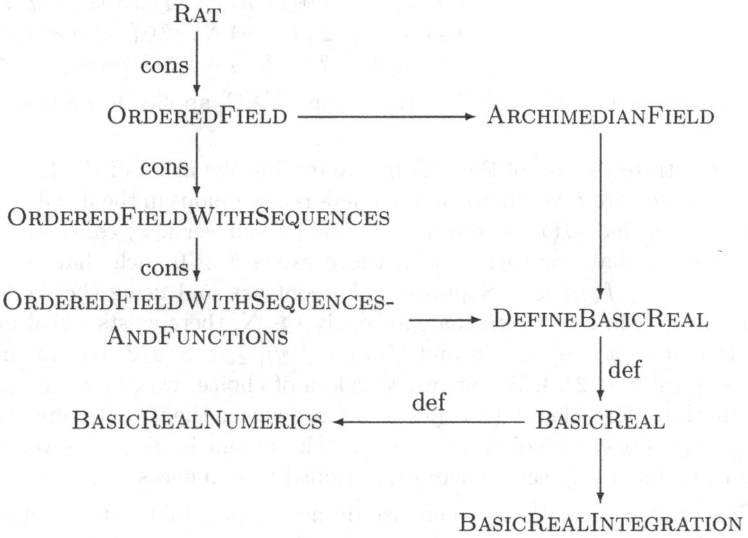

1.3 Axiomatization

As indicated above, the main issues in the axiomatization of the weak real numbers concern weak variants of the axioms of choice and various completeness properties. In the form chosen here, these axioms serve to ensure the existence of certain sequences or real numbers, resp. There are no existence axioms for functions, which arise purely from the associated construction operators, most importantly as Taylor series.

To cover the requirements concerning choice, we have chosen a single (first order) axiom scheme, parametrized over $n \in \mathbb{N}$, stating informally that, whenever $f_1, \ldots, f_n$ are functions and $s^1, \ldots, s^n, t^1, \ldots, t^n$ are sequences such that, for each $m \in \mathbb{N}$, there exists a real number x such that $s^i_m < f_i(x) < t^i_m$, $i = 1, \ldots, n$, then there exists a sequence r such that $s^i_m < f_i(r_m) < t^i_m$, for all i, m. Axiom schemes are not a feature of CASL. However, organizing the functions f_i and the sequences s^i, t^i as lists, the above scheme can be expressed as a single axiom in CASL, cf. Figure 1. The datatype LIST is provided by the CASL standard library [RMS00]. Within LIST, $\sharp s$ denotes the lenght of list s (the empty list has lenght 0), and $s!i$ is the ith element of list s, $1 \leq i \leq \sharp s$. The resulting formula %[AC] is rather complex. Thus we present here the (hopefully better readable) instance $n = 3$ of this scheme – avoiding lists:

vars $s\_1, s\_2, s\_3, t\_1, t\_2, t\_3 : \mathit{Sequence};$
$\quad f\_1, f\_2, f\_3 : \mathit{Fun}$

- %[AC_3]

$$
\begin{aligned}
(\forall n : \mathit{Nat} \bullet \exists x : \mathit{Real} \bullet\ & s\_1@n < f\_1@x \wedge f\_1@x < t\_1@n \wedge \\
& s\_2@n < f\_2@x \wedge f\_2@x < t\_2@n \wedge \\
& s\_3@n < f\_3@x \wedge f\_3@x < t\_3@n) \\
\Rightarrow \exists r : \mathit{Sequence} \bullet\ & \forall n : \mathit{Nat} \bullet \\
& s\_1@n < f\_1@(r@n) \wedge f\_1@(r@n) < t\_1@n \wedge \\
& s\_2@n < f\_2@(r@n) \wedge f\_2@(r@n) < t\_2@n \wedge \\
& s\_3@n < f\_3@(r@n) \wedge f\_3@(r@n) < t\_3@n
\end{aligned}
$$

As *Sequence* is a subtype of *Fun*, the axiom %[AC] applies to sequences f_i as well.

To illustrate the use of this axiom, we outline the proof of the fact that any function which preserves limits of sequences is continuous in the usual 'ε-δ-sense': Given f such that $(f(x_n))$ converges to $f(x)$ whenever (x_n) converges to x, we have to show that, for each $\varepsilon > 0$, there exists $\delta > 0$ such that $|x - y| < \delta$ implies $|f(x) - f(y)| < \varepsilon$. Supposing the contrary and using the Archimedian axiom, we obtain $\varepsilon > 0$ such that, for each $n \in \mathbb{N}$, there exists a real number y such that $0 < |x - y| < 1/n$ and $|f(x) - f(y)| \geq \varepsilon > \varepsilon/2$ (equivalently: $0 < |f(x) - f(y)|^{-1} < 2/\varepsilon$). By our weak axiom of choice, we can write x_n instead of y in these formulae, where (x_n) is a sequence; then (x_n) converges to x, but $(f(x_n))$ does not converge to $f(x)$. The axiom is used in several similar arguments, including cases where it is applied to sequences f_i.

Concerning completeness, there are numerous possibilities to select theorems from real analysis that are equivalent to Cauchy completeness in the usual setting in order to arrive at a set of completeness properties that is reasonably concise and at the same time covers as many applications as possible. At present, there are three completeness axioms: The first one is of algebraic nature and states that each polynomial of odd degree has a root:

- %[Real_closed_1]
  $\forall p : \mathit{Polynomial} \bullet \mathit{odd}(\mathit{degree}(p)) \Rightarrow \exists r : \mathit{Real} \bullet p@r = 0$

It is included in order to improve the algebraic properties of the field of weak real numbers, to wit, to make them a real-closed field [Lan84]. Of course, this axiom follows from the Intermediate Value Theorem; however, it is unclear whether or not this theorem can be deduced in our setting, and it has as yet not been included as an axiom since it is not required for the proofs of the statements listed in DEFINEBASICREAL.

The other two axioms are topological in content: One is a variant of the Theorem of Bolzano and Weierstraß, stating that each bounded sequence has a largest point of accumulation; the other asserts the existence of suprema of images of functions:

vars $s : \mathit{Sequence}; f : \mathit{Fun}; a, b : \mathit{Real}$
- %[Bolzano-Weierstraß] $\mathit{isBounded}(s) \Rightarrow \mathit{hasLargestPointOfAcc}(s)$
- %[lub_Fun] $\mathit{hasUpperBound}(f, a, b) \Rightarrow \exists l : \mathit{Real} \bullet l = \mathit{lub}(f, a, b)$

It must be said that it is unclear whether these statements are actually independent.

Given these axioms, several other completeness properties known from real analysis can actually be deduced; this includes in particular Cauchy completeness in the usual sense (every Cauchy sequence converges), existence of suprema of sequences with upper bounds, and existence of maxima and minima of continuous functions on compact intervals. The latter statement implies Rolle's Theorem and hence, crucially, the Mean Value Theorem. Whether other important properties such as some form of the Theorem of Heine and Borel (closed and bounded equals compact) or the above-mentioned Intermediate Value Theorem can be derived as well remains an open question (cf. the concluding section).

2 Concepts Definable in BasicReal

A theory of the real numbers should permit the study of continuity, differentiation and integration. In this section we discuss to what extent this is possible within the specification DEFINEBASICREAL: For continuity and the derivation of functions we obtain the usual calculus. We develop the beginnings of a theory of integration up to the definition of the integral; further research will lead to the usual calculus of integration.

2.1 Continuity

The definition of continuity in BASICREAL is as usual: A function f of type *Fun* is continuous at some point a of type *Real*, a property denoted as $\mathit{cont}(a, f)$ in BASICREAL, iff

$\mathit{def}\ f@a \wedge (\forall \mathit{epsilon} : \mathit{Real} \bullet \mathit{epsilon} > 0 \Rightarrow (\exists \mathit{delta} : \mathit{Real} \bullet \mathit{delta} > 0 \wedge$
$(\forall x : \mathit{Real} \bullet (\mathit{abs}(x - a) < \mathit{delta} \wedge \mathit{def}\ f@x) \Rightarrow \mathit{abs}(f@x - f@a) < \mathit{epsilon})))$

As an alternative, we introduce the concept of sequential continuity:
- %[contSeq_local_def] $\mathit{contSeq}(a, f) \Leftrightarrow \mathit{def}\ f@a \wedge$
  $(\forall s : \mathit{Sequence} \bullet (\mathit{lim}\ s = a \wedge \mathit{def}\ f \diamond s) \Rightarrow \mathit{lim}(f \diamond s) = f@\mathit{lim}(s))$

While continuity implies sequential continuity, the equivalence of the two concepts depends on the weak axiom of choice %[AC]; cf. Figure 1 and the discussion of the axiom %[AC] in Section 1.3.

Within BASICREAL we can prove that sums, products, composites etc. of continuous functions and, by consequence, polynomials are continuous; cf. [RSM00].

2.2 Derivability

We define the derivation $der(a, f)$ of a function f of type *Fun* at given number a of type *Real* as the limit

$$\lim_{x \to a} \frac{f(x) - f(a)}{x - a}.$$

For the derivation $der(f)$ of a whole function, one has the choice between two possibilities: The operator *der* can be total or partial. If **op** $der : Fun \to Fun$ is *total*, the concept of derivation becomes a construction principle for the function type *Fun*, i.e. the derivation of a function f of type *Fun* may lead to a new function $g = der(f)$. In this case, the introduction of derivation fails to be a definitional extension. Therefore, it has been decided to define the operator **op** $der : Fun \to? Fun$ as a *partial* function:

then %**def**
  op $der : Fun \to? Fun$
  var $f, g : Fun$
  • %[der_global_def] $der(f) = g \Leftrightarrow \forall a : Real \bullet der(a, f) = g@a$

Independently of this decision, we can prove within DEFINEBASICREAL

- the usual calculus for $f \odot g$, where f, g are of type *Fun* and $\odot \in \{+, -, *, /\}$,
- the usual calculus for polynomials, and
- the chain rule.

These results can be found in [RSM00].

2.3 Towards Integrability

To define the integral of a function within BASICREAL it is necessary to add another completeness axiom; currently we use

- %[existence_UpperIntegral] $isBounded(f \diamond idClosed(a, b)) \wedge a < b$
  $\Rightarrow \exists l : Real \bullet isUpperIntegral(l, f, a, b)$

I.e. for any function f of our function type *Fun* that is bounded on the closed interval $[a, b]$ and that is defined on all elements of the interval $[a, b]$, the upper integral, i.e. the greatest lower bound of all upper sums, exists. In contrast to the situation in classical analysis, where any set with a lower bound also has a greatest lower bound, it is improbable that the completeness axioms stated so far imply this axiom in our setting.

Using the axiom %[existence_UpperIntegral], we can define the integral of a function:

spec BASICREALINTEGRATION = BASICREAL[DEFINEBASICREAL]
then ... %% define **preds** isPartion, isUpperSum, isUpperIntergral, ...
then %% Completeness Axiom
  vars $f : \mathit{Fun}; a, b : \mathit{Real}$
  • %[existence_UpperIntegral]
    $\mathit{isBounded}(f \diamond \mathit{idClosed}(a, b)) \wedge a < b \Rightarrow$
    $\exists l : \mathit{Real} \bullet \mathit{isUpperIntegral}(l, f, a, b)$
then %**implies** ... %% %[existence_LowerIntegral]
then %**def**
  ops $\mathit{lowerIntegral}, \mathit{upperIntegral},$
    $\mathit{integral} : \mathit{Fun} \times \mathit{Real} \times \mathit{Real} \rightarrow ?\ \mathit{Real};$
  vars $f : \mathit{Fun}; a, b, x : \mathit{Real}$
  • %[lowerIntegral_def]
    $\mathit{lowerIntegral}(f, a, b) = x \Leftrightarrow \mathit{isLowerIntegral}(x, f, a, b)$
  • %[upperIntegral_def]
    $\mathit{upperIntegral}(f, a, b) = x \Leftrightarrow \mathit{isUpperIntegral}(x, f, a, b)$
  • %[integral_def_1] $\mathit{integral}(f, a, b) = \mathit{upperIntegral}(f, a, b)$
    if $\mathit{upperIntegral}(f, a, b) = \mathit{lowerIntegral}(f, a, b) \wedge a < b$
  • %[integral_def_2] $\mathit{integral}(f, a, a) = 0$
  • %[integral_def_3] $\mathit{integral}(f, a, b) = \mathit{integral}(f, -b, -a)$ *if* $a > b$

3 Newton's Method – a Numerical Application

To demonstrate that our weak theory of the real numbers is both strong enough for practical purposes and easy to handle, we study Newton's Method as an application of BASICREAL. First we deal with Banach's Fixed Point Theorem. Based on this theorem we can define Newton's Method and prove its usual properties. Finally we discuss how this example leads towards a methodology for the development of numerical algorithms in CASL as a first step.

3.1 Banach's Fixed Point Theorem

Banach's fixed point theorem is formulated for complete metric spaces $(M, d : M \times M \rightarrow \mathbb{R}_{\geq 0})$. Here we replace the set M as well as the positive real numbers $\mathbb{R}$ by our sort *Real* and specify the distance function as

  ops $d : \mathit{Real} \times \mathit{Real} \rightarrow \mathit{Real}$
  axiom $\forall x, y : \mathit{Real} \bullet d(x, y) = \mathit{abs}(x - y)$

In this setting we can prove within the specification BASICREAL the propositions of Banach's theorem:

var $a, b, x : \mathit{Real}; f : \mathit{Fun}$
• %[Iteration_Method_for_FixedPoint]
  $\mathit{isContracting}(f \diamond \mathit{idClosed}(a, b)) \wedge a \leq x \wedge x \leq b$
  $\Rightarrow f@\mathit{lim}(\mathit{induct}(x, f)) \stackrel{e}{=} \mathit{lim}(\mathit{induct}(x, f))$
• %[Uniqueness_of_Fixed_Point]
  $\mathit{isContracting}(f) \Rightarrow \forall y, z : \mathit{Real} \bullet f@y = y \wedge f@z = z \Rightarrow y = z$

I.e. for any element f of our function type that is contracting the sequence $x, f(x), f^2(x), \ldots$ converges to a fixed point of f, and this fixed point is unique.

The usual proof of Banach's theorem can easily be carried out within the specification BASICREAL; of course the construction requires the iteration operator *induct*.

3.2 Newton's Method

Given a function $f : [a, b] \to \mathbb{R}$ such that $f(x) = 0$ for some $x \in [a, b] \subset \mathbb{R}$, Newton's Method computes – under certain assumptions – an approximation of x up to a given precision. The idea is to iterate the function $g(x) = x - f(x)/f'(x)$. Provided g is contracting on $[a, b]$, Banach's Theorem ensures that for any $x \in [a, b]$ the limit of the sequence $x, g(x), g^2(x), \ldots$ is a fixed point of g; such a fixed point is a zero of f. By the Mean Value Theorem, the function g is contracting on $[a, b]$ if $|g'(x)| = |f(x) * f''(x)/f^2(x)| < 1$ for all $x \in [a, b]$.

Since both the Mean Value Theorem (cf. Figure 1) and Banach's Theorem (cf. Subsection 3.1) can be proved within the specification BASICREAL, we can conclude

then %**implies**
var f : *Fun*; a, b, x : *Real*
• *hasNewtonProperties*$(f, a, b) \wedge (a \leq x \wedge x \leq b)$
$\wedge\ (\forall y : Real \bullet a \leq y \wedge y \leq b$
$\Rightarrow (f * der(der(f))/(der(f) * der(f)))@y < 1)$
$\Rightarrow converges(induct(x, id - f/der(f))) \wedge$
$f@lim(induct(x, id - f/der(f))) = 0$

I.e. Newton's Method is definable within BASICREAL and computes the desired root.

3.3 Development of Algorithms with Numerical Aspects

The specification BASICREAL allows for the following formal development of algorithms with numerical aspects within CASL:

theory of	object	example for an object
$\mathbb{R}$	formula specifying an element	x such that $f(x) = 0$
$\mathbb{R}$	abstract algorithm	Newton's Method: approximate x by x', where $\lvert x - x'\rvert < \epsilon$
FPS	concrete algorithm	modified Newton's Method: • $<$ 1000 iterations • iterate until $\lvert g(x_n) - g(x_{n+1})\rvert < \delta$ • transform towards zero

- First write a *requirement specification,* which specifies the object to be computed in a theory $\mathbb{R}$ of the real numbers. For example, specify the root of a function f within BasicReal.
- In the next step refine this requirement specification by the choice of a specific algorithm that computes the desired object or an approximation of this object up to a given precision, resp. Usually such an *abstract algorithm* is only correct within a theory $\mathbb{R}$ of the real numbers: Most iteration methods depend on Banach's fixed point theorem; Gauß Elimination needs the structure of a vector space. For example, choose Newton's Method as an abstract algorithm to approximate a root of a function (cf. Section 3.2).
- Finally, formulate a *concrete algorithm* in a floating point system (FPS). The concrete algorithm modifies the abstract algorithm in accordance with the specific properties of the FPS. In the example above, the concrete algorithm may restrict the number of iterations to ensure the termination of the algorithm; or it restricts the precision of the approximation due to the possible precision within the FPS; or it transforms computations towards zero in order to use the higher precision of the FPS near zero.

Thus it is possible to capture all aspects of such a development in Casl. It is important to note that we do not provide a full methodology for this engineering process: While numerical analysis and computer algebra deal with the question how to choose a suitable abstract algorithm for a given requirement specification, it is an open problem how to deal in a formal way with the step from an abstract algorithm to a concrete algorithm. For the latter [Moo88] presents some solutions. Based on [KM81] we provide some ideas for a relation between a floating point system specified in Casl and the specification BasicReal in [RSM00]. [Har99] discusses a different approach to this problem in more detail.

4 Relating BasicReal with other Theories of $\mathbb{R}$

The standard approaches to the specification of real numbers use either set theory or higher-order logic. In fact, we have reconstructed the standard approaches to the real numbers within Casl or extensions of Casl.

Within HOCasl, the higher-order extension of Casl [MHKB], it is easy to specify the real numbers using some form of the (second-order) completeness axiom. This specification can be found in [RSM00].

Moreover, as indicated in Section 1, it is possible to specify set theory within (first-order) Casl. The standard basic datatypes of Casl [RMS00] provide such a specifiation based on the axiom system of von Neumann-Bernays-Gödel. This axiom system is finite thanks to Gödels trick of replacing the (infinite) comprehension axiom scheme of Zermelo-Fraenkel set theory by a number of its instances [Göd40]. This specification can then be definitionally extended by one of the usual set-theoretic constructions or axiomatizations of the real numbers, yielding a specification VNBGReal which is equivalent to the standard axiomatizations of the real numbers ZFCReal in ZFC; the latter can be specified in Schematic-Casl, an extension of Casl that allows axiom schemes.

In the rest of this section, we demonstrate how these alternative approaches relate to our (weaker) first-order theory of real numbers.

4.1 BasicReal and HOReal

To be able to compare our specification BasicReal with the specification HOReal of reals in HOCasl, we consider BasicReal as a HOCasl specification. Fortunately, this is possible without changing the model class. The relation of BasicReal and HOReal can now be expressed as a **view** in HOCasl:

spec HOReal = ... **sorts** $HOSequence = Nat \rightarrow HOReal$;
$HOFun = HOReal \rightarrow ?\ HOReal$

view BasicReal_To_HOReal: BasicReal **to** HOReal =
sorts $Real \mapsto HOReal$,
$Sequence \mapsto HOSequence$,
$Fun \mapsto HOFun$
...

This **view** expresses that BasicReal indeed is a subtheory of HOReal. In particular, we have the following

Fact: *Given a* BasicReal*-formula* φ,
BasicReal $\vdash \varphi$ *implies* HOReal $\vdash$ BasicReal_To_HOReal(φ)

This also implies that each HOReal-model can be reduced to a BasicReal-model along the view. We also can show that BasicReal is strictly weaker than HOReal: BasicReal admits less definable numbers than HOReal.

4.2 Countability

Concerning countability, we have to carefully distinguish the object language from the meta language. From an *external point of view*, that is, within the meta language, all of BasicReal, HOReal[1], ZFCReal and VNBGReal have a countable model, due to the theorem of Löwenheim and Skolem.

On the other hand, *internally*, that is, within the object language, we can prove the uncountability even of the sort *Real* in BasicReal: The formula

(1) $\neg\ \exists s : Sequence \bullet \forall r : Real \bullet \exists n : Nat \bullet s@n = r$

expressing uncountability of the real numbers is provable within BasicReal, using Cantor's argument (cf. [RSM00] for a proof sketch). By the above fact, this translates to HOReal:

(1') $\neg\ \exists s : HOSequence \bullet \forall r : HOReal \bullet \exists n : Nat \bullet s@n = r$

However, the BasicReal-*definable* reals are a countable set in HOReal:

(2') $\exists s : HOSequence \bullet \forall r : HOReal \bullet isBRdef(r) \Rightarrow \exists n : Nat \bullet s@n = r$

[1] Note that HOCasl uses a Henkin model semantics.

4.3 Comprehension vs. Constructors

The different approaches to the specification of real numbers can be summarized in the following table:

Theory	Language	Techniques
BasicReal	Casl	sequence and function constructors
⊂ VNBGReal	Casl	Gödel's set constructors
ZFCReal	Schematic-Casl	comprehension as an axiom scheme
HOReal	HOCasl	λ-abstraction

Generally, the weakness of first-order logic is the lack of variable binding mechanisms (like λ-abstraction or comprehension) in the formation of terms. This weakness can be overcome by working with constructors (like in Curry's theory of combinators) instead, at the price of getting a clumsier theory: we think this is manageable in our specification BasicReal, while we have doubts in the case of VNBGReal.

5 Conclusion

We have presented a weak theory BasicReal of the real numbers in the first order algebraic specification language Casl that

- is easy to handle,
- uses standard mathematical notation,
- allows the deduction of the central results of basic real analysis,
- is strong enough for many practical purposes, in particular certain numerical applications,
- has a proper connection to the reals as specified e.g. in HOCasl via a HOCasl **view**, and
- is suitable for specifying and verifying computer arithmetic (c.f. [RSM00]), e.g. the floating point standards IEEE 754 or 854 that are becoming rapidly accepted by commercial hardware manufacturers.

The difficulties presented by the fact that many of the concepts used in classical analysis are second order have turned out to be serious, but not insurmountable in theory as well as in practice. The obstacle regarding countability mentioned in the introduction has been shown to be insubstantial: The associated argument is in fact based on a misunderstanding regarding internal and external countability; we have shown in Section 4 that the weak real numbers as specified here are indeed internally uncountable, although externally countable.

Nevertheless, the specification BasicReal being to our knowledge the first attempt to specify the real numbers in a first order setting, there remain several open problems, which will be addressed in future research:

- It has to be decided which concepts that are equivalent to Cauchy completeness in the usual analysis of real numbers follow from the given axioms and which are needed as further axioms. This includes in particular the Theorem of Heine and Borel and the Intermediate Value Theorem. If the latter theorem were either proved or added as an axiom, the real closedness axiom could be removed. Moreover, it is open whether a more general completeness axiom can be found which encompasses the ones given here, possibly including the completeness axiom introduced specifically for integration; a relevant option in this context is the introduction of further quasi 'higher order types', such as a type representing subsets of the real line.
- The calculus of integration has to be proven; this concerns in particular the Main Theorem of Calculus.
- Continuity, derivation and integration of the concrete functions *sin*, *cos*, ... defined in BasicReal has to be studied.
- Although constructive analysis is a quite different approach, its results may very well prove to be helpful in our setting; in particular, it has to be explored how constructive methods can be applied to deal with the substitutes for the higher order types.
- It is left as an open problem to determine how the numbers definable within the specification BasicReal are related to the concept of computable numbers in the sense of [Tur37]. This question opens up an interesting connection to domain theory.

Besides this conceptual research that will improve and extend the specification BasicReal, we plan to reprove the existing results with the Casl tools developed at Bremen, i.e. our Casl encoding [MKK98] in Isabelle/HOL.

Acknowledgement

The authors wish to thank Bernd Krieg-Brückner, Magne Haveraaen, and Horst Herrlich for useful comments and suggestions.

References

CoF. CoFI. The Common Framework Initiative for algebraic specification and development, electronic archives. Notes and Documents accessible by WWW[2] and FTP[3]. 146, 160, 161

CoF99. CoFI Language Design Task Group. Casl – The CoFI Algebraic Specification Language – Summary, version 1.0. Documents/CASLSummary, in [CoF], July 1999. 146

Göd40. K. Gödel. *The Consistency of the Continuum Hypothesis.* Number 3 in Annals of Math. Studies. Princeton University Press, 1940. 157

[2] http://www.brics.dk/Projects/CoFI

[3] ftp://ftp.brics.dk/Projects/CoFI

Har99. John R. Harrison. A machine-checked theory of floating point arithmetic. In *The 12th International Conference on Theorem Proving in Higher Order Logics, TPHOLs'99*, volume 1690 of *LNCS*, pages 113-130. Springer, 1999. 157

KM81. Ulrich W. Kulisch and Willard L. Miranker. *Computer Arithmetic in Theory and Practice.* Academic Press, 1981. 157

Lan84. Serge Lang. *Algebra.* Addison-Wesley, 2nd edition, 1984. 153

MHKB. T. Mossakowski, A. Haxthausen, and B. Krieg-Brückner. Subsorted partial higher-order logic as an extension of CASL. In *14th International Workshop on Algebraic Development Techniques, WADT'99*, volume 1827 of *LNCS*. Springer, 2000. 157

MKK98. T. Mossakowski, Kolyang, and B. Krieg-Brückner. Static semantic analysis and theorem proving for CASL. In F. Parisi Presicce, editor, *Recent trends in algebraic development techniques. Proc. 12th International Workshop*, volume 1376 of *LNCS*, pages 333–348. Springer, 1998. 160

Moo88. R.E. Moore, editor. *Reliability in Computing, The Role of Interval Methods in Scientific Computations.* Academic Press, 1988. 157

RSM00. Markus Roggenbach, Lutz Schröder, and Till Mossakowski. The datatypes REAL and COMPLEX in CASL. Note M-7, version 0.3, in [CoF], 2000. 147, 154, 157, 158, 159

RMS00. Markus Roggenbach, Till Mossakowski, and Lutz Schröder. Basic Datatypes in CASL. Note L-12, version 0.4, in [CoF], March 2000. 147, 148, 150, 152, 157

RM00. Markus Roggenbach and Till Mossakowski. Rules of Methodology. Note M-6, version 0.3, in [CoF], 2000. 147

Tur37. Alan M. Turing. On computable numbers, with an application to the Entscheidungsproblem. *Proceedings of the London Mathematical Society*, 42:230 – 265, 1936/37. 160

Specification Refinement with System F – The Higher-Order Case

Jo Erskine Hannay

LFCS, Division of Informatics, University of Edinburgh, Scotland, U.K.
joh@dcs.ed.ac.uk

Abstract. A type-theoretic counterpart to the notion of algebraic specification refinement is discussed for abstract data types with higher-order signatures. The type-theoretic setting consists of System F and the logic for parametric polymorphism of Plotkin and Abadi. For first-order signatures, this setting immediately gives a natural notion of specification refinement up to observational equivalence via the notion of simulation relation. Moreover, a proof strategy for proving observational refinements formalised by Bidoit, Hennicker and Wirsing can be soundly imported into the type theory. In lifting these results to the higher-order case, we find it necessary firstly to develop an alternative simulation relation and secondly to extend the parametric PER-model interpretation, both in such a way as to observe data type abstraction barriers more closely.

1 Introduction

One framework in algebraic specification that has particular appeal and applicability is that of *stepwise specification refinement*. The idea is that a program is the end-product of a step-wise refinement process starting from an abstract high-level specification. At each refinement step some design decisions and implementation issues are resolved, and if each refinement step is proven correct, the resulting program is guaranteed to satisfy the initial specification. This formal methodology for software development, although in principle first-order, is supported *e.g.* by the wide-spectrum language EML for SML result programs [17].

The motivation for our present work is a wish to transfer this concept and its theoretical rigour to a wider spectrum of language principles, and to go beyond the first-order boundaries inherent in the universal algebra approach.

In this paper we look at Girard/Reynolds' polymorphic λ-calculus System F. The accompanying logic of Plotkin and Abadi [30] asserts *relational parametricity* in Reynolds' sense [34,21]. This setting allows an elegant formalisation of abstract data types as existential types [25], and the relational parametricity axiom enables one to derive in the logic that two concrete data types are equal if and only if there exists a simulation relation between their operational parts. At first order, this in turn corresponds to a notion of observational equivalence. Thus, the type-theoretic formalism of refinement due to Luo [20] automatically gives a notion in the logic of specification refinement up to observational equivalence; a key issue in program development.

D. Bert, C. Choppy, and P. Mosses (Eds.): WADT'99, LNCS 1827, pp. 162–182, 2000.

In [11] a formal connection is shown at first order between an account of algebraic specification refinement due to Sannella and Tarlecki [37,36] and the type-theoretic refinement notion above. Issues in algebraic specification refinement, such as input-sort choice [35] and constructor stability [38,36,9], are automatically resolved in the type-theoretic setting. Also, a proof method for proving observational refinements due to Bidoit, Hennicker and Wirsing [4,3,5] is soundly imported into the type-theory logic. The soundness of the logic as a whole is with reference to the parametric PER-model of Bainbridge *et al.* [2].

This paper now generalises the concepts established at first order and treats data types whose operations may be higher-order and polymorphic. At higher order we run into two problems, both of which are solvable by simply observing more closely the abstraction barrier supplied by existential types. Firstly, at higher order, the formal link between the existence of a simulation relation and observational equivalence breaks down. By analysing the existential-type abstraction barrier, one can devise an alternative notion of simulation relation in the logic [12]. This notion composes at higher-order, thus relating the syntactic level to on-going work on the semantic level remedying the fact that logical relations traditionally used to describe refinement do not compose at higher order [15,16,19,18,31]. Now, using an alternative simulation relation means that parametricity is not applicable in the needed form. This is solved soundly w.r.t. the parametric PER-model by augmenting the logical language with a new basic predicate Closed with predefined semantics, so as to restrict observable computations to be closed, and then asserting the needed variant of parametricity [12].

The second problem arises when attempting to validate the proof method of Bidoit *et al.* at higher order w.r.t. the parametric PER-model. Again, observing abstraction barriers more acutely, this problem is solved by supplying an interpretation for encapsulated operations that exactly mirror their applicability.

The theoretical foundations in universal algebra are formidable, see [8]. But there has been substantial development for refinement in type theory as well, and other relevant work include [32,28,29,27,33,1,40,39].

Section 2 outlines the type theory, the logic, and the standard PER semantics. In Sect. 3 specification refinement is introduced. Simulation relations and the proof method for proving observational refinements are introduced for first order. In Sect. 4 we present the alternative simulation relation in the logic to cope with higher-order and polymorphism, and in Sect. 5 we develop the semantics to validate the proof method also at higher order.

2 Parametric Polymorphism

2.1 Syntax

The polymorphic λ-calculus System F has types and terms given by grammars

$$T ::= X \mid T \to T \mid \forall X.T \qquad\qquad t ::= x \mid \lambda x{:}T.t \mid tt \mid \Lambda X.t \mid tT$$

where X and x range over type and term variables respectively. Judgements for type and term formation involve type contexts, and term-contexts depending on type contexts, *e.g.* $X, x{:}X \rhd x{:}X$. The logic in [30,22] for relational parametricity on System F has formulae built using the standard connectives, but now basic predicates are not only equations, but also relation membership statements:

$$\phi ::= (t =_A u) \mid R(t,u) \mid \cdots \mid \forall R\subset A\times B.\phi \mid \exists R\subset A\times B.\phi$$

where R ranges over relation symbols. We write $\alpha[R,X,x]$ to indicate possible occurrences of R, X and x in type, term or formula α, and may write $\alpha[\rho,A,t]$ for the result of substitution, following the appropriate rules concerning capture. We also write $t\ R\ u$ in place of $R(t,u)$. Judgements for formula formation now involve relation symbols, so contexts are augmented with relation variables, depending on the type context, and obeying standard conventions for contexts. The judgements are as expected. Relation definition is accommodated,

$$\frac{\Gamma, x{:}A, y{:}B \rhd \phi \ \mathsf{prop}}{\Gamma \rhd (x{:}A, y{:}B)\ .\ \phi \quad \subset A\times B}$$

by syntax as indicated. For example $\mathsf{eq}_A \stackrel{def}{=} (x{:}A, y{:}A).(x =_A y)$.

If $\rho\subset A\times B$, $\rho'\subset A'\times B'$ and $\rho''[R]\subset A[Y]\times B[Z]$, then complex relations are built by $\rho\to\rho' \subset (A\to A')\times(B\to B')$ where

$$(\rho\to\rho') \stackrel{def}{=} (f{:}A\to A', g{:}B\to B').(\forall x{:}A\forall x'{:}B.(x\rho x' \ \Rightarrow\ (fx)\rho'(gx')))$$

and $\forall(Y,Z,R\subset Y\times Z)\rho''[R] \subset (\forall Y.A[Y])\times(\forall Z.B[Z])$ where

$$\forall(Y,Z,R\subset Y\times Z)\rho'' \stackrel{def}{=} (y{:}\forall Y.A[Y], z{:}\forall Z.B[Z]).(\forall Y\forall Z\forall R\subset Y\times Z.((yY)\rho''[R](zZ)))$$

One acquires further relations by substituting relations for type variables in types. For $\boldsymbol{X} = X_1,\ldots,X_n$, $\boldsymbol{B} = B_1,\ldots,B_n$, $\boldsymbol{C} = C_1,\ldots,C_n$ and $\boldsymbol{\rho} = \rho_1,\ldots,\rho_n$, where $\rho_i\subset B_i\times C_i$, we get $T[\boldsymbol{\rho}]\subset T[\boldsymbol{B}]\times T[\boldsymbol{C}]$, the *action* of $T[\boldsymbol{X}]$ on $\boldsymbol{\rho}$, defined by cases on $T[\boldsymbol{X}]$ as follows:

$$\begin{array}{ll} T[\boldsymbol{X}] = X_i : & T[\boldsymbol{\rho}] = \rho_i \\ T[\boldsymbol{X}] = T'[\boldsymbol{X}] \to T''[\boldsymbol{X}] : & T[\boldsymbol{\rho}] = T'[\boldsymbol{\rho}] \to T''[\boldsymbol{\rho}] \\ T[\boldsymbol{X}] = \forall X'.T'[\boldsymbol{X},X'] : & T[\boldsymbol{\rho}] = \forall(Y,Z,R\subset Y\times Z).T'[\boldsymbol{\rho},R] \end{array}$$

The proof system is natural deduction over formulae now involving relation symbols, and is augmented with inference rules for relation symbols, for example we have for Φ a finite set of formulae:

$$\frac{\Phi \vdash_{\Gamma,R\subset A\times B} \phi[R]}{\Phi \vdash_\Gamma \forall R\subset A\times B\ .\ \phi[R]},\ \text{no } R \text{ in } \Phi \qquad \frac{\Phi \vdash_\Gamma \forall R\subset A\times B.\phi[R],\quad \Gamma\rhd\rho\subset A\times B}{\Phi\vdash_\Gamma \phi[\rho]}$$

One has axioms for equational reasoning and $\beta\eta$ equalities. And now finally, the following relational parametricity axiom schema is asserted:

$$\textsc{Param}:\ \forall Y_1,\ldots,\forall Y_n\forall u{:}(\forall X.T[X,Y_1,\ldots,Y_n])\ .\ u(\forall X.T[X,\mathsf{eq}_{Y_1},\ldots,\mathsf{eq}_{Y_n}])u$$

To understand, it helps to ignore the parameters Y_i and expand the definition to get $\forall u{:}\,(\forall X.T[X])\ .\forall Y\forall Z\forall R{\subset}Y{\times}Z\ .\ u(Y)\ T[R]\ u(Z)$ *i.e.* if one instantiates a polymorphic inhabitant at two related types then the results are also related. This logic is sound w.r.t. the parametric PER-model of [2] and also w.r.t. the syntactic parametric models of [13]. The following link to equality is essential.

Theorem 1 (Identity Extension Lemma [30]**).** *For any* $T[\boldsymbol{Z}]$*, the following sequent is derivable using* PARAM.

$$\forall \boldsymbol{Z}.\forall u,v{:}T[\boldsymbol{Z}]\ .\ (u\ T[\mathsf{eq}_{\boldsymbol{Z}}]\ v \quad\Leftrightarrow\quad (u =_{T[\boldsymbol{Z}]} v))$$

For abstract data types (ADTs), encapsulation is provided in the style of [25] by the following encoding of existential types and pack and unpack combinators. Parameters in existential types are omitted from the discussion, since we will not be dealing with parameterised specifications.

$$\exists X.T[X] \stackrel{def}{=} \forall Y.(\forall X.(T[X] \to Y) \to Y)$$

$$\mathsf{pack}_{T[X]}{:}\forall X.(T[X] \to \exists X.T[X])$$
$$\mathsf{pack}_{T[X]}(A)(opns) \stackrel{def}{=} \Lambda Y.\lambda f{:}\forall X.(T[X] \to Y).f(A)(opns)$$

$$\mathsf{unpack}_{T[X]}{:}\,(\exists X.T[X]) \to \forall Y.(\forall X.(T[X] \to Y) \to Y)$$
$$\mathsf{unpack}_{T[X]}(package)(B)(client) \stackrel{def}{=} package(B)(client)$$

We omit subscripts to pack and unpack as much as possible. Operationally, pack packages a data representation and an implementation of operations on that data representation to give an instance of the ADT given by the existential type. The resulting package is a polymorphic functional that given a client computation and its result domain, instantiates the client with the particular elements of the package. The unpack combinator is the application operator for pack.

Existential types together with the pack and unpack combinators embody a crucial abstraction barrier. Any client computation $f : \forall X.(T[X] \to Y)$ is η-equivalent to a term of the form $\Lambda X.\lambda x{:}\,T[X]\ .\ t[X,x]$. Notice then that a client computation cannot have free variables of types involving the bound (viz. existentially quantified) type variable X. The only way a client computation may compute over types involving X is by accessing virtual operations in the supplied collection x of operations. Notice also that the only way a package can be used is through client computations for which the above holds. The result of all this is the following crucial fact that will be instrumental for our results later:

***abs-bar*:** Operations from a in a package $(\mathsf{pack}Aa){:}\,\exists X.T[X]$ will only be applied to terms $t[\boldsymbol{E}/\boldsymbol{Y}, A/X, a/x]$ s.t. $\boldsymbol{Y}, X, x{:}\,T[X] \rhd t[\boldsymbol{Y}, X, x]\ :\ U[\boldsymbol{Y}, X]$ where the vector $\boldsymbol{Y}$ accounts for instances of polymorphic operations.

Theorem 2 (Characterisation by Simulation Relation [30]**).** *The following sequent schema is derivable using* PARAM.

$$\forall u,v{:}\,\exists X.T[X]\ .\quad u =_{\exists X.T[X]} v \quad\Leftrightarrow$$
$$\exists A,B.\exists a{:}T[A],b{:}T[B].\exists R{\subset}A{\times}B\ .\ u = (\mathsf{pack}Aa)\ \wedge\ v = (\mathsf{pack}Bb)\ \wedge\ a(T[R])b$$

Theorem 2 states the equivalence of equality at existential type with the existence of a simulation relation in the sense of [23]. From this we also get

Theorem 3. $\forall u{:}\,\exists X.T[X].\exists A.\exists a{:}\,T[A]\ .\ u = (\mathsf{pack}Aa)$

Weak versions of standard constructs such as products, sums, initial and final (co-)algebras are encodable in System F [6]. With PARAM, these constructs are provably universal constructions. We can *e.g.* freely use product types. Given $\rho \subset A{\times}B$ and $\rho' \subset A'{\times}B'$, $(\rho\times\rho)$ is defined as the action $(X\times X')[\rho,\rho']$. One derives $\forall u{:}\,A\times A', v{:}\,B\times B'\ .\ u(\rho\times\rho')v \ \Leftrightarrow\ (\mathsf{fst}(u)\ \rho\ \mathsf{fst}(v)\ \wedge\ \mathsf{snd}(u)\ \rho\ \mathsf{snd}(v))$. We use the abbreviations $\mathsf{bool} \stackrel{def}{=} \forall X.X \to X \to X$, $\mathsf{nat} \stackrel{def}{=} \forall X.X \to (X \to X) \to X$, and $\mathsf{list}(A) \stackrel{def}{=} \forall X.X \to (A \to X \to X) \to X$.

2.2 Semantics

We very briefly overview the parametric PER-model of [2] for the logic.

Let **PER** denote the universe of all partial equivalence relations (PERs) over the natural numbers $\mathbb{N}$. Types are interpreted as PERs, but intuitively it helps to think of the associated quotient instead, whose elements are equivalence classes. Terms are thus interpreted as functions mapping equivalence classes from one PER to another. Relations between PERs relate equivalence classes of the PERs.

Formally this is expressed in elementary terms as follows. A PER $\mathcal{A}$ is a symmetric and transitive binary relation on $\mathbb{N}$. The domain $dom(\mathcal{A})$ of $\mathcal{A}$ contains those $a \in \mathbb{N}$ for which $a\ \mathcal{A}\ a$. For any $a \in dom(\mathcal{A})$ we can form the equivalence class $[a]_{\mathcal{A}}$. A morphism from $\mathcal{A}$ to $\mathcal{B}$ is given by $n \in \mathbb{N}$ if for any $a, a' \in \mathbb{N}$, $a \in dom(\mathcal{A}) \ \Rightarrow\ n(a)\downarrow$ and $a\ \mathcal{A}\ a' \ \Rightarrow\ n(a)\ \mathcal{B}\ n(a')$. Here, $n(a)$ denotes the result of evaluating the nth partial recursive function on a, and $n(a)\downarrow$ denotes that this function is defined for a. We can form a PER $(\mathcal{A} \to \mathcal{B})$ by defining $n\ (\mathcal{A} \to \mathcal{B})\ n' \stackrel{def}{\Leftrightarrow}$ for any $a, a' \in \mathbb{N}$, $a \in dom(\mathcal{A}) \ \Rightarrow\ n(a)\downarrow$ and $n'(a)\downarrow$, and $a\ \mathcal{A}\ a' \ \Rightarrow\ n(a)\ \mathcal{B}\ n'(a')$. That is, the equivalence classes in $(\mathcal{A} \to \mathcal{B})$ contain functions that are extensionally equal w.r.t. $\mathcal{A}$ and $\mathcal{B}$. Each such equivalence class is then a morphism between $\mathcal{A}$ and $\mathcal{B}$, with application defined as $[n]_{\mathcal{A}\to\mathcal{B}}[a]_{\mathcal{A}} \stackrel{def}{=} [n(a)]_{\mathcal{B}}$. Products are given by $n\ (\mathcal{A}\times\mathcal{B})\ n' \stackrel{def}{\Leftrightarrow} n.1\ \mathcal{A}\ n'.1\ \wedge\ n.2\ \mathcal{B}\ n'.2$, where $m.i$ decodes the pairing encoding of natural numbers. A relation between $\mathcal{A}$ and $\mathcal{B}$ is given by a relation S between $dom(\mathcal{A})$ and $dom(\mathcal{B})$ that is *saturated*, *i.e.* $(m\ \mathcal{A}\ n$ and $n\ S\ n'$ and $n'\ \mathcal{B}\ m') \ \Rightarrow\ m\ S\ m'$. Thus S preserves, and can be seen to relate equivalence classes. Any member n of an equivalence class q is called a *realiser* for q.

Type semantics are now defined denotationally w.r.t. to an environment γ.

$$\begin{aligned}
[\![\Gamma, X \rhd X]\!]_\gamma &\stackrel{def}{=} \gamma(X)\\
[\![\Gamma \rhd U \to V]\!]_\gamma &\stackrel{def}{=} ([\![\Gamma \rhd U]\!]_\gamma \to [\![\Gamma \rhd V]\!]_\gamma)\\
[\![\Gamma \rhd \forall X.U[X]]\!]_\gamma &\stackrel{def}{=} (\textstyle\bigcap_{\mathcal{A}\in\mathbf{PER}}[\![\Gamma, X \rhd U[X]]\!]_{\gamma[X\mapsto\mathcal{A}]})^\flat
\end{aligned}$$

where $(\bigcap_{\mathcal{A}\in\mathbf{PER}}[\![\Gamma, X \rhd U[X]]\!]_{\gamma[X\mapsto\mathcal{A}]})^\flat$ is the indicated intersection but trimmed down to only those elements invariant over all saturated relations. This trimming is what makes the model relational parametric.

For brevity we omit the details of term interpretation, since these are not extensively needed in our discussion. The fact we will need, is that the term semantics yields realisers that encode partial recursive functions according to term structure. One is thus justified in viewing a realiser as being generated freely over a set of realisers representing free variables, using term-formation rules. This can be done independently of typing information.

In the parametric PER-model initial constructs interpret to objects isomorphic to interpretations of corresponding inductive types, *e.g.* let $T[X] = 1 + X$. Then $[\![\triangleright\forall X.((T[X] \to X) \to X)]\!] \cong [\![\triangleright\forall X.(X \to (X \to X) \to X)]\!] \cong \mathbb{N}$.

3 Abstract Data Type Specification Refinement

We describe ADT specification refinement up to observational equivalence. The latter is defined w.r.t. a finite set *Obs* of observable types, *viz.* closed inductive types. Examples are bool and nat. Henceforth we reserve $\mathfrak{T}[X]$ for the *body* part of abstract data type $\exists X.\mathfrak{T}[X]$. Parameterised specifications are outside the scope of this paper, so we assume X to be the only free type variable in $\mathfrak{T}[X]$.

Reflecting notions from algebraic specification and [23], we define observational equivalence in terms of observable computations in the logic as follows.

Definition 1 (Observational Equivalence (ObsEq) **[11,12]).** *Define* observational equivalence ObsEq w.r.t. observable types *Obs in the logic by*

$$\begin{aligned}&\mathsf{ObsEq}^{Obs} \stackrel{def}{=} (u{:}\,\exists X.\mathfrak{T}[X], v{:}\,\exists X.\mathfrak{T}[X]).\\ &(\exists A, B.\exists \mathfrak{a}{:}\,\mathfrak{T}[A], \mathfrak{b}{:}\,\mathfrak{T}[B]\ .\ u = (\mathsf{pack}A\mathfrak{a})\ \wedge\ v = (\mathsf{pack}B\mathfrak{b})\ \wedge\\ &\qquad\qquad \textstyle\bigwedge_{D\in Obs} \forall f{:}\,\forall X.(\mathfrak{T}[X] \to D)\ .\ (fA\,\mathfrak{a}) = (fB\,\mathfrak{b}))\end{aligned}$$

Now we define ADT specification up to observational equivalence. ADT bodies may contain higher-order and polymorphic types. In our setting, there is always a current set *Obs* of observable types. We assume the following:

***adt*:** A product $T_1[\boldsymbol{Y}, X] \times \cdots \times T_m[\boldsymbol{Y}, X]$ is on *ADT-body form* if each $T_i[\boldsymbol{Y}, X]$ is in uncurried form, *i.e.* of the form $T_{i1}[\boldsymbol{Y}, X] \times \cdots \times T_{n_i}[\boldsymbol{Y}, X] \to T_{c_i}[\boldsymbol{Y}, X]$, where $T_{c_i}[\boldsymbol{Y}, X]$ is not an arrow type, and secondly, $T_{c_i}[\boldsymbol{Y}, X]$ is either X or some $D \in Obs$ or a universal type $\forall Y'.T[\boldsymbol{Y}, Y', X]$ where $T[\boldsymbol{Y}, Y', X]$ is on ADT-body form. If $n_i = 0$, then $T_i[\boldsymbol{Y}, X] = T_{c_i}[\boldsymbol{Y}, X]$. At top level, then, we assume for the body $\mathfrak{T}[X]$ of $\exists X.\mathfrak{T}[X]$ that $\mathfrak{T}[X] \stackrel{def}{=} T_1[X] \times \cdots \times T_k[X]$ is on ADT-body form. We will write $\mathfrak{T}[X]$ as *Record*$(f_1{:}T_1[X], \ldots, f_k{:}T_k[X])$.

The uncurried form and the record-type notation are merely notational conveniences aiding discourse. The restriction on universal types is however a proper restriction. We do not know exactly how severe this restriction is in practice.

Definition 2 (Abstract Data Type Specification). *An* abstract data type specification *SP is a tuple* $\langle\langle Sig_{SP}, \Theta_{SP}\rangle, Obs_{SP}\rangle$ *where*

$$\begin{aligned}&Sig_{SP} \stackrel{def}{=} \exists X.\mathfrak{T}_{SP}[X],\\ &\Theta_{SP}(u) \stackrel{def}{=} \exists X.\exists \mathfrak{x}{:}\,\mathfrak{T}_{SP}[X]\ .\ u\ \mathsf{ObsEq}^{Obs_{SP}}\ (\mathsf{pack}X\mathfrak{x})\ \wedge\ \Phi_{SP}[X, \mathfrak{x}],\end{aligned}$$

where $\Phi_{SP}[X, \mathfrak{x}]$ *is a finite set of formulae in the logic. If* $\Theta_{SP}(u)$ *is derivable, then* u *is said to be a* realisation of SP.

Consider for example the specification Set $\stackrel{def}{=}$ $\langle\langle Sig_{\mathsf{Set}}, \Theta_{\mathsf{Set}}\rangle, \{\mathsf{bool}, \mathsf{nat}\}\rangle$, where

$$\begin{aligned}
&Sig_{\mathsf{Set}} = \exists X.\mathfrak{T}_{\mathsf{Set}}[X],\\
&\mathfrak{T}_{\mathsf{Set}}[X] = Record(\mathsf{empty}{:}\,X,\ \mathsf{add}{:}\,\mathsf{nat}\times X{\to}X,\ \mathsf{remove}{:}\,\mathsf{nat}\times X{\to}X,\\
&\qquad\qquad \cap{:}\,X\times X\to X,\ \mathsf{in}{:}\,\mathsf{nat}\times X{\to}\mathsf{bool},\ \mathsf{prsrv}\cap{:}\,(X\to X)\to\mathsf{bool}),\\
&\Theta_{\mathsf{Set}}(u) = \exists X.\exists\mathfrak{x}{:}\,\mathfrak{T}_{\mathsf{Set}}[X]\ .\ u\ \mathsf{ObsEqC}^{\{\mathsf{bool},\mathsf{nat}\}}\ (\mathsf{pack}X\mathfrak{x})\ \wedge\\
&\quad \forall x{:}\,\mathsf{nat}, s{:}\,X\ .\ \mathfrak{x}.\mathsf{add}(x, \mathfrak{x}.\mathsf{add}(x,s)) = \mathfrak{x}.\mathsf{add}(x,s)\ \wedge\\
&\quad \forall x,y{:}\,\mathsf{nat}, s{:}\,X\ .\ \mathfrak{x}.\mathsf{add}(x, \mathfrak{x}.\mathsf{add}(y,s)) = \mathfrak{x}.\mathsf{add}(y, \mathfrak{x}.\mathsf{add}(x,s))\ \wedge\\
&\quad \forall x{:}\,\mathsf{nat}\ .\ \mathfrak{x}.\mathsf{in}(x, \mathfrak{x}.\mathsf{empty}) = \mathsf{false}\ \wedge\\
&\quad \forall x,y{:}\,\mathsf{nat}, s{:}\,X\ .\ \mathfrak{x}.\mathsf{in}(x, \mathfrak{x}.\mathsf{add}(y,s)) = \mathsf{if}\ x =_{\mathsf{nat}} y\ \mathsf{then\ true\ else}\ \mathfrak{x}.\mathsf{in}(x,s)\ \wedge\\
&\quad \forall x{:}\,\mathsf{nat}, s{:}\,X\ .\ \mathfrak{x}.\mathsf{in}(x, \mathfrak{x}.\mathsf{remove}(x,s)) = \mathsf{false}\ \wedge\\
&\quad \forall s,s{:}\,X, x{:}\,\mathsf{nat}\ .\ \mathfrak{x}.\mathsf{in}(x,s)\ \wedge\ \mathfrak{x}.\mathsf{in}(x,s')\ \Leftrightarrow\ \mathfrak{x}.\mathsf{in}(x, \mathfrak{x}.\cap(s,s'))\ \wedge\\
&\quad \forall f{:}\,X\to X, s, s'{:}\,X\ .\ \mathfrak{x}.\mathsf{prsrv}\cap(f) = \mathsf{true}\ \Leftrightarrow\ \mathfrak{x}.\cap(s,s') = \mathfrak{x}.\cap(fs, fs')
\end{aligned}$$

This higher-order specification also illustrates the notion of *input types/sorts.* Consider the package LI $\stackrel{def}{=}$ (pack list(nat) $\mathfrak{l}$): Sig_{Set}, where $\mathfrak{l}$.empty gives the empty list, $\mathfrak{l}$.add adds a given element to the end of a list only if the element does not occur in the list, $\mathfrak{l}$.in is the occurrence function, $\mathfrak{l}$.remove removes the first occurrence of a given element, and $\mathfrak{l}.\cap$ takes two lists and generates a non-repeating list of common elements. By ***abs-bar***, typing allows users of LI to only build lists using operations of $\mathfrak{l}$, such as $\mathfrak{l}$.empty and $\mathfrak{l}$.add, and on such lists the efficient $\mathfrak{l}$.remove gives the intended result. By the same token, any observable computation $f{:}\,\forall X.(\mathfrak{T}_{\mathsf{Set}}[X] \to D)$, $D \in \{\mathsf{bool}, \mathsf{nat}\}$ can only refer to such lists, and not to arbitrary lists. This is the crucial point that admits LI as a realisation of Set according to Def. 2. In the world of algebraic specification, there is no formal restriction on the set In of so-called input-sorts. Thus, if one chooses the set of input sorts to be $In = \{\mathsf{set}, \mathsf{bool}, \mathsf{nat}\}$, then $\mathsf{in}(x, \mathsf{remove}(x, s))$ where s is a variable, is an observable computation. This computation might give true, since s ranges over all lists. One has to explicitly restrict input sorts to not include the abstract sort, in this case set, when defining observational equivalence [35], whereas the type-theoretic formalism here deals with this automatically.

The realisation predicate $\Theta_{SP}(u)$ of Def. 2 expresses u *is observationally equivalent to a package* (pack$X\mathfrak{x}$) *that satisfies the axioms* Φ_{SP}. Hence specification is up to observational equivalence. Specification refinement up to observational equivalence can now be expressed in the logic as follows.

Definition 3 (Specification Refinement). *A specification* SP' *is a* refinement *of a specification* SP, via constructor $F{:}\,Sig_{SP'} \to Sig_{SP}$ *if*

$$\forall u{:}\,Sig_{SP'}\ .\ \Theta_{SP'}(u)\ \Rightarrow\ \Theta_{SP}(Fu)$$

is derivable. We write $SP \underset{F}{\rightsquigarrow} SP'$ *for this fact.*

The notion of constructor in Def. 3 is based on the notion of parameterised program [9]. Given a program P that is a realisation of SP', the instantiation

$F(P)$ is then a realisation of SP. Constructors correspond to refinement maps in [20] and derived signature morphisms in [15]. It is evident that the refinement relation of Def. 3 is transitive, *i.e.* for $F \circ F' \stackrel{def}{=} \lambda u{:}\, Sig_{SP''}.F(F'u)$:

$$SP \underset{F}{\rightsquigarrow} SP' \quad \text{and} \quad SP' \underset{F'}{\rightsquigarrow} SP'' \quad \Rightarrow \quad SP \underset{F \circ F'}{\rightsquigarrow} SP''$$

If $\mathfrak{T}[X]$ is first-order, we get a string of interesting results in the logic.

Theorem 4 ([11]). *Suppose* $\langle\langle \exists X.\mathfrak{T}[X], \Theta\rangle, Obs\rangle$ *is a specification where* $\mathfrak{T}[X]$ *only contains first-order function profiles. With* PARAM *we derive that the existence of a simulation relation is equivalent to observational equivalence, i.e.*

$$\begin{array}{l}\forall A, B.\forall \mathfrak{a}{:}\,\mathfrak{T}[A], \mathfrak{b}{:}\,\mathfrak{T}[B]\ .\\ \quad \exists R \subset A \times B\ .\ \mathfrak{a}(\mathfrak{T}[R])\mathfrak{b} \quad \Leftrightarrow \quad \bigwedge_{D \in Obs} \forall f{:}\,\forall X.(\mathfrak{T}[X] \to D)\ .\ (f A\, \mathfrak{a}) = (f B\, \mathfrak{b})\end{array}$$

Proof: $\Rightarrow$: This follows from PARAM.

$\Leftarrow$: We must exhibit an R such that $\mathfrak{a}(\mathfrak{T}[R])\mathfrak{b}$. Semantically, [23,24,38] relate elements iff they are denotable by some common term. We mimic this: For R give $\mathsf{Dfnbl} \stackrel{def}{=} (a{:}\,A, b{:}\,B).(\exists f{:}\,\forall X.(\mathfrak{T}[X] \to X).(f A\, \mathfrak{a}) = a\ \wedge\ (f B\, \mathfrak{b}) = b)$. □

Together with Fact 2 this gives:

Theorem 5 ([11]). *Let* $\exists X.\mathfrak{T}[X]$ *be as in Theorem 5. With* PARAM *we derive*

$$\forall u, v{:}\, \exists X.\mathfrak{T}[X]\ .\ u =_{\exists X.\mathfrak{T}[X]} v \quad \Leftrightarrow \quad u\ \mathsf{ObsEq}\ v$$

By Theorem 5 we can substitute equality for $\mathsf{ObsEq}^{Obs_{SP}}$ in Def. 2, the definition of specification. This reduces our formalisms of specification and specification refinement to those of Luo's [20], with the important difference that parametricity lifts the formalisms to observational equivalence. Also any constructor F is now inherently stable, *i.e.* $u\ \mathsf{ObsEq}^{Obs_{SP'}}\ v \ \Rightarrow\ F(u)\ \mathsf{ObsEq}^{Obs_{SP}}\ F(v)$, simply by congruence for equality. Stability simplifies observational proofs significantly.

Theorem 4 means that we can explain observational equivalence, and thus also specification refinement up to observational equivalence, in terms of the existence of simulation relations. At first order, theorems 5 and 4 give the essential property that the existence of simulation relations is transitive, but we can actually give a more constructive result:

Theorem 6 (Composability of Simulation Relations[12]**).** *Suppose* $\mathfrak{T}[X]$ *only contains first-order function profiles. Then we can derive*

$$\begin{array}{l}\forall A, B, C, R \subset A \times B, S \subset B \times C, \mathfrak{a}{:}\,\mathfrak{T}[A], \mathfrak{b}{:}\,\mathfrak{T}[B], \mathfrak{c}{:}\,\mathfrak{T}[C].\\ \qquad\qquad \mathfrak{a}(\mathfrak{T}[R])\mathfrak{b}\ \wedge\ \mathfrak{b}(\mathfrak{T}[S])\mathfrak{c} \ \Rightarrow\ \mathfrak{a}(\mathfrak{T}[S \circ R])\mathfrak{c}\end{array}$$

Thus simulation relations explain stepwise refinement, but methodologically this is not enough. Given instances u and v and constructor F one can check that there is a simulation relation relating (Fu) and v. But this point-wise method of verifying a refinement step is impractical, since it involves choosing candidates v at best heuristically, and then specialised verification is employed for each pair u, v. One would prefer a general method for proving refinement.

Such a universal method exists in algebraic specification, using only abstract information. One proves observational refinements by considering quotients w.r.t. a possibly partial congruence [4], and then one uses an axiomatisation of this congruence to prove relativised versions of the axioms of the specification to be refined. If the congruence is partial, clauses restricting to the domain of the congruence must also be incorporated [5,3].

As observed in [32,11], this method is not expressible in the type theory or the logic of [30]. The simple solution of [32,11] is to soundly add axioms in order to axiomatise partial congruences. We give the axiom schemata below. Rather than being fundamental, they are tailored to suit refinement-proof purposes.

Definition 4 (Existence of Sub-objects (SUB) [11]**).**

$$\begin{array}{l}\forall X\,.\,\forall\mathfrak{x}\colon\mathfrak{T}[X]\,.\,\forall R\subset X\times X\,.\quad (\mathfrak{x}\ \mathfrak{T}[R]\ \mathfrak{x})\ \Rightarrow\\ \exists S\,.\,\exists\mathfrak{s}\colon\mathfrak{T}[S]\,.\,\exists R'\subset S\times S\,.\,\exists\mathsf{mono}\colon S\to X\,.\qquad \forall s\colon S\,.\ s\ R'\ s \hfill \wedge\\ \qquad\qquad \forall s.s'\colon S\,.\ s\ R'\ s' \ \Leftrightarrow\ (\mathsf{mono}\,s)\ R\ (\mathsf{mono}\,s') \ \wedge\\ \qquad\qquad \mathfrak{x}\ (\mathfrak{T}[(x\colon X, s\colon S).(x =_X (\mathsf{mono}\,s))])\ \mathfrak{s}\end{array}$$

Definition 5 (Existence of Quotients (QUOT) [32]**).**

$$\begin{array}{l}\forall X\,.\,\forall\mathfrak{x}\colon\mathfrak{T}[X]\,.\,\forall R\subset X\times X\,.\quad (\mathfrak{x}\ \mathfrak{T}[R]\ \mathfrak{x}\ \wedge\ equiv(R))\ \Rightarrow\\ \quad\exists Q\,.\,\exists\mathfrak{q}\colon\mathfrak{T}[Q]\,.\,\exists\mathsf{epi}\colon X\to Q\,.\ \forall x,y\colon X\,.\ xRy\ \Leftrightarrow\ (\mathsf{epi}\,x) =_Q (\mathsf{epi}\,y)\ \wedge\\ \qquad\qquad \forall q\colon Q.\exists x\colon X\,.\ q =_Q (\mathsf{epi}\,x)\ \wedge\\ \qquad\qquad \mathfrak{x}\ (\mathfrak{T}[(x\colon X, q\colon Q).((\mathsf{epi}\,x) =_Q q)])\ \mathfrak{q}\end{array}$$

where $equiv(R)$ specifies R to be an equivalence relation.

Theorem 7. *If $\mathfrak{T}[X]$ adheres to* ***adt*** *and contains only first-order function profiles, then* SUB *and* QUOT *are valid in the parametric PER-model of* [2].

We refer to [32,41] for concrete examples using QUOT and SUB and to the vast amount of specification examples in the literature, *e.g.* [14] for other examples using this framework. In [11] the axioms are instrumental for the correspondence between refinement in type theory and refinement in algebraic specification.

4 The Simulation Relation at Higher Order

If $\mathfrak{T}[X]$ has higher-order function profiles, theorems 4 and 6 fail, and indeed we cannot even derive that the existence of simulation relations is transitive.

We here take the view that the current notion of simulation relation is unduly demanding, and fails to observe closely enough the abstraction barrier provided by existential types. Consider $\mathsf{prsrv}\cap\colon (X \to X) \to \mathsf{bool}$ from specification Set. For $R \subset A\times B$ to be respected by two implementations $\mathfrak{a}$ and $\mathfrak{b}$, one demands $\forall\alpha\colon A \to A, \forall\beta\colon B \to B\ .\ \alpha(R \to R)\beta\ \Rightarrow\ \mathfrak{a}.\mathsf{prsrv}\cap(\alpha) =_{\mathsf{bool}} \mathfrak{b}.\mathsf{prsrv}\cap(\beta)$. But according to ***abs-bar***, $\mathfrak{a}.\mathsf{prsrv}\cap$ and $\mathfrak{b}.\mathsf{prsrv}\cap$ can only be applied to arguments expressible by the supplied operations in $\mathfrak{a}$ and $\mathfrak{b}$. One solution is therefore to alter the relational proof criteria accordingly. Depending on what type of model one is interested in, this can be done in several ways [12]. We here recapture a solution that works in the parametric PER-model. For this we must first refine our notion of observational equivalence.

4.1 Closed Computations

Semantically, observational equivalence is usually defined w.r.t. contexts that when filled, are closed terms. A reasonable alternative definition in the logic of observational equivalence is therefore the following.

Definition 6 (Closed Context Observational Equivalence (ObsEqC) [12]**).** *Define* closed context observational equivalence ObsEqC w.r.t. *Obs by*

$$\begin{array}{l}\mathsf{ObsEqC}^{Obs} \stackrel{def}{=} (u{:}\exists X.\mathfrak{T}[X], v{:}\exists X.\mathfrak{T}[X]).\\ (\exists A, B.\exists \mathfrak{a}{:}\mathfrak{T}[A], \mathfrak{b}{:}\mathfrak{T}[B]\ .\ u = (\mathsf{pack} A \mathfrak{a})\ \wedge\ v = (\mathsf{pack} B \mathfrak{b})\ \wedge\\ \qquad \bigwedge_{D\in Obs} \forall f{:}\forall X.(\mathfrak{T}[X] \to D)\ .\ \mathsf{Closed}_{\Gamma^{In}}(f)\ \Rightarrow\ (f A\, \mathfrak{a}) = (f B\, \mathfrak{b}))\end{array}$$

where $\mathsf{Closed}_{\Gamma^{In}}(f)$ *is derivable iff* $\Gamma^{In} \rhd f$.

Closedness is qualified by a given context Γ^{In} so as to allow for variables of input types *In* in observable computations. This is automatically taken care of in the notion of general observable computations of Def 1, but now we are compelled to explicitly specify *In*. We set $In = Obs$ as a sensible choice [35,11].

The predicate $\mathsf{Closed}_{\Gamma^{In}}(f)$ is intractable in the existing logic, but we can easily circumvent this problem by introducing $\mathsf{Closed}_{\Gamma^{In}}$ as a family of new basic predicates together with a predefined semantics as follows.

Definition 7 ([12])**.** *The logical language is extended with families of predicates* $\mathsf{Closed}_{\hat{\Gamma}}(T)$ *ranging over types* T, *and* $\mathsf{Closed}_{\hat{\Gamma}}(t, T)$ *ranging over terms* $t{:}T$, *both relative to a given environment* $\hat{\Gamma}$. *This syntax is given a predefined semantics as follows. For any type* $\Gamma \rhd T$, *term* $\Gamma \rhd t{:}T$, *and valuation* γ *on* $[\![\Gamma]\!]$,

$$\models_{\Gamma,\gamma} \mathsf{Closed}_{\hat{\Gamma}}(T) \stackrel{def}{\Leftrightarrow} \textit{exists some type } \hat{\Gamma} \rhd A, \textit{ some } \hat{\gamma} \textit{ on } [\![\hat{\Gamma}]\!] \quad \textit{s.t. } [\![\Gamma \rhd T]\!]_{\gamma} = [\![\hat{\Gamma} \rhd A]\!]_{\hat{\gamma}}$$

$$\models_{\Gamma,\gamma} \mathsf{Closed}_{\hat{\Gamma}}(t, T) \stackrel{def}{\Leftrightarrow} \textit{exists some type } \hat{\Gamma} \rhd A, \textit{ term } \hat{\Gamma} \rhd a{:}A, \textit{ some } \hat{\gamma} \textit{ on } [\![\hat{\Gamma}]\!] \quad \textit{s.t. } [\![\Gamma \rhd T]\!]_{\gamma} = [\![\hat{\Gamma} \rhd A]\!]_{\hat{\gamma}} \textit{ and } [\![\Gamma \rhd t{:}T]\!]_{\gamma} = [\![\hat{\Gamma} \rhd a{:}A]\!]_{\hat{\gamma}}$$

We will usually omit the type argument in the term family of Closed.

4.2 The Alternative Simulation Relation

For a k-ary vector $\boldsymbol{Y}$, we write $\forall \boldsymbol{Y}$ for the string $\forall Y_1.\forall Y_2.\dots.\forall Y_k$. If $k = 0$ this denotes the empty string. The first l components of $\boldsymbol{Y}$ are denoted by $\boldsymbol{Y}|_l$.

Definition 8 (Data Type Relation [12]**).** *For* $\mathfrak{T}[X]$, *for* k*-ary* $\boldsymbol{Y}$, l*-ary*, $l \geq k$, $\boldsymbol{E}$, $\boldsymbol{F}$, $\boldsymbol{\rho} \subset \boldsymbol{E} \times \boldsymbol{F}$, A, B, $R \subset A \times B$, $\mathfrak{a}{:}\,\mathfrak{T}[A]$, $\mathfrak{b}{:}\,\mathfrak{T}[B]$, *we define the* data type relation $U[\boldsymbol{\rho}, R]^{\varsigma}_{\mathsf{C}}$ *for the string* $\varsigma = \boldsymbol{E}, \boldsymbol{F}, A, B, \mathfrak{a}, \mathfrak{b}$ *inductively on* $U[\boldsymbol{Y}, X]$ *by*

$$\begin{array}{ll} U = X & : U[\boldsymbol{\rho}, R]^{\varsigma}_{\mathsf{C}} \stackrel{def}{=} R\\ U = Y_i & : U[\boldsymbol{\rho}, R]^{\varsigma}_{\mathsf{C}} \stackrel{def}{=} \rho_i\\ U = \forall X'.U'[\boldsymbol{Y}, X', X] & : U[\boldsymbol{\rho}, R]^{\varsigma}_{\mathsf{C}} \stackrel{def}{=}\\ & \quad \forall (E_{l+1}, F_{l+1}, \rho_{l+1} \subset E_{l+1} \times F_{l+1})(U'[\boldsymbol{\rho}, \rho_{l+1}, R]^{E_{l+1}, F_{l+1}, \varsigma}_{\mathsf{C}})\\ U = U' \to U'' & : U[\boldsymbol{\rho}, R]^{\varsigma}_{\mathsf{C}} \stackrel{def}{=} \end{array}$$

$$(g{:}\,U'[\boldsymbol{E},A] \to U''[\boldsymbol{E},A],\ h{:}\,U'[\boldsymbol{F},B] \to U''[\boldsymbol{F},B])\ .\ (\forall x{:}\,U'[\boldsymbol{E},A], \forall y{:}\,U'[\boldsymbol{F},B]\ .$$
$$(x\ U'[\boldsymbol{\rho},R]^{\varsigma}_{\mathsf{C}}\ y\ \ \wedge\ \ \mathsf{DfnblC}^{\varsigma}_{U'[\boldsymbol{Y},X]}(x,y))\ \ \Rightarrow\ \ (gx)\ U''[\boldsymbol{\rho},R]^{\varsigma}_{\mathsf{C}}\ (hy))$$

where

$$\mathsf{DfnblC}^{\varsigma}_{U'[\boldsymbol{Y},X]}(x,y) \stackrel{def}{=} \exists f{:}\forall \boldsymbol{Y}.\forall X.(\mathfrak{T}[X] \to U'[\boldsymbol{Y},X])\ .$$
$$\mathsf{Closed}_{\Gamma^{In}}(f)\ \wedge\ (f\boldsymbol{E}|_k A\,\mathfrak{a}) = x\ \wedge\ (f\boldsymbol{F}|_k B\,\mathfrak{b}) = y$$

for $\Gamma^{In} = x_1{:}\,U_1, \ldots, x_m{:}\,U_m$, $U_i \in In$, $1 \le i \le m$.

We usually omit the type subscript to the $\mathsf{DfnblC}^{\varsigma}$ clause. The essence of Def. 8 is the weakened arrow-type relation via the $\mathsf{DfnblC}^{\varsigma}$ clause; an extension of the relation exhibited for proving Theorem 4. We have conveniently:

Lemma 8 ([12]). *For* $\mathfrak{T}[X]$ *satisfying* **adt**, *we have the derivability of*

$$\mathfrak{a}(\mathfrak{T}[R]^{\varsigma}_{\mathsf{C}})\mathfrak{b}\ \ \Leftrightarrow\ \ \wedge_{1\le i\le k}\ \mathfrak{a}.f_i\ (T_i[R]^{\varsigma}_{\mathsf{C}})\ \mathfrak{b}.f_i$$

Lemma 9 ([12]). *With respect to the parametric PER-model of* [2] *it is sound to assert the following axiom schema for* $D \in Obs$.

$$\text{IDENTC:}\ \ \forall x,y{:}\,D\ .\ x =_D y\ \ \Leftrightarrow\ \ x(D[\rho]^{\varsigma}_{\mathsf{C}})y$$

4.3 Special Parametricity

With the alternative simulation relation in place we should now be able to re-establish versions of theorems 4 and 6 valid for $\mathfrak{T}[X]$ of any order. However, since we do not alter the parametricity axiom schema, we can no longer rely directly on parametricity as in Lemma 4, when deriving observational equivalence from the existence of a simulation relation. However, the needed instance of alternative parametricity can be validated semantically.

We write $f\ \ (\forall X.\mathfrak{T}[X]^{\epsilon}_{\mathsf{C}}\ \ \to\ \ U[X]^{\epsilon}_{\mathsf{C}})\ \ f$, meaning $\forall A,B,R{\subset}A{\times}B.\forall \mathfrak{a}{:}\,\mathfrak{T}[A], \mathfrak{b}{:}\,\mathfrak{T}[B]$.
$\mathfrak{a}(\mathfrak{T}[R]^{\varsigma}_{\mathsf{C}})\mathfrak{b}\ \Rightarrow\ (fA\,\mathfrak{a})(U[R]^{\varsigma}_{\mathsf{C}})(fB\,\mathfrak{b}))$, for $\varsigma = A, B, \mathfrak{a}, \mathfrak{b}$.

Lemma 10 ([12]). *For* $\mathfrak{T}[X]$ *adhering to* **adt**, *for* $f{:}\,\forall X.(\mathfrak{T}[X] \to U[X])$, *for any* $U[X]$, *and where free term variables of* f *are of types in* In, *we can derive*

$$f\ (\forall X.\mathfrak{T}[X]^{\epsilon}_{\mathsf{C}} \to U[X]^{\epsilon}_{\mathsf{C}})\ f$$

By Lemma 10 the following schema is sound w.r.t. the parametric PER-model.

$$\text{SPPARAMC:}\ \ \forall f{:}\forall X.(\mathfrak{T}[X] \to U[X])\ .\ \mathsf{Closed}_{\Gamma^{In}}(f) \Rightarrow f\ (\forall X.\mathfrak{T}[X]^{\epsilon}_{\mathsf{C}} \to U[X]^{\epsilon}_{\mathsf{C}})\ f$$

We can now show the higher-order polymorphic generalisation of Theorem 4 validated w.r.t. the parametric PER-model:

Theorem 11. *With* SPPARAMC, *for* $\mathfrak{T}[X]$ *adhering to* **adt**, *the following is derivable, for* $\Gamma^{In} = x_1{:}\,U_1, \ldots, x_m{:}\,U_m$, $U_i \in In$, $1 \le i \le m$.

$$\forall A,B.\forall \mathfrak{a}{:}\,\mathfrak{T}[A], \mathfrak{b}{:}\,\mathfrak{T}[B]\ .$$
$$\exists R{\subset}A{\times}B\ .\ \mathfrak{a}(\mathfrak{T}[R]^{\varsigma}_{\mathsf{C}})\mathfrak{b}\ \ \Leftrightarrow$$
$$\bigwedge_{D\in Obs} \forall f{:}\forall X.(\mathfrak{T}[X] \to D)\ .\ \mathsf{Closed}_{\Gamma^{In}}(f)\ \ \Rightarrow\ \ (fA\,\mathfrak{a}) = (fB\,\mathfrak{b})$$

We regain not only transitivity of the existence of simulation relations, but also composability of simulation relations. This is akin to recent notions on the semantic level, *i.e. pre-logical relations* [15,16], *lax logical relations* [31,19], and *L-relations* [18].

Theorem 12 (Composability of Simulation Relations). *For $\mathfrak{T}[X]$ adhering to* ***adt****, let $\varsigma = A, B, \mathfrak{a}, \mathfrak{b}$, $\varsigma' = B, C, \mathfrak{b}, \mathfrak{c}$, $\varsigma'' = A, C, \mathfrak{a}, \mathfrak{c}$. Given* sPPARAMC,

$$\forall A, B, C, R \subset A \times B, S \subset B \times C, \mathfrak{a}: \mathfrak{T}[A], \mathfrak{b}: \mathfrak{T}[B], \mathfrak{c}: \mathfrak{T}[C]. \\ \mathfrak{a}(\mathfrak{T}[R]^{\varsigma}_{\mathsf{C}})\mathfrak{b} \ \wedge \ \mathfrak{b}(\mathfrak{T}[S]^{\varsigma'}_{\mathsf{C}})\mathfrak{c} \ \Rightarrow \ \mathfrak{a}(\mathfrak{T}[S \circ R]^{\varsigma''}_{\mathsf{C}})\mathfrak{c}$$

If one is content with syntactic models, one may drop the Closed clause everywhere in the previous discussion. One thus obtains relations $U[\rho, R]^{\varsigma}$ in place of $U[\rho, R]^{\varsigma}_{\mathsf{C}}$, and axioms sPPARAM in place of sPPARAMC, and IDENT in place of IDENTC. These axiom schema are valid in the parametric term model and the parametric second-order minimum model of Hasegawa [13], based on the polymorphic extensionally collapsed syntactic models of [7] and the second-order maximum consistent theory of [26]. In fact, with sPPARAM we can show that the existence of an alternative simulation relation coincides with the existence of a standard simulation relation. Let $(\exists X.\mathfrak{T}[X])^{\epsilon}$ be the relation defined by

$$(\exists X.\mathfrak{T}[X])^{\epsilon} \stackrel{def}{=} (u{:}\, \exists X.\mathfrak{T}[X], v{:}\, \exists X.\mathfrak{T}[X]) \ . \\ (\ \forall Y.\forall Z.\forall S \subset Y \times Z \ . \ \ \forall f{:}\forall X.\mathfrak{T}[X] \to Y.\ \forall g{:}\forall X.\mathfrak{T}[X] \to Z \ . \\ f\ (\forall X'.\mathfrak{T}[X']^{\epsilon} \to S)\ g \ \Rightarrow \ (uYf)\ \ S\ \ (vZg)\ )$$

Theorem 13. *The following is derivable using* sPPARAM.

$$\forall u, v{:}\, \exists X.\mathfrak{T}[X]\ .\ u =_{\exists X.\mathfrak{T}[X]} v \ \Leftrightarrow \ u\ (\exists X.\mathfrak{T}[X])^{\epsilon}\ v$$

Theorem 14 (Characterisation by Alternative Simulation Relation). *The following is derivable.*

$$\forall u, v{:}\, \exists X.\mathfrak{T}[X]\ . \quad u\ (\exists X.\mathfrak{T}[X])^{\epsilon}\ v \quad \Leftrightarrow \\ \exists A, B.\exists \mathfrak{a}{:}\, \mathfrak{T}[A], \mathfrak{b}{:}\, \mathfrak{T}[B].\exists R \subset A \times B\ .\ u = (\mathsf{pack} A \mathfrak{a}) \wedge v = (\mathsf{pack} B \mathfrak{b}) \ \wedge\ \mathfrak{a}(\mathfrak{T}[R]^{\varsigma})\mathfrak{b}$$

5 The Refinement Proof Strategy at Higher Order

We now have that composable simulation relations explain specification refinement via observational equivalence—for arbitrary order function profiles and limited polymorphism. But what now about the general proof method for proving observational refinement? We do not know whether or not SUB and QUOT with higher-order $\mathfrak{T}[X]$ are valid in the parametric PER-model. It is conjectured in [41] but not proven, that QUOT and an extension of SUB is valid. In this paper we are however in possession of some additional insight, and we are able to validate versions of SUB and QUOT using the alternative simulation relation in an interpretation using the parametric PER-model that reflects ***abs-bar***. Again, observing existing abstraction barriers more closely, offers a solution.

To motivate, suppose we attempt to validate QUOT as is, w.r.t. the parametric PER-model. Immediately there is a definitional problem. For any PER $\mathcal{X}$ and element $\mathsf{x} \in [\![X \rhd \mathfrak{T}[X]]\!]_{[X \mapsto \mathcal{X}]}$, we should display a quotienting PER $\mathcal{Q}$ and element $\mathsf{q} \in [\![X \rhd \mathfrak{T}[X]]\!]_{[X \mapsto \mathcal{Q}]}$ with the desired characteristics. Quotients over an algebra A are usually constructed directly from A with the new operations derived from the original operations. Thus, the natural approach to constructing the operations of q is to use the same realisers that give the operations of x.

At first order this is straight-forward, but at higher order this is problematic. Suppose $\mathsf{x} = \langle [e_0]_{\mathcal{X}}, [e_1]_{\mathcal{X} \to \mathcal{X}}, [e_2]_{(\mathcal{X} \to \mathcal{X}) \to \mathcal{X}}, \ldots \rangle$. We would now like to simply define q as $\langle [e_0]_{\mathcal{Q}}, [e_1]_{\mathcal{Q} \to \mathcal{Q}}, [e_2]_{(\mathcal{Q} \to \mathcal{Q}) \to \mathcal{Q}}, \ldots \rangle$. But to be able to do this we must check that the indicated equivalence classes actually exist. Suppose we want to show $e_2\ ((\mathcal{Q} \to \mathcal{Q}) \to \mathcal{Q})\ e_2$. First we must show that if $n\ (\mathcal{Q} \to \mathcal{Q})\ n$ then $e_2(n)\downarrow$. However, this does not follow from the running assumption that $n\ (\mathcal{X} \to \mathcal{X})\ n$ implies $e_2(n)\downarrow$; indeed it is easy to find counter-examples.

The angle of approach we take to this problem is simply a natural continuation of tactics so far, namely we refine the interpretation of ADT-instance operations to reflect exactly their actual applicability as captured in ***abs-bar***. For example, above we need clearly only consider arguments n expressible over supplied ADT-instance operations e_0, e_1, e_2, *etc.*

5.1 Observing the ADT-Abstraction Barrier in the Semantics

We now implement this idea. We keep the parametric PER-model as structure, but supply a modified interpretation for ADT operations.

Definition 9 (ADT Semantics). *For any PER $\mathcal{X}$ and $x, y \in \mathbb{N}$,*

$$x\ [\![X \rhd \mathfrak{T}[X]]\!]_{[X \mapsto \mathcal{X}]}\ y \overset{def}{\Leftrightarrow} \text{for all components } g_i{:}T_i[X] \text{ in } \mathfrak{T}[X]$$
$$x.i\ ([\![X \rhd T_i[X]]\!]^{x,y,X,\mathfrak{x}:\mathfrak{T}[X]}_{[X \mapsto \mathcal{X}]})\ y.i$$

where, for $\varrho = x, y, \Gamma$ for $\Gamma = \boldsymbol{Y}, X, \mathfrak{x}{:}\mathfrak{T}[X]$, k-ary $\boldsymbol{Y}$, γ a valuation on $\boldsymbol{Y}, X$,

$$[\![\boldsymbol{Y}, X \rhd X]\!]^{\varrho}_{\gamma} \overset{def}{=} \gamma(X)$$
$$[\![\boldsymbol{Y}, X \rhd Y_j]\!]^{\varrho}_{\gamma} \overset{def}{=} \gamma(Y_j)$$
$$[\![\boldsymbol{Y}, X \rhd \forall X'.U[X', X]]\!]^{\varrho}_{\gamma} \overset{def}{=}$$
$$(\textstyle\bigcap_{A \in \mathbf{PER}} [\![\boldsymbol{Y}, Y_{k+1}, X \rhd U[\boldsymbol{Y}, Y_{k+1}, X]]\!]^{\varrho, Y_{k+1}}_{\gamma[Y_{k+1} \mapsto A]})^{\flat}$$
$$[\![\boldsymbol{Y}, X \rhd U[\boldsymbol{Y}, X] \to V[\boldsymbol{Y}, X]]\!]^{\varrho}_{\gamma} \overset{def}{=}$$
$$(([\![\boldsymbol{Y}, X \rhd U[\boldsymbol{Y}, X]]\!]^{\varrho}_{\gamma} \cap \mathcal{D}^{\varrho;\gamma}_{U[\boldsymbol{Y}, X]}) \to [\![\boldsymbol{Y}, X \rhd V[\boldsymbol{Y}, X]]\!]^{\varrho}_{\gamma})$$

where

$$n\ \mathcal{D}^{\varrho;\gamma}_{U[\boldsymbol{Y}, X]}\ n' \overset{def}{\Leftrightarrow} \text{there exist terms } t, t' \text{ s.t.}$$
$$\Gamma \rhd t{:}U[\boldsymbol{Y}, X] \quad \text{and} \quad \Gamma \rhd t'{:}U[\boldsymbol{Y}, X], \quad \text{and}$$
$$t[x] = n \quad \text{and} \quad t'[y] = n'$$

where $u[z]$ denotes the realiser freely generated over z, according to term u.

The special semantics defined in Def. 9 simply reflects the actual use of ADT operations captured by ***abs-bar***. The essence is the weakened condition for arrow-type semantics. All relevant instances of PARAM and SPPARAMC hold under this semantics, and previous results hold.

It would be nice to have special types or annotated types for use in ADTs. However, this does not seem feasible without involving recursive (domain-)equations, the solutions of which are not obvious. In the current approach, when to apply ADT semantics is not given by the type system; one simply has to know when to do this. This applies to the logic as well. Moreover, issues of co-existence of ADT semantics and normal semantics have not been thoroughly explored. The presented ADT semantics is thus an interesting solution utilising ***abs-bar***, but more work may be necessary in order that this approach be fitted properly.

Here then, are the new versions of SUB and QUOT. Besides referring to the alternative simulation relation, there are also other changes: We need to treat higher-order variables in propositions, so the statements are generalised accordingly. Unfortunately, we cannot yet deal with variables of open universal types in propositions. Below, $U \in \Phi$ ranges over all types U, except open universal types, involving the existentially bound type variable, that occur in the axioms Φ of the relevant specification.

Definition 10 (Existence of Sub-objects (SUBG)**).** *For* $\varsigma = X, S, \mathfrak{x}, \mathfrak{s}$,

$$\begin{array}{l} \forall X . \forall \mathfrak{x}{:}\, \mathfrak{T}[X] . \forall R \subset X \times X . \quad (\mathfrak{x}\ \mathfrak{T}[R]\ \mathfrak{x}) \;\Rightarrow \\ \quad \exists S . \exists \mathfrak{s}{:}\, \mathfrak{T}[S] . \exists R' \subset S \times S . \exists_{U \in \Phi} \mathsf{mono}_U{:}\, U[S] \to U[X] . \\ \qquad \bigwedge_{U\in\Phi} \forall s{:}\, U[S] \ .\ s\ U[R']\ s \hfill \wedge \\ \qquad \bigwedge_{U\in\Phi} \forall s.s'{:}\, U[S] \ .\ s\ U[R']\ s' \;\Leftrightarrow\; (\mathsf{mono}_U\ s)\ U[R]\ (\mathsf{mono}_U\ s') \;\; \wedge \\ \qquad \mathfrak{x}\ (\mathfrak{T}[(x{:}\,X, s{:}\,S).(x =_X (\mathsf{mono}\ s))]^{\varsigma}_{\mathsf{C}})\ \mathfrak{s} \end{array}$$

Definition 11 (Existence of Quotients (QUOTG)**).** *For* $\varsigma = X, Q, \mathfrak{x}, \mathfrak{q}$,

$$\begin{array}{l} \forall X . \forall \mathfrak{x}{:}\, \mathfrak{T}[X] . \forall R \subset X \times X . \quad (\mathfrak{x}\ \mathfrak{T}[R]\ \mathfrak{x} \wedge \mathit{equiv}(R)) \;\Rightarrow \\ \quad \exists Q . \exists \mathfrak{q}{:}\, \mathfrak{T}[Q] . \exists_{U\in\Phi} \mathsf{epi}_U{:}\, U[X] \to U[Q] . \\ \qquad \bigwedge_{U\in\Phi} \forall x, y{:}\, U[X] \ .\ x\ U[R]\ y \;\Leftrightarrow\; (\mathsf{epi}_U\ x) =_{U[Q]} (\mathsf{epi}_U\ y) \;\; \wedge \\ \qquad \bigwedge_{U\in\Phi} \forall q{:}\, U[Q] . \exists x{:}\, U[X] \ .\ q =_{U[Q]} (\mathsf{epi}_U\ x) \hfill \wedge \\ \qquad \mathfrak{x}\ (\mathfrak{T}[(x{:}\,X, q{:}\,Q).((\mathsf{epi}\ x) =_Q q)]^{\varsigma}_{\mathsf{C}})\ \mathfrak{q} \end{array}$$

where $\mathit{equiv}(R)$ *specifies* R *to be an equivalence relation.*

Theorem 15. SUBG *and* QUOTG *are valid in the parametric PER-model of* [2], *under the assumption of ADT semantics.*

In the following, we will write *e.g.* $[\![U[\mathcal{X}]]\!]$ in place for $[\![X \rhd U[X]]\!]_{[X \mapsto \mathcal{X}]}$. In the following $\Gamma \stackrel{def}{=} X, \mathfrak{x}{:}\, \mathfrak{T}[X]$.

5.2 Validating SUBG (proof of Theorem 15)

Definition 12 (Sub-object PER). *Let* $\mathcal{X}$ *be any PER, and* $\mathfrak{R}$ *any relation on* $\mathcal{X}$. *Define the* sub-object $R_{\mathfrak{R}}(\mathcal{X})$ restricted on $\mathfrak{R}$ *by*

$$n\ R_{\mathfrak{R}}(\mathcal{X})\ m \;\stackrel{def}{\Leftrightarrow}\; n\ \mathcal{X}\ m \;\; and \;\; [n]_{\mathcal{X}}\ \mathfrak{R}\ [m]_{\mathcal{X}}$$

As expected we do not in general have $n\ R_{\Re}(\mathcal{X})\ m \ \Leftarrow\ [n]_{\mathcal{X}}\ \Re\ [m]_{\mathcal{X}}$. We do have by definition and symmetry $n\ R_{\Re}(\mathcal{X})\ m \ \Rightarrow\ [n]_{\mathcal{X}}\ \Re\ [m]_{\mathcal{X}}$, and also $n\ \mathcal{X}\ m \ \Leftarrow\ n\ \mathcal{S}\ m$, but not necessarily the converse implication.

To validate SubG, consider an arbitrary PER $\mathcal{X}$, $\mathsf{x} \in [\![\mathfrak{T}[\mathcal{X}]]\!]$, and relation $\Re$ on $\mathcal{X}$. We must exhibit a PER $\mathcal{S}$, a relation $\Re'$ on $\mathcal{S}$, an $\mathsf{s} \in [\![\mathfrak{T}[\mathcal{S}]]\!]$, and maps $mono_U \colon [\![U[\mathcal{S}]]\!]^{\varrho} \to [\![U[\mathcal{X}]]\!]^{\varrho'}$, where $\varrho = s, \Gamma$, for s a realiser of s, and $\varrho' = x, \Gamma$, for x a realiser of x, all satisfying the following properties,

Sub-1. For all $s \in [\![U[\mathcal{S}]]\!]^{\varrho}$, $s\ [\![U[\Re']]\!]^{\varrho}\ s$
Sub-2. For all $s, s' \in [\![U[\mathcal{S}]]\!]^{\varrho}$, $s\ [\![U[\Re']]\!]^{\varrho}\ s' \ \Leftrightarrow\ mono_U(s)\ [\![U[\Re]]\!]^{\varrho'}\ mono_U(s')$
Sub-3. $\mathsf{x}\ [\![\mathfrak{T}[(x{:}\mathcal{X}, s{:}\mathcal{S}).(x =_{\mathcal{X}} (mono\ s))]^{\varsigma}_{\mathsf{C}}]\!]\ \mathsf{s}$

We exhibit $\mathcal{S} \stackrel{def}{=} R_{\Re}(\mathcal{X})$, define $mono_U([n]_{[\![U[\mathcal{S}]]\!]^{\varrho}}) \stackrel{def}{=} [n]_{[\![U[\mathcal{X}]]\!]^{\varrho'}}$, and define $\Re'$ by $s\ \Re'\ s' \stackrel{def}{\Leftrightarrow} mono(s)\ \Re\ mono(s')$. Well-definedness and (Sub-1) and (Sub-2) follow by definition and from Lemma 18 below.

We now postulate that we can construct s as the k-tuple where the ith component is $[e_i]_{[\![T_i[\mathcal{S}]]\!]^{\varrho}}$ derived from the ith component $[e_i]_{[\![T_i[\mathcal{X}]]\!]^{\varrho'}}$ of x. For each component $g_i \colon (U[X] \to V[X])$ in $\mathfrak{T}[X]$ we must show for all n, n' s.t. there exist terms t, t' s.t. $\Gamma \rhd t{:}U[X]$, $\Gamma \rhd t'{:}U[X]$, and $t[s] = n$, $t'[s] = n'$, that

verSub-1. $n\ [\![U[\mathcal{S}]]\!]^{\varrho}\ n \ \Rightarrow\ (e_i(n)\!\downarrow\ \wedge\ e_i(n)\!\downarrow)$,
verSub-2. $n\ [\![U[\mathcal{S}]]\!]^{\varrho}\ n' \ \Rightarrow\ e_i(n)\ [\![V[\mathcal{S}]]\!]^{\varrho}\ e_i(n')$.

The crucial observation that now lets us show the well-definedness of s, is that the realiser s can be assumed to be a realiser x for the existing x. It therefore suffices to show (verSub-1) and (verSub-2) for n, n' s.t. $t[x] = n$ and $t'[x] = n'$.

Lemma 16. *For any PER $\mathcal{X}$, realiser x of x, and relation $\Re$ on $\mathcal{X}$ s.t. $\mathsf{x}\ [\![\mathfrak{T}[\Re]]\!]\ \mathsf{x}$, for any n s.t. there exists a term t s.t. $\Gamma \rhd t{:}X$, and $t[x] = n$,*

$$[n]_{\mathcal{X}}\ \Re\ [n]_{\mathcal{X}}$$

Proof: This follows from a variant of Lemma 10. □

Lemma 17. *For any n, n' s.t. there exist terms t, t' s.t. $\Gamma \rhd t{:}X$, $\Gamma \rhd t'{:}X$, and $t[x] = n$, $t'[x] = n'$, where x is a realiser of x,*

$$n\ \mathcal{X}\ n' \ \Leftrightarrow\ n\ \mathcal{S}\ n'$$

Proof: Suppose $n\ \mathcal{X}\ n'$. It suffices to show $[n]_{\mathcal{X}}\ \Re\ [n']_{\mathcal{X}}$. By Lemma 16 we get $[n']_{\mathcal{X}}\ \Re\ [n']_{\mathcal{X}}$, and $n\ \mathcal{X}\ n'$ gives $[n]_{\mathcal{X}} = [n']_{\mathcal{X}}$. Suppose $n\ \mathcal{S}\ n'$. By definition this gives $n\ \mathcal{X}\ n'$. □

Lemma 18. *For any n, n' s.t. there exist terms t, t' s.t. $\Gamma \rhd t{:}U[X]$, $\Gamma \rhd t'{:}U[X]$, and $t[x] = n$, $t'[x] = n'$, where x is a realiser of x,*

$$n\ [\![U[\mathcal{X}]]\!]^{\varrho}\ n' \ \Leftrightarrow\ n\ [\![U[\mathcal{S}]]\!]^{\varrho}\ n'$$

Proof: This follows from Lemma 17 by induction on type structure. □

So let n, n' be as proposed, and recall that we are assuming the existence of χ, thus we have e_i $[\![(U[\mathcal{X}] \to V[\mathcal{X}])]\!]^{\varrho}$ e_i. We may now use Lemma 18 directly and immediately get what we want since e_i satisfies its conditions. However, for illustrative purposes we go a level down. By assumption we have

assmpSUB-1. n $[\![U[\mathcal{X}]]\!]^{\varrho}$ $n \Rightarrow (e_i(n)\downarrow \;\wedge\; e_i(n)\downarrow)$,
assmpSUB-2. n $[\![U[\mathcal{X}]]\!]^{\varrho}$ $n' \Rightarrow e_i(n)$ $[\![V[\mathcal{X}]]\!]^{\varrho}$ $e_i(n')$.

Showing (verSUB-1) is now easy. By assumption on n, we can use Lemma 18, and then (assmpSUB-1) yields $(e_i(n)\downarrow \;\wedge\; e_i(n)\downarrow)$. For (verSUB-2) assume n $[\![U[\mathcal{S}]]\!]^{\varrho}$ n'. Lemma 18 gives n $[\![U[\mathcal{X}]]\!]^{\varrho}$ n', and (assmpSUB-2) gives $e_i(n)$ $[\![V[\mathcal{X}]]\!]^{\varrho}$ $e_i(n')$, and then Lemma 18 gives $e_i(n)$ $[\![V[\mathcal{S}]]\!]^{\varrho}$ $e_i(n')$. This concludes the definition of $\mathfrak{s}$.

It is time to verify χ $[\![\mathfrak{T}[(x{:}\mathcal{X}, s{:}\mathcal{S}).(x =_{\mathcal{X}} (mono\ s))]]\!]$ $\mathfrak{s}$. First we have

Lemma 19. *For any* $D \in Obs$, $n\ (D)^{\varrho}\ m \;\Leftrightarrow\; n\ (D)\ m$

Let $\rho \overset{def}{=} (x{:}\mathcal{X}, s{:}\mathcal{S}).(x =_{\mathcal{X}} (mono\ s))$. For any component $g_i{:}\,(U[X] \to V[X])$ in $\mathfrak{T}[X]$. we must show for all $[n] \in [\![U[\mathcal{X}]]\!]^{\varrho}$ and $[m] \in [\![U[\mathcal{S}]]\!]^{\varrho}$ that

$$[n]\ [\![U[\rho]]\!]^{\varrho}\ [m] \;\wedge\; [\![\mathsf{DfnblC}^{\varsigma}([n],[m])]\!] \;\Rightarrow\; [e_i(n)]\ [\![V[\rho]]\!]^{\varrho}\ [e_i(m)]$$

Let e be the realiser of the polymorphic functional of which $\mathsf{DfnblC}^{\varsigma}$ asserts the existence. This realiser is the same for all instances of this functional, and by construction the realiser for χ and the realiser for $\mathfrak{s}$ are the same, say x. Hence the $\mathsf{DfnblC}^{\varsigma}$ clause asserts that $e(x) = n$ and $e(x) = m$, thus $n = m$. If $V[X]$ is X we must show $[e_i(n)]_{\mathcal{X}} = mono([e_i(m)]_{\mathcal{S}})$, *i.e.* $[e_i(n)]_{\mathcal{X}} = [e_i(m)]_{\mathcal{X}}$, and if $V[X]$ is some $D \in Obs$ we must show $[e_i(n)]_D = [e_i(m)]_D$. Both cases follow since $n = m$. To deal with $V[X]$ a universal type according to ***adt***, generalise the proof to incorporate quantifier-introduced $\boldsymbol{Y}$, omitted here for clarity.

5.3 Validating QUOTG (proof of Theorem 15)

Definition 13 (Quotient PER). *Let* $\mathcal{X}$ *be any PER, and* $\mathfrak{R}$ *any equivalence relation on* $\mathcal{X}$. *Define the* quotient $\mathcal{X}/\mathfrak{R}$ *of* $\mathcal{X}$ w.r.t. $\sim$ *by*

$$n\ \mathcal{X}/\mathfrak{R}\ m \;\overset{def}{\Leftrightarrow}\; n\ \mathcal{X}\ n \;\; and \;\; m\ \mathcal{X}\ m \;\; and \;\; [n]_{\mathcal{X}}\ \mathfrak{R}\ [m]_{\mathcal{X}}$$

The following lemma follows immediately by definition.

Lemma 20. *For all* n, m, *we have, provided that* $[n]_{\mathcal{X}}$ *and* $[m]_{\mathcal{X}}$ *exist,*

$$n\ \mathcal{X}/\mathfrak{R}\ m \;\Leftrightarrow\; [n]_X\ \mathfrak{R}\ [m]_X$$

We also have by definition and reflexivity of $\mathfrak{R}$, $n\ \mathcal{X}\ m \;\Rightarrow\; n\ \mathcal{Q}\ m$, but not necessarily the converse implication.

To validate QUOTG, consider any PER $\mathcal{X}$, $\chi \in [\![\mathfrak{T}[\mathcal{X}]]\!]$, and equivalence relation $\mathfrak{R}$ on $\mathcal{X}$. We must exhibit a PER $\mathcal{Q}$, a $q \in [\![\mathfrak{T}[\mathcal{Q}]]\!]$, and maps $epi_U :$ $[\![U[\mathcal{X}]]\!]^{\varrho} \to [\![U[\mathcal{Q}]]\!]^{\varrho}$, where $\varrho = q, \Gamma$, for q a realiser of q, and $\varrho' = x, \Gamma$, for x a realiser of χ, all satisfying the following properties.

QUOT-1. For all $x, y \in [\![U[\mathcal{X}]]\!]^{\varrho'}$, $x\ [\![U[\mathfrak{R}]]\!]^{\varrho'}\ y \quad \Leftrightarrow \quad epi_U(x) =_{[\![U[\mathcal{Q}]]\!]^{\varrho}} epi_U(y)$
QUOT-2. For all $q \in [\![U[\mathcal{Q}]]\!]^{\varrho}$, there exists $x \in [\![U[\mathcal{X}]]\!]^{\varrho'}$ s.t. $q =_{[\![U[\mathcal{Q}]]\!]} epi_U(x)$
QUOT-3. $\times\ [\![\mathfrak{T}[(x{:}\,\mathcal{X}, s{:}\,\mathcal{Q}).(epi(x) =_{\mathcal{X}} q)]^{\varsigma}_{\mathsf{C}}]\!]\ q$

We exhibit $\mathcal{Q} \stackrel{def}{=} \mathcal{X}/\mathfrak{R}$, and define $epi_U([n]_{[\![U[\mathcal{X}]]\!]^{\varrho'}}) \stackrel{def}{=} [n]_{[\![U[\mathcal{Q}]]\!]^{\varrho}}$. Well-definedness, (QUOT-1) and (QUOT-2) follow by definition and Lemma 20.

Both the construction of q and the rest of the proof follow analogously to the case for SUBG. Things are a bit simpler, because we have lemma 20.

5.4 Using QUOTG and SUBG

We illustrate the general use of QUOTG and SUBG in proving a refinement $SP \rightsquigarrow SP'$. For clarity we omit constructors, and then $\mathfrak{T}_{SP}[X] = \mathfrak{T}_{SP'}[X]$. We denote both by $\mathfrak{T}[X]$. We also assume $Obs = Obs_{SP} = Obs_{SP'}$, and for brevity we assume equational axioms. As mentioned before, QUOTG and SUBG cannot as yet deal with variables of open universal types in the axioms of specifications.

The task is to derive $\forall u{:}\, Sig_{SP'} \,.\, \Theta_{SP'}(u) \;\Rightarrow\; \Theta_{SP}(u)$, in other words, for $u{:}\, Sig_{SP'}$, assuming $\exists A.\exists \mathfrak{a}{:}\,\mathfrak{T}[A] \,.\, (\mathsf{pack}A\mathfrak{a})\ \mathsf{ObsEqC}^{Obs}\ u \wedge \Phi_{SP'}[A, \mathfrak{a}]$ we must derive $\exists B.\exists \mathfrak{b}{:}\,\mathfrak{T}[B] \,.\, (\mathsf{pack}B\mathfrak{b})\ \mathsf{ObsEqC}^{Obs}\ u \wedge \Phi_{SP}[B, \mathfrak{b}]$.

Following the strategy of algebraic specification, we attempt to define a (partial) congruence $\sim$ on A and show $\Phi_{SP}[A, \mathfrak{a}]_{rel}$, where $\Phi_{SP}[A, \mathfrak{a}]_{rel}$ is obtained from $\Phi_{SP}[A, \mathfrak{a}]$ by replacing all occurrences of $=_{U[A]}$ by $U[\sim]$ (justified by extensionality), and in case $\sim$ is partial, also conditioning every formula ϕ whose free variables of types $U_i[A]$ are among $x_1, \ldots, x_n$, by $\wedge_i(x_i\ U_i[\sim]\ x_i) \;\Rightarrow\; \phi$.

Suppose this succeeds. Then since $\sim$ is an axiomatisation of a partial congruence, we have $\mathfrak{a}\ \mathfrak{T}[\sim]\ \mathfrak{a}$. We use SUBG to get S_A, $\mathfrak{s}_{\mathfrak{a}}$ and $\sim' \subset S_A \times S_A$, and maps $\mathsf{mono}_U{:}\, U[S_A] \to U[A]$ such that we can derive

$$(s1)\ \textstyle\bigwedge_{U \in \Phi_{SP}} \forall s{:}\, U[S_A] \,.\, s\ U[\sim']\ s$$
$$(s2)\ \textstyle\bigwedge_{U \in \Phi_{SP}} \forall s.s'{:}\, U[S_A] \,.\, s\ U[\sim']\ s' \;\Leftrightarrow\; (\mathsf{mono}_U\ s)\ U[\sim]\ (\mathsf{mono}_U\ s')$$
$$(s3)\ \mathfrak{a}\ (\mathfrak{T}[(a{:}\, A, s{:}\, S_A).(a =_A (\mathsf{mono}\ s))]^{\varsigma}_{\mathsf{C}})\ \mathfrak{s}_{\mathfrak{a}}$$

By $(s2)$ we get $\mathfrak{s}_{\mathfrak{a}}\ \mathfrak{T}[\sim']\ \mathfrak{s}_{\mathfrak{a}}$. We also get $equiv(\sim')$ by $(s1)$. We now use QUOTG to get Q and $\mathfrak{q}{:}\,\mathfrak{T}[Q]$ and maps $\mathsf{epi}_U{:}\, U[S_A] \to U[Q]$ s.t.

$$(q1)\ \textstyle\bigwedge_{U \in \Phi_{SP}} \forall s, s'{:}\, U[S_A] \,.\, s\ U[\sim']\ s' \;\Leftrightarrow\; (\mathsf{epi}_U\ s) =_{U[Q]} (\mathsf{epi}_U\ s')$$
$$(q2)\ \textstyle\bigwedge_{U \in \Phi_{SP}} \forall q{:}\, U[Q].\exists s{:}\, U[S_A] \,.\, q =_{U[Q]} (\mathsf{epi}_U\ s)$$
$$(q3)\ \mathfrak{s}_{\mathfrak{a}}\ (\mathfrak{T}[(s{:}\, S_A, q{:}\, Q).((\mathsf{epi}\ s) =_Q q)]^{\varsigma'}_{\mathsf{C}})\ \mathfrak{q}$$

Thus we should exhibit Q for B, and $\mathfrak{q}$ for $\mathfrak{b}$; and it then remains to derive 1. $(\mathsf{pack}Q\mathfrak{q})\ \mathsf{ObsEqC}^{Obs}(\mathsf{pack}A\mathfrak{a})$, and 2. $\Phi_{SP}[Q, \mathfrak{q}]$. To show the derivability of (1), it suffices to observe that, through Theorem 11, $(s3)$ and $(q3)$ give $(\mathsf{pack}A\mathfrak{a})\ \mathsf{ObsEqC}^{Obs}\ (\mathsf{pack}S_A\mathfrak{s}_{\mathfrak{a}})\ \mathsf{ObsEqC}^{Obs}\ (\mathsf{pack}Q\mathfrak{q})$. For (2) we must show the derivability of $\forall \boldsymbol{x}_Q.u[Q, \mathfrak{q}] =_{V[Q]} v[Q, \mathfrak{q}]$ for every $\forall \boldsymbol{x}_X.u =_{V[X]} v$ in $\Phi_{SP}[X, \mathfrak{x}]$.

We may by extensionality assume that V is X or some $D \in Obs$. For any variable $q : U[Q]$ in $u[Q, \mathfrak{q}]$ or $v[Q, \mathfrak{q}]$, we may by $(q2)$ assume an $s_q{:}\, U[S_A]$ s.t. $(\mathsf{epi}_U\ s_q) =_{U[Q]} q$. Since we succeeded in deriving $\Phi_{SP}[A, \mathfrak{a}]_{rel}$, we can derive $((\mathsf{mono}_U\, s_q)\ \ U[\sim]\ \ (\mathsf{mono}_U\, s_q)) \ \Rightarrow\ u[A,\mathfrak{a}][(\mathsf{mono}_U\, s_q)]\ V[\sim]v[A,\mathfrak{a}][(\mathsf{mono}_U\, s_q)]$ (for clarity only displaying one variable). By ($s2$) and ($s3$) this is equivalent to $s_q\ U[\sim']\ s_q \ \Rightarrow\ u[S_A,\mathfrak{s}_\mathfrak{a}][s_q]\ V[\sim']\ v[S_A,\mathfrak{s}_\mathfrak{a}][s_q]$, which by ($s1$) is equivalent to $u[S_A,\mathfrak{s}_\mathfrak{a}][s_q]\ \ V[\sim']\ \ v[S_A,\mathfrak{s}_\mathfrak{a}][s_q]$. Then from ($q1$), or if $V = D \in \mathit{Obs}$ we have this immediately, we can derive $(\mathsf{epi}_V\, u[S_A,\mathfrak{s}_\mathfrak{a}][s_q]) =_{V[Q]} (\mathsf{epi}_V\, v[S_A,\mathfrak{s}_\mathfrak{a}][s_q])$. By ($q3$) we get $(\mathsf{epi}_V\, u[S_A,\mathfrak{s}_\mathfrak{a}][s_q]) = u[Q,\mathfrak{q}]$ and $(\mathsf{epi}_V\, v[S_A,\mathfrak{s}_\mathfrak{a}][s_q]) = v[Q,\mathfrak{q}]$.

This illustration is somewhat oversimplified. In most concrete examples where SubG would be necessary, one would at least find useful the hiding constructor

$$\lambda u{:}\, \mathit{Sig}_{SP'}.(\mathsf{unpack}(u)(\mathit{Sig}_{SP})$$
$$(\Lambda X.\lambda\mathfrak{x}{:}\,\mathfrak{T}_{SP'}[X].(\mathsf{pack}\ X\ \mathit{record}(\texttt{those items of } \mathfrak{x} \texttt{ matching } \mathit{Sig}_{SP})))$$

6 Final Remarks

This paper has described specification refinement up to observational equivalence for specifications involving operations of any order and a limited form of polymorphism. This was done in System F using extensions of Plotkin and Abadi's logic for parametric polymorphism, which are sound w.r.t. the parametric PER-model. We established in the logic a common general method for proving observational refinements, and we established in the logic a simulation relation that composes at any order.

The main stratagem of this paper was to observe more closely existing abstraction barriers provided by existential types. This is fruitful both in devising the alternative simulation relation, and in providing a semantics to validate the higher-order version of the proof method for showing observational refinement.

In future work, one should clarify how the ADT semantics outlined in this paper should be integrated into a wider semantical framework. One should also try to find a counterpart in the syntax for the ADT-semantics. An interesting alternative to all of this would perhaps be to impose suitable abstraction barriers in the logical deduction part of the system instead, extending ideas in [10].

Obvious links to ongoing work on the semantic level concerning data refinement and specification refinement should be clarified. This promises interesting results in both directions. For example in System F and the logic, semantic notions such as applicative structures and combinatory algebras can be internalised in syntax. The semantic notion of pre-logical relations could therefore also be internalised. The problem posed by an infinite family of relations might be solved by using definability w.r.t. the relevant ADT according to ***abs-bar***.

We have added axioms to the logic, but we have not made any model-theoretical deliberations outside relating the discussion mainly to the parametric PER-model. It is for example highly relevant to investigate the general power of these axioms in restricting the class of models. This would especially comes into play if one were to consider consistency w.r.t. related type systems.

Acknowledgements

Many thanks to John Longley for a crucial hint concerning the ADT semantics. Thanks also to Martin Hofmann, Furio Honsell, and Don Sannella for valuable discussions. Thanks to the referees for helpful comments.

References

1. D. Aspinall. *Type Systems for Modular Programs and Specifications.* PhD thesis, University of Edinburgh, 1998. 163
2. E. S. Bainbridge, P. J. Freyd, A. Scedrov, and P. J. Scott. Functorial polymorphism. *Theoretical Computer Science*, 70:35–64, 1990. 163, 165, 166, 170, 172, 175
3. M. Bidoit and R. Hennicker. Behavioural theories and the proof of behavioural properties. *Theoretical Computer Science*, 165:3–55, 1996. 163, 170
4. M. Bidoit, R. Hennicker, and M. Wirsing. Behavioural and abstractor specifications. *Science of Computer Programming*, 25:149–186, 1995. 163, 170
5. M. Bidoit, R. Hennicker, and M. Wirsing. Proof systems for structured specifications with observability operators. *Theoretical Computer Sci.*, 173:393–443, 1997. 163, 170
6. C. Böhm and A. Beraducci. Automatic synthesis of typed λ-programs on term algebras. *Theoretical Computer Science*, 39:135–154, 1985. 166
7. V. Breazu-Tannen and T. Coquand. Extensional models for polymorphism. *Theoretical Computer Science*, 59:85–114, 1988. 173
8. M. Cerioli, M. Gogolla, H. Kirchner, B. Krieg-Brückner, Z. Qian, and M. Wolf. *Algebraic System Specification and Development. Survey and Annotated Bibliography, 2nd Ed.*, volume 3 of *Monographs of the Bremen Institute of Safe Systems.* Shaker, 1997. 1st edition available in *LNCS* 501, Springer, 1991. 163
9. J. A. Goguen. Parameterized programming. *IEEE Transactions on Software Engineering*, SE-10(5):528–543, 1984. 163, 168
10. J. E. Hannay. Abstraction barriers in equational proof. In *Proc. of AMAST'98*, volume 1548 of *LNCS*, pages 196–213, 1998. 179
11. J. E. Hannay. Specification refinement with System F. In *Proc. CSL'99*, volume 1683 of *LNCS*, pages 530–545, 1999. 163, 167, 169, 170, 171
12. J. E. Hannay. A higher-order simulation relation for System F. In *Proc. FOSSACS 2000*, volume 1784 of *LNCS*, pages 130–145, 2000. 163, 167, 169, 170, 171, 172
13. R. Hasegawa. Parametricity of extensionally collapsed term models of polymorphism and their categorical properties. In *Proc. TACS'91*, volume 526 of *LNCS*, pages 495–512, 1991. 165, 173
14. R. Hennicker. Structured specifications with behavioural operators: Semantics, proof methods and applications. Habilitationsschrift, LMU, München, 1997. 170
15. F. Honsell, J. Longley, D. Sannella, and A. Tarlecki. Constructive data refinement in typed lambda calculus. In *Proc. FOSSACS 2000*, volume 1784 of *LNCS*, pages 161–176, 2000. 163, 169, 173
16. F. Honsell and D. Sannella. Pre-logical relations. In *Proc. CSL'99*, volume 1683 of *LNCS*, pages 546–561, 1999. 163, 173
17. S. Kahrs, D. Sannella, and A. Tarlecki. The definition of Extended ML: a gentle introduction. *Theoretical Computer Science*, 173:445–484, 1997. 162

18. Y. Kinoshita, P. W. O'Hearn, A. J. Power, M. Takeyama, and R. D. Tennent. An axiomatic approach to binary logical relations with applications to data refinement. In *Proc. of TACS'97*, volume 1281 of *LNCS*, pages 191–212, 1997. 163, 173
19. Y. Kinoshita and A. J. Power. Data refinement for call-by-value programming languages. In *Proc. CSL'99*, volume 1683 of *LNCS*, pages 562–576, 1999. 163, 173
20. Z. Luo. Program specification and data type refinement in type theory. *Math. Struct. in Comp. Sci.*, 3:333–363, 1993. 162, 169
21. Q. Ma and J. C. Reynolds. Types, abstraction and parametric polymorphism, part 2. In *Proc. 7th MFPS*, volume 598 of *LNCS*, pages 1–40, 1991. 162
22. H. Mairson. Outline of a proof theory of parametricity. In *ACM Symposium on Functional Programming and Computer Architecture*, volume 523 of *LNCS*, pages 313–327, 1991. 164
23. J. C. Mitchell. On the equivalence of data representations. In V. Lifschitz, editor, *Artificial Intelligence and Mathematical Theory of Computation: Papers in Honor of John McCarthy*, pages 305–330. Academic Press, 1991. 166, 167, 169
24. J. C. Mitchell. *Foundations for Programming Languages.* MIT Press, 1996. 169
25. J. C. Mitchell and G. D. Plotkin. Abstract types have existential type. *ACM Trans. on Programming Languages and Systems*, 10(3):470–502, 1988. 162, 165
26. E. Moggi and R. Statman. The maximum consistent theory of the second order lambda calculus. e-mail to Types list. Available at `ftp://ftp.disi.unige.it/person/MoggiE/papers/maxcons`, 1986. 173
27. N. Mylonakis. Behavioural specifications in type theory. In *Recent Trends in Data Type Spec., 11th WADT*, volume 1130 of *LNCS*, pages 394–408, 1995. 163
28. A. M. Pitts. Parametric polymorphism and operational equivalence. In *Proc. 2nd Workshop on Higher Order Operational Techniques in Semantics*, volume 10 of *ENTCS*. Elsevier, 1997. 163
29. A. M. Pitts. Existential types: Logical relations and operational equivalence. In *Proc. ICALP'98*, volume 1443 of *LNCS*, pages 309–326, 1998. 163
30. G. Plotkin and M. Abadi. A logic for parametric polymorphism. In *Proc. of TLCA 93*, volume 664 of *LNCS*, pages 361–375, 1993. 162, 164, 165, 170
31. G. D. Plotkin, A. J. Power, and D. Sannella. Lax logical relations. To appear in *Proc. ICALP 2000, LNCS*, 2000. 163, 173
32. E. Poll and J. Zwanenburg. A logic for abstract data types as existential types. In *Proc. TLCA'99*, volume 1581 of *LNCS*, pages 310–324, 1999. 163, 170
33. B. Reus and T. Streicher. Verifying properties of module construction in type theory. In *Proc. MFCS'93*, volume 711 of *LNCS*, pages 660–670, 1993. 163
34. J. C. Reynolds. Types, abstraction and parametric polymorphism. *Information Processing*, 83:513–523, 1983. 162
35. D. Sannella and A. Tarlecki. On observational equivalence and algebraic specification. *Journal of Computer and System Sciences*, 34:150–178, 1987. 163, 168, 171
36. D. Sannella and A. Tarlecki. Toward formal development of programs from algebraic specifications: Implementations revisited. *Acta Inform.*, 25(3):233–281, 1988. 163
37. D. Sannella and A. Tarlecki. Essential concepts of algebraic specification and program development. *Formal Aspects of Computing*, 9:229–269, 1997. 163
38. O. Schoett. *Data Abstraction and the Correctness of Modular Programming.* PhD thesis, University of Edinburgh, 1986. 163, 169
39. T. Streicher and M. Wirsing. Dependent types considered necessary for specification languages. In *Recent Trends in Data Type Spec.*, volume 534 of *LNCS*, pages 323–339, 1990. 163

40. J. Underwood. Typing abstract data types. In *Recent Trends in Data Type Spec., Proc. 10th WADT*, volume 906 of *LNCS*, pages 437–452, 1994. 163
41. J. Zwanenburg. *Object-Oriented Concepts and Proof Rules: Formalization in Type Theory and Implementation in Yarrow.* PhD thesis, Technische Universiteit Eindhoven, 1999. 170, 173

Guarded Algebras: Disguising Partiality so You Won't Know Whether Its There*

Magne Haveraaen[1] and Eric G. Wagner[2]

[1] Institutt for Informatikk, Universitetet i Bergen, HiB
N-5020 Bergen, Norway
`http://www.ii.uib.no/~magne`
[2] Wagner Mathematics,
1058 Old Albany Post Road, Garrison, NY 10524, USA
`http://www.ii.uib.no/~wagner`

Abstract. Motivated by considerations from program semantics, we suggest the notion of guarded algebras. These make explicit the significant arguments to functions, and prevent involuntary capture of error values and undefined cases in specifications. Here we show that guarded reasoning disguises whether the underlying models are partial or total.

1 Introduction

When using algebraic technology to specify software we run into the problem of partiality in the operators. Partiality can be inherent in an operation itself, or be an artifact of certain models, such as the finite size of our computational models. An example of the former is division by zero. Examples of the latter are limits on the applicability of arithmetic operators due to size limitations on computer representation of numbers.

These issues are addressed by *guarded algebras* [HW95]. The carrier sets of the sorts are partitioned, using sort-guards, into "significant" and "insignificant" elements, and the arguments of the operations are partitioned, using operator-guards, into "significant" and "insignificant" arguments. Guards are ordinary operations which are being used to describe the limitations of sorts and other operations. The notion of significance is built into the semantics of the specifications by an appropriate choice for the satisfaction relation between models and specifications. These modifications have two desirable effects:

1. Guarded algebras may be used to model detectable error conditions by having error values as insignificant elements in the carriers.
2. Undetectable error situations may be represented by partiality in the guarded models.

* This work has been partially supported by the research council of Norway, by the EU through the COMPASS and CoFI networks, by the Department of Informatics at the University of Bergen, and the Department of Computer Science at the University of Wales Swansea.

D. Bert, C. Choppy, and P. Mosses (Eds.): WADT'99, LNCS 1827, pp. 182–201, 2000.

If we distinguish models solely by their significant elements, we find that there is an isomorphism between the category of care-distinct guarded total models (all errors are detectable) and the category of care-distinct guarded partial models (undetectable errors are allowed). Thus we may fully disguise whether total or partial models are being used. In this paper we restrict our attention to conditional equational logic.

Several approaches have been developed to handle error situations using total algebras. Among these are error algebras [GTW78], which identify error elements for every sort, or *OK*-algebras [GDLE84,HL89], which use predicates to designate the safe arguments of ordinary operators. Surveys with further references for many of these and various other approaches, also involving partiality, can be found in [Mos93] and [Mos95]. We restrict our more detailed comparison to three approaches: Reichel's equoids [Rei87], Kreowski's based algebras [Kre87,KM95], and Meseguer's membership algebras [Mes98]. These approaches have in common the feature that within a specification special sets are defined (akin to the guards in guarded specifications) which are, or can be, used to define the "significant" elements and/or arguments, or can be used to define the domains of definition of the operations in a partial algebra interpretation.

Reichel's equoids are similar to guarded algebras in that for each operator σ a set of equations, *def* σ, is used to specify the domains of the operators – the domain of $A(\sigma)$ in an algebra A being required to be exactly the set of solutions for *def* σ. This differs from the guarded framework in which the satisfaction of operator-guards is only a sufficient condition for definedness (significance). Reichel's framework does not include a counterpart to the sort-guards of the guarded framework. Equoids are specified using existential satisfaction of conditional equations with an emphasis on partiality, but a similar approach could be taken within the framework of total conditional equational logic. Another difference is that equoids have hierarchically structured signatures rather than the simple two-level partition into UF and PF employed in this paper. The use of hierarchical signatures increases expressiveness but having *def* σ tightly determine the domain of definition appears to restrict the model class.

Kreowski's based algebras provide a means for defining certain classes of partial algebras within the framework of total conditional equational logic. A based specification is a pair $BASP = (BASE, SPEC)$ of plain specifications, where $BASE$ is a subspecification of $SPEC$. A $BASP$-algebra is a triple (B, C, h) where B is a $BASE$-algebra, C is a $SPEC$-algebra and $h : B \rightarrow C|_{BASE}$ is a homomorphism from B to the $BASE$-reduct of C (a slightly more general definition is given in [KM95]). The partiality is achieved by means of the `PART` constructions which restricts and corestricts the operations of C to the image of B under h. While the emphasis in [Kre87] is on partiality, the same idea could be used to define a notion akin to that of significant arguments in guarded algebras. The results in [KM95] show that the based algebra framework is equivalent in expressiveness to total conditional equational logic. A similar result can be shown for the guarded algebra framework. However this proof (and definition) of equivalent expressiveness does not take into account the difference in how the transition is made from total to partial algebras. While based algebras can be used to produce many pleasing specifications (including one for the standard example: stacks), the technique does not seem applicable to examples such as bounded stacks. The reason is that the sets of "significant elements" in a based algebra are always a subset of the carrier generated by a subset of the operators starting from a subset of the carriers. This is not as general as what can be done in the other approarches.

Messquer's membership algebras [Mes98], while apparently developed primarily as general framework for dealing with subsorting issues, can also be used to define partiality within a total algebra framework. Roughly speaking, specifications of membership algebras employ membership predicates to specify the sortedness of terms and the relationships between sorts. By decreeing certain sorts to be "significant" one can simulate guarded algebras, but at the cost of losing the brevity of guarded satisfaction since the guards must be explicitly stated in the conditional equations. Membership algebras are shown, in [Mes98], to have the same expressive power as Horn Clause Logic (with equality and predicates) which is a more expressively powerful framework than that used for guarded algebras. Conversely, it is possible to approximate the membership predicates within the framework of guarded algebras. We are still investigating the effects of this difference in power on actual specifications.

This paper is organized as follows: In section two we recapitulate some definitions and results about institutions and general logics. Then we define total, partial and guarded algebras. Section four defines the corresponding institutions, relates these, and contains our main result on guardedness and partiality. Finally we discuss further theoretical development of the notion of guarded algebras.

2 Institutions and Logics

The general concept of a logic [Mes89] has three facets: model theory, entailment, and proof calculus, all sharing the same notions of signature and sentence. The model-theoretic aspect is captured by the concept of an institution: signatures, sentences, models and satisfaction. An entailment system captures the syntactic notions of a logic: signatures, sentences and syntactic derivability (entailment). A proof calculus is on top of an entailment system and provides the structural aspects of how to actually prove a derivation of the entailment system.

Let **Set** be the category of sets and total functions.

Definition 1 (Institution). *An* institution *is given by a quadruple* $\mathcal{INST} = (\mathbf{Sign}, \mathit{Sen}, \mathit{Mod}, \models)$, *where*

- **Sign** *is a category of* signatures,
- $\mathit{Sen} : \mathbf{Sign} \to \mathbf{Set}$ *is a functor giving the* sentences
- $\mathit{Mod} : \mathbf{Sign}^{\mathsf{op}} \to \mathbf{CAT}$ *is a functor giving the category of* models
- $\models$ *is a family, indexed by* $\mathsf{Obj}(\mathbf{Sign})$, *of* satisfaction relations, $\models_\Theta \subseteq \mathit{Mod}(\Theta) \times \mathit{Sen}(\Theta)$ *for each* $\Theta \in \mathsf{Obj}(\mathbf{Sign})$

such that, for each morphism $\theta \in \mathbf{Sign}(\Theta, \Theta')$, *the* satisfaction condition,

$$M' \models_{\Theta'} Sen(\theta)(\varphi) \Leftrightarrow Mod(\theta)(M') \models_{\Theta} \varphi,$$

holds for each $M' \in \mathsf{Obj}(Mod(\Theta'))$ *and each* $\varphi \in Sen(\Theta)$.

An *entailment* system defines an entailment relation between sets of sentences (axioms) and sentences (facts) for any given signature. Using entailment one may derive, on a syntactic level, new facts as consequences of axioms. An entailment system coupled with an institution forms a *logic*. A logic coupled with a *proof calculus*, taking into account the structural aspects in how facts are derived from axioms, forms a *logical system*[1]. If the entailment system of a logic only derives facts satisfied by the models of the axioms, it is *sound*. The entailment system is *complete* if, for the models satisfying a set of axioms, all sentences satisfied by the models are derivable from the axioms.

There are forgetful functors from logical systems and logics to institutions. These functors are adjoint to several functors going from institutions to logics and logical systems. Given an institution, entailment systems and proof calculi may be generated using these functors. In most cases such systems will be of little use as they will not be efficient to work with. Instead one wants an independently developed proof calculus with an entailment system which is efficient, sound and, if possible, complete.

Institutions can be related by many different kinds of morphisms. Certain of these morphisms transport entailment systems and proof calculi between institutions. This allows reuse of useful entailment systems and proof calculi, and also the reuse of tools developed for one logical system for the entailment system and proof calculus of a different institution.

The following definitions and theorems are adapted from [Mes89]. See also [Cer93] which investigates their use in relating various partial algebra approaches.

Definition 2 (Theory). *Given an institution* $\mathcal{INST} = (\mathbf{Sign}, Sen, Mod, \models)$.
The axiom-preserving theory *of* $\mathcal{INST}$ *is the category* $\mathbf{Th}_0(\mathcal{INST})$ *with*

- presentations *as objects* $(\Theta, \Phi) \in \mathsf{Obj}(\mathbf{Th}_0(\mathcal{INST}))$ *where* $\Theta \in \mathsf{Obj}(\mathbf{Sign})$ *and* $\Phi \subseteq Sen(\Theta)$, *and*
- *morphisms* $\theta : (\Theta, \Phi) \to (\Theta', \Phi') \in \mathsf{Mor}(\mathbf{Th}_0(\mathcal{INST}))$ *where* $\theta \in \mathbf{Sign}(\Theta, \Theta')$ *such that* $Sen(\theta)(\Phi) \subseteq \Phi'$.

Definition 3. *Given an institution* $\mathcal{INST} = (\mathbf{Sign}, Sen, Mod, \models)$.
The varieties *of* $\mathcal{INST}$ *are the categories given by the functor* $Vmod_{\mathcal{INST}} : \mathbf{Th}_0(\mathcal{INST})^{\mathsf{op}} \to \mathbf{CAT}$, *where* $Vmod_{\mathcal{INST}}(\Theta, \Phi)$, *for* $\Phi \subseteq Sen(\Theta)$, *is the full subcategory of* $Mod(\Theta)$ *with objects* $\mathsf{Obj}(Vmod_{\mathcal{INST}}(\Theta, \Phi)) = \{M \in \mathsf{Obj}(Mod(\Theta)) \mid M \models_{\Theta} \Phi\}$.

[1] Readers are referred to [Mes89] for a proper treatment of these concepts. Lack of space prohibits a more in depth presentation here, and further technical details are not needed in this paper.

Definition 4 (Simple map of institutions). *Let* $sign : \mathbf{Th}_0(\mathcal{INST}) \rightarrow \mathbf{Sign}$ *and* $sign' : \mathbf{Th}_0(\mathcal{INST}') \rightarrow \mathbf{Sign}'$ *be projection functors on theories for institutions* $\mathcal{INST} = (\mathbf{Sign}, Sen, Mod, \models)$ *and* $\mathcal{INST}' = (\mathbf{Sign}', Sen', Mod', \models')$.

A simple map of institutions *is given by* $(\zeta, \alpha, \beta) : \mathcal{INST} \rightarrow \mathcal{INST}'$, *where*

- $\zeta : \mathbf{Th}_0(\mathcal{INST}) \rightarrow \mathbf{Th}_0(\mathcal{INST}')$ *is a functor with a related functor on signatures* $\zeta_1 : \mathbf{Sign} \rightarrow \mathbf{Sign}'$ *such that*
  - $sign' \circ \zeta = \zeta_1 \circ sign$
  - $\zeta(\Theta, \Phi) = \zeta(\Theta, \emptyset) \cup (\zeta_1(\Theta), \alpha_\Theta(\Phi))$ *for all* $(\Theta, \Phi) \in \mathsf{Obj}(\mathbf{Th}_0(\mathcal{INST}))$
- $\alpha : Sen \rightarrow Sen' \circ \zeta_1$ *is a natural transformation in* **Set** *indexed by the signatures in* **Sign**,
- $\beta : Vmod_{\mathcal{INST}'} \circ \zeta^{op} \rightarrow Vmod_{\mathcal{INST}}$ *is a natural transformation in* **CAT** *indexed by the presentations in* $\mathbf{Th}_0(\mathcal{INST})$,

such that for each $\Theta \in \mathsf{Obj}(\mathbf{Sign})$, $\varphi \in Sen(\Theta)$ *and* $M' \in Vmod_{\mathcal{INST}'}(\zeta(\Theta, \emptyset))$,

$$M' \models'_{\zeta_1(\Theta)} \alpha_\Theta(\varphi) \Leftrightarrow \beta_{(\Theta,\emptyset)}(M') \models_\Theta \varphi.$$

If the functors $\beta_{(\Theta,\emptyset)}$ are surjective for every $(\Theta, \emptyset) \in \mathsf{Obj}(\mathbf{Th}_0(\mathcal{INST}))$, then the simple map of institutions is said to be surjective.

Theorem 1. *Given institutions* $\mathcal{INST} = (\mathbf{Sign}, Sen, Mod, \models)$ *and* $\mathcal{INST}' = (\mathbf{Sign}', Sen', Mod', \models')$ *where* $\mathcal{INST}'$ *is part of the logical system* $\mathcal{L}'$ *with an entailment system and corresponding proof calculus.*

If there is a simple map of institutions $(\zeta, \alpha, \beta) : \mathcal{INST} \rightarrow \mathcal{INST}'$ *then we get a logical system* $\mathcal{L}$, *containing* $\mathcal{INST}$, *with entailment system and corresponding proof calculus from* $\mathcal{L}'$.

If $\mathcal{L}'$ *has a complete entailment system, then* $\mathcal{L}$ *will have a complete entailment system. Moreover, if* $\mathcal{L}'$ *has a sound entailment system and the simple map of institutions is surjective, then* $\mathcal{L}$ *will have a sound entailment system.*

3 Algebraic Concepts

We write $[n]$ for the set $\{1, \ldots, n\}$. We view a string of length n of elements of a set S as a mapping $u : [n] \rightarrow S$. We write ϵ for the empty string and S^* for the set of all strings over S. We write $|w|$ for the length of a string w. A partial function $f : A \xrightarrow{p} B$ consists of a set $\partial(f)$ together with total function $\underline{f} : \partial(f) \xrightarrow{t} B$.

3.1 Signatures

Definition 5 (Plain signatures). *A* plain signature Σ *is given by the data of a 4-tuple,* $\Sigma = (S, F, \mathrm{dom}, \mathrm{cod})$, *for* S *a set of sorts,* F *a set of operators, a function* $\mathrm{dom} : F \xrightarrow{t} S^*$ *giving the domain, and a function* $\mathrm{cod} : F \xrightarrow{t} S$ *giving the codomain of every operator. A* plain signature morphism $\mu : \Sigma \rightarrow \Sigma'$, *for plain signatures* $\Sigma = (S, F, \mathrm{dom}, \mathrm{cod})$ *and* $\Sigma' = (S', F', \mathrm{dom}', \mathrm{cod}')$, *is a pair of functions* $\mu_1 : S \xrightarrow{t} S'$ *and* $\mu_2 : F \xrightarrow{t} F'$ *such that* $\mathrm{dom}' \circ \mu_2 = \mu_1 \circ \mathrm{dom}$, *and* $\mathrm{cod}' \circ \mu_2 = \mu_1 \circ \mathrm{cod}$.

Plain signatures with signature morphisms form a category **Sig**. For an operator $\sigma \in F$ the pair, $\langle \mathrm{dom}(\sigma), \mathrm{cod}(\sigma) \rangle$ is called the *profile* of σ.

Example 1. The plain signature for the mathematical concept of a Group can be given using the following, slightly sugared, syntax.

$$
\begin{array}{lll}
\textbf{sig } \Sigma_{\mathsf{Group}} = & & \\
& \textbf{sorts} & \mathsf{group} \\
& \textbf{opns} & \odot : \rightarrow \mathsf{group} \\
& & \oplus : \mathsf{group} \times \mathsf{group} \rightarrow \mathsf{group} \\
& & \ominus : \mathsf{group} \rightarrow \mathsf{group}
\end{array}
$$

Definition 6 (Guarded signatures). *A* guarded signature Γ *is given by the data of a 7-tuple,* $\Gamma = (S, UF, PF, \mathrm{dom}, \mathrm{cod}, \delta, \gamma)$*, for* S *a set of sorts;* UF *a set of unprotected operators;* PF *a set of protected operators, such that* $(UF \cap PF) = \emptyset$*; a function* $\mathrm{dom} : (UF \cup PF) \xrightarrow{t} S^*$ *giving the domain and a function* $\mathrm{cod} : (UF \cup PF) \xrightarrow{t} S$ *giving the codomain of every operator;* $\delta : S \xrightarrow{t} (S \times UF \times UF)$ *the sort-guard and* $\gamma : PF \xrightarrow{t} (S \times UF \times UF)$ *the operator-guard, with the requirement that for every* $s \in S$ *and for every* $\psi \in PF$

$$
\begin{array}{lll}
\delta(s)_1 = \mathrm{cod}(\delta(s)_2) = \mathrm{cod}(\delta(s)_3), & \mathrm{dom}(\delta(s)_2) = \epsilon, & \mathrm{dom}(\delta(s)_3) = s, \\
\gamma(\psi)_1 = \mathrm{cod}(\gamma(\psi)_2) = \mathrm{cod}(\gamma(\psi)_3), & \mathrm{dom}(\gamma(\psi)_2) = \epsilon, & \mathrm{dom}(\gamma(\psi)_3) = \mathrm{dom}(\psi).
\end{array}
$$

A closed guarded signature morphism $\mu : \Gamma \rightarrow \Gamma'$*, for guarded signatures* $\Gamma = (S, UF, PF, \mathrm{dom}, \mathrm{cod}, \delta, \gamma)$ *and* $\Gamma' = (S', UF', PF', \mathrm{dom}', \mathrm{cod}', \delta', \gamma')$*, is a triple of functions* $\mu_1 : S \xrightarrow{t} S'$*,* $\mu_2 : UF \xrightarrow{t} UF'$ *and* $\mu_3 : PF \xrightarrow{t} PF'$ *such that the profiles and guard structure are preserved, that is:*

$$
\begin{array}{rr}
\mathrm{dom}' \circ \mu_2 = \mu_1 \circ \mathrm{dom}, & \mathrm{cod}' \circ \mu_2 = \mu_1 \circ \mathrm{cod}, \\
\mathrm{dom}' \circ \mu_3 = \mu_1 \circ \mathrm{dom}, & \mathrm{cod}' \circ \mu_3 = \mu_1 \circ \mathrm{cod}, \\
\delta' \circ \mu_1 = (\mu_1 \times \mu_2 \times \mu_2) \circ \delta, & \gamma' \circ \mu_3 = (\mu_1 \times \mu_2 \times \mu_2) \circ \gamma.
\end{array}
$$

Guarded signatures with closed signature morphisms form a category **CGSig**.

Let PL : **CGSig**$\rightarrow$**Sig** be the functor taking each guarded signature to the corresponding plain signature, i.e., $PL(S, UF, PF, \mathrm{dom}, \mathrm{cod}, \delta, \gamma) = (S, (UF \cup PF), \mathrm{dom}, \mathrm{cod})$ and $PL(\mu_1, \mu_2, \mu_3) = (\mu_1, \mu_2 \cup \mu_3)$.

Example 2. The guarded signature for the mathematical concept of a Group is the same as the plain signature for Group (see Example 1), but extended with the declaration of sorts and functions for the sort- and operator-guards.

$$
\begin{array}{lll}
\textbf{sig } \Gamma_{\mathsf{Group}} = & & \\
& \textbf{sorts} & \mathsf{group} \\
& \textbf{opns} & \odot : \rightarrow \mathsf{group} \\
& & \oplus : \mathsf{group} \times \mathsf{group} \rightarrow \mathsf{group} \\
& & \ominus : \mathsf{group} \rightarrow \mathsf{group} \\
& \textbf{delta}(\mathsf{group}) & = (B, t, \mathsf{dgroup}) \\
& \textbf{delta}(B) & = (B, t, \mathsf{dB})
\end{array}
$$

Here the line "**delta**(group) = (B, t, dgroup)" signals the definition of sort-guard for sort group, and implicitly declares B as a sort name and operations $t : \to B$ and dgroup : group$\to B$ in accordance with the requirements on δ. The line "**delta**(B) = (B, t, dB)" declares sort-guard for the sort B, naming B as the sort, reusing the operation $t : \to B$, and introduces the operation $\mathsf{dB} : B \to B$. In [HW95] it was shown that the sort-guards may be added in a canonical way using an additional sort B, a fixed constant t and a fresh operation name ds for every sort s. Thus we will normally not include explicit sort-guards as part of the sugared signature declarations.

Example 3. The situation becomes more interesting if we create a guarded group with an operator-guard on the inverse-operation (omitting the sort-guards):

sig Γ_{GGroup} =
  sorts group
  opns $\odot : \to \mathsf{group}$
    $\oplus : \mathsf{group} \times \mathsf{group} \to \mathsf{group}$
    $\ominus : \mathsf{group} \to \mathsf{group}$
  guard($\ominus$) = (Bool, true, invertible)

The line "**guard**($\ominus$) = (Bool, true, invertible)" defines the operator-guard for $\ominus$, and implicitly declares Bool as a sort name and operations true : $\to$Bool and invertible : group$\to$Bool in accordance with the requirements on γ. An operation in the target of a **guard** cannot be used as the argument for a guard in order to provide the necessary partitioning of operators for guarded signatures. The declaration Γ_{GGroup} defines sorts group and Bool, and an anonymous sort B as target for δ. Unprotected operators are $\odot$, $\oplus$, true, invertible, the anonymous constant t into B and anonymous operations dgroup, dBool and dB from each sort into B, as required for δ. In this example there is only one protected operator, namely $\ominus$.

3.2 Algebras

We use the standard notions of plain total and partial algebras. For every plain signature Σ the *category of plain total algebras*, $\mathbf{TAlg}(\Sigma)$, has plain total algebras for Σ as objects and plain homomorphisms between them as morphisms. The *categories of plain partial algebras*, $\mathbf{PAlg}(\Sigma)$, has plain partial algebras for Σ as objects and weak homomorphisms between them as morphisms.

Definition 7 (Significant elements). *Let* $\Sigma = PL(\Gamma)$ *for a guarded signature* $\Gamma = (S, UF, PF, \mathrm{dom}, \mathrm{cod}, \delta, \gamma)$.

The set of significant elements *for a sort* $s \in S$ *of a plain total algebra* A *for* Σ *is given by*

$$D(A, s) = \{a \in A(s) \mid A(\delta(s)_2) = A(\delta(s)_3)(a)\}$$

The set of significant elements *for a sort* $s \in S$ *of a plain partial algebra* A *for* Σ *is given by*

$$D(A,s) = \begin{cases} \{a \in \partial(A(\delta(s)_3)) \mid A(\delta(s)_2) = A(\delta(s)_3)(a)\} & \text{if } \partial(A(\delta(s)_2)) \neq \emptyset \\ \emptyset & \text{if } \partial(A(\delta(s)_2)) = \emptyset \end{cases}$$

For $w \in S^*$ *define* $D(A,w) = D(A,w_1) \times \cdots \times D(A,w_{|w|})$.

Definition 8 (Significant arguments). *Let* $\Gamma = (S, UF, PF, \mathrm{dom}, \mathrm{cod}, \delta, \gamma)$ *be a guarded signature and let* $\Sigma = PL(\Gamma)$.

The set of significant arguments *for an operator* $\sigma \in (UF \cup PF)$ *in the plain total algebra* A *for* Σ *is given by*

$$G(A,\sigma) = \begin{cases} D(A,\mathrm{dom}(\sigma)) & \text{if } \sigma \in UF \\ \{a \in D(A,\mathrm{dom}(\sigma)) \mid A(\gamma(\sigma)_2) = A(\gamma(\sigma)_3)(a)\} & \text{if } \sigma \in PF, \end{cases}$$

The significant arguments *for an operator* $\sigma \in UF \cup PF$ *in the plain partial algebra* A *for* Σ *are given by*

$$G(A,\sigma) = \begin{cases} D(A,\mathrm{dom}(\sigma)) & \text{if } \sigma \in UF \\ \{a \in D(A,\mathrm{dom}(\sigma)) \mid \\ \quad A(\gamma(\sigma)_2) = A(\gamma(\sigma)_3)(a)\} & \text{if } \sigma \in PF, \\ & \quad \partial(A(\gamma(\sigma)_2)) \neq \emptyset \text{ and} \\ & \quad D(A,\mathrm{dom}(\sigma)) \subseteq \partial(A(\gamma(\sigma)_3)) \\ \emptyset & \text{otherwise} \end{cases}$$

Definition 9 (Guarded algebras). *Let* $\Sigma = PL(\Gamma)$ *for guarded signature* $\Gamma = (S, UF, PF, \mathrm{dom}, \mathrm{cod}, \delta, \gamma)$.

A guarded total algebra A *for* Γ *is a plain total algebra* A *for* Σ, *such that for every operator* $\sigma \in (UF \cup PF)$, *we have* $A(\sigma)\,(G(A,\sigma)) \subseteq D(A,\mathrm{cod}(\sigma))$.

A guarded partial algebra A *for* Γ *is a plain partial algebra* A *for* Σ, *such that for every operator* $\sigma \in (UF \cup PF)$, *we have* $G(A,\sigma) \subseteq \partial(A(\sigma))$ *and* $\underline{A(\sigma)}\,(G(A,\sigma)) \subseteq D(A,\mathrm{cod}(\sigma))$.

For a guarded partial algebra A we have that $\partial(A(\delta(s)_2)) \neq \emptyset$ for every $s \in S$ and $\partial(A(\gamma(\sigma)_2)) \neq \emptyset$ for every $\sigma \in PF$ since $D(A,\epsilon) \neq \emptyset$. Also, $D(A,\mathrm{dom}(\sigma)) \subseteq \partial(A(\gamma(\sigma)_3))$ for every $\sigma \in PF$ since $D(A,\mathrm{dom}(\sigma)) = D(A,\mathrm{dom}(\gamma(\sigma)_3)) = G(A,\gamma(\sigma)_3)$ and $G(A,\gamma(\sigma)_3) \subseteq \partial(A(\gamma(\sigma)_3))$.

The *category of guarded total algebras* **GTAlg**(Γ) is the full subcategory of **TAlg**(Σ) with guarded total algebras as objects. The *category of guarded partial algebras* **GPAlg**(Γ) is the full subcategory of **PAlg**(Σ) with guarded partial algebras as objects.

Defining reducts (on algebras and homomorphisms) in the usual way, we may extend the notion of a category of algebras for every signature to a functor from the dual of the signature category into **CAT**. Then we get functors **TAlg** : $\mathbf{Sig}^{op} \to \mathbf{CAT}$ and **PAlg** : $\mathbf{Sig}^{op} \to \mathbf{CAT}$ for plain algebras and **GTAlg** : $\mathbf{CGSig}^{op} \to \mathbf{CAT}$ and **GPAlg** : $\mathbf{CGSig}^{op} \to \mathbf{CAT}$ for guarded algebras.

The intuition behind guarded algebras is that if A is a guarded algebra with plain signature Σ, then, for each $s \in S$, we only "really care" about those elements of the carrier $a \in A(s)$ which are in $D(A,s)$, and, for each $\sigma \in (UF \cup PF)$, we only care about the values of $A(\sigma)$ for the arguments $a \in G(A,\sigma) \subseteq A(\mathrm{dom}(\sigma))$. This suggests that if we have two guarded algebras, A and B, in which the elements and arguments about which we "really care" are the same and whose operations behave the same on those arguments, then these algebras are equivalent.

Definition 10. *Given guarded, total or partial, algebras A and B with the same guarded signature $\Gamma = (S, UF, PF, \mathrm{dom}, \mathrm{cod}, \delta, \gamma)$ we say they are* care-equivalent, *and write $A \equiv_\Gamma B$, if*

1. *$D(A,s) = D(B,s)$ for every $s \in S$.*
2. *$G(A,\sigma) = G(B,\sigma)$ for every $\sigma \in (UF \cup PF)$.*
3. *For every $\sigma \in (UF \cup PF)$ we have $A(\sigma)(a)|_{G(A,\sigma)} = B(\sigma)(a)|_{G(A,\sigma)}$.*

Algebras which are not care-equivalent are care-distinct.

3.3 Terms, Sentences and Satisfaction

Definition 11. *A* finite collection of variables *$\chi = (X, v, \overline{x})$ for a plain signature $\Sigma = (S, F, \mathrm{dom}, \mathrm{cod})$, consists of a finite set X of variable names, where $X \cap F = \emptyset$, a function $v : X \to S$ typing the variables and a bijective function $\overline{x} : [|X|] \to X$ defining a string of all the variables in X.*

The function v gives the sort of each variable, the function $\overline{x}$ orders the variables, permitting us, among other things, to speak of the i'th variable. The use of a finite collection of variables is insufficient for certain constructions, but is sufficient when considering ordinary terms and axioms composed from finite sets of terms.

The S-indexed family $T(\Sigma, \chi)$ of terms with variables χ for Σ is defined in the normal way. We extend the functions dom and cod to derived operators $\chi.t \in T(\Sigma,\chi)_s$ for $s \in S$ by taking $\mathrm{dom}(\chi.t) = v \circ \overline{x}$, and $\mathrm{cod}(\chi.t) = s$. The result is a derived function $A(\chi.t) : A(v \circ \overline{x}) \to A(s)$, for each total or partial algebra A for Σ, defined recursively in the normal way on the structure of t.

We define the semantics of a guarded total (respectively partial) function with variables $\chi = (X, v, \overline{x})$ over Γ with $(S, F, \mathrm{dom}, \mathrm{cod}) = PL(\Gamma)$ as for a total (partial) derived operation. In addition we define the significant arguments, $G(A, \chi.t) \subseteq D(A, \mathrm{dom}(\chi.t))$ by

$$G(A,\chi.t) = \begin{cases} D(A,\mathrm{dom}(\chi.t)) & \text{If } t = \overline{x}_i \\ \big\{a \in D(A,\mathrm{dom}(\chi.t)) \mid a \in G(A,\chi.t_i)), i \in [n], & \\ \quad \langle A(\chi.t_1)(a), \dots, A(\chi.t_n)(a)\rangle \in G(A,\sigma)\big\} & \text{If } t = \sigma(t_1, \dots, t_n) \end{cases}$$

Proposition 1. *Given a guarded partial algebra A and variables* $\chi = (X, v, \overline{x})$ *for guarded signature* Γ *with* $\Sigma = PL(\Gamma)$*, then* $G(A, \chi.t) \subseteq \partial(A(\chi.t))$*.*

Proof. Easily shown by structural induction on the form of t by observing it holds for t a variable and is preserved for every operation in the signature. □

The sentences, given by the functor Sen : **CGSig**→**Set**, define the kind of axioms we have. In this paper we focus on conditional equational logics, so our axiom schemata will only allow for this.

Definition 12 (Conditional equation). *Given a plain signature* Σ*.*

A conditional equation $\chi.\,(\{(t_1, u_1), \ldots, (t_k, u_k)\}, (t_{k+1}, u_{k+1}))$*, for* $k \geq 0$*, consists of terms* $\chi.t_i, \chi.u_i \in T(\Sigma, \chi)_{s_i}$*,* $i \in [k+1]$*,* $s_i \in S$*, for a finite collection of variables* $\chi = (X, v, \overline{x})$ *over* Σ*.*

The set of all conditional equations for Σ is denoted $CE(\Sigma)$. Different conditional equations in $CE(\Sigma)$ may have different collections of variables.

We may now extend CE to a functor CE : **Sig**→**Set** by defining $CE(\mu : \Sigma \to \Sigma')$ as the normal substitution of operations (and variables) generated by μ. This also gives us a functor $CE \circ PL$: **CGSig**→**Set**, which we sometimes will denote as just CE.

We can define a translation from guarded conditional equations to plain conditional equations that follows the same pattern as that of defining the significant arguments for a derived operator.

Definition 13. *Given a guarded signature* $\Gamma = (S, UF, PF, \mathrm{dom}, \mathrm{cod}, \delta, \gamma)$*, and a finite collection of variables* $\chi = (X, v, \overline{x})$*.*

The domain-set $\mathbf{d}(\Gamma, \chi, t)$*, for a term* $\chi.t \in T(PL(\Gamma), \chi)_s$ *for some* $s \in S$*, is defined by*

$$\mathbf{d}(\Gamma, \chi, t) = \begin{cases} \{(\delta(v(x))_2, \delta(v(x))_3(x)) | x \in X\} & \textit{If } t \in X \\ \{(\delta(v(x))_2, \delta(v(x))_3(x)) | x \in X\} & \\ \quad \bigcup \left(\cup_{i \in [n]} (\mathbf{d}(\Gamma, \chi, t_i)) \right) & \textit{If } v \in UF,\ t = v(t_1, \ldots, t_n) \\ \{(\delta(v(x))_2, \delta(v(x))_3(x)) | x \in X\} & \\ \quad \bigcup \left(\cup_{i \in [n]} (\mathbf{d}(\Gamma, \chi, t_i)) \right) & \\ \quad \bigcup \{(\gamma(\psi)_2, \gamma(\psi)_3(t_1, \ldots, t_n))\} & \textit{If } \psi \in PF,\ t = \psi(t_1, \ldots, t_n) \end{cases}$$

The *generating principle* for an operation $\sigma \in UF \cup PF$ from a guarded signature $\Gamma = (S, UF, PF, \mathrm{dom}, \mathrm{cod}, \delta, \gamma)$ is the $CE(\Gamma)$ equations

$$\mathbf{d}(\Gamma, \sigma) = \chi.\left(\mathbf{d}(\Gamma, \chi, \sigma(\overline{x})), (\delta(\mathrm{cod}(\sigma))_2, \delta(\mathrm{cod}(\sigma))_3(\sigma(\overline{x})))\right)$$

for some $\chi = (X, v, \overline{x})$ such that $v \circ \overline{x} = \mathrm{dom}(\sigma)$.

The *fully guarded-equation* $\mathbf{d}(\Gamma, \varphi)$ for a sentence $\varphi \in CE(PL(\Gamma))$, where $\varphi = \chi.(\{(t_i, u_i) | i \in [k]\}, (t_{k+1}, u_{k+1}))$ for $k \geq 0$, is defined by

$$\mathbf{d}(\Gamma, \varphi) = \chi.\left(\cup_{i \in [k+1]} (\mathbf{d}(\Gamma, \chi, t_i) \cup \mathbf{d}(\Gamma, \chi, u_i)) \bigcup \{(t_i, u_i) | i \in [k]\}, (t_{k+1}, u_{k+1})\right)$$

Definition 14 (Plainification). *For $\Gamma = (S, UF, PF, \mathrm{dom}, \mathrm{cod}, \delta, \gamma)$, a guarded signature, and $\Phi \subseteq CE(\Gamma)$, a set of sentences, define the* plainification *of presentation (Γ, Φ) by*

$$PL(\Gamma, \Phi) = (PL(\Gamma), \{\mathbf{d}(\Gamma, \sigma) \mid \sigma \in UF \cup PF\} \cup \{\mathbf{d}(\Gamma, \varphi) \mid \varphi \in \Phi\}).$$

The plainified specification consists of two parts: one generated from the signature, and the other generated from each of the equations of the presentation. Note the overloading of PL as a functor $PL : \mathbf{CGSig} \to \mathbf{Sig}$ and a translation on presentations (pairs consisting of a signature and a set of axioms).

A satisfaction relation relates models and sentences by defining when a sentence holds in an algebra. We will define satisfaction relations for the three cases of total, partial and guarded algebras.

Definition 15 (Plain satisfaction). *Let $\Sigma = (S, F, \mathrm{dom}, \mathrm{cod})$ be a plain signature, $\varphi = \chi.(\{(t_1, u_1), \ldots, (t_k, u_k)\}, (t_{k+1}, u_{k+1})) \in CE(\Sigma)$ a conditional equation.*

The total satisfaction relation *for Σ, $\overset{t}{\models}_\Sigma \subseteq \mathsf{Obj}(\mathbf{TAlg}(\Sigma)) \times CE(\Sigma)$, is defined by* $A \overset{t}{\models}_\Sigma \varphi \Leftrightarrow \left(\forall \alpha \in A(v \circ \overline{x}) \cdot \bigwedge_{i \in [k]} \{A(\chi.t_i)(\alpha) = A(\chi.u_i)(\alpha)\} \Rightarrow A(\chi.t_{k+1})(\alpha) = A(\chi.u_{k+1})(\alpha)\right)$.

The existential satisfaction relation, $\overset{e}{\models}_\Sigma \subseteq \mathsf{Obj}(\mathbf{PAlg}(\Sigma)) \times CE(\Sigma)$, *is defined by* $A \overset{e}{\models}_\Sigma \varphi \Leftrightarrow \left(\forall \alpha \in \left\{a \in A(v \circ \overline{x}) \mid a \in \bigcap_{i \in [k]} (\partial(A(\chi.t_i)) \cap \partial(A(\chi.u_i)))\right\} \cdot \bigwedge_{i \in [k]} \{A(\chi.t_i)(\alpha) = A(\chi.u_i)(\alpha)\} \Rightarrow \alpha \in \partial(A(\chi.t_{k+1})) \wedge \alpha \in \partial(A(\chi.u_{k+1})) \wedge A(\chi.t_{k+1})(\alpha) = A(\chi.u_{k+1})(\alpha)\right)$.

The *weak satisfaction relation*, which is the same as the existential satisfaction relation, except that $\alpha \in \bigcap_{i \in [k+1]} (\partial(A(\chi.t_i)) \cap \partial(A(\chi.u_i)))$, is closer to the notion of guarded satisfaction, being defined below. Using weak satisfaction will not change any of the results presented here. Existential satisfaction is considered more versatile than weak satisfaction, and is the one most commonly used.

Definition 16 (Guarded satisfaction). *Let $\Gamma = (S, UF, PF, \mathrm{dom}, \mathrm{cod}, \delta, \gamma)$ be a guarded signature and let $\varphi = \chi.(\{(t_1, u_1), \ldots, (t_k, u_k)\}, (t_{k+1}, u_{k+1})) \in CE(PL(\Gamma))$ be a conditional equation.*

The guarded satisfaction relation *for Γ, $\overset{g}{\models}_\Gamma \subseteq \mathsf{Obj}(\mathbf{GAlg})(\Gamma) \times CE(\Gamma)$, where* **GAlg** *is* **GTAlg** *or* **GPAlg** *as appropriate, is defined by* $A \overset{g}{\models}_\Gamma \varphi \Leftrightarrow \left(\forall \alpha \in \bigcap_{i \in [k+1]} (G(A, \chi.t_i) \cap G(A, \chi.u_i)) \cdot \bigwedge_{i \in [k]} \{A(\chi.t_i)(\alpha) = A(\chi.u_i)(\alpha)\} \Rightarrow A(\chi.t_{k+1})(\alpha) = A(\chi.u_{k+1})(\alpha)\right)$.

Example 4. We may now provide the standard group axioms for the signature Σ_{Group} from Example 1.

$$\begin{array}{lll} \textbf{spec}\ \mathsf{Group} = & & \\ & \textbf{sorts} & \mathsf{group} \\ & \textbf{opns} & \odot : \to \mathsf{group} \\ & & \oplus : \mathsf{group} \times \mathsf{group} \to \mathsf{group} \\ & & \ominus : \mathsf{group} \to \mathsf{group} \\ & \textbf{vars} & a, b, c : \mathsf{group} \\ & \textbf{axioms} & \odot \oplus a = a = a \oplus \odot \\ & & (a \oplus b) \oplus c = a \oplus (b \oplus c) \\ & & a \oplus (\ominus a) = \odot = (\ominus a) \oplus a \end{array}$$

This identifies $\odot$ as the unit element of the group, $\oplus$ as associative, and $\ominus$ as the inverse operation with respect to $\oplus$. The Group variety for total satisfaction includes the integers and the rationals with 0 as unit element, addition as $\oplus$ and minus for $\ominus$. It does not include the integers with 1, multiplication and division, since only 1 and -1 have multiplicative inverses among the integers. It does not include the rationals with 1, multiplication and division either, since 0 does not have a multiplicative inverse. Using existential satisfaction and partial algebras will change this, since letting $\ominus$ be undefined on the problematic elements will be inconsistent with the third axiom which implicitly ensures definedness of $\ominus$ on all arguments.

Using weak satisfaction would circumvent the forced definedness of $\ominus$ on all values, so we could then make $\ominus$ undefined on the problematic values and permit the last two models. However, weak satisfaction does not allow error recovery, as any value, even an error value, returned by $\ominus$ must obey all axioms of the specification.

Example 5. We may also provide the guarded signature Γ_{GGroup} from Example 3 with the group axioms.

$$\begin{array}{lll} \textbf{spec}\ \mathsf{GGroup} = & & \\ & \textbf{sorts} & \mathsf{group} \\ & \textbf{opns} & \odot : \to \mathsf{group} \\ & & \oplus : \mathsf{group} \times \mathsf{group} \to \mathsf{group} \\ & & \ominus : \mathsf{group} \to \mathsf{group} \\ & \textbf{guard}(\ominus) = & (\mathsf{Bool}, \mathsf{true}, \mathsf{invertible}) \\ & \textbf{vars} & a, b, c : \mathsf{group} \\ & \textbf{axioms} & \odot \oplus a = a = a \oplus \odot \\ & & (a \oplus b) \oplus c = a \oplus (b \oplus c) \\ & & a \oplus (\ominus a) = \odot = (\ominus a) \oplus a \end{array}$$

The axioms for $\ominus$ are now protected, and may not be relevant for all elements in the carrier for group. The quantification on the variable a in the last axiom is restricted to values such that $\mathsf{invertible}(a) = \mathsf{true}$. Models of this specification includes those for the plain group for the sort group and operators $\odot$, $\oplus$ and $\ominus$, irrespectively of the models for Bool, true and invertible. This holds, e.g., when the carrier for Bool has only one element. If the carrier for Bool has at least two elements, and invertible($\odot$) is distinct from true, then the rationals with 1, multiplication and division will be a model for GGroup. Also, if invertible only takes on the value true for 1 and -1, the integers with 1, multiplication and division will also be a model.

In this example, as in general, a sort like Bool will not have a two-valued carrier. Any value that is distinct from true will implicitly be understood as false when guarding $\ominus$. These non-true values may be significant or non-significant (error values), and the implicit sort-guards will automatically distinguish between these. This also goes for the carrier for group. For the last two models mentioned, $\ominus(0)$ will be an insignificant error value or a significant recovery value, as determined by the sort-guard, if $\ominus(0)$ is defined. In any case, this value need not obey the third axiom since $\ominus$ is protected by invertible. If the value returned by $\ominus$ is non-significant, it will in fact not have to obey any of the axioms of the specification, since the axioms are only relevant for significant values and significant arguments. Note that guarded satisfaction will behave the same way whether a total or a partial algebra is chosen as the model for GGroup.

Proposition 2. *For* $z = t, e, g, g$, *for* $\mathbf{Sign} = \mathbf{Sig}, \mathbf{Sig}, \mathbf{CGSig}, \mathbf{CGSig}$ *and for* $\mathbf{Alg} = \mathbf{TAlg}, \mathbf{PAlg}, \mathbf{GTAlg}, \mathbf{GPAlg}$, *respectively:*

Given a signature morphism $\theta \in \mathbf{Sign}(\Theta, \Theta')$, *a conditional equation* $\varphi \in CE(\Theta)$, *and an algebra* $A' \in \mathsf{Obj}(\mathbf{Alg}(\Theta'))$, *then* $A' \overset{z}{\models}_{\Theta'} CE(\theta)(\varphi)$ *if and only if* $\mathbf{Alg}(\theta)(A') \overset{z}{\models}_{\Theta} \varphi$.

The proof is standard and follows the same pattern in all cases.

In each of the cases above, let $\overset{z}{\models}$ denote the family of satisfaction relations $\overset{z}{\models}_{\Theta}$ for $\Theta \in \mathsf{Obj}(\mathbf{Sign})$.

Proposition 3. *If* A *and* B *are care-equivalent guarded, total or partial, algebras over a guarded signature* Γ, *then* $A \overset{g}{\models}_{\Gamma} \varphi$ *if and only if* $B \overset{g}{\models}_{\Gamma} \varphi$.

Proof. Guarded satisfaction only relates to the significant arguments. Since care-equivalent algebras are identical on the significant arguments, they must satisfy the same axioms.

4 Institutions of Algebras

The concepts we developed in the previous section give us several institutions.

Proposition 4. *There exist institutions* $\mathcal{TCEL}$ *(Total Conditional Equational Logic),* $\mathcal{PCEL}$ *(Partial Conditional Equational Logic),* $\mathcal{GTCEL}$ *(Guarded Total*

Conditional Equational Logic), and $\mathcal{GPCEL}$ (Guarded Partial Conditional Equational Logic) given by

$$\begin{aligned}\mathcal{TCEL} &= (\mathbf{Sig}, CE, \mathbf{TAlg}, \overset{t}{\models})\\ \mathcal{PCEL} &= (\mathbf{Sig}, CE, \mathbf{PAlg}, \overset{e}{\models})\\ \mathcal{GTCEL} &= (\mathbf{CGSig}, CE \circ PL, \mathbf{GTAlg}, \overset{g}{\models})\\ \mathcal{GPCEL} &= (\mathbf{CGSig}, CE \circ PL, \mathbf{GPAlg}, \overset{g}{\models}).\end{aligned}$$

Note that $\mathbf{Th}_0(\mathcal{TCEL}) = \mathbf{Th}_0(\mathcal{PCEL})$ and $\mathbf{Th}_0(\mathcal{GTCEL}) = \mathbf{Th}_0(\mathcal{GPCEL})$.

Both $\mathcal{TCEL}$ and $\mathcal{PCEL}$ have extensively studied entailment systems and proof calculi, and there also exist quite a lot of useful support tools for the corresponding logical systems.

4.1 Theories and Varieties

Given a plain signature Σ. The *inclusion functor* $\mathcal{I}_\Sigma : \mathbf{TAlg}(\Sigma) \to \mathbf{PAlg}(\Sigma)$ takes a total algebra to the partial algebra with the same carriers and functions. The functor $\mathcal{I}_\Sigma$ has a left adjoint $\mathcal{T}_\Sigma : \mathbf{PAlg}(\Sigma) \to \mathbf{TAlg}(\Sigma)$ (see [Bur86] or [HW95] for a proof). We call $\mathcal{T}_\Sigma$ the *free totalisation functor for* Σ.

The next functor relating total and partial model classes is defined on guarded signatures since it exploits the extra structure provided by the guards.

Definition 17 (Partialisation functor). *Given a guarded signature Γ.*

The partialisation functor $\mathcal{P}_\Gamma : \mathbf{GTAlg}(\Gamma) \to \mathbf{GPAlg}(\Gamma)$ *takes a guarded total algebra to the guarded partial algebra resulting from removing all insignificant elements from each carrier and restricting the domain of each operation to its significant arguments.*

It is easy to verify that $\mathcal{T} \circ \mathcal{P}(A) \equiv_\Gamma A$ for every $A \in \mathsf{Obj}(\mathbf{GTAlg}(\Gamma))$ and that $\mathcal{P} \circ \mathcal{T}(A) \equiv_\Gamma A$ for every $A \in \mathsf{Obj}(\mathbf{GPAlg}(\Gamma))$.

The inclusion, totalisation and partialisation functors all form natural transformations, indexed by the signatures, in $\mathbf{CAT}$.

The inclusion functor restricts covariantly for plain and guarded presentations, e.g., for $(\Sigma, \Phi) \in \mathsf{Obj}(\mathbf{Th}_0(\mathcal{TCEL}))$ we have that $\mathcal{I}_\Sigma|_{Vmod_{\mathcal{TCEL}}(\Sigma,\Phi)} : Vmod_{\mathcal{TCEL}}(\Sigma, \Phi) \to Vmod_{\mathcal{PCEL}}(\Sigma, \Phi)$. The totalisation functor does not restrict nicely for plain presentations. The new elements being added to the carriers and domains of the operations will in general not obey the axioms.

Proposition 5. *Given a guarded signature Γ.*

The totalisation functor $\mathcal{T}_{PL(\Gamma)} : \mathbf{GPAlg}(\Gamma) \to \mathbf{GTAlg}(\Gamma)$ and the the partialisation functor $\mathcal{P}_\Gamma : \mathbf{GTAlg}(\Gamma) \to \mathbf{GPAlg}(\Gamma)$ both restrict covariantly for presentations.

Proof. For any $\varphi \in CE(\Gamma)$, $A \in \mathsf{Obj}(\mathbf{GTAlg}(\Gamma))$ and $M \in \mathsf{Obj}(\mathbf{GPAlg}(\Gamma))$ we have that $(A \overset{g}{\models}_\Gamma \varphi) \Leftrightarrow (\mathcal{P}(A) \overset{g}{\models}_\Gamma \varphi)$ and $(M \overset{g}{\models}_\Gamma \varphi) \Leftrightarrow (\mathcal{P}(M) \overset{g}{\models}_\Gamma \varphi)$ since $\overset{g}{\models}_\Gamma$ only relates to the significant arguments of the operations of Γ, and these are preserved (and reflected) by both $\mathcal{P}$ and $\mathcal{T}$. □

We define the following algebra functors $\mathbf{IGTAlg} = \mathcal{T} \circ \mathcal{P} \circ \mathbf{GTAlg} : \mathbf{CGSig}^{\mathsf{op}} \rightarrow \mathbf{CAT}$ and $\mathbf{IGPAlg} = \mathcal{P} \circ \mathcal{T} \circ \mathbf{GPAlg} : \mathbf{CGSig}^{\mathsf{op}} \rightarrow \mathbf{CAT}$. Using these functors we get institutions of initial guarded total conditional equational logic $\mathcal{IGTCEL} = (\mathbf{CGSig}, CE \circ PL, \mathbf{IGTAlg}, \overset{g}{\models})$ and of initial guarded partial conditional equational logic $\mathcal{IGPCEL} = (\mathbf{CGSig}, CE \circ PL, \mathbf{IGPAlg}, \overset{g}{\models})$. The name derives from the fact that these varieties contain the initial algebra from each care-equivalence class as the unique representative of that care-equivalence class (see [HW95] for details).

All the guarded institutions share the same syntactic notions (guarded signatures and sentences), i.e., $\mathbf{Th}_0(\mathcal{GTCEL}) = \mathbf{Th}_0(\mathcal{GPCEL}) = \mathbf{Th}_0(\mathcal{IGTCEL}) = \mathbf{Th}_0(\mathcal{IGPCEL})$ all represent the same guarded theory.

We may relate the guarded theories to the plain theories using plainification. We have already defined plainification on signature categories and on presentations. Plainification on guarded theory-morphisms reduces to plainification of the underlying signature morphism. This gives us a plainification functor $PL : \mathbf{Th}_0(\mathcal{GTCEL}) \rightarrow \mathbf{Th}_0(\mathcal{TCEL})$ on theories. If we let $cgsig : \mathbf{Th}_0(\mathcal{GTCEL}) \rightarrow \mathbf{CGSig}$ and $sig : \mathbf{Th}_0(\mathcal{TCEL}) \rightarrow \mathbf{Sig}$ be the obvious first projection functors on theories, we get $sig \circ PL = PL \circ cgsig$ relating plainification of theories and plainification of signatures.

Proposition 6. *Plainification of guarded theories preserves varieties, i.e.,*

$$Vmod_{\mathcal{TCEL}} \circ PL^{\mathsf{op}} = Vmod_{\mathcal{GTCEL}} \text{ and } Vmod_{\mathcal{TCEL}} \circ PL^{\mathsf{op}} = Vmod_{\mathcal{GTCEL}}.$$

Proof. See [HW95]. □

Proposition 7.

$$\mathcal{T} \circ \mathcal{P} \circ Vmod_{\mathcal{GTCEL}} = Vmod_{\mathcal{IGTCEL}}$$
$$\mathcal{P} \circ \mathcal{T} \circ Vmod_{\mathcal{GPCEL}} = Vmod_{\mathcal{IGPCEL}}.$$

Proof. Follows from the observation that care-equivalent algebras satisfy the same axioms, and that, for every $(\Gamma, \Phi) \in \mathsf{Obj}(\mathbf{Th}_0(\mathcal{GTCEL}))$ we have that $Vmod_{\mathcal{IGTCEL}}(\Gamma, \Phi)$ is a full subcategory of $Vmod_{\mathcal{GTCEL}}(\Gamma, \Phi)$. Likewise for the varieties $Vmod_{\mathcal{IGPCEL}}$ and $Vmod_{\mathcal{GPCEL}}$. □

Proposition 8. *The categories $Vmod_{\mathcal{IGTCEL}}(\Gamma, \Phi)$ and $Vmod_{\mathcal{IGPCEL}}(\Gamma, \Phi)$ are isomorphic for every $(\Gamma, \Phi) \in \mathsf{Obj}(\mathbf{Th}_0(\mathcal{GTCEL}))$.*

Proof. Given an arbitrary guarded signature Γ. For $A \in \mathsf{Obj}(\mathbf{IGTAlg}(\Gamma))$ we easily see that $\mathcal{T} \circ \mathcal{P}(A) = A$ and that for $h \in \mathbf{IGTAlg}(\Gamma)(A, A')$ we have that $\mathcal{T} \circ \mathcal{P}(h) = h$. Likewise, $\mathcal{P} \circ \mathcal{T}(M) = M$ and $\mathcal{P} \circ \mathcal{T}(w) = w$ for $M \in \mathsf{Obj}(\mathbf{IGPAlg}(\Gamma))$ and $w \in \mathbf{IGPAlg}(\Gamma)(M, M')$. □

Obviously, **IGTAlg** is isomorphic to **IGPAlg** with $\mathcal{P}$ and $\mathcal{T}$ as the isomorphisms.

4.2 Relating the Institutions

The next series of theorems lead to the main claim of this paper, that in the context of a guarded specification, we will not be able to distinguish between total or partial models from a logical viewpoint.

Theorem 2. *There is a simple map of institutions* $(\zeta, \alpha, \beta) : \mathcal{GTCEL} \to \mathcal{TCEL}$ *which is surjective.*

Proof. We need to define the functor ζ on theories (and ζ_1 on signatures), and the natural transformations α indexed by guarded signatures and β indexed by guarded presentations, and show that they have the necessary properties.

- Define the functor $\zeta = PL : \mathbf{Th}_0(\mathcal{GTCEL}) \to \mathbf{Th}_0(\mathcal{TCEL})$ and the functor $\zeta_1 = PL : \mathbf{CGSig} \to \mathbf{Sig}$.
- Define the natural transformation $\alpha : (CE \circ PL) \to CE \circ PL$ by $\alpha_\Gamma(\varphi) = \mathbf{d}(\Gamma, \varphi)$, the "translation of axioms" part of PL on presentations.
- Define the natural transformation $\beta : Vmod_{\mathcal{TCEL}} \circ PL^{\mathsf{op}} \to Vmod_{\mathcal{GTCEL}}$ as the identity natural transformation since $Vmod_{\mathcal{TCEL}} \circ PL^{\mathsf{op}} = Vmod_{\mathcal{GTCEL}}$.

This satisfies the necessary conditions:

- We have that $sig \circ \zeta = \zeta_1 \circ cgsig$ since $sig \circ \zeta = sig \circ PL = PL \circ cgsig$ (with PL on signatures) and $\zeta_1 \circ cgsig = PL \circ cgsig$.
- $\zeta(\Gamma, \Phi) = PL(\Gamma, \Phi) = PL(\Gamma, \emptyset) \cup (PL(\Gamma), \alpha_\Gamma(\Phi)) = \zeta(\Gamma, \emptyset) \cup (\zeta_1(\Gamma), \alpha_\Gamma(\Phi))$.
- Let $sp : \mathbf{Th}_0(\mathcal{TCEL}) \to \mathbf{Set}$ be the obvious second projection. For each $\Gamma \in \mathsf{Obj}(\mathbf{CGSig})$, $\varphi \in CE(PL(\Gamma))$ and $M' \in Vmod_{\mathcal{TCEL}}(PL(\Gamma, \emptyset))$, we have that $\beta_{(\Gamma,\emptyset)}(M') \overset{g}{\models}_\Gamma \varphi \Leftrightarrow M' \overset{g}{\models}_\Gamma \varphi \Leftrightarrow M' \overset{t}{\models}_{PL(\Gamma)} sp \circ PL(\Gamma, \varphi) \Leftrightarrow M' \overset{t}{\models}_{PL(\Gamma)} sp(PL(\Gamma, \emptyset) \cup (PL(\Gamma), \alpha_\Gamma(\varphi))) \Leftrightarrow M' \overset{t}{\models}_{PL(\Gamma)} sp(PL(\Gamma, \emptyset)) \cup sp(PL(\Gamma), \alpha_\Gamma(\varphi)) \Leftrightarrow M' \overset{t}{\models}_{PL(\Gamma)} sp(PL(\Gamma), \alpha_\Gamma(\varphi)) \Leftrightarrow M' \overset{t}{\models}_{PL(\Gamma)} \alpha_\Gamma(\varphi)$ since $M' \overset{t}{\models} sp(PL(\Gamma, \emptyset))$ by default.
- Since β is the identity natural transformation it is automatically surjective.

□

Theorem 3. *There is a simple map of institutions* $(\zeta, \alpha, \beta) : \mathcal{GPCEL} \to \mathcal{PCEL}$ *which is surjective.*

Proof. Let sp, ζ, ζ_1 and α be as above.

- Define the natural transformation $\beta : Vmod_{\mathcal{PCEL}} \circ PL^{\mathsf{op}} \to Vmod_{\mathcal{GPCEL}}$ as the identity natural transformation since $Vmod_{\mathcal{PCEL}} \circ PL^{\mathsf{op}} = Vmod_{\mathcal{GPCEL}}$.

This satisfies the necessary conditions:

- The constraints on syntax have been shown for $\mathcal{GTCEL}$.

- For each $\Gamma \in \mathsf{Obj}(\mathbf{CGSig})$, $\varphi \in CE(PL(\Gamma))$ and $M' \in Vmod_{\mathcal{PCEL}}(PL(\Gamma,\emptyset))$ we get: $\beta_{(\Gamma,\emptyset)}(M') \overset{g}{\models}_{\Gamma} \varphi \Leftrightarrow M' \overset{e}{\models}_{PL(\Gamma)} sp(PL(\Gamma,\emptyset)) \cup sp(PL(\Gamma),\alpha_{\Gamma}(\varphi)) \Leftrightarrow M' \overset{e}{\models}_{PL(\Gamma)} \alpha_{\Gamma}(\varphi)$ since $M' \overset{e}{\models} sp(PL(\Gamma,\emptyset))$ by default.
- Since β is the identity natural transformation it is automatically surjective.

□

Theorem 4. *There is a simple map of institutions* $(\zeta,\alpha,\beta) : \mathcal{IGTCEL}{\rightarrow}\mathcal{GTCEL}$ *which is surjective.*

Proof. Let *sp* be as before. Since the theories are the same, ζ, ζ_1 are identity functors and α is the identity natural transformation.

- Define $\beta = \mathcal{T} \circ \mathcal{P} : Vmod_{\mathcal{GTCEL}} \circ \zeta^{\mathsf{op}} {\rightarrow} Vmod_{\mathcal{IGTCEL}}$.

This satisfies the necessary conditions:

- We have that $cgsig \circ \zeta = \zeta_1 \circ cgsig$ since ζ and ζ_1 are identities.
- $\zeta(\Gamma,\Phi) = (\Gamma,\Phi) = \zeta(\Gamma,\emptyset) \cup (\zeta_1(\Gamma),\alpha_{\Gamma}(\Phi))$ since all these functions and functors are identities.
- For each $\Gamma \in \mathsf{Obj}(\mathbf{CGSig})$, $\varphi \in CE(\Gamma)$ and $M' \in Vmod_{\mathcal{GTCEL}}(PL(\Gamma,\emptyset))$, we have that $\beta_{(\Gamma,\emptyset)}(M') \overset{g}{\models}_{\Gamma} \varphi \Leftrightarrow \mathcal{T}(\mathcal{P}(M')) \overset{g}{\models}_{\Gamma} \varphi \Leftrightarrow M' \overset{g}{\models}_{\Gamma} \varphi \Leftrightarrow M' \overset{g}{\models}_{\Gamma} \alpha_{\Gamma}(\varphi)$ since $M' \equiv_{\Gamma} \mathcal{T}(\mathcal{P}(M'))$ and by Proposition 3 they will satisfy the same formulas.
- Since $\beta = \mathcal{T} \circ \mathcal{P}$ it is surjective.

□

Theorem 5. *There is a simple map of institutions* $(\zeta,\alpha,\beta) : \mathcal{IGPCEL}{\rightarrow}\mathcal{GPCEL}$*, which is surjective.*

Proof. Similar to the previous proof. □

Theorem 6. *There is an isomorphism from* $\mathcal{IGTCEL}$ *to* $\mathcal{IGPCEL}$ *which is a surjective, simple map of institutions* $(\zeta,\alpha,\beta) : \mathcal{IGTCEL}{\rightarrow}\mathcal{IGPCEL}$.

Proof. Let *cgsig* and *sp* be as before. Since the theories are the same, ζ, ζ_1 are identity functors and α is the identity natural transformation.

- Define the natural transformation $\beta = \mathcal{T} : Vmod_{\mathcal{IGPCEL}} \circ \zeta^{\mathsf{op}} {\rightarrow} Vmod_{\mathcal{IGTCEL}}$, which is also an isomorphism between the categories.

This satisfies the necessary conditions. For the theories this has already been proved.

- For each $\Gamma \in \mathsf{Obj}(\mathbf{CGSig})$, $\varphi \in CE(\Gamma)$ and $M' \in Vmod_{\mathcal{IGPCEL}}(PL(\Gamma,\emptyset))$, we have that $\beta_{(\Gamma,\emptyset)}(M') \overset{g}{\models}_{\Gamma} \varphi \Leftrightarrow \mathcal{T}(M') \overset{g}{\models}_{\Gamma} \varphi \Leftrightarrow M' \overset{g}{\models}_{\Gamma} \varphi \Leftrightarrow M' \overset{g}{\models}_{\Gamma} \alpha_{\Gamma}(\varphi)$ since $\mathcal{T}$ preserves and reflects satisfaction.
- Since $\beta = \mathcal{T}$ is an isomorphism it is surjective.

Since all components of (ζ, α, β) are identities or isomorphisms, the map itself is an isomorphism. □

This allows us to prove our main theorem.

Theorem 7. *We may use entailment systems and proof calculi for $\mathcal{TCEL}$ for $\mathcal{IGTCEL}$ and use entailment systems and proof calculi for $\mathcal{PCEL}$ for $\mathcal{IGPCEL}$.*

Further, in the context of $\mathcal{IGTCEL}$ and $\mathcal{IGPCEL}$ entailment systems and proof calculi for $\mathcal{TCEL}$ and $\mathcal{PCEL}$ are indistinguishable.

Proof. The first two statements follow from composing the institution maps of the previous theorems. The last statement follows from the isomorphism institution maps between the institutions $\mathcal{IGTCEL}$ and $\mathcal{IGPCEL}$. □

This result can be extended to $\mathcal{GTCEL}$ and $\mathcal{GPCEL}$, but the proof will be more involved since the maps upwards from $\mathcal{IGTCEL}$ and $\mathcal{IGPCEL}$ are not surjective on model classes. We should also be able to allow weak guarded signature morphisms, i.e., guarded signature morphisms which also may map protected operators to unprotected operators.

The model classes of $\mathcal{IGTCEL}$ and $\mathcal{IGPCEL}$ contain exactly one representative from each of the care-equivalence classes, a representative that is canonical in the sense that it is initial in the care-equivalence class [HW95]. A care-equivalence class does not contain final algebras, but there are other choices, such as error-algebras, which may be interesting for certain purposes. How to select these, and how those classes relate back to $\mathcal{GTCEL}$ and $\mathcal{GPCEL}$ is open for investigation.

5 Conclusion

We have shown that the concept of guarded algebra provides a very nice correspondence between total and partial varieties using the inclusion, totalisation and partialisation model functors. Further, it allows a logical framework insensitive to the choice of total or partial models. We may choose the entailment systems and proof calculi which are most simple to work with, irrespectively of whether total models or partial models are best suited to understand the problem domain. This may be useful when, for example, investigating program semantics with detectable and undetectable errors.

The practical use may be hampered by the number of conditions generated by plainification, the translation from guarded to plain presentations. Other translation schemes that yield plain presentations that are more efficient to work with are being considered. Such a scheme may not yield the full model classes of $\mathcal{GTCEL}$ or $\mathcal{GPCEL}$ after the translation, but it seems that as long as each care-equivalence class is represented, the translation will be adequate from the logical aspect.

Further investigation of the relationship between guarded algebras and similar specification formalisms, such as membership algebras [Mes98], may allow the transferal of additional useful logical reasoning and rewrite tools to the guarded context.

We also want to extend the notion of guardedness beyond conditional equational specifications. First-order logic is especially interesting. A positive result here may be useful in the context of the algebraic specification language CASL [Mos97], which admits both partial and total models.

References

Bur86. Peter Burmeister. *A Model Theoretic Oriented Approach to Partial Algebras.* Akademie-Verlag, 1986. 195

Cer93. Maura Cerioli. *Relationships between Logical Formalism.* PhD thesis, Università de Pisa–Genova–Udine, 1993. 185

GDLE84. M. Gogolla, K. Drosten, U. Lipeck, and H.-D. Ehrich. Algebraic and operational semantics of specifications allowing exceptions and errors. *Theoretical Computer Science*, 34:289–313, 1984. 183

GTW78. Joseph A. Goguen, J. W. Thatcher, and Eric G. Wagner. An initial algebra approach to the specification, correctness, and implementation of abstract data types. In R. T. Yeh, editor, *Current Trends in Programming Methodology, IV, Data Structuring*, pages 80–149. Prentice-Hall, 1978. 183

HL89. Ivo Van Horebeek and Johan Lewi. *Algebraic Specifications in Software Engineering – an introduction.* International Series of Monographs on Computer Science. Springer–Verlag, Berlin, 1989. 183

HW95. Magne Haveraaen and Eric G. Wagner. Guarded algebras and data type specification. Technical Report 108, Department of Informatics, University of Bergen, P.O.Box 7800, N-5020 Bergen, Norway, October 1995. 182, 188, 195, 196, 199

Kre87. Hans-Jörg-Kreowski. Partial algebras flow from algebraic specifications. In *Proc. ICALP 87*, volume 267 of *Lecture Notes in Computer Science*, pages 521–530. Springer Verlag, 1987. 183

KM95. Hans-Jörg-Kreowski and Till Mossakowski. Equivalence and difference between institutions: simulating Horn Clause Logic with based algebras. *Math Struct. in Comp. Science* 5:189–215, 1995. 183

Mes89. J. Meseguer. General logics. In *Proc. Logic Colloquium '87.* North-Holland, 1989. 184, 185

Mes98. José Meseguer. Membership algebra as a logical framework for equational specification. In Francesco Parisi Presicce, editor, *Recent Trends in Algebraic Development Techniques*, volume 1376 of *Lecture Notes in Computer Science*, pages 18–61. Springer Verlag, 1998. 183, 184, 199

Mos95. Till Mossakowski. Equivalences among various logical frameworks of partial algebras. Bericht Nr, 4/95, Universität Bremen, Fachbereich Mathematik und Informatik, 1995. 183

Mos93. Peter D. Mosses. The use of sorts in algebraic data type specification. In *Recent Trends in Data Type Specification*, pages 66–91. LNCS 655, 1993. 183

Mos97. Peter D. Mosses. CoFI: The common framework initiative for algebraic specification and development. In Michel Bidoit and Max Dauchet, editors, *TAPSOFT'97: Theory and Practice of Software Development*, volume 1214 of *Lecture Notes in Computer Science*, pages 115–137. Springer-Verlag, 1997. 200

Rei87. Horst Reichel. *Initial Computability Algebraic Specifications, and Partial Algebras*. Clarendon Press, Oxford, 1987 183

A General Completeness Result in Refinement*

Yoshiki Kinoshita[1] and John Power[2]

[1] Computer Science Division, ETL
Amagasaki, 661–0974 Japan
[2] LFCS, Division of Informatics, Edinburgh University
King's Buildings, Edinburgh, EH9 3JZ Scotland

Abstract. In a paper in 1986, Hoare, He and Sanders proposed a formulation of refinement for a system equivalent to the ν-calculus using a relation based semantics. To give a proof method to show that one program is a refinement of another, they introduced downward simulation and upward simulation, but the proof method based upon either of them is not complete with respect to their notion of refinement, so they claimed "joint" completeness based upon both notions of simulation with respect to their notion of refinement.
We give a new definition of refinement in terms of structure respecting lax transformations, and show that the proof method based upon downward simulation is complete with respect to this notion of refinement. Although our theory works for the ν-calculus, we present the result for the μ-calculus to make the presentation simpler. We use results in enriched category theory to show this, and the central notion here is that of algebraic structure on locally ordered categories, not on sets. Our definition of refinement is neither a restriction nor a generalisation of Hoare, He and Sanders' definition, but we include all their important examples.

1 Introduction

Hoare, He and Sanders [6,7] introduced the notion of downward simulation and upward simulation between interpretations of base statements and showed *joint* completeness of downward and upward simulations with respect to data refinement in the ν-calculus, in the sense that every data refinement arises as an extension of a composite of upward *and* downward simulations. They did not show the completeness of downward simulation alone. In the setting of the μ-calculus, de Roever and Engelhardt explicitly gave an example of data refinement which cannot arise as an extension of downward simulation in [2]. Later, Gardiner and Morgan [3,4] worked on predicate transformer semantics and obtained a *single* completeness result for simulation and cosimulation, providing the operators preserve some properties.

* The authors acknowledge the support of STA through the COE budget for Global Information Processing Project and a British Council grant. The second author also acknowledges the support of EPSRC grants GR/J84205 and GR/M56333. A part of this work was done while the first author was staying at McGill University funded by an NSERC grant.

D. Bert, C. Choppy, and P. Mosses (Eds.): WADT'99, LNCS 1827, pp. 201–218, 2000.

The aim of our paper is to give a completeness result for downward simulation in a more general setting. Our definition of downward simulation can be specialised to that in [7], as well as the notion of simulation in the sense of [4] and L-simulation in [2]. We analyse why we obtained completeness hitherto unfound. Our result characterises the power of downward simulation as a method of proving refinement. Downward simulation gives a restrictive class of refinements, and ultimately one may want a broader class, but we defer such investigation to later work.

We also give a criterion for deciding which language constructs allow completeness of downward simulations. So, our result applies to a much wider class of languages than we present in this paper which is focused on the μ-calculus.

The paper is organised as follows. In Section 2, we give the syntax for our example language, which is a mild generalisation of the μ-calculus presented in [1]. Our example language has the least fixpoint construct in contrast to the greatest fixpoint provided in the ν-calculus studied in [7]. Our theory works both for the μ-calculus and the ν-calculus, but we concentrate on the former since the latter needs a lengthier presentation. In fact, our theory is applicable to any calculus whose semantic domain is given by algebraic structure on LocOrd_ℓ, hence the word "general" in the title of this paper. In Section 3, we give basic definitions on locally ordered categories, which provides the mathematical background of our work. In Section 4, we define models (semantics) of our example language in terms of Fix-algebras, which are given by algebraic structure on locally ordered categories. The technique we use here is an enriched version of functorial semantics as originated by Lawvere [10] (see also [11].) In Section 5, we define refinement as a structure respecting lax transformation between models and prove soundness and completeness of lax transformations with respect to refinements. The fundamental mathematical fact we need here is that the adjunction between the category LocOrd of small locally ordered categories and locally ordered functors and $\mathsf{Fix\text{-}Alg}_\circ$ is enriched over LocOrd_ℓ, so not only the locally ordered functors but also the lax transformations are extended uniquely. In Section 6, we give concluding remarks and outline further work.

2 Fixpoint Commands Presented by Judgments

We consider a simple programming language which has sequencer, nondeterministic choice and least fixpoint operators. This is a mild generalisation of the language considered in [1] and [2] in that ours allows commands to change the *set* of states; a command operating on a state σ in a set S of states may result in a state σ' belonging to a different set S' of states.

We give a natural deduction style presentation for our syntactic definition of commands as that makes it easier to keep track of free command variables, which we need for a rigorous treatment of fixpoint operators.

Definition 1 (Graph). *A graph is a quadruple $\langle N, E, d_0, d_1\rangle$ of sets N and E and functions $d_0, d_1\colon E \to N$.*

Let Γ be a graph. We write $\emptyset$ for the empty graph, $\mathrm{Node}(\Gamma)$ for the set of nodes of Γ, $\mathrm{Edge}(\Gamma)$ for the set of edges, and $\mathrm{d}_0(\Gamma)$ and $\mathrm{d}_1(\Gamma)$ for the source and target functions, respectively.

Definition 2 (Context). *By an* $(\mathcal{S},\mathcal{V})$-context, *we mean a graph whose nodes are at most countable and taken from* $\mathcal{S}$, *and whose edges are also at most countable and taken from* $\mathcal{V}$.

Example 1. Let the set $\mathcal{S}$ of symbols for state sets be $\{*\}$, a singleton set with $*$ as its unique element. Then an $(\mathcal{S},\mathcal{V})$-context amounts to a set A of edges.

Example 2. Let the set $\mathcal{S}$ consist of three symbols $*$, S and $\star$, and consider a context Γ with a unique edge I from $*$ to S, a unique edge F from S to $\star$ with all other edges being from S to itself. $(\mathcal{S},\mathcal{V})$-contexts for this $\mathcal{S}$ are used in Example 5.

In the following, we fix the sets $\mathcal{S}$ and $\mathcal{V}$; *contexts* will always mean $(\mathcal{S},\mathcal{V})$-contexts for these particular sets, unless otherwise stated.

Notation 1. If Γ is a context

$$\Gamma \uplus \{X\colon S \to S'\} \stackrel{\mathrm{def}}{=} \langle N \cup \{S, S'\},\, E \uplus X,\, d'_0,\, d'_1\rangle,$$

where $E \uplus X$ is the disjoint union of E and X, d'_i $(i = 1,2)$ extends d_i by $d'_0(X) = S$ and $d'_1(X) = S'$. For two graphs Γ and Γ', we write $\Gamma \subseteq \Gamma'$ to mean $\mathrm{Node}(\Gamma) \subseteq \mathrm{Node}(\Gamma')$, $\mathrm{Edge}(\Gamma) \subseteq \mathrm{Edge}(\Gamma')$, and $\mathrm{d}_i(\Gamma')$ is an extension of $\mathrm{d}_i(\Gamma)$, for $i = 0, 1$.

Note that, in the above notation, S and S' may or may not be elements of N; but usually, when we use this notation, they are elements of N.

We define *judgments* to be of the form:

$$\Gamma \vdash C\colon S {\to} S',$$

where Γ is a context and $S, S' \in \mathcal{S}$. The derivation rules for such judgments follow.

axiom

$$\frac{}{X\colon S{\to}S' \vdash X\colon S{\to}S'}$$

skip

$$\frac{S \in \mathrm{Node}(\Gamma)}{\Gamma \vdash \mathbf{skip}\colon S{\to}S}$$

abort

$$\frac{S, S' \in \mathrm{Node}(\Gamma)}{\Gamma \vdash \mathbf{abort}\colon S{\to}S'}$$

sequencer

$$\frac{\Gamma \vdash C\colon S \to S' \quad \Gamma \vdash C'\colon S' \to S''}{\Gamma \vdash C; C'\colon S \to S''}$$

nondeterministic choice

$$\frac{\Gamma \vdash C\colon S \to S' \quad \Gamma \vdash C'\colon S \to S'}{\Gamma \vdash C \,\mathbf{or}\, C'\colon S \to S'}$$

fixpoint

$$\frac{\Gamma \uplus \{X\colon S \to S'\} \vdash C\colon S \to S' \quad S, S' \in \mathrm{Node}(\Gamma)}{\Gamma \vdash \mathbf{fix} X.C\colon S \to S'}$$

We also have the following structural rule.

Thinning

$$\frac{\Gamma' \vdash C\colon S \to S' \quad \Gamma' \subseteq \Gamma}{\Gamma \vdash C\colon S \to S'}$$

We say that C is a *well-formed Γ-command* with source S and target S' if $\Gamma \vdash C\colon S \to S'$ is derived by means of the above rules finitely many times in the usual way.

The intuition behind the definition of Γ-command C is that, if one assigns a set of states to each node of Γ and a command to each edge of Γ preserving sources and targets, a Γ-command C is assigned a meaning. This will be formulated in Section 5.

3 Locally Ordered Categories

In this section, we give basic definitions and facts about locally ordered categories.

A *locally ordered category* is a category for which each homset is equipped with a partial order and the partial order is preserved by composition. So,

$$f \leq g, f' \leq g' \Longrightarrow f \circ f' \leq g \circ g'$$

always holds, whenever f and f' are composable. Since homsets of a locally ordered category are posets, we use the term *homposets*.

Example 3. Let **Rel** be the category whose objects are small sets and arrows from a to b are binary relations from a to b, with the identity being the diagonal and the composition being the usual composition of relations. Regarding relations as subsets of product sets, $\mathbf{Rel}(a, b)$ is equipped with the partial order $\subseteq$ of set inclusion. Composition of relations preserves this order, so **Rel** with $\subseteq$ is a locally ordered category. This is a category used in relational semantics of fixpoint programs in, say, [2,7]

Example 4. Let **Poset** be the category of small partially ordered sets and monotone functions. The homset $\mathbf{Poset}(a, b)$ can be ordered pointwise: for f, $g \in \mathbf{Poset}(a, b)$, $f \sqsubseteq g$ if and only if, for each $x \in a$, $f(x) \leq g(x)$. By monotonicity of homomorphisms, it can easily be shown that $\sqsubseteq$ is preserved by composition. So, **Poset** with $\sqsubseteq$ is a locally ordered category. This argument also shows that the subcategory **cBa** of complete Boolean algebras and their homomorphisms makes a locally ordered category.

A *locally ordered functor* is a functor between locally ordered categories which preserves the order. Small locally ordered categories and locally ordered functors between them form a category, which we call LocOrd.

It is well-known that a graph extends freely to a category. There is an analogue to locally ordered categories. Let a *locally ordered graph* be defined as a graph $G = \langle N, E, d_0, d_1 \rangle$ with an $N \times N$-indexed family of partial orders $\leq_{n,m}$ on $G(n, m) = \{ e \in E \mid d_0(e) = n, d_1(e) = m \}$. Morphisms of locally ordered graphs are graph morphisms preserving these orders. So, we have a category $\mathsf{LOGraph}$ of locally ordered graphs and their morphisms. There is an obvious forgetful functor $U\colon \mathsf{LocOrd} \to \mathsf{LOGraph}$.

Proposition 1 (Free locally ordered category). *Given a locally ordered graph G, there is a locally ordered category $F(G)$ and a locally ordered graph morphism $\eta_G\colon G \to U(F(G))$ such that, for each locally ordered category C and each locally ordered graph morphism $f\colon G \to U(C)$, there is a unique locally ordered functor $\overline{f}\colon F(G) \to C$ such that $f = U(\overline{f}) \circ \eta_G$.*

Given two locally ordered functors $F, G\colon A \to B$ from a locally ordered category A to B, a *lax transformation* from F to G is an $\mathrm{ob}(A)$-indexed family α of arrows in B, which satisfies the following conditions. For each $a \in \mathrm{ob}(A)$, $\alpha_a \in B(F(a), G(a))$; moreover, for each arrow $f \in A(a, a')$ of A, $G(f) \circ \alpha_a \leq \alpha_{a'} \circ F(f)$. This is depicted as follows.

$$\begin{array}{ccccc} a & \qquad & F(a) & \xrightarrow{\alpha_a} & G(a) \\ {\scriptstyle \forall f}\downarrow & & {\scriptstyle F(f)}\downarrow & \geq & \downarrow{\scriptstyle G(f)} \\ a' & & F(a') & \xrightarrow[\alpha_{a'}]{} & G(a') \end{array}$$

Similarly, an *oplax transformation* from F to G is an $\mathrm{ob}(A)$-indexed family of arrows of B with the order condition reversed:

$$\begin{array}{ccccc} a & \qquad & F(a) & \xrightarrow{\alpha_a} & G(a) \\ {\scriptstyle \forall f}\downarrow & & {\scriptstyle F(f)}\downarrow & \leq & \downarrow{\scriptstyle G(f)} \\ a' & & F(a') & \xrightarrow[\alpha_{a'}]{} & G(a') \end{array}$$

One cannot define lax transformations between morphisms of locally ordered graphs in general. One can, however, think of them if the codomain of the morphisms is a locally ordered category, that is, of the form $U(C)$. For such, we have the following proposition.

Proposition 2. *Given a locally ordered category M and morphisms of ordered graphs $F_0, F_0' \colon \Gamma \to U(M)$. There is a one-one onto correspondence between the set of lax transformations between F_0 and F_0', and the set of lax transformations between locally ordered functors:*

$$\mathsf{LOGraph}(\Gamma, U(M))(F_0, F_0') \cong \mathsf{LocOrd}_\ell([\![\Gamma]\!], M)(\overline{F_0}, \overline{F_0'})$$

There is no reasonable definition of horizontal composition of lax transformations. But they can be composed vertically and we can define an analogue of functor category. We define $\mathrm{Lax}(A, B)$ to be a locally ordered category whose objects are locally ordered functors from A to B, and arrows are lax transformations, with the obvious domain and codomain. $\mathrm{Oplax}(A, B)$ is defined similarly.

4 Semantics

In this section, we first introduce Fix-algebras as small locally ordered categories whose homposets are equipped with least upper bounds of any countable set, with those upper bounds preserved by composition. We use the term Fix-algebra because, as we shall see later, Fix-algebra structure is necessary and sufficient to interpret our example language. We write $\mathsf{Fix\text{-}Alg}_\circ$ for the category of Fix-algebras and structure preserving locally ordered functors. $\mathsf{Fix\text{-}Alg}_\circ$ is an ordinary category, rather than a LocOrd_ℓ-enriched category as will soon appear. An important observation is that the forgetful (ordinary) functor $\mathcal{U} \colon \mathsf{Fix\text{-}Alg}_\circ \to \mathsf{LocOrd}$ has a left adjoint $\mathcal{F} \colon \mathsf{LocOrd} \to \mathsf{Fix\text{-}Alg}_\circ$ where LocOrd is the (ordinary) category of small locally ordered categories and locally ordered functors. The image of a locally ordered category X under $\mathcal{F}$ may be explicitly described as follows: $\mathrm{ob}(\mathcal{F}(X)) = \mathrm{ob}(X)$, and $\mathcal{F}(X)(S, S')$ is the countably complete upper semilattice freely generated by the homposet $X(S, S')$.

Next, we establish a semantics for our example language by defining denotations of contexts and derivable judgments. A context Γ is modeled by a locally ordered category $[\![\Gamma]\!]$ freely generated by the graph Γ, and a derivable judgment $\Gamma \vdash C \colon S \to S'$ is modeled by an arrow from S to S' in the Fix-algebra $\mathcal{F}([\![\Gamma]\!])$.

We close this section by a brief justification of our semantics by means of provable equations and orderings between denotations of commands.

4.1 Semantics in Fix-Algebra

We state some properties of the algebraic structure Fix on locally ordered categories, introduced in Section 3. The reason for introducing Fix-algebras is that we shall later give our semantics of our example language introduced in Section 2.

We define the algebraic structure $\mathsf{Fix} = (S, E)$ on locally ω-presentable categories in Example 6 of Appendix.

Proposition 3. *A* Fix*-algebra is a small locally ordered category whose hom-posets have least upper bounds of any countable subset, with the least upper bounds preserved by composition. A morphism between* Fix*-algebras is a locally ordered functor which preserves least upper bounds.*

This immediately follows from the definition of Fix. Hence, given a Fix-algebra with base locally ordered category M, we write $\mathrm{lub}_{M(A,B)}(X)$ or $\mathrm{lub}(X)$ for a countable subset X of some homposet $M(A,B)$. Then $\mathrm{lub}_{M(A,B)}(\emptyset)$ is the least element of $M(A,B)$, and we write $\bot_{M(A,B)}$ for this. We further write $f \sqcup g$ for $\mathrm{lub}(\{f, g\})$.

Remark 1. The operators we need are only $\bot$, $\sqcup$ and lub_ω's of ω-chains (increasing sequences of length ω), but these operators exist if and only if one has the same structure as Fix, i.e., all least upper bounds of countable sets. If we have $\bot$, $\sqcup$ and lub_ω, the lub of any countable set $\{a_0, a_1, a_2, \ldots\}$ is given by $\mathrm{lub}_\omega(a_0 \sqsubseteq a_0 \sqcup a_1 \sqsubseteq a_0 \sqcup a_1 \sqcup a_2 \sqsubseteq \ldots)$.

The forgetful functor $\mathcal{U}$ from $\mathsf{Fix\text{-}Alg}_\circ$ to the category LocOrd of small locally ordered categories and locally ordered functors has a left adjoint $\mathcal{F}\colon \mathsf{LocOrd} \to \mathsf{Fix\text{-}Alg}_\circ$. This may be spelled out by the following theorem.

Theorem 1 (Ordinary adjunction). *For each small locally ordered category A, there is a* Fix*-algebra $\mathcal{F}(A)$ and a locally ordered functor $\eta_A\colon A \to \mathcal{U}(\mathcal{F}(A))$ which satisfies the following universality property: for each* Fix*-algebra M and locally ordered functor $F\colon A \to \mathcal{U}(M)$, there exists a unique* Fix*-algebra morphism $\overline{F}\colon \mathcal{F}(A) \to M$ which satisfies $F = \mathcal{U}(\overline{F}) \circ \eta_A$.*

The theorem can be depicted by the following diagram.

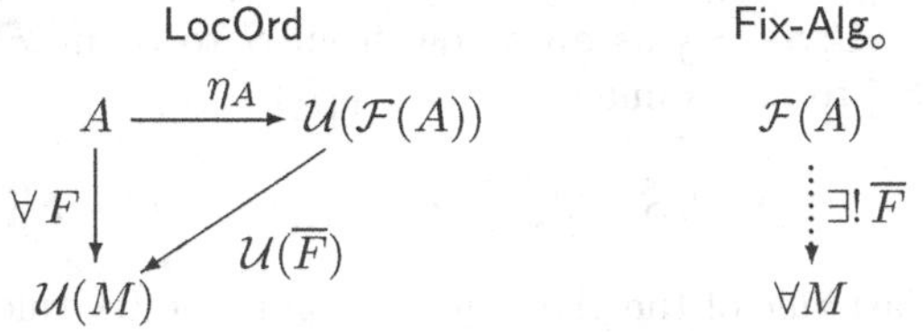

A standard argument shows the Theorem is equivalent to the following Corollary.

Corollary 1. *There is a bijection between the set of locally ordered functors from A to $\mathcal{U}(M)$ and the set of* Fix*-algebra morphisms from $\mathcal{F}(A)$ to M.*

$$\mathsf{LocOrd}(A, \mathcal{U}(M)) \cong \mathsf{Fix\text{-}Alg}_\circ(\mathcal{F}(A), M)$$

Moreover, this bijection is natural in A and M.

4.2 Denotations

Let $\Gamma = \langle N, E, d_0, d_1 \rangle$ be a context. We define $[\![\Gamma]\!]$ to be the locally ordered category freely generated by Γ: it is in fact a mere category freely generated by Γ, whose homsets are considered to be discrete posets. The "free generation" implies the following

Proposition 4. *For any locally ordered category M, there is a one-one onto mapping between the set $\mathsf{LOGraph}(\Gamma, U(M))$ of locally ordered graph morphisms from Γ to the underlying graph $U(M)$ of M and the set $\mathsf{LocOrd}([\![\Gamma]\!], M)$ of locally ordered functors from $[\![\Gamma]\!]$ to M.*

Given a derivation of a judgment $\Gamma \vdash C\colon S \to S'$ according to the rules in Section 2, we define its denotation $[\![\Gamma \vdash C\colon S \to S']\!]$ to be an arrow from S to S' in $\mathcal{F}([\![\Gamma]\!])$. The definition is given by induction on the construction of the derivation. We write η for the unit of the adjunction $\mathcal{F} \dashv \mathcal{U}$, so that, for each $X \in [\![\Gamma]\!](S, S')$, $\eta_{[\![\Gamma]\!]}(X)$ is an arrow in the homset $\mathcal{F}([\![\Gamma]\!])(\eta_{[\![\Gamma]\!]}(S), \eta_{[\![\Gamma]\!]}(S'))$.

1. $[\![X\colon S \to S' \vdash X\colon S \to S']\!] \stackrel{\text{def}}{=} \eta_{[\![X:S\to S']\!]}(X)$.
2. $[\![\Gamma \vdash \mathbf{skip}\colon S \to S]\!] \stackrel{\text{def}}{=} \mathrm{id}_{\eta_{[\![\Gamma]\!]}(S)}$.
3. $[\![\Gamma \vdash \mathbf{abort}\colon S \to S']\!] \stackrel{\text{def}}{=} \bot_{M(\eta_{[\![\Gamma]\!]}(S), \eta_{[\![\Gamma]\!]}(S'))}$.
4. $[\![\Gamma \vdash C; C'\colon S \to S'']\!] \stackrel{\text{def}}{=} [\![\Gamma \vdash C'\colon S' \to S'']\!] \circ [\![\Gamma \vdash C\colon S \to S']\!]$, using composition $\circ$ in $\mathcal{F}([\![\Gamma]\!])$.
5. $[\![\Gamma \vdash C \,\mathbf{or}\, C'\colon S \to S']\!] \stackrel{\text{def}}{=} [\![\Gamma \vdash C\colon S \to S']\!] \sqcup [\![\Gamma \vdash C'\colon S \to S']\!]$, using the lub operator $\sqcup$ of $\mathcal{F}([\![\Gamma]\!])(S, S')$.
6. Assume the last rule of the given derivation is the **Thinning** rule

$$\frac{\Gamma' \vdash C\colon S' \to S'}{\Gamma \vdash C\colon S \to S'}\,.$$

   Send the graph inclusion $j\colon \Gamma' \hookrightarrow \Gamma$ first by $[\![-]\!]$, and then by $\mathcal{F}$ to obtain $\mathcal{F}([\![j]\!])\colon \mathcal{F}([\![\Gamma']\!]) \to \mathcal{F}([\![\Gamma]\!])$. By the induction hypothesis, we have already defined $[\![\Gamma' \vdash C\colon S \to S']\!]$ as an arrow from S to S' in $\mathcal{F}([\![\Gamma']\!])$. We define $[\![\Gamma \vdash C\colon S \to S']\!]$ to be its image under $\mathcal{F}([\![j]\!])$:

$$[\![\Gamma \vdash C\colon S \to S']\!] \stackrel{\text{def}}{=} \mathcal{F}([\![j]\!])([\![\Gamma \vdash C\colon S \to S']\!])$$

7. Assume the last rule of the given derivation is the **fix** rule

$$\frac{\Gamma \uplus \{X\colon S \to S'\} \vdash C\colon S \to S'}{\Gamma \vdash \mathbf{fix}X.C\colon S \to S'}$$

   From the derivation of the upper judgment $\Gamma \uplus \{X\colon S \to S'\} \vdash C\colon S \to S'$, we define an endofunction $\Phi_{\Gamma \uplus \{X:S\to S'\} \vdash C:S \to S'}$ on $\mathcal{F}([\![\Gamma]\!])(S, S')$ as follows. Assuming there is no confusion, we write Φ_C for $\Phi_{\Gamma \uplus \{X:S\to S'\} \vdash C:S\to S'}$.

$$\begin{array}{ccccc} [\![\Gamma]\!] & & [\![\Gamma \uplus \{X\}]\!] & & \mathcal{F}([\![\Gamma \uplus \{X\}]\!]) \\ \downarrow \eta_\Gamma & \xmapsto{\text{extension by } X \mapsto Y} & \downarrow \rho_Y & \xmapsto{\text{Theorem 1}} & \downarrow \overline{\rho_Y} \\ \mathcal{U}(\mathcal{F}([\![\Gamma]\!])) & & \mathcal{U}(\mathcal{F}([\![\Gamma]\!])) & & \mathcal{F}([\![\Gamma]\!]) \end{array}$$

   Given $Y \in \mathcal{F}([\![\Gamma]\!])(S, S')$, define $\rho_Y\colon [\![\Gamma \uplus \{X\}]\!] \to \mathcal{U}(\mathcal{F}([\![\Gamma]\!]))$ to be the extension of $\eta_{[\![\Gamma]\!]}\colon [\![\Gamma]\!] \to \mathcal{F}([\![\Gamma]\!])$ satisfying $\rho_Y(X) = Y$. By Theorem 1, ρ_Y

extends uniquely to $\overline{\rho_Y}: \mathcal{F}([\![\Gamma \uplus \{X\}]\!]) \to \mathcal{F}([\![\Gamma]\!])$. There occur at most $N-1$ applications of the **fix** rule in our subderivation of $\Gamma \uplus \{X\} \vdash C: S \to S'$, so we have already defined $[\![\Gamma \uplus \{X\} \vdash C: S \to S']\!]$ by the induction hypothesis, and it is an arrow in $\mathcal{F}([\![\Gamma \uplus \{X\}]\!])(S, S')$. So, we define $\Phi_C(Y) \stackrel{\text{def}}{=} \overline{\rho_Y}([\![\Gamma \uplus \{X\} \vdash C: S \to S']\!])$.

With this apparatus, we define

$$[\![\Gamma \vdash \mathbf{fix}X.C: S \to S']\!] \stackrel{\text{def}}{=} \mathrm{lub}(\{(\Phi_C)^n(\bot_{\mathcal{F}([\![\Gamma]\!])(S,S')}) \mid n \in \omega\}),$$

This completes our definition of $[\![\Gamma \vdash C: S \to S']\!]$.

Remark 2. As for Φ_C introduced in the definition, we can show that $\{(\Phi_C)^n(\bot) \mid n \in \omega\}$ is an increasing ω-chain, and this corresponds to the chain used in the usual Tarski fixpoint argument. But we do not have to check that it is an ω-chain to get the lub, since we have all lub's of countable sets here. See Remark 1.

Remark 3. Coherence holds for our language in the sense that judgments are given the same denotation regardless of their derivations, but we do not go into detail about this point in this paper.

We can prove the following equations and partial orderings between denotations of derivations of judgment. This should justify our semantics, or definition of denotations of judgments. We write as if equations and orderings are between judgments, but strictly speaking, we mean they are equations and orderings between derivations of those judgments.

Proposition 5 (Equations). *The following equations hold.*

1. **skip** *is a unit with respect to the sequencer*

$$[\![\Gamma \vdash (\mathbf{skip}; C): S \to S']\!] = [\![\Gamma \vdash C: S \to S']\!] = [\![\Gamma \vdash (C; \mathbf{skip}): S \to S']\!]$$

2. *Sequencer is associative*

$$[\![\Gamma \vdash (C; C'); C'': S \to S']\!] = [\![\Gamma \vdash C; (C'; C''): S \to S']\!]$$

3. **fix**$X.C$ *gives the fixpoint*

$$[\![\Gamma \vdash \mathbf{fix}X.C: S \to S']\!] = \Phi_{\Gamma \uplus \{X:S \to S'\} \vdash C:S \to S'}([\![\Gamma \vdash \mathbf{fix}X.C: S \to S']\!])$$

Proposition 6 (Ordering). *The following orderings hold.*

1. **abort** *is the least element*

$$[\![\Gamma \vdash \mathbf{abort}: S \to S']\!] \sqsubseteq [\![\Gamma \vdash C: S \to S']\!]$$

2. **or** *is the least upper bound*
   - $[\![\Gamma \vdash C: S \to S']\!] \sqsubseteq [\![\Gamma \vdash C \,\mathbf{or}\, C': S \to S']\!]$,
   - $[\![\Gamma \vdash C': S \to S']\!] \sqsubseteq [\![\Gamma \vdash C \,\mathbf{or}\, C': S \to S']\!]$,

– *If* $[\![\Gamma \vdash C\colon S{\to}S']\!] \sqsubseteq [\![\Gamma \vdash C''\colon S{\to}S']\!]$ *and* $[\![\Gamma \vdash C'\colon S{\to}S']\!] \sqsubseteq [\![\Gamma \vdash C''\colon S{\to}S']\!]$, *then*

$$[\![\Gamma \vdash C \,\mathbf{or}\, C'\colon S{\to}S']\!] \sqsubseteq [\![\Gamma \vdash C''\colon S{\to}S']\!]$$

3. $\mathbf{fix}X.C$ *gives the* least *fixpoint. If* $\Gamma \vdash C'\colon S{\to}S'$ *is well-formed and it is a fixpoint of* Φ_C *in the sense that*

$$\Phi_C([\![\Gamma \vdash C'\colon S{\to}S']\!]) = [\![\Gamma \vdash C'\colon S{\to}S']\!],$$

then

$$[\![\Gamma \vdash \mathbf{fix}X.C\colon S{\to}S']\!] \sqsubseteq [\![\Gamma \vdash C'\colon S{\to}S']\!].$$

5 Soundness and Completeness

We shall show the main theorem of this paper in this section. We start by stating the basic fact about enriched adjunction. Then we define interpretations of contexts. We use Theorem 1 to show that an interpretation of context Γ always extends to an interpretation of Γ-commands uniquely.

We then proceed to the definition of downward simulation of interpretations of contexts by means of lax transformations. As soon as these lax transformations arise, the ordinary categories LocOrd and $\mathsf{Fix\text{-}Alg}_\circ$ become insufficient, as they do not contain lax transformations among their data, which is why we consider *enrichment* in Theorem 2. We refer the reader to Appendix and [9,8] for the background mathematical setting and proofs. Theorem 2 is the key to prove our main theorem, which states the soundness and completeness result. Soundness says that any downward simulation between interpretations of contexts extends to refinement of interpretation of commands. Completeness says that every refinement of a Γ-command is obtained as an extension of a downward simulation of Γ.

We start by stating the basic fact about enriched adjunctions, which give the mathematical background to soundness and completeness.

5.1 Enriched Adjunction

Each homset $\mathsf{LocOrd}_\ell(A, B)$ of the category LocOrd_ℓ is not a mere set, but it has the structure of a locally ordered category. It is the locally ordered category whose objects are locally ordered functors from A to B, and whose arrows are lax transformations, where the order between lax transformations is determined pointwise.

At first glance, it looks as though locally ordered categories, locally ordered functors and lax transformations make a 2-category, but they do not: one cannot give a reasonable horizontal composition of lax transformations, because the usual square does not commute but is only related by the order. However, the fact that each homset has locally ordered category structure can be formulated by an enrichment in the monoidal biclosed category LocOrd_ℓ, as shown in Appendix.

Accordingly, the above adjunction is also enriched, resulting in the following theorem.

Theorem 2 (LocOrd$_\ell$-enriched adjunction). *As in Theorem 1, let A be a small locally ordered category, M a* Fix*-algebra, and $\alpha\colon F \overset{\text{lax}}{\Rightarrow} G\colon A \to \mathcal{U}(M)$ be a lax transformation from a locally ordered functor F to G. Then there exists a unique structure respecting lax transformation $\overline{\alpha}$ from the unique extension $\overline{F}$ of F (which exists by Theorem 1) to the unique extension $\overline{G}$ of G, which satisfies $\alpha_a = \overline{\alpha}_{\eta_A(a)}$ for each object a of A, where η is the unit for the ordinary adjunction as in the Theorem 1.*

Again, the situation may be depicted as follows.

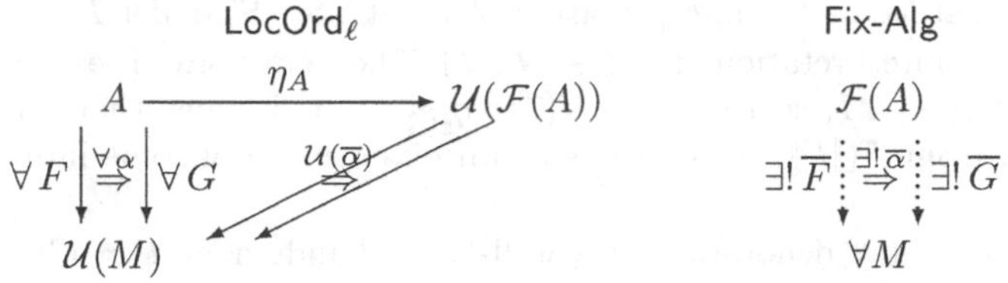

Corollary 2. *There is an isomorphism in the monoidal biclosed category* LocOrd$_\ell$ *between* LocOrd$(A,\mathcal{U}(M))$ = Lax$(A,\mathcal{U}(M))$ *and* Fix-Alg$(\mathcal{F}(A), M)$.

$$\mathsf{Lax}(A,\mathcal{U}(M)) \cong \mathsf{Fix\text{-}Alg}(\mathcal{F}(A), M)$$

This enrichment of the adjunction plays the essential role in this section in showing soundness and completeness of lax transformations with respect to refinements of commands.

5.2 Simulations and Refinements

Definition 3 (Interpretation of Contexts). *Let Γ be a context and M be a* Fix*-algebra. An interpretation of Γ in M is a locally ordered functor from $[\![\Gamma]\!]$ to $\mathcal{U}(M)$.*

By Proposition 4, an interpretation of Γ in M is in one-one correspondence with a graph morphism from Γ to $U(M)$, the underlying graph of M. In the case of Example 1, where Γ has a unique node $*$, such a graph morphism amounts to the image S of $*$ and the indexed set $A = \{\, A_i \mid i \in \mathrm{Edge}(\Gamma) \,\}$ of arrows in $M(S,S)$. This index set A is called the set of "atomic operations" in the literature.

Example 5. If Γ is of the form described in Example 2, its interpretation ρ in **Rel**, the locally ordered category of small sets and binary relations ordered by inclusion, amounts to a program over the set $P = \{\rho(A) \mid A \text{ is an edge of } \Gamma \text{ from } A \text{ to } A\}$ of endorelations on the interpretation of S. Moreover, the triple $(\rho(I), P, \rho(F))$ exactly amounts to what is called a data type in [7].

Definition 4 (Downward Simulation). *Given two interpretations $\rho, \psi\colon [\![\Gamma]\!] \to \mathcal{U}(M)$ of a context Γ in M. A downward simulation from ρ to ψ is defined to be a lax transformation from ρ to ψ.*

Proposition 4 shows that our definition matches precisely the definition in [7], in the setting of Example 1, with M being **Rel**, the category of sets and binary relations.

Definition 5 (Interpretation of Γ-commands). *An interpretation of Γ-commands in M is defined to be a* Fix*-algebra morphism from $\mathcal{F}(\llbracket\Gamma\rrbracket)$ to M.*

If $\Gamma \vdash C\colon S \to S'$ is a Γ-command, the denotation $\llbracket\Gamma \vdash C\colon S \to S'\rrbracket$ is an arrow in $\mathcal{F}(\llbracket\Gamma\rrbracket)$, so an interpretation I in M maps it to an arrow in $M(I(S), I(S'))$, which is regarded as the interpretation of $\Gamma \vdash C\colon S \to S'$ under I.

Given an interpretation $\rho\colon \llbracket\Gamma\rrbracket \to \mathcal{U}(M)$, Theorem 1 says it extends uniquely to $\overline{\rho}\colon \mathcal{F}(\llbracket\Gamma\rrbracket) \to M$, so that $\rho = \mathcal{U}(\overline{\rho}) \circ \eta_{\llbracket\Gamma\rrbracket}$. This implies that any μ-algebra morphism from $\mathcal{F}(\llbracket\Gamma\rrbracket)$ to M arises as an extension $\overline{\rho}$ of some interpretation ρ of Γ in M.

So $\overline{\rho}$ maps any denotation of a well-formed judgment $\Gamma \vdash C\colon S \to S'$ to an arrow in $M(S, S')$.

Definition 6 (Refinement of Interpretations of Γ-commands). *Given two interpretations $F, G\colon \mathcal{F}(\llbracket\Gamma\rrbracket) \to M$ of Γ-commands in M, a refinement of commands from F to G is defined to be a lax transformation from F to G.*

One of the central problems in refinement is to seek a good method of obtaining a refinement between two interpretations of Γ-commands. Here, we propose obtaining such a refinement from downward simulation via Theorem 2.

We state two theorems to support this proposal. One is about the soundness of our method, and the other is about completeness.

Theorem 3 (Soundness). *To each downward simulation α from an interpretation H of Γ to K, our method gives a Γ-command refinement from $\overline{H}$ to $\overline{K}$.*

Proof. Let α be a downward simulation from an interpretation H of Γ to K. By definition, α is a lax transformation from H to K. So Theorem 2 says that there is a lax transformation $\overline{\alpha}$ from $\overline{H}$ to $\overline{K}$, but this is defined to be a Γ-command refinement.

Theorem 4 (Completeness). *Let γ be a Γ-command refinement from an interpretation H of the Γ-command to K. Then H is given by our method from some interpretation H' of Γ; that is, there is such H' with $\overline{H'} = H$. Similarly, there is also K' such that $\overline{K'} = K$. Moreover, γ is given by our method from some downward simulation γ' from H' to K'.*

Proof. Corollary 1 says the mapping of a locally ordered functor F to $\overline{F}$ is (one-one and) onto. So, there are H' and K' such that $\overline{H'} = H$ and $\overline{K'} = K$. Moreover, Corollary 2 says the mapping of a lax transformation $\alpha\colon H' \stackrel{\text{lax}}{\Rightarrow} K'$ to $\overline{\alpha}\colon H \stackrel{\text{lax}}{\Rightarrow} K$ is onto, as was required.

6 Conclusions and Further Work

In this paper, we have concentrated on downward simulations. Upward simulations could be defined by means of oplax transformations.

As we mentioned in various parts in the paper, Hoare He and Sanders' work [7] corresponds to the case, modulo the difference of the least and the greatest fixpoints, where $\mathcal{S}$ is given as in Example 2 and the semantic domain is the locally ordered category **Rel** of sets and binary relations. Although the definition of downward simulation exactly coincides, [7] did not obtain completeness. It is because our notion of refinement is a restriction of theirs. We restrict refinement to the case where the abstract program can be shown to be larger *respecting the structure* (this is what the existence of a structure respecting lax transformation tells us,) while [7] did not require refinements to respect the structure. The computational effect of this restriction should be investigated, but we have at least given a precise characterisation of the range of refinements that the class of downward simulations generates.

The relationship with work based on predicate transformers remains a very interesting topic. Our approach may also work with predicate transformer semantics, letting the semantic domain category be that of complete Boolean algebras or complete Heyting algebras, as in Example 4. Gardiner and Morgan [3,4] gave a completeness result not restricting [7]'s sense of data refinement, but restricting the operations by postulating some properties, not necessarily coming from the structure of data or programs.

Our theory gives a criterion for programming language constructs that allows soundness and completeness of simulation for refinement. In this paper, we gave one definition of commands, but for any language construct that can be modeled by algebraic structure on LocOrd, we have the same completeness result. In particular, glb's of descending chains, as [7] used, or glb's of a finite number of programs are within this framework.

References

1. Jaco de Bakker and Erik de Vink. *Control Flow Semantics.* Foundations of Computing Series. The MIT Press, 1996. 202
2. Willem-Paul de Roever and Kai Engelhardt. *Data Refinement: Model-Oriented Proof Methods and their Comparison.* Number 47 in Cambridge Tracts in Theoretical Computer Science. Cambridge University Press, 1998. 201, 202, 204
3. Paul Gardiner and Carroll Morgan. Data refinement of predicate transformers. *Theoretical Computer Science*, 87:142–162, 1991. 201, 213
4. Paul Gardiner and Carroll Morgan. A single complete rule for data refinement. *Formal Aspects of Computing*, 5:367–382, 1993. 201, 202, 213
5. R. Gordon and A. J. Power. Algebraic structure for bicategory enriched categories. *Journal of Pure and Applied Algebra*, 130:119–132, 1998. 218
6. J. He, C. A. R. Hoare, and J . W. Sanders. Data refinement refined. volume 213 of *Springer Lecture Notes in Computer Science*, pages 186–196, 1986. 201
7. C. A. R. Hoare, He Jifeng, and Jeff W. Sanders. Prespecification in data refinement. *Information Processing Letters*, 25:71–76, 1987. 201, 202, 204, 211, 212, 213

8. Y. Kinoshita and A.J. Power. Data refinement and algebraic structure. ETL Technical Report TR96–2, Electrotechnical Laboratory, January 1996. to appear in Acta Informatica. 210
9. Y. Kinoshita and A.J. Power. Lax naturality through enrichment. *Journal of Pure and Applied Algebra*, 112(1):53–72, 1996. 210, 214, 215, 218
10. F. William Lawvere. Functorial semantics of algebraic theories. *Proc. Nat. Acad. Sci. U.S.A.*, 50:869–873, 1963. 202
11. F. E. J. Linton. An outline of functorial semantics. In *Seminar on triples and categorical homology theory*, number 80 in Springer Lecture Notes in Computer Science, pages 7–52. Springer-Verlag, 1966. 202

Appendix

A Algebraic Structures on Locally Ordered Categories

Biclosed Monoidal category LocOrd_ℓ *enriched by itself.* Let LocOrd be the category of small locally ordered categories and locally ordered functors. This category is equipped with the following monoidal structure $\otimes$, called Gray tensor in [9]. For A, $B \in \mathrm{ob}(\mathsf{LocOrd})$, $A \otimes B$ is the locally ordered category

- whose objects are pairs $\langle a, b\rangle \in \mathrm{ob}(A) \times \mathrm{ob}(B)$,
- where an arrow from $\langle a, b\rangle$ to $\langle a', b'\rangle$ is a finite sequence of non-identity arrows alternating between arrows in A and arrows in B such that the subsequence of arrows in A is a directed path in A from a to a' and the subsequence of arrows in B is a directed path in B from b to b',
- whose identity on $\langle a, b\rangle$ is the empty sequence,
- whose composition is given by concatenating the sequences, then factoring according to the composition and identities in A and B; and
- whose local order is generated by the local order on A and that on B and

$$\begin{array}{ccc} \langle a, b\rangle & \xrightarrow{\langle f, b\rangle} & \langle a', b\rangle \\ {\scriptstyle \langle a, g\rangle}\downarrow & \geq & \downarrow{\scriptstyle \langle a', g\rangle} \\ \langle a, b'\rangle & \xrightarrow[\langle f, b'\rangle]{} & \langle a', b'\rangle \end{array}$$

for any $f \in A(a, a')$ and $g \in B(b, b')$.

This $\otimes$ is trivially extended to a binary functor on LocOrd, and we obtain a monoidal structure on LocOrd with the unit being the singleton. We shall write LocOrd_ℓ for this monoidal category. This is not symmetric, but it is biclosed in the sense that both the functors $- \otimes A$ and $A \otimes -$ from LocOrd to itself has a right adjoint. In fact, $\mathrm{Lax}(A, -)$ is right adjoint to $- \otimes A$, and $\mathrm{Oplax}(A, -)$ is right adjoint to $A \otimes -$.

By raising the cardinal number one up in our argument in [9], LocOrd_ℓ is a locally ω-presentable LocOrd_ℓ-category.

Algebraic Structures on ω-presentable LocOrd_ℓ-categories. Here, we present a definition of algebraic structures on ω-presentable LocOrd_ℓ-categories, restricting the general case in the same way as [9] restricts the case to finite case. In the sequel, we write ω_1 for the first uncountable ordinal.

Let $\mathsf{LocOrd}_{\ell\omega}$ denote the full sub-LocOrd_ℓ-category of LocOrd_ℓ determined by the isomorphism class of the locally ordered categories with at most ω arrows, and let $|\mathsf{LocOrd}_{\ell\omega}|$ denote its set of objects as a discrete LocOrd_ℓ-category. We define a *signature* on LocOrd_ℓ to be a LocOrd_ℓ-functor $S\colon |\mathsf{LocOrd}_{\ell\omega}| \to \mathsf{LocOrd}_\ell$, and call $S(c)$ the locally ordered category of *basic operations of arity* c. We then define

$$\begin{aligned} S_0 &= J, \qquad \text{the inclusion of } \mathsf{LocOrd}_{\ell\omega} \text{ in } \mathsf{LocOrd}_\ell. \\ S_{n+1} &= J + \textstyle\sum_{d\in|\mathsf{LocOrd}_{\ell\omega}|} \mathrm{Lax}(d, S_n(-)) \otimes S(d), \\ \sigma_0 &= \text{the injection to the left from } S_0 = J \text{ to } S_1 = J + \textstyle\sum_d \mathrm{Lax}(d,c) \otimes S(d), \\ \sigma_{n+1} &= J + \textstyle\sum_{d\in|\mathsf{LocOrd}_{\ell\omega}|} \mathrm{Lax}(d, \sigma_n(-)) \otimes S(d) \colon S_{n+1} \to S_{n+2} \end{aligned}$$

and for a limit ordinal λ,

$$\begin{aligned} S_\lambda &= \operatorname*{Colim}_{n<\lambda}(S_n, \sigma_n) \\ \sigma_\lambda &= \text{the mediating arrow from the colimiting cone } S_\lambda \text{ to the cone } \gamma_\lambda, \end{aligned}$$

Here, the colimiting cone S_λ is defined to be the colimiting cone which defines S_λ. We call the injections of this colimiting cone $\iota_n\colon S_n \to S_\lambda$. Then the cone γ_λ has the same base, has the pivot $S_{\lambda+1}$ and the injections $j_n\colon S_n \to S_{\lambda+1}$ are defined inductively as follows.

$$\begin{aligned} j_0 &= \text{the injection to the left from } S_0 = J \text{ to } S_{\lambda+1} = J + \textstyle\sum_d \mathrm{Lax}(d, S_\lambda(c)) \\ &\quad \otimes S(d), \\ j_{n+1} &= 1_J + \textstyle\sum_{d\in|\mathsf{LocOrd}_{\ell\omega}|} \mathrm{Lax}(d, \iota_n) \otimes S(d), \\ j_\mu &= \text{the mediating arrow from the colimiting cone } S_\mu \text{ to the cone} \\ &\quad \{\, S_n, j_n \mid n < \mu \,\} \end{aligned}$$

We say *algebraic structure* on LocOrd_ℓ consists of a signature S together with a LocOrd_ℓ-functor $E\colon |\mathsf{LocOrd}_{\ell\omega}| \to \mathsf{LocOrd}_\ell$ of *equations* and two LocOrd_ℓ-natural transformations $\tau_1, \tau_2\colon E \to S_{\omega_1}(K(-))$, where $K\colon |\mathsf{LocOrd}_{\ell\omega}| \to \mathsf{LocOrd}_{\ell\omega}$ is the inclusion. We denote such an algebraic structure by $\langle S, E\rangle$.

Remark 4. In practice, the image of $(\tau_1)_c$ and $(\tau_2)_c$ are often restricted to $S_n(c)$ for some $n < \omega_1$, and in that case, it is easier to define the codomain of τ_1 and τ_2 to be S_n, rather than S_{ω_1}.

Given a signature S, an *S-algebra* consists of a small locally ordered category A together with a locally ordered functor $\nu_c\colon \mathrm{Lax}(c, A) \to \mathrm{Lax}(S(c), A)$ for each $c \in |\mathsf{LocOrd}_{\ell\omega}|$. An S-algebra extends to an S_n-algebra by induction as follows.

- $(\nu_0)_c$: $\mathrm{Lax}(c, A) \to \mathrm{Lax}(S_0(c), A)$ is the identity.
- $(\nu_{n+1})_c$: $\mathrm{Lax}(c, A) \to \mathrm{Lax}(S_{n+1}(c), A)$ is given using the inductive definition of S_{n+1}, by identity functor from $\mathrm{Lax}(c, A)$ to $\mathrm{Lax}(c, A)$, and for each d with at most countable arrows, the functor

$$\mathrm{Lax}(c, A) \to \mathrm{Lax}(\mathrm{Lax}(d, S_n(c)), \mathrm{Lax}(S(d), A))$$

given by

$$\mathrm{Lax}(c, A) \xrightarrow{(\nu_n)_c} \mathrm{Lax}(S_n(c), A) \xrightarrow{\text{postcomposition}} \mathrm{Lax}(\mathrm{Lax}(d, S_n(c)), \mathrm{Lax}(d, A)) \xrightarrow{\mathrm{Lax}(\mathrm{id}, \nu_d)} \mathrm{Lax}(\mathrm{Lax}(d, S_n(c)), \mathrm{Lax}(S(d), A)).$$

So, this takes a functor $h: c \to A$ to the functor from $\mathrm{Lax}(d, S_n(c))$ to $\mathrm{Lax}(S(d), A)$, taking $\varphi: d \to S_n(c)$ to $\nu_d((\nu_n)_c(h) \circ \varphi): S(d) \to A$.
- For a limit ordinal λ, $(\nu_\lambda)_c$: $\mathrm{Lax}(c, A) \to \mathrm{Lax}(S_\lambda, A)$ is defined to be the mediating arrow from the cone
  - whose base consists of $\mathrm{Lax}(S_n(c), A)$ and $\mathrm{Lax}((\sigma_n)_c, A)$,
  - whose pivot is $\mathrm{Lax}(c, A)$,
  - and whose projection to $\mathrm{Lax}(S_n(c), A)$ is $(\nu_n)_c$: $\mathrm{Lax}(c, A) \to \mathrm{Lax}(S_n(c), A)$,

  to the limiting cone
  - whose base is the same as that of the cone above,
  - whose pivot is $\mathrm{Lax}(S_\lambda(c), A)$,
  - and whose projection to $\mathrm{Lax}(S_n(c), A)$ is $\mathrm{Lax}(\iota_n, A)$: $\mathrm{Lax}(S_\lambda(c), A) \to \mathrm{Lax}(S_n(c), A)$.

An $\langle S, E\rangle$-algebra is an S-algebra such that both legs of

$$\mathrm{Lax}(c, A) \xrightarrow{(\nu_n)_c} \mathrm{Lax}(S_n(K(c)), A) \underset{\mathrm{Lax}((\tau_2)_c, A)}{\overset{\mathrm{Lax}((\tau_1)_c, A)}{\rightrightarrows}} \mathrm{Lax}(E(c), A)$$

agree.

Example 6 (Algebraic structure Fix*).* In this example, we describe the algebraic structure $\langle S, E\rangle$.

Let Ω be the locally ordered category freely generated by the locally ordered graph

$$\Omega_0 = \langle \{ a, b \}, \{ f_n \mid n \in \omega \}, \delta_0, \delta_1 \rangle,$$

which has the discrete order in the set of edges, and $\delta_0(f_n) = a$, $\delta_1(f_n) = b$ for all $n \in \omega$. Locally ordered categories Ω' and Ω'' are similarly obtained from the locally ordered graph

$$\Omega'_0 = \langle \{ a', b' \}, \{ g_n \mid n \in \omega + 1 \}, \delta'_0, \delta'_1 \rangle$$

with the order on edges defined by

$$g_m \leq g_n \qquad \text{iff} \qquad (m \in \omega \wedge n = \omega) \vee (m = n),$$

and with the domain and codomain functions defined by $\delta'_0(g_n) = a$, $\delta'_1(g_n) = b$ for all $n \in \omega + 1$, and the locally ordered graph

$$\Omega''_0 = \langle \{ a'', b'' \}, \{ h_n \mid n \in \omega + 1 \}, \delta''_0, \delta''_1 \rangle$$

with the order on edges defined by

$$h_m \leq h_n \qquad \text{iff} \qquad (m \in \omega \wedge (n = \omega \vee n = \omega + 1)) \vee (m = \omega \wedge (n = \omega + 1) \vee m = n$$

and with the domain and codomain functions defined by $\delta'_0(g_n) = a$, $\delta'_1(g_n) = b$ for all $n \in \omega + 2$,

Each of Ω, Ω' and Ω'' is an object of $\mathsf{LocOrd}_{\ell\omega}$. Then we define the signature S by

$$S(c) = \begin{cases} \Omega' \text{ if } c = \Omega, \\ \Omega'' \text{ if } c = \Omega', \\ \emptyset \quad \text{otherwise.} \end{cases}$$

The next task is to define equations. For each object c of $\mathsf{LocOrd}_{\ell\omega}$, we define the locally ordered category $E(c)$ of equations of arity c by

$$E(c) = \begin{cases} \Omega' & \text{if } c = \Omega, \\ \Omega' + \Omega' & \text{if } c = \Omega', \\ \emptyset & \text{otherwise.} \end{cases}$$

Furthermore, we must define the natural transformations τ_1 and τ_2. Remark 4 applies to our case and, we define their codomain to be S_1, so $\tau_1, \tau_2 \colon E \Rightarrow S_1$. We start by computing S_1 for our signature S. For each c,

$$\begin{aligned} S_1(c) &= c + \sum_{d \in |\mathsf{LocOrd}_{\ell\omega}|} \mathrm{Lax}(d, S_0(c)) \otimes S(d) \\ &= c + \sum_{d \in |\mathsf{LocOrd}_{\ell\omega}|} \mathrm{Lax}(d, c) \otimes S(d) \\ &= c + \mathrm{Lax}(\Omega, c) \otimes \Omega' + \mathrm{Lax}(\Omega', c) \otimes \Omega'' \end{aligned}$$

We write $\mathrm{inj}_1 \colon c \to S_1(c)$, $\mathrm{inj}_2 \colon \mathrm{Lax}(\Omega, c) \otimes \Omega'$, and $\mathrm{inj}_3 \colon \mathrm{Lax}(\Omega', c) \otimes \Omega''$ to denote the injections to $S_1(c)$. Since $E(c) =$ if c is neither Ω nor Ω', we have only to define $(\tau_i)_\Omega$ and $(\tau_i)_{\Omega'}$, for $i = 1, 2$.

- $(\tau_1)_\Omega, (\tau_2)_\Omega \colon E(\Omega) = \Omega \longrightarrow S_1(\Omega) = \Omega + \mathrm{Lax}(\Omega, \Omega) \otimes \Omega' + \mathrm{Lax}(\Omega', \Omega) \otimes \Omega''$ are defined by

$$\begin{aligned} (\tau_1)_\Omega(a) &= \mathrm{inj}_1(a), \\ (\tau_1)_\Omega(b) &= \mathrm{inj}_1(b), \\ (\tau_1)_\Omega(f_n) &= \mathrm{inj}_1(f_n), \end{aligned}$$

$$(\tau_2)_\Omega(a) = \mathrm{inj}_2(\langle \mathrm{id}_\Omega, a'\rangle),$$
$$(\tau_2)_\Omega(b) = \mathrm{inj}_2(\langle \mathrm{id}_\Omega, b'\rangle),$$
$$(\tau_2)_\Omega(f_n) = \mathrm{inj}_2(\langle 1_{\mathrm{id}_\Omega}, f_n\rangle),$$

- Let $j\colon \Omega \to \Omega'$ be the obvious inclusion, and we use inj_1 and inj_2 to denote the two injections $\Omega' \to \Omega' + \Omega'$, as well as the injections to $S_1(c)$. Then $(\tau_1)_{\Omega'}, (\tau_2)_{\Omega'}\colon E(\Omega') = \Omega' + \Omega' \longrightarrow S_1(\Omega') = \Omega' + \mathrm{Lax}(\Omega, \Omega') \otimes \Omega' + \mathrm{Lax}(\Omega', \Omega') \otimes \Omega''$ are defined by

$$(\tau_1)_{\Omega'}(\mathrm{inj}_1(a')) = \mathrm{inj}_2(\langle j, a'\rangle),$$
$$(\tau_1)_{\Omega'}(\mathrm{inj}_1(b')) = \mathrm{inj}_2(\langle j, b'\rangle),$$
$$(\tau_1)_{\Omega'}(\mathrm{inj}_1(g_n)) = \mathrm{inj}_2(\langle 1_j, g_n\rangle),$$
$$(\tau_1)_{\Omega'}(\mathrm{inj}_2(a')) = \mathrm{inj}_1(a'),$$
$$(\tau_1)_{\Omega'}(\mathrm{inj}_2(b')) = \mathrm{inj}_1(b'),$$
$$(\tau_1)_{\Omega'}(\mathrm{inj}_2(g_n)) = \mathrm{inj}_1(g_n),$$
$$(\tau_2)_{\Omega'}(\mathrm{inj}_1(a')) = \mathrm{inj}_3(\langle \mathrm{id}_{\Omega'}, a''\rangle),$$
$$(\tau_2)_{\Omega'}(\mathrm{inj}_1(b')) = \mathrm{inj}_3(\langle \mathrm{id}_{\Omega'}, b''\rangle),$$
$$(\tau_2)_{\Omega'}(\mathrm{inj}_1(g_n)) = \mathrm{inj}_3(\langle 1_{\mathrm{id}_{\Omega'}}, h_n\rangle),$$
$$(\tau_2)_{\Omega'}(\mathrm{inj}_2(a')) = \mathrm{inj}_3(\langle \mathrm{id}_{\Omega'}, a''\rangle),$$
$$(\tau_2)_{\Omega'}(\mathrm{inj}_2(b')) = \mathrm{inj}_3(\langle \mathrm{id}_{\Omega'}, b''\rangle),$$
$$(\tau_2)_{\Omega'}(\mathrm{inj}_2(g_n)) = \begin{cases} \mathrm{inj}_3(\langle 1_{\mathrm{id}_{\Omega'}}, h_n\rangle), & \text{if } n < \omega, \\ \mathrm{inj}_3(\langle 1_{\mathrm{id}_{\Omega'}}, h_{\omega+1}\rangle), & \text{if } n = \omega, \end{cases}$$

This completes the description of the equational presentation $\langle S, E\rangle$. Observe that an $\langle S, E\rangle$-algebra $\langle A, \nu\rangle$ is exactly a locally ordered category A whose homset has arbitrary countable least upper bounds. We call an $\langle S, E\rangle$-algebra to be a Fix-algebra.

As shown in [9], we further define homobjects $\langle S, E\rangle\text{-}\mathsf{Alg}(\langle A, \nu\rangle, \langle B, \mu\rangle)$ by taking the appropriate equaliser. In the case of Example 6, this homobject amounts to the locally ordered category whose objects are locally ordered functors from A to B which strictly preserves the countable least upper bounds of homsets. It is easy to see that these data make a LocOrd_ℓ-category Fix-Alg.

The main result of [5] is specialised to LocOrd_ℓ-setting as follows.

Theorem 5. *The forgetful* LocOrd_ℓ*-functor* $\mathcal{U}\colon \langle S, E\rangle\text{-}\mathsf{Alg} \to \mathsf{LocOrd}_\ell$ *is* LocOrd_ℓ*-monadic over* LocOrd_ℓ*.*

Therefore, $\mathcal{U}$ has a LocOrd_ℓ-left adjoint $\mathcal{F}\colon \mathsf{LocOrd}_\ell \to \langle S, E\rangle\text{-}\mathsf{Alg} \to \mathsf{LocOrd}_\ell$. In particular, when the algebraic structure $\langle S, E\rangle$ is one given in Example 6, this amounts to saying that the forgetful LocOrd_ℓ-functor from Fix-Alg to LocOrd_ℓ has a LocOrd_ℓ-left adjoint

$$\mathcal{F}\colon \mathsf{LocOrd}_\ell \to \text{Fix-}\mathsf{Alg},$$

and this $\mathcal{F}$ gives the essential mathematical basis for this paper.

An Institution of Hybrid Systems*

Hugo Lourenço and Amílcar Sernadas

Logic and Computation Group, CMA, Dep. Matemática,
IST, Av. Rovisco Pais, 1049-001 Lisboa, Portugal
{hlouren,acs}@math.ist.utl.pt

Abstract. Hybrid systems are systems that intermix discrete and continuous behavior. Interest in hybrid systems has grown in recent years, mainly because of their relation with embedded systems (systems that interact with the *continuously* changing real-world). In order to deal with complex problems, compositional specification and verification methods are needed. Using the specification language of HyTech as a starting point, an institution of hybrid systems is established. Generalizing the results for classical systems, free aggregation, interconnection and abstraction of hybrid systems are presented as categorial constructions within the proposed institution, at both the specification and the model levels. The HyTech parallel composition constructor is shown to be a particular case of interconnection. Compositional model checking of a complex system is shown to be possible by capitalizing on categorial structure. A class of properties that can be verified with HyTech is identified.

1 Introduction

A *hybrid system* is a system that intermixes discrete and continuous components (typically a digital computer interacting with the analog physical world). Hybrid system are everywhere: they arise in air traffic control, automobiles, robotics, consumer electronics (e.g. VCR, microwave oven, heater)...

Hybrid systems exhibit a phased evolution: discrete steps alternate with continuous evolution. We can describe such a system in terms of its (real-valued) attributes, modes of operation and action symbols. Each mode of operation describes how the attributes evolve and the actions label discrete transitions.

While a discrete transition does not occur the hybrid system remains in the same mode of operation and the attributes values change continuously according to the evolution law of the mode of operation. When a discrete transition takes place both the mode of operation and the attributes values may change. Each discrete transition is (possibly) labelled with an action symbol. Action symbols are useful for interconnecting hybrid systems.

* This work was partially supported by *Fundação para a Ciência e a Tecnologia*, the PRAXIS XXI Projects PCEX/P/MAT/46/96 ACL, PRAXIS/P/MAT/10002/1998 ProbLog and 2/2.1/TIT/1658/95 LogComp, as well as by the ESPRIT IV Working Groups 22704 ASPIRE and 23531 FIREworks.

D. Bert, C. Choppy, and P. Mosses (Eds.): WADT'99, LNCS 1827, pp. 219–236, 2000.

As an example, consider a heater. A possible attribute is the current temperature. We can consider an "heating" mode of operation during which the heater is on and the temperature is continuously increasing, and a "cooling" mode of operation during which the heater is off and temperature decreases. Also, we can act on the heater by turning it on or off. A mode of operation can also be seen as a particular valuation of a set of boolean attributes. In the previous example, we would say that the heater is in an "heating" mode whenever "heating=true". At every instant, the state of the heater is described by a pair of values: the temperature and the current mode of operation.

Interest in hybrid systems has grown in recent years, mainly because of their relation with embedded systems. These systems often arise in safety critical situations, so formal verification methods for hybrid systems have been the subject of intense research [1,2,6,9,7,4,3,5].

However, in order to deal with real world problems compositional verification methods are known to be needed. We thus seek to construct an institution of hybrid system and characterize categorially some forms of combining hybrid systems. Namely, we seek to characterize free aggregation as a product, restriction as a cartesian lifting and abstraction as a cocartesian lifting. Interconnection is seen as a two-step process: free aggregation followed by restriction. These constructions extend to hybrid systems the well known definitions of aggregation and interconnection of transition systems as presented in [13].

The paper is organized as follows. First, we briefly describe HyTech, upon which the syntax for our institution is based. We then proceed with the definition of the institution of hybrid computations, from which we build the institution of hybrid systems (preliminary work on the semantic component of the institution can be found in [11,10]). Then we present the already referred forms of combining hybrid systems. Finally, we look at model checking procedures for hybrid systems and show how the categorial structure of a complex system can be used to ease the verification process.

We assume familiarity with some basic concepts of category theory (namely, (co)products and (co)cartesian morphisms - see [12]).

2 HyTech

HyTech [8] is a tool for model checking hybrid systems. A hybrid system is described in terms of its attributes, modes of operation (which are also referred to as *locations*) and action symbols. The user then describes the discrete behavior of the system (stating when is each action enabled and what are the effects of its occurrence) and the continuous behavior of the system (by providing a constraint on the values of the derivatives of the attributes for each location). Additionally, the user can also supply an *invariant* for each location (a constraint on the values of the attributes). These are usually used to trigger discrete transitions, as the system cannot evolve into a state not satisfying the invariant.

A typical input file for HyTech consists of the description of several hybrid systems. The tool then enables the user to verify the *parallel composition* of the

```
var T, C: analog;
automaton c
   synclabs: heat, cool;
   loc off:
      while True wait {dC=0}
      when T<=40 sync heat do {C'=0} goto on;
   loc on:
      while 0<=C & C<=10 wait {dC=1}
      when True sync cool goto off;
end
automaton h
   synclabs: heat, cool;
   ...
end
```

Fig. 1. The heater and its controller in HyTech

component systems: the system obtained by sharing attributes and actions. The sharing of actions means that the component systems synchronize on discrete transitions labelled with the same action symbol.

Not all hybrid systems can be input into HyTech: the syntax restricts the user to *linear hybrid systems* - systems in which the constraints are (in)equalities between linear combinations of attributes or their derivatives (but not mixing attributes with derivatives).

Before presenting a concrete example, consider the following examples of hybrid systems.

Example 1. Consider a heater. The heater can be either on or off. When it is on, the temperature T *rises according to the law* $\mathbf{D}T = 4 - T/20$*; when it is off,* T *follows* $\mathbf{D}T = -T/20$*. The heater can be turned on and off by its heat and cool actions.*

Example 2. Consider a controller for the preceding heater. For safety reasons, the heater cannot be turned on if the temperature is over 40*. Also, the heater cannot stay on for more than* 10 *time units, so this controller has a clock* C *to measure how long the heater has been on. If the clock reaches* 10 *without the heater being turned off in the meantime, then the controller forces the heater to turn off.*

In fig. 1 a partial description of these two systems is presented.[1] The statement `var` introduces the attributes of the systems (remember that they are shared). In each system (or `automaton`) the statement `synclabs` enumerates the available action symbols. For each location a statement of the form `while` *`invariant_cond`* `wait` {*`deriv_constr`*} provides the location invariant and the

[1] Note that the heater of example 1 cannot be described in HyTech because it is not a linear hybrid system. Some simplified version would have to be used.

constraint on the derivatives. In *deriv_constr* the derivative of an attribute x is denoted dx. Discrete transitions departing from each location are denoted by statements of the form **when** ***pre_cond*** **sync** ***action*** **do** $\{$***post_cond***$\}$ **goto** ***end_loc***. In *post_cond* a primed attribute x' refers to the value of x just after the discrete transition. Despite the somewhat misleading syntax, a system can is not obliged to take a discrete transition when it becomes enabled - it may remain in the current location as long as the invariant is satisfied.

HYTECH does not provide a logic for specifying the properties to be verified. Instead, given a input file describing a hybrid system and a condition defining a set of initial states, HYTECH provides operators for calculating the set of reachable states and comparing sets. Thus, to verify a property the user has to express it in terms of (un)reachability. Later on these concepts will be clarified.

3 The Institution of Hybrid Computations

In this section we establish the institution $I^b = \langle Sig, Sen, Int^b, \Vdash^b \rangle$ of hybrid computations. In the sequel, *Fin* denotes the category of finite sets and maps and *PFin* denotes the category of finite sets and partial maps.

3.1 The Signature Category

A hybrid system is described in terms of its attributes, modes of operation and action symbols. We thus have the objects for *Sig*. As for the signature morphisms, lets look at what we want to get as signature coproducts.

If we take the signatures of two systems, we want their coproduct to correspond to the signature of the free aggregation of the two systems. So we want to have all the attributes together but keeping the distinction between attributes with the same name, a mode of operation will be a pair of modes of operation, and an action of the resulting system can either be an action from only one of the components or a pair of actions (again, actions with the same name are kept distinct).

Definition 1. *Sig* is the category $Fin \times Fin^{op} \times PFin^{op}$.

Given a signature $\langle X, V, A \rangle$, X is a set of real-valued attributes, V is a set of vertices and A is a set of action symbols. Each vertex corresponds to a mode of operation. The action symbols are used to label discrete transitions. Together, a vertex $v \in V$ and a valuation $\alpha \in \mathbb{R}^X$ define a state of the hybrid system. We use St_Σ for the set $V \times \mathbb{R}^X$ (of Σ-states). A morphism $\sigma : \Sigma \to \Sigma'$ has the form $\langle \overrightarrow{\sigma}_{\text{att}} : X \to X', \overleftarrow{\sigma}_{\text{vtx}} : V' \to V, \overleftarrow{\sigma}_{\text{act}} : A' \rightharpoonup A \rangle$.[2] For a signature op-morphism $f : \Sigma' \to \Sigma$ we reverse the arrows: $\langle \overleftarrow{f}_{\text{att}} : X \to X', \overrightarrow{f}_{\text{vtx}} : V' \to V, \overrightarrow{f}_{\text{act}} : A' \rightharpoonup A \rangle$.

Example 3. Consider again the heater of example 1. A possible signature for the heater is $\Sigma_h = \langle X_h, V_h, A_h \rangle$ *with* $X_h = \{T\}$, $V_h = \{on, off\}$ *and* $A_h = \{heat, cool\}$.

[2] Sometimes we omit the subscripts in σ.

Example 4. If we hide the attribute T in the preceding system, we retain only the discrete behavior of the heater. A possible signature for this simplified system is $\Sigma_{h'} = \langle X_{h'}, V_{h'}, A_{h'} \rangle$ *with* $X_{h'} = \emptyset$, $V_{h'} = \{\text{on}, \text{off}\}$ *and* $A_{h'} = \{\text{heat}, \text{cool}\}$.

Example 5. Consider again the controller of example 2. A possible signature for the controller is $\Sigma_C = \langle X_C, V_C, A_C \rangle$ *with* $X_C = \{T, C\}$, $V_C = \{\text{on}, \text{off}\}$ *and* $A_C = \{\text{heat}, \text{cool}\}$. *A simplified version c' of c can be defined as we did for the heater. In this case,* $\Sigma_{c'} = \Sigma_{h'}$.

3.2 The Semantic Functor

In the hybrid systems literature, a hybrid system run (or computation) is usually seen as an alternating sequence of *continuous phases* and *discrete jumps*.

Definition 2. Let $\Sigma = \langle X, V, A \rangle \in |Sig|$. A *$\Sigma$-phase* is a triple $p = \langle v, h, Dh \rangle$ with $v \in V$ and $h, Dh : I \to \mathbb{R}^X$, where $I \subseteq \mathbb{R}_0^+$ is a closed interval and such that (*i*) $0 \in I$, (*ii*) for each $x \in X$, $Dh^x \stackrel{\text{def}}{=} \lambda t.Dh(t)(x)$ is continuous and (*iii*) for each $x \in X$, $h^x \stackrel{\text{def}}{=} \lambda t.h(t)(x)$ satisfies $h^x(t) = h^x(0) + \int_0^t Dh^x(t)dt$.

We use I_p for denoting the interval I and P_Σ for the set of Σ-phases.

In the following definition, $\overline{\mathbb{N}}_0$ stands for $\mathbb{N}_0 \cup \{+\infty\}$, and a range $0..n$ denotes the set $\{i \in \mathbb{N}_0 \mid i \leq n\}$ (note that $+\infty \notin 0..+\infty$).

Definition 3. Let $\Sigma = \langle X, V, A \rangle$ be a signature. A *Σ-computation* is a triple $\langle n, p, a \rangle$ with $n \in \overline{\mathbb{N}}_0$, $p : 0..n \to P_\Sigma$ and $a : 0..(n-1) \rightharpoonup A$ such that (*i*) if $I_{p_i} = \mathbb{R}_0^+$ then $i = n$ and (*ii*) $\sum length(I_{p_i}) = +\infty$.

We denote the length of I_{p_i} by d_i, and use Ξ_Σ for the set of Σ-computations.

The number of phases in the computation is given by $n + 1$, the phases by p and the action symbols (possibly) labelling the end of the phases by a.[3] We can have a finite number of phases, but in that case the last phase is of infinite length. All computations are infinite in time. We usually refer to the phase p_i by $\langle v_i, h_i, Dh_i \rangle$.

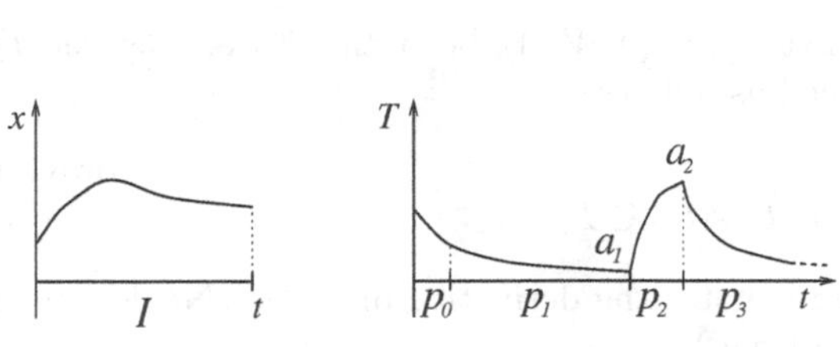

Fig. 2. A phase and a computation. Note the absence of label a_0

[3] The possibility to have discrete jumps without labels will become clear when we discuss the aggregation of hybrid systems

Definition 4. A morphism $\sigma : \Sigma \to \Sigma'$ induces the maps $\overleftarrow{\sigma}_{\text{asg}} : \mathbb{R}^{X'} \to \mathbb{R}^{X}$, $\overleftarrow{\sigma}_{\text{st}} : St_{\Sigma'} \to St_{\Sigma}$, $\overleftarrow{\sigma}_{\text{ph}} : P_{\Sigma'} \to P_{\Sigma}$ and $\overleftarrow{\sigma}_{\text{cmp}} : \Xi_{\Sigma'} \to \Xi_{\Sigma}$ defined as follows:

- $\overleftarrow{\sigma}_{\text{asg}}(\alpha') = \alpha' \circ \overrightarrow{\sigma}_{\text{att}}$;
- $\overleftarrow{\sigma}_{\text{st}}(\langle v', \alpha' \rangle) = \langle \overleftarrow{\sigma}_{\text{vtx}}(v'), \overleftarrow{\sigma}_{\text{asg}}(\alpha') \rangle$;
- $\overleftarrow{\sigma}_{\text{ph}}(\langle v', h', Dh' \rangle) = \langle \overleftarrow{\sigma}_{\text{vtx}}(v'), \overleftarrow{\sigma}_{\text{asg}} \circ h', \overleftarrow{\sigma}_{\text{asg}} \circ Dh' \rangle$;
- $\overleftarrow{\sigma}_{\text{cmp}}(\langle n', p', a' \rangle) = \langle n', \overleftarrow{\sigma}_{\text{ph}} \circ p', \overleftarrow{\sigma}_{\text{act}} \circ a' \rangle$.

So a signature morphism enables us to (backward)translate assignments, states, phases and computations.

As remarked before, we reverse the arrows for morphisms in Sig^{op} so that the direction of the arrow reflects the "translation" direction. So we write $\overleftarrow{\sigma}_{\text{cmp}}$ for a signature morphism σ but $\overrightarrow{f}_{\text{cmp}}$ for a computation morphism f.

Prop/Definition 1. Let Σ, Σ' be signatures and $\xi \in \Xi_{\Sigma}$, $\xi' \in \Xi_{\Sigma'}$. A computation morphism $f : \xi' \to \xi$ is a Sig^{op} morphism $\Sigma' \to \Sigma$[4] such that $\overrightarrow{f}_{\text{cmp}}(\xi') = \xi$. Computations and their morphisms constitute a category *Comp*.

In order to establish the semantic functor $Int^b : Sig \to Cat^{op}$ we start by defining a cofibration $cS : Comp \to Sig^{op}$ that has a splitting cocleavage. Then we obtain Int^b in a canonical way (see [12] for details).

Prop/Definition 2. We obtain a (forgetful) functor $cS : Comp \to Sig^{op}$ by defining that $cS(\xi) = \Sigma$ for every $\xi \in \Xi_{\Sigma}$ and $cS(f : \xi \to \xi') = f$.

We have that cS is a cofibration: given $\sigma : \Sigma' \to \Sigma$ in Sig^{op} and $\xi' \in \Xi_{\Sigma'}$, the computation morphism $\sigma : \xi' \to \overrightarrow{\sigma}_{\text{cmp}}(\xi')$ is cocartesian by cS for σ on ξ'. Moreover, cS has a splitting cocleavage.

We write $Comp_{\Sigma}$ for $cS^{-1}(\Sigma)$ (the fiber of *Comp* over Σ).

Prop/Definition 3. We obtain the functor $Int^b : Sig \to Cat^{op}$ from cS. Namely, $Int^b(\Sigma) = Comp_{\Sigma}$ and $Int^b(\sigma : \Sigma \to \Sigma')(\xi') = \overleftarrow{\sigma}_{\text{cmp}}(\xi')$.

3.3 The Syntactic Functor

Definition 5. Let $\Sigma = \langle X, V, A \rangle$ be a signature. The set T_{Σ} of Σ-terms is inductively defined as follows:

- $q, x, \mathbf{D}x \in T_{\Sigma}$ provided $q \in \mathbb{Q}, x \in X$;
- $\mathbf{N}t_1, (t_1 + t_2), (t_1 \times t_2) \in T_{\Sigma}$ provided $t_1, t_2 \in T_{\Sigma}$.

The term $\mathbf{D}x$ denotes the derivative of x, and $\mathbf{N}t$ denotes the value of t at the next point in time.[5]

Definition 6. Let $\Sigma = \langle X, V, A \rangle$ be a signature. The set L_{Σ} of Σ-formulae is inductively defined as follows:

[4] That is, $f^{op} : \Sigma \to \Sigma'$ is a *Sig* morphism.

[5] Because we are dealing with a continuous time domain, it may seem strange to talk about a "next point in time". Later on, the meaning will become clear.

- $t_1 \leq t_2 \in L_\Sigma$ provided $t_1, t_2 \in T_\Sigma$;
- $@W, \mathbf{N}@W \in L_\Sigma$ provided $W \subseteq V$;
- $\nabla B \in L_\Sigma$ provided $B \subseteq A$;
- $(\neg \varphi), (\varphi \Rightarrow \psi) \in L_\Sigma$ provided $\varphi, \psi \in L_\Sigma$;
- $(\varphi \mathbf{U}^{\alpha..\beta} \psi), (\varphi \mathbf{S}^{\alpha..\beta} \psi) \in L_\Sigma$ provided $\varphi, \psi \in L_\Sigma$, $\alpha \in \mathbb{Q}_0^+$ and $\beta \in \overline{\mathbb{Q}_0^+}$.

A formula $@W$ is intended to mean that the current mode of operation (or vertex) is in W (we omit the braces when W is a singleton), whereas $\mathbf{N}@W$ means that at the next point in time the vertex will be in W. A formula ∇B states that an action in B is occurring. In order to be able to specify precise timing constraints, the "until" (**U**) and "since" (**S**) operators have a time bound. The usual operators arise if we use $0.. + \infty$ as the time bound.

We use the usual abbreviations: $\mathbf{F}\varphi \stackrel{\text{def}}{=} (\varphi \vee \neg \varphi)\ \mathbf{U}\ \varphi$ for "sometime in the future", $\mathbf{G}\varphi \stackrel{\text{def}}{=} \neg(\mathbf{F}(\neg \varphi))$ for "always in the future", etc. The following formula is true precisely at the points where the system is behaving continuously:

$$\mathbf{Cnt}_\Sigma \stackrel{\text{def}}{=} (\bigwedge_{x \in X} x = \mathbf{N}x) \wedge (\bigwedge_{x \in X} \mathbf{D}x = \mathbf{ND}x) \wedge (\bigwedge_{v \in V} @v \Leftrightarrow \mathbf{N}@v)$$

Example 6. Recall the systems described in examples 3, 4 and 5. Let us now see a possible specification of such systems:

- $\Gamma_h = \{\ @on \Rightarrow \mathbf{D}T = 4 - T/20,$
  $@off \Rightarrow \mathbf{D}T = -T/20,$
  $\nabla heat \Rightarrow (@off \wedge \mathbf{N}@on \wedge \mathbf{N}T = T),$
  $(\neg \nabla A_h) \Rightarrow \mathbf{Cnt}_{\Sigma_h},$
  $\nabla cool \Rightarrow (@on \wedge \mathbf{N}@off \wedge \mathbf{N}T = T)\}$
- $\Gamma_{h'} = \{\ \nabla heat \Rightarrow (@off \wedge \mathbf{N}@on),$
  $(\neg \nabla A_{h'}) \Rightarrow \mathbf{Cnt}_{\Sigma_{h'}},$
  $\nabla cool \Rightarrow (@on \wedge \mathbf{N}@off)\}$
- $\Gamma_C = \{\ @on \Rightarrow \mathbf{D}C = 1,$
  $@off \Rightarrow \mathbf{D}C = 0,$
  $\nabla heat \Rightarrow (@off \wedge T \leq 40 \wedge \mathbf{N}@on \wedge \mathbf{N}C = 0),$
  $\nabla cool \Rightarrow (@on \wedge \mathbf{N}@off),$
  $(\neg \nabla A_C) \Rightarrow \mathbf{Cnt}_{\Sigma_C},$
  $@on \Rightarrow (0 \leq C \leq 10)\}$

A signature morphism $\sigma : \Sigma \to \Sigma'$ induces the maps $\overrightarrow{\sigma}_{\text{trm}} : T_\Sigma \to T_{\Sigma'}$ and $\overrightarrow{\sigma}_{\text{lng}} : L_\Sigma \to L_{\Sigma'}$ defined as expected. Namely, $\overrightarrow{\sigma}_{\text{lng}}(@W) = @\overleftarrow{\sigma}_{\text{vtx}}^{-1}(W)$, $\overrightarrow{\sigma}_{\text{lng}}(\mathbf{N}@W) = \mathbf{N}@\overleftarrow{\sigma}_{\text{vtx}}^{-1}(W)$ and $\overrightarrow{\sigma}_{\text{lng}}(\nabla B) = \nabla \overleftarrow{\sigma}_{\text{act}}^{-1}(B)$. We thus have:

Prop/Definition 4. The (syntactic) functor $Sen : Sig \to Set$ is defined by $Sen(\Sigma) = L_\Sigma$ and $Sen(\sigma : \Sigma \to \Sigma') = \overrightarrow{\sigma}_{\text{lng}}$.

3.4 The Satisfaction Relation

In order to define the satisfaction relation, we start by defining the term interpretation map. Terms are interpreted at "points" in computations.

Definition 7. Let $\xi = \langle n, p, a\rangle$ be a computation. The *point space* associated with ξ is the set $spa_\xi = \{\langle i,t\rangle \in \mathbb{N}_0 \times \mathbb{R}_0^+ \mid i \le n, 0 \le t \le d_i\}$. For $\langle i,t\rangle \in spa_\xi$, i corresponds to number of the phase and t to time elapsed since the beginning of the phase. We obtain a total ordering over spa_ξ by defining that $\langle i,t\rangle \le \langle i',t'\rangle$ iff $i < i'$ or ($i = i'$ and $t \le t'$), and write $\xi(\langle i,t\rangle)$ for the Σ-state $\langle v_i, h_i(t)\rangle$.

Also, a function $T_\xi : spa_\xi \to \mathbb{R}_0^+$ mapping points in spa_ξ to the real-time axis can be defined by $T_\xi(\langle i,t\rangle) = t + \sum_{j<i} d_j$.

Definition 8. Let $\Sigma = \langle X, V, A\rangle$ be a signature, $\xi \in \Xi_\Sigma$ a computation and $\langle i,t\rangle \in spa_\xi$. Then the *term interpretation map* $[\![\_]\!]_\Sigma^{\xi,\langle i,t\rangle} : T_\Sigma \to \mathbb{R}$, mapping Σ-terms to their value, is inductively defined as follows:

- $[\![x]\!]_\Sigma^{\xi,\langle i,t\rangle} = h_i^x(t)$ for $x \in X$;
- $[\![\mathbf{D}x]\!]_\Sigma^{\xi,\langle i,t\rangle} = Dh_i^x(t)$ for $x \in X$;
- $[\![\mathbf{N}t]\!]_\Sigma^{\xi,\langle i,t\rangle} = \begin{cases} [\![t]\!]_\Sigma^{\xi,\langle i+1,0\rangle} & \text{pt } t = d_i \\ [\![t]\!]_\Sigma^{\xi,\langle i,t\rangle} & \text{otherwise} \end{cases}$ for $t \in T_\Sigma$;
- etc.

Note the interpretation of the term $\mathbf{N}t$. Here it is clear what we mean by "next point in time": if we are at the end of a phase, then the next point in time is the first point of the *next* phase; otherwise, it is just the current point.

Definition 9. Let $\Sigma = \langle X, V, A\rangle$ be a signature. The satisfaction relation $\Vdash^b \subseteq \Xi_\Sigma \times L_\Sigma$ is defined by $\xi \Vdash^b_\Sigma \varphi$ iff $\xi, \langle i,t\rangle \Vdash^b_\Sigma \varphi$ for all $\langle i,t\rangle \in spa_\xi$ where:

- $\xi, \langle i,t\rangle \Vdash_\Sigma t_1 \le t_2$ iff $[\![t_1]\!]_\Sigma^{\xi,\langle i,t\rangle} \le [\![t_2]\!]_\Sigma^{\xi,\langle i,t\rangle}$
- $\xi, \langle i,t\rangle \Vdash_\Sigma @W$ iff $v_i \in W$
- $\xi, \langle i,t\rangle \Vdash_\Sigma \mathbf{N}@W$ iff $(t = d_i, v_{i+1} \in W)$ or $(t < d_i, v_i \in W)$
- $\xi, \langle i,t\rangle \Vdash_\Sigma \nabla B$ iff $t = d_i$, a_i is defined and $a_i \in B$
- $\xi, \langle i,t\rangle \Vdash_\Sigma (\varphi \mathbf{U}^{\alpha..\beta}\psi)$ iff for some $\langle i',t'\rangle \ge \langle i,t\rangle$ $T_\xi(\langle i',t'\rangle) - T_\xi(\langle i,t\rangle) \in [\alpha,\beta]$, $\xi, \langle i',t'\rangle \Vdash_\Sigma \psi$ and $\xi, \langle i'',t''\rangle \Vdash_\Sigma \varphi$ for all $\langle i,t\rangle \le \langle i'',t''\rangle < \langle i',t'\rangle$

3.5 The Satisfaction Condition

Proposition 1. Let $\sigma : \Sigma \to \Sigma'$ be a signature morphism, $\xi' \in \Xi_{\Sigma'}$ and $\varphi \in L_\Sigma$. Then $\xi' \Vdash^b_{\Sigma'} \overrightarrow{\sigma}_{\mathrm{lng}}(\varphi)$ iff $\overleftarrow{\sigma}_{\mathrm{cmp}}(\xi') \Vdash^b_\Sigma \varphi$.

4 The Institution of Hybrid Systems

Capitalizing on the previous institution I^b, we build the institution of hybrid systems, $I = \langle Sig, Sen, Int, \Vdash\rangle$.

We define a hybrid systems to be a set of computations (with some additional properties). Thus I is easily obtained: the *Sig* category and the *Sen* functor are just as in I^b; the *Int* functor is built upon Int^b; the satisfaction relation $\Vdash$ is just an extension of $\Vdash^b$; finally, the satisfaction condition is a consequence of the satisfaction condition for I^b.

4.1 The Semantic Functor

A hybrid system consists of a set of computations. However, not every set of computations will do, because our logic cannot distinguish every two sets of computations. We thus start by considering a notion of *pre-computation system* that is then refined into the desired notion of *computation system.*

Definition 10. Let Σ be a signature. A *Σ-pre-computation system* is a pair $\langle\Sigma, \Xi\rangle$ where $\Xi \subseteq \Xi_\Sigma$.

Given $\Xi \subseteq \Xi_\Sigma$, we can determine the set of formulae satisfied by Ξ. Reciprocally, given $\Gamma \subseteq L_\Sigma$, we can determine the set of computations that satisfy Γ. These notions are captured in the following definition where, as usual, we define that $\Xi \Vdash^b_\Sigma \varphi$ iff $\xi \Vdash^b_\Sigma \varphi$ for every $\xi \in \Xi$ and $\xi \Vdash^b_\Sigma \Gamma$ iff $\xi \Vdash^b_\Sigma \varphi$ for every $\varphi \in \Gamma$.

Definition 11. Let Σ be a signature. We define the maps $S_\Sigma : 2^{L_\Sigma} \rightarrow 2^{\Xi_\Sigma}$ and $T_\Sigma : 2^{\Xi_\Sigma} \rightarrow 2^{L_\Sigma}$ by $S_\Sigma(\Gamma) = \{\xi \in \Xi_\Sigma \mid \xi \Vdash^b_\Sigma \Gamma\}$ and $T_\Sigma(\Xi) = \{\varphi \in L_\Sigma \mid \Xi \Vdash^b_\Sigma \varphi\}$. Given $\Xi \subseteq \Xi_\Sigma$, we write $\Xi^\equiv$ for $S_\Sigma(T_\Sigma(\Xi))$. Thus $\Xi^\equiv$ consists of all computations that satisfy the same formulae that are satisfied by Ξ.

Definition 12. Let Σ be a signature. A *Σ-computation system* is a Σ-pre-computation system $\langle\Sigma, \Xi\rangle$ such that $\Xi = \Xi^\equiv$.

We denote by $|Sys_\Sigma|$ the set of Σ-computation systems.

Prop/Definition 5. A computation system morphism $f : \langle\Sigma', \Xi'\rangle \rightarrow \langle\Sigma, \Xi\rangle$ is a signature morphism $f : \Sigma \rightarrow \Sigma'$ such that $\overrightarrow{f}_{\mathrm{cmp}}(\Xi') \subseteq \Xi$. Computation systems and their morphisms constitute a category *Sys*.

A signature morphism $\sigma : \Sigma \rightarrow \Sigma'$ induces a map $\overleftarrow{\sigma}_{\mathrm{cs}} : |Sys_{\Sigma'}| \rightarrow |Sys_\Sigma|$ defined by $\overleftarrow{\sigma}_{\mathrm{cs}}(\langle\Sigma', \Xi'\rangle) = \langle\Sigma, \overleftarrow{\sigma}_{\mathrm{cmp}}(\Xi')^\equiv\rangle$.

Prop/Definition 6. We obtain a (forgetful) functor $sS : Sys \rightarrow Sig^{op}$ by defining that $sS(\langle\Sigma, \Xi\rangle) = \Sigma$ and $sS(f : s \rightarrow s') = f$.

We have that sS is a cofibration: given $\sigma : \Sigma' \rightarrow \Sigma$ in Sig^{op} and s' in $|Sys_{\Sigma'}|$, the computation system morphism $\sigma : s' \rightarrow \overrightarrow{\sigma}_{\mathrm{cs}}(s')$ is cocartesian by sS for σ on s'. Moreover, sS has a splitting cocleavage.

We write Sys_Σ for $sS^{-1}(\Sigma)$ (the fiber of *Sys* over Σ).

Prop/Definition 7. The functor $Int : Sig \rightarrow Cat^{op}$ is obtained from sS. Namely, $Int(\Sigma) = Sys_\Sigma$ and $Int(\sigma : \Sigma \rightarrow \Sigma')(s') = \overleftarrow{\sigma}_{\mathrm{cs}}(s')$.

4.2 The Satisfaction Relation

Definition 13. Let Σ be a signature. The relation $\Vdash_\Sigma \subseteq Sys_\Sigma \times L_\Sigma$ is defined by $\langle\Sigma, \Xi\rangle \Vdash_\Sigma \varphi$ iff $\Xi \Vdash^b_\Sigma \varphi$.

4.3 The Satisfaction Condition

Proposition 2. For every $\sigma : \Sigma \to \Sigma'$, $s' \in |Sys_{\Sigma'}|$ and $\varphi \in L_\Sigma$, $\overleftarrow{\sigma}_{cs}(s') \Vdash_\Sigma \varphi$ iff $s' \Vdash_{\Sigma'} \overrightarrow{\sigma}_{lng}(\varphi)$.

Corollary 1. System morphisms reflect properties, that is, for $f : s' \to s$ in *Sys*, with $s \in |Sys_\Sigma|$, and $\varphi \in L_\Sigma$, if $s \Vdash_\Sigma \varphi$ then $s' \Vdash_{\Sigma'} \overleftarrow{f}_{lng}(\varphi)$.

5 Theories versus Interpretation Structures

The concept of "theory" is well known and understood in the institutional setting. For the sake of completeness, we present below the definitions and results required to carry on.

Let Σ be a signature, $\Gamma \subseteq L_\Sigma$ and $\varphi \in L_\Sigma$. As usual, $\Gamma \models_\Sigma \varphi$ states that for every Σ-computation system s, if $s \Vdash_\Sigma \Gamma$ then $s \Vdash_\Sigma \varphi$. Also, we use $\Gamma^{\models}$ for denoting the set $\{\varphi \in L_\Sigma \mid \Gamma \models_\Sigma \varphi\}$ (the semantic closure of Γ).

A Σ-specification is a pair $\langle \Sigma, \Gamma \rangle$ with $\Gamma \subseteq L_\Sigma$, and a Σ-theory is a Σ-specification $\langle \Sigma, \Gamma \rangle$ such that $\Gamma = \Gamma^{\models}$. A theory morphism $\sigma : \langle \Sigma, \Gamma \rangle \to \langle \Sigma', \Gamma' \rangle$ is a signature morphism $\sigma : \Sigma \to \Sigma'$ such that $\overrightarrow{\sigma}_{lng}(\Gamma) \subseteq \Gamma'$. Theories and their morphisms constitute a category *Th*. We obtain a (forgetful) functor $tS : Th \to Sig$ by defining that $tS(\langle \Sigma, \Gamma \rangle) = \Gamma$ and $tS(\sigma : th \to th') = \sigma$.

Theories and interpretation structures can be related by the two following functors (recall the maps S_Σ and T_Σ presented in def. 11.)

Prop/Definition 8. We obtain a functor $S : Th^{op} \to Sys$ (the *semantics* functor) by defining that $S(\langle \Sigma, \Gamma \rangle) = \langle \Sigma, S_\Sigma(\Gamma) \rangle$ and $S(f : th \to th') = f$.

Prop/Definition 9. We obtain a functor $T : Sys \to Th^{op}$ (the *theory* functor) by defining that $T(\langle \Sigma, \Xi \rangle) = \langle \Sigma, T_\Sigma(\Xi) \rangle$ and $T(f : s \to s') = f$.

Proposition 3. The pair $\langle T, S \rangle$ is a concrete isomorphism over Sig^{op} wrt $\langle tS, sS \rangle$. Thus T and S preserve (co)limits and (co)cartesian morphisms.

Note that the functor S assigns to each theory its *maximal model*, i.e., the system consisting of all the computations that satisfy the theory.

6 Combining Hybrid Systems

In this section we present several forms of combining hybrid systems. All these operations can be expressed as categorial constructions.

In the following examples we will refer recurrently to the heater, its simplified version and the controller. Let $th_h = \langle \sigma_h, \Gamma_h^{\models} \rangle$, $th_{h'} = \langle \sigma_{h'}, \Gamma_{h'}^{\models} \rangle$ and $th_c = \langle \sigma_c, \Gamma_c^{\models} \rangle$ be the theories obtained from the already presented specifications, and $h = S(th_h)$, $h' = S(th_{h'})$ and $c = S(th_c)$ be the corresponding maximal models.

6.1 Free Aggregation

In this section we characterize free aggregation of two hybrid systems as a product in *Sys* and a coproduct in *Th*. By "free aggregation" we mean the composition of two systems without any form of interaction.

Because *Th* and *Sys* are concrete over *Sig*, it is useful to start by looking at coproducts in *Sig*. Coproducts in *Sig* are straightforward obtained from the (co)products in *Fin* and *PFin*.

Proposition 4. Let $\Sigma' = \langle X', V', A' \rangle$, $\Sigma'' = \langle X'', V'', A'' \rangle$ be signatures. The triple $\langle \Sigma' + \Sigma'', i', i'' \rangle$ where $\Sigma' + \Sigma'' = \langle X' + X'', V' \times V'', A' \times A'' \rangle$[6] and $i' : \Sigma' \to \Sigma' + \Sigma''$, $i'' : \Sigma' \to \Sigma' + \Sigma''$ are obtained from the injection/projection morphism in *Fin*/*PFin* is a coproduct of Σ' and Σ'' in *Sig*.

Example 7. We have that $\Sigma_{h \times c} = \langle X_{h \times c}, V_{h \times c}, A_{h \times c} \rangle$, *with* $X_{h \times c} = \{T_1, T_2, C_2\}$, $V_{h \times c} = \{\langle on, on \rangle, \langle off, on \rangle, \langle on, off \rangle, \langle off, off \rangle\}$ *and* $A_{h \times c} = \{heat_1,\ cool_1,\ heat_2,\ cool_2,\ \langle heat, cool \rangle,\ \langle cool, cool \rangle,\ \langle heat, heat \rangle,\ \langle cool, heat \rangle\}$, *is the signature of the free aggregation of h and c.*

Proposition 5. Let $th' = \langle \Sigma', \Gamma' \rangle$ and $th'' = \langle \Sigma'', \Gamma'' \rangle$ be theories. The triple $\langle th' + th'', i', i'' \rangle$ where $th' + th'' = \langle \Sigma' + \Sigma'', (\vec{i'}_{\text{lng}}(\Gamma') \cup \vec{i''}_{\text{lng}}(\Gamma''))^{\models} \rangle$ and i', i'' are the injection morphisms defined in 4 is a coproduct of th' and th'' in *Th*.

Example 8. We have that $\langle \Sigma_{h \times c}, \Gamma_{h \times c} \rangle$ *with*

$$\Gamma_{h \times c} = \{\ @\{\langle on, on \rangle, \langle on, off \rangle\} \Rightarrow \mathbf{D}T_1 = 4 - T_1/20, ...,\\ @\{\langle on, on \rangle, \langle off, on \rangle\} \Rightarrow (0 \leq C_2 \leq 10)\}$$

is a specification of the free aggregation of h and c.

Proposition 6. Let $s' = \langle \Sigma', \Xi' \rangle$, $s'' = \langle \Sigma'', \Xi'' \rangle$ be computation systems and $s' \times s'' = \langle \Sigma' + \Sigma'', \{\xi \in \Xi_{\Sigma' + \Sigma''} \mid \vec{i'}_{\text{cmp}}(\xi) \in \Xi', \vec{i''}_{\text{cmp}}(\xi) \in \Xi''\} \rangle$. The triple $\langle s' \times s'', i', i'' \rangle$ where i', i'' are the injection morphisms defined in 4 is a product of s' and s'' in *Sys*.

The products in *Sys* are what we wanted: a computation ξ is in $s' \times s''$ iff we can extract from ξ a computation $\vec{i'}_{\text{cmp}}(\xi)$ of s' and a computation $\vec{i''}_{\text{cmp}}(\xi)$ of s''. So, we can think of the computations of $s' \times s''$ as being pairs of computations from s' and s''. Coproducts in *Th* correspond to products in *Sys* (and vice-versa), so $th_h + th_c$ is a specification of $h \times c$.[7]

6.2 Restriction

Consider two systems s' and s'' that we want to interconnect. Two typical forms of interconnection are attribute and action sharing. These can be expressed as restrictions on the signature of $s' \times s''$. If we use a signature morphism $\sigma : \Sigma' + \Sigma'' \to \Sigma$ where Σ is the desired signature, then we can obtain the desired system in a canonical way. The same is true for theories.

[6] Note that the product $A' \times A''$ is computed in *PFin*.

[7] Or, reciprocally, $h \times c$ is a model of $th_h + th_c$.

Proposition 7. Let $\sigma : \Sigma \to \Sigma'$ be a morphism in *Sig*, $th = \langle \Sigma, \Gamma \rangle \in |Th_\Sigma|$ and $s = \langle \Sigma, \Xi \rangle \in |Sys_\Sigma|$. Also, let $\overrightarrow{\sigma}_{\text{thr}}(th) = \langle \Sigma', \overrightarrow{\sigma}_{\text{lng}}(\Gamma)^{\models} \rangle$ and $\overrightarrow{\sigma}_{\text{cs}}^{-1}(s) = \langle \Sigma', \overrightarrow{\sigma}_{\text{cmp}}^{-1}(\Xi) \rangle$. Then the *Th* morphism $\sigma : th \to \overrightarrow{\sigma}_{\text{thr}}(th)$ is cocartesian by *tS* for σ on *th* and the *Sys* morphism $\sigma : \overrightarrow{\sigma}_{\text{cs}}^{-1}(s) \to s$ is cartesian by *sS* for σ on *s*:

$$\langle \Sigma, \Gamma \rangle \xrightarrow{\sigma} \langle \Sigma', \overrightarrow{\sigma}_{\text{lng}}(\Gamma)^{\models} \rangle \qquad\qquad \Sigma \xrightarrow{\sigma} \underline{\Sigma'}$$
$$\langle \Sigma, \Xi \rangle \xleftarrow{\sigma} \langle \Sigma', \overrightarrow{\sigma}_{\text{cmp}}^{-1}(\Xi) \rangle$$

Thus, given a system *s* (theory *th*) with signature Σ and a desired signature Σ', we have a canonical way of obtaining from *s* (*th*) a system *s'* (theory *th'*) with signature Σ' by resorting to a signature morphism $\sigma : \Sigma \to \Sigma'$.

The HyTech parallel composition operation arises a special case of restriction. The following definition shows how to obtain such operation via an adequate signature morphism.

Definition 14. Let $\Sigma' = \langle X', V', A' \rangle$ and $\Sigma'' = \langle X'', V'', A'' \rangle$ be signatures. We then define $\Sigma' || \Sigma''$, $\sigma_{\Sigma'||\Sigma''}^{\Sigma'+\Sigma''} : \Sigma' + \Sigma'' \to \Sigma' || \Sigma''$, $\sigma_{\Sigma'||\Sigma''}^{\Sigma'} : \Sigma' \to \Sigma' || \Sigma''$ and $\sigma_{\Sigma'||\Sigma''}^{\Sigma''} : \Sigma'' \to \Sigma' || \Sigma''$ as follows (using σ for $\sigma_{\Sigma'||\Sigma''}^{\Sigma'+\Sigma''}$):

- $\Sigma' || \Sigma'' = \langle X' \cup X'', V' \times V'', A' \cup A'' \rangle$;
- $\overrightarrow{\sigma}_{\text{att}}(\overrightarrow{i'}_{\text{att}}(x')) = x'$ for every $x' \in X'$ (similarly for $x'' \in X''$);
- $\overleftarrow{\sigma}_{\text{vtx}} = id_{V' \times V''}$;
- $\overleftarrow{\sigma}_{\text{act}}(a') = \overleftarrow{i'}_{\text{act}}(a')$ for every $a' \in A' \setminus A''$ (similarly for $a'' \in A'' \setminus A'$);
- $\overleftarrow{\sigma}_{\text{act}}(a) = \langle a, a \rangle$ for every $a \in A' \cap A''$;
- $\sigma_{\Sigma'||\Sigma''}^{\Sigma'} = \sigma \circ i'$, $\sigma_{\Sigma'||\Sigma''}^{\Sigma''} = \sigma \circ i''$;

where i', i'' are the injection morphisms of the coproduct of Σ' and Σ'' (see prop. 4). Thus in $\Sigma' || \Sigma''$ we share attributes and actions.

Example 9. Consider again h *and* c*. Suppose that we want to share the attribute* T *and actions heat,cool, thus obtaining a new system* h||c *and specification* $th_h || th_c$*. This system has signature* $\Sigma_{h||c} = \Sigma_h || \Sigma_c = \langle \{T, C\}, V_{h \times c}, \{\text{heat}, \text{cool}\} \rangle$*. Then* $\sigma = \sigma_{\Sigma_{h||c}}^{\Sigma_{h \times c}} : \Sigma_{h \times c} \to \Sigma_{h||c}$ *is such that* $\overrightarrow{\sigma}_{\text{att}} = \{T_1 \mapsto T, T_2 \mapsto T, C_2 \mapsto C\}$, $\overleftarrow{\sigma}_{\text{vtx}} = id_{V_{h \times c}}$ *and* $\overleftarrow{\sigma}_{\text{act}} = \{\text{heat} \mapsto \langle \text{heat}, \text{heat} \rangle, \text{cool} \mapsto \langle \text{cool}, \text{cool} \rangle\}$*. We have that* $h||c = \overrightarrow{\sigma}_{\text{cs}}^{-1}(h \times c)$ *and* $th_h || th_c = \overrightarrow{\sigma}_{\text{thr}}(th_h + th_c)$*. Namely:*

$$\Gamma_{h||c} = \{\ @\{\langle on, on \rangle, \langle on, off \rangle\} \Rightarrow \mathbf{D}T = 4 - T/20, ...,$$
$$@\{\langle on, on \rangle, \langle off, on \rangle\} \Rightarrow (0 \leq C \leq 10)\}$$

6.3 Abstraction

In some cases it is desirable to abstract away certain details of a system. For instance, we may be interested in hiding attributes and actions or representing a set of operation modes by a more general mode of operation. This construction can be carried out in a way similar to the restriction operation.

Proposition 8. Let $\sigma : \Sigma \to \Sigma'$ be a morphism in *Sig*, $th' = \langle \Sigma', \Gamma' \rangle \in |Th_{\Sigma'}|$ and $s' = \langle \Sigma', \Xi' \rangle \in |Sys_{\Sigma'}|$. Also, let $\overrightarrow{\sigma}_{\text{thr}}^{-1}(th') = \langle \Sigma, \overrightarrow{\sigma}_{\text{lng}}^{-1}(\Gamma') \rangle$ and $\overrightarrow{\sigma}_{\text{cs}}(s') = \langle \Sigma, \overrightarrow{\sigma}_{\text{cmp}}(\Xi')^{\equiv} \rangle$. Then the *Th* morphism $\sigma : \overrightarrow{\sigma}_{\text{thr}}^{-1}(th') \to th'$ is cartesian by *tS* for σ on th' and the *Sys* morphism $\sigma : s' \to \overrightarrow{\sigma}_{\text{cs}}(s')$ is cocartesian by *sS* for σ on s':

$$\begin{array}{ccc} \langle \Sigma, \overrightarrow{\sigma}_{\text{lng}}^{-1}(\Gamma') \rangle & \xrightarrow{\ \sigma\ } & \langle \Sigma', \Gamma' \rangle \\ \langle \Sigma, \overrightarrow{\sigma}_{\text{cmp}}(\Xi')^{\equiv} \rangle & \xleftarrow{\ \sigma\ } & \langle \Sigma', \Xi' \rangle \end{array} \qquad \underline{\Sigma} \xrightarrow{\ \sigma\ } \Sigma'$$

Thus, given a system s' (theory th') with signature Σ' and a desired signature Σ, we have a canonical way of obtaining from s' (th') a system s (theory th) with signature Σ by resorting to a signature morphism $\sigma : \Sigma \to \Sigma'$.

Example 10. Consider an abstraction of h in which we hide T. This can be done by considering the signature morphism $h^a : \Sigma_{h'} \to \Sigma_h$ *such that* $\overleftarrow{h^a}_{\text{vtx}} = id_{V_h}$ *and* $\overleftarrow{h^a}_{\text{act}} = id_{A_h}$. *Then* $\overrightarrow{h^a}_{\text{thr}}^{-1}(th_h) = th_{h'}$ *and* $\overrightarrow{h^a}_{\text{cs}}(h) = h'$. *Similarly, we can simplify c to get c' by hiding T and C, using a morphism* $c^a : \Sigma_{c'} \to \Sigma_c$.

6.4 Putting it All Together

The following serves as an usage example of the operations presented above.

Suppose we have two pairs of systems a, b and a', b' that we interconnect by using signature morphisms $q : \Sigma_a + \Sigma_b \to \Sigma$, $r : \Sigma_{a'} + \Sigma_{b'} \to \Sigma'$ thereby obtaining systems $s = \overrightarrow{q}_{\text{cs}}^{-1}(a \times b)$ and $s' = \overrightarrow{k}_{\text{cs}}^{-1}(a' \times b')$. Consider also that there are morphisms $h_a : a \to a'$, $h_b : b \to b'$. We might then ask if there is any relation between s and s'.[8] First of all, because $h_a \circ p_a : a \times b \to a'$ and $h_b \circ p_b : a \times b \to b'$ (p_a, p_b are the product projection morphisms) we conclude that h_a, h_b uniquely determine a morphism $u : a \times b \to a' \times b'$:

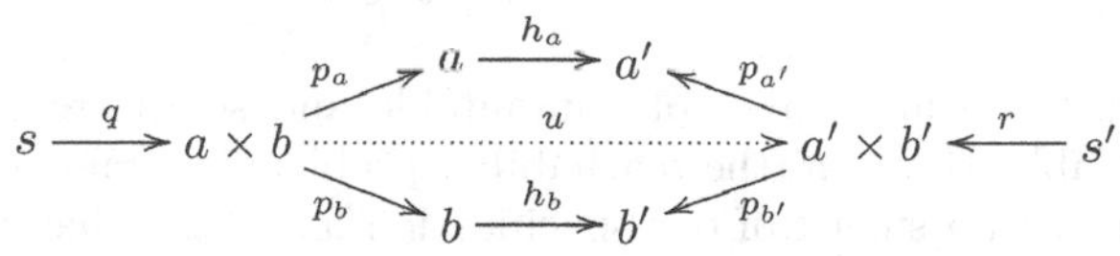

Let $k = u \circ q$. *In the case* that there is $t : \Sigma' \to \Sigma$ such that $k = t \circ r$, then the universal property of the cartesian morphism $r : s' \to a' \times b'$ guarantees that $t : s \to s'$ is a morphism in *Sys*:[9]

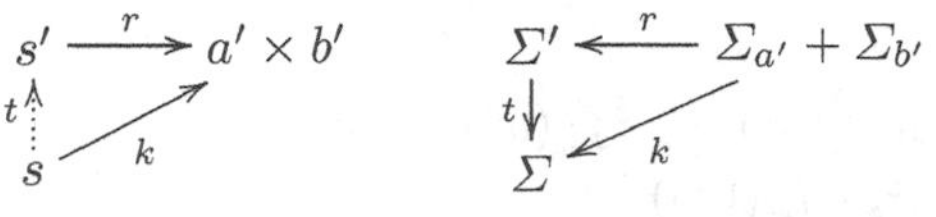

---

[8] In the particular case that a' and b' are abstractions of a and b, we are then asking if s' is an abstraction of s.

[9] Informally speaking, the existence of t means that the restriction morphisms q and r are *compatible*.

Example 11. We have a morphism $t : h||c \longrightarrow h'||c'$ *obtained from* $q = \sigma_{\Sigma_{h||c}}^{\Sigma_{h\times c}}$ *and* $r = \sigma_{\Sigma_{h'||c'}}^{\Sigma_{h'\times c'}}$: $t = \langle \emptyset, id_{V_h \times V_c}, id_{A_h \cup A_c} \rangle$.

7 Compositional Model Checking

In this section we present the main concepts of a model checking procedure for hybrid systems. The main result here is that the model checking procedure of HYTECH can be extended to take advantage of the categorial structure of a complex system.

7.1 Reachability

The reachability problem is the following: given a hybrid system s and two sets of states W and W', is it possible for s to reach a state in W' starting from a state in W? Certain interesting classes of properties (namely safety and some liveness properties) can be expressed as reachability problems.

Definition 15. Let $s = \langle \Sigma, \Xi \rangle$ be a computation system. Then s induces the (reachability) relation $\longrightarrow_s \subset St_\Sigma \times St_\Sigma$ defined by $w \longrightarrow_s w'$ iff $\xi(\langle i, t \rangle) = w$ and $\xi(\langle i', t' \rangle) = w'$ for some $\xi \in \Xi$ and $\langle i, t \rangle, \langle i', t' \rangle \in spa_\xi$ s.t. $\langle i, t \rangle \leq \langle i', t' \rangle$.[10]

Definition 16. Let $s = \langle \Sigma, \Xi \rangle$ be a computation system. We define the (forward and backward reachability) maps $\mathcal{F}_s, \mathcal{B}_s : 2^{St_\Sigma} \longrightarrow 2^{St_\Sigma}$ as

- $\mathcal{F}_s(W) = \{w' \in St_\Sigma \mid w \longrightarrow_s w' \text{ for some } w \in W\}$
- $\mathcal{B}_s(W') = \{w \in St_\Sigma \mid w \longrightarrow_s w' \text{ for some } w' \in W'\}$

In general, these maps are not computable and so the reachability problem is undecidable. However, the reachability problem is semi-decidable for systems specified with a subset of our specification language (that corresponds to HYTECH's language).

Proposition 9. Let Σ, Σ' be signatures, $s \in |Sys_\Sigma|$ and $s' \in |Sys_{\Sigma'}|$. Also, let $f : s \longrightarrow s'$ be a morphism in *Sys*. Then f preserves reachability, that is, for every $w, w' \in S_\Sigma$ and $W \subseteq S_\Sigma$:

- if $w \longrightarrow_s w'$ then $\overrightarrow{f}_{st}(w) \longrightarrow_{s'} \overrightarrow{f}_{st}(w')$;
- $\overrightarrow{f}_{st}(\mathcal{F}_s(W)) \subseteq \mathcal{F}_{s'}(\overrightarrow{f}_{st}(W))$
- $\overrightarrow{f}_{st}(\mathcal{B}_s(W)) \subseteq \mathcal{B}_{s'}(\overrightarrow{f}_{st}(W))$

[10] That is, w' can be reached from w iff there is some computation where w' occurs after w.

7.2 Verification

The notions presented in the previous subsection enable us to verify certain classes of properties. Because the notions presented are semantic ones, we start by defining their syntactic counterpart.

Definition 17. Let Σ be a signature. The set of *Σ-state terms*, sT_Σ, is the set of Σ-terms that can be written without the $\mathbf{D}$ and $\mathbf{N}$ operators. Likewise, the set of *Σ-state formulae*, sL_Σ, is the set of Σ-formulae that can be written without the $\mathbf{N}$, ∇, $\mathbf{U}$ and $\mathbf{S}$ operators.

A state is all we need to interpret state formulae.

Definition 18. Let Σ be a signature. The *state formula interpretation map* $[\![\text{-}]\!]_\Sigma : sL_\Sigma \to 2^{St_\Sigma}$ is defined by $[\![\varphi]\!]_\Sigma = \{w \in St_\Sigma \mid w \text{ satisfies } \varphi\}$.

Safety properties can be easily represented as reachability problems, as the following proposition shows.

Proposition 10. Let $\Sigma \in |Sig|$, $s \in |Sys_\Sigma|$ and $\varphi_0, \varphi \in sL_\Sigma$. Then
$s \Vdash_\Sigma \varphi_0 \Rightarrow \mathbf{G}\varphi$ iff $\mathcal{F}_s([\![\varphi_0]\!]_\Sigma) \cap [\![\neg\varphi]\!]_\Sigma = \emptyset$ iff $[\![\varphi_0]\!]_\Sigma \cap \mathcal{B}_s([\![\neg\varphi]\!]_\Sigma) = \emptyset$

Example 12. We can prove that $h \Vdash 0 < T < 80 \Rightarrow \mathbf{G}(0 < T < 80)$, *from which we can conclude that* $h \Vdash 0 < T < 80 \Rightarrow \mathbf{G}(-4 < \mathbf{D}T < 4 \wedge \mathbf{D}T \neq 0)$.

Some "bounded" safety and liveness properties can also be dealt with by composing the system to be verified with an auxiliary one.

Definition 19. A *clock C* is a system $Ck_C = S(\langle\Sigma_C\rangle, \Gamma_C^{\models})$ where Σ_C is the signature $\langle\{C\}, \{v\}, \emptyset\rangle$ and $\Gamma_C = \{\mathbf{D}C = 1\}$

Definition 20. A *monitor for action "a" using clock C* is a system $m_{a,C} = S(\langle\Sigma_{a,C}\rangle, \Gamma_{a,C}^{\models})$ where $\Sigma_{a,C}$ is the signature $\langle\{C\}, \{n, y\}, \{a\}\rangle$ and $\Gamma_{a,C}$ is the set $\{@n \Rightarrow \mathbf{D}C = 1, @y \Rightarrow \mathbf{D}C = 0, \nabla a \Rightarrow \mathbf{N}@y, (\neg\nabla a) \Rightarrow \mathbf{Cnt}_{\Sigma_{a,C}}\}$.

We use $\star_{m_{a,C}}$ for the formula $C = 0 \wedge @n$. Note that if $m_{a,C}$ starts in a state satisfying $\star_{m_{a,C}}$, then it will record the time of the first occurrence of a or keep running the clock forever if a never occurs.

Proposition 11. Let $\Sigma = \langle X, V, A\rangle$ be a signature, s a Σ-computation system, φ_0 a Σ-state formula and $C \notin X$. Then

$$s \Vdash \varphi_0 \Rightarrow \mathbf{G}^{\leq\delta}\varphi \quad\text{iff}\quad s||Ck_C \Vdash (\varphi_0' \wedge C = 0) \Rightarrow \mathbf{G}(C \leq \delta \Rightarrow \varphi)$$
$$s \Vdash \varphi_0 \Rightarrow \mathbf{F}^{\leq\delta}\nabla a \quad\text{iff}\quad s||m_{a,C} \Vdash (\varphi_0' \wedge \star_{m_{a,C}}') \Rightarrow \mathbf{G}(C \leq \delta)$$
$$s \Vdash \varphi_0 \Rightarrow \mathbf{G}^{\leq\delta}(\neg\nabla a) \quad\text{iff}\quad s||m_{a,C} \Vdash (\varphi_0' \wedge \star_{m_{a,C}}') \Rightarrow \mathbf{G}(@y' \Rightarrow C > \delta)$$

where $\varphi_0' = \overrightarrow{\sigma}^{\Sigma}_{\Sigma||\Sigma_{a,C}}(\varphi)$, $\star_{m_{a,C}}' = \overrightarrow{\sigma}^{\Sigma_{a,C}}_{\Sigma||\Sigma_{a,C}}(\star_{m_{a,C}})$ and $y' = \overrightarrow{\sigma}^{\Sigma_{a,C}}_{\Sigma||\Sigma_{a,C}}(y)$.

Example 13. We can prove[11] *that* $c \Vdash @on \Rightarrow \mathbf{F}^{\leq 10}\nabla cool$, *from which we can conclude that* $c \Vdash \nabla heat \Rightarrow (T \leq 40 \wedge \mathbf{F}^{\leq 10}\nabla cool)$.

[11] Using HYTECH!

7.3 Compositional Verification

In this subsection we show (by means of some examples) that it is possible to take advantage of the categorial structure of a complex system to ease the verification of properties of the system.

Suppose we have two systems $s \in |Sys_\Sigma|$, $s' \in |Sys_{\Sigma'}|$ related by a morphism $f : s \rightarrow s'$ and a formula $\varphi \in L_\Sigma$. In some cases, we may prove that $s \Vdash \varphi$ by executing the following steps (this method is particularly advantageous if s' is "simpler" than s):

1. Find $\varphi' \in L_{\Sigma'}$ such that $\varphi = \overleftarrow{f}_{\mathrm{lng}}(\varphi')$.[12]
2. Prove that $s' \Vdash \varphi'$.
3. Conclude that $s \Vdash \varphi$ because morphisms in Sys reflect properties.

The three systems considered so far can be related in the following way (h^a, c^a are the morphism introduced in example 10, t is the morphism introduced in example 11, p_h and p_c are projection morphisms and $q = \sigma_{\Sigma_{h||c}}^{\Sigma_{h \times c}}$):

$$h||c \xrightarrow{\ q\ } h \times c \ \begin{array}{c} \nearrow^{p_h} \\ \searrow_{p_c} \end{array} \ \begin{array}{c} h \xrightarrow{\ h^a\ } h' \\ \\ c \xrightarrow{\ c^a\ } c' \end{array} \qquad\qquad h||c \xrightarrow{\ t\ } h'||c'$$

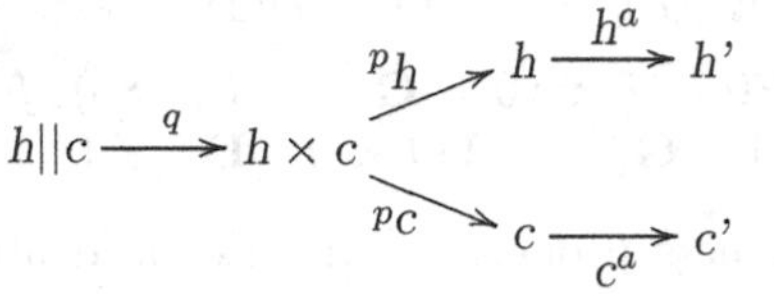

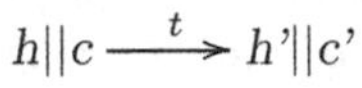

Consider the formulae $\varphi_1 = @\{\langle on, on\rangle, \langle off, off\rangle\} \Rightarrow \mathbf{G}@\{\langle on, on\rangle, \langle off, off\rangle\}$ and $\varphi_2 = \nabla heat \Rightarrow \mathbf{F}^{\leq 10}\nabla cool$. Using the above strategy we can prove that $h||c \Vdash \varphi_i$ $(i = 1, 2)$:

1. Find $\varphi_1' \in L_{\Sigma_{h'||c'}}$, such that $\varphi = \overleftarrow{t}_{\mathrm{lng}}(\varphi_1')$. We can choose $\varphi_1' = \varphi_1$.
2. Prove that $h'||c' \Vdash \varphi_1'$. We can use HyTech to prove this.
3. Conclude that $h||c \Vdash \varphi_1$.

and

1. Find $\varphi_2' \in L_{\Sigma_c}$ such that $\varphi_2 = \overleftarrow{p_c \circ q}_{\mathrm{lng}}(\varphi_2')$. We can choose $\varphi_2' = \varphi_2$.
2. Prove that $c \Vdash \varphi_2'$. We have already seen that this is the case.
3. Conclude that $h||c \Vdash \varphi_2$.

8   Concluding Remarks

The main goal of this paper has been achieved: we were able to construct an institution of hybrid systems and provide a categorial characterization of free aggregation, restriction and abstraction of such systems, thus providing a basis for compositional specification and verification of hybrid systems.

---

[12] Of course, this is not always possible.

Namely, we showed that in the category of hybrid systems free aggregation corresponds to a product, restriction to a cartesian lifting and abstraction to a cocartesian lifting. The lifting is done from the category of signatures, where the desired signatures and morphisms are chosen. The (co)cartesian lifting obtained are very general, not being restricted to inclusion of attributes or action symbols. Also, because of the isomorphism between theories and hybrid systems, these semantic constructions have a well defined syntactic counterpart.

Interconnection of two systems was shown to be possible by doing a restriction operation on the free aggregation of the systems. Standard interconnection constructions (such as HYTECH's parallel composition) appear as special cases on our framework.

It was also shown (by the mean of some examples) that compositional verification of hybrid systems is possible. Namely, the categorial structure of complex systems can be used to ease the verification process. More work is ongoing in this direction.

The reachability calculation problem is the issue most addressed by the hybrid system community, as it is the basis of the verification process. Efforts are targeted at algorithms for systems as general as possible (and not only linear hybrid systems), even if that means that only approximations can be computed. Of course, if doing approximations then care must be taken, because then reachability can no longer be used to assert validity. Nevertheless, if only under (resp. over) approximation is used, then the positive answer to reachability (resp. unreachability) can be trusted.

Because research is targeted at the reachability problem, the hybrid system community has not properly looked at the benefits of modular specification and verification. Typically, the only available form of combining systems is parallel composition *a la* HYTECH. Nevertheless, more general combination mechanism such as those presented are surely needed in order to model large systems and enable reusability.

References

1. R. Alur, C. Courcoubetis, N. Halbwachs, T. A. Henzinger, P.-H. Ho, X. Nicollin, A. Olivero, J. Sifakis, and S. Yovine. The algorithmic analysis of hybrid systems. *Theoretical Computer Science*, 138:3–34, 1995. 220
2. R. Alur, T. A. Henzinger, and P.-H. Ho. Automatic symbolic verification of embedded systems. *IEEE Transactions on Software Engineering*, 22(3):181–201, 1996. 220
3. R. Alur, T. A. Henzinger, and E. D. Sontag, editors. *Hybrid Systems III: Verification and Control*. Lecture Notes in Computer Science 1066. Springer-Verlag, 1996. 220
4. P. Antsaklis, W. kohn, A. Nerode, and S. Sastry, editors. *Hybrid Systems II*. Lecture Notes in Computer Science 999. Springer-Verlag, 1995. 220
5. P. Antsaklis, W. Kohn, A. Nerode, and S. Sastry, editors. *Hybrid Systems IV*. Lecture Notes in Computer Science 1273. Springer-Verlag, 1997. 220
6. L. de Alfaro, A. Kapur, and Z. Manna. Hybrid diagrams: A deductive-algorithmic approach to hybrid system verification. In R. Reischuk and M. Morvan, editors,

STACS'97, volume 1200 of *Lecture Notes in Computer Science*, pages 153–164. Springer Verlag, 1997. 220

7. R. Grossman, A. Nerode, A. Ravn, and H. Rischel, editors. *Hybrid Systems*. Lecture Notes in Computer Science 736. Springer-Verlag, 1993. 220
8. T. A. Henzinger, P.-H. Ho, and H. Wong-Toi. A user guide to HyTech. In E. Brinksma, W. R. Cleaveland, K. G. Larsen, T. Margaria, and B. Steffen, editors, *TACAS 95: Tools and Algorithms for the Construction and Analysis of Systems*, Lecture Notes in Computer Science 1019, pages 41–71. Springer-Verlag, 1995. 220
9. A. Kapur, T. A. Henzinger, Z. Manna, and A. Pnueli. Proving safety properties of hybrid systems. In H. Langmaack, W.-P. de Roever, and J. Vytopil, editors, *FTRTFT 94: Formal Techniques in Real-time and Fault-tolerant Systems*, Lecture Notes in Computer Science 863, pages 431–454. Springer-Verlag, 1994. 220
10. H. Lourenço and A. Sernadas. Combining hybrid systems. Research report, Section of Computer Science, Department of Mathematics, Instituto Superior Técnico, 1096 Lisboa, Portugal, 1999. Submitted for publication. 220
11. H. Lourenço, A. Sernadas, and C. Sernadas. Aggregation and interconnection of hybrid automata: Categorial characterization. Research report, Section of Computer Science, Department of Mathematics, Instituto Superior Técnico, 1096 Lisboa, Portugal, 1998. Presented at FIREworks Meeting, Magdeburg, May 15-16. 220
12. A. Sernadas, C. Sernadas, and C. Caleiro. Denotational semantics of object specification. *Acta Informatica*, 35:729–773, 1998. 220, 224
13. Glynn Winskel and Mogens Nielsen. *Semantics and Logics of Computation*, chapter Categories in Concurrency, pages 299–354. Publications of the Newton Institute. 1997. 220

Realization of Probabilistic Automata: Categorical Approach

Paulo Mateus, Amílcar Sernadas, and Cristina Sernadas

CMA - Departamento de Matemática, Instituto Superior Técnico
Av. Rovisco Pais, 1049-001 Lisboa, Portugal

Abstract. We present a categorical framework to study probabilistic automata starting by obtaining aggregation and interconnection as universal constructions. We also introduce the notion of probabilistic behavior in order to get adjunctions between probabilistic behavior and probabilistic automata. Thus we are able to extend to the probabilistic setting free and minimal realization as universal constructions.

1 Introduction

Probabilistic automata [12,11] are central in the theory of unreliable systems, namely for providing the appropriate semantic domain (see for instance [4,9,14]). In particular we adopt the Moore model, that is, the outputs are assigned to the states.

In [10,13] we provided a (pre)categorical characterization for several combinations of probabilistic automata. However, we had to work with structures weaker than categories [6,5] because composition of morphisms was not always defined. Herein we adopt a different approach by considering that the random source (probability space) is fixed, avoiding the notion of morphism between probability spaces. Of course this option is more restrictive but it allow us to stay in the categorical setting. Incidentally it is also the perspective usually adopted in probability theory.

We start by characterizing aggregation and interconnection (by input calling) as universal constructions, that is, free aggregation corresponds to product and interconnection to Cartesian lifting in the same style as presented in [15].

We also introduce the notion of probabilistic behavior allowing us to establish adjunctions between automata and behavior. In this way, we are able to extend to the probabilistic setting the classical result about the universality of minimal and free realizations [7,1].

In section 2 of the paper we present the category of (Moore) probabilistic automata. We go on in section 3 showing that finite products and Cartesian liftings exist. We also analyze the probabilistic meaning of aggregating independent automata. Section 4 is dedicated to showing that free realization is universal. For this purpose we introduce the concepts of accessible state and probabilistic behavior. Then we show that there is an adjunction between the categories of

D. Bert, C. Choppy, and P. Mosses (Eds.): WADT'99, LNCS 1827, pp. 237–251, 2000.

probabilistic behavior and probabilistic automata. In section 5 we prove that minimal realization is also universal.

We assume that the reader is familiar with basic aspects of category theory namely Cartesian liftings (see [2]) and fibred adjunctions (see [3]).

2 Probabilistic Automata

We start by recalling a few notions of basic measure and probability theory (for further details see for instance [8]). A *probability space* is a triple $\langle \Omega, \mathcal{F}, P\rangle$ where Ω is a non-empty set (of outcomes); $\mathcal{F}$ is a σ-algebra (each element is an event) over Ω and P is a measure (a probability) over $\langle \Omega, \mathcal{F}\rangle$ such that $P(\Omega) = 1$.

In the sequel we need to use the n-th product probability space of a probability space $\mathcal{P} = \langle \Omega, \mathcal{F}, P\rangle$ for each $n \in \mathbb{N}$ defined as follows: $\mathcal{P}^n = \langle \Omega^n, \mathcal{F}^n, P^n\rangle$ where $\mathcal{F}^n$ is the smallest σ-algebra containing $\prod_{i=1}^n \mathcal{F}$ and P^n is the extension of $P^* : \prod_{i=1}^n \mathcal{F} \to [0,1]$ such that $P^*(\mathcal{F}_1 \ldots \mathcal{F}_n) = \prod_{i=1}^n P(\mathcal{F}_i)$ (see [8] for details). Observe that $\mathcal{P}^0 = \langle \{*\}, 2^{\{*\}}, P^0\rangle$ where P^0 is uniquely defined.

Whenever Ω is a countable set we usually take $\mathcal{F}$ to be 2^Ω. Then, it is enough to work with the notion of *probability presentation* as a pair $\langle \Omega, p\rangle$ where Ω is non-empty countable set of outcomes and $p : \Omega \to [0,1]$ is a map such that $\sum_{\omega\in\Omega} p(\omega) = 1$. This map can be extended to a probability $P : 2^\Omega \to [0,1]$ where $P(B) = \sum_{\omega\in B} p(\omega)$. Once again we need the n-product of a probability presentation $\mathcal{P} = \langle \Omega, p\rangle$ for each $n \in \mathbb{N}$ defined as follows: $\mathcal{P}^n = \langle \Omega^n, p^n\rangle$ where $p^n(\omega_1 \ldots \omega_n) = \prod_{i=1}^n p(\omega_i)$. The n-product can be extended to a probability space $\mathcal{P}^n = \langle \Omega^n, 2^{\Omega^n}, P^n\rangle$ where P^n is the extension of p^n.

A *random quantity* over a probability presentation $\langle \Omega, p\rangle$ and a set Q is a map $f : \Omega \to Q$. In the particular case of Q being $\mathbb{R}$, the random quantity is a random variable. Two random quantities f_1, f_2 over $\mathcal{P}$ and Q are *independent* iff $P(f_1^{-1}(q_1) \cap f_2^{-1}(q_2)) = P(f_1^{-1}(q_1)) \times P(f_2^{-1}(q_2))$ for all $q_1, q_2 \in Q$.

A (Moore) probabilistic automaton is, roughly speaking, a device with an internal state that receiving an input (from a specified set I, the input alphabet) changes probabilistically its state to another and emits an output signal (from a specified set O, the output alphabet).

Definition 2.1. A *(Moore) probabilistic automaton* over a probabilistic presentation $\mathcal{P} = \langle \Omega, p\rangle$ is a tuple $m = \langle I, O, S, \delta, \Lambda\rangle$ where:

- I is a finite pointed set with a distinguished element $\perp$;
- O is a finite set;
- S is a countable pointed set with a distinguished element s_0;
- $\delta = \{\delta_s^i\}_{i\in I, s\in S}$ where each δ_s^i is a random quantity over $\mathcal{P}$ and S;
- $\Lambda : S \to O$ is a map;

such that $\delta_s^\perp = \lambda\omega \in \Omega.\ s$ for all $s \in S$.

The set I is the *input alphabet* and $\perp$ is the *idle input* that we will need later on when dealing with interconnection. An input different from $\perp$ is called a *proper input*. The set O is the *output alphabet*. The elements of S are called *states* and s_0 is the *initial state*. The random quantity δ_s^i is the *random transition map* from state s on input i. The map Λ is the *output map*.

For instance, the probability $p_{s_1}^i(s_2)$ of reaching a state s_2 from s_1 on input i is $P(\{\omega \in \Omega \ : \ \delta_{s_1}^i(\omega) = s_2\})$. Observe that $\sum_{s_2 \in S} p_{s_1}^i(s_2) = 1$ for all $s_1 \in S$ and $i \in I$.

Example 2.2. Consider an unreliable binary discrete channel (with memory) that sends bits without any error except if it has just sent 00. In this case if a 0 is received it will be successfully transmitted. However if a 1 is received, it will be transmitted successfully with probability q. The probability space that we have to fix has two outcomes, one representing success ω_1 (1 is received after 00 and transmitted successfully) and ω_2 represents the other case. Therefore $\mathcal{P} = \langle\{\omega_1, \omega_2\}, p\rangle$ with $p(\omega_1) = q$. The set of states is $S = \{s_0, s_1, s_2\}$.

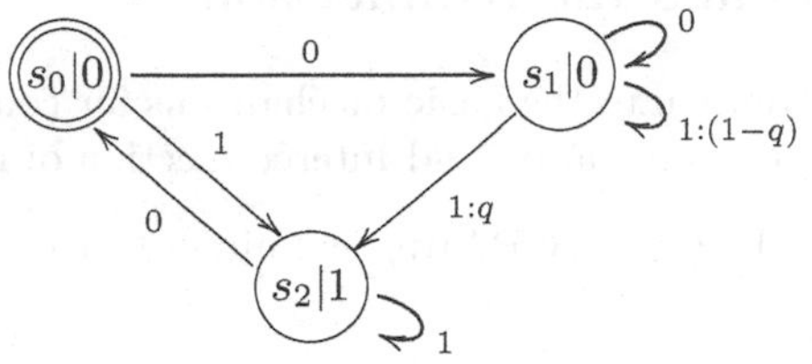

The random transition maps are as follows:

- $\delta_{s_0}^0 = \lambda\omega.s_1$;
- $\delta_{s_0}^1 = \lambda\omega.s_2$;
- $\delta_{s_1}^0 = \lambda\omega.s_1$;
- $\delta_{s_1}^1(\omega_1) = s_2$ and $\delta_{s_1}^1(\omega_2) = s_1$;
- $\delta_{s_2}^0 = \lambda\omega.s_0$;
- $\delta_{s_2}^1 = \lambda\omega.s_2$.

That is, all quantities are deterministic with the exception of $\delta_{s_1}^1$, which is a Bernoulli random quantity with success probability q.

In the sequel it is useful to consider the full subcategories of $\mathbf{Set}_*$, $\mathbf{cSet}_*$ and $\mathbf{fSet}_*$ spanned, respectively, by all countable and by all finite sets.

Definition 2.3. Let m and m' be probabilistic automata over the same $\mathcal{P} = \langle\Omega, p\rangle$. A *probabilistic automaton morphism* $f : m \to m'$ is a tuple

$$f = \langle\overline{f}, \overline{\overline{f}}, \underline{f}\rangle$$

where:

- $\overline{f} : I \to I'$ is a morphism in $\mathbf{fSet}_*$;
- $\overline{\overline{f}} : O \to O'$ is a map;
- $\underline{f} : S \to S'$ is a morphism in $\mathbf{cSet}_*$

such that for all $i \in I$, $s \in S$ and $\omega \in \Omega$:

- $\delta'^{\overline{f}(i)}_{\underline{f}(s)}(\omega) = \underline{f}(\delta^i_s(\omega))$;
- $\Lambda'(\underline{f}(s)) = \overline{\overline{f}}(\Lambda(s))$.

The notion of probabilistic automaton morphism implies the following relationship between probabilities

$$P(\{\omega \in \Omega : \delta'^{\overline{f}(i)}_{\underline{f}(s)}(\omega) = s'\}) = \sum_{r \in \underline{f}^{-1}(s')} P(\{\omega \in \Omega : \delta^i_s(\omega) = r\}).$$

Prop/Definition 2.4. Probabilistic automata over $\mathcal{P}$ and their morphisms constitute the category $\mathbf{PAut}_{\mathcal{P}}$.

3 Aggregation and Interconnection

We now turn our attention to the basic mechanisms for combining probabilistic automata, that is, free aggregation and interconnection of inputs.

Proposition 3.1. The category $\mathbf{PAut}_{\mathcal{P}}$ is finitely Cartesian.

Proof.
(i) Terminal object:
Consider the automaton with a singleton input alphabet, a singleton output alphabet and a singleton state space. Note that δ and Λ are uniquely defined.

(ii) Binary products:
A product of m_1 and m_2 is $m_1 \times m_2 = \langle I_1 \times I_2, O_1 \times O_2, S_1 \times S_2, \delta, \Lambda_1 \times \Lambda_2\rangle$ endowed with the obvious projections $\pi_k : m \to m_k$ with $k \in \{1,2\}$ and where

$$\delta^{i_1 i_2}_{s_1 s_2} = \langle {\delta_1}^{i_1}_{s_1}, {\delta_2}^{i_2}_{s_2}\rangle : \Omega \to S_1 \times S_2.$$

It is straightforward to check that each π_k is a morphism.

Universal property:
Let $f_k : m' \to m_k$ be a morphism for $k \in \{1,2\}$, then the morphism $f : m' \to m_1 \times m_2$ where:

- $\overline{f} = \langle \overline{f_1}, \overline{f_2}\rangle : I' \to I_1 \times I_2$;
- $\overline{\overline{f}} = \langle \overline{\overline{f_1}}, \overline{\overline{f_2}}\rangle : O' \to O_1 \times O_2$;
- $\underline{f} = \langle \underline{f_1}, \underline{f_2}\rangle : S' \to S_1 \times S_2$;

Clearly f is the only morphism such that $\pi_k \circ f = f_k$ with $k \in \{1,2\}$; therefore we only show that f is a morphism, indeed :

- $\delta^{\overline{f}(i')}_{\underline{f}(s')}(\omega) = \delta^{\langle \overline{f}_1(i'), \overline{f}_2(i')\rangle}_{\langle \overline{f}_1(i'), \overline{f}_2(i')\rangle}(\omega) = \langle {\delta_1}^{\overline{f}_1(i')}_{\underline{f}_1(s')}(\omega), {\delta_2}^{\overline{f}_2(i')}_{\underline{f}_2(s')}(\omega)\rangle =$
$\langle \underline{f}_1(\delta'^{i'}_{s'}(\omega)), \underline{f}_2(\delta'^{i'}_{s'}(\omega))\rangle = \underline{f}(\delta'^{i'}_{s'}(\omega))$;

– $\Lambda(\underline{f}(s')) = \Lambda(\langle \underline{f}_1(s'), \underline{f}_2(s')\rangle) = \langle \Lambda_1(\underline{f}_1(s')), \Lambda_2(\underline{f}_2(s'))\rangle = \langle \overline{\overline{f}}_1(\Lambda'(s')), \overline{\overline{f}}_2(\Lambda'(s'))\rangle = \overline{\overline{f}}(\Lambda'(s'))$. □

Observe that:

$$P(\{\omega \in \Omega \,:\, \delta_k{}^{i_k}_{s_k}(\omega) = s'_k\}) = \sum_{s \in \underline{\pi}_k^{-1}(s'_k)} P(\{\omega \in \Omega \,:\, \delta^i_s(\omega) = r\})$$

for all $\overline{\pi}(i) = i_k$, $\underline{\pi}(s) = s_k$ and $k \in \{1, 2\}$.

Definition 3.2. Let m_1 and m_2 be probabilistic automata. The *free aggregation* of m_1 with m_2 is the automaton $m_1 || m_2 = m_1 \times m_2$, i. e., the vertex of the product of m_1 and m_2.

Note that, since our automata share the same probability presentation it maybe the case that two different automata have dependent random transition maps, meaning that they are not totally independent from a probabilistic point of view. The result bellow provides a necessary and sufficient condition for achieving probabilistic independence.

Proposition 3.3. Let m_1 and m_2 be probabilistic automata over $\mathcal{P}$. Then $p^{i_1 i_2}_{s_1 s_2}(s'_1 s'_2) = p_1{}^{i_1}_{s_1}(s'_1) \times p_2{}^{i_2}_{s_2}(s'_2)$ iff $\delta_1{}^{i_1}_{s_1}$ is independent from $\delta_2{}^{i_2}_{s_2}$ for all $s_1 \in S_1$, $s_2 \in S_2$, $i_1 \in I_1$ and $i_2 \in I_2$.

Proof. Straightforward by definition of independence. □

Example 3.4. Consider the following two independent probabilistic automata. Assume that $\langle\{\omega_1, \omega_2, \omega_2, \omega_4\}, p\rangle$ with $p(\omega_1) = q^2$ and $p(\omega_2) = p(\omega_3) = q(1 - q)$. For the sake of simplicity we only present the random transition map of the initial states:

	ω_1	ω_2	ω_3	ω_4
$\delta'^{\perp'}_{s'_0}$	s'_0	s'_0	s'_0	s'_0
$\delta'^{0'}_{s'_0}$	s'_0	s'_0	s'_1	s'_1
$\delta'^{1'}_{s'_0}$	s'_1	s'_1	s'_0	s'_0

	ω_1	ω_2	ω_3	ω_4
$\delta''^{\perp''}_{s''_0}$	s''_0	s''_0	s''_0	s''_0
$\delta''^{0''}_{s''_0}$	s''_0	s''_1	s''_0	s''_1
$\delta''^{1''}_{s''_0}$	s''_1	s''_0	s''_1	s''_0

if we aggregate these two automata we obtain an automaton with nine inputs. The random transition map for the state $s'_0 s''_0$ of the combined automaton is:

	ω_1	ω_2	ω_3	ω_4
$\delta^{\perp'\perp''}_{s'_0 s''_0}$	$s'_0 s''_0$	$s'_0 s''_0$	$s'_0 s''_0$	$s'_0 s''_0$
$\delta^{\perp'0''}_{s'_0 s''_0}$	$s'_0 s''_0$	$s'_0 s''_1$	$s'_0 s''_0$	$s'_0 s''_1$
$\delta^{\perp'1''}_{s'_0 s''_0}$	$s'_0 s''_1$	$s'_0 s''_0$	$s'_0 s''_1$	$s'_0 s''_0$
$\delta^{0'\perp''}_{s'_0 s''_0}$	$s'_0 s''_0$	$s'_0 s''_0$	$s'_1 s''_0$	$s'_1 s''_0$
$\delta^{0'0''}_{s'_0 s''_0}$	$s'_0 s''_0$	$s'_0 s''_1$	$s'_1 s''_0$	$s'_1 s''_1$
$\delta^{0'1''}_{s'_0 s''_0}$	$s'_0 s''_1$	$s'_0 s''_0$	$s'_1 s''_1$	$s'_1 s''_0$
$\delta^{1'\perp''}_{s'_0 s''_0}$	$s'_1 s''_0$	$s'_1 s''_0$	$s'_0 s''_0$	$s'_0 s''_0$
$\delta^{1'0''}_{s'_0 s''_0}$	$s'_1 s''_0$	$s'_1 s''_1$	$s'_0 s''_0$	$s'_0 s''_1$
$\delta^{1'1''}_{s'_0 s''_0}$	$s'_1 s''_1$	$s'_1 s''_0$	$s'_0 s''_1$	$s'_0 s''_0$

Interaction can be achieved by restricting the pairing of actions from each component. To this end we use the following universal construction over the obvious forgetful functor $Inp : \mathbf{PAut}_{\mathcal{P}} \to \mathbf{fSet}_*$ that maps each probabilistic automaton to its input space.

Proposition 3.5. The functor *Inp* is a fibration with splitting cleavage

$$k = \{k(\overline{f}, m')\}_{m' \in \mathbf{PAut}_{\mathcal{P}}, \overline{f} \in \hom(I, Inp(m'))}$$

where:

- $k(\overline{f}, m') = \langle \overline{f}, \mathrm{id}_{O'}, \mathrm{id}_{S'} \rangle : m \to m'$;
- $m = \langle I, O', S', \delta, \Lambda' \rangle$;
- $\delta^i_{s'} = \delta'^{\overline{f}(i)}_{s'}$.

Proof. It is easy to see that m is indeed an automaton and that $k(\overline{f}, m')$ is a morphism in $\mathbf{PAut}_{\mathcal{P}}$.

Universal property:

Let $h : m'' \to m' \in \mathbf{PAut}_{\mathcal{P}}$ and $\overline{g} : I'' \to I \in \mathbf{fSet}_*$ such that $\overline{f} \circ \overline{g} = \overline{h}$. Consider now $\overline{\overline{g}} = \overline{\overline{h}}$ and $\underline{g} = \underline{h}$ where $g : m'' \to m'$; clearly g is the only triple such that $f \circ g = h$ and therefore we only show that g is a morphism in $\mathbf{PAut}_{\mathcal{P}}$:

- $\delta^{\overline{g}(i'')}_{\underline{g}(s'')}(\omega) = \delta'^{\overline{f}(\overline{g}(i''))}_{\underline{g}(s'')}(\omega) = \delta'^{\overline{h}(i'')}_{\underline{h}(s'')}(\omega) = \underline{h}(\delta''^{i''}_{s''}(\omega)) = \underline{g}(\delta''^{i''}_{s''}(\omega))$;
- $\Lambda(\underline{g}(s'')) = \Lambda'(\underline{h}(s'')) = \overline{\overline{h}}(\Lambda''(s'')) = \overline{\overline{g}}(\Lambda''(s''))$.

Finally k is a splitting cleavage:

- $k(\mathrm{id}_I, m) = \mathrm{id}_m$;
- $k(\overline{f}, m'') \circ k(\overline{g}, m') = \langle \overline{f} \circ \overline{g}, \mathrm{id}_{O''}, \mathrm{id}_{S''} \rangle : m \to m''$ where $\delta^i_{s''} = \delta'^{\overline{g}(i)}_{s''} = \delta''^{\overline{f}(\overline{g}(i))}_{s''}$ and so $k(\overline{f}, m') \circ k(\overline{g}, m) = k(\overline{f} \circ \overline{g}, m'')$. □

Definition 3.6. Let m' and m'' be probabilistic automata, i' an input in I' and i'' an input in I''. Then, the *interconnection of* m' *and* m'' *by* i' *calling* i'' is

$$m'||_{i'>>i''}m'' = \mathrm{dom}(k(\overline{f}, m'||m''))$$

where $\overline{f} : ((I' \setminus \{i'\}) \times I'') \cup \{\langle i', i''\rangle\} \hookrightarrow I' \times I''$;

Example 3.7. Recall the automaton obtained in Example 3.4 and suppose that now we impose that $0'$ calls $0''$. To define $\delta||_{0'>>0''}$ for the initial state we just drop the random quantities $\delta^{0'\perp''}_{s'_0s''_0}$, $\delta^{0'1''}_{s'_0s''_0}$ of δ, that is:

	ω_1	ω_2	ω_3	ω_4
$\delta\|\|_{0'>>0''}{}^{\perp'\perp''}_{s'_0s''_0}$	$s'_0s''_0$	$s'_0s''_0$	$s'_0s''_0$	$s'_0s''_0$
$\delta\|\|_{0'>>0''}{}^{\perp'0''}_{s'_0s''_0}$	$s'_0s''_0$	$s'_0s''_1$	$s'_0s''_0$	$s'_0s''_1$
$\delta\|\|_{0'>>0''}{}^{\perp'1''}_{s'_0s''_0}$	$s'_0s''_1$	$s'_0s''_0$	$s'_0s''_1$	$s'_0s''_0$
$\delta\|\|_{0'>>0''}{}^{0'0''}_{s'_0s''_0}$	$s'_0s''_0$	$s'_0s''_1$	$s'_1s''_0$	$s'_1s''_1$
$\delta\|\|_{0'>>0''}{}^{1'\perp''}_{s'_0s''_0}$	$s'_1s''_0$	$s'_1s''_0$	$s'_0s''_0$	$s'_0s''_0$
$\delta\|\|_{0'>>0''}{}^{1'0''}_{s'_0s''_0}$	$s'_1s''_0$	$s'_1s''_1$	$s'_0s''_0$	$s'_0s''_1$
$\delta\|\|_{0'>>0''}{}^{1'1''}_{s'_0s''_0}$	$s'_1s''_1$	$s'_1s''_0$	$s'_0s''_1$	$s'_0s''_0$

4 Unfolding

In this section we examine the notion of probabilistic behavior of an automaton. Furthermore, we study what is the relationship between the behavior of a combined automaton with the behavior of its components, capitalizing in the universal characterizations provided in the last section. As in classical sequential automaton, only accessible states are relevant for determining the behavior of an automaton.

Definition 4.1. The set of *accessible states* of an automaton m, A_m, is inductively defined in the following way: $s_0 \in A_m$; $s_2 \in A_m$ provided that $s_2 \in \mathrm{cod}(\delta^i_{s_1})$ for some $i \in I$ and $s_1 \in A_m$. An automaton m is *accessible* iff $A_m = S$. Finally, we call $\mathbf{aPAut}_{\mathcal{P}}$ the full subcategory of $\mathbf{PAut}_{\mathcal{P}}$ spanned by all accessible automata.

From the probabilistic point of views it seems more natural to say that the set of probabilistically accessible states is defined as follows: $s_0 \in pA_m$; $s_2 \in pA_m$ provided that $p^i_{s_1}(s_2) > 0$ for some $i \in I$ and $s_1 \in pA_m$. Of course $pA_m \subseteq A_m$. Whenever $p(\omega) > 0$ for all $\omega \in \Omega$ then the two notions coincide. Nothing is lost if we consider that the probability presentation we work with has this property.

Proposition 4.2. Morphisms in $\mathbf{PAut}_{\mathcal{P}}$ preserve accessibility, that is, if $f : m \to m'$ is a morphism and $s \in A_m$ then $\underline{f}(s) \in A_{m'}$.

Proof. By induction on the structure of A_m:
base: $\underline{f}(s_0) = s'_0 \in A_{m'}$;
induction step: $s_2 = \delta^i_{s_1}(\omega)$ with $s_1 \in A_m$ then, by definition of morphism,

$$\underline{f}(s_2) = \delta'^{\overline{f}(i)}_{\underline{f}(s_1)}(\omega).$$

By induction hypothesis, $\underline{f}(s_1) \in A_{m'}$ and therefore $\underline{f}(s_2) \in A_{m'}$. □

It is easy to see taking into account the probabilistic transfer properties of morphisms that morphisms also preserve probabilistic accessibility.

Corollary 4.3. $\mathbf{aPAut}_{\mathcal{P}}$ is a coreflexive subcategory of $\mathbf{PAut}_{\mathcal{P}}$.

Proof. Let m be a probabilistic automaton, consider the accessible automaton $m_A = \langle I, O, A_m, \delta|_{I \times A_m}, \Lambda|_{A_m}\rangle$ endowed with the morphism

$$\iota = \langle \mathrm{id}_I, \mathrm{id}_O, \underline{\iota}\rangle : m_A \to m,$$

where $\underline{\iota} : A_m \hookrightarrow S$. It is easy to see that m_A is a probabilistic automaton and that ι is a morphism.

Universal property:

Let m' be a accessible automaton and $h : m' \to m \in \mathbf{PAut}_{\mathcal{P}}$. Then by Proposition 4.2, $\mathrm{cod}(\underline{f}) \subseteq A_{m'}$, and therefore $f : m \to m'_A$ is a morphism. Furthermore $h : m' \to m_A$ is the only morphism such that $\iota \circ h = h$ by definition of ι. □

The above result asserts the existence a functor *Acc* : $\mathbf{PAut}_{\mathcal{P}} \to \mathbf{aPAut}_{\mathcal{P}}$ that is right adjoint to the inclusion functor from $\mathbf{aPAut}_{\mathcal{P}}$ to $\mathbf{PAut}_{\mathcal{P}}$. Roughly speaking, this functor maps each automaton to its "subautomaton" containing just the accessible states. Since *Acc* is right adjoint, its preserves limits and in particular products; hence $Acc(m' || m'') = Acc(m') || Acc(m'')$. With respect to the other construction a further result is relevant:

Proposition 4.4. The coreflection presented in Corollary 4.3 is fibred with respect to *Inp*.

Proof. Let m be an automaton, its coreflection $\iota : m \to m_A$ as defined in Corollary 4.3 is such that $Inp(\iota) = \mathrm{id}_I$ and furthermore, $Inp \circ Acc = Inp$. □

Hence *Acc* preserves Cartesian morphisms by *Inp*. Moreover *Inp* :$\mathbf{aPAut}_{\mathcal{P}} \to \mathbf{fSet}_*$ is a fibration. In what concerns runs, a Moore probabilistic automata over $\mathcal{P}$ with input alphabet I can be seen as a sequential automata, or even a F-automata [1], if we set the sequential input alphabet to be $I\Omega$ and forget the probabilities. This observation motivates the following definition of probabilistic behavior:

Definition 4.5. A *probabilistic behavior* over a probability presentation $\mathcal{P}$ is a tuple $B = \langle I, O, \beta\rangle$ where:

- I is a finite pointed set with a distinguished element $\perp$;
- O is a finite set;
- $\beta = \{\beta_x\}_{x \in I^*}$ where each β_x is a random quantity over $\mathcal{P}^{|x|}$ and O;

such that $\beta_{x_1 \perp x_2}(\boldsymbol{\omega_1} \omega \boldsymbol{\omega_2})) = \beta_{x_1 x_2}(\boldsymbol{\omega_1}\boldsymbol{\omega_2})$ for all $x_1, x_2 \in I^*$, $\omega \in \Omega$, $\boldsymbol{\omega_1} \in \Omega^{|x_1|}$ and $\boldsymbol{\omega_2} \in \Omega^{|x_2|}$.

The sets I and O have the same meaning as before. The random quantity β_x, called *random behavior*, gives the output on sequence of inputs x. The probability of obtaining output o on sequence of inputs x is $P^{|x|}(\{\boldsymbol{\omega} \in \Omega^{|x|} : \beta_x(\boldsymbol{\omega}) = o\})$.

We introduce some useful notation. The elements of $(I\Omega)^*$ are called *runs*. The elements of $((I \setminus \{\perp\})\Omega)^*$ are called *proper runs* over $\mathcal{P}$ and I and we denote this set by $\text{pRun}_{\mathcal{P},I}$. Given $i_1\omega_1 \ldots i_n\omega_n \in (I\Omega)^*$ and $\overline{f} : I \to I'$, we denote $\overline{f}(i_1)\omega_1 \ldots \overline{f}(i_n)\omega_n$ by $\overline{f}(i_1\omega_1 \ldots i_n\omega_n)$.

Definition 4.6. A *probabilistic behavior morphism* is a pair

$$f = \langle \overline{f}, \overline{\overline{f}} \rangle : \langle I, O, \beta \rangle \to \langle I', O', \beta' \rangle$$

where:

- $\overline{f} : I \to I'$ is a morphism in $\mathbf{fSet}_*$;
- $\overline{\overline{f}} : O \to O'$ is a map;

such that $\overline{\overline{f}}(\beta_x) = \beta'_{\overline{f}(x)}$ for all $x \in I^*$ and $\boldsymbol{\omega} \in \Omega^{|x|}$.

Prop/Definition 4.7. Probabilistic behaviors over $\mathcal{P}$ and their morphisms constitute the category $\mathbf{PBeh}_{\mathcal{P}}$.

We call the obvious forgetful functor that maps each probabilistic behavior to its input alphabet by $bInp : \mathbf{PBeh}_{\mathcal{P}} \to \mathbf{fSet}_*$. We want to establish and adjunction between the category of probabilistic behaviors and the category of probabilistic automata. For this purpose is is important to note that the random transition map of an automaton m can be generalized to sequence of inputs. That is, let m be an automaton then $\delta^* = \{{\delta^*}^x_s\}_{x \in I^*, s \in S}$ where ${\delta^*}^x_s : \Omega^{|x|} \to S$ is inductively defined in the following way:

- ${\delta^*}^\epsilon_s = s$;
- ${\delta^*}^{xi}_s(\boldsymbol{\omega}\omega) = \delta^i_{{\delta^*}^x_s(\boldsymbol{\omega})}(\omega)$.

It is easy to see that a state s of an automaton m is accessible iff there exists a $x \in I^*$ and $\boldsymbol{\omega} \in \Omega^{|x|}$ such that ${\delta^*}^x_{s_0}(\boldsymbol{\omega}) = s$. Therefore, the preservation of accessibility by probabilistic automaton morphisms, Proposition 4.2, is a simple corollary of the following lemma:

Lemma 4.8. Let $f : m \to m'$ be a morphism in $\mathbf{PAut}_{\mathcal{P}}$, then for all $i \in I^*$ and $\boldsymbol{\omega} \in \Omega^{|x|}$:

$$\underline{f}({\delta^*}^x_s(\boldsymbol{\omega})) = {\delta'^*}^{\overline{f}(x)}_{\underline{f}(s)}(\boldsymbol{\omega}).$$

Proof. By induction on the size of σ:
base: $\underline{f}({\delta^*}^{\epsilon}_{s}) = \underline{f}(s) = {\delta'^*}^{\epsilon}_{\underline{f}(s)}$;
induction step:
$\underline{f}({\delta^*}^{xi}_{s}(\boldsymbol{\omega}\omega)) = \underline{f}(\delta^{i}_{{\delta^*}^{x}_{s}(\boldsymbol{\omega})}(\omega)) = {\delta'}^{\overline{f}(i)}_{\underline{f}({\delta^*}^{x}_{s}(\boldsymbol{\omega}))}(\omega) = {\delta'}^{\overline{f}(i)}_{{\delta'^*}^{\overline{f}(x)}_{\underline{f}(s)}(\boldsymbol{\omega})}(\omega) = {\delta'^*}^{\overline{f}(xi)}_{\underline{f}(s)}(\boldsymbol{\omega}\omega)$. □

We now can establish the unfolding functor from probabilistic automata to probabilistic behaviors.

Prop/Definition 4.9. The functor *Unf* : $\mathbf{aPAut}_{\mathcal{P}} \to \mathbf{PBeh}_{\mathcal{P}}$ is defined as follows:

- $\mathit{Unf}(m) = \langle I, O, \{\Lambda \circ {\delta^*}^{x}_{s_0}\}_{x \in I^*}\rangle$;
- $\mathit{Unf}(\langle \overline{f}, \overline{\overline{f}}, \underline{f}\rangle) = \langle \overline{f}, \overline{\overline{f}}\rangle$.

Proof.

- $\mathit{Unf}(m)$ is a probabilistic behavior:
  It is easy to see by induction on the length of x_2 that:
  $${\delta^*}^{x_1 \perp x_2}_{s}(\boldsymbol{\omega}_1 \omega \boldsymbol{\omega}_2) = {\delta^*}^{x_1 x_2}_{s}(\boldsymbol{\omega}_1 \boldsymbol{\omega}_2)$$
  and therefore $\Lambda({\delta^*}^{x_1 \perp x_2}_{s}(\boldsymbol{\omega}_1 \omega \boldsymbol{\omega}_2)) = \Lambda({\delta^*}^{x_1 x_2}_{s}(\boldsymbol{\omega}_1 \boldsymbol{\omega}_2))$;
- $\mathit{Unf}(f)$ is a probabilistic behavior morphism:
  $\overline{\overline{f}}(\Lambda({\delta^*}^{x}_{s_0}(\boldsymbol{\omega}))) = \Lambda'(\underline{f}({\delta^*}^{x}_{s_0}(\boldsymbol{\omega})))$ (by Lemma 4.8)
  $= \Lambda'({\delta'^*}^{\overline{f}(x)}_{\underline{f}(s_0)}(\boldsymbol{\omega})$. □

Theorem 4.10. The functor *Unf* has a left adjoint. Furthermore the adjunction is fibred with respect to *Inp* and *bInp*.

Proof.
Left adjoint:
Let *Free* : $\mathbf{PBeh}_{\mathcal{P}} \to \mathbf{aPAut}_{\mathcal{P}}$ be such that:

- $\mathit{Free}(\langle I, O, \beta\rangle) = \langle I, O, \mathrm{pRun}_{\mathcal{P},I}, \delta, \Lambda\rangle$ where:
  - $\delta^{i}_{\sigma}(\omega) = \sigma i \omega$ for all $i \in I \setminus \{\perp\}$, $\omega \in \Omega$ and $\sigma \in \mathrm{pRun}_{\mathcal{P},I}$;
  - $\Lambda(i_1\omega_1 \ldots i_n\omega_n) = \beta_{i_1 \ldots i_n}(\omega_1 \ldots \omega_n)$.

  It is clear that $\mathit{Free}(\langle I, O, \beta\rangle)$ is an accessible automaton.
- $\mathit{Free}(\langle \overline{f}, \overline{\overline{f}}\rangle) = \langle \overline{f}, \overline{\overline{f}}, \overline{f}\rangle$. We proceed by checking that $\mathit{Free}(f)$ is a probabilistic automata morphism:
  - $\overline{f}(\delta^{i}_{\sigma}(\omega)) = \overline{f}(\sigma i \omega) = \overline{f}(\sigma)\overline{f}(i)\omega = {\delta'}^{\overline{f}(i)}_{\overline{f}(\sigma)}(\omega)$ for all $i \in I \setminus \{\perp\}$;
  - $\underline{f}(\delta^{\perp}_{\sigma}(\omega)) = \underline{f}(\sigma) = {\delta'}^{\perp'}_{\underline{f}(\sigma)}(\omega) = {\delta'}^{\overline{f}(\perp)}_{\underline{f}(\sigma)}(\omega)$;
  - $\overline{\overline{f}}(\Lambda(i_1\omega_1 \ldots i_n\omega_n)) = \overline{\overline{f}}(\beta_{i_1 \ldots i_n}(\omega_1 \ldots \omega_n)) =$
    $\beta'_{\overline{f}(i_1 \ldots i_n)}(\omega_1 \ldots \omega_n) = \Lambda'(\overline{f}(i_1\omega_1 \ldots i_n\omega_n))$.

Counit:
Let δ' and Λ' be the random transition map and the output map of *Free*(*Unf*(m)) respectively. The counit of the adjunction is the family

$$\varepsilon_m = \langle \mathrm{id}_I, \mathrm{id}_O, \underline{\varepsilon}_m \rangle : \mathit{Free}(\mathit{Unf}(m)) \to m$$

where $\underline{\varepsilon}_m(i_1\omega_1 \dots i_n\omega_n) = \delta{*}^{i_1 \dots i_n}_{s_0}(\omega_1 \dots \omega_n)$ for every $m \in \mathbf{aPAut}_{\mathcal{P}}$. We verify that ε_m is a morphism in $\mathbf{aPAut}_{\mathcal{P}}$:

- $\delta^i_{\underline{\varepsilon}_m(i_1\omega_1 \dots i_n\omega_n)}(\omega) = \delta^i_{\delta{*}^{i_1 \dots i_n}_{s_0}(\omega_1 \dots \omega_n)}(\omega) = \delta{*}^{i_1 \dots i_n i}_{s_0}(\omega_1 \dots \omega_n\omega) =$
  $\underline{\varepsilon}_m(i_1\omega_1 \dots i_n\omega_n i\omega) = \underline{\varepsilon}_m(\delta'^i_{i_1\omega_1 \dots i_n\omega_n}(\omega))$;
- $\Lambda(\underline{\varepsilon}_m(i_1\omega_1 \dots i_n\omega_n i\omega)) = \Lambda(\delta{*}^{i_1 \dots i_n}_{s_0}(\omega_1 \dots \omega_n)) = \Lambda'(i_1\omega_1 \dots i_n\omega_n)$.

Finally we check that ε is a natural transformation:
$\underline{f}(\underline{\varepsilon}_{m_1}(i_1\omega_1 \dots i_n\omega_n)) = \underline{f}(\delta{*}^{i_1 \dots i_n}_{1\,s_0}(\omega_1 \dots \omega_n)) =$
$\quad \delta{*}^{\overline{f}(i_1) \dots \overline{f}(i_n)}_{2\,\underline{f}(s_0)}(\omega_1 \dots \omega_n) = \underline{\varepsilon}_{m_2}(\overline{f}(i_1\omega_1 \dots i_n\omega_n))$.

Universal Property:
Let $\langle \overline{f}, \overline{\overline{f}}, \underline{f} \rangle : \mathit{Free}(B) \to m_1$ be a morphism in $\mathbf{PAut}_{\mathcal{P}}$. The pair

$$\langle \overline{f}, \overline{\overline{f}} \rangle : B \to \mathit{Unf}(m_1)$$

is a morphism in $\mathbf{PBeh}_{\mathcal{P}}$:
$\overline{\overline{f}}(\beta_{i_1 \dots i_n}(\omega_1 \dots \omega_n)) = \overline{\overline{f}}(\Lambda(i_1\omega_1 \dots i_n\omega_n)) = \Lambda_1(\underline{f}(i_1\omega_1 \dots i_n\omega_n)) =$
$\quad \Lambda_1(\underline{f}(\delta{*}^{i_1 \dots i_n}_{s_0}(\omega_1 \dots \omega_n))) = \Lambda_1(\delta{*}^{\overline{f}(i_1 \dots i_n)}_{1\,\underline{f}(s_0)}(\omega_1 \dots \omega_n)))$.
Clearly $\varepsilon_{m'} \circ \mathit{Free}(\langle \overline{f}, \overline{\overline{f}} \rangle) = \langle \overline{f}, \overline{\overline{f}}, \underline{f} \rangle$:
$\underline{\varepsilon}_{m_1}(\overline{f}(i_1\omega_1 \dots i_n\omega_n)) = \delta{*}^{\overline{f}(i_1 \dots i_n)}_{1\,s_{10}}(\omega_1 \dots \omega_n) =$
$\quad \underline{f}(\delta{*}^{i_1 \dots i_n}_{\epsilon}(\omega_1 \dots \omega_n)) = \underline{f}(i_1\omega_1 \dots i_n\omega_n)$.
The uniqueness requirement is straightforward.

Fibred adjunction:
Clearly we have that *Inp*∘*Free* = *bInp* and *bInp*∘*Unf* = *Inp*. Furthermore we also have $\mathit{Inp}(\varepsilon_m) = \mathrm{id}_I$. □

A simple corollary of this theorem is that all constructs presented in Section 3 are preserved by *Unf*. Furthermore it is easy to show that *bInp* is a fibration.

5 Minimal Realization

Now we show that there is a universal minimal realization for each probabilistic behavior. For this purpose, we fix an input alphabet, that is, we work with the fibers induced by *Inp* and *bInp*. Thus, let I be some finite pointed set we call $\mathbf{PAut}_{\mathcal{P},I}$ the fiber of $\mathbf{PAut}_{\mathcal{P}}$ induced by *Inp* and I. We also call $\mathbf{aPAut}_{\mathcal{P},I}$ the co-reflexive subcategory of $\mathbf{PAut}_{\mathcal{P},I}$ spanned by all accessible automata. In a similar way we call $\mathbf{PBeh}_{\mathcal{P},I}$ the fiber of $\mathbf{PBeh}_{\mathcal{P}}$ induced by $bInp$ and I. The first step of minimization is to merge states that are indistinguishable.

Definition 5.1. Let m be an accessible automaton over a probability presentation $\mathcal{P}$. We say that $\rho \subseteq S^2$ is a congruence relation over m iff ρ is an equivalence relation; $\delta^i_{s_1}(\omega)\rho\delta^i_{s_2}(\omega)$ for all $i \in I$ and $\omega \in \Omega$ whenever $s_1\rho s_2$; $\Lambda(s_1) = \Lambda(s_2)$ whenever $s_1\rho s_2$.

Prop/Definition 5.2. Let m be a probabilistic automaton and ρ a congruence relation over m. The quotient automaton $m/\rho = \langle I, O, S/\rho, \delta_\rho, \Lambda_\rho\rangle$ is such that: $S/\rho = \{[s]_\rho \mid s \in S\}$ where $[s]_\rho = \{s' \mid s'\rho s\}$; $\delta_{\rho}{}^{i}_{[s]_\rho}(\omega) = [\delta^i_s(\omega)]_\rho$; $\Lambda_\rho([s]_\rho) = \Lambda(s)$.

The next step is to find the greatest congruence relation over an automaton.

Proposition 5.3. Let m be a probabilistic automaton and consider $\approx \subseteq S^2$ defined as follows: $s_1 \approx s_2$ iff $\Lambda(\delta*^{i_1\ldots i_n}_{s_1}(\omega_1\ldots\omega_n)) = \Lambda(\delta*^{i_1\ldots i_n}_{s_2}(\omega_1\ldots\omega_n))$. Then $\approx$ is a congruence relation over m and for any congruence relation ρ over m, $\rho \subseteq \approx$.

Proof. We verify that $\approx$ is a congruence (clearly it is an equivalence relation):

- If $s_1 \approx s_2$ then $\Lambda(\delta*^{i_1\ldots i_n}_{\delta^i_{s_1}(\omega)}(\omega_1\ldots\omega_n)) = \Lambda(\delta*^{ii_1\ldots i_n}_{s_1}(\omega\omega_1\ldots\omega_n)) =$
  $\Lambda(\delta*^{ii_1\ldots i_n}_{s_2}(\omega\omega_1\ldots\omega_n)) = \Lambda(\delta*^{i_1\ldots i_n}_{\delta^i_{s_2}(\omega)}(\omega_1\ldots\omega_n))$.
- If $s_1 \approx s_2$ then $\Lambda(s_1) = \Lambda(\delta*^{\epsilon}_{s_1}) = \Lambda(\delta*^{\epsilon}_{s_2}) = \Lambda(s_2)$.

Moreover consider now another congruence over m, ρ, we show that $\rho \subseteq \approx$, that is, if $s_1\rho s_2$ then $s_1 \approx s_2$: (By induction on n)

- $\Lambda(\delta*^{\epsilon}_{s_1}) = \Lambda(s_1) = \Lambda(s_2) = \Lambda(\delta*^{\epsilon}_{s_2})$;
- $\Lambda(\delta*^{ii_1\ldots i_n}_{s_1}(\omega\omega_1\ldots\omega_n)) = \Lambda(\delta*^{i_1\ldots i_n}_{\delta^i_{s_1}(\omega)}(\omega_1\ldots\omega_n)) =$
  $\Lambda(\delta*^{i_1\ldots i_n}_{\delta^i_{s_2}(\omega)}(\omega_1\ldots\omega_n)) = \Lambda(\delta*^{ii_1\ldots i_n}_{s_2}(\omega\omega_1\ldots\omega_n))$. □

Clearly an automaton m is minimal iff $\approx_m = \Delta_S$, that is $s_1 \approx_m s_2$ iff $s_1 = s_2$. We can present the main theorem of this section but before we need an auxiliary result:

Lemma 5.4. Let $f : m \to m'$ be a morphism in $\mathbf{aPAut}_{\mathcal{P},I}$, then $\underline{f}([s]_\approx) \subseteq [\underline{f}(s)]_{\approx'}$ for all $s \in S$.

Proof.
Suppose that $s_1 \approx s_2$ then:
$\Lambda'(\delta'*^{i_1\ldots i_n}_{\underline{f}(s_1)}(\omega_1\ldots\omega_n)) = \Lambda'(\underline{f}(\delta*^{i_1\ldots i_n}_{s_1}(\omega_1\ldots\omega_n))) =$
$\overline{\overline{f}}(\Lambda(\delta*^{i_1\ldots i_n}_{s_1}(\omega_1\ldots\omega_n))) =$
$\overline{\overline{f}}(\Lambda(\delta*^{i_1\ldots i_n}_{s_2}(\omega_1\ldots\omega_n))) = \Lambda'(\underline{f}(\delta*^{i_1\ldots i_n}_{s_2}(\omega_1\ldots\omega_n))) = \Lambda'(\delta'*^{i_1\ldots i_n}_{\underline{f}(s_2)}(\omega_1\ldots\omega_n))$.
Hence $\underline{f}(s_1) \approx' \underline{f}(s_2)$. □

Theorem 5.5. The functor $Unf\colon \mathbf{aPAut}_{\mathcal{P},I} \to \mathbf{PBeh}_{\mathcal{P},I}$ has a right adjoint.

Proof.
Right adjoint:
Let $Min : \mathbf{PBeh}_{\mathcal{P},I} \to \mathbf{aPAut}_{\mathcal{P},I}$ be such that:

- $Min(B) = Free(B)/\approx$. Clearly, $Min(B)$ is an accessible automaton.
- $Min(\overline{\overline{f}}) = \langle \overline{\overline{f}}, \underline{f}_{\approx} \rangle$ where $\underline{f}_{\approx} = \mathrm{id}_{\mathrm{pRun}_{\mathcal{P},I}\approx}$ that is, $\underline{f}_{\approx}([\sigma]_{\approx}) = [\sigma]_{\approx'}$. Note that $Free(\overline{\overline{f}}) = \langle \overline{\overline{f}}, \mathrm{id}_{\mathrm{pRun}_{\mathcal{P},I}} \rangle$ and therefore, by Lemma 5.4, $[\sigma]_{\approx} \subseteq [\sigma]_{\approx'}$. Hence, $\underline{f}_{\approx}$ is well defined. Moreover $Min(\overline{\overline{f}})$ is a morphism :
  - $\underline{f}_{\approx}(\delta_{\approx}{}^{i}_{[\sigma]_{\approx}}(\omega)) = \underline{f}_{\approx}([\sigma i\omega]_{\approx}) = [\sigma i \omega]_{\approx'} = \delta'_{\approx'}{}^{i}_{[\sigma]_{\approx'}}(\omega) =$ $\delta'_{\approx'}{}^{i}_{\underline{f}_{\approx}([\sigma]_{\approx})}(\omega)$ for all $i \in I \setminus \{\bot\}$ and $\omega \in \Omega$;
  - $\underline{f}_{\approx}(\delta_{\approx}{}^{\bot}_{[\sigma]_{\approx}}(\omega)) = \underline{f}_{\approx}([\sigma]_{\approx}) = [\sigma]_{\approx'} = \delta'_{\approx'}{}^{\bot}_{[\sigma]_{\approx'}}(\omega) = \delta'_{\approx'}{}^{\bot}_{\underline{f}_{\approx}([\sigma]_{\approx})}(\omega)$ for all $\omega \in \Omega$;
  - $\overline{\overline{f}}(\Lambda_{\approx}([\sigma]_{\approx})) = \overline{\overline{f}}(\Lambda(\sigma)) = \Lambda'(\sigma) = \Lambda'([\sigma]_{\approx'})$.

Unit:
Let δ' and Λ' be the random transition map and the output map of $Free(Unf(m))$ respectively. The unit of the adjunction is the family

$$\eta_m = \langle \mathrm{id}_O, \underline{\eta}_m \rangle : m \to Min(Unf(m))$$

where $\underline{\eta}_m : S \to \mathrm{pRun}_{\mathcal{P},I}/\approx$ is such that $\underline{\eta}_m(s) = [\sigma]_{\approx}$ for any $\sigma = i_1\omega_1 \ldots i_n\omega_n$ such that $\delta^{*}{}^{i_1 \ldots i_n}_{s_0}(\omega_1 \ldots \omega_n) = s$. The automaton m is accessible and hence for all $s \in S$ there exists at least one $\sigma \in \mathrm{pRun}_{\mathcal{P},I}$ fulfilling the previous condition. We now check the good definition of $\underline{\eta}_m$. Consider $\rho \subseteq (\mathrm{pRun}_{\mathcal{P},I})^2$ where

$$\rho = \{\langle i_1\omega_1 \ldots i_n\omega_n, i'_1\omega'_1 \ldots i'_k\omega'_k\rangle \;:\; \delta^{*}{}^{i_1\ldots i_n}_{s_0}(\omega_1 \ldots \omega_n) = \delta^{*}{}^{i'_1\ldots i'_k}_{s_0}(\omega'_1 \ldots \omega'_k)\}.$$

We verify that ρ is a congruence over $Free(Unf(m))$. Clearly it is an equivalence relation, moreover if $i_1\omega_1 \ldots i_n\omega_n \,\rho\, i'_1\omega'_1 \ldots i'_k\omega'_k$ then:

- $i_1\omega_1 \ldots i_n\omega_n i\omega \,\rho\, i'_1\omega'_1 \ldots i'_k\omega'_k i\omega$, hence $\delta'^{i}_{i_1\omega_1\ldots i_n\omega_n}(\omega) \,\rho\, \delta'^{i}_{i'_1\omega'_1\ldots i'_k\omega'_k}(\omega)$;
- $\Lambda'(i_1\omega_1 \ldots i_n\omega_n) = \Lambda(\delta^{*}{}^{i_1\ldots i_n}_{s_0}(\omega_1 \ldots \omega_n)) =$
  $\Lambda(\delta^{*}{}^{i'_1\ldots i'_k}_{s_0}(\omega'_1 \ldots \omega'_k)) = \Lambda'(i'_1\omega'_1 \ldots i'_k\omega'_k)$.

Assume that $\sigma_1, \sigma_2 \in \mathrm{pRun}_{\mathcal{P},I}$ are such that $\underline{\eta}_m(s) = [\sigma_1]_{\approx}$ and $\sigma_1\rho\sigma_2$ (i.e. $\underline{\eta}_m(s)$ is also equal to $[\sigma_2]_{\approx}$); then since $\rho \subseteq\approx$ we have $[\sigma_1]_{\approx} = [\sigma_2]_{\approx}$ and hence $\underline{\eta}_m$ is well defined. In the sequel we denote by σ_s a proper run such that $\sigma_s = i_1\omega_1 \ldots i_n\omega_n$ and $\delta^{*}{}^{i_1\ldots i_n}_{s_0}(\omega_1 \ldots \omega_n) = s$. We now check that η_m is a morphism:

- $\underline{\eta}_m(\delta^{i}_{s}(\omega)) = \underline{\eta}_m(\delta^{i}_{\delta^{*}{}^{i_1\ldots i_n}_{s_0}(\omega_1\ldots\omega_n)}(\omega)) = \underline{\eta}_m(\delta^{*}{}^{i_1\ldots i_n i}_{s_0}(\omega_1 \ldots \omega_n\omega)) =$
  $[\sigma_s i\omega]_{\approx} = \delta'_{\approx}{}^{i}_{[\sigma_s]_{\approx}}(\omega) = \delta_{\approx}{}^{i}_{\underline{\eta}_m(s)}(\omega)$;

– $\Lambda(s) = \Lambda(\delta^{*i_1 \dots i_n}_{s_0}(\omega_1 \dots \omega_n)) = \Lambda'(\sigma_s) = \Lambda'_\approx([\sigma_s]_\approx) = \Lambda'_\approx(\underline{\eta}_m(s))$.

Furthermore we show that η is a natural transformation:
$(\mathrm{id}_{\mathrm{pRun}_{\mathcal{P},I\approx}} \circ \underline{\eta}_{m_1})(s_1) = (\mathrm{id}_{\mathrm{pRun}_{\mathcal{P},I\approx}} \circ \underline{\eta}_{m_1})(\delta^{*i_1 \dots i_n}_{1\,s_0^1}(\omega_1 \dots \omega_n)) =$
$\mathrm{id}_{\mathrm{pRun}_{\mathcal{P},I\approx}}([\sigma_{s_1}]_{\approx_1}) = [\sigma_{s_1}]_{\approx_2} = \underline{\eta}_{m_2}(\delta^{*i_1 \dots i_n}_{2\,s_0^2}(\omega_1 \dots \omega_n)) = (\underline{\eta}_{m_2} \circ \underline{f})(s_1)$.
Universal Property:
Let $\langle \overline{\overline{f}}, \underline{f} \rangle : m_1 \to \mathit{Min}(B)$ be a morphism in $\mathbf{aPAut}_{\mathcal{P},I}$. Then, $\overline{\overline{f}} : \mathit{Unf}(m_1) \to B$ is a morphism in $\mathbf{PBeh}_{\mathcal{P},I}$:

– $\overline{\overline{f}}(\Lambda_1(\delta^{*i_1 \dots i_n}_{1\,s_0}(\omega_1 \dots \omega_n))) = \Lambda_\approx(\underline{f}(\delta^{*i_1 \dots i_n}_{1\,s_0}(\omega_1 \dots \omega_n))) =$
$\Lambda_\approx(\delta_\approx{}^{*i_1 \dots i_n}_{[\varepsilon]_\approx}(\omega_1 \dots \omega_n)) = \beta(i_1\omega_1 \dots i_n\omega_n)$.

Clearly $\mathit{Min}(\overline{\overline{f}}) \circ \eta_m = \langle \overline{\overline{f}}, \underline{f} \rangle$:
$\mathrm{id}_{\mathrm{pRun}_{\mathcal{P},I\approx}}(\underline{\eta}_m(s)) = \mathrm{id}_{\mathrm{pRun}_{\mathcal{P},I\approx}}(\underline{\eta}_m(\delta^{*i_1 \dots i_n}_{1\,s_0}(\omega_1 \dots \omega_n))) =$
$\mathrm{id}_{\mathrm{pRun}_{\mathcal{P},I\approx}}([\sigma_s]_{\approx_1}) = [\sigma_s]_\approx = \delta_\approx{}^{*i_1 \dots i_n}_{[\epsilon]_\approx}(\omega_1 \dots \omega_n) =$
$\underline{f}(\delta^{*i_1 \dots i_n}_{s_0}(\omega_1 \dots \omega_n)) = \underline{f}(s)$.
The uniqueness requirement is straightforward. □

As usual, the minimal realization is obtained by applying the minimization procedure to the free realization. The congruence $\approx$ over $\mathit{Free}(B)$ is called the (probabilistic) Nerode equivalence for the behavior B. The preservation of aggregation and interconnection via *Min* is meaningless since we have fixed the input alphabet and these constructs are only defined when we change the input alphabets of the automata.

6 Conclusions

We have characterized both aggregation and interconnection of probabilistic automata by means of universal constructs. Furthermore we have shown that minimal and free realization for probabilistic behavior are both universal. Finally we also have shown that *Unf*, the functor that maps each probability automaton to its behavior, preserves the constructions in mind.

We manage to achieve the results above by assuming that the random source (probability presentation) is fixed. Otherwise we have to define the notion of morphism between probability spaces and work with weaker structures than categories [10]. However certain constructions can not be explained with a single random source, such as state constraints. We intend to extend the work to a generic random source (probability space where the σ-algebra is not the 2^Ω and Ω is not countable). Another interesting research direction that we intend to pursue is the study of probabilistic properties like first passage times (of an output, of a state) and how they propagate over aggregation and interconnection as well as free and minimal realizations.

Acknowledgements

This work was partially supported by Fundação para a Ciência e a Tecnologia, the PRAXIS XXI Projects PRAXIS/P/MAT/10002/1998 ProbLog, PCEX/P /MAT/46/96 ACL and 2/2.1/TIT/1658/95 LogComp, as well as by the ESPRIT IV Working Groups 22704 ASPIRE and 23531 FIREworks.

References

1. J. Adámek and V. Trnková. *Automata and Algebras in Categories.* Kluwer Academic Publishers, Dordrecht/Boston/London, 1989. 237, 244
2. M. Barr and C. Wells. *Category Theory for Computing Science.* Prentice-Hall International Series in Computer Science. Prentice-Hall, 1990. 238
3. J. Bénabou. Fibred categories and the foundations of naive category theory. *Journal of Symbolic Logic*, 50:10–37, 1985. 238
4. R. Blute, J. Desharnais, A. Edalat, and P. Panangaden. Bisimulation for labelled Markov processes. In *Proceedings, Twelth Annual IEEE Symposium on Logic in-Computer Science*, pages 149–158, Warsaw, Poland, 29 June–2 July 1997. IEEE Computer Society Press. 237
5. L. Coppey. Quelques problèmes typiques concernant les graphes. *Diagrammes*, 3:C1–C46, 1980. 237
6. C. Ehresmann. *Catégories et structures.* Dunod, 1965. 237
7. J. Goguen. Realization is universal. *Mathematical Systems Theory*, 6:359–374, 1973. 237
8. P. Halmos. *Measure Theory.* Van Nostrand, New York, NY, 1969. (July 1969 reprinting). 238
9. K. Larsen and A. Skou. Bisimulation through probabilistic testing. *Information and Computation*, 94(1):1–28, September 1991. 237
10. P. Mateus, A. Sernadas, and C. Sernadas. Precategories for combining probabilistic automata. *Electronic Notes in Theoretical Computer Science*, 1999. Early version presented at FIREworks Meeting, Magdeburg, May 15-16, 1998. Presented at CTCS'99, Edinburgh, September 10-12, 1999. In print. 237, 250
11. A. Paz. Some aspects of probabalistic automata. *Information and Control*, 9(1):26–60, February 1966. 237
12. M. Rabin. Probabilistic automata. *Information and Control*, 6(3):230–245, September 1963. 237
13. L. Schröder and P. Mateus. Universal aspects of probabilistic automata. Research report, Section of Computer Science, Department of Mathematics, Instituto Superior Técnico, 1049-001 Lisboa, Portugal, 1999. Submitted for publication. 237
14. R. van Glabbeek, S. Smolka, B. Steffen, and C. Tofts. Reactive, generativem and stratified models for probabilistic processes. *Information and Computation*, 121(1):59–80, 1995. 237
15. G. Winskel and M. Nielsen. Models of concurrency. In D. Gabbay S. Abramsky and T. Maibaum, editors, *Handbook of Logic in Computer Science 4*, pages 1–148. Oxford Science Publications, 1995. 237

Specifications in an Arbitrary Institution with Symbols

Till Mossakowski

Department of Computer Science and Bremen, Institute for Safe Systems,
University of Bremen, Germany

Abstract. We develop a notion of institution with symbols and a kernel language for writing structured specifications in CASL. This kernel language has a semantics in an arbitrary but fixed institution with symbols. Compared with other institution-independent kernel languages, the advantage is that translations, hidings etc. can be written in a symbol-oriented way (rather than being based on signature morphisms as primitive notion), while still being institution-independent. The semantics of the kernel language has been used as the basis for the semantics of structured specifications in CASL.

1 Introduction

Formal specification of software systems can typically be split into specification-in-the-small, dealing with the specification of individual datatypes, and specification-in-the-large, dealing with the combination of specifications and/or datatypes in a structured way. The framework of institutions, a formalization of the model-theoretic aspects of the notion of logical system, allows a clean separation of these issues: while specification-in-the-small is based on a particular institution, a number of formalisms for specification-in-the-large such as Clear, ACT TWO, ASL and ASL+ have been developed largely for an arbitrary (but fixed) institution.

However, the institution-independent setting as used in the above formalism has some important drawbacks:

- signature morphisms are taken as primitives. This implies that one cannot rename or hide just a symbol, but rather has to construct the resulting signature in advance, together with the corresponding signature morphism;
- pushouts (in some formalisms necessary for instance to instantiate generic specifications) are defined only up to isomorphism; thus, the user does not have full control over the name space of the specification constructed;
- unions can be taken only of specifications over the same signature (unless an extra inclusion system is specified).

In this work, to resolve these problems, we propose a notion of institution with symbols. Roughly, an institution with symbols is an institution where each signature has an underlying set of symbols, and each signature morphism has

D. Bert, C. Choppy, and P. Mosses (Eds.): WADT'99, LNCS 1827, pp. 252–270, 2000.

an underlying symbol translation function. Within this setting, we can define renamings, hidings, unions and pushouts in an explicit, symbol-oriented way that overcomes the above drawbacks. We also define a notion of institution with qualified symbols to deal with the problems of overloading.

To show that these extra complications can be avoided when not needed, we show that an institution with qualified symbols can be constructed out of any institution with symbols in a trivial way (with no overloading possible).

These notions provide a proper institutional framework for the semantics of CASL, a specification formalism developed within the CoFI initiative. In particular, the semantics of structured specifications in CASL can be based on an arbitrary institution with qualified symbols.

The paper is organized as follows. In section 2, we recall the notion of institution and a kernel language allowing to write specifications over an arbitrary institutions. We discuss the problems with this approach, which leads to the definition of institution with symbols in section 3 and of a new kernel language (together with its semantics) in section 4. Institutions with qualified symbols are introduced in section 5, and the CASL institution is shown to be an institution with qualified symbols in section 6. Finally, section 7 contains conclusions and future work. An extended version of this paper (including all proofs) is available as CoFI study note S-10 in [4].

2 Specifications in an Arbitrary Institution

The theory of *institutions* [7] takes a predominantly model-theoretic view of logic, with the satisfaction relation between models and logical sentences adopted as a primary notion. Somewhat unlike in the classical model-theory though, a family of such relations is considered at once, indexed by a category of signatures.

Definition 2.1. An *institution* **I** consists of:

- a category $\mathbf{Sign_I}$ of *signatures*;
- a functor $\mathbf{Sen_I}: \mathbf{Sign_I} \to \mathbf{Set}$, giving a set $\mathbf{Sen}(\Sigma)$ of *Σ-sentences* for each signature $\Sigma \in |\mathbf{Sign_I}|$;
- a functor $\mathbf{Mod_I}: \mathbf{Sign_I}^{op} \to \mathbf{Cat}^1$, giving a class $\mathbf{Mod}(\Sigma)$ of *Σ-models* for each signature $\Sigma \in |\mathbf{Sign_I}|$; and
- for $\Sigma \in |\mathbf{Sign_I}|$, a *satisfaction relation* $\models_{\mathbf{I},\Sigma} \subseteq \mathbf{Mod_I}(\Sigma) \times \mathbf{Sen_I}(\Sigma)$

such that for any signature morphism $\sigma: \Sigma \to \Sigma'$, Σ-sentence $\varphi \in \mathbf{Sen_I}(\Sigma)$ and Σ'-model $M' \in \mathbf{Mod_I}(\Sigma')$ the following *satisfaction condition* holds:

$$M' \models_{\mathbf{I},\Sigma'} \mathbf{Sen_I}(\sigma)(\varphi) \iff \mathbf{Mod_I}(\sigma)(M') \models_{\mathbf{I},\Sigma} \varphi$$

We write $M'|_\sigma$ for $\mathbf{Mod}(\sigma)(M')$, where $\sigma: \Sigma \longrightarrow \Sigma' \in \mathbf{Sign}$ and $M' \in \mathbf{Mod}(\Sigma')$.

The notion of institution emerged as a formalisation of the concept of logical system underlying algebraic specification formalisms. Given an institution **I**,

[1] **Cat** is the (quasi-)category of all categories.

the rough idea is that signatures determine the syntax of the systems to be specified, models of the institution represent (the semantics of) the systems themselves, and sentences are used to specify the desired system properties. Whatever specifications are, they should ultimately describe a signature and a class of models over this signature, called *models of the specifications*, to capture the admissible realizations of the specified system. Consequently, any specification formalism over **I** determines a class of specifications, and then, for any specification SP, its signature $Sig[SP] \in |\mathbf{Sign}|$ and the collection of its models $Mod[SP] \subseteq \mathbf{Mod}(Sig[SP])$. If $Sig[SP] = \Sigma$, we refer to SP as Σ-specification.

In [9], the following kernel language for specifications in an arbitrary institution **I** has been proposed:

***presentations*:** For any signature $\Sigma \in |\mathbf{Sign}|$ and set $\Phi \subseteq \mathbf{Sen}(\Sigma)$ of Σ-sentences, the *presentation* $\langle \Sigma, \Phi \rangle$ is a specification with:
$$Sig[\langle \Sigma, \Phi \rangle] = \Sigma$$
$$Mod[\langle \Sigma, \Phi \rangle] = \{M \in \mathbf{Mod}(\Sigma) \mid M \models \Phi\}$$

***union*:** For any signature $\Sigma \in |\mathbf{Sign}|$, given Σ-specifications SP_1 and SP_2, their *union* $SP_1 \cup SP_2$ is a specification with:
$$Sig[SP_1 \cup SP_2] = \Sigma$$
$$Mod[SP_1 \cup SP_2] = Mod[SP_1] \cap Mod[SP_2]$$

***translation*:** For any signature morphism $\sigma: \Sigma \to \Sigma'$ and Σ-specification SP, **translate** SP **by** σ is a specification with:
$$Sig[\textbf{translate } SP \textbf{ by } \sigma] = \Sigma'$$
$$Mod[\textbf{translate } SP \textbf{ by } \sigma] = \{M' \in \mathbf{Mod}(\Sigma') \mid M'|_\sigma \in Mod[SP]\}$$

***hiding*:** For any signature morphism $\sigma: \Sigma \to \Sigma'$ and Σ'-specification SP', **derive from** SP' **by** σ is a specification with:
$$Sig[\textbf{derive from } SP' \textbf{ by } \sigma] = \Sigma$$
$$Mod[\textbf{derive from } SP' \textbf{ by } \sigma] = \{M'|_\sigma \mid M' \in Mod[SP']\}$$

The above *specification-building operations*, although extremely simple, already provide flexible mechanisms for expressing basic ways of putting specifications together and so for building specifications in a structured manner. Further, perhaps rather more convenient-to-use operations may be built on this basis. See for instance [9] for examples and much further discussion.

However, the institution-independent setting as used in this and other similar formalisms has some important drawbacks:

- signature morphisms are taken as primitives. This implies that one cannot rename or hide just a symbol, but rather has to construct the resulting signature in advance, together with the corresponding signature morphism;
- pushouts (in some formalisms necessary for instance to instantiate generic specifications) are defined only up to isomorphism; thus, the user does not have full control over the name space of the specification constructed;
- unions can be taken only of specifications with the same signature.

The third problem (concerning unions) can be overcome by working with signature categories having associated inclusion systems [3]. However, the other problems still remain in such an approach.

3 Institution with Symbols

To resolve the problems mentioned at the end of the last section, we propose a notion of institution with symbols. Roughly, an institution with symbols is an institution where each signature has an underlying set of symbols, and each signature morphism has an underlying symbol translation function. Within this setting, we can define renamings, hidings, unions and pushouts in an explicit, symbol-oriented way that overcomes the above problems.

Consider an institution $(\mathbf{Sign}, \mathbf{Sen}, \mathbf{Mod}, \models)$ additionally equipped with a faithful functor $|\_|: \mathbf{Sign} \longrightarrow \mathbf{Set}$ that extracts from each signature the set of (fully qualified) symbols that occur in it (i.e. $(\mathbf{Sign}, |\_|)$ is a concrete category [1]). We assume that there is some fixed "universe" of *Sym* of symbols that may be used by the specifier when writing symbol mappings. The latter are the means for the user to specify signature morphisms in a convenient way. A symbol map should be some kind of map on *Sym*. We cannot expect this map to be total, because not all symbols may be mapped. Moreover, we even cannot expect it to be total on the set of symbols of a given source signature, since we want to free the user from specifying identically mapped symbols. Finally, it turns out to be much more convenient even not to require symbol maps to be functions – a user may erroneously map one and the same symbol to two different symbols (of course, in such a case, there will be no signature morphism induced by the symbol map). So we arrive at the following:

A symbol map h is a finite *relation* $h \subseteq \mathit{Sym} \times \mathit{Sym}$.

The *domain* of a symbol map is defined as

$$\mathit{dom}(h) = \{SY \in \mathit{Sym} \mid \exists (SY, SY') \in h\}$$

We further assume that some function $\mathit{Ext}: |\mathbf{Sign}| \times |\mathbf{Sign}| \times \mathit{FinSet}(\mathit{Sym} \times \mathit{Sym}) \longrightarrow \mathit{FinSet}(\mathit{Sym} \times \mathit{Sym})$ is given. Its use is as follows. Consider a parameterized specification; and let h be a symbol map fitting the formal parameter (having signature Σ) with the actual parameter (having signature Σ'). Then $\mathit{Ext}(\Sigma, \Sigma', h)$ extends h to a translation of compound identifiers in the body (for example, in CASL, a fitting of sort *Elem* to sort Nat leads to the renaming of sort *List*[*Elem*] into the sort *List*[Nat]). If one is not interested in compound identifiers, $\mathit{Ext}(\Sigma, \Sigma', h)$ can be taken to be just h. In section 5, we will propose a particular definition of *Ext*. Now we are ready for our central definition:

Definition 3.1. An *institution with symbols* $(\mathbf{Sign}, \mathbf{Sen}, \mathbf{Mod}, \models, \mathit{Sym}, |\_|)$ consists of

- an institution $(\mathbf{Sign}, \mathbf{Sen}, \mathbf{Mod}, \models)$,
- a set of (fully qualified) symbols *Sym*,
- a faithful functor $|\_|: \mathbf{Sign} \longrightarrow \mathbf{Set}$ giving, for each signature Σ, a set of symbols $|\Sigma| \subseteq \mathit{Sym}$, and for each signature morphism $\sigma: \Sigma \longrightarrow \Sigma'$, a translation of symbols $|\sigma|: |\Sigma| \longrightarrow |\Sigma'|$,
- a function $\mathit{Ext}: |\mathbf{Sign}| \times |\mathbf{Sign}| \times \mathit{FinSet}(\mathit{Sym} \times \mathit{Sym}) \longrightarrow \mathit{FinSet}(\mathit{Sym} \times \mathit{Sym})$,

such that

$$h \subseteq Ext(\Sigma, \Sigma', h)$$

for each $h \subseteq Sym \times Sym$ and $\Sigma, \Sigma' \in |\mathbf{Sign}|$.

In the sequel, we will, by abuse of notation, identify σ and $|\sigma|$ (this is legitimated by faithfulness of $|\_|$). In particular, we say that a map $\sigma: |\Sigma| \longrightarrow |\Sigma'|$ is a signature morphism if there exists a signature morphism $\theta: \Sigma \longrightarrow \Sigma'$ with $|\theta| = \sigma$. By faithfulness of $|\_|$, such a θ is unique. By abuse of notation, we will also denote it by $\sigma: \Sigma \longrightarrow \Sigma'$.

4 A New Kernel Language

In this section, we define a new kernel language for structured specifications, which can be seen as an underlying kernel language for CASL. It is defined over an arbitrary institution with symbols and allows to write specifications in a more concise and convenient way in comparison with the kernel language introduced in section 2. For simplicity, we include not all the constructs of CASL structured specification in the kernel language, but leave out those like local specifications that can be expressed using other constructs. Moreover, we do not allow signature fragments as in CASL, since allowing these would lead to a more complex semantics of the language without giving much more insight into the concepts that we want to present. The kernel language for institutions with symbols consists of the following (the function Sig, computing the signature of a specification, as well as the constructions $h|_{\Sigma}$, $\Sigma|_{SYs}$, $\Sigma|^{SYs}$ and $h|^{\Sigma}_{\Sigma'}$, will be defined in the subsections below):

presentations: For any signature $\Sigma \in |\mathbf{Sign}|$ and set $\Phi \subseteq \mathbf{Sen}(\Sigma)$ of Σ-sentences, the *presentation* $\langle \Sigma, \Phi \rangle$ is a specification,

union: For any specifications SP_1 and SP_2 with the corresponding signature union $Sig[SP_1] \cup Sig[SP_2]$ defined, their *union* SP_1 **and** SP_2 is a specification,

translation: For any symbol map $h \subseteq Sym \times Sym$ and specification SP with $h|_{Sig[SP]}$ defined, SP **with** h is a specification

revealing: For any specification SP and set of symbols $SYs \subseteq Sym$ with $Sig[SP]|_{SYs}$ defined, SP **reveal** SYs is a specification,

hiding: For any specification SP and set of symbols $SYs \subseteq Sym$ with $Sig[SP]|^{SYs}$ defined, SP **hide** SYs is a specification,

instantiation: For any three specifications SP, SP' and SP_A and a symbol map $h \subseteq Sym \times Sym$ such that $Sig[SP]$ is a subsignature of $Sig[SP']$ and $h|^{Sig[SP]}_{Sig[SP_A]}$ is defined, **instantiate** (SP, SP') **by** SP_A **fit** h is a specification.

The side conditions on the well-formedness of a specification are explained in the following subsections. For typical institutions with symbols, they can be checked statically. Thus, it makes sense to impose them on the language.

The semantics of the new kernel language is given by translating it to the old kernel language, using a translation function $[\![\_]\!]$. Using this translation function, we can easily lift the semantic functions *Sig* and *Mod* from the old to the new kernel language by putting, for a specification SP written in the new kernel language:

$$Sig[SP] = Sig[[\![SP]\!]] \qquad Mod[SP] = Mod[[\![SP]\!]]$$

Note that even for well-formed specifications, the translation function $[\![\_]\!]$ will be a partial function, and so will be *Sig* and *Mod*. This means that the semantics of some specifications of the new kernel language will be undefined (this will happen only for specifications involving instantiations). Checking definedness involves checking model class inclusions, which is undecidable in general. In contrast, the function *Sig* will be decidable for those institutions with symbols having the constructions $h|_\Sigma$, $\Sigma|_{SYs}$, $\Sigma|^{SYs}$ and $h|^{\Sigma}_{\Sigma'}$ computable.

For presentations, the clause of the inductive definition of the translation function is trivial:

$$[\![\langle \Sigma, \Phi \rangle]\!] = \langle \Sigma, \Phi \rangle$$

4.1 Revealings and Hidings

To be able to interpret the revealing of a set of symbols of a given signature, we need to be able to construct a subsignature generated by these symbols. This can be formalized within an arbitrary but fixed institution with symbols as follows, directly following [10].

We say that a signature morphism $\iota: \Sigma \longrightarrow \Sigma'$ is a *signature inclusion* if $|\iota|$ is an inclusion (of $|\Sigma|$ into $|\Sigma'|$). If there exists a signature inclusion from Σ to Σ', we call Σ a *subsignature* of Σ', and write $\Sigma \subseteq \Sigma'$. Notice that then the signature inclusion is unique, since the functor $|\_|$ is faithful; we denote it by $\iota_{\Sigma \subseteq \Sigma'}$.

A subsignature Σ of Σ' is said to be *full*[2] if every subsignature of Σ' with the same set of symbols as Σ is a subsignature of Σ. Notice that for standard many-sorted signatures, the notions of signature and full subsignature coincide — every subsignature is full. A subsorted subsignature Σ of Σ' is full if and only if Σ inherits from Σ' all the subsort requirements concerning the sorts of Σ.

We call a set of symbols $SYs \subseteq |\Sigma|$ *closed* in Σ if there is a subsignature Σ' of Σ with the set of symbols SYs, i.e. such that $|\Sigma'| = SYs$.

For any set $SYs \subseteq |\Sigma|$, a *signature generated in Σ by SYs* is a full subsignature Σ' of Σ such that $|\Sigma'|$ is the smallest set containing SYs and closed in Σ. It is denoted by $\Sigma|_{SYs}$.

Dually, to be able to interpret hiding, we need: For any set $SYs \subseteq |\Sigma|$, a *signature co-generated in Σ by SYs* is a full subsignature Σ' of Σ such that $|\Sigma'|$ is the largest set disjoint from SYs and closed in Σ. It is denoted by $\Sigma|^{SYs}$.

With this, we can give a (translational) semantics of revealing and hiding:

$[\![SP$ **reveal** $SYs]\!] =$ **derive from** $[\![SP]\!]$ **by** σ

where $\Sigma = Sig[SP]$ and $\sigma: \Sigma|_{SYs} \longrightarrow \Sigma$ is the inclusion.

[2] To be more uniform with section 4.2, we could replace fullness by initiality. $\iota: \Sigma \longrightarrow \Sigma'$ is initial if for any function $\sigma: |\Sigma''| \longrightarrow |\Sigma|$, σ is a signature morphism provided $\iota \circ \sigma$ is. Initiality implies fullness, but not conversely, although the converse is true for the standard examples.

$[\![SP \textbf{ hide } SYs]\!] = \textbf{derive from } [\![SP]\!] \textbf{ by } \sigma$
where $\Sigma = Sig[SP]$ and $\sigma\colon \Sigma\,|^{SYs} \longrightarrow \Sigma$ is the inclusion.

4.2 Translations

For translations, the main problem is the following: Given a signature Σ and a symbol map h, construct a signature morphism $\sigma\colon \Sigma \longrightarrow \Sigma'$ that is in some sense compatible with h. Generally, there are many different choices for the target signature Σ' with the same underlying symbol map $|\sigma|$: one can arbitrarily extend Σ' with some stuff that is not in the image of $|\sigma|$. We therefore want Σ' to be minimal in a certain sense. This is achieved by the notion of finality[3].

A signature morphism $\sigma\colon \Sigma \longrightarrow \Sigma'$ is said to be *final* [1][4] if for any function $\sigma'\colon |\Sigma'| \longrightarrow |\Sigma''|$, σ' is a signature morphism provided that $\sigma' \circ \sigma$ is. In the category of many-sorted algebraic signatures, a signature morphism is final iff it is surjective. For morphisms between subsorted signatures, finality additionally means that Σ' has the minimal subsorting relation making σ into a signature morphism (i.e. Σ' inherits the subsorting relation from Σ along σ), see proposition 6.5 below.

Next, we have to specify the exact relation between a symbol map h and the corresponding signature morphism σ. We want to free the user from specifying the mapping of symbols that are mapped identically. This is achieved by the following: Given a signature Σ and a symbol map h, if there is a unique signature morphism $\sigma\colon \Sigma \longrightarrow \Sigma'$ such that $h \subseteq graph(|\sigma|)$ and σ is final, then σ is called *the signature morphism from* Σ *induced by* h, written $h|_\Sigma$ (otherwise, $h|_\Sigma$ is undefined). Given a signature Σ, a symbol map h is called *admissible for* Σ, if there is some signature morphism $\sigma\colon \Sigma \longrightarrow \Sigma'$ with $h \subseteq graph(|\sigma|)$ and σ is final. Let $Admissible(\Sigma)$ be the set of symbol maps admissible for Σ.

With this, we can specify how translations are mapped to the old kernel language:

$$[\![SP \textbf{ with } h]\!] = \textbf{translate } [\![SP]\!] \textbf{ by } h|_{Sig[SP]}$$

Note that definedness of $h|_{Sig[SP]}$ is already required by the well-formedness condition of the translation.

[3] The reader may be surprised that finality corresponds to some minimality principle here, while final algebras usually satisfy some *maximality* principle. The reason is that the notion of finality comes from categorical topology, and final continuous maps indeed have a *maximal* topology on their target (while final signature morphisms typically have a *minimal* target).

[4] In the theory of co-fibrations, these morphisms as called *co-cartesian* [2], and they are defined in a slightly more general setting, namely, faithfulness of the functor is not required. We nevertheless stick to finality here, because finality is also defined for sinks, see below.

4.3 Unions

Concerning unions, the main feature that we have added to the old kernel language is the ability to unite specifications having different signatures. Therefore, we need to be able to unite signatures. We will do this using so-called minimal lifts of sinks.

A *sink* is a pair of morphisms with common codomain.

A *lift* of a $|\_|$-structured sink $(\sigma_1: |\Sigma_1| \longrightarrow SYs, \sigma_2: |\Sigma_2| \longrightarrow SYs)$ is a sink $(\sigma_1: \Sigma_1 \longrightarrow \Sigma, \sigma_2: \Sigma_2 \longrightarrow \Sigma)$ such that $|\Sigma| = SYs$.[5]

A lift $(\sigma_1: \Sigma_1 \longrightarrow \Sigma, \sigma_2: \Sigma_2 \longrightarrow \Sigma)$ of a $|\_|$-structured sink $(\sigma_1: |\Sigma_1| \longrightarrow SYs, \sigma_2: |\Sigma_2| \longrightarrow SYs)$ is said to be *minimal*, if for every other lift $(\sigma_1: \Sigma_1 \longrightarrow \Sigma', \sigma_2: \Sigma_2 \longrightarrow \Sigma')$ of the same sink, the function $id_{|\Sigma|}: \Sigma \longrightarrow \Sigma'$ is a signature morphism.

Given two signatures Σ_1 and Σ_2, if the sink $(\iota_{|\Sigma_1| \subseteq |\Sigma_1| \cup |\Sigma_2|}, \iota_{|\Sigma_2| \subseteq |\Sigma_1| \cup |\Sigma_2|})$ has a unique minimal lift, the latter is called the *union* of Σ_1 and Σ_2, denoted by $\Sigma_1 \cup \Sigma_2$. This enables us to define the semantics of unions:

$$[\![SP_1 \textbf{ and } SP_2]\!] = (\textbf{translate } [\![SP_1]\!] \textbf{ by } \sigma_1) \cup (\textbf{translate } [\![SP_2]\!] \textbf{ by } \sigma_2)$$

where $\Sigma_1 = Sig[SP_1]$, $\Sigma_2 = Sig[SP_2]$, $\Sigma = \Sigma_1 \cup \Sigma_2$, and $\sigma_1: \Sigma_1 \longrightarrow \Sigma$ and $\sigma_2: \Sigma_2 \longrightarrow \Sigma$ are the inclusions.

4.4 Instantiations

For instantiations of generic specifications, usually a pushout semantics is used [6]. The problem with this approach is that the user does not have full control over the name space of the specification constructed: generally, new names have to be created in the pushout. In contrast, CASL follows a "same name–same thing" philosophy, which leaves the control over the name space to the user: instantiations are constructed in a naive set-theoretic way. The pushout approach and the set-theoretic approach can be reconciled by requiring the set-theoretic construction to actually be a pushout (and letting the instantiation being undefined if this requirement is not fulfilled). In this section, we show how to perform the set-theoretic construction of an instantiation and formulate conditions that guarantee this construction to be a pushout. Both the construction and the conditions can be formulated in an institution-with-symbols-independent way. Again, the crucial notion is that of finality.

A sink $(\sigma_1: \Sigma_1 \longrightarrow \Sigma, \sigma_2: \Sigma_2 \longrightarrow \Sigma)$ is called *final*, if for each function $\sigma: |\Sigma| \longrightarrow |\Sigma'|$, σ is a signature morphism provided that $\sigma \circ \sigma_1$ and $\sigma \circ \sigma_2$ are. Again, a sink of many-sorted algebraic signature morphisms is final iff the signature morphisms are jointly surjective. For subsorted signature morphisms, additionally the subsorting relation on Σ has to be minimal w.r.t. making both

[5] Recall that by abuse of notation, we use the same names for a signature morphism and its underlying symbol map.

σ_1 and σ_2 signature morphisms, and the transitive closure of the overloading relation has to be the transitive closure of the union of the translated overloading relations (for a related result, see proposition 6.8).

A *final lift* of a $|\_|$-structured sink $(\sigma_1: |\Sigma_1| \longrightarrow SYs, \sigma_2: |\Sigma_2| \longrightarrow SYs)$ is a final sink $(\sigma_1: \Sigma_1 \longrightarrow \Sigma, \sigma_2: \Sigma_2 \longrightarrow \Sigma)$ such that $|\Sigma| = SYs$.

A union of two signatures is said to be *final* if the sink consisting of the two inclusions is final.

The notions of final sink and final lift can be generalized to an arbitrary number of morphisms with common codomain. The concept gains its importance from the following (note that cocones and colimits are special cases of sinks):

Proposition 4.1. *In a concrete category, a final lift of a colimit is again a colimit.*

Since we use final signature morphisms and final unions in the stepwise construction of an instantiation of a generic specification, we can use the above proposition to show that the instantiation is a pushout.

The construction assumes that the formal parameter signature of the generic specification is included in the body signature (so we do not allow an arbitrary signature morphism between formal parameter and body).

Our construction now works as follows: Given a signature inclusion $\Delta: \Sigma \longrightarrow \Sigma'$ (which acts as the inclusion of the formal parameter into the body) and a signature morphism $\sigma: \Sigma \longrightarrow \Sigma_A$ (which acts as the fitting morphism from the formal to the actual parameter), if

- the signature morphism $h|_{\Sigma'}$ from Σ' induced by

$$h = Ext(\Sigma', \Sigma_A, graph(|\sigma|))$$

  exists[6] (let its target be denoted by $\Sigma_A(\Delta)$),
- the union $\Sigma_A \cup \Sigma_A(\Delta)$ exists[7], and moreover, it is final[8],
- $|\Sigma_A| \cap |\Sigma_A(\Delta)| \subseteq |\sigma|(|\Sigma|)$[9], and
- $ker(|(h|_{\Sigma'})|) \subseteq ker(|\sigma|)$[10],

[6] This may fail to exist for several reasons. One is that the symbol map h is not a function because of the definition of *Ext* (see section 5 for an example). Another one is that h is a function, but there is no signature morphism induced by it. In the CASL institution, the latter can happen for example if h does not preserve the overloading relations. An example is given in [8].

[7] The union may fail to exist in the CASL institution because a total and a partial operation symbol with the same profile get united.

[8] The union may fail to be final in the CASL institution if symbols newly get into the overloading relation, cf. Proposition 6.8.

[9] This property may fail if the actual parameter and the body share symbols that are not in the formal parameter.

[10] For the standard definition of *Ext* described in section 5, this property may fail if the fitting morphism σ is not injective (say, it maps both *Elem*1 and *Elem*2 to *nat*) and this leads to new identifications in the extension (say, both *List*[*Elem*1] and *List*[*Elem*2] occur in the body, so $\sigma(\Delta)$ maps both to *List*[*Nat*]).

then $\iota_{\Sigma_A(\Delta) \subseteq \Sigma_A \cup \Sigma_A(\Delta)} \circ h|_{\Sigma'}$ is called the *extension of σ along Δ*, denoted by $\sigma(\Delta) \colon \Sigma' \longrightarrow \Sigma_A \cup \Sigma_A(\Delta)$.

Here, the kernel of a function $f \colon A \longrightarrow B$ is defined as usual:

$$ker(f) = \{(x, y) \in A \times A | f(x) = f(y)\}.$$

Proposition 4.2. *If the extension of $\sigma \colon \Sigma \longrightarrow \Sigma_A$ along $\Delta \colon \Sigma \longrightarrow \Sigma'$ exists, then*

$$\begin{array}{ccc} \Sigma & \subseteq & \Sigma' \\ \downarrow{\scriptstyle \sigma} & & \downarrow{\scriptstyle \sigma(\Delta)} \\ \Sigma_A & \subseteq & \Sigma_A \cup \Sigma_A(\Delta) \end{array}$$

is a pushout in Sig.

Before we can use the above construction to define the semantics of instantiations, we first have to specify how the fitting morphism is obtained from a symbol map. Given signatures Σ and Σ' and a symbol map $h \subseteq Sym \times Sym$, if there is a unique signature morphism $\sigma \colon \Sigma \longrightarrow \Sigma'$ with

$$h \subseteq graph(|\sigma|)$$

we call it *the signature morphism from Σ to Σ' induced by h*, denoted by $h|^{\Sigma}_{\Sigma'}$. Given signatures Σ and Σ', a symbol map $h \subseteq Sym \times Sym$ is called *admissible for Σ and Σ'*, if there is some signature morphism $\sigma \colon \Sigma \longrightarrow \Sigma'$ with $h \subseteq graph(|\sigma|)$. $Admissible(\Sigma, \Sigma')$ denotes the set of all symbol maps admissible for Σ and Σ'.

With this, the semantics of instantiations (given by a translation to the old kernel language) is as follows:

$$[\![\textbf{instantiate } (SP, SP') \textbf{ by } SP_A \textbf{ fit } h]\!] = [\![SP_A]\!] \cup (\textbf{translate } [\![SP']\!] \textbf{ by } \sigma(\Delta))$$

where $\Sigma = Sig[SP]$, of $\Sigma' = Sig[SP']$, $\Delta \colon \Sigma \longrightarrow \Sigma'$ is the inclusion, $\Sigma_A = Sig[SP_A]$ and $\sigma = h|^{\Sigma}_{\Sigma_A}$. The semantics is undefined whenever it is not the case that

1. $\mathbf{Mod}(SP')|_{\iota_{Sig[SP] \subseteq Sig[SP']}} \subseteq \mathbf{Mod}(SP)$, and
2. $\mathbf{Mod}(SP_A)|_{\sigma} \subseteq \mathbf{Mod}(SP)$.

which means that $\iota_{Sig[SP] \subseteq Sig[SP']}$ and σ are both specification morphisms.

5 Institutions with Qualified Symbols

In this section, we define a notion of institution with qualified symbols to deal with the problems of overloading and qualification.

In the CASL institution, the natural choice for $|\Sigma|$ is the set of *fully qualified* symbols of Σ (if we omit qualifications, $|\_|$ is no longer faithful, because symbols may be overloaded with different profiles). Now in CASL symbol mappings, one may (either partially or completely) omit qualifications of symbols. This leads to the notion of *raw symbol*, which in the case of the CASL institution can be a qualified symbol, an unqualified symbol or a partially qualified symbol. The link between symbols and raw symbols is given by a *matching relation* specifying which symbols correspond to which raw symbols. In order to be able to construct the extension map *Ext* explicitly, we further assume that there is a set of *compound identifiers*.

The following notion abstracts this to an institution-independent setting:

Definition 5.1. An *institution with qualified symbols* $(\mathbf{Sign}, \mathbf{Sen}, \mathbf{Mod}, \models, \mathit{Sym}, |\_|, \mathtt{ID}, \mathit{RawSym}, \mathit{IDAsRawSym}, \mathit{SymAsRawSym}, \mathit{matches})$ consists of

- an institution $(\mathbf{Sign}, \mathbf{Sen}, \mathbf{Mod}, \models)$,
- a set of (fully qualified) symbols Sym,
- a faithful functor $|\_|: \mathbf{Sign} \longrightarrow \mathbf{Set}$,
- a set $\mathtt{ID}$ of compound identifiers,
- a set of raw symbols RawSym together with two injections $\mathit{IDAsRawSym}: \mathtt{ID} \longrightarrow \mathit{RawSym}$ and $\mathit{SymAsRawSym}: \mathit{Sym} \longrightarrow \mathit{RawSym}$,
- a matching relation $\mathit{matches} \subseteq \mathit{Sym} \times \mathit{RawSym}$ specifying which qualified symbols match which raw symbols,

such that

- $|\Sigma| \subseteq \mathit{Sym}$ for each $\Sigma \in |\mathbf{Sign}|$,
- for $id, ci_1, \ldots, ci_n \in \mathtt{ID}$, also $id[ci_1, \ldots, ci_n] \in \mathtt{ID}$ (i.e. we can form compound identifiers)
- SY matches $\mathit{SymAsRawSym}(SY')$ iff $SY = SY'$ for $SY, SY' \in \mathit{Sym}$[11] and
- for each $SY \in \mathit{Sym}$, there is a unique $\mathit{Ident} \in \mathtt{ID}$ with SY matching $\mathit{IDAsRawSym}(\mathit{Ident})$ (called the *name* of SY)

Raw symbol maps are defined like symbol maps: they are finite binary relations $r \subseteq \mathit{RawSym} \times \mathit{RawSym}$. In the kernel language of section 4, we now can replace symbol maps by raw symbols maps and thus obtain more conciseness when writing specifications. In most cases, the kernel language just remains the same as before (note that $\mathit{Sig}[\_]$, $\{\{\_\}\}$ and $\{\{\_\}\}^-$ are defined later on):

***presentations*:** For any signature $\Sigma \in |\mathbf{Sign}|$ and set $\Phi \subseteq \mathbf{Sen}(\Sigma)$ of Σ-sentences, the *presentation* $\langle \Sigma, \Phi \rangle$ is a specification,

***union*:** For any specifications SP_1 and SP_2 with the corresponding signature union $\mathit{Sig}[SP_1] \cup \mathit{Sig}[SP_2]$ defined, their *union* SP_1 **and** SP_2 is a specification,

***translation*:** For any raw symbol map $r \subseteq \mathit{RawSym} \times \mathit{RawSym}$ and specification SP with $\{\{r\}\}^{\mathit{Admissible}(\mathit{Sig}[SP])}|_{\mathit{Sig}[SP]}$ defined, SP **with** r is a specification

***revealing*:** For any specification SP and set of raw symbols $RSYs \subseteq \mathit{RawSym}$ with $\mathit{Sig}[SP]|_{\{\{RSYs\}\} \cap \mathit{Sig}[SP]}$ defined, SP **reveal** SYs is a specification,

[11] This property is not technically needed in the semantics, but it is desirable since it means that for each ambiguity there is a qualification to resolve it.

***hiding*:** For any specification SP and set of raw symbols $RSYs \subseteq RawSym$ with $Sig[SP] |^{\{\{RSYs\}\} \cap Sig[SP]}$ defined, SP **hide** SYs is a specification,

***instantiation*:** For any three specifications SP, SP' and SP_A and a raw symbol map $r \subseteq RawSym \times RawSym$ such that $Sig[SP]$ is a subsignature of $Sig[SP']$ and $\{\{r\}\}^{Admissible(Sig[SP'],Sig[SP_A])} |^{ISig[SP]}_{Sig[SP_A]}$ is defined,

$$\textbf{instantiate } (SP, SP') \textbf{ by } SP_A \textbf{ fit } r$$

is a specification.

To be able to interpret this modified kernel language and explain its well-formedness conditions, we need to construct a symbols out of raw symbols somehow. At the symbol level this is easy: just put

$$\{\{RSYs\}\} = \{SY \in Sym | SY \text{ matches some } RSY \in RSYs\}$$

Now let us concern the level of maps. A first step is to extend the matching relation from symbols to maps as follows: Given a symbol map $h \subseteq Sym \times Sym$ and a raw symbol map $r \subseteq RawSym \times RawSym$, we say that *h matches r* if

- For all $RSY \in dom(r)$, there exists some $SY \in dom(h)$ matching RSY
- For all $(RSY, RSY') \in r$ and $(SY, SY') \in h$, SY matches RSY implies SY' matches RSY'.

However, the matching relation between symbol maps and raw symbol maps does not suffice to achieve our goal. This is illustrated by an example that lives in the CASL institution (this institution is formally defined in section 6). Consider the signatures

Signature	sorts	operation symbols
Σ	$s,\ u$	$f : s \to s,\ f : u \to u$
Σ'	$t,\ v$	$g : t \to t,\ f : v \to v$
Σ''	$t,\ v$	$g : t \to t,\ g : v \to v$

Let r be the raw symbol map $\{(s,t); (u,v); (f\colon s \longrightarrow s, g)\}$. We are looking for a symbol map that both matches r and is admissible for Σ (admissibility has been defined in section 4.2). Now there are at least two symbol maps satisfying these constraints, namely

$$h = \{(sort\ s, sort\ t); (sort\ u, sort\ v); (f\colon s \longrightarrow s, g\colon t \longrightarrow t); (f\colon u \longrightarrow u, f\colon v \longrightarrow v)\}$$

$$k = \{(sort\ s, sort\ t); (sort\ u, sort\ v); (f\colon s \longrightarrow s, g\colon t \longrightarrow t); (f\colon u \longrightarrow u, g\colon v \longrightarrow v)\}$$

Admissibility of h and k can be seen by noticing that h indeed is a signature morphism from Σ to Σ', while k is a signature morphism from Σ to Σ''.

How to distinguish h as the symbol map that we want? Neither of h and k map $f\colon u \longrightarrow u$ identically, but h maps it to a symbol with the same name. This can be formalized in an arbitrary institution with qualified symbols as follows: The *core* of a symbol map is defined to be

$$core(h) := \{(SY, SY') \in h \mid SY \text{ does not have the same name as } SY'\}$$

(Note that by the definition of institution with qualified symbols, each symbol has a unique name.) With this, we can define a pre-order relation on the set of symbol maps by putting

$$h \leq h' \text{ iff } core(h) \subseteq core(h')$$

For the above example, we have $h \leq k$ but not vice versa, since $(f\colon u \longrightarrow u, g\colon v \longrightarrow v) \in core(k) \setminus core(h)$.

Given a set of admissible symbol maps Ad and a raw symbol map r, we now can define the associated symbol map $\{\{r\}\}^{Ad}$ to be the least element of the set of all symbols maps that match r and are in Ad, provided this least element exists and is unique. Otherwise, $\{\{r\}\}^{Ad}$ is undefined. (Note that in a pre-order, there may be several least elements.) The function $\{\{\_\}\}^{Ad}$ now admits to interpret the modified kernel language, by just replacing each raw symbol map r by the corresponding symbol map $\{\{r\}\}^{Ad}$.

Before doing this, however, we first have to construct an institution with symbols out of an institution with raw symbols. We do this by defining, for a given institution with qualified symbols, the map Ext which is required in the definition of institution with symbols. Recall that Ext is needed for the semantics of instantiations of generic specifications (see section 4.4). We here define Ext in such a way that it implements the automatic renaming of compound identifiers that is used in CASL to prevent name clashes between different instantiations of one and the same generic specification.

The function Ext takes two signatures (the formal and the actual parameter signature) and a symbol map (the fitting symbol map) and delivers a symbol map again (the symbol map modified by the mechanism to rename compound identifiers). We want to rename the components of compound identifiers according to the fitting map. Since the fitting map is a symbol map, while the component of compound identifiers are just identifiers, we need the machinery of raw symbols to link these concepts properly:

Given a symbol map $h \subseteq Sym \times Sym$, define

$$Ext(\Sigma, \Sigma', h) = \{\{r\}\}^{Admissible(\Sigma,\Sigma')}$$

where

$$r = (SymAsRawSym \times SymAsRawSym)(h)$$

$$\cup\{(IDAsRawSym(id[ci_1, \ldots, ci_n]), IDAsRawSym(id[ci'_1, \ldots, ci'_n]))$$

$$\mid \text{some } SY \in |\Sigma| \text{ matches } IDAsRawSym(id[ci_1, \ldots, ci_n])$$

$$\text{and } (ci_i, ci'_i) \in h' \text{ for } i = 1, \ldots, n\}^{12}$$

[12] The union may lead to non-functionality (and, therefore, undefinedness of the instantiation of the generic extension, because the raw symbol map does not induce a signature morphism), if a compound identifier is mapped both explicitly by the fitting morphism and implicitly by the extension mechanism.

and

$$\begin{aligned} h' = \{(Ident, Ident') \mid\ & Ident, Ident' \in \mathtt{ID}, \\ & (SY, SY') \in h, \\ & SY \text{ matches } IDAsRawSym(Ident), \\ & SY' \text{ matches } IDAsRawSym(Ident')\}^{13}. \end{aligned}$$

It is obvious that $h \subseteq Ext(\Sigma, \Sigma', h)$, thus we get:

Proposition 5.1. *From each institution with qualified symbols, we get an institution with symbols by letting Ext be defined in the above way and by forgetting the sets of raw symbols and of identifiers and the functions associated with them.*

With this, we now can interpret kernel language with raw symbols in an arbitrary institution with qualified symbols. Most constructs are the same as for institution with symbols; thus we interpret them in the associated institution with symbols (see proposition 5.1). Translation and instantiation have a new form; we interpret them by translating them to the kernel language for institutions with symbols:

$$\{\{\langle \Sigma, \Phi \rangle\}\} = \langle \Sigma, \Phi \rangle$$

$$\{\{SP_1 \textbf{ and } SP_2\}\} = \{\{SP_1\}\} \textbf{ and } \{\{SP_2\}\}$$

$$\{\{SP \textbf{ with } r\}\} = SP \textbf{ with } \{\{r\}\}^{Admissible(Sig[SP])}$$

$$\{\{SP \textbf{ reveal } RSYs\}\} = \{\{SP\}\} \textbf{ reveal } \{\{RSYs\}\} \cap Sig[SP]$$

$$\{\{SP \textbf{ hide } RSYs\}\} = \{\{SP\}\} \textbf{ hide } \{\{RSYs\}\} \cap Sig[SP]$$

$$\begin{gathered} \{\{\textbf{instantiate } (SP, SP') \textbf{ by } SP_A \textbf{ fit } r\}\} = \\ \textbf{instantiate } (SP, SP') \textbf{ by } SP_A \textbf{ fit } \{\{r\}\}^{Admissible(Sig[SP'], Sig[SP_A])} \end{gathered}$$

Again, we can define *Sig* and *Mod* on the kernel language with raw symbols using the above translation:

$$Sig[SP] = Sig[\{\{SP\}\}] \ (= Sig[[\![\{\{SP\}\}]\!]])$$

$$Mod[SP] = Mod[\{\{SP\}\}] \ (= Mod[[\![\{\{SP\}\}]\!]])$$

What if we want to use the kernel language for institution with qualified symbols, but only have an institution with symbols at hand?

---

[13] Notice that h' may fail to be a function even if h is one, destroying the definedness of the instantiation of a generic extension. In the CASL institution, this may happen, for example, if two different profiles of a function are mapped to different names, and the function name occurs in a compound identifier.

Proposition 5.2. *For each institution with symbols closed under compound symbols, i.e.*

$$\textit{for } id, ci_1, \ldots, ci_n \in Sym, \ \textit{also } id[ci_1, \ldots, ci_n] \in Sym,$$

there is an institution with qualified symbols corresponding to no possible qualifications.

Note that the *Ext* component is forgotten during this constructions; it gets replaced by a specific *Ext* as defined above when interpreting the kernel language for institutions with qualified symbols.

6 CASL as an Institution with (Qualified) Symbols

We here concentrate on the category of CASL signatures and signature morphisms, together with the symbol functor. Sentences, models and satisfaction are described in the CASL semantics [5] in detail, we leave them out here since they do not really matter in this context.

6.1 CASL as an Institution with Symbols

Let ID be a fixed set of identifiers. A *CASL signature* $\Sigma = (S, TF, PF, P, \leq)$ consists of:

- a set $S \subseteq \mathtt{ID}$ of *sorts*, together with a pre-order $\leq$
- two $S^* \times S$-sorted families $TF = (TF_{w,s})_{w \in S^*, s \in S}$ and $PF = (PF_{w,s})_{w \in S^*, s \in S}$ of *total function symbols* and *partial function symbols*, respectively, with $TF_{w,s} \subseteq \mathtt{ID}$ $PF_{w,s} \subseteq \mathtt{ID}$ and such that $TF_{w,s} \cap PF_{w,s} = \{\}$, for each $(w, s) \in S^* \times S$ (constants are treated as functions with no arguments)
- a family $P = (P_w)_{w \in S^*}$ of *predicate symbols* with $P_w \subseteq \mathtt{ID}$

We write $f : w \longrightarrow s \in TF$ for $f \in TF_{w,s}$, $f : w \longrightarrow s \in PF$ for $f \in PF_{w,s}$ and $p : w \in P$ for $p \in P_w$.

For a subsorted signature, $\Sigma = (S, TF, PF, P, \leq_S)$, we define *overloading relations* σ_F and $\sim_P$, for function and predicate symbols, respectively:

Let $f : w_1 \to s_1, f : w_2 \to s_2 \in TF \cup PF$, then $f : w_1 \to s_1 \sim_F f : w_2 \to s_2$ iff there exist $w \in S^*$ with $w \leq w_1$ and $w \leq w_2$ and a common supersort s of s_1 and s_2.

Let $p : w_1, p : w_2 \in P$, then $p : w_1 \sim_P p : w_2$ iff there exists $w \in S^*$ with $w \leq w_1$ and $w \leq w_2$.

Given signatures $\Sigma = (S, TF, PF, P, \leq)$ and $\Sigma' = (S', TF', PF', P', \leq')$, a signature morphism $\sigma : \Sigma \longrightarrow \Sigma'$ consists of

- a map $\sigma^S : S \longrightarrow S'$,
- a map $\sigma^{TF}_{w,s} : TF_{w,s} \longrightarrow TF'_{\sigma^{S^*}(w), \sigma^S(s)}$ [14] for each $w \in S^*, s \in S$,

[14] σ^{S^*} is the extension of σ^S to finite strings

- a map $\sigma^{PF}_{w,s}: PF_{w,s} \longrightarrow PF'_{\sigma^{S*}(w),\sigma^S(s)} \cup TF'_{\sigma^{S*}(w),\sigma^S(s)}$, and
- a map $\sigma^P_w: P_w \longrightarrow P'_{\sigma^{S*}(w)}$ for each $w \in S^*$,

such that the subsort relation $\leq$ and the overloading relations $\sim_F$ and $\sim_P$ are preserved by σ^S.

Let the set *Sym* of symbols be the set

$$\mathtt{ID} \cup \{f^{\mathsf{t}}_{ws} \mid f, s \in \mathtt{ID}, w \in \mathtt{ID}^*\} \cup \{f^{\mathsf{p}}_{ws} \mid f, s \in \mathtt{ID}, w \in \mathtt{ID}^*\} \cup \{p_w \mid p \in \mathtt{ID}, w \in \mathtt{ID}^*\}$$

The functor $|\_|$ maps a signature $\Sigma = (S, TF, PF, P, \leq)$ to the set $|\Sigma| =$

$$\{s \mid s \in S\} \cup \{f^{\mathsf{t}}_{ws} \mid f \in TF_{w,s}\} \cup \{f^{\mathsf{p}}_{ws} \mid f \in PF_{w,s}\} \cup \{p_w \mid p \in P_w\}$$

Given a signature morphism $\sigma: \Sigma \longrightarrow \Sigma'$, $|\sigma|$ maps a symbol of form $s \in \mathtt{ID}$ to $\sigma^S(s)$, a symbol of form f^{t}_{ws} to $\sigma^{TF}_{w,s}(f)^{\mathsf{t}}_{\sigma^{S*}(w)\Sigma^S(s)}$, a symbol of form f^{p}_{ws} to $\sigma^{PF}_{w,s}(f)^{\mathsf{p}}_{\sigma^{S*}(w)\Sigma^S(s)}$, and a symbol of form p_w to $\sigma^P_w(p)_{\sigma^{S*}(w)}$.

For simplicity, let $Ext(\Sigma, \Sigma', h)$ just be h (a better Ext will emerge when considering CASL as an institution with qualified symbols).

Proposition 6.1. *The above gives us CASL as an institution with symbols.*

Let us now examine how the various constructions needed for the semantics of the kernel language look in CASL.

Proposition 6.2. *In the CASL institution, the following are equivalent for a subsignature Σ of Σ':*

1. *Σ is a full subsignature of Σ'.*
2. *Σ inherits from Σ' all the subsort requirements concerning the sorts of Σ, i.e. $\leq = \leq' \cap (S \times S)$.*

We now have the following

Proposition 6.3. *In the CASL institution, for any set $SYs \subseteq |\Sigma|$, there is a signature generated in Σ by SYs.*

Proposition 6.4. *In the CASL institution, for any set $SYs \subseteq |\Sigma|$, there is a signature co-generated in Σ by SYs.*

Proposition 6.5. *In the CASL institution, given two signatures $\Sigma = (S, TF, PF, P, \leq)$ and $\Sigma' = (S', TF', PF', P', \leq')$ and a signature morphism $\sigma: \Sigma \longrightarrow \Sigma'$, the following are equivalent:*

1. *σ is final.*
2. *$|\sigma|$ is surjective, detects totality (i.e. $f': w' \longrightarrow s' \in TF$ implies that there is some $f: w \longrightarrow s \in TF$ with $\sigma^{TF}_{w,s}(f) = f'$); and $\leq'$ is the least pre-order on S' satisfying*

$$\sigma^S(s_1) \leq' \sigma^S(s_2) \text{ if } s_1 \leq s_2$$

Given two signatures $\Sigma_1 = (S_1, TF_1, PF_1, P_1, \leq_1)$ and $\Sigma_2 = (S_2, TF_2, PF_2, P_2, \leq_2)$ their *union* $\Sigma_1 \cup \Sigma_2 = (S, TF, PF, P, \leq)$, is defined by

- $S = S_1 \cup S_2$
- $XF(ws) = XF_1(ws) \cup XF_2(ws)$ for $XF \in \{TF, PF\}$ and $ws \in S^* \times S$. Here, if in $XF_1(ws) \cup XF_2(ws)$ one of both sides is undefined, it counts as the empty set.
- $P(ws) = P_1(w) \cup P_2(w)$ for $w \in S^*$. Again, if in $P_1(w) \cup P_2(w)$ one of both sides is undefined, it counts as the empty set.
- $\leq = \leq_1 \cup \leq_2$

The union exists iff $\Sigma_1 \cup \Sigma_2$ is a signature iff $TF(ws) \cap PF(ws) = \emptyset$ for all $ws \in S^* \times S$. Otherwise, the union is undefined.

Proposition 6.6. *In the CASL institution, given two signatures Σ_1 and Σ_2 such that $\Sigma_1 \cup \Sigma_2$ exists, the sink $(\iota_{|\Sigma_1| \subseteq |\Sigma_1| \cup |\Sigma_2|}, \iota_{|\Sigma_2| \subseteq |\Sigma_1| \cup |\Sigma_2|})$ has a unique minimal lift, namely $(\iota_{\Sigma_1 \subseteq \Sigma_1 \cup \Sigma_2}, \iota_{\Sigma_2 \subseteq \Sigma_1 \cup \Sigma_2})$.*

Let $\equiv_F$ and $\equiv_P$ denote the transitive closures of the overloading relations $\sim_F$ and $\sim_P$, respectively.

Proposition 6.7. *In the CASL institution, signature morphisms preserve $\equiv_F$ and $\equiv_P$.*

Proposition 6.8. *In the CASL institution, for a union $\Sigma_1 \cup \Sigma_2$, the following are equivalent:*

1. *The union is final.*
2. *The relation $\equiv_F^{\Sigma_1 \cup \Sigma_2}$ of $\Sigma_1 \cup \Sigma_2$ is the transitive closure of the union of the relations $\equiv_F^{\Sigma_1}$ and $\equiv_F^{\Sigma_2}$ (and similarly for $\equiv_P$).*

6.2 Alternative Definition of a CASL Institution with Symbols

The above definition is not the only natural way to turn the CASL institution into an institution with symbols. The other natural way would we to throw out symbols of form $f^{\mathtt{p}}_{ws}$, and use symbols of form $f^{\mathtt{t}}_{ws}$ for both total and partial operation symbols.

The effect would be the following:

- Subsignature inclusions may change a partial operation symbol in the subsignature to a total operation symbol in the supersignature, and only full subsignatures inherit totality.
- Unions of signatures are always defined. An operation symbol in the union is total iff it is total in one of the signatures that are united.

Whether one choses the first or second variant of CASL as an institution with symbols, is mainly a matter of taste. In the CASL semantics, the first version is chosen. The second version has the nice consequence that unions are always defined.

6.3 CASL as an Institution with Qualified Symbols

The set of compound identifiers in CASL is defined by just closing some given set SIMPLE-ID of simple identifiers under formation of compound identifiers, i.e. ID is the least set with

$$\texttt{SIMPLE-ID} \subseteq \texttt{ID}$$

$$\text{for } id, ci_1, \ldots, ci_n \in \texttt{ID}, \text{ also } id[ci_1, \ldots, ci_n] \in \texttt{ID},$$

The set of raw symbols is defined by

$$RawSym = Sym \uplus (SymKind \times \texttt{ID})$$

where $SymKind = \{implicit, sort, fun, pred\}$. We write $SY^{sym} \in RawSym$ for $SY \in Sym$ and $(k, Ident) \in RawSym$ for $k \in SymKind$ and $Ident \in \texttt{ID}$.

Both identifiers and symbols can be regarded as raw symbols using the injections $IDAsRawSym \colon \texttt{ID} \longrightarrow RawSym$ and $SymAsRawSym \colon Sym \longrightarrow RawSym$ defined by

$$IDAsRawSym(Ident) = (implicit, Ident)$$

and

$$SymAsRawSym(SY) = SY^{sym}$$

The matching relation

$$matches \subseteq Sym \times RawSym$$

between symbols and raw symbols is the least relation satisfying

$$\begin{array}{ll} s \text{ matches } (implicit, s), & s \text{ matches } (sort, s), \text{ for } s \in \textbf{sort}, \\ f^{\mathsf{t}}_{ws} \text{ matches } (implicit, f), & f^{\mathsf{t}}_{ws} \text{ matches } (fun, f), \\ f^{\mathsf{p}}_{ws} \text{ matches } (implicit, f), & f^{\mathsf{p}}_{ws} \text{ matches } (fun, f), \\ p_w \text{ matches } (implicit, f), & p_w \text{ matches } (pred, f), \\ \multicolumn{2}{c}{SY \text{ matches } SY^{sym} \text{ for } SY \in Sym.} \end{array}$$

Proposition 6.9. *The above definition turns CASL into an institution with qualified symbols.*

Note that by Proposition 5.1, we also get an institution with symbols out of this. It is the same institution with symbols as the one defined in section 6.1, except from the function *Ext*. The *Ext* function in the present case ensures a treatment of compounf identifiers within instantiations as it is in CASL.

7 Conclusion and Future Work

We have defined a kernel language for CASL structured specifications, which allows us to deal with symbols and symbol maps in a convenient way, instead of taking signature morphisms as a primitive notion. This has the advantage that the user has full control over the name space, and the transition from a symbol map to a signature morphism can be described in an institution-independent way.

The kernel language can be interpreted over an arbitrary but fixed institution with symbols. For coping with overloading, we also have defined a notion of institution with qualified symbols. We show how these notions specialize to the CASL institution. Since the structure required by an institution of (qualified) symbols is just a bit of syntax, it can be expected that nearly any institution can be extended to an institution with (qualified) symbols.

The work presented here has been the basis of the semantics of CASL structured specifications [5]. Thus, it is possible to use CASL structured specifications practically for any institution, the only easy-to-fulfill requirement being to equip the institution with a symbol structure.

Future work (jointly with Andrzej Tarlecki) will extend the kernel language and the notion of institution developed here to deal with the problems of *sharing*, which occurs in (the semantics of) CASL architectural specifications. It is also planned to implement an institution-with-symbols static analysis of CASL structured specifications.

Acknowledgements

Thanks to all participants of the CoFI semantics group (and the first reader of the semantics, Sasha Zamulin). In particular, I wish to thank Andrzej Tarlecki for numerous fruitful discussions and comments.

References

1. J. Adámek, H. Herrlich, and G. Strecker. *Abstract and Concrete Categories.* Wiley, New York, 1990. 255, 258
2. F. Borceux. *Handbook of Categorical Algebra I – III.* Cambridge University Press, 1994. 258
3. V. E. Căzănescu and G. Roşu. Weak inclusion systems. *Mathematical Structures in Computer Science*, 7(2):195–206, Apr. 1997. 254
4. CoFI. The Common Framework Initiative for algebraic specification and development, electronic archives. Notes and Documents accessible from http://www.brics.dk/Projects/CoFI. 253, 270
5. CoFI Semantics Task Group. CASL – The CoFI Algebraic Specification Language – Semantics. Note S-9 (version 0.95), in [4], Mar. 1999. 266, 270
6. H. Ehrig and B. Mahr. *Fundamentals of Algebraic Specification 1.* Springer Verlag, Heidelberg, 1985. 259
7. J. A. Goguen and R. M. Burstall. Institutions: Abstract model theory for specification and programming. *Journal of the Association for Computing Machinery*, 39:95–146, 1992. Predecessor in: LNCS 164, 221–256, 1984. 253
8. T. Mossakowski. Cocompleteness of the CASL signature category. Note S-7, in [4], Feb. 1998. 260
9. D. Sannella and A. Tarlecki. Specifications in an arbitrary institution. *Information and Computation*, 76:165–210, 1988. 254
10. D. T. Sannella and A. Tarlecki. Extended ML: an institution-independent framework for formal program development. In *Proc. Workshop on Category Theory and Computer Programming*, volume 240 of *Lecture Notes in Computer Science*, pages 364–389. Springer, 1986. 257

A General Algebraic Framework for Studying Modular Systems

Fernando Orejas, Elvira Pino

Dept. de L.S.I., Universitat Politècnica de Catalunya, Barcelona, SPAIN
{orejas, pino}@lsi.upc.es

Abstract. In this paper, we propose a general algebraic framework that serves as a basis for the semantic definition of modular systems. It is general in two senses. First, it is independent of the specification (or programming) formalism used to build modules as long as the formalism satisfies some algebraic properties. Moreover, we can combine modules built over different such formalisms. Secondly, our setting enables us to define compositional semantics for modular systems at any stage of development, including the case of non-hierarchical systems.

1 Introduction

Algebraic techniques are a very powerful tool to study the semantics and to reason about modular systems. The basic idea is to separate the study of the semantics of the modules from the semantics of the operations for putting modules together. Being specific, the semantics of a given module, which depends on the specification or programming formalism used "inside" the module is defined in terms of some algebraic constructions associated to the underlying formalism. Conversely, the semantics of the operations for combining modules is defined, independently from the formalism used in the modules, as some kind of combination of the algebraic constructions used to define the semantics of the modules. In this way, one can study and obtain general results about modular systems which can be applicable to a large class of specification or programming languages. This approach has its origin in the notion of *institution* [6,7] developed by Burstall and Goguen to define the logic-independent semantics of the Clear specification language [2]. Moreover, the approach was successfully used by the authors to study the semantics of modular constructions in logic programming languages [13,10].

The standard approach used to define the semantics of a modular system consists in, first, defining the meaning of a modular system by putting together (usually, by means of some form of amalgamation) the meaning of the given modules, according to the semantics of the combination operations involved. In [12] an alternative approach was defined consisting in, first, seeing a modular system just as a collection of modules linked together by an implicit binding mechanism and, then, seeing a module in a modular system as a constraint (similar to data constraints [18]) that

D. Bert, C. Choppy, and P. Mosses (Eds.): WADT'99, LNCS 1827, pp. 271-290, 2000.

imposes how a given part of a system has to be defined. In this sense, the semantics of a system, defined by a set of modules, is just the class of models that satisfy all these constraints. This approach was very useful for studying the development and certain correctness issues of modular systems, since it allowed us not to be bound to a specific set of combination operations and to give meaning to incomplete systems. This is an advantage from the standard technique based on explicitly composing the component modules (as done, for instance, in [5]) since, in an early stage of development, when a system is still incomplete, it may not be sensible to assume that all modules in the system can be composed.

In this paper, we show how this approach can be used in two situations where the standard one poses some problems. On the one hand we consider heterogeneous systems, i.e., systems where different modules may use different underlying specification formalisms. On the other hand, we consider the combination of modules which use circularly each other, e.g. a module M1 uses or imports definitions from module M2 and vicecersa. This situation may be quite common in certain contexts. For instance, it may often be found in object-oriented approaches or in logic programming [8] and is difficult to treat using the standard approach.

Moreover, in [14,17] it was shown how this approach could be used to define the semantics of most operations used for combining modules. In this sense, we can also prove the equivalence between the semantics obtained by composing the modules in a given system and the constraint-based definition. This result is called compatibility. In particular, we prove compatibility for a general composition operation called *circular combination*. This operation can be considered as a categorical abstraction of the composition operation in [8] (where a compositionality result is not provided) and, it is quite similar to the mutual recursive composition operation defined in [16, 5]. By this means, it can be considered that our approach provides a modular semantic constructor for circular combinations of modules.

The rest of the paper is structured as follows: In section 2, some basic notation used in the rest of the paper is introduced. In section 3, we define and study the notions of module and heterogeneous modular system. Finally, in section 4, we study an operation of circular combination of modules.

2 Preliminaries

In this section we introduce some basic notation and concepts. For further details see e.g. [1].

Our specifications will be built over an arbitrary *institution* I = (Sig, Sent, Mod, $\models$) equipped with some notion of signature inclusion (see e.g. [3]). I is an *exact* (*semiexact*) institution iff Sig has finite colimits (pushouts) and, in addition, Mod transforms finite colimits (pushouts) in Sig into limits (pullbacks) in Cat^{op}.

An institution I = (Sig, Sent, Mod, $\models$) *has differences with respect to monomorphisms* if for any signatures $\Sigma 0$, $\Sigma 1$ and $\Sigma 2$ in Sig such that there exist monomorphisms i: $\Sigma 1 \rightarrow \Sigma 2$ and k: $\Sigma 0 \rightarrow \Sigma 1$ in Sig, there exists a signature $\Sigma 3$, called the Σ0-*difference of* Σ1 *and* Σ2 *with respect to* i *and* k, and a monomorphism h: Σ0→Σ3 such that the following diagram of signatures is both a pushout and a pullback:

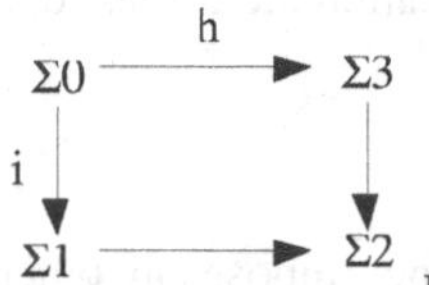

Fig. 1.

To fix notation in what follows we will write $b \cup_{a,f,g} c$ to denote the pushout of objects b and c with respect to an object a and morphisms f: a→b and g: a→c. As well, we may write $b \cap_{a,f,g} c$ to denote the pullback of b and c with respect to a, f: b→a and g: c→a. Moreover, we may write $b \cup_a c$, respectively, $b \cap_a c$, if f and g are clear from the context.

Given an institution *I*, we consider that a specification over *I* is a pair consisting of a signature and a set of axioms. We could also have dealt with institutions more semantically, as pairs formed by a signature and a set of models over this signature. Anyhow, the results obtained would have been essentially the same. The class of specifications can be made into a category by defining a notion of specification morphism as follows:

$\underline{\text{Spec}}_I$ ($\underline{\text{Spec}}$ if *I* is clear from the context) is the category of specifications whose objects are all pairs (Σ, Ax), where Σ is a signature in $\underline{\text{Sig}}$ and Ax is a set of Σ-sentences (called the *axioms* of the specification), i.e. Ax ⊆ Sen(Σ), and whose morphisms h: (Σ, Ax) → (Σ', Ax') are signature morphisms h: Σ → Σ' satisfying Sen(h)(Ax) ⊆ Ax'.

Given a specification SP, we will assume that Σ_{SP} denotes the signature of the specification SP, i.e. if SP = (Σ, Ax) ∈ $\underline{\text{Spec}}$ then $\Sigma_{SP} = \Sigma$.

3 Modular Systems over a Heterogeneous Institutional Framework

In this section we introduce the syntactic and semantic definition of the notions of module and heterogeneous modular system considered.

The notion of module that we consider is inspired in the one defined in [8] and is quite close to the notion studied in [5] (also used in [14]) and to other module notions (e.g. [19]). In particular, the intuition behind this module concept is the following one: a module MOD is some kind of specification (or program) unit that not only consists of a specification BOD of the "objects" specified in the unit, but also includes two additional interface specifications: the first one, the import specification IMP, specifies the part of BOD that "is needed to know" about the rest of the system; the second one, the export specification EXP, specifies what the module "offers", that is, EXP is the visible part of BOD. In addition, BOD may contain an internal (non-visible) part specifying some auxiliary components.

Definition 3.1 A *module specification* in a given institution I is a 5-tuple MOD = (IMP, EXP, BOD, s: IMP→BOD, v: EXP→BOD), where EXP is the export interface specification, IMP is the import interface specification, BOD is the body specification and, s and v are specification inclusions representing the relations among these specifications in $\underline{\mathrm{Spec}}_I$.

Remarks and definition 3.2

1. For the sake of generality, we do not impose any other condition but that IMP and EXP are subspecifications of BOD. For instance, IMP and EXP do not have to be disjoint, so IMP can be a subspecification of EXP.
2. We have not explicitly considered, as it is done for instance in [5], a sixth component corresponding to the common part of IMP and EXP. Instead, we consider that the common part of IMP and EXP is just the specification COM resulting of the pullback COM = $\mathrm{IMP}\cap_{\mathrm{BOD,s,v}}\mathrm{EXP}$. That is, COM specifies all what is shared by IMP and EXP. Accordingly, since IMP specifies what "is still needed to know", it can be considered that a module of this kind *defines* all what is specified in EXP except what is in IMP (i.e., COM).

Now, a modular system, where all the modules are defined over the same institution, is seen as a collection of modules together with some *global description* of the system, e.g. the facilities or operations offered by the system. In our case we regard this description just as a signature. The modules are bound to this global signature by means of fitting (signature) morphisms, matching the services or operations imported and exported by a module with the global operations offered by the system. In this context, these signature morphisms play the role of (implicitly) interconnecting the modules of a given system. However, if each module is defined over a different institution and the system itself (i.e. its global signature) is also defined over a different institution then there should be a well-defined relation between all these institutions allowing to relate the signatures of the modules with the signature of the system and the semantics of the modules with the semantics of the system.

An heterogeneous institutional framework consists of a collection of institutions $\{I_j\}_{1\leq j\leq n}$ used for writing the modules together with an institution I which represents the logic language used for describing the "services" that are specified by the global system. Then, the institutions $\{I_j\}_{1\leq j\leq n}$ are mapped into I. At this point, we have to say that the aim of this paper is not to contribute with a new study of mappings between institutions. On the contrary, as we have introduced in section 1, our proposal is to define a semantic framework based on seeing modules as constraints that solves the difficulties presented there. As a consequence, we borrow a proper notion of mapping from the existing proposal. The idea behind a map r_j: $I_j \rightarrow I$ of such institutions $\{I_j\}_{1\leq j\leq n}$ into I, is that r_j shows how the constructions in an institution I_j can be encoded or represented in the institution I. This is the idea of the kind of map of institutions called *institution representation* by Tarlecki [20] and, *plain map of institutions* by Meseguer [11]. Indeed, we use a simpler notion called *semi-representation* defined by Tarlecki in [21] because we do not need to represent the sentences from institutions $\{I_j\}_{1\leq j\leq n}$ into the institution I.

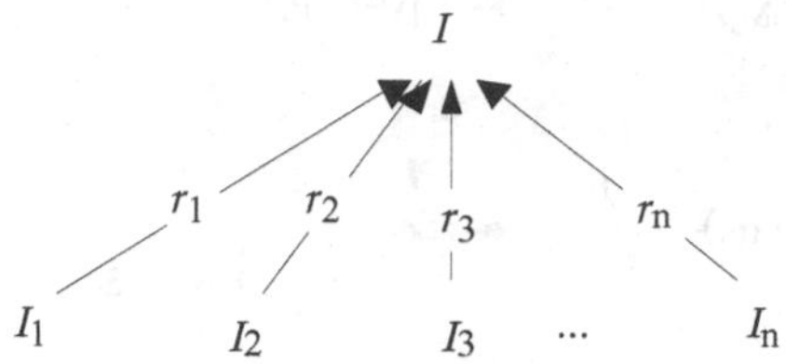

Fig. 2.

Definitions 3.3 We say that $(I, \{I_j, r_j\}_{1\leq j\leq n})$ is an *institutional framework* if

1. I = (Sig, Sent, Mod, $\models$) and I_j = (Sig$_j$, Sent$_j$, Mod$_j$, $\models^j$) for every j, $1\leq j\leq n$, are liberal semi-exact institutions having differences and pullbacks of signatures with respect to monomorphisms.
2. For every j, $1\leq j\leq n$, $r_j = (\mathcal{S}_j, m_j)$: $I_j \rightarrow I$ is a map consisting of:
   - a functor $\mathcal{S}_j$: Sig$_j$$\rightarrow$Sig, and
   - a monic natural transformation m_j: Mod$\circ\mathcal{S}_j^{op}\rightarrow$Mod$_j$, that is a collection of functors $m_j(\Sigma)$: Mod$(\mathcal{S}_j(\Sigma))\rightarrow$Mod$_j(\Sigma)$ for every signature Σ in Sig$_j$.

Remark 3.4 In the above definition the natural transformations m_j are required to be monic to guarantee that there is not more than one representation in I of a model interpreting a component specified in one of the institutions I_j.

Now, we define the notion of modular system over a heterogeneous institutional framework as above. Every module of such a kind of system is written in an institution of the collection $\{I_j, r_j\}_{1\leq j\leq n}$. The additional institution I describes the operations exported by the system. More specifically, a heterogeneous modular system consists of a global signature of the global institution I and a collection of modules defined over the non-global institutions. The signatures of the export and import interfaces are mapped to the global signature such that common elements are mapped to the same elements:

Definition 3.5 A (heterogeneous) *modular system over a global signature Σ_G and an institutional framework* $(I, \{I_j, r_j\}_{1\leq j\leq n})$, is a pair

$$\mathcal{SM} = (\Sigma_G, \{(\text{MODj}, i_j, e_j)\}_{1\leq j\leq n})$$

where Σ_G is a signature in Sig of I, and for each j, $1\leq j\leq n$,

- MODj = (IMPj, EXPj, BODj, s_j, v_j) is a module in the institution I_j, and

- i_j: $\mathcal{S}_j(\Sigma_{IMPj}) \rightarrow \Sigma_G$ and e_j: $\mathcal{S}_j(\Sigma_{EXPj}) \rightarrow \Sigma_G$ are two signature monomorphisms in Sig such that $\mathcal{S}_j(\Sigma_{COMj}) = \mathcal{S}_j(\Sigma_{IMPj}) \cap_{\Sigma_G, i_j, e_j} \mathcal{S}_j(\Sigma_{EXPj})$ is a pullback in Sig:

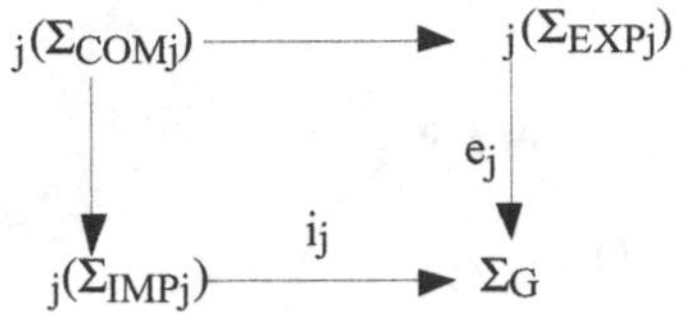

Fig. 3.

Remarks 3.6

(1) Since the specifications COMj include the common elements of IMPj and EXPj, then the above pullbacks for $\mathcal{S}_j(\Sigma_{COMj})$ state that these common elements must be bound to the same elements of the global signature Σ_G through i_j and e_j. Moreover, the mappings i_j and e_j are defined to be monomorphisms. The reason is that we consider that a given operation offered by a system cannot be internally defined in terms of two different operations within the same module.

(2) It may be noted that a modular system of this kind may be "incomplete" in the sense that there may be "elements" in the global signature which are not exported or not "defined" by any module of the system in the sense of remark 3.4(2).

(3) Moreover, this kind of modular system may contain circular definitions in the sense that a module MOD1 may import a definition exported by MOD2 which itself imports another definition exported by MOD1, unless we impose an additional syntactic restriction on the implicit interconnection of modules.

3.1 Modules as Constraints over a System

Similar to what is done in [12], we can define the semantics of a modular system as the class of all models (of the global signature) which satisfy each component module. Therefore, the resulting semantics can be considered really modular, in the sense that the meaning of the whole system is given in terms of the meaning of its parts without having to "compute" the composition of all modules:

Definitions 3.1.1 Given a modular system $\mathcal{SM} = (\Sigma_G, \{(MODj, i_j, e_j)\}_{1 \leq j \leq n})$ over a global signature Σ_G and an institutional framework $(I, \{I_j, r_j\}_{1 \leq j \leq n})$, *the semantics of* $\mathcal{SM}$, denoted $[\![\mathcal{SM}]\!]$, is defined as:

$$[\![\mathcal{SM}]\!] = \{A \in Mod(\Sigma_G) \mid \forall (MODj, i_j, e_j)\ A \models_{<i_j, e_j>} MODj\},$$

where $A \in Mod(\Sigma_G)$ *satisfies MODj with respect to* i_j *and* e_j, $A \models_{<i_j, e_j>} MODj$, iff

- $\mathit{m}_j(\Sigma_{IMPj})(V_{i_j}(A)) \in Mod(IMPj)$ and
- $\mathit{m}_j(\Sigma_{EXPj})(V_{e_j}(A)) = V_{v_j} \circ F_{s_j}(\mathit{m}_j(\Sigma_{IMPj})(V_{i_j}(A)))$

being F_{s_j}: Mod(IMPj)→Mod(BODj) and V_{v_j}: Mod(BODj)→Mod(EXPj) the free and forgetful functors corresponding to s_j and v_j, respectively. A module specification is *correct* if the free functor F_{s_j} is strongly persistent, i.e. $V_{s_j} \circ F_{s_j} = ID_{Mod_j(IMPj)}$.

The idea in this definition is that the semantics of a given system is the class of those models of the global signature Σ_G in *I* containing, for every j, a part $V_{e_j}(A)$ which represents via r_j an EXPj-model, $m_j(\Sigma_{EXPj})(V_{e_j}(A))$, which is the EXPj-part over its IMPj-part. It may be argued that this kind of semantics is only useful if modules are intended to have free semantics (and, consequently, specifications have initial semantics). However, in [14] it is shown how this can be generalized to other kind of semantics by considering that the semantics of a module is any arbitrary constructor.

The following example aims to illustrate that this kind of semantics is adequate for describing the incremental design of systems:

Example 3.1.2 Let us consider Σ_G = {p,q,r,s} a signature of predicate symbols and the following modules over the institution *PHCL* (Propositional Horn Clause Logic):

MOD1 = (Ø, {r}, {r.}), MOD2 = ({p}, {q}, {q←p}),
MOD3 = ({r}, {p}, {p←r}), MOD4 = ({p,q}, {s}, {s←p∧q})

where the modules are represented as MODj = (Ij, Ej, BODj) such that Ij, Ej are just signatures of predicate symbols corresponding, respectively, to the import and the export of the module; and, the specification BODj, written as a set of propositional Horn clauses, is assumed to contain as signature all the predicate symbols occurring in the module. The following are the semantics, in terms of classes of Herbrand structures, of some subsystems of the (hierarchical) system $\mathcal{SM} = (\Sigma_G, \{MODj\}_{1\leq j\leq 4})$:

- $[\![\Sigma_G, \{MOD1, MOD2\}]\!] = [\![\Sigma_G, \{MOD1\}]\!] \cap [\![\Sigma_G, \{MOD2\}]\!]$ = {{r}, {r, s}, {r, p, q}, {r, p, q, s}}
- $[\![\Sigma_G, \{MOD1, MOD2, MOD3\}]\!]$ = {{r, p, q}, {r, p, q, s}}
- $[\![\Sigma_G, \{MOD1, MOD2, MOD3, MOD4\}]\!]$ = {{r, p, q, s}}

On the one hand, note that the semantics of the system consisting of the modules MOD1 and MOD2 is defined even though these modules could not be composed if an operation of union is not available. On the other, it can be seen that the process of adding modules to the system restricts the class of its models reflecting the idea that the system is becoming more complete.

Actually, in the above example the system $\mathcal{SM} = (\Sigma_G, \{MODj\}_{1\leq j\leq 4})$ can be considered complete since its component modules define (export) all the pedicates in the global signature. In what follows we prove that when the a system is complete and hierarchical then there exists a unique model in $[\![\mathcal{SM}]\!]$. The following defines that a modular system is hierarchical and (SP0, Σ_G)-complete if it is possible to define a chain of pushouts of the representations of all the export interfaces such that this result in a signature containing all the elements in the global signature Σ_G, maybe except those in a specification, SP0, of some components considered predefined. Recall that we consider that a module defines all what it exports except what it imports.

Definition 3.1.3 A modular system $\mathcal{SM} = (\Sigma_G, \{(\text{MODj}, i_j, e_j)\}_{1 \le j \le n})$ over a global signature Σ_G and an institutional framework $(I, \{I_j, r_j\}_{1 \le j \le n})$, is *hierarchical and (SP0, Σ_G)-complete* iff we can define the following sequence of pushouts of signatures for some family of morphisms f_j, g_j, e_j', h_j, j = 1,..,n:

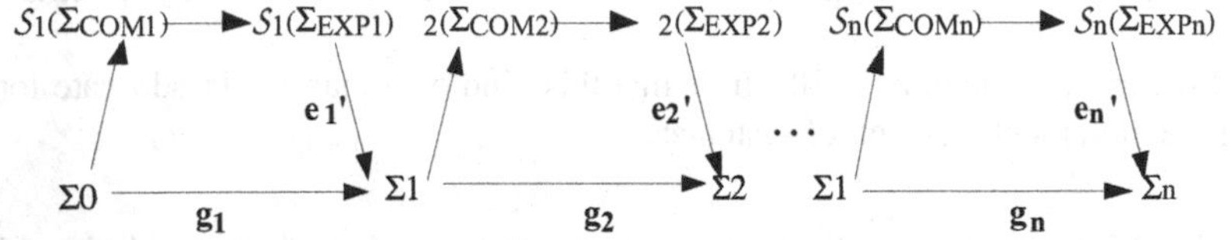

Fig. 4.

such that $\Sigma 0 = \Sigma_{SP0}$, $h_n(\Sigma n) = \Sigma_G$ and, for every j =1,..,n:

- f_j: $S_j(\Sigma_{IMPj}) \rightarrow \Sigma j\text{-}1$
- $e_j = h_n \circ g_n \circ \ldots \circ g_{j+1} \circ e_j'$ and
- $i_j = h_n \circ g_n \circ \ldots \circ g_j \circ f_j$.

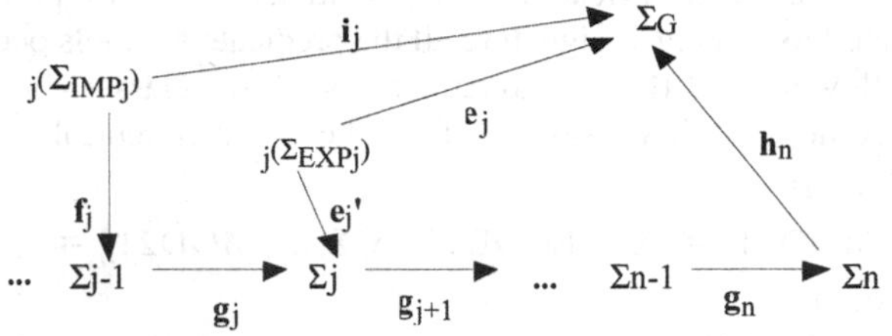

Fig. 5.

The conditions on the relations among morphisms, guarantee that the representation of the import and export interfaces are preserved under the composition of signatures. When the empty specification Ø exists in the category of syntactical specifications of *I* and SP0 = Ø then, we just say that *$\mathcal{SM}$ is Σ_G-complete.*

Theorem 3.1.4 If $\mathcal{SM} = (\Sigma_G, \{(MODj, i_j, e_j)\}_{1\le j\le n})$ is a $(SP0, \Sigma_G)$-complete system of modules for a given sequences of pushouts as in definition 3.1.3, then for some prefixed interpretation A0 of SP0 there is at most one model (up to isomorphism) A in $[\![\mathcal{SM}]\!]$ such that $V_{\Sigma_{SP0}}(A) = A0$.

Sketch of the Proof To prove that if A and B are models in $[\![\mathcal{SM}]\!]$ such that $V_{\Sigma_{SP0}}(A) = V_{\Sigma_{SP0}}(B)$ then they are isomorphic, one can use induction on the number of modules (that is of pushouts in the chain in 3.1.3) involved. The base case (0 modules) is trivial. For the induction step, it is enough to use the universal property of amalgamation, which can be used since the institution *I* is semiexact. ■

The previous theorem shows that, at the end of the design process, when the modular system is complete, the semantics of the system is either monomorphic or empty. It must be clear that we cannot ensure the existence of a model of the system since we have not imposed any condition ensuring that the modules are consistent, nor any form of persistence.

In addition, in [14,17] it was shown compatibility of this semantics with respect to several (hierarchical) operations for (explicitly) composing modules. This means that the semantics obtained by explicitly composing the modules in a given system and the semantics obtained by just "putting its modules together" are equivalent. In this sense, in most cases, the two approaches only differ in the tools used to define the compositional semantics.

In section 4, we will present a similar result with respect to a circular combination of modules. For this purpose we have first to solve the problems related to the compositional semantic definition of non-hierarchical systems that is led to the following subsection.

3.2 Generalization to the General Case

The following examples show that neither the semantic definition 3.1.1 nor 3.1.3 and 3.1.4 work unless we impose a hierarchical structure on the interconnections between modules: On the one hand, as a consequence of the circularities occurring between the modules, there may exist more than one possible interpretation of those parts involved in the circular definitions. On the other, it should be obvious that it is not possible to define chains as in 3.1.3. Even though, the example aims to provide some intuition about what we consider to be the "import" and the "export" part of a general modular system.

Example 3.2.1 Let $\mathcal{SM} = (\Sigma_G, \{MOD1, MOD2\})$ over $\Sigma_G = \{p,q,r,s\}$ and $\mathcal{PHCL}$:

$MOD1 = (\{q,r,s\}, \{p,s\}, \{p \leftarrow q \wedge r \wedge s\})$ and

$MOD2 = (\{p,s\}, \{q,s\}, \{q \leftarrow p \wedge s\})$.

Following the idea of the mutual recursive composition operation defined in [15], we can assume that this system can be represented as a module MOD that exports all the predicates that are exported by the modules in the system, that is: E = {p, q, s}; whereas, it has to import all the predicates that are imported by every module but are not exported by any other, that is: I = {r, s}. Note that the predicate s is considered to be imported but also exported. This is because it is both imported and exported in the same module MOD2, so, according to what we consider to be defined by a module (see remark 3.4), MOD2 does not completely define s. Note that the signatures I and E can be computed by means of the following operations:

$$E = E1 \cup E2 = \{p,q,s\} \text{ and } I = I1'' \cup I2'' = \{r,s\} \text{ where}$$
$$I1'' = (I1 \setminus E2) \cup COM0 = \{r,s\},$$
$$I2'' = (I2 \setminus E1) \cup COM0 = \{s\} \text{ and}$$
$$COM0 = COM1 \cap COM2 = (I1 \cap E1) \cap (I2 \cap E2).$$

Then, MOD = ({r,s}, {p,q,s}, {p←q∧r∧s; q←p∧s}).

Note that the model A = {r,p,q,s} satisfies MOD1 and MOD2 but it does not satisfy MOD2 because: $V_{\{p,q,s\}} \circ F_{\{p \leftarrow q \wedge r \wedge s;\, q \leftarrow p \wedge s\}}(V_{\{r,s\}}(A)) = \emptyset$ but $V_{\{p,q,s\}}(A) = \{p,q,s\}$. As we said, in that system there exists more than one possible interpretation of those parts involved in the circular definitions. In particular, MOD1 defines p using q, whereas, MOD2 defines q in terms of p, and, as a consequence {r,s} and {p,q,r,s} are two models of MOD1 and MOD2 having the same I1"∪I2"-part.

Concerning this situation, in some stages of development of modular systems it may be sensible to assume having more than one interpretation of some parts but, it does not in a final stage. However, models such as {p,q,r,s} that (over-)interprets the indefinition on p and q will never be removed from the semantics by adding new modules to the system. Then, the semantic definition ⟦ ⟧ is not adequate enough and, in order to eliminate these models considered "over-interpretations" we need to define a more restrictive semantics.

For instance, a reasonable choice for defining the meaning of the above system $\mathcal{SM} = (\Sigma_G, \{MOD1, MOD2\})$, is to interpret that p and q should not be true, so, its semantics is {Ø, {r,s}}. In this sense, the model {r, p, q, s} can be considered an "over-interpretation" of the system. Note that A = {r, p, q, s} can be removed from the semantics if we impose the models to satisfy $\mathcal{SM}$ in the same sense they satisfy each module in the system, that is, to be a free construction over its I1"∪I2"-part. In what follows we will show how this new constraint for obtaining a proper semantics, is formulated in categorical terms. First of all, notice that I1" = (I1\E2)∪COM0 is defined as the difference of I1 and I1∩E2 preserving the common part COM0, thus, in categorical terms, we can say that I1" is the COM0-difference of I1 and I1∩E2 as defined in section 2, since:

$$I1 = I1'' \cup (I1 \cap E2) \cup COM0 \text{ and } COM0 = I1'' \cap ((I1 \cap E2) \cup COM0).$$

Following this idea we can construct the signatures corresponding to the exported and the imported part of a modular system as follows:

Definition 3.2.2 Let MODj = (IMPj, EXPj, BODj, s_j, v_j), j = 1,2, be two module specifications over an institutional framework $(I, \{I_j, r_j\}_{1 \le j \le n})$. Let i_j: $S_j(\Sigma_{IMPj}) \to \Sigma_G$ and e_j: $S_j(\Sigma_{EXPj}) \to \Sigma_G$ be the monomorphisms that bind the modules to a global signature Σ_G in Sig. We define the operation $*_{\Sigma_G}$:

$$((\Sigma_{IMP1}, \Sigma_{EXP1}, i_1, e_1), (\Sigma_{IMP2}, \Sigma_{EXP2}, i_2, e_2))*_{\Sigma_G} = (\Sigma_{IMP}, \Sigma_{EXP}, i, e)$$

that constructs the signatures of the *imported* and the *exported parts* of the system $(\Sigma_G, \{(MODj, i_j, e_j)\}_{1 \le j \le 2})$, Σ_{IMP} and Σ_{EXP}, respectively, as the following pushouts in Sig:

- $\Sigma_{IMP1} = \Sigma_{IMP1''} \cup_{\Sigma_{IMP0}} \Sigma_{IMP2''}$
- $\Sigma_{EXP} = S1(\Sigma_{EXP1}) \cup_{\Sigma_{EXP0}} S2(\Sigma_{EXP2})$,

where

- $\Sigma_{IMP0} = \Sigma_{IMP1''} \cap_{\Sigma_G} \Sigma_{IMP2''}$,
- $\Sigma_{EXP0} = S_1(\Sigma_{EXP1}) \cap_{\Sigma_G} S_2(\Sigma_{EXP2})$,
- and, the signatures $\Sigma_{IMPj''}$ are the subsignatures of $S_j(\Sigma_{IMPj})$ for j = 1,2, defined as follows: Let $\Sigma_{IMPj'}$ for j = 1,2, be the following pullback signatures in Sig:

  $\Sigma_{IMP1'} = S_1(\Sigma_{IMP1}) \cap_{\Sigma_G, i_1, e_2} S_2(\Sigma_{EXP2})$ and

  $\Sigma_{IMP2'} = S_2(\Sigma_{IMP2}) \cap_{\Sigma_G, i_2, e_1} S_1(\Sigma_{EXP1})$.

  Then, for every j = 1,2, $\Sigma_{IMPj''}$ is the subsignature of $S_j(\Sigma_{IMPj})$ defined as the Σ_{COM0}-difference of $\Sigma_{IMPj'}$ and $S_j(\Sigma_{IMPj})$), where

  $\Sigma_{COM0} = S_1(\Sigma_{COM1}) \cap_{\Sigma_G} S_2(\Sigma_{COM2})$ and

  $\Sigma_{COMj} = \Sigma_{IMPj} \cap_{\Sigma_{BODj}} \Sigma_{EXPj}$, for j = 1,2.

Finally, i and e are the unique (universal) monomorphisms going from the pushout objects Σ_{IMP} and Σ_{EXP} into Σ_G, respectively.

Remarks 3.2.3

(1) In the above definition, the signature $\Sigma_{IMPj'}$, for each j = 1,2, represents the part of the corresponding $S_j(\Sigma_{IMPj})$ which is exported by the other module. Note that the existence of a morphism from $\Sigma_{IMP1'}$ to $S_2(\Sigma_{EXP2})$ (or, from $\Sigma_{IMP2'}$ to $S_1(\Sigma_{EXP1})$) is uniquely determined (as a pullback) by the binding morphisms i_1 and e_2 to the global signature Σ_G. Then, the signature $\Sigma_{IMPj''}$ is uniquely determined as a difference operation and represents the part of $S_j(\Sigma_{IMPj})$ which has to be still imported. In addition, $\Sigma_{IMPj''}$ must contain all components which are exported but also imported by the other module. As we saw in example 3.2.1, this is because we consider that those components which are imported and exported within the same module are not completely defined yet.

(2) Notice that the operation $*_{\Sigma_G}$ is commutative. Moreover, $*_{\Sigma_G}$ is associative as a direct consequence of the fact that pushouts and pullbacks are closed under composition of diagrams. Therefore, the result of (iteratively) applying $*_{\Sigma_G}$ to all the

modules in a system will be independent of the order we choose to combine all the modules.

Let $\mathcal{SM}*_{\Sigma_G}$ denote the result of any iterative application of $*_{\Sigma_G}$ to all the modules in a system $\mathcal{SM}$. Now, we can define the new semantics in the following terms:

Definition 3.2.4 Let $\mathcal{SM} = (\Sigma_G, \{(MODj, i_j, e_j)\}_{1\leq j\leq n})$ be a modular system over $(I, \{I_j, r_j\}_{1\leq j\leq n})$ and let $\mathcal{SM}*_{\Sigma_G} = (\Sigma_{IMP}, \Sigma_{EXP}, i, e)$. Then, the *semantics of* $\mathcal{SM}$ is defined as:

$$[\![\mathcal{SM}]\!]_{\mathcal{G}} = \{A\in Mod(\Sigma_G) \mid A\in [\![\mathcal{SM}]\!] \text{ and } A \models R(\Sigma_{IMP}, \Sigma_{EXP}, [\![\mathcal{SM}]\!])\},$$

where $A \models R(\Sigma_{IMP}, \Sigma_{EXP}, [\![\mathcal{SM}]\!])$ iff for each other model $B\in [\![\mathcal{SM}]\!]$ such that there exists a Σ_{IMP}-homomorphism $f: V_i(A)\rightarrow V_i(B)$, then there exists a Σ_{EXP}-homomorphism $f^*: V_e(A)\rightarrow V_e(B)$, such that $V_{\Sigma_{COM}}(f^*) = V_{\Sigma_{COM}}(f)$, being $\Sigma_{COM} = \Sigma_{IMP} \cap_{\Sigma_G} \Sigma_{EXP}$.

The additional constraint states a slightly weaker condition than asking the EXP-part of A to be free with respect to its IMP-part.

Examples 3.2.5

(1) The model $\{p, q, r, s\}\in [\![\mathcal{SM}]\!]$, being $\mathcal{SM}$ the modular system in example 3.2.1, does not satisfy $R(\{r, s\}, \{p, q, s\}, [\![\mathcal{SM}]\!])$ due to the fact that $\{r, s\}$ also belongs to $[\![\mathcal{SM}]\!]$ and $V_I(\{r\}) = V_I(\{r, p, q, s\}) = \emptyset$ but there is not a homomorphism (inclusion) from $V_E(\{p, q, r, s\}) = \{p, q, s\}$ to $V_E(\{r, s\}) = \{s\}$. Indeed, it is not difficult to see that $[\![\mathcal{SM}]\!]_{\mathcal{G}} = \{\emptyset, \{r, s\}\}$.

(2) Let us consider a global signature consisting of three constants a, b and c, FS = {a, b, c}. Consider the following equational modules:

MOD1 = ({a,c}, {b,c}, ({a,b,c}, a=b)),

MOD2 = ({b}, {a}, ({a,b}, a=b)).

As above, since morphisms are inclusions, the components of the modules are presented as a 3-tuple: (IMPj, EXPj, BODj). Let $\mathcal{SM} = (\Sigma_G, \{MOD1, MOD2\})$ and notice that $\mathcal{SM}*_{\Sigma_G} = (\{c\}, \{a,b,c\})$.

It is not difficult to see that, the FS-structure A = ({0,1}, a=b=0, c=1) satisfies MOD1 and MOD2 but it does not the new constraint $R(\{c\}, \{a,b,c\}, [\![\mathcal{SM}]\!])$. In particular, let us consider the FS-structure $B = (\{0,1,2\}, c=1, a=b=2)\in [\![\mathcal{SM}]\!]$. Then,

$V_i(A) = (\{0,1\}, c=1)$, $V_e(A) = A$

$V_i(B) = (\{0,1,2\}, c=1)$, $V_e(B) = B$

thus there exists an {c}-homomorphism f: $V_i(A) \rightarrow V_i(B)$ defined as $f(0) = 0$ and $f(1) = 1$. However, there does not exist any {a,b,c}-homomorphism f*: $V_e(A) \rightarrow V_e(B)$, such that $V_{\Sigma_{COM}}(f^*) = V_{\Sigma_{COM}}(f)$.
Moreover, B neither satisfies $R(\{c\}, \{a,b,c\}, [\![\mathcal{SM}]\!])$ since $g(0) = 0$ and $g(1) = g(2) = 1$ is a {c}-homomorphism g: $V_i(B) \rightarrow V_i(A)$, and again there does not exist any {a,b,c}-homomorphism g*: $V_e(A) \rightarrow V_e(B)$, such that $V_{\Sigma_{COM}}(g^*) = V_{\Sigma_{COM}}(g)$.
Indeed, there does not exist any FS-structure satisfying $R(\{c\}, \{a,b,c\}, [\![\mathcal{SM}]\!])$. The reason is that models satisfying MOD1 and MOD2 cannot be a free construction in Mod({a,b,c}, a=b)) over its {c}-restriction.

As we will see in the next section (see Counterexample 4.4), the situation in the above example (2) is not really a problem but just agree with the fact that correctness preserving with respect to circular combinations cannot be guaranteed in general ([15, 5]).

To end this section, we will show that imposing the new constraint is enough to show that complete system (that is, defining all the components in Σ_G) of correct modules has a unique model. The same result was proved in [12, 17] for the (homogeneous) hierarchical case. There, the key was that models in $[\![\mathcal{SM}]\!]$ are free constructions over some Σ_{IMP}-part when $\mathcal{SM}$ is hierarchical. Although, the above example 3.2.5(2) shows that in the non-hierarchical case the models in $[\![\mathcal{SM}]\!]$ are not necessarily free constructions over a Σ_{IMP}-part, now the key is the same because the new constraint removes the models that do not satisfy this condition.

First, we define when a system is (SP0, Σ_G)-complete:

Definition 3.2.6 Let $\mathcal{SM} = (\Sigma_G, \{(MODj, i_j, e_j)\}_{1 \le j \le n})$ be a modular system over $(I, \{I_j, r_j\}_{1 \le j \le n})$ and let $\mathcal{SM}^*_{\Sigma_G} = (\Sigma_{IMP}, \Sigma_{EXP}, i, e)$. Then, $\mathcal{SM}$ is *(SP0, Σ_G)-complete* if $\Sigma_{IMP} = \Sigma_{SP0}$ and $V_e(\Sigma_{EXP}) = \Sigma_G$.
Again when SP0 = Ø (if the empty specification in *I* exists) we just say that $\mathcal{SM}$ is *Σ_G-complete*.

Theorem 3.2.7 Let $\mathcal{SM} = (\Sigma_G, \{(\text{MODj}, i_j, e_j)\}_{1\leq j\leq n})$ be a $(\text{SP0}, \Sigma_G)$-complete system of modules over $(I, \{I_j, r_j\}_{1\leq j\leq n})$. Then, for some prefixed interpretation A0 of SP0, there exists at most one (up to isomorphism) model $A \in [\![\mathcal{SM}]\!]_{\mathcal{G}}$ such that $V_i(A) = A0$.

Sketch of the Proof If A and B are models in $[\![\mathcal{SM}]\!]$ satisfying $R(\Sigma_{SP0}, [\![\mathcal{SM}]\!])$ and $V_i(A) = V_i(B)$, then, by the definition of $R(\Sigma_{SP0}, [\![\mathcal{SM}]\!])$ we can guarantee the existence of unique homomorphisms $f^*: A \rightarrow B$ and $g^*: B \rightarrow A$ with $V_i(f^*) = V_i(g^*) = id_{A0}$. Then, we have to prove that f* and g* are unique. For doing so, we use the fact that A and B can be built amalgamating A0 with all the $\mathcal{S}_j(\Sigma_{EXPj}) \cap \Sigma_G$-parts of A (resp. B) and the fact that each of these parts satisfies a universal property, as a consequence of its free generation in the corresponding constraint. ■

4 Circular Combination of Modules

At the syntactic level, the *circular combination of modules* can be defined as an extension to specifications of the operation $*_{\Sigma_G}$. Note that this operation has to be defined in a homogeneous framework (i.e., in a single institution).

Definition 4.1 Let $\text{MODj} = (\text{IMPj}, \text{EXPj}, \text{BODj}, s_j, v_j)$, $j = 1,2$, be two module specifications over a global signature Σ_G and a homogeneous institutional framework I. Let $i_j: \Sigma_{IMPj} \rightarrow \Sigma_G$ and $e_j: \Sigma_{EXPj} \rightarrow \Sigma_G$ be monomorphisms that bind the modules to Σ_G. Let $(\Sigma_G, \{(\text{MODj}, i_j, e_j)\}_{1\leq j\leq 2})*_{\Sigma_G} = (\Sigma_{IMP}, \Sigma_{EXP}, i, e)$ and consider the following specifications:

(a) Let $\text{IMPj} = \text{IMPj}' \cup_{\Sigma_{COM0}} \text{IMPj}''$, for j = 1,2, be such that

$$\Sigma_{COM0} = \Sigma_{IMPj'} \cap_{\Sigma_{IMPj}} \Sigma_{IMPj''},$$

$$\text{IMP1}' = \text{IMP1} \cap_{\Sigma_G} \text{EXP2},$$

$$\text{IMP2}' = \text{IMP2} \cap_{\Sigma_G} \text{EXP1}.$$

(b) Let IMP, EXP and BOD be the following pushouts of specifications:

$$\text{IMP} = \text{IMP1}'' \cup_{\Sigma_{IMP0}} \text{IMP2}'',$$

$$\text{EXP} = \text{EXP1} \cup_{\Sigma_{EXP0}} \text{EXP2},$$

$$\text{BOD} = \text{BOD1} \cup_{\Sigma_{BOP0}} \text{BOD2},$$

such that:

$$\Sigma_{IMP0} = \Sigma_{IMP1''} \cap_{\Sigma_G} \Sigma_{IMP2''},$$

$$\Sigma_{EXP0} = \Sigma_{EXP1} \cap_{\Sigma_G} \Sigma_{EXP2},$$

$$\Sigma_{BOD0} = \Sigma_{BOD1} \cap_{\Sigma_G} \Sigma_{BOD2}.$$

Then, the *circular combination of MOD1 and MOD2 via f_1 and f_2* is defined, at the specification level, as the module:

$$(\text{MOD1}, \text{MOD2})*_{f_1,f_2} = \text{MOD} = (\text{IMP}, \text{EXP}, \text{BOD}, s, v),$$

being the morphisms f_1: IMP1'→EXP2 and f_2: IMP2'→EXP1 such that $e_2 \circ f_1 = i_1'$ and $e_1 \circ f_2 = i_2'$, where for every j =1,2, i_j' and i_j'' stand for the restricted morphisms i_j': $\Sigma_{IMP'} \to \Sigma_G$ and i_j'': $\Sigma_{IMPj''} \to \Sigma_G$, respectively.

The specification IMPj', for each j =1,2, is assumed to be the part of the corresponding import specification IMPj which is defined by the other module. In addition, the definitions of the common export part EXP0, implies that EXP1 and EXP2 are disjoint except on those parts belonging to IMP1' and IMP2'.

The circular combination operation defined in [15] can be seen as a particular case of the above definition insofar as conditions $e_2 \circ f_1 = i_1'$ and $e_1 \circ f_2 = i_2'$ are satisfied.

As a consequence of the situation presented and discused in section 3, here it cannot be expected to obtain a general result of compatibility of $[\![\ ]\!]$ with $*_{f_1,f_2}$, unless we impose a hierarchical relation between the composed modules. Counterexample 4.3 and example 4.4 aim to illustrate this situation. Instead, in this section, we will prove compatibility of $*_{f_1,f_2}$ with $[\![\ ]\!]_G$ for the general case.

First, the following theorem shows that models of $(\text{MOD1}, \text{MOD2})*_{f_1,f_2}$ satisfy MOD1 and MOD2 (of course, the converse is not true in general):

Theorem 4.2 Given correct modules (MODj, i_j, e_j) over a global signature Σ_G and a homogeneous institutional framework *I*. Then for each A∈Mod(Σ_G),

$$A \models_{<i,e>} (\text{MOD1}, \text{MOD2})*_{f_1,f_2} \Rightarrow A \in [\![(\Sigma_G, \{(\text{MODj}, i_j, e_j)\}_{1\le j\le 2})]\!]$$

but the converse is not true in general.

Sketch of the Proof The theorem is proved making use of amalgamation and extension properties associated to the following pushout diagrams (a), (b) and (c):

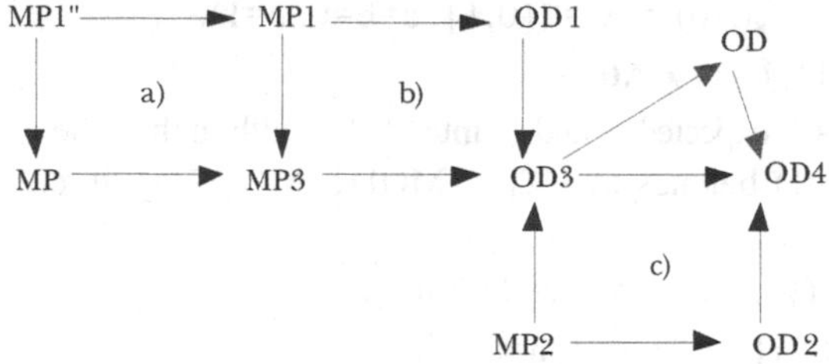

Fig. 6.

And, the corresponding diagrams of model classes:

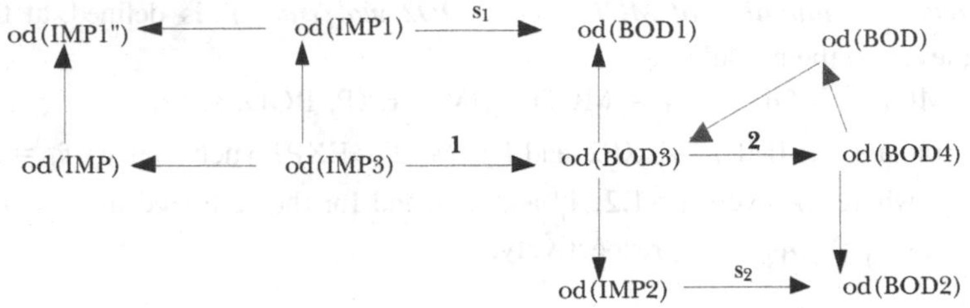

Fig. 7.

where F1 and F2 are, respectively, the free extensions of F_{s_1} and F_{s_2} and the rest of the arrows correspond to forgetful functors.
Counterexample 4.3 shows that the converse is not true in general. ■

Counterexample 4.3 Let (Σ_G, {MOD1, MOD2}) be the modular system in example 3.2.1 and 3.2.5(1): The model A = {p, q, r, s} $\in [\![(\Sigma_G, \{MOD1, MOD2\})]\!]$ does not satisfy (MOD1, MOD2)* = ({r,s}, {p,q,s}, {p←q∧r∧s; q←p∧s}) because

$V_v \circ F_s(V_i(A)) = \{s\}$ but

$V_e(A) = \{p,q,s\}$.

Indeed, as shown in 3.2.5(1), (and was intended) A is neither in $[\![\mathcal{SM}]\!]_{\mathcal{G}} = \{\emptyset, \{r, s\}\}$. In contrast, it is easy to see that models Ø, {r, s} satisfy (MOD1, MOD2)*.

Moreover, as we pointed out in section 3, correctness preserving is not guaranteed with respect to circular combinations of (correct) modules ([15, 5]):

Counterexample 4.4 Consider again example 3.2.5(2). It should be obvious that MOD1 and MOD2 are correct. However, the module

$$MOD = (MOD1, MOD2)^* = (\{c\}, \{a,b,c\}, (\{a,b,c\}, a=b))$$

is not. For instance, the free construction over the initial IMP-model A0 = ({1}, c=1) will be the initial BOD-model

$$F_s(A0) = A = (\{0,1\}, a=b=0, c=1),$$

but $V_s \circ F_s(A0) = (\{0,1\}, c=1) \neq A0$.

Again, as it was expected and intended, although the FS-structure A = ({0,1}, a=b=0, c=1) belongs to $[\![(\Sigma_G, \{MOD1, MOD2\})]\!]$, it does not satisfy (MOD1, MOD2)*:

$V_e(A) = A = (\{0,1\}, a=b=0, c=1)$ but

$V_v \circ F_s(V_i(A)) = (\{0,1,2\}, c=1, a=b=2)$.

Let's go back to what 3.2.5(2) aimed to illustrate. Now we can argue that it was impossible that A satisfies $R(\{c\}, \{a,b,c\}, [\![(\Sigma_G, \{MOD1, MOD2\}]\!])$ because it is initial in Mod(BOD): Let B and f: $V_i(A) \to V_i(B)$ be the same model and IMP-homorphism considered there. Now we know h(0) = 2 and h(1) = 1, is the unique

BOD-homorphism h: A→B but, since $\Sigma_{BOD} = \Sigma_{EXP}$, it is also the unique EXP-homorphism h: $V_e(A)\to V_e(B)$ and it is obvious that $V_{\Sigma_{COM}}(h) \neq V_{\Sigma_{COM}}(f)$. Moreover, according to the fact that $[\![\mathcal{SM}]\!]_{\mathcal{G}} = \emptyset$, there does not exist any FS-structure satisfying (MOD1, MOD2)* because for each IMP-restriction of a model, the free functor F_s defines a BOD-model containing one more value interpreting the constants a=b.

To prove compatibility of $*_{f_1,f_2}$ with $[\![\ ]\!]_{\mathcal{G}}$ we need the following lemma:

Lemma 4.5 Let (MODj, i_j, e_j) be correct modules over a global signature Σ_G, for j = 1,2, and let MOD = (MOD1, MOD2)$*_{f_1,f_2}$. If there exists a model $A\in[\![(\Sigma_G, \{(\text{MODj}, i_j, e_j)\}_{1\leq j\leq 2})]\!]_{\mathcal{G}}$ then

1. $F_s(V_i(A)) = F_{s_1}(V_{i_1}(A)) +_{V_{\Sigma BOD0}(A)} F_{s_2}(V_{i_2}(A)) \in \text{Mod(BOD)}$
2. MOD is persistent on $V_i(A)$

Sketch of the Proof To prove 1, assuming $A\in[\![(\Sigma_G, \{(\text{MODj}, i_j, e_j)\}_{1\leq j\leq 2})]\!]_{\mathcal{G}}$, we know that

$$A' = F_{s_1}(V_{i_1}(A)) +_{V_{\Sigma BOD0}(A)} F_{s_2}(V_{i_2}(A)) \in \text{Mod(BOD)}$$

is well-defined since, as a consequence of persistence and $V_{e_j}(A) = V_{v_j}\circ F_{s_j}(V_{i_j}(A))$ for j = 1,2, we have

$$V_{\Sigma_{BOD0}}\circ F_{s_1}(V_{i_1}(A)) = V_{\Sigma_{BOD0}}\circ F_{s_2}(V_{i_2}(A)) = V_{\Sigma_{BOD0}}(A).$$

To prove that A' is free over $V_i(A)$ with respect to s: IMP→BOD, we make use of the universal properties of amalgamation and extension.

2 follows from the following chain of equalities:

$$V_s\circ F_s(V_i(A)) = V_s(F_{s_1}(V_{i_1}(A)) +_{V_{\Sigma BOD0}(A)} F_{s_2}(V_{i_2}(A))) =$$
$$(V_{s_1}" +_{V_{\Sigma IMP0}(A)} V_{s_2}")(F_{s_1}(V_{i_1}(A)) +_{V_{\Sigma BOD0}(A)} F_{s_2}(V_{i_2}(A))) =$$
$$V_{s_1}"\circ F_{s_1}(V_{i_1}(A)) +_{V_{\Sigma IMP0}(A)} V_{s_2}"\circ F_{s_2}(V_{i_2}(A)) = V_i(A).$$ ■

Now we can state compatibility of $*_{f_1,f_2}$ with $[\![\ ]\!]_{\mathcal{G}}$ in the general case:

Theorem 4.6 Given correct modules (MODj, i_j, e_j) over a global signature Σ_G and a homogeneous institutional framework *I*, and let MOD = (MOD1, MOD2)$*_{f_1,f_2}$, then:

$$A\in[\![(\Sigma_G, \{(\text{MODj}, i_j, e_j)\}_{1\leq j\leq 2})]\!]_{\mathcal{G}} \Leftrightarrow A \models_{<i,e>} (\text{MOD1, MOD2})*_{f_1,f_2}.$$

Sketch of the Proof (i) For the left-to-right implication note that A $\models_{<i,e>}$(MOD1, MOD2)$*_{f_1,f_2}$ directly follows from lemma 4.5 and the following chain of equalities:

$$V_v \circ F_s(V_i(A)) = V_v(F_{s_1}(V_{i_1}(A)) +_{V_{\Sigma BODO}(A)} F_{s_2}(V_{i_2}(A))) =$$
$$(V_{v_1} +_{V_{\Sigma EXPO}} V_{v_2})(F_{s_1}(V_{i_1}(A)) +_{V_{\Sigma BODO}(A)} F_{s_2}(V_{i_2}(A))) =$$
$$V_{v_1} \circ F_{s_1}(V_{i_1}(A)) +_{V_{\Sigma EXPO}(A)} V_{v_2} \circ F_{s_2}(V_{i_2}(A)) = V_e(A).$$

(ii) To prove the right-to-left implication, assume that A $\models_{<i,e>}$(MOD1, MOD2)$*_{f_1,f_2}$. First as a consequence of theorem 4.2. we have that $A \in [\![(\Sigma_G, \{(MODj, i_j, e_j)\}_{1 \leq j \leq 2})]\!]$, so, F_s is persistent on $V_i(A)$ as a consequence of lemma 4.5. Finally, to prove that A satisfies $R(\Sigma_{IMP}, [\![(\Sigma_G, \{(MODj, i_j, e_j)\}_{1 \leq j \leq 2})]\!])$ notice that, as a consequence of the universal property of F_s, we know that for every model $B' \in Mod(BOD)$ such that there exists a IMP-homomorphism $f: V_i(A) \rightarrow V_s(B')$, there exists a unique BOD-homomorphism $g: F_s(V_i(A)) \rightarrow B'$ such that $V_s(g) = f$. In particular, this will hold for every $B \in [\![(\Sigma_G, \{(MODj, i_j, e_j)\}_{1 \leq j \leq 2})]\!]$ because, as in lemma 4.5, the amalgamated sum $F_{s_1}(V_{i_1}(B)) +_{V_{\Sigma BODO}(B)} F_{s_2}(V_{i_2}(B)) \in Mod(BOD)$ is well-defined. ■

As a consequence, we can prove that the following partial correctness preservation with respect to $*_{f_1,f_2}$ is required for the existence of a non-empty semantics:

Corollary 4.7 Let $(MODj, i_j, e_j)$ be correct modules over a global signature Σ_G, for j = 1,2 and if there exists a model A in $Mod(\Sigma_G)$ such that A $\models_{<i,e>}$(MOD1, MOD2)$*_{f_1,f_2}$ then (MOD1, MOD2)$*_{f_1,f_2}$ is correct on $V_i(A)$.

In fact the above partial correctness preservation was a key for obtaining the compatibility result. However, it is important to notice that the above corollary cannot be generalized to "if A $\models_{<i,e>}$MOD then MOD is correct on $V_i(A)$" because it is not true in general unless MOD has been built as combination of two correct modules. It is enough to consider the module MOD = ({p}, {q}, p., q.}) (that cannot be obtained from two correct modules) and the model A = {q}. A satisfies MOD but $V_s \circ F_s(V_i(A)) = \{p\} \neq V_i(A) = \emptyset$.

Acknowledgements This work has been partially supported by the Spanish CICYT project HEMOSS (ref. TIC98-0949-C02-01) and, CIRIT *Grup de Recerca Consolidat* 1999SGR-150.

References

[1] E. Astesiano, H-J. Kreoski, B. Krieg-Brückner (editors), *Algebraic Foundations for System Specification*, IFIP State-of-the-art Reports, Springer-Verlag 1999.

[2] R.M. Burstall, J.A.Goguen: The semantics of Clear, a specification language, Proc. Copenhagen Winter School on Abstract Software Specification, Springer LNCS 86, pp. 292-332, 1980.

[3] R. Diaconescu, J. A. Goguen, P. Stefaneas. Logical support for modularisation, Report Prog. Res. Group, Oxford University, 1991

[4] H. Ehrig, B. Mahr: *Fundamentals of Algebraic Specification 1*, Springer 1985.

[5] H. Ehrig, B. Mahr: *Fundamentals of Algebraic Specification 2*, Springer 1989.

[6] J.A. Goguen, R.M. Burstall: Introducing institutions. *Proc. Logics of Programming Workshop*, Carnegie-Mellon. Springer LNCS 164, 221-256 (1984).

[7] J.A. Goguen, R.M. Burstall, Institutions: Abstract model theory for specification and programming, *Journal of the ACM* 39, 1 (1992) 95-146.

[8] H. Gaifman, and E. Shapiro. Fully abstract compositional semantics for logics programs. *In Proc. Sixteenth Annual ACM Symp. on Principles of Programming Languages*, (1989) 134-142.

[9] Heinrich Hussmann, Maura Cerioli, Gianna Reggio and Françoise Tort, Abstract Data Types and UML Models, WADT 99, Chateau de Bonas (France), Sept. 1999.

[10] P. Lucio, F. Orejas, E. Pino. An algebraic framework for the definition of compositional semantics of Normal Logic Programs. *Journal of Logic Programming*. 40(1):89-124, july 1999.

[11] J. Meseguer. General logic. *Logic Colloq.'87*. H.-D. Ebbinghaus et al. eds. 279-329, North Holland 1989.

[12] M. Navarro, F. Orejas, A. Sánchez. On the Correctness of Modular Systems. In *Theoretical Computer Science*, 140 (1995) 139-177.

[13] F. Orejas, E. Pino, H. Ehrig: Institutions for Logic Programming *Theoretical Computer Science* 173:485-511 (1997).

[14] F. Orejas. *Chapter 6: Structuring and Modularity*. In [AKK99].

[15] F. Parisi-Presicce. Product and iteration of module specification.. In *Proc. Joint Conf. on Theory and Practice of Software Development*, Pisa LNCS 249, 217-231, Springer-Verlag, 1987.

[16] F. Parisi-Presicce. Partial Composition and Recursion of Module Specifications. In *Proc. Colloq. on trees in Algebra and Programming'88*, Nancy 299, 149-164, Springer LNCS, 1988.

[17] E. Pino. *Algebraic study of modularity in logic programming*. Ph. D. Thesis. Software Department. Technical University of Catalonia.

[18] H. Reichel. Initiallity restricting algebraic theories, in: *Proc. Mathematical Foundations of Computer Science 80*, *Lectures Notes in Computer Science*, Vol. 88 (Springer, Berlin, 1980) 504-514.

[19] D.T. Sannella, A. Tarlecki. Toward Formal Development of ML Programs: Foundations And Methodology. In *Proc. TAPSOFT'89*, Barcelona, Springer LNCS 352 (1989) 375-389.

[20] A. Tarlecki. Moving between logical systems. In Recent Trends in Algebraic Development Taechniques. Springer LNCS 1130,478-502, 1996.

[21] A. Tarlecki. Towards heterogeneous specifications. In *Proc. Workshop on Frontiers of Combining Systems* FroCoS'98, Amsterdam, October 1998, *Applied Logic Series, Kluwer Academic Publishers* 1998.

History Preserving Bisimulation for Contextual Nets*

Paolo Baldan, Andrea Corradini, and Ugo Montanari

Dipartimento di Informatica
Università di Pisa

Abstract. We investigate the notion of *history preserving bisimulation* [15,18,3] for *contextual P/T nets*, a generalization of ordinary P/T Petri nets where a transition may check for the presence of tokens without consuming them (non-destructive read operations). A first equivalence, simply called *HP-bisimulation*, is based on Winskel's prime event structures. A finer equivalence, called *RHP-bisimulation* (where "R" stands for "read"), relies on *asymmetric event structures* [1], a generalization of prime event structures which gives a more faithful account of the dependencies among transition occurrences arising in contextual net computations. Extending the work in [11,19], we show that HP-bisimulation is decidable for finite n-safe contextual nets. Moreover by resorting to *causal automata* [12] — a variation of ordinary automata introduced to deal with history dependent formalisms — we can obtain an algorithm for deciding HP-bisimulation and for getting a minimal realization. Decidability of RHP-bisimulation, instead, remains an open question.

1 Introduction

Contextual nets [14], also called nets with test arcs in [5], with activator arcs in [9] or with read arcs in [20], are a generalization of classical P/T Petri nets where transitions may check for the presence of tokens in the places of the net, without consuming such tokens. More precisely, a transition of a contextual net, besides the usual preconditions and postconditions, may also have some context conditions. The transition is enabled if the current marking covers its preconditions and context conditions. Then the firing of the transition consumes its preconditions, leaves the context unchanged and produces its postconditions. The possibility of faithfully representing a "read-only" access to resources allows contextual nets to model many concrete situations more naturally than classical nets. In recent years they have been used to model concurrent accesses to shared data [16], to provide concurrent semantics to concurrent constraint (CC) programs [13] and to model priorities [8].

Several concurrent semantics for contextual nets based on processes and event structures have been defined in the literature [9,21,7,1]. Relying on such concurrent descriptions of contextual net computations, the aim of this paper is to

* Research partially supported by MURST project Tecniche Formali per Sistemi Software, by TMR Network GETGRATS and by Esprit WG APPLIGRAPH.

D. Bert, C. Choppy, and P. Mosses (Eds.): WADT'99, LNCS 1827, pp. 291–310, 2000.

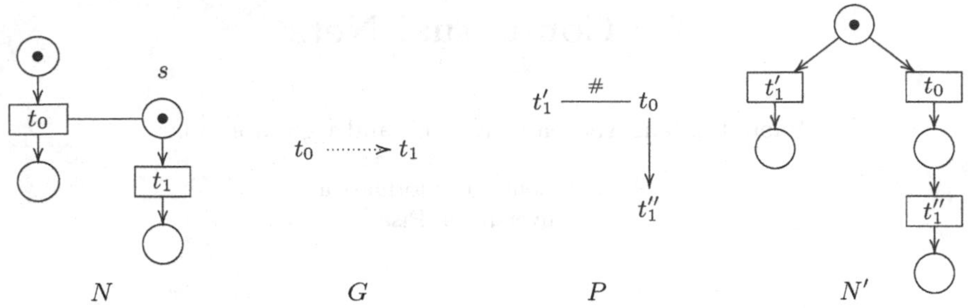

Fig. 1. A contextual net N with its AES G and PES P semantics, and a net N' with the same PES semantics.

discuss more abstract semantics by introducing suitable notions of bisimulation, inspired by the classical *history preserving bisimulation* [15,18,3]. The reason why the extension to contextual nets is not straightforward is that, as noticed in [1], a new kind of dependency between transitions, different from causality and symmetric conflict arises in contextual nets, which cannot be represented faithfully in traditional event structures. The new kind of dependency is related to the possibility of reading part of the state without changing it, and thus it is common to all computational formalisms where a step may preserve part of the state. Consider the contextual net N in Fig. 1 with two transitions t_0 and t_1 such that the same place s is a context for t_0 and a precondition for t_1. As for a conflict of ordinary nets, the firing of t_1 prevents t_0 to be executed, so that t_0 can never follow t_1 in a computation. But the converse is not true, since t_0 *can* fire before t_1. This situation can be naturally interpreted as an *asymmetric conflict* between the two transitions. Equivalently, since t_0 precedes t_1 in any computation where both fire, in such computations t_0 acts as a cause of t_1, but, differently from a cause, t_0 is not necessary for the firing of t_1. Hence we can also think of the relation between t_0 and t_1 as a *weak* form of *causal dependency*.

A reasonable way of encoding a situation of asymmetric conflict in Winskel's prime event structures (PES's) consists of representing the firing of t_1 with two distinct events (see the PES P in Fig. 1): t_1' representing the execution of t_1 that prevents t_0, thus mutually exclusive with t_0, and t_1'' representing the execution of t_1 after t_0 (thus caused by t_0). Besides this phenomenon of "duplication" of events, which increases the complexity of the structures, what may be unsatisfactory in such encoding is the fact that it looses the information on weak causality. For instance, the net N' in Fig. 1 has the same PES semantics of N. In [1] we proposed a solution based on *asymmetric event structures* (AES's), a generalization of prime event structures where the symmetric binary conflict relation is replaced by a relation $\nearrow$ modeling asymmetric conflict. In an AES a situation of asymmetric conflict as in the net N of Fig. 1 is faithfully represented simply by $t_0 \nearrow t_1$. The AES G corresponding to the net N is depicted in the same figure (asymmetric conflict is represented by a dotted arrow).

History preserving bisimulation on ordinary P/T nets relies on the notion of process and of deterministic PES $ev(\pi)$ associated to a process π. Roughly speaking, two nets N_0 and N_1 are history preserving bisimilar if for any process π_0 of N_0 we can find a process π_1 of N_1 such that the underlying deterministic PES's are isomorphic. Moreover whenever π_0 can perform an action becoming a process π_0', also π_1 can perform the same action becoming π_1' and vice versa. The isomorphism between $ev(\pi_0)$ and $ev(\pi_1)$ is required to be extensible to an isomorphism between $ev(\pi_0')$ and $ev(\pi_1')$. Informally this means that each event in N_1 can be simulated by an event in N_2 with the same causal history.

When trying to reformulate this notion for contextual nets, we have more than one possibility according to what we decide to observe as history. We can decide that the history of an event e in a process is given by the set of events that precede e in the process, with their relative ordering and without any additional information on the origin of the precedences among events. This amounts to associate to a process π a deterministic PES. The corresponding notion of bisimulation is called *history preserving bisimulation* (*HP-bisimulation*). As already noticed, the PES semantics and thus HP-bisimulation loose the information on weak causality (asymmetric conflict) between events which, working with deterministic processes, is confused with causality. For instance the nets N and N' in Fig. 1, are HP-bisimilar since they have the same PES semantics. In some situations this level of abstraction may be not appropriate: the firing sequence $t_0; t_1$ in N is simulated by $t_0; t_1''$ in N', but in N', differently from what happens in N, there is a flow of information from t_0 to t_1''. Imagine that tokens represent pieces of data and transitions are functions operating on such data. Then changing the function computed by t_0 in the net N' we influence the output of t_1'', while in N the output of t_1 does not depend on t_0. A different notion of bisimulation, discriminating the nets N and N', arises by assuming that the history of an event in a process should record complete information on causality and weak causality. Formally, this is obtained by associating to a process π a deterministic AES. The corresponding finer equivalence is called *read history preserving bisimulation* (*RHP-bisimulation*). Both HP-bisimulation and RHP-bisimulation coincide with the classical notion when restricted to ordinary P/T nets.

Generalizing the results proved in [11,19] for ordinary P/T nets, we show that HP-bisimulation is decidable for finite n-safe contextual nets. To this aim we resort to *causal automata* [11], a variation of ordinary automata suited to deal with history-dependent formalisms like CCS with causal or location semantics and the π-calculus with the ordinary or non-interleaving semantics. The (possibly infinite) transition system of processes of a contextual net, which is used to define HP-bisimulation, is abstracted to a causal automaton via a construction which respects (preserves and reflects) bisimilarity. The automaton is finite for finite n-safe contextual nets. Hence the HP-bisimilarity of any two finite n-safe contextual nets can be checked by applying the general algorithm proposed in [11] to the corresponding causal automata. Since such algorithm relies on the translation of causal automata into ordinary automata, the standard techniques for ordinary transition systems can be used, allowing, for instance, to obtain a minimal realization for a contextual net up to HP-bisimulation. Our attempt of extending the described approach to RHP-bisimulation instead fails. In principle, we are still able to build a (generalized) causal automaton corresponding to a contextual net in a way that respects RHP-bisimulation. However such an automaton is in general infinite also for finite n-safe nets and thus the translation does not suggest an immediate way of checking RHP-bisimulation. The decidability of RHP-bisimulation on contextual nets is left as an open question.

2 Contextual Nets, Processes and Asymmetric Event Structures

In this section, after introducing the basics of marked contextual P/T nets [16], we present the notions of deterministic occurrence contextual net and process. Then we briefly review prime event structures, and asymmetric event structures as defined in [1].

2.1 Contextual Nets

We first recall some notation for multisets. Let A be a set; a *multiset* of A is a function $M : A \to \mathbb{N}$. It is called finite if $\{a \in A : M(a) > 0\}$ is finite. The set of finite multisets of A is denoted by $\mu_* A$. The usual operations and relations on multisets, like multiset union $+$ or multiset difference $-$, are used. We write $M \leq M'$ if $M(a) \leq M'(a)$ for all $a \in A$. If $M \in \mu_* A$, we denote by $[\![M]\!]$ the multiset defined, for all $a \in A$, as $[\![M]\!](a) = 1$ if $M(a) > 0$, and $[\![M]\!](a) = 0$ otherwise. With abuse of notation we will write $a \in M$ for $M(a) > 0$ and $M \cap M'$ for the set $\{a \in A : M(a) > 0 \wedge M'(a) > 0\}$. A *multirelation* $f : A \to B$ is a multiset of $A \times B$. It is called *finitary* if $\{b \in B : f(a, b) > 0\}$ is a finite set for all $a \in A$. A finitary multirelation f induces in an obvious way a function $\mu f : \mu_* A \to \mu_* B$, defined as $\mu f(M)(b) = \sum_{a \in A} M(a) \cdot f(a, b)$ for $M \in \mu_* A$ and $b \in B$. In the sequel we will implicitly assume that all multirelations are finitary.

Definition 1 ((labelled, marked) contextual net). *A* (marked) contextual Petri net (c-net) *is a tuple* $N = \langle S, T, F, C, m \rangle$, *where*

- S *is a set of* places *and* T *is a set of* transitions*;*
- $F = \langle F_{pre}, F_{post} \rangle$ *is a pair of multirelations from* T *to* S*;*
- C *is a multirelation from* T *to* S, *called the* context relation*;*
- m *is a finite multiset of* S, *called the* initial marking.

The c-net is called finite *if* T *and* S *are finite sets. Without loss of generality, we assume* $S \cap T = \emptyset$. *Moreover, we require that for each transition* $t \in T$, *there exists a place* $s \in S$ *such that* $F_{pre}(t, s) > 0$. *A* labelled c-net *is a pair* $\langle N, l_N \rangle$ *where* N *is a c-net and* $l_N : T \to \mathsf{Act}$ *is a function from* T *to a set of labels* Act.

In the following when considering a c-net N, we implicitly assume that $N = \langle S, T, F, C, m \rangle$ and, if N is labelled, we denote by l_N its labelling function. Furthermore, throughout the paper we consider a fixed set of labels Act.

As usual, given a finite multiset of transitions $A \in \mu_* T$ we write $^\bullet A$ for its *pre-set* $\mu F_{pre}(A)$ and $A^\bullet$ for its *post-set* $\mu F_{post}(A)$. Moreover, by $\underline{A}$ we denote the *context* of A, defined as $\underline{A} = \mu C(A)$. The same notation is used to denote the functions from S to the powerset $\mathcal{P}(T)$ defined as, for $s \in S$, $^\bullet s = \{t \in T : F_{post}(t,s) > 0\}$, $s^\bullet = \{t \in T : F_{pre}(t,s) > 0\}$, $\underline{s} = \{t \in T : C(t,s) > 0\}$.

Let N be a contextual net. For a finite multiset of transitions A to be enabled by a marking M, it is sufficient that M contains the pre-set of A and at least one *additional* token in each place of the context of A. This corresponds to the intuition that a token in a place can be used as context concurrently by many transitions and with multiplicity greater than one by the same transition. Formally, a finite multiset of transitions $A \in \mu_* T$ is *enabled* by a marking $M \in \mu_* S$ if $^\bullet A + [\![\underline{A}]\!] \leq M$. In this case, to indicate that the execution of A in M produces the new marking $M' = M - {}^\bullet A + A^\bullet$ we write $M\,[A\rangle\, M'$. We call $M\,[A\rangle\, M'$ a *step* (or a *firing* when it involves just one transition).

A marking M of a c-net N is called *reachable* if there is a finite step sequence in N leading to M from the initial marking, i.e., $m\,[A_0\rangle\, M_1\,[A_1\rangle\, M_2 \ldots [A_n\rangle\, M$. A c-net is called *$n$-safe* if for any reachable marking M each place contains at most n tokens, namely $M(s) \leq n$ for all $s \in S$. A 1-safe net will be often called simply *safe*.

2.2 Deterministic Occurrence C-Nets and Processes

As for ordinary nets a process of a c-net is defined as an occurrence c-net with a mapping to the original net. Occurrence c-nets are safe c-nets such that the dependency relations between transitions satisfy suitable acyclicity and well-foundedness requirements.

Definition 2 (causality). *Let N be a safe c-net. The* causality relation $<_N$ *is the least transitive relation on $S \cup T$ such that*

1. *if $s \in {}^\bullet t$ then $s <_N t$;*
2. *if $s \in t^\bullet$ then $t <_N s$;*
3. *if $t^\bullet \cap \underline{t'} \neq \emptyset$ then $t <_N t'$.*

Given $x \in S \cup T$, we write $\lfloor x \rfloor$ for the set of causes *of x in T, defined as $\lfloor x \rfloor = \{t \in T : t \leq_N x\} \subseteq T$, where $\leq_N$ is the reflexive closure of $<_N$.*

Note that causality is defined as for ordinary nets, with an additional clause stating that transition t causes t' if it generates a token in a context place of t'.

Definition 3 (asymmetric conflict). *Let N be a safe c-net. The* asymmetric conflict relation $\nearrow_N$ *is defined as*

$$t \nearrow_N t' \quad \text{iff} \quad \underline{t} \cap {}^\bullet t' \neq \emptyset \;\; \text{or} \;\; (t \neq t' \wedge {}^\bullet t \cap {}^\bullet t' \neq \emptyset) \;\; \text{or} \;\; t <_N t'.$$

In our interpretation, $t \nearrow_N t'$ if t' prevents t to be fired or, equivalently, if t must precede t' in each computation where both transitions fire. Informally, if $\mathit{fire}_C(t)$ indicates that t fires in a computation C and $\mathit{prec}_C(t,t')$ indicates that t precedes t' in C, then $t \nearrow t'$ means that

$$\text{for all computations } C, \text{ if } \mathit{fire}_C(t) \text{ and } \mathit{fire}_C(t') \text{ then } \mathit{prec}_C(t,t') \qquad (\dagger)$$

The discussion in the introduction suggests that, in an acyclic safe net, (†) is surely satisfied when the same place s appears as context for t and as precondition for t'. But (†) is trivially true (with t and t' in interchangeable roles) when t and t' have a common precondition, since they never fire in the same computation. This corresponds to the intuition that an ordinary symmetric conflict amounts to an asymmetric conflict in both directions. Finally, (†) is weaker than the condition expressing causality and thus it is satisfied when $t < t'$.

We are now able to introduce deterministic occurrence c-nets.

Definition 4 ((deterministic) occurrence c-nets). *A* deterministic occurrence c-net *is a safe c-net* $O = \langle S, T, F, C, m \rangle$ *such that*

1. *each place* $s \in S$ *is in the post-set of at most one transition, i.e.* $|{}^\bullet s| \leq 1$*;*
2. $\nearrow_O$ *is well-founded and finitary; thus* $(\nearrow_O)^*$ *and* $\leq_O$ *are finitary partial orders;*[1]
3. $m = \{s \in S : {}^\bullet s = \emptyset\}$.

While conditions (1) and (3) are standard, condition (2) deserves some comments. First, it implies the acyclicity of $\nearrow_O$, which can be interpreted as a conflict freeness property. In fact, if some transitions $t_0, \ldots, t_n$ form a $\nearrow_O$-cycle $t_0 \nearrow_O t_1 \nearrow_O \ldots \nearrow_O t_n \nearrow_O t_0$ then they cannot fire together in the same computation since each one should precede the others. Hence cycles of asymmetric conflict can be thought of as a kind of conflicts on sets of events. Condition (2) also requires the absence of infinite descending chains of $\nearrow_O$, ensuring that each transition must be preceded only by finitely many other transitions.

We will denote by $\min(O)$ and $\max(O)$ the sets of minimal and maximal places of O w.r.t. the partial order $\leq_O$. An occurrence c-net O will be often denoted as $\langle S, T, F, C \rangle$, not mentioning the initial marking m which is uniquely determined as $\min(O)$.

In a deterministic occurrence c-net *all* transitions can fire in a single computation, in any order compatible with the asymmetric conflict relation. Hence, as for ordinary nets, a deterministic process of a c-net, representing a concurrent computation of the net, is defined as a deterministic occurrence c-net with a mapping to the original net. Such a mapping allows one to transform each firing (step) sequence of the occurrence net into a firing sequence of the original net.

Definition 5 ((deterministic) process). *A* deterministic process *of a c-net N is a mapping* $\pi : O_\pi \to N$*, where O_π is a deterministic occurrence c-net and π is a strong c-net morphism, namely a pair of total functions* $\pi = \langle \pi_S : S_N \to S_{O_\pi}, \pi_T : T_N \to T_{O_\pi} \rangle$ *such that the pre-set, post-set and context of each transition are preserved. A process π is called* marked *if π_S preserves also the initial marking of the net.*

[1] A relation $r \subseteq X \times X$ is called *finitary* if for any $x \in X$ the set $\{y \in X : y\, r\, x\}$ is finite. Furthermore r^* denotes the reflexive and transitive closure of a relation r.

We will denote by $\min(\pi)$ and $\max(\pi)$ the sets of places $\min(O_\pi)$ and $\max(O_\pi)$. Similarly the relations $\leq_{O_\pi}$ and $\nearrow_{O_\pi}$ will be denoted simply as $\leq_\pi$ and $\nearrow_\pi$. Any marked process of the net N having an empty set of transitions is called an *initial process* of N (observe that all the initial processes of a net are isomorphic). Since in this paper we will only deal with deterministic occurrence c-nets and processes, the qualification "deterministic" will be often omitted. Some examples of deterministic marked processes of a c-net can be found in Fig. 2 (for the moment ignore the fact that processes are partly dotted).

Hereinafter we will consider only finite processes, i.e., processes with a finite underlying occurrence net. It is possible to show that a marking M of a c-net N is reachable iff there is some finite marked process π such that $M = \mu\pi_S(\max(\pi))$.

2.3 Prime and Asymmetric Event Structures

Event structures [22] are a simple event based model of concurrent computations in which events are considered as atomic and instantaneous steps, which can appear only once in a computation. Recall that a (labelled) *prime* event structure with *binary conflict* (PES) is a tuple $\langle E, \leq, \#, l\rangle$ consisting of a set E of events endowed with two binary relations: the partial order $\leq$ modelling *causality* and the relation $\#$ modeling *conflict*, which is symmetric, irreflexive and hereditary w.r.t. causality. The last component $l : E \to \mathsf{Act}$ is the labelling function over the fixed set of labels Act.

To faithfully model the dependencies in c-net computations, in [1] we introduced *asymmetric event structures*, a generalization of PES's where the symmetric conflict relation is replaced by a relation $\nearrow$ representing *weak causality* or *asymmetric conflict*.

Definition 6 (asymmetric event structure). *A* (labelled) asymmetric event structure (AES) *is a tuple* $G = \langle E, \leq, \nearrow, l\rangle$, *where* E *is a set of* events, $l : E \to \mathsf{Act}$ *is the labelling function (with* Act *fixed set of labels) and* $\leq$, $\nearrow$ *are binary relations on* E *called* causality *and* asymmetric conflict, *respectively, such that:*

1. $\leq$ *is a partial order and* $\lfloor e\rfloor = \{e' \in E : e' \leq e\}$ *is finite for all* $e \in E$;
2. $< \subseteq \nearrow$ *and* $\nearrow$ *is acyclic on* $\lfloor e\rfloor$ *for all* $e \in E$.

We do not discuss in detail the notion of AES. It is basically a "stateless" counterpart of (possibly nondeterministic) occurrence c-nets and most of the considerations done for occurrence c-nets also apply to AES's. In particular the conflict relation is induced by cycles of asymmetric conflict.

In this paper we are interested only in finite deterministic event structures. A *(deterministic) prime event structure* is a conflict free PES, namely a PES $\langle E, \leq, \#, l\rangle$ such that $\# = \emptyset$. It will be always denoted simply by $\langle E, \leq, l\rangle$. Similarly a *(deterministic) asymmetric event structure* is an AES $\langle E, \leq, \nearrow, l\rangle$ such that the asymmetric conflict relation is well-founded and finitary (in particular the relation $\nearrow$ is acyclic, a property corresponding to conflict freeness). Observe that for finite AES's such conditions reduce to the acyclicity of $\nearrow$. For both deterministic PES's and AES's the entire set E of events is a configuration of the event structure, meaning that all the events in E can be executed in a single computation of the modelled system.

The notion of isomorphism for PES's and AES's is defined in the obvious way.

3 History Preserving Bisimulation on Contextual Nets

As mentioned in the introduction, history preserving bisimulation is a behavioural equivalence which takes into account the dependencies among events. Roughly speaking it equates two ordinary nets if each action of the first net can be simulated by an action of the second net with the same history, and vice versa. This section generalizes this idea to the setting of contextual nets, where, according to the chosen notion of history, two different formulations of history preserving bisimulation arise: HP-bisimulation, relying on PES's, which observes only the precedences between events, and RHP-bisimulation, based on AES's, which instead distinguishes causality from weak causality.

A basic ingredient for the definition of history preserving bisimulation is a transition system, associated to each c-net, where states are processes.

Definition 7 (process moves). *Given two processes π and π' of a labelled c-net N, we write $\pi \xrightarrow[e]{a} \pi'$, saying that π* moves to π' performing action a, *if*

- *$T_{\pi'} = T_\pi \cup \{e\}$, with $e \notin T_\pi$ and $l_N(\pi'_T(e)) = a$;*
- *$S_\pi \subseteq S_{\pi'}$;*
- *π_S, π_T, F_π and C_π are the restrictions to O_π of the components of π'.*

Fig. 2 represents a sequence of processes of a c-net N such that each π_i moves to π_{i+1}. For example, $\pi_0 \xrightarrow[e_0]{c} \pi_1$ and $\pi_1 \xrightarrow[e_1]{b} \pi_2$.

To each process π of a c-net we can naturally associate a (deterministic) PES having the transitions of the underlying occurrence net as events and the transitive closure of the asymmetric conflict relation as causality: this corresponds to confuse the weak causality determined by the precedences induced by contexts and the "strong" causality deriving from the flow of information. Alternatively, we can associate to the process a deterministic AES, which keeps weak causality and "strong" causality distinct.

Definition 8 (event structures for processes). *Let π be a process of a labelled c-net N. The* PES associated to π *is defined as:*

$$ev(\pi) = \langle T_\pi, (\nearrow_\pi)^*, l_N \circ \pi_T \rangle$$

The AES associated to π *is instead*

$$aev(\pi) = \langle T, \leq_\pi, \nearrow_\pi, l_N \circ \pi_T \rangle$$

Based on the notions of process and of (asymmetric) event structure associated to a process, *history preserving (HP-) bisimulation* and *read history preserving (RHP-) bisimulation* are readily defined.

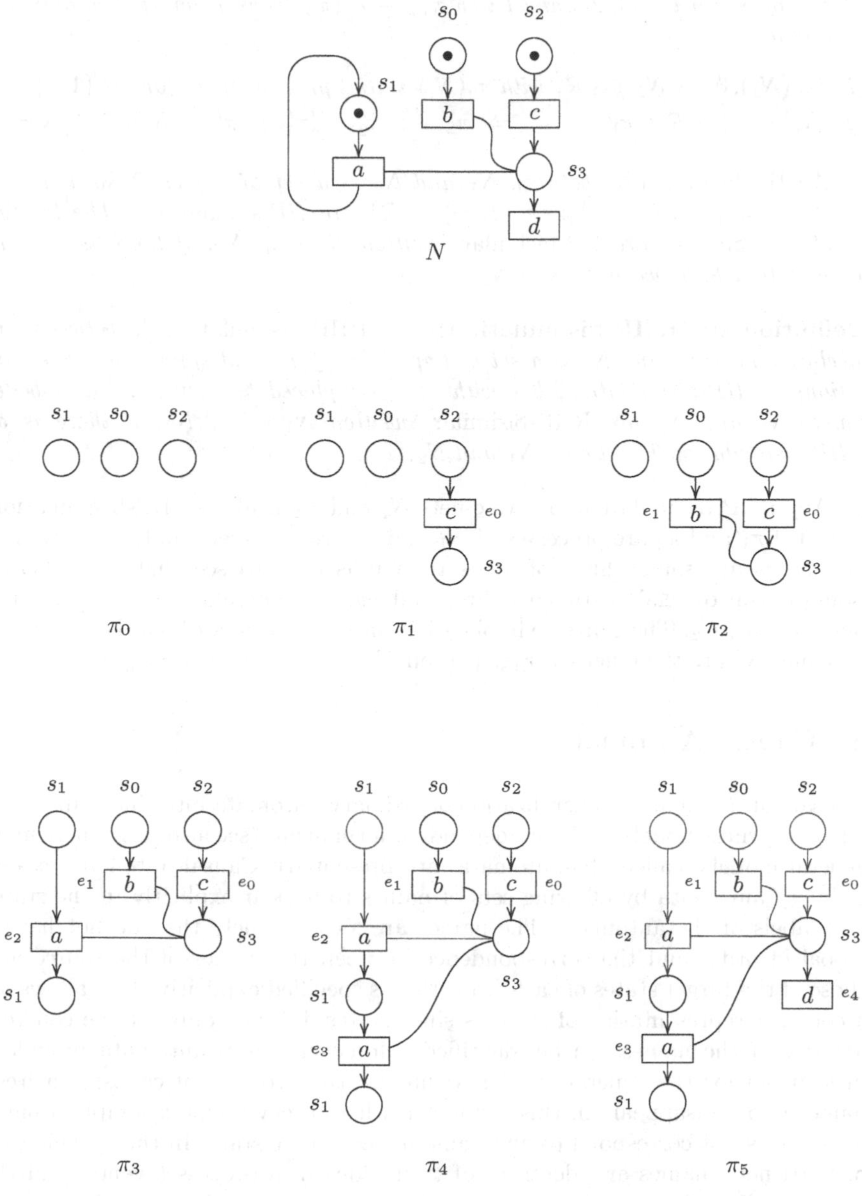

Fig. 2. A contextual net N and a sequence of process moves starting from an initial process. The process mappings are specified by the labelling of the items. For any process the non dotted part represents the corresponding partial process.

Definition 9 (HP-bisimulation). *Let N_1 and N_2 be labelled c-nets. An* HP-simulation $\mathcal{R}$ *of N_1 in N_2 is a set of triples $\langle \pi_1, f, \pi_2 \rangle$ where π_i is a marked process of N_i for $i \in \{1,2\}$, and $f : ev(\pi_1) \to ev(\pi_2)$ is an isomorphism of* PES*'s, such that*

1. $\langle \pi_0(N_1), \emptyset, \pi_0(N_2) \rangle \in \mathcal{R}$, *with $\pi_0(N_i)$ initial process of N_i for $i \in \{1,2\}$;*
2. $\langle \pi_1, f, \pi_2 \rangle \in \mathcal{R} \wedge \pi_1 \xrightarrow[e_1]{a} \pi_1' \Rightarrow \pi_2 \xrightarrow[e_2]{a} \pi_2' \wedge \langle \pi_1', f', \pi_2' \rangle \in \mathcal{R} \wedge f'_{|ev(\pi_1)} = f$.

An HP-bisimulation *between N_1 and N_2 is a set of triples $\mathcal{R}$ such that $\mathcal{R}$ and $\mathcal{R}^{-1} = \{\langle \pi_2, f^{-1}, \pi_1 \rangle : \langle \pi_1, f, \pi_2 \rangle \in \mathcal{R}\}$ are HP-simulations. The labelled c-nets N_1 and N_2 are* HP-bisimilar, *written $N_1 \sim_{hp} N_2$, if there is an HP-bisimulation $\mathcal{R}$ between N_1 and N_2.*

Definition 10 (RHP-bisimulation). *An* RHP-bisimulation $\mathcal{R}$ *between two labelled c-nets N_1 and N_2 is a set of triples $\langle \pi_1, f, \pi_2 \rangle$ satisfying the same conditions as HP-bisimulation, but with $ev(\pi_i)$ replaced by $aev(\pi_i)$. The labelled c-nets N_1 and N_2 are* RHP-bisimilar, *written $N_1 \sim_{rhp} N_2$, if there is an RHP-bisimulation $\mathcal{R}$ between N_1 and N_2.*

Any RHP-bisimulation for two c-nets N_1 and N_2 is also an HP-bisimulation. In fact if π_1 and π_2 are processes of N_1 and N_2, respectively, and $f : aev(\pi_1) \to aev(\pi_2)$ is an isomorphism of AES's then it is easy to see that f is also an isomorphism of PES's between $ev(\pi_1)$ and $ev(\pi_2)$. Therefore $N_1 \sim_{rhp} N_2$ implies $N_1 \sim_{hp} N_2$. The converse implication, instead, does not hold. For instance, if N and N' are the c-nets in Fig. 1, then $N \sim_{hp} N'$, while $N \not\sim_{rhp} N'$.

4 Causal Automata

Causal automata are a generalization of ordinary automata introduced in [11] as an appropriate model for history dependent formalisms (see also [12], where more general models, called HD-automata, are presented). Causal automata extend ordinary automata by allowing sets of names to appear explicitly in the states and labels of the automata. The names are local, namely they do not have a global identity, and the correspondence between the names of the source and those of the target states of each transition is specified explicitly. This allows for a compact representation of systems since states differing only for the concrete identity of the names can be identified. Moreover causal automata provide a mechanism for the generation of new names: the problem of choosing a fresh name simply disappears in this formalism where a new name is simply a name which does not correspond to any name in the source state. In the specific case of Petri nets, names are identities of transitions in a process (events) and the correspondence between names allows to represent causal dependencies.

Definition 11 (causal automaton). *Let $\mathcal{N}$ be a fixed infinite countable set of names (event names) and let* Act *be a fixed set of labels. A* causal automaton *is a tuple $\mathcal{A} = \langle Q, n, \longmapsto, q_0 \rangle$, where*

– *Q is the set of* states*;*
– *$n : Q \to \mathcal{P}_{fin}(\mathcal{N})$ is a function associating to each state a finite set of names;*
– *$\longmapsto$ is a set of transitions, each of the form $q \overset{a}{\underset{M}{\longmapsto}}_\sigma q'$, with*
  - *q, q' the source and target states;*
  - *$a \in \mathsf{Act}$ the label;*
  - *$M \subseteq n(q)$ the set of dependencies of the transition;*
  - *$\sigma : n(q') \hookrightarrow n(q) \cup \{\star\}$ the injective inverse renaming function;*
– *$q_0 \in Q$ is the initial state; it is required that $n(q_0) = \emptyset$.*

For each state $q \in Q$ the set of names $n(q)$ is used to represent the past events which can (but not necessarily will) be referenced by future transitions. Conceptually, each transition $q \overset{a}{\underset{M}{\longmapsto}}_\sigma q'$ depends on the past events mentioned in M. Due to the local scope of names, the function $\sigma : n(q') \hookrightarrow n(q) \cup \{\star\}$ is needed to relate the names of the target state to those of the source. The event mapped to $\star$ (if any) represents the new event generated by the considered transition. In the following the components of a causal automaton will be often denoted by using the name of the automaton as subscript.

The notion of bisimulation on causal automata (CA-bisimulation) takes into account the fact that a state has attached a set of local names. Hence a bisimulation not only relates states, but also the corresponding sets of local names.

Definition 12 (CA-bisimulation). *Let $\mathcal{A}$ and $\mathcal{B}$ be two causal automata. A* CA-simulation *$\mathcal{R}$ of $\mathcal{A}$ in $\mathcal{B}$ is a set of triples $\langle q, \delta, p\rangle$, where $q \in Q_\mathcal{A}$, $p \in Q_\mathcal{B}$ and δ is a partial injective function from $n_\mathcal{A}(q)$ to $n_\mathcal{B}(p)$, such that*

1. *$\langle q_{0\mathcal{A}}, \emptyset, q_{0\mathcal{B}}\rangle \in \mathcal{R}$;*
2. *if $\langle q, \delta, p\rangle \in \mathcal{R}$ and $q \overset{a}{\underset{M}{\longmapsto}}_\sigma q'$ in $\mathcal{A}$ then*
   – *$p \overset{a}{\underset{\delta(M)}{\longmapsto}}_\rho p'$ in $\mathcal{B}$ for some p' and*
   – *$\langle q', \delta', p'\rangle \in \mathcal{R}$ for some δ' such that $\delta^\star \circ \sigma = \rho \circ \delta'$, where $\delta^\star$ is defined as $\delta \cup \{(\star, \star)\}$ (see the diagram below).*

$$\begin{array}{ccc} n_\mathcal{A}(q) \cup \{\star\} & \xrightarrow{\delta^\star} & n_\mathcal{B}(p) \cup \{\star\} \\ {\scriptstyle\sigma}\uparrow & & \uparrow{\scriptstyle\rho} \\ n_\mathcal{A}(q') & \xrightarrow[\delta']{} & n_\mathcal{B}(p') \end{array}$$

A CA-bisimulation *between $\mathcal{A}$ and $\mathcal{B}$ is a set of triples $\mathcal{R}$ such that $\mathcal{R}$ and $\mathcal{R}^{-1} = \{\langle p, \delta^{-1}, q\rangle : \langle q, \delta, p\rangle \in \mathcal{R}\}$ are CA-simulations. The automata $\mathcal{A}$ and $\mathcal{B}$ are* CA-bisimilar*, written $\mathcal{A} \sim_{ca} \mathcal{B}$, if there exists a bisimulation $\mathcal{R}$ between $\mathcal{A}$ and $\mathcal{B}$.*

In [11] an algorithm has been proposed for checking the CA-bisimilarity of (finite) causal automata. Given a causal automaton $\mathcal{A}$, after removing the "unnecessary" names from the states of the automaton, the basic step of the algorithm constructs an ordinary labelled transition system $\mathit{Unf}(\mathcal{A})$, called the

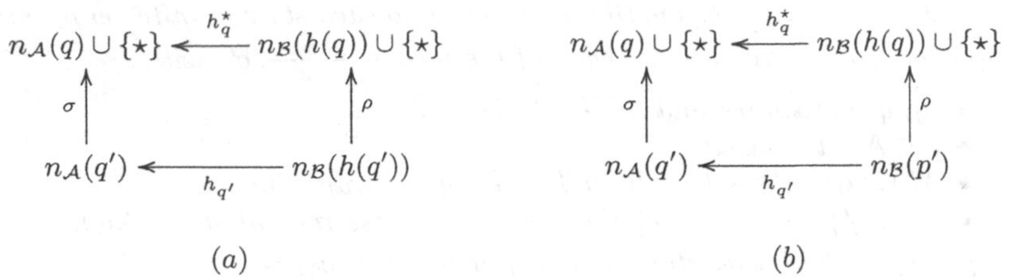

Fig. 3. Diagrams for abstraction homomorphisms.

unfolding of $\mathcal{A}$, such that $\mathcal{A} \sim_{ca} \mathcal{B}$ iff the associated transition systems $Unf(\mathcal{A})$ and $Unf(\mathcal{B})$ are bisimilar. Then standard algorithms (e.g., a partition/refinement algorithm) can be used to verify bisimilarity on the ordinary transition systems or to obtain a minimal equivalent transition system.

Abstraction homomorphisms [4], also called zig-zag morphisms [17] or transition preserving homomorphisms [6], are defined in the setting of ordinary automata as morphisms which "preserve" and "reflect" transitions. The existence of an abstraction homomorphism ensures that the source an target automata are bisimilar. The next definition generalizes this idea to causal automata.

Definition 13 (abstraction homomorphism). *Let $\mathcal{A}$ and $\mathcal{B}$ be causal automata. An* abstraction homomorphism $\mathsf{h} : \mathcal{A} \to \mathcal{B}$ *is a pair* $\mathsf{h} = \langle h, \{h_q\}_{q \in Q_\mathcal{A}} \rangle$ *where $h : Q_\mathcal{A} \to Q_\mathcal{B}$ is a function and for all $q \in Q_\mathcal{A}$, $h_q : n_\mathcal{B}(h(q)) \to n_\mathcal{A}(q)$ is an injective function, such that $h(q_{0\mathcal{A}}) = q_{0\mathcal{B}}$ and*

- *if $q \overset{a}{\underset{M}{\longmapsto}}_\sigma q'$ in $\mathcal{A}$ then $h(q) \overset{a}{\underset{h_q^{-1}(M)}{\longmapsto}}_\rho h(q')$ in $\mathcal{B}$, with $\sigma \circ h_{q'} = h_q^\star \circ \rho$ (see Fig. 3.(a));*
- *if $h(q) \overset{a}{\underset{M}{\longmapsto}}_\rho p'$ in $\mathcal{B}$ then $q \overset{a}{\underset{h_q(M)}{\longmapsto}}_\sigma q'$ in $\mathcal{A}$ for some q', with $h(q') = p'$ and $\sigma \circ h_{q'} = h_q^\star \circ \rho$ (see Fig. 3.(b)).*

Intuitively, via an abstraction homomorphism $\mathsf{h} : \mathcal{A} \to \mathcal{B}$ several states of $\mathcal{A}$ can collapse into a single state of $\mathcal{B}$, in a way that respects the behaviour and the naming. Also in this setting, the existence of an abstraction homomorphism $\mathsf{h} : \mathcal{A} \to \mathcal{B}$ is sufficient to conclude the bisimilarity of $\mathcal{A}$ and $\mathcal{B}$.

Lemma 1. *Let $\mathcal{A}$ and $\mathcal{B}$ be causal automata. If there exists an abstraction homomorphism $\mathsf{h} : \mathcal{A} \to \mathcal{B}$ then $\mathcal{A} \sim_{ca} \mathcal{B}$.*

It is worth observing that, as for ordinary automata, the above lemma does not provide a necessary condition. Indeed, in [12], following the approach of [10], abstraction homomorphisms have been described as open maps in a category of causal automata, and CA-bisimilarity has been given a characterization by means of spans of open maps.

5 Causal Automata for Contextual Net Bisimulations

As in the ordinary case, the definition of (R)HP-bisimulation for contextual nets relies on the transition system of marked processes and process moves, which is infinite for any non-trivial net exhibiting a cyclic behaviour. In the case of ordinary nets, the solution proposed in the literature for deciding history preserving bisimulation on significant subclasses of nets consists of recording only the part of a process which is, in a sense, relevant for the current state. More precisely, the techniques in [19] for safe nets and in [11] for n-safe P/T nets, basically rely on the idea of restricting the attention only to the set of events which produced at least one token in the current state and to the causal ordering among them. The corresponding structures are called *configurations* in [11] and *ordered markings* in [19]. The bisimulation relation defined on the transition system having such configurations as states, called incremental bisimulation, is shown to coincide with history preserving bisimulation. Since a finite n-safe net only has finitely many configurations (up to isomorphism), incremental bisimulation (and thus also history preserving bisimulation) is decidable for this class of nets. Furthermore, the paper [11] shows how it is possible to associate to each finite n-safe net N a finite causal automaton $\mathcal{A}(N)$ such that two nets N_1 and N_2 are bisimilar if and only if $\mathcal{A}(N_1) \sim_{ca} \mathcal{A}(N_2)$. Then the general algorithm for causal automata mentioned in Section 4 can be used to check the bisimilarity of nets and to construct a minimal realization.

In this section we address the problem of extending such a method to contextual nets. We prove that HP-bisimulation is still decidable for finite n-safe contextual nets by showing how a finite causal automaton can be associated to such nets via a construction which respects HP-bisimilarity. Instead, when considering RHP-bisimulation some serious problems arise: the natural extension of the described approach produces a causal automaton which may be infinite also for finite safe c-nets. Hence the decidability of RHP-bisimulation remains an open question.

5.1 HP-Bisimulation

As mentioned before, to construct a finite causal automaton, or, in general, a finite transition system allowing to decide history preserving bisimulation for ordinary nets the leading idea is that not all the information carried by a process is relevant for deciding bisimulation. Hence processes may be replaced by more compact structures where part of the past history is discarded.

As one would expect, when considering HP-bisimulation on c-nets, one must keep information not only about the events which produced a token in the current marking ("producers"), but also about the events which read a token in the current marking ("readers"). Fortunately, among the readers, which can be unbounded even for a safe net, only the maximal ones play a significant role, while the others can be safely discarded.

Definition 14 (producers and (maximal) readers). *Given a process π of a c-net N, we define*

- *the set of* producers
  $p(\pi) = \{t \in T_\pi : t^\bullet \cap \max(\pi) \neq \emptyset\}$;
- *the set of* readers
  $r(\pi) = \{t \in T_\pi : \underline{t} \cap \max(\pi) \neq \emptyset\}$;
- *the set of* maximal readers
  $mr(\pi) = \{t \in r(\pi) : \exists s \in \underline{t} \cap \max(\pi).\ t \text{ is } \leq_\pi -\text{maximal in } \underline{s}\}$.

For instance the set of producers of the process π_4 in Fig. 2 is $p(\pi_4) = \{e_0, e_3\}$, its set of readers is $r(\pi_4) = \{e_1, e_2, e_3\}$, while the set of maximal readers is $mr(\pi_4) = \{e_1, e_3\}$.

As expressed by the proposition below, for a finite n-safe c-net N the sets $p(\pi)$ and $mr(\pi)$, with π ranging over the marked processes of N, are bounded.

Proposition 1. *Let N be a finite n-safe c-net. Then, for any marked process π of N, we have $|p(\pi)| \leq n \cdot |S_N|$ and $|mr(\pi)| \leq (n \cdot |S_N|)^2$.*

We next define partial processes, which are aimed at representing truncations of marked processes where only a relevant part for discriminating non HP-bisimilar states is kept, namely the producers and the maximal readers.

Definition 15 (partial process). *A* partial process *γ of a c-net N is an unmarked process $\gamma : O_\gamma \to N$, where $T_\gamma = p(\gamma) \cup mr(\gamma)$.*

Observe that any initial process for a c-net N is a partial process of N, since it has an empty set of productions.

To each (marked or unmarked) process π of a net N we associate in the obvious way a partial process which is obtained by keeping only the producers and the maximal readers of π (see Fig. 2).

Definition 16. *Each process π of a c-net N naturally induces a partial process, denoted $\gamma(\pi)$, such that $O_{\gamma(\pi)} = \langle S', T', F', C' \rangle$, where*

- *$T' = p(\pi) \cup mr(\pi)$;*
- *$S' = \max(\pi) \cup \bigcup\{{}^\bullet t : t \in T'\}$;*
- *F', C' and the mapping to N are the restrictions of F_π, C_π and π.*

We next introduce the *move relation* on partial processes, leading to a transition system of partial processes which is then exploited in the construction of the causal automaton associated to a c-net.

Definition 17 (partial processes moves). *Given two partial processes γ and γ' we write $\gamma \xrightarrow[e]{a} \gamma'$, and we say that γ* moves to *γ'* performing the action *a, iff $\gamma \xrightarrow[e]{a} \pi$ (as a generic process, according to Definition 7) and $\gamma(\pi) = \gamma'$.*

The process move $\gamma \xrightarrow[e]{a} \pi$ is called the process move underlying the partial process move $\gamma \xrightarrow[e]{a} \gamma'$. Considering only the non-dotted parts, Fig. 2 represents a sequence of partial process moves starting from the initial process π_0.

To each (partial) process move we associate the set of maximal (weak or strong) causes of the executed transition, which will play a basic role in the definition of the automaton. In fact, to observe the partial order associated to an evolving computation it is sufficient to look, step by step, only at the immediate maximal causes of each single transition (the other dependencies being implicitly given by the transitivity of the partial order).

Definition 18 (immediate and maximal causes). *The set of* immediate (weak or strong) causes *of a process move* $\pi \xrightarrow[e]{a} \pi'$ *is defined as* $\mathsf{IC}(\pi \xrightarrow[e]{a} \pi') = \{t \in T_\pi : t^\bullet \cap (\underline{e} \cup {}^\bullet e) \neq \emptyset \ \vee\ \underline{t} \cap {}^\bullet e \neq \emptyset\}$. *We denote by* $\mathsf{MC}(\pi \xrightarrow[e]{a} \pi')$ *the set of* maximal (immediate) causes, *namely the subset of* $\nearrow_\pi$*-maximal elements of* $\mathsf{IC}(\pi \xrightarrow[e]{a} \pi')$. *The sets of immediate and maximal causes of a partial process move are defined in the obvious way by resorting to the underlying process move.*

For example, for the move $\pi_4 \xrightarrow[e_4]{d} \pi_5$ we have that $\mathsf{IC}(\pi_4 \xrightarrow[e_4]{d} \pi_5) = \{e_0, e_1, e_2, e_3\}$, while $\mathsf{MC}(\pi_4 \xrightarrow[e_4]{d} \pi_5) = \{e_0, e_1, e_3\}$.

It is possible to show that if a partial process γ of a c-net N is reachable from an initial process via a finite sequence of moves, then $\gamma = \gamma(\pi)$ for some marked process π of N. When the c-net N is n-safe and finite, the definition of $\gamma(\pi)$ and Proposition 1 allow us to conclude the validity of the following result.

Lemma 2. *For any n-safe finite c-net the set of partial processes reachable from the initial process (and taken up to isomorphism) is finite.*

We are now ready to present the construction of the causal automaton associated to a c-net for checking HP-bisimilarity. To obtain a "compact" automaton (with a finite number of states for finite n-safe c-nets) we must consider partial processes up to isomorphism. To this aim we fix a standard representative in each class of isomorphic partial processes. Furthermore we consider a normalization function `norm` such that for any partial process γ, $\mathtt{norm}(\gamma) = \langle \gamma', i \rangle$, where γ' is the standard representative in the isomorphism class of γ and $i : \gamma' \to \gamma$ is a chosen process isomorphism. We assume that the names of the transitions in any (partial) process γ are taken from $\mathcal{N}$, namely that $T_\gamma \subseteq \mathcal{N}$.

Definition 19 (causal automaton for HP-bisimulation). *Let N be a labelled contextual net. The* HP-causal automaton *associated to N is the automaton $\mathcal{A}_{hp}(N) = \langle Q, n, \longmapsto, q_0 \rangle$, having (standard representatives of) partial processes as states. The initial state q_0 is the standard representative γ_0 of the initial processes of N and whenever $\gamma \in Q$ then*

- $n(\gamma) = T_\gamma$;
- *if* $\gamma \xrightarrow[e]{a} \gamma'$ *and* $\mathtt{norm}(\gamma') = \langle \gamma'', i \rangle$ *then* $\gamma'' \in Q$ *and* $\gamma \overset{a}{\underset{M}{\longmapsto}}_\sigma \gamma''$ *where*
  - $\sigma : T_{\gamma''} \hookrightarrow T_\gamma \cup \{\star\}$ *is defined as* $\sigma = (id_{T_\gamma} \cup \{(e, \star)\}) \circ i_T$;
  - $M = \mathsf{MC}(\gamma \xrightarrow[e]{a} \gamma')$.

Observe that the renaming function in a transition of the causal automaton is obtained from the isomorphism given by the normalization function `norm`, simply by redirecting the new name e to $\star$. As anticipated, the maximal causes of a process move are used as dependencies in the automaton transition.

The states of the automaton are standard representatives of partial processes reachable from the initial partial process. Hence by Lemma 2 we derive that for any finite n-safe c-net the above defined automaton has a finite number of states (and clearly, being the net finite, it has also a finite number of transitions leaving from each state). Vice versa, if the net is not n-safe for some n, then the automaton will have an infinite number of states.

To effectively build the automaton we can perform an inductive construction based on Definition 19. The only thing to observe is that, given a partial process γ, there might be infinitely many moves $\gamma \xrightarrow[e]{a} \gamma'$ since the event e can be chosen arbitrarily among the unused events in $\mathcal{N}$. However, without loss of generality, we can limit our attention only to some partial process moves, called the *representative* moves, where the newly generated name is chosen in a canonical way. For instance we can suppose that the set of names $\mathcal{N}$ is well-ordered and call a transition $\gamma \xrightarrow[e]{a} \gamma'$ representative if $e = \min(\mathcal{N} - T_\gamma)$.

Proposition 2. *Let N be a finite c-net. Then N is n-safe for some n iff the automaton $\mathcal{A}_{hp}(N)$ is finite.*

The main result now states that there is a precise correspondence between HP-bisimulation on contextual nets and CA-bisimulation on causal automata. Hence HP-bisimilarity of contextual nets can be checked on the corresponding automata.

Theorem 1. *Let N_1 and N_2 be two c-nets. Then $N_1 \sim_{hp} N_2$ if and only if $\mathcal{A}_{hp}(N_1) \sim_{ca} \mathcal{A}_{hp}(N_2)$.*

Proof (sketch). The proof is organized in two steps. First observe that the transition system of marked processes of a c-net N can be seen itself as a causal automaton $\mathcal{A}_{pr}(N) = \langle Q, n, \longmapsto, q_0 \rangle$, where

- Q is the set of marked processes π of N and $n(\pi) = T_\pi$ for any process π;
- $\pi \overset{a}{\underset{M}{\longmapsto}}_\sigma \pi'$ if, according to Definition 7, $\pi \xrightarrow[e]{a} \pi'$, $M = \mathsf{MC}(\pi \xrightarrow[e]{a} \pi')$, and the naming $\sigma : T_{\pi'} \to T_\pi \cup \{\star\}$ is defined as the identity for $x \in T_{\pi'} - \{e\}$, while $\sigma(e) = \star$;
- the initial state q_0 is any initial process of N.

Then, it is possible to prove that HP-bisimulation on c-nets coincides with CA-bisimulation on the causal automata of processes, namely $N_1 \sim_{hp} N_2$ iff $\mathcal{A}_{pr}(N_1) \sim_{ca} \mathcal{A}_{pr}(N_2)$.

The second step of the proof shows that, for any c-net N there exists an abstraction homomorphism $\mathsf{h} : \mathcal{A}_{pr}(N) \to \mathcal{A}_{hp}(N)$, and thus, by Lemma 1, $\mathcal{A}_{pr}(N) \sim_{ca} \mathcal{A}_{hp}(N)$. The abstraction homomorphism $\mathsf{h} = \langle h, \{h_\pi\}_\pi \rangle$ can be defined as follows: for any marked process π (state of $\mathcal{A}_{pr}(N)$), if $\mathtt{norm}(\gamma(\pi)) = \langle\gamma', i\rangle$ then $h(\pi) = \gamma'$ and $h_\pi : T_{\gamma'} \to T_\pi$ is simply i_T.

Summing up, by the above considerations we have that $\mathcal{A}_{pr}(N_i) \sim_{ca} \mathcal{A}_{hp}(N_i)$ for $i \in \{1, 2\}$, and moreover $\mathcal{A}_{pr}(N_1) \sim_{ca} \mathcal{A}_{pr}(N_2)$ iff $N_1 \sim_{hp} N_2$. Hence the thesis easily follows. □

By Proposition 2 and Theorem 1 we immediately conclude the desired decidability result.

Corollary 1. *HP-bisimulation is decidable on finite n-safe contextual nets.*

To conclude the discussion on HP-bisimulation it is worth observing that the configurations in [11] and the ordered markings in [19] are slightly more abstract than our partial processes essentially for the fact that they do not record the correspondence between events in the process and transitions in the original net. We have used partial processes only because they allow for a simpler presentation, since partial processes are still (unmarked) processes of the given net and no new notion has to be introduced. Concretely, the drawback of our choice is that dealing with configurations the number of states of the causal automaton associated to a net may result significantly smaller. Therefore, although conceptually the two approaches are very similar, when one is interested in complexity and efficiency issues working with configurations is the better choice.

5.2 RHP-Bisimulation

Let us turn our attention to RHP-bisimulation, the finer equivalence introduced in Definition 10. Since asymmetric event structures and thus RHP-bisimulation distinguish (strong) causality from weak causality (asymmetric conflict), for each step of computation we must observe *separately* the maximal causes and the weak causes (namely the events in the current state which are in asymmetric conflict with the considered transition). It is easy to realize that keeping information only about the producers and maximal readers of processes is no more adequate and thus the partial processes defined in the previous section are not sufficiently informative to discriminate c-nets which differ according to RHP-bisimulation.

Consider for instance the net N and the process π_4 in Fig. 2. Since $e_2 \leq e_3$ and both transitions read the same token, the corresponding partial process records only the transition e_3. However, in this way, when the transition labelled by d fires, the partial process allows us to recover only the weak dependency from transition e_3, while the dependency from e_2 is lost.

To extend the technique described in the previous section to deal with RHP-bisimulation we must change the notion of partial process in order to keep trace of *all* events, maximal or not, which read a token in the current marking.

Definition 20 (read partial processes). *A* read partial process (R-partial process) χ *of a net* N *is an unmarked process* $\chi : O_\chi \to N$, *where* $T_\chi = p(\chi) \cup r(\chi)$.

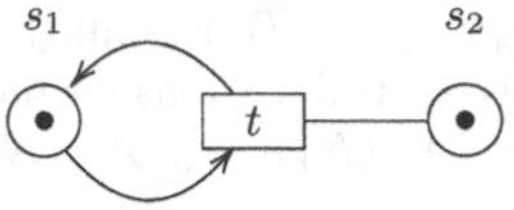

Fig. 4. A finite safe c-net where the number of readers in a marked process is unbounded.

The notion of R-partial process move can be defined in the obvious way, and relying on the transition system of R-partial processes of a c-net N we can construct a causal automaton $\mathcal{A}_{rhp}(N)$. The only difference with respect to the case of HP-bisimulation is that the transitions of the causal automaton must be labeled with two sets of names, i.e., they must have the form $q \overset{a}{\underset{M,W}{\longmapsto}}_{\sigma} q'$. In fact for each transition we must observe separately the set of maximal (strong) causes $\mathsf{MC}(\chi \xrightarrow[e]{a} \chi') = \{t \in T_\chi : t^\bullet \cap ({}^\bullet e \cup \underline{e}) \neq \emptyset \ \wedge \ t \text{ is } \leq_\chi\text{-maximal}\}$ and the set of all weak causes $\mathsf{WC}(\chi \xrightarrow[e]{a} \chi') = \{t \in T_\chi : \underline{t} \cap {}^\bullet e \neq \emptyset\}$. For example, in Fig. 2, for the move $\pi_4 \xrightarrow[e_4]{d} \pi_5$ we have $\mathsf{MC}(\pi_4 \xrightarrow[e_4]{d} \pi_5) = \{e_0\}$, while $\mathsf{WC}(\pi_4 \xrightarrow[e_4]{d} \pi_5) = \{e_1, e_2, e_3\}$.

Generalizing the notion of CA-bisimulation for causal automata where transitions are labelled by two sets of names, it is still possible to prove that given two c-nets N_1 and N_2, $N_1 \sim_{rhp} N_2$ iff $\mathcal{A}_{rhp}(N_1) \sim_{ca} \mathcal{A}_{rhp}(N_2)$.

Unfortunately, as anticipated, such translation into causal automata does not help in checking RHP-bisimulation. The states of the automaton $\mathcal{A}_{rhp}(N)$, which are normalized R-partial processes reachable from the initial process, can be infinitely many also for a finite safe net. In fact, the number of readers $r(\pi)$ in a marked process of very simple finite safe c-nets is easily seen to be unbounded, as shown, for instance by the net in Fig. 4.

6 Conclusions

We have provided contextual nets with abstract semantics inspired by the classical notion of history preserving bisimulation. The presence of asymmetric conflicts (weak causalities) between events in contextual net computations naturally suggests two different formulations of history preserving bisimulation. HP-bisimulation, relying on deterministic PES's, observes only the precedences between events, while the finer RHP-bisimulation observes both causality and weak causality by exploiting deterministic AES's. We have shown that, as for ordinary nets, HP-bisimulation is decidable for finite n-safe contextual nets, and we have provided a "translation" of such kind of nets into finite state causal automata, which allows us to reuse the algorithms existing for this general formalism in order to decide the bisimulation equivalence and to obtain a minimal realization. Such a translation can be adapted to deal with RHP-bisimulation.

However in this case the construction may produce an infinite state automaton also for finite n-safe nets and thus it is not helpful to conclude the decidability of RHP-bisimulation, which remains a matter of future investigation.

An alternative solution to the problem of deciding HP-bisimulation on finite n-safe c-nets could be to find a procedure which translates each finite n-safe c-net into an HP-bisimilar ordinary net, and then to exploit the corresponding algorithm for ordinary nets. It should not be difficult to see that the translation proposed in [14], which maps each 1-safe c-net into an ordinary 1-safe net, respects HP-bisimulation and thus is appropriate for this aim. However, such translation does not extends naturally to general n-safe nets with weighted contexts. A preliminary investigation reveals that, if a translation exists, probably it would transform a c-net into a significantly more complex ordinary net. Hence, the direct algorithm proposed in this paper could still be preferable.

In [10] the hereditary (or strong) version of history preserving bisimulation on PES's is given an abstract characterization in terms of open maps, by taking as experiments finite deterministic PES's. It would be interesting to investigate the notions of bisimulation on AES's arising when one takes as experiments the deterministic PES's and the deterministic AES's. We conjecture that such equivalences gives, respectively, the hereditary variations of HP- and RHP-bisimulations.

Finally, a more general direction of future research is the development of Hennessy-Milner style logics to be interpreted over formalisms endowed with a causal semantics, with particular interest in the general model of causal automata. Such logics would be particularly appropriate for concurrent systems, allowing to express properties on their causal behaviour, like the existence of a computation where an action can be executed with a given set of causes. Some preliminary studies [2] have led to a logic for causal automata, which has been shown to be adequate with respect to CA-bisimulation in the sense that two automata are bisimilar iff they satisfies the same set of formulae.

Acknowledgments

We are grateful to the anonymous referees for their comments on the submitted version of this paper.

References

1. P. Baldan, A. Corradini, and U. Montanari. An event structure semantics for P/T contextual nets: Asymmetric event structures. In M. Nivat, editor, *Proceedings of FoSSaCS '98*, volume 1378 of *LNCS*, pages 63–80. Springer Verlag, 1998. 291, 292, 294, 297
2. R. Bartolini. Model checking di proprietà causali di reti di Petri. MSc Thesis, University of Pisa, 1999. 309
3. E. Best, R. Devillers, A. Kiehn, and L. Pomello. Concurrent bisimulations in Petri nets. *Acta Informatica*, 28(3):231–264, 1991. 291, 292
4. I. Castellani. Bisimulations and abstraction homomorphisms. *Journal of Computer and System Sciences*, 34(2/3):210–235, 1987. 302

5. S. Christensen and N. D. Hansen. Coloured Petri nets extended with place capacities, test arcs and inhibitor arcs. In M. Ajmone-Marsan, editor, *Applications and Theory of Petri Nets*, volume 691 of *LNCS*, pages 186–205. Springer Verlag, 1993. 291
6. G. Ferrari and U. Montanari. Towards the unification of models of concurrency. In A. Arnold, editor, *Proceedings of CAAP '90*, volume 431 of *LNCS*, pages 162–176. Springer-Verlag, 1990. 302
7. F. Gadducci and U. Montanari. Axioms for contextual net processes. In *Proceedings of ICALP'98*, LNCS, pages 296–308. Springer Verlag, 1998. 291
8. R. Janicki and M. Koutny. Invariant semantics of nets with inhibitor arcs. In *Proceedings of CONCUR '91*, volume 527 of *LNCS*. Springer Verlag, 1991. 291
9. R. Janicki and M. Koutny. Semantics of inhibitor nets. *Information and Computation*, 123:1–16, 1995. 291
10. A. Joyal, M. Nielsen, and G. Winskel. Bisimulation from open maps. *Information and Computation*, 127(2):164–185, 1996. 302, 309
11. U. Montanari and M. Pistore. Minimal transition systems for history-preserving bisimulation. In *14th Annual Symposium on Theoretical Aspects of Computer Science*, volume 1200 of *LNCS*, pages 413–425. Springer Verlag, 1997. 291, 293, 300, 301, 303, 307
12. U. Montanari and M. Pistore. History-dependent automata. Technical Report TR-98-11, Dipartimento di Informatica, 1998. Available as ftp://ftp.di.unipi.it/pub/techreports/TR-98-11.ps.Z. 291, 300, 302
13. U. Montanari and F. Rossi. Contextual occurrence nets and concurrent constraint programming. In H.-J. Schneider and H. Ehrig, editors, *Proceedings of the Dagstuhl Seminar 9301 on Graph Transformations in Computer Science*, volume 776 of *LNCS*. Springer Verlag, 1994. 291
14. U. Montanari and F. Rossi. Contextual nets. *Acta Informatica*, 32, 1995. 291, 309
15. A. Rabinovich and B. A. Trakhtenbrot. Behavior Structures and Nets. *Fundamenta Informaticæ*, 11(4):357–404, 1988. 291, 292
16. G. Ristori. *Modelling Systems with Shared Resources via Petri Nets.* PhD thesis, Department of Computer Science - University of Pisa, 1994. 291, 294
17. J. van Bentham. Correspondence theory. In *Handbook of Philosophical Logic*, volume II. Reidel, 1984. 302
18. R. van Glabbeek and U. Goltz. Equivalence notions for concurrent systems and refinement of actions. In A. Kreczmar and G. Mirkowska, editors, *Proceedings of MFCS'89*, volume 39 of *LNCS*, pages 237–248. Springer Verlag, 1989. 291, 292
19. W. Vogler. Deciding history preserving bisimilarity. In J. Leach Albert, B. Monien, and M. Rodríguez-Artalejo, editors, *Proceedings of ICALP'91*, volume 510 of *LNCS*, pages 495–505. Springer-Verlag, 1991. 291, 293, 303, 307
20. W. Vogler. Efficiency of asynchronous systems and read arcs in Petri nets. In *Proceedings of ICALP'97*, volume 1256 of *LNCS*, pages 538–548. Springer Verlag, 1997. 291
21. W. Vogler. Partial Order Semantics and Read Arcs. In *Proceedings of MFCS'97*, volume 1295 of *LNCS*, pages 508–518. Springer Verlag, 1997. 291
22. G. Winskel. Event Structures. In *Petri Nets: Applications and Relationships to Other Models of Concurrency*, volume 255 of *LNCS*, pages 325–392. Springer Verlag, 1987. 297

A Model for Interaction of Agents and Environments

Alexander Letichevsky[1] and David Gilbert[2]

[1] Glushkov Institute of Cybernetics, National Academy of Sciences of Ukraine
let@d105.icyb.kiev.ua
[2] Department of Computing, City University
London EC1V 0HB, UK
drg@soi.city.ac.uk

Abstract. A new abstract model of interaction between agents and environments considered as objects of different types is introduced. Agents are represented by means of labelled transition systems considered up to bisimilarity. The equivalence of agents is characterised in terms of an algebra of behaviours which is a continuous algebra with approximation and two operations: nondeterministic choice and prefixing. Environments are introduced as agents supplied with an insertion function which takes the behaviour of an agent and the behaviour of an environment as arguments and returns the new behaviour of an environment. Arbitrary continuous functions can be used as insertion functions, and we use functions defined by means of rewriting logic as computable ones. The transformation of environment behaviours defined by the insertion function also defines a new type of agent equivalence — insertion equivalence. Two behaviours are insertion equivalent if they define the same transformation of an environment. The properties of this equivalence are studied. Three main types of insertion functions are used to develop interesting applications: one-step insertion, head insertion, and look-ahead insertion functions.

Keywords: agents, behaviour, environments, interaction, continuous algebras, semantics

1 Introduction

The majority of traditional theories of interaction including CCS [24], CSP [13], ACP [5], TLA [22], and more recent theories such as game semantics [3], and the tile model [8], consider interaction between agents in the environment. However the notion of an environment is used implicitly or its elements are introduced as elements of process algebra expressions undistinguished from agent expressions. In those models where the environment is considered explicitly such as programs over shared memory (including constraint store as in ccp [26]) or Linda based models [9], the notion of an environment is very special. Actually the environment in these cases is considered only as a space for keeping and processing data structures, constraints, or the elements of tuple spaces. Actor languages [4]

D. Bert, C. Choppy, and P. Mosses (Eds.): WADT'99, LNCS 1827, pp. 311–328, 2000.

have a more abstract model, but still use special message passing and interface mechanisms.

In this paper we consider agents and environments as objects of different types. Agents are represented by means of labelled transition systems with divergence and termination, considered up to bisimilarity. The equivalence of agents is characterised in terms of an algebra of behaviours which is a two sorted (actions and behaviours) continuous algebra with approximation and two operations: nondeterministic choice and prefixing (like basic ACP). The notion of an abstract agent can be introduced as a transition closed set of behaviours. All known compositions in various kinds of process algebras can be then defined by means of continuous functions over agents.

Environments are introduced as agents supplied with functions used for the insertion of other agents into these environments. An insertion function has two arguments: the behaviour of an agent and the behaviour of an environment. The value of an insertion function is a new behaviour of an environment. The notion of an environment gives the possibility of defining a new type of agent equivalence — insertion equivalence. Two behaviours are insertion equivalent if they define the same transformation of an environment. Most of the known equivalences for processes can be characterised as insertion equivalence.

In earlier publications [18,19,21] the model has been considered in the context of language representation. The generic (Parameterised) Action Language (AL), introduced there was considered as a general model of computation and interaction covering a wide class of nondeterministic concurrent programming languages. The interaction semantics of AL has been defined in terms of transformations of environment behaviours and has been used for the definition of a computational semantics as well. In [20] a new, more abstract model of interaction between agents and environments has been introduced. This paper generalises the approach of previous ones, allowing the use of arbitrary continuous functions for the definition of the insertion of an agent into an environment.

Three main types of insertion functions are used to develop interesting applications: one-step insertion, head insertion, and look-ahead insertion functions. They are introduced by means of inference rules, axioms and rewrite rules in the style of rewriting logic [15]. We study insertion equivalence for one-step insertion using an algebraic representation of agents and prove the congruence property for the main operations of the behaviour algebra. We also show that head and look-ahead insertions can be reduced to a one-step insertion. The implementation of the model using the algebraic programming system APS is described.

2 Preliminaries

2.1 Transition Systems

Definition 1. *(Park [7]) A transition system over a set of actions A is a set S of states with a transition relation $s \xrightarrow{a} s'$, $s, s' \in S$, $a \in A$, and two subsets S_Δ and $S_\perp$ called correspondingly sets of terminal and divergent states.*

The original definition of D.Park does not contain terminal and divergent states. The former is used for the definition of computational semantics of agents, and the latter for introducing the approximation relation and the technically important construction of infinite objects from finite ones by passing to limits.

Definition 2. *A binary relation $R \subseteq S \times S$ is called a partial bisimulation if for all s and t such that sRt and for all $a \in A$*

- $s \in S_\Delta \Rightarrow t \in S_\Delta$
- $s \xrightarrow{a} s' \Rightarrow \exists t'.t \xrightarrow{a} t' \wedge s'Rt'$
- $s \notin S_\perp \Rightarrow (t \notin S_\perp \wedge (t \xrightarrow{a} t' \Rightarrow \exists s'.s \xrightarrow{a} s' \wedge s'Rt'))$

This definition is a slight modification of the definition in [2]. A state s of a transition system S is called a *bisimilar approximation* of t denoted as $s \sqsubseteq_B t$ if there exists a partial bisimulation R such that sRt. The relation $s \sqsubseteq_B t \wedge t \sqsubseteq_B s$ is a *bisimulation equivalence* denoted $s \sim_B t$. The definition of partial bisimulation can be easily extended to the case when R is defined as a relation between the states of two different systems, considering the disjoint union of their sets of states. Two transition systems are bisimilarly equivalent (or bisimilar) if each state of one of them is bisimilarly equivalent to some state of another.

We give some consequences from this definition in order to help the reader to understand it better. The divergent state without transitions approximates an arbitrary other state if it is not terminal. If s approximates t and s is convergent (not divergent) then t is also convergent, s and t have transitions for the same sets of actions and satisfy the same conditions as for usual bisimulation without divergence. Otherwise if s is divergent the set of actions for which s has transitions is only included in the set of actions for which t has transitions, i.e. s is less defined than t.

2.2 Behaviour Algebra

A behaviour algebra (or an algebra of behaviours) over an action set A is a continuous algebra [12] or an algebra with approximation (a poset with a least element and continuous operations [17]). It has two operations, the first being denoted by $+$ is an internal binary aci-operation (idempotent associative and commutative operation); this operation corresponds to nondeterministic choice. The second operation is prefixing $a.u$, a being an action, u being a behaviour. The least element of a behaviour algebra is denoted $\perp$. The empty behaviour Δ performs no actions and usually denotes the successful termination of a (computational) process. The impossible behaviour 0 is the neutral element for nondeterministic choice. There is also the impossible (empty) action $\emptyset$ in A. The identities of a behaviour algebra are shown in Figure 1.

The approximation relation of the algebra of behaviours over A is a partial order which satisfies the relations presented in Figure 2.

If all relations of a behaviour algebra are consequences of those presented in Figure 1 and the approximation relation is the least partial order satisfying the relations in Figure 2 then this algebra is called a free algebra. The elements

$$u + v = v + u$$
$$(u + v) + w = u + (v + w)$$
$$u + u = u$$
$$u + 0 = 0 + u = u$$

$$\emptyset.u = 0$$

Fig. 1. Relations of an algebra of behaviours

$$\bot \sqsubseteq u$$

$$u \sqsubseteq v \Rightarrow u + w \sqsubseteq v + w$$
$$u \sqsubseteq v \Rightarrow a.u \sqsubseteq a.v$$

Fig. 2. Approximation for behaviours

of the minimal (initial) sub-algebra $F_{\mathtt{fin}}(A)$ of a free behaviour algebra over A (i.e. a sub-algebra generated by the empty behaviour, the impossible behaviour and the bottom element) are called *finite behaviours.* All other behaviours (of a free behaviour algebra) are assumed to be the limits (least upper bounds) of the directed sets of finite elements. The free continuous behaviour algebra which includes all such limits is denoted $F(A)$. This algebra is an algebraic cpo and is defined uniquely up to a continuous isomorphism. Note that we do not restrict ourselves to ω-continuity and consider directed sets of arbitrary cardinality.

Note that in $F(A)$ the fixed point theorem is true, so we can use it for constructing new behaviours from those already built by means of equations of the form $X = \Phi(X)$, where X is a vector of variables (possibly infinite) and $\Phi(X)$ is an algebraic functional, that is a functional constructed from variables and constants Δ, $\bot$ and 0 by means of nondeterministic choice and prefixing.

An alternative approach is to consider $F(A)$ as a final coalgebra and use coinduction for reasoning and constructing behaviours [6,23]. The advantage of continuous algebras is that we can use not only coinductive reasoning based on bisimulation but also ordinary induction for finite elements and extend this to infinite elements by passing to limits. We could also use power domains for constructing behaviours as has been done by S.Abramsky in [2], but the algebraic approach seems to be more abstract and simpler.

Each behaviour $u \in F(A)$ can be represented in the form

$$u = \sum_{i \in I} a_i.u_i + \varepsilon \tag{1}$$

where a_i are different from the impossible action, u_i are behaviours, I is a finite (for finite elements) or infinite set of indices, $\varepsilon = \Delta, \bot, \Delta + \bot, 0$ (*termination constants*). To represent a behaviour arbitrary sets of indices I can be used, but because of the idempotence law, the cardinality of I can be bounded by the cardinality of $F(A)$. If all summands in representation (1) are different then this representation is unique up to the associativity and commutativity of nondeterministic choice. A behaviour u is called *divergent* if $\varepsilon = \perp, \Delta + \perp$ and *convergent* otherwise. Note that u is always divergent for infinite I as a limit of finite divergent sums. Convergent infinite sums can be introduced by extending the notion of a finite element. Namely, termination constants, prefixed extended finite elements, and arbitrary (finite or infinite) sums of extended finite elements are also considered as extended finite elements.

2.3 Behaviours and Transition Systems

For each state $s \in S$ of a transition system let us consider a behaviour $\mathtt{beh}(s) = u_s$ (of a system in a given state s) defined as a component of a minimal solution of a system

$$u_s = \sum_{s \xrightarrow{a} s'} a.u_{s'} + \varepsilon_s \tag{2}$$

where termination constants ε_s are defined in Figure 3.

$$s \notin S_\Delta \cup S_\perp \Rightarrow \varepsilon_s = 0$$

$$s \in S_\Delta \setminus S_\perp \Rightarrow \varepsilon_s = \Delta$$

$$s \in S_\perp \setminus S_\Delta \Rightarrow \varepsilon_s = \perp$$

$$s \in S_\Delta \cap S_\perp \Rightarrow \varepsilon_s = \Delta + \perp$$

Fig. 3. Termination constants for the behaviour of a system in a given state

A set U of behaviours is called *transition closed* if from $a.u+v \in U$ and $a \neq \emptyset$ it follows that also $u \in U$. Each transition closed set U can be considered as a set of states of a transition system with transitions $a.u+v \xrightarrow{a} u, a \neq \emptyset$, the set of terminal states $U_\Delta = \{u | u = u + \Delta\}$, and divergent states $U_\perp = \{u | u = u + \perp\}$. Therefore the relations $\sqsubseteq_B$ and $\sim_B$ can be considered for behaviours as well as for the states of a transition system. Note that when two behaviours are compared they should be considered as elements of some transition closed set of behaviours (the minimal set that is a set of all reachable behaviours is sufficient because partial bisimulation defined for this set can be extended to a larger one in a trivial way).

Theorem 1. *Let s and s' are states of a transition system, u and v are behaviours. Then:*

1. $s \sqsubseteq_B s' \Leftrightarrow u_s \sqsubseteq u_{s'}$;
2. $s \sim_B s' \Leftrightarrow u_s = u_{s'}$;
3. $u = v \Leftrightarrow u \sim_B v$.

Proof. The first follows from the bisimilarity of s and u_s (considered as a state), $1 \Rightarrow 2$ because $\sqsubseteq$ is a partial order and $2 \Rightarrow 3$ because $\mathtt{beh}(u) = u$. □

In the following we shall use $\sim$ instead of $\sim_B$.

2.4 Compositions of Behaviours

There are many useful compositions defined in concurrency theory as operations on processes or agents represented as transition systems. The majority of them are defined independently on the representation of states. These operations preserve bisimilarity and can therefore be defined as operations on behaviours. Another useful property of these compositions is continuity. To define a continuous function over behaviours it is sufficient to define it on finite behaviours and extend to all others by passing to limits. Definitions in the style of SOS semantics [25] or employing conditional rewriting systems always produce continuous functions (at least when they use the operations expressed in terms of termination constants, prefixing and nondeterministic choice only). In this section two main compositions – sequential and parallel – will be defined.

Sequential composition of behaviours u and v is a new behaviour denoted as $(u; v)$ and defined by means of the inference rules and equations presented in Figure 4.

$$\frac{u \xrightarrow{a} u'}{(u; v) \xrightarrow{a} (u'; v)}$$

$$((u + \Delta); v) = (u; v) + v$$

$$((u + \perp); v) = (u; v) + \perp$$

$$(0; u) = 0$$

Fig. 4. Sequential composition of behaviours

This definition must be understood in the following way. First we consider a transition system with states which are expressions built from arbitrary behaviours over A by means of operations of the behaviour algebra and new operation denoted as $(u; v)$. Expressions are considered up to the equivalence defined by equations (the extension of a behaviour algebra by this operation is conservative). Inference rules define a transition relation on a set of equivalence classes (the independence from the choice of representatives is obvious).

In the following we shall also use the notation uv instead of $(u; v)$ and (au) instead of $(a.u)$. This notation is not ambiguous if we identify an action a with the behaviour $a.\Delta$.

From the first rule and the second equation it follows that $(\Delta; v) = v$ and $(\perp; v) = \perp$ (take $u = 0$). To prove that $(u; \Delta) = u$ it is sufficient to prove that the expressions $(u; \Delta)$ and u are bisimilarly equivalent. Using bisimilarity one can also prove that sequential composition is associative and it is also left distributive:

$$(u+v)w = uw + vw$$

Parallel composition of behaviours. Up to now the set of actions A was considered as a flat set without any structure. Now we define an algebraic structure on this set introducing the combination $a \times b$ of actions a and b. This operation is commutative and associative with the empty action as annulator ($a \times \emptyset = \emptyset$). Thus the set A becomes an algebra of actions. The simplest examples of action algebras are those of Hoare ($a \times a = a, a \times b = \emptyset$ if $a \neq b$) and Milner ($a \times \overline{a} = \tau, a \times b = \emptyset$ if $b \neq \overline{a}$). Relations on some set of states or transformations defined by assignments on a set of memory states are also the examples of action algebras.

The inference rules and equations for the definition of the parallel composition $u \| v$ of behaviours u and v are presented in Figure 5.

$$\frac{u \xrightarrow{a} u',\ \ v \xrightarrow{b} v',\ \ a \times b \neq \emptyset}{u \| v \xrightarrow{a \times b} u' \| v'}$$

$$u \xrightarrow{a} u' \vdash u \| v \xrightarrow{a} u' \| v, \quad u \| (v + \Delta) \xrightarrow{a} u'$$

$$v \xrightarrow{a} v' \vdash u \| v \xrightarrow{a} u \| v', \quad (u + \Delta) \| v \xrightarrow{a} v'$$

$$(u + \Delta) \| (v + \Delta) = (u + \Delta) \| (v + \Delta) + \Delta$$

$$(u + \bot) \| v = (u + \bot) \| v + \bot$$

$$u \| (v + \bot) = u \| (v + \bot) + \bot$$

Fig. 5. Parallel composition of behaviours

The following equations for termination constants are direct consequences from these definitions:

$$\Delta \| \varepsilon = \varepsilon \| \Delta = \varepsilon, \ \ \bot \| \varepsilon = \varepsilon \| \bot = \bot$$

$$0 \| \varepsilon = \varepsilon \| 0 = 0 \ \ if \ \ \varepsilon \neq \varepsilon + \bot$$

$$0 \| \varepsilon = \varepsilon \| 0 = \bot \ \ if \ \ \varepsilon = \varepsilon + \bot$$

Here ε is an arbitrary termination constant. Commutativity and associativity of parallel composition can be proved using the bisimilarity of corresponding expressions. The difference of our definition from the usual definition for the process algebras is in the equations for the termination constants.

3 Agents and Environments

The previous section contains fairly standard definitions and constructions which are used as the mathematical foundation of concurrency theory. Our approach is close to that of ACP [5], and we use the continuous algebra of behaviours as a domain for the characterisation of transition systems up to bisimilarity instead of power-domains as in [2] or [11]. In this section we introduce the main construction of our theory, namely the insertion of an agent into an environment.

An *abstract agent* U over an action algebra A is a transition closed set of behaviours over A. An agent can be initialized by distinguishing the set $U_0 \subseteq U$ of possible initial states so that each other state of an agent is reachable from some of the initial states.

Usually agents are represented by transition systems and are identified with these systems. In this case the corresponding abstract agent is the set of all behaviours of the states of its representation. Two representations of the same agent are therefore bisimilarly equivalent.

The set of behaviours of an agent can be considered as a transition system as well (the standard representation of an agent) and we can speak about the set of states when considering the behaviours of an agent. We should distinguish between an agent as a set of states or behaviours and an agent in a given state. In the latter case we consider each individual state or behaviour of an agent as the same agent in a given state.

An *Environment* E is an agent over an *environment algebra of actions* C with an *insertion function*. The insertion function $\mathtt{Ins}$ of an environment is a function of two arguments: $\mathtt{Ins}(e, u) = e[u]$. The first argument e is a behaviour of an environment, the second is a behaviour of an agent over an action algebra A in a given state u (the action algebra of agents can be a parameter of an environment). An insertion function is an arbitrary function continuous in both of its arguments. The result is a new behaviour of the same environment.

For the definition of insertion functions we can use the same methods as for the definition of operations over behaviours, but the semantics of agents is different. They are considered up to an equivalence which is in general weaker than bisimilarity. This is *insertion equivalence* which depends on an environment and its insertion function. Two agents (in given states) or behaviours u and v are *insertion equivalent* with respect to an environment E, written $u \sim_E v$ if for all $e \in E$ $e[u] = e[v]$. Each agent u defines the transformation $\mathtt{Tr}_u^E : E \to E$ of its environment: $\mathtt{Tr}_u^E(e) = e[u]$ and $u \sim_E v$ iff $\mathtt{Tr}_u^E = \mathtt{Tr}_v^E$. We shall also use the notation $[u]$ for $\mathtt{Tr}_u^E$.

After inserting an agent into an environment, the new environment can accept new agents to be inserted, and the insertion of several agents is something that we will often wish to describe. We shall use the notation

$$e[u_1, \ldots, u_n] = e[u_1] \ldots [u_n]$$

for the insertion of several agents.

Note that in this expression $u_1, \ldots, u_n$ are agents inserted into the environment simultaneously, but the order can be essential for some environments. If you want agent u to be inserted after agent v, you must compute some transition $e[u] \xrightarrow{a} s$ and consider expression $s[v]$. Some environments can move independently, suspending the movement of an agent inserted into them. In this case if

$e[u] \xrightarrow{a} e'[u]$ then $e'[u, v]$ describes the simultaneous insertion of v and u into the environment in a state e' as well as the insertion of u at the moment when an environment is in state e and after this the insertion of v.

An environment $e[u]$ containing an inserted agent u can be used for the insertion of another agent using the insertion function $\mathtt{Ins}$, or can be considered as a new agent which can be inserted into a new environment e' with another insertion function $\mathtt{Ins}'$. In this case $e'[e[u]] = \mathtt{Ins}'(e', \mathtt{Ins}(e, u))$, and we can associate with the behaviour u not only transformation $\mathtt{Tr}_u^E$ but also a function $F = \mathtt{Tr}_u^{E\times E' \to E'} : E \times E' \to E'$ defined by equation $F(e, e') = e'[e[u]]$.

In the sequel the notation $e[u]$ will be used not only for the case when u and e are behaviours (or expressions which take values in the behaviour algebra) but also states of transition systems used to represent corresponding behaviours. In this case we must prove the correctness of an expression, or its independence from the representation of a state, that is $e \sim e' \Rightarrow e[u] \sim e'[u]$.

Let us now consider some important cases of environments and insertion functions.

3.1 Parallel and Sequential Environments

The insertion function for a parallel environment is

$$e[u] = e \| u$$

In this case all agents inserted into an environment interact in parallel and $e[u_1, \ldots, u_n]$ does not depend on the order of insertion.

Another important case is a sequential environment:

$$e[u] = eu$$

In this case the performance of agents is sequential.

If $\Delta \in E$ then the insertion equivalence of agents is a bisimulation. A weaker equivalence can be obtained if the definition of the insertion function is modified in the following way:

$$e[u] = \varphi(e \| u)$$

for a parallel environment or

$$e[u] = \varphi(eu)$$

for a sequential one. In this modification φ is an arbitrary continuous transformation of E. The restriction function of CCS or the hiding function of CSP or their combinations are useful special cases of φ.

3.2 One-Step Insertion

The class of one-step insertion functions consists of insertion functions that define the interaction between environment and inserted agents in such a way that the current observable action of a resulting environment depends on the behaviour of an environment and agents in the current moment of time only (one-step behaviour). This dependency is defined by means of a *hiding function* $h : A \times C \to 2^C$ (in [21] the similar function was called a residual function). The formal definition is presented in Figure 6. In this figure ε_u is a termination constant in the canonical representation of $u = \sum a_i.u_i + \varepsilon_u$, ε is an arbitrary termination constant.

$$\frac{u \xrightarrow{a} u',\ e \xrightarrow{c} e',\ d \in h(a,c)}{e[u] \xrightarrow{d} e'[u']}$$

$$e \xrightarrow{c} e' \vdash e[u] \xrightarrow{c} e'[u]$$

$$e[u+\Delta] = e[u+\Delta] + e,\ e[u+\perp] = e[u+\perp] + e \| \perp,\ (e+\perp)[u] = e[u]+\perp$$

$$\varepsilon[u] = \varepsilon \| \varepsilon_u$$

Fig. 6. One-step insertion function

The second rule shows that an environment can move independently suspending the movement of an inserted agent. In this case the action of the environment can be used by an agent inserted later. Each state of a one-step environment can be presented as $e[u]$ because $e = e[\Delta]$. In this section $[u]$ means the transformation of a one-step environment defined by a hiding function h.

In order to prove the properties of one-step insertion it is useful to introduce its algebraic representation. Let us consider the canonical forms of the state (behaviour) $e = \sum_{i \in I} c_i.e_i + \varepsilon_e$ of an environment and the state $u = \sum_{j \in J} a_j.u_j + \varepsilon_u$ of an agent. The following representation of $e[u]$ is a consequence of its definition in Figure 6:

$$e[u] = \sum_{d \in h(a_j,c_i)} d.e_i[u_j] + \sum_{i \in I} c_i.e_i[u] + \beta(\varepsilon_u, e) \tag{3}$$

where $\beta(\varepsilon+\varepsilon', e) = \beta(\varepsilon, e) + \beta(\varepsilon', e)$, $\beta(0, e) = 0 \| \varepsilon_e$, $\beta(\Delta, e) = e$, $\beta(\perp, e) = e \| \perp$. This representation provides the computation of prefixing and nondeterministic choice:

$$e[a.u] = \sum_{d \in h(a,c_i)} d.e_i[u] + \sum_{i \in I} c_i.e_i[a.u] + \beta(0, e) \tag{4}$$

$$e[u+v] = e \times [u] + e \times [v] + \sum_{i \in I} c_i.e_i[u+v] + \beta(\varepsilon_u, e) + \beta(\varepsilon_v, e) \tag{5}$$

where

$$e \times [u] = \sum_{d \in h(a_j,c_i)} d.e_i[u_j]$$

The equations (4) and (5) show that transformations $[a.u]$ and $[u+v]$ can be expressed in terms of $[u]$ and $[v]$ (as a minimal fixed point). Thus one-step insertion equivalence is a congruence (with respect to prefixing and nondeterministic choice) and these equations can be used for the definition of prefixing $a.[u] = [a.u]$ and nondeterministic choice $[u] + [v] = [u + v]$ on the set of continuous transformations of E. As a result the mapping $u \rightarrow [u]$ is a continuous homomorphism.

A natural special case of a one-step insertion environment is a *memory* over some set R of names or variables. A state of this environment is a mapping $e : D^R \rightarrow D^R$ where D is a data domain. Actions $c \in C$ correspond to statements over R such as (parallel) assignments and conditions. If c is a statement then $e \xrightarrow{c} e'$ is a functional relation on E, and if c is a condition then $e \xrightarrow{c} e$ iff c is true on e. A combination over the set of actions $c \times c'$ can be defined as an action equivalent to the simultaneous performance of c and c'. In this case $c \times c' \neq \emptyset$ iff c and c' are consistent. Consistency can be defined for the synchronous or asynchronous combination of actions, and for synchronous combination consistency means that each of two statements c and c' do not change the same variables. For asynchronous combination a stronger condition is used: neither of two statements can use the variables changed by the other one.

A hiding function h for a memory environment can be defined in the following way: $h(a, c) = \{d | c = a \times d\}$, if $a \neq c$ and $h(a, a) = \{\delta\}$, where δ is a special atomic action (empty statement) such that $\delta \times a = a \times \delta = a$ for an arbitrary action a and $e \xrightarrow{\delta} e$. It can be proved that for a memory environment $e[u, v] = e[u \| v]$. A memory environment extended by input/output and interface (send/receive) statements can be used for modeling (deterministic or nondeterministic) parallel imperative programs over shared memory.

A useful extension of one-step insertion can be obtained by introducing tools for making some of the interactions of agents and environments unobservable. For this purpose let us introduce a special symbol o to denote the unobservable action and let $h : A \times C \rightarrow C \cup \{o\}$. Define the unlabeled transitions on the set of states $e[u]$:

$$\frac{u \xrightarrow{a} u', \; e \xrightarrow{c} e', \; o \in h(a, c)}{e[u] \rightarrow e'[u']}$$

and the rule:

$$\frac{e[u] \xrightarrow{*} e'[u'], \; e'[u'] \xrightarrow{d} e''[u'']}{e[u] \xrightarrow{d} e''[u'']}$$

A one-step environment with these two extra rules is called an *extended* one-step environment. For this environment a summand $\sum_{o \in h(a_j, c_i)} e_i[u_j]$ must be added to the representation (3) and the congruence properties for the operations of behaviour algebra are still valid.

3.3 Head Insertion

When we study the interaction of a client and a server the latter can be considered as the main part of an environment into which several clients can be inserted. An environment in this case can observe only the current action of a client (query, message, pushing buttons and so on). At the same time the server knows its internal state and can make a decision by analysing its future behaviour. This situation can be captured by head insertion.

A head insertion function is defined by means of three systems of rewriting rules. The rules of the first system have the form

$$(a, G(x_1, x_2, \ldots)) \to (d, G'(x_1, x_2, \ldots))$$

where $a \in A,\ d \in C$, $G(x_1, x_2, \ldots)$ and $G'(x_1, x_2, \ldots)$ are terms of a behaviour algebra over C with variables $x_1, x_2, \ldots$ considered up to the identities of this algebra. The relation defined by this system is called the *interaction move* and is denoted by $(a, e) \overset{\texttt{interact}}{\to} (d, e')$. The rules of the second system have the form

$$(a, G(x_1, x_2, \ldots)) \to G'(x_1, x_2, \ldots)$$

They define the *hidden move* relation which is denoted as $(a, e) \overset{\texttt{hidden}}{\to} e'$ The rules of the third system have the form

$$G(x_1, x_2, \ldots) \to (d, G'(x_1, x_2, \ldots))$$

They define the *environment move* which is denoted as $e \overset{\texttt{env-move}}{\to} (d, e')$. The number of rules can be infinite but all of them are assumed to be left linear (each variable has only one occurrence in the left hand side). In the case of infinite sets of rules they must be enumerable if we want to have a computable insertion function.

The rules for transitions of $e[u]$ are presented in Figure 7. They include the unlabeled transitions defined by the hidden moves. An expression of the type $s \not\to$ means that there is no transitions $s \xrightarrow{d} s'$ or $s \to s'$. The third rule combines three different rules with the same assumption.

The insertion function defined by the rules of Figure 7 is continuous. In order to prove this statement note that the knowledge of all finite approximations of e and u is sufficient for computing the transition $e[u] \xrightarrow{d} e'[u']$.

3.4 Look-Ahead Insertion

A more general situation occurs in comparison with head insertion if an environment contains the interpreter for some programming language and an agent is a software agent written in this language. In this case an environment can analyse not only its own future behaviour but the behaviour of an interpreted program as well. This situation can be described by means of look-ahead insertion. This function is also defined by means of a left linear system of rewriting rules of only one type, namely interaction rules

$$(F(x_1, x_2, \ldots), G(y_1, y_2, \ldots)) \to (d, F'(x_1, x_2, \ldots), G'(x_1, x_2, \ldots))$$

These rules define an interaction relation denoted as

$$(u, e) \overset{\texttt{interact}}{\to} (d, u', e')$$

$$\frac{u \xrightarrow{a} u',\ (a,e) \overset{\texttt{interact}}{\longrightarrow} (d,e')}{e[u] \xrightarrow{d} e'[u']}$$

$$\frac{u \xrightarrow{a} u',\ (a,e) \overset{\texttt{hidden}}{\longrightarrow} e'}{e[u] \rightarrow e'[u']}$$

$$\frac{e \overset{\texttt{env-move}}{\longrightarrow} (d,e')}{e[u] \xrightarrow{d} e'[u],\ e[u+\Delta] \xrightarrow{d} e',\ e[u+\perp] \xrightarrow{d} e' \| \perp}$$

$$\frac{e[u] \xrightarrow{*} e'[u'],\ e'[u'] \xrightarrow{d} e''[u'']}{e[u] \xrightarrow{d} e''[u'']}$$

$$\frac{e[u] \xrightarrow{d} e'[u'] \vee e[u] \xrightarrow{*} e'[u'],\ f \sqsubseteq e,\ f[u] \not\rightarrow}{f[u] = \perp}$$

$$\varepsilon[u] = \varepsilon \| \varepsilon_u$$

Fig. 7. Head insertion function

It can be proved that this general type of rewriting rules also covers hidden and environment moves (if we admit the possibility of an infinite number of rules which may be required to implement the transitive closure of unlabeled transitions).

$$\frac{(u,e) \overset{\texttt{interact}}{\longrightarrow} (d,u',e')}{e[u] \xrightarrow{d} e'[u']}$$

$$\frac{e[u] \xrightarrow{d} e'[u'],\ v \sqsubseteq u,\ f \sqsubseteq e,\ f[v] \not\rightarrow}{f[v] = \perp}$$

$$\varepsilon[u] = \varepsilon \| \varepsilon_u$$

Fig. 8. Look-ahead insertion function

The rules for look-ahead insertion function are presented in Figure 8. A look-ahead insertion function is also continuous; the proof is the same as that for a head insertion.

3.5 Distributed Environments

We can obtain multilevel distributed structures by recursive insertion and the use of different environments on different levels. Let E_1 be some environment used as a local environment shared by several agents (shared memory or constraint store, for instance). An environment $e[u_1, \ldots, u_n]$ can be closed by the application of some continuous function φ, changing it to an agent which can be inserted into the environment E_2 of the next level. Several agents $v_1, \ldots, v_m$ constructed this way can be inserted into E_2 and a new environment $e[v_1, \ldots, v_m]$ can be considered as a distributed environment with local components (environments) $v_1, \ldots, v_m$. This construction can be repeated recursively. Look-ahead insertion can use the low level insertion function for the computation of transitions of low level components.

4 Insertion Equivalence

4.1 One-Step Insertion

In this section we shall study a one-step insertion equivalence. First the notion of normalised behaviour representation will be introduced and the criteria of one-step insertion equivalence of agents will be established. Then we shall study the congruence properties of sequential and parallel composition of agents.

Let E be a one-step environment with a hiding function h. First, let us note that if $u \sim_E v$, i.e. $[u] = [v]$, then $[au + bv] = [(a + b)u]$. This relation is also valid for an infinite number of summands:

$$[\sum_{i \in I} a_i.u_i] = [(\sum_{i \in I} a_i)u]$$

if all u_i are equivalent to u. A behaviour which is a sum of actions will be called a *one-step behaviour*. An arbitrary behaviour can be represented up to equivalence (wrt E) as the sum:

$$\sum_{i \in I} p_i u_i + \varepsilon \tag{6}$$

where p_i are one-step behaviours and $[u_i] \neq [u_j]$ if $i \neq j$. To obtain this representation for the behaviour $\sum_{i \in I} a_i.u_i + \varepsilon$ it is sufficient to partition all summands $a_i.u_i$, collecting together those for which u_i are mutually equivalent, and apply the equation above.

Let us extend the hiding function to one-step behaviours by defining $h(p, c) = \bigcup_{i \in I} h(a_i, c)$ and $h(p) = \bigcup_{c \in C} h(p, c)$ for $p = \sum_{i \in I} a_i$. For a one-step behaviour p if $h(p) = \emptyset$ then $[pu] = [0]$ and $[pu + v] = [v]$. Therefore representation (6) can be restricted so that for all $i \in I$ $h(p_i) \neq \emptyset$. Such a representation is called a *normal form* of an agent for the environment E.

Definition 3. *A one-step environment is called* regular *if:*

1. *For all $a \in A$ and $c \in C$ $c \notin h(a, c)$;*
2. *For all $e \in E$ and $c \in C$ $c.e \in E$ (E is an "ideal" of $F(C)$).*

One-step behaviours p and q are called equivalent wrt a hiding function h ($p \sim_h q$) if for all $c \in C$ $h(p, c) = h(q, c)$. If p and q are equivalent then $[pu] = [qu]$.

Theorem 2. *For a regular one-step environment the normal form of a behaviour is unique up to the commutativity of nondeterministic choice and equivalence of the one-step behaviour coefficients.*

To prove the theorem let us first prove that if $h(p) \neq \emptyset$ and $[pu] = [qv]$ then $p \sim_h q$ and $[u] = [v]$ (the inverse is evident). Let $d \in h(p)$, then for some $a \in A$ and $c \in C$, $d \in h(a, c)$. Let us take an arbitrary state (behaviour) $e \in E$. Since E is regular, $ce \in E$ and $c \neq d$. Therefore $(ce)[pu] \xrightarrow{d} e[u]$. From the equivalence of pu and qv it follows that $(ce)[pu] \sim (ce)[qv] \Rightarrow (ce)[qv] \xrightarrow{d} e[v]$ and this is the only transition from $(ce)[qv]$ labelled by d. Therefore $d \in h(q)$ and $e[u] \sim e[v]$. From the arbitrariness of e we have $[u] = [v]$. Symmetric reasoning gives also $d \in h(q) \Rightarrow d \in h(p) \Rightarrow p \sim_h q$.

Next we show that if $u = \sum_{i \in I} p_i u_i + \varepsilon_u$, $v = \sum_{j \in J} q_j v_j + \varepsilon_v$ are two normal forms and $[u] = [v]$ then for each $i \in I$ there exists $j \in J$ such that $[p_i u_i] = [q_j v_j]$ and from symmetry these forms are the same up to the commutativity and equivalence of coefficients. Again, as above if $(ce)[p_i u_i] \xrightarrow{d} e[u_i], c \neq d$ there exists only one j such that $(ce)[q_j v_j] \xrightarrow{d} e[v_j]$ and vice versa. Therefore $p_i \sim_h q_j$, $[u_i] = [v_j]$ and $[p_i u_i] = [q_j u_j]$. The equality of ε_u and ε_v is obvious. □

Sequential composition has a congruence property for regular one-step environments, as shown by the following theorem.

Theorem 3. *Let E be a regular one-step environment. Then $[u] = [u']$, $[v] = [v'] \Rightarrow [uv] = [u'v']$.*

To prove this theorem we prove that the relation $e[uv] \sim_R e[u'v']$ defined for an arbitrary $e \in E$, $u, v, u', v' \in F(A)$ by the condition $[u] = [u']$, $[v] = [v']$ is a bisimilarity. In order to compute transitions, normal forms for the representation of agent behaviours must be used. We omit the details of this proof. □

Parallel composition does not in general have a congruence property. To find the condition when it does, let us extend the combination of actions to one-step behaviours assuming that

$$p \times q = \sum_{p=a+p',\ q=b+q'} a \times b$$

The equivalence of one-step behaviours is a congruence if $h(p) = h(q) \Rightarrow h(p \times r) = h(q \times r)$.

Theorem 4. *Let E be a regular one-step environment and the equivalence of one-step behaviours be a congruence. Then $[u] = [u']$, $[v] = [v'] \Rightarrow [u \| v] = [u' \| v']$.*

As for the previous theorem we prove that the relation $e[u \| v] \sim_R e[u' \| v']$ defined for an arbitrary $e \in E$, $u, v, u', v' \in F(A)$ by the condition $[u] = [u']$, $[v] = [v']$ is a bisimilarity. To compute transitions, normal forms for the representation of agent behaviours must be used as well as the algebraic representation of parallel composition:

$$u \| v = u \times v + u \lfloor\lfloor v + v \lfloor\lfloor u$$

where $\times$ denotes a communication merge and $\lfloor\lfloor$ the left merge operations used in ACP [5] for the equational definition of parallel composition (some difference is in the use of termination constants). The details are also omitted. □

5 Implementation

The model described in the paper has been implemented in the algebraic programming system APS [16] which is based on rewriting logic, and the Action Language has been used as a language for the description of agents. The main compositions in the Action Language (AL) are nondeterministic choice, parallel and sequential compositions. Actions are considered as primitive statements. The syntax and semantics of combinations and other operations in the algebra of actions are parameters of the AL which is considered as a generic model for a class of nondeterministic concurrent programming languages. Procedure calls are another kind of primitive statement. The syntax of these kind of statements is also a parameter of the AL as well as their intensional semantics which is defined by means of the *unfold operator* represented in the form of a rewriting system (recursion). The intensional semantics of a program is defined as the behaviour of an agent, and the interaction semantics is a parameter of a language and defined by means of rewriting rules for the insertion function for a given environment.

The language can also describe variables, localising them within local program components which can be used for the description of distributed agents. Variables are considered as variables of a memory state or a constraint store considered as a local environment for agents, and the meaning of a local component is that of an agent inserted into its local environment. The parallel composition of local components is considered as a set of agents inserted into the higher level environment which is a shared memory or a shared constraint store.

The first implementation of the AL by means of an interpreter written in APLAN (the source language of APS) has been described in [10]. The next step was the development of a simulator which has been used to study the semantics of concurrent constraint and probabilistic concurrent constraint languages [27]. These early implementations used one-step insertion only. The current implementation is based on head insertion and can be easily extended to look-ahead insertion.

The simulator is an interactive program which can explore the behaviour of an environment with agents inserted into it step-by-step, with branching at nondeterministic points and and the ability to return back to previous states. In automatic mode it can search for states with specific properties, such as successful termination or dead-lock states.

6 Conclusions

A model of interacting of agents and environments based on insertion functions has been presented in this paper. The set of behaviour transformations has been introduced as a domain for the semantic description of agents inserted into a corresponding environment. This description reflects the interaction of agents and environments and mathematically is represented by a continuous mapping from behaviours to transformations. This mapping is a continuous homomorphism for a regular one-step insertion. We can also prove the theorems about the reduction of head insertion to one-step insertion and look-ahead insertion to head insertion.

Recently there have been several attempts to unify different programming paradigms and to construct theories to give a better understanding of contemporary software development processes. The book of C.A.R.Hoare and He Jifeng [14] is relevant in this context, as well as the approaches based on rewriting [15].

Our model can also be used for the development of a new methodology of programming. This methodology considers the transformation of an environment behaviour as the main semantic invariant of a software agent inserted into this environment. The model has been implemented in the algebraic programming system APS and this implementation is being used to study interaction and computation in declarative programming paradigms as well as for the development of some application projects. One of these projects is a mathematical information environment [1] designed as an environment for mathematical agents capable to read mathematical texts, check their correctness prove and solve mathematical problems.

References

1. A. A.Letichevsky, J. V.Kapitonova, V. A.Volkov, A.Chugajenko, V.Chomenko, and D. R.Gilbert. The development of interactive algorithms for a mathematical environment. In Alessandro Armando and Tudor Jebelean, editors, *CALCULEMUS 99, Systems for Integrated Computtion and Deduction*, Electronic Notes in Theoretical Computer Sciences http://www.elsevier.nl/locate/entcs, pages 33–50, 1999. 327
2. S. Abramsky. A domain equation for bisimulation. *Information and Computation*, 92(2):161–218, 1991. 313, 314, 318
3. Samson Abramsky. Semantics of interaction. In *Trees in Algebra and Programming – CAAP'96, Proc. 21st Int. Coll., Linköping*, volume 1059 of *Lecture Notes in Computer Science*, page 1. Springer-Verlag, 1996. 311
4. Ian A.Mason and Carolyn L.Talkott. Actor languages their syntax, semantics, translation, and equivalence. *Theoretical Computer Science*, 220(2):409–467, 1999. 311
5. J. A. Bergstra and J. W. Klop. Process algebra for synchronous communication. *Information and Control*, 60(1/3):109–137, 1984. 311, 318, 325
6. B.Jacobs and J.Rutten. A tutorial on (co)algebras and (co)induction. *Bulletin of the EATCS*, 62:222–259, 1997. 314
7. D. M. R.Park. Concurrency and automata on infinite sequences. In *Proc. 5th GI Conf*, volume 104 of *Lecture Notes in Computer Science*. Springer-Verlag, 1981. 312
8. U.Montanari F.Gadducci. The tile model. Technical Report TR-96-27, Department of Computer Science, University of Pisa, 1996. 311
9. D. Gelernter and L. Zuck. On What Linda is: Formal Description of Linda as a reactive system. In D. Garlan and D. LeMetayer, editors, *Proc. 2nd Int. Conf. on Coordination Models and Languages*, volume 1282 of *Lecture Notes in Computer Science*, pages 187–204, Berlin, Germany, September 1997. Springer-Verlag, Berlin. 311

10. D. R. Gilbert and A. A. Letichevsky. A universal interpreter for nondeterministic concurrent programming languages. In Maurizio Gabbrielli, editor, *Fifth Compulog network area meeting on language design and semantic analysis methods*, Sep 1996. 326
11. G.Milne and R.Milner. Concurrent processes and their syntax. *J.Assoc.Comput.Mach.*, 26(2):302, 1979. 318
12. I. Guessarian. *Algebraic semantics*. Lecture Notes in Computer Science v.99. Springer-Verlag, 1981. 313
13. C. A. R. Hoare. *Communicating Sequential Processes*. Prentice Hall, UK, 1985. 311
14. C. A. R. Hoare and He Jifeng. *Unifying Theories of Programming*. Prentice Hall, 1999. 327
15. J.Meseguer. Conditional rewriting logic as a unified model of concurrency. *Theoretical Computer Science*, 96:73–155, 1992. 312, 327
16. J. V. Kapitonova, A. A. Letichevsky, and S. V. Konozenko. Computations in aps. *Theoretical Computer Science*, 119:145–171, 1993. 326
17. A. A. Letichevsky. Algebras with approximation and recursive data structures. *Kibernetika*, (5):32–37, September-October 1987. 313
18. A. A. Letichevsky and D. R. Gilbert. Toward an implementation theory of nondeterministic concurrent languages. Technical Report 1996/09. ISSN 1364-4009, Department of Computer Science, City University, 1996. Also presented at the Second workshop of the INTAS-93-1702 project Efficient Symbolic Computing St Petersburg, Russia, October 1996. 312
19. A. A. Letichevsky and D. R. Gilbert. A general theory of action languages. Technical report, Department of Computer Science, City University, London, UK, Aug 1997. 312
20. A. A. Letichevsky and D. R. Gilbert. Agents and environments. In *1st International scientific and practical conference on programming, Proceedings 2-4 September, 1998*. Glushkov Institute of Cybernetics, National Academy of Sciences of Ukraine, 1998. 312
21. A. A. Letichevsky and D. R. Gilbert. A general theory of action languages. *Cybernetics and System Analysis*, (1):16–36, January-February 1998. 312, 320
22. L.Lamport. The temporal logic of actions. *acm Transactions on Programming Languages and Systems*, 16(3):872–923, 1994. 311
23. M.Barr. Terminal coalgebras in well-founded set theory. *Theoretical Computer Science*, 114(2):299–315, 1993. 314
24. R. Milner. *Communication and Concurrency*. Prentice Hall, 1989. 311
25. G. Plotkin. A structured approach to operational semantics. Technical Report DAIMI FN-19, Computer Science Dept., Aarhus University, 1981. 316
26. V. Saraswat. *Concurrent Constraint Programming*. MIT Press, 1993. 311
27. T. Valkevych, D. R. Gilbert, and A. A. Letichevsky. A generic workbench for modelling the behaviour of concurrent and probabilistic systems. In *Workshop on Tool Support for System Specification, Development and Verification, at TOOLS98*, Malente, Germany, June 2–4, 1998. 326

Algebra-Coalgebra Structures and Bialgebras

Ataru T. Nakagawa

SRA Software Engineering Laboratory

Abstract. A recent paper by Hennicker and Kurz[4] gives a formulation of algebraic operations which respect behavioural equivalence as a pair of an algebra and a coalgebra structures on the same carrier set. The conditions on such a pair are simple but elegant and intuitive. Another elegant formulation, given by Turi and Plotkin[18], uses a similar pair of an algebra and a coalgebra structures, which fits in a certain diagram that involves a natural transformation with distributive property. The paper investigates a relationship between these two similar formulations, and shows when they can be interchangeable and when they cannot.

1 Introduction

One of the recent advances in behavioural semantics developed ways to formalise algebraic structures on top of behavioural structures, defined in various ways: coalgebras in the case of Rutten and Turi '94[16] and Turi and Plotkin '97[18]; hidden algebras in the case of Diaconescu '98[3] and Rosu '98[14]; observational equivalence in the case of Bidoit and Hennicker '98[2].

There are two principal motivations behind these trends: process algebras and algebraic specifications. On one hand, one would like to ensure that SOS rules of process algebras are congruent with operators. One the other hand, one would like to ensure that non-observational operators respect observational equivalence defined in algebraic specification frameworks. According to these motivations, the formulations, restrictions, and conditions take different guises.

One recent paper, Hennicker and Kurz '99[4], gives yet another formulation, this time based on coalgebraic structures but from the perspective of algebraic specifications. Although not stated explicitly, this approach could be seen as a step toward finding relations between two trends and exploiting merits from both. Encouraged by their results, we would like to probe a little further into how and to what extent the results from the process algebraic perspective are relevant to the algebraic specification perspective.

2 Preliminaries

2.1 Basic Facts and Assumptions

The following facts, remarks, notations and assumptions are implicit thoughout the paper. The relevant references are [10,11,15,16], and [17].

D. Bert, C. Choppy, and P. Mosses (Eds.): WADT'99, LNCS 1827, pp. 329–347, 2000.

- For brevity and simplicity, the underlying category is fixed to be *Set* of sets and functions. Some of the results can be generalised to other categories. In particular, all the results hold for the product category Set^n, based on the recent results in [8].
- Endofunctors Σ, B : $Set \to Set$. The former is used to obtain algebraic structures $\Sigma X \to X$ for sets X's, while the latter is to obtain coalgebraic structures $X \to BX$.
- The categories Set^Σ, Set_B of Σ-algebras and B-coalgebras respectively. A Σ-algebra is just a function $\Sigma X \xrightarrow{f} X$ for some set X, and Set^Σ-morphism is a function that respects the Σ-algebraic structure, i.e. such h that makes the diagram below commute.

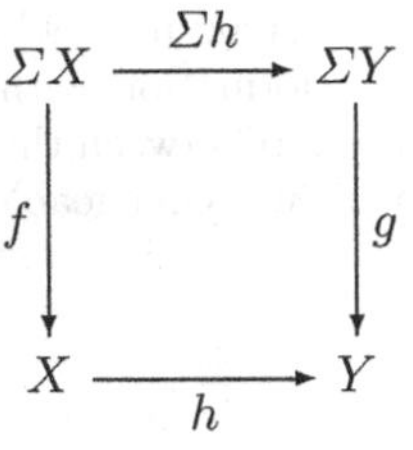

  B-coalgebras and Set_B-morphisms are defined dually.
- Σ and B preserve weak pullbacks.
- The final B-coalgebra, written $\nu B \xrightarrow{\beta} B\nu B$, exists.
- Σ and B are also used to denote signatures defining endofunctors. In such a case, Σ, B are restricted to a plain algebraic specification style: they consist of operators equipped with rank from $S^* \to S$ for some sort set S, with the following restrictions.
  - A single sort $s \in S$, called *sort in focus*, is marked out.
  - Each operator (symbol) in B has exactly one s in its arity.
  - The coarity of each operator in Σ is s.

  The sorts other than s is called *data sorts*. The data sorts are treated as in hidden algebras[5]: the data universe is fixed once and for all, and to treat terms correctly, we assume the signature contains a constant for each element of the universe (or we so expand the signature in defining term algebras).
- The forgetful functor $Set^\Sigma \xrightarrow{U^\Sigma} Set$ has a left adjoint F^Σ that sends X to the term algebra $\Sigma TX \xrightarrow{ev_X} TX$. We denote the unit and counit of the adjunction as η, ε.

The adjunction defines a monad $\langle T = U^\Sigma F^\Sigma, \eta, \mu = U^\Sigma \varepsilon F^\Sigma \rangle$, which in turn defines an algebraic structure. We say that T is induced by Σ, and call an algebra for this monad a T-algebra. A T-algebra is a function $TX \xrightarrow{f} X$ that makes the diagrams below commute.

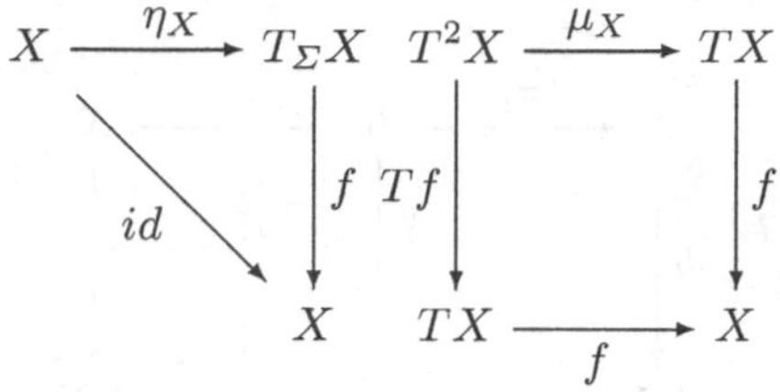

A morphism between T-algebra is a function that fits in the commutative diagram below.

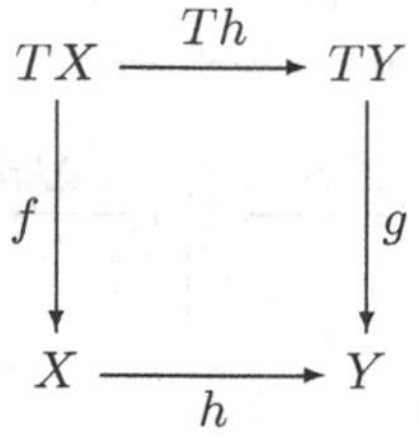

The categories of T-algebras, written Set^T, is isomorphic to Set^Σ: the isomorphism is given by

$$Set^\Sigma \underset{\Psi}{\overset{\Phi}{\rightleftarrows}} Set^T$$

with $\Phi f = \varepsilon_f$ and $\Psi g = g \circ ev \circ \Sigma \eta$.

$$\begin{array}{ccc}
\Sigma TX + X & \xrightarrow{\Sigma\Phi f + id} & \Sigma X + X \\
\downarrow{\scriptstyle [ev_X, \eta_X]} & & \downarrow{\scriptstyle [f, id]} \\
TX & \xrightarrow{\Phi f} & X
\end{array}$$

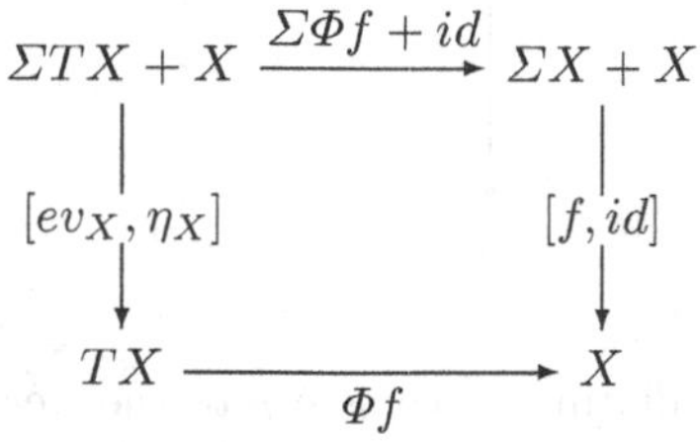

– Dually, the forgetful functor $Set_B \overset{U_B}{\to} Set$ has a right adjoint R_B that sends X to the cofree B-coalgebra over X (whose existence is an assumption), written $\nabla X \overset{ve_X}{\to} B\nabla X$. The unit and counit is written η', ε'. The adjunction defines a comonad $\langle \nabla = U_B R_B, \varepsilon', \delta = U_B \eta' R_B \rangle$, which in turn defines the category Set_∇ of ∇-coalgebras. Set_B and Set_∇ are isomorphic via

$$Set_B \underset{\Psi}{\overset{\Phi}{\rightleftarrows}} Set_\nabla$$

with $\Phi f = \eta'_f$ and $\Psi g = B\varepsilon' \circ ve \circ g$.

– A B-bisimulation on $X \xrightarrow{h} BX$ is a relation $R \subseteq X \times X$ that can be equipped with a B-coalgebra structure r that makes the diagram below commute.

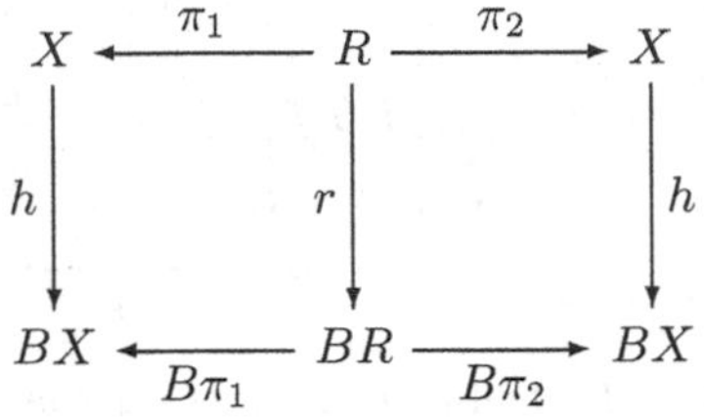

Similarly, a Σ-congruence on $\Sigma X \xrightarrow{h} X$ is a relation R such that there is an s that makes the diagram below commute.

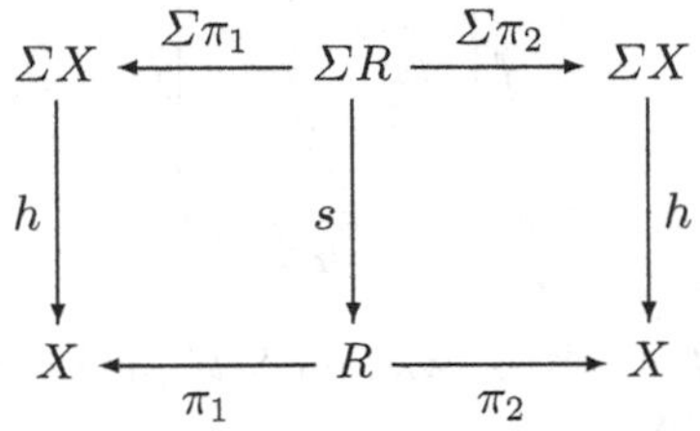

– The largest B-bisimulation (B-bisimilarity) is the kernel P of the terminal Set_B-morphism, as in

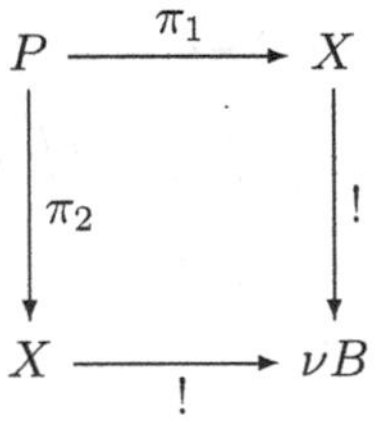

equipped with a mediating morphism p to the weak pullback BP.

2.2 Σ,B-Structures

The following definitions and results are from Hennicker and Kurz[4].

Definition 2.1 (Σ,B-Structures.). *Given endofunctors Σ and B, a Σ,B-structure is a pair $\Sigma X \xrightarrow{h} X \xrightarrow{k} BX$ of a Σ-algebra and a B-coalgebra such that the terminal Set_B-morphism $X \xrightarrow{!} \nu B$ is a Set^{Σ}-morphism to some Σ-algebra $\Sigma \nu B \xrightarrow{\alpha} \nu B$, called* a witness.

Pictorially, Σ,B-structure is a pair such that there is α that makes the diagram below commute.

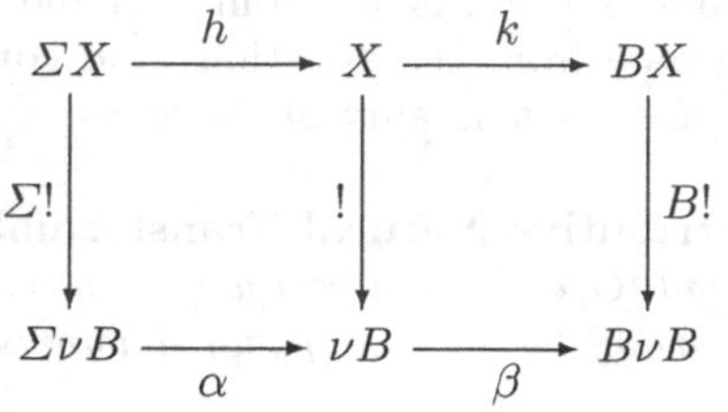

Definition 2.2 (Σ-Congruent B-Bisimulation.). *Given a pair $\Sigma X \xrightarrow{h} X \xrightarrow{k} BX$ of a Σ-algebra and a B-coalgebra, a B-bisimulation R on k is Σ-congruent (wrt h) iff R may be equipped with a Σ-structure that makes it a Σ-congruence on h.*

The pair h, k is Σ-congruent iff B-bisimilarity on k is Σ-congruent.

Pictorially, R is Σ-congruent iff there is s that makes the top half of the diagram below commute.

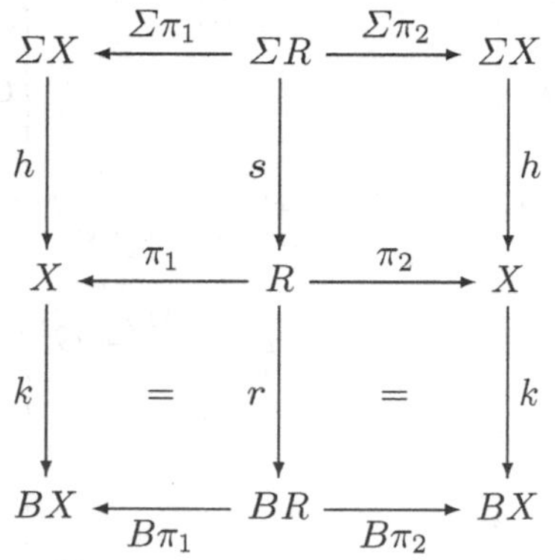

Theorem 2.3 (Hennicker & Kurz 99). *For a pair $\Sigma X \xrightarrow{h} X \xrightarrow{k} BX$, the followings are equivalent.*

(1) It is a Σ,B-structure.
(2) It is Σ-congruent.

[4] gave a sufficient condition for a pair to be a Σ,B-structure. It also showed that an observer complete specification in the sense of [2] has only Σ,B-structures as models. B-bisimilarity identifies elements indistinguishable by any observations in B. When Σ, B are derived from a signature, Σ-congruence means that the operations in Σ map any two indistinguishable elements to indistinguishables: such a model, therefore, is an intuitively correct one. By the above theorem, an observer complete specification can be regarded as correct (at least in this sense).

2.3 λ-Bialgebras

The following definitions and results are from Turi and Plotkin[18]. In this subsection we slightly deviate from the notations and conventions established in Section 2.1, to emphasise the generality of the ideas.

Definition 2.4 (Distributive Natural Transformation.). *Given a monad* $\langle T, \eta, \mu \rangle$ *and a comonad* $\langle G, \epsilon, \delta \rangle$ *on a category* $\mathcal{C}$*, a natural transformation* $\lambda : TG \Rightarrow GT$ *is distributive iff the following four diagrams commute.*

$$
\begin{array}{ccc}
GX & & \\
\downarrow{\scriptstyle \eta_{GX}} & \searrow^{G\eta_X} & \\
TGX & \xrightarrow[\lambda_X]{} & GTX
\end{array}
\qquad\qquad
\begin{array}{ccc}
TGX & \xrightarrow{\lambda_X} & GTX \\
& \searrow_{T\epsilon_X} & \downarrow{\scriptstyle \epsilon_{TX}} \\
& & TX
\end{array}
$$

$$
\begin{array}{ccccc}
T^2GX & \xrightarrow{\mu_{GX}} & TGX & \xrightarrow{\lambda_X} & GTX \\
\downarrow{\scriptstyle T\lambda_X} & & & & \uparrow{\scriptstyle G\mu_X} \\
TGTX & & \xrightarrow[\lambda_{TX}]{} & & GT^2X
\end{array}
$$

$$
\begin{array}{ccccc}
TGX & \xrightarrow{\lambda_X} & GTX & \xrightarrow{\delta_{TX}} & G^2TX \\
\downarrow{\scriptstyle T\delta_X} & & & & \uparrow{\scriptstyle G\lambda_X} \\
TG^2X & & \xrightarrow[\lambda_{GX}]{} & & GTGX
\end{array}
$$

Definition 2.5 (λ-Bialgebra.). *Given a monad, a comonad, and a distributive natural transformation as above, a* λ*-bialgebra is a pair* $TX \xrightarrow{h} X \xrightarrow{k} GX$ *of a* T*-algebra and a* G*-coalgebra that makes the diagram below commute.*

$$
\begin{array}{ccccc}
TX & \xrightarrow{h} & X & \xrightarrow{k} & GX \\
\downarrow{\scriptstyle Tk} & & & & \uparrow{\scriptstyle Gh} \\
TGX & & \xrightarrow[\lambda_X]{} & & GTX
\end{array}
$$

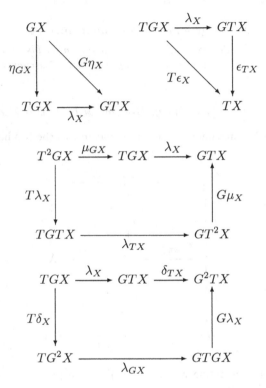

Let λ-**Bialg** be the category of λ-bialgebras, whose morphisms are functions that are both T-algebra morphisms and G-coalgebra morphisms. The following theorems exploit the isomorphisms between λ-**Bialg** and the category G_λ-**Coalg** of G_λ-coalgebras (the category T_λ-**Alg** of T_λ-algebras resp.), where G_λ (T_λ resp.) is a "lifted" comonad on Set^T (a monad on Set_G) defined as

$$G_\lambda(TX \xrightarrow{h} X) = TGX \xrightarrow{\lambda_X} GTX \xrightarrow{Gh} GX$$

(

$$T_\lambda(X \xrightarrow{k} GX) = TX \xrightarrow{Tk} TGX \xrightarrow{\lambda_X} GTX$$

), and a theorem in [7].

Theorem 2.6 (Turi & Plotkin 97). *The forgetful functor* U^λ : λ-**Bialg** $\to$ Set_G *has a left adjoint* F^λ

$$F^\lambda(X \xrightarrow{k} GX) = T^2X \xrightarrow{\mu_X} TX \xrightarrow{T_\lambda k} GTX$$

Since Set_G has the initial object $0 \xrightarrow{!} G0$ and the left ajoint preserves it, we have

Corollary 2.7. λ-**Bialg** *has the initial object.*

Specifically, the initial object is the image $0 \xrightarrow{!} G0$ under F^λ. Dually,

Theorem 2.8 (Turi & Plotkin 97). *The forgetful functor* U_λ : λ-**Bialg** $\to$ Set^T *has a right adjoint* R_λ

$$R_\lambda(TX \xrightarrow{h} X) = TGX \xrightarrow{G_\lambda h} GX \xrightarrow{\delta_X} G^2X$$

Corollary 2.9. λ-**Bialg** *has the final object.*

Specifically, it is the image of $T1 \xrightarrow{!} 1$ under R_λ.

Going back to the notations of Section 2.1, in the rest of the paper, we abuse the terminology and say that a pair $\Sigma X \xrightarrow{h} X \xrightarrow{k} BX$ of a Σ-algebra and a B-coalgebra is a λ-bialgebra if the corresponding $TX \xrightarrow{\varepsilon_h} X \xrightarrow{\eta'_k} \nabla X$ is.

3 Running Examples

For illustration we use two simple examples Σ, B, both coming from algebraic specification style signatures. In this paper we say nothing on the actual shape axioms take, and give informal verbal explanations.

3.1 Piggy Bank Accounts

In the sequel we call this example EX-1.

Let $(N, 0, +)$ be the natural numbers with addition (a data sort), and X be a sort (symbol). Define B to be the signature

```
crash : X -> N
```

and Σ to be the signature

```
new : -> X
add : X N -> X
```

where `X` is the sort in focus. This example is meant to depict piggy bank accounts, where the only possible observation is to inspect the total amount in them (by `crash`ing). Operations in Σ correspond to buying new piggy banks and to depositing coins in them.

The final B-coalgebra is very simple: it is just the identity $N \overset{id}{\to} N$ on N.

3.2 EX-2: Streams

In the sequel we call this example EX-2.

Let $A = \{a, b\}$ be a doubleton set (a data sort), and X be a sort. Define B to be the signature

```
head : X -> A
rest : X -> X
```

and Σ to be the signature

```
all-a : -> X
all-b : -> X
merge : X X -> X
comb : X -> X
```

where `X` is the sort in focus as before. This example is meant to depict infinite streams of A's elements. The observations consist of looking at the head and the rest of streams. Operations in Σ correspond to an infinite a-constant stream, to a b-constant stream, to merging (or "zip"ping) two streams into one, and combing streams to create ones consisting of only elements of odd indices.

The final B-coalgebra is

$$A^\omega \xrightarrow{\langle head, rest \rangle} A \times A^\omega$$

which is indeed the set of infinite streams of A's elements. *head* returns the head element and *rest* returns the rest.

4 λ-Bialgebras as Σ,B-Structures

Theorem 4.1 (Bialgebras are Σ,B-Structures.). *Given endofunctors Σ, B on Set, let T, ∇ be the monad and the comonad induced by Σ and B respectively, and let $\lambda : T\nabla \Rightarrow \nabla T$ be a distributive natural transformation. For such a λ, there is a witness $\Sigma\nu B \xrightarrow{\alpha} \nu B$ that makes any λ-bialgebra a Σ,B-structure: for any λ-bialgebra $\Sigma X \xrightarrow{h} X \xrightarrow{k} BX$, the diagram*

$$\begin{array}{ccccc}
\Sigma X & \xrightarrow{h} & X & \xrightarrow{k} & BX \\
\downarrow{\scriptstyle \Sigma !} & & \downarrow{\scriptstyle !} & & \downarrow{\scriptstyle B!} \\
\Sigma\nu B & \xrightarrow[\alpha]{} & \nu B & \xrightarrow[\beta]{} & B\nu B
\end{array}$$

commutes, where $!$ is the unique terminal morphism to the final coalgebra $\nu B \xrightarrow{\beta} B\nu B$.

Proof. By Corollary 2.9, the category of λ-bialgebras has the terminal object given by

$$T\nabla 1 \xrightarrow{\lambda_1} \nabla T1 \xrightarrow{\nabla t} \nabla 1 \xrightarrow{\delta_1} \nabla^2 1$$

where $T1 \xrightarrow{t} 1$ is the terminal T-algebra. This means, for any λ-bialgebra $\Sigma X \xrightarrow{h} X \xrightarrow{k} BX$, that there is a unique function $X \xrightarrow{!} \nabla 1$ that makes the following diagram commute.

$$\begin{array}{ccccccc}
TX & & \xrightarrow{\varepsilon_h} & & X & \xrightarrow{\eta'_k} & \nabla X \\
\downarrow{\scriptstyle T!} & & & & \downarrow{\scriptstyle !} & & \downarrow{\scriptstyle \nabla !} \\
T\nabla 1 & \xrightarrow[\lambda_1]{} & \nabla T1 & \xrightarrow[\nabla t]{} & \nabla 1 & \xrightarrow[\delta_1]{} & \nabla^2 1
\end{array}$$

Whence we get a commutative diagram

$$\begin{array}{ccccc}
\Sigma X & \xrightarrow{h} & X & \xrightarrow{k} & BX \\
\downarrow{\scriptstyle \Sigma !} & & \downarrow{\scriptstyle !} & & \downarrow{\scriptstyle B!} \\
\Sigma\nabla 1 & \xrightarrow[\nabla t \circ \lambda_1 \circ ev_{\nabla 1} \circ \Sigma\eta_{\nabla 1}]{} & \nabla 1 & \xrightarrow[B\varepsilon'_{\nabla 1} \circ ve_{\nabla 1} \circ \delta_1]{} & B\nabla 1
\end{array}$$

by the isomorphism between the categories of T-algebras and Σ-algebras, and the one between those of ∇-coalgebras and B-coalgebras. We then observe that

- $\nabla 1$, which is the carrier of the terminal $B \times 1$-coalgebra, is just νB.
- δ_1 is by definition η'_{ve_1}, so that, by the isomorphism between Set_B and Set_∇ (cf. Section 2.1), the bottom right composition is just ve_1 which in turn, by the above observation, is just the terminal B-coalgebra β.
- Commutativity of the right square means, therefore, that ! is indeed the unique terminal arrow from B-coalgebra k.

QED

This gives yet another proof that λ-bialgebras have bisimilarity preserving algebraic structures, in cases when the comonads are derived from signature functors.

5 Σ,B-Structures as λ-Bialgebras

To get a converse result, we have to impose various restrictions. The first restriction is on the type of functors Σ and B. This is essentially the same restriction as imposed by Hennicker and Kurz [4], when they introduced a concrete language.

5.1 Σ,B from Signatures

B from a signature. we restrict B, Σ to be polynomials induced by algebraic specification style signatures. The general form of such a B is given by

$$\prod_{i=1}^{n} -^{A_i} \times \prod_{j=1}^{m} E_j^{C_j}$$

where E_j's are fixed sets and A_i, C_j's are finite products of fixed sets. For the sake of brevity, we write E for $\prod_j E_j^{C_j}$.

For example, in the case of `EX-1`, $BX = N$ for any set X, and $Bf = id_N$ for any function f. In the case of `EX-2`, $BX = E \times X$ and $Bf = id_E \times f$.

Such a B is ω^{op}-continuous and the final B-coalgebra may be obtained as the limit of the chain

$$1 \stackrel{!}{\leftarrow} B1 \stackrel{B!}{\leftarrow} B^2 1 \stackrel{B^2!}{\leftarrow} \dots$$

We may construct the carrier of the final B-coalgebra explicitly as

$$\nu B (= \nabla 1) = \prod_l E^l$$

where l ranges over finite products of A_i's.

Similarly, the (carrier of the) cofree B-coalgebra over a set X, which is in fact the final $B \times X$-coalgebra ([15]), may be obtained as the limit of the chain

$$1 \stackrel{!}{\leftarrow} B1 \times X \stackrel{B! \times id}{\leftarrow} B(B1 \times X) \times X \stackrel{B(B! \times id) \times id}{\leftarrow} \dots$$

and the carrier may be written as

$$\nabla X = \zeta E \times \zeta X = \nabla 1 \times \zeta X$$

where $\zeta\_ = \prod_l \_^l$ with l as above. The counit ε'_X is the projection to X as a multiplicand of ζX (with l the empty product), and ve_X is the projection to the rest of the multiplicands.

Using these notations, we may put

$$T\nabla X = T(\nabla 1 \times \zeta X)$$

and

$$\nabla TX = \nabla 1 \times \zeta TX$$

Remark 5.1 (Projections from ζ.). In the sequel, an element of ζX may be denoted as $(x_l)_l$, where l ranges over products of A_i's, and x_l is a function of rank $l \to X$. A projection $\zeta X \to X^l$ may be denoted as π_l. π_1 is the projection to X.

Remark 5.2 (ζ as a functor.). For a function $X \xrightarrow{f} Y$, we have the usual definition for $\zeta X \xrightarrow{\zeta f} \zeta Y$ via exponentials. This extension makes ζ a functor on *Set*.

Σ from a signature. Σ is of the form

$$\sum_{i=1}^{n} \_^{k_i} \times U_i$$

where U_i's are finite products of fixed sets.

For example, in the case of EX-1, $\Sigma X = 1 + X \times N$ for a set X and $\Sigma f = id_1 + f \times id_N$ for a function f. In the case of EX-2, $\Sigma X = 1+1+X\times X+X$ and $\Sigma f = id_1 + id_1 + f \times f + f$.

Given such a Σ, define $\Sigma\zeta X \xrightarrow{\rho_X} \zeta\Sigma X$ as a unique mediating function from the coproduct associated with the following function for each summand.

$$(\zeta X)^{k_i} \times U_i \xrightarrow{id \times c} (\zeta X)^{k_i} \times \zeta U_i \xrightarrow{\simeq} \zeta(X^{k_i} \times U_i) \xrightarrow{\zeta\iota} \zeta \sum_i X^{k_i} \times U_i = \zeta\Sigma X$$

where

1. $U_i \xrightarrow{c} \zeta U_i$ is the "constant" function: for any $u \in U_i$, $cu = (cu_l)_l$ consists of functions that send every $(a_1, \ldots, a_j) \in l$ to u, for all l.
2. $\simeq$ juggles products: it is the mapping

$$((x_{1,l})_l, \ldots, (x_{k_i,l})_l, (u_l)_l) \mapsto (x_{1,l}, \ldots, x_{k_i,l}, u_l)_l$$

3. ι is the injection to the coproduct.

ζ-lifting of Σ-algebras. Given a Σ-algebra $\Sigma X \xrightarrow{f} X$, define $\Sigma\zeta X \xrightarrow{\theta f} \zeta X$ to be the composition

$$\Sigma\zeta X \xrightarrow{\rho_X} \zeta\Sigma X \xrightarrow{\zeta f} \zeta X$$

where ρ_X is given as above.

Remark 5.3. For a Σ-algebra $\Sigma X \xrightarrow{h} X$ and for an operation σ in Σ (as a signature), we write h_σ for the component of h corresponding to σ.

5.2 Construction of λ

Given a Σ-algebra $\Sigma\nabla 1 \xrightarrow{\hat{r}} \nabla 1$, let $r = \varepsilon_{\hat{r}}$ be the corresponding T-algebra. Then we have functions

$$T(\nabla 1 \times \zeta X) \xrightarrow{T\pi_1} T\nabla 1 \xrightarrow{\quad r \quad} \nabla 1$$

and

$$T(\nabla 1 \times \zeta X) \xrightarrow{T\pi_2} T\zeta X \xrightarrow{\zeta\eta_X{}^{\#}} \zeta TX$$

where $\zeta\eta_X{}^{\#}$ is the unique Set^{Σ}-morphism to the ζ-lifting θev_X that makes the diagram below commute.

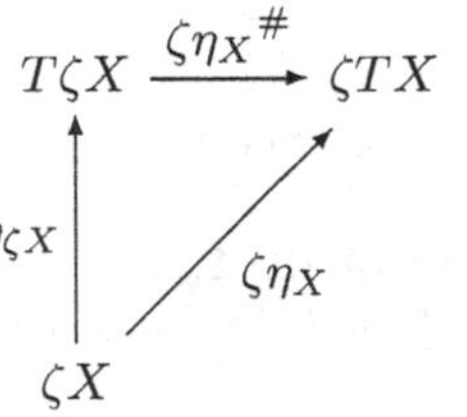

These functions combine to a function

$$T\nabla X = T(\nabla 1 \times \zeta X) \xrightarrow{\lambda_X} \nabla 1 \times \zeta TX = \nabla TX$$

Remark 5.4. The above construction is not unique. Especially, the function $T\zeta X \xrightarrow{\zeta\eta_X{}^{\#}} \zeta TX$ may be replaced by a function induced by the projections from ζX. We chose the above definition since it makes proofs much simpler.

The first leg, however, cannot be replaced by other functions. On one hand, to make λ natural, this leg must be independent of the underlying set X, which implies that it may be written as a composition with the (image of the) projection $T\pi_1$. On the other hand, to recover a definition from any Σ,B-structure, we are forced to use a witness (see the diagram below Theorem 5.11).

5.3 Assumption on r

For the above definition of λ to be distributive — more specifically, for the diagram involving δ to commute —, we need a certain assumption on the Σ-algebra $\hat{r}$.

Assumption 5.5 (Uniformity under projection.). *We require that the following diagram commute.*

$$\begin{array}{ccc} \Sigma\nabla 1 & \xrightarrow{\Sigma\xi_E} & \Sigma\zeta\nabla 1 \\ \downarrow \hat{r} & & \downarrow \theta\hat{r} \\ \nabla 1 & \xrightarrow[\xi_E]{} & \zeta\nabla 1 \end{array}$$

where ξ_E is defined as follows. Let l_1, l_2 be products of A_i's, $x = (x_l)_l \in \zeta E$, $\overline{a_1} \in l_1$, and $\overline{a_2} \in l_2$. Then

$$((\xi_E(x)_{l_1}(\overline{a_1}))_{l_2}(\overline{a_2}) = x_{l_1 \times l_2}(\overline{a_1}, \overline{a_2})$$

Remark 5.6. The assumption is very strong. Consider `EX-2`. The operation `merge` interleaves two streams smoothly. For example, it merges

```
aaaaa...
bbbbb...
```

into

```
ababababab...
```

This operation cannot be part of $\hat{r}$. Note that in this case l may taken to be a natural number and the projection to l sends a stream $(e_l)_l$ to the stream stripped of the top lth elements. Thus, if we write 1-th projection as `p1`, we get

```
p1(merge(aba...,aba...)) = abbaa...
merge(p1(aba...),p1(aba...)) = bbaa...
```

so that the assumption does not hold.

Similarly, the operation `comb` cannot be part of $\hat{r}$.

Remark 5.7. The assumption is necessary: for example, the operations `merge` and `comb` fail to satisfy the coherence condition for comultiplication δ in Definition 2.4.

Remark 5.8. Nevetheless, there are many examples where the assumption is reasonable. If the coarity of every operation in B is a data sort, as is the case of `EX-1`, the terminal algebra $\nabla 1$ is simply a product of data sorts, and both ζ

and ξ are shrinked to the identities. Therefore the assumption holds trivially.

Even if there are operations in B that violate the assumption, it is often the case that B can be replaced by a signature that does satisfy the condition, and which defines the same bisimilarity. In the case of **EX-2**, instead of **head** and **rest**, we may have a single observer

```
inspect : X N -> A
```

(`N` is taken to be the natural number) that checks every element of streams. This signature engenders the same (carrier of the) final coalgebra and the same bisimilarity.

5.4 This λ is What We Want

We say that λ defined by the above construction for each X is *induced* by $\hat{r}$.

Theorem 5.9 (Naturality.). *$\lambda : T\nabla \Rightarrow \nabla T$ induced by* any *Σ-algebra $\Sigma\nabla 1 \xrightarrow{\hat{r}} \nabla 1$ is a natural transformation.*

The proof is by simple diagram chasings and by universality of η.

Theorem 5.10 (Distributivity.). *If $\Sigma\nabla 1 \xrightarrow{\hat{r}} \nabla 1$ satisfies Assumption 5.5, the induced natural transformation λ is distributive.*

The proof consists of simple diagram chasings, and relies heavily on the universality of the unit η. Of the four coherence diagrams, those that involve η, μ and ε' can be shown to commute without any condition on $\hat{r}$.

Assumption 5.5 is used to prove the coherence condition that involves the comultiplication δ. In a simplified form, the critical part is to show that the diagram

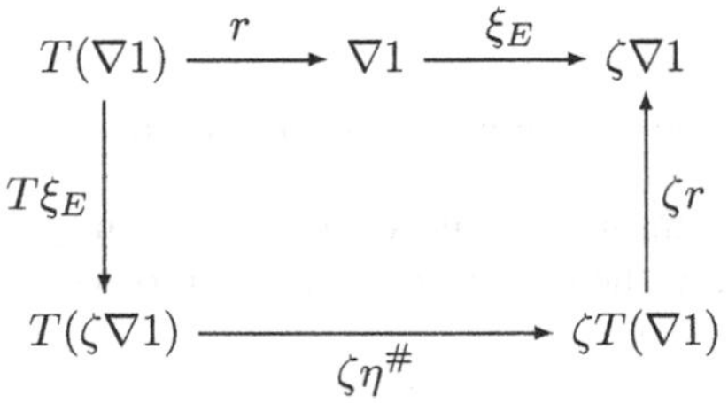

commutes. The proof itself uses the assumption purely technically (to establish that certain functions are Set^{Σ}-morphisms).

5.5 (Some) Σ,B-Structures are λ-Bialgebras

Theorem 5.11 (Σ,B-structures as bialgebras.). *Suppose that $\Sigma\nabla 1 \xrightarrow{\hat{r}} \nabla 1$ is a witness to a Σ,B-structure $\Sigma X \xrightarrow{h} X \xrightarrow{k} BX$. Then the structure is a λ-bialgebra for the induced natural transformation λ,* provided *one of the following conditions holds.*

(Cond 1.) B is a constant functor in the sense of Remark 5.8.
(Cond 2.) Assumption 5.5 holds for $\hat{r}$, and the terminal Set_B-morphism from $X \xrightarrow{k} BX$ is injective.

The proof again consists of simple diagram chasings, using universality of η and the fact that, by definition of Σ,B-structures and by the the isomorphism between Set^{Σ} (Set_B resp.) and Set^{T} (Set_{∇} resp.), the diagram

$$\begin{array}{ccccc} TX & \xrightarrow{\varepsilon_h} & X & \xrightarrow{\eta'_k} & \nabla 1 \times \zeta X \\ \big\downarrow{\scriptstyle T!} & & \big\downarrow{\scriptstyle !} & & \big\downarrow{\scriptstyle id \times \zeta !} \\ T\nabla 1 & \xrightarrow[r]{} & \nabla 1 & \xrightarrow[\delta_1]{} & \nabla^2 1 \end{array}$$

commutes for the terminal Set_B-morphism !. When Cond 1. holds, the required commutativity comes easily since the diagram collapses into a simple identity and Assumption 5.5 holds automatically.

In cases when B is not a constant functor, Assumption 5.5 and injectivity of the terminal morphism are used to show that some functions are Set^{Σ}-morphisms so that we may resort to the universality of η[1].

When the assumption of the theorem holds, a Σ,B-structure may be put in a category of λ-bialgebras where both the initial and final objects exist. By construction these objects are made out of the initial Σ-algebra and final B-coalgebra. Which implies, in turn, that it makes sense to talk about minimal and/or simple Σ,B-structure, and proofs by induction and coinduction may be used as appropriate to reason about the structure.

In the rest of the section, suppose that Cond 1. does not hold. The theorem need not hold if the (coalgebra-part of the) Σ,B-structure is not a subcoalgebra of the terminal.

(Counter)example. If you remove `all-b`, `merge`, and `comb` from `EX-2`, you do get a Σ-algebra $\hat{r}$ on A^w, defined as $\hat{r}(*) = (a)_{i\in\omega}$, that satisfies Assumption 5.5, so that $\hat{r}$ induces a distributive λ. Further, if you define a

[1] Injectivity is a sufficient, but not necessary, condition.

Σ-algebra and a B-coalgebra on the carrier $2 = \{0, 1\}$ as

$$\begin{aligned} h(*) &= 0 \\ k(0) &= \langle a, 1\rangle \\ k(1) &= \langle a, 0\rangle \end{aligned}$$

you get a commutative diagram

$$\begin{array}{ccccc} 1 & \xrightarrow{h} & 2 & \xrightarrow{k} & A \times 2 \\ \Big\downarrow{\scriptstyle id} & & \Big\downarrow{\scriptstyle f} & & \Big\downarrow{\scriptstyle id \times f} \\ 1 & \xrightarrow[\hat{r}]{} & A^{\omega} & \xrightarrow[\langle head, rest\rangle]{} & A \times A^{\omega} \end{array}$$

where the terminal morphism f sends both 0, 1 to the constant stream $(a)_{i\in\omega}$.

The pair h, k is not a λ-bialgebra: in the diagram

$$\begin{array}{ccccc} \{\texttt{all}-\texttt{a}\} & \xrightarrow{\varepsilon_h} & 2 & \xrightarrow{\eta'_k} & A^{\omega} \times 2^{\omega} \\ \Big\downarrow{\scriptstyle id} & & & & \Big\uparrow{\scriptstyle id \times \varepsilon_h} \\ \{\texttt{all}-\texttt{a}\} & & \xrightarrow[\lambda_2]{} & & A^{\omega} \times \{\texttt{all}-\texttt{a}\}^{\omega} \end{array}$$

the second leg of one arrow composition sends **all-a** to the alternating sequence $0, 1, 0, 1\ldots$ while the second leg of the other composition sends that term to the constant sequence of 0's.

Finally, recall from [4] that a pair $\Sigma X \xrightarrow{h} X \xrightarrow{k} BX$ is a Σ,B-structure iff it factors through its (unique) "behavioural image" as in the commutative diagram below

$$\begin{array}{ccccc} \Sigma X & \xrightarrow{h} & X & \xrightarrow{k} & BX \\ \Big\downarrow{\scriptstyle \Sigma e} & & \Big\downarrow{\scriptstyle e} & & \Big\downarrow{\scriptstyle Be} \\ \Sigma\overline{X} & \xrightarrow{\overline{h}} & \overline{X} & \xrightarrow{\overline{k}} & B\overline{X} \\ \Big\downarrow{\scriptstyle \Sigma\iota} & & \Big\downarrow{\scriptstyle \iota} & & \Big\downarrow{\scriptstyle B\iota} \\ \Sigma\nu B & \xrightarrow[\alpha]{} & \nu B & \xrightarrow[\beta]{} & B\nu B \end{array}$$

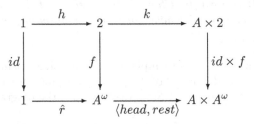

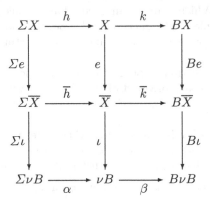

where $\iota \circ e$ is the epi-mono factorisation of the terminal B-coalgebra morphism from k. (The bottom left square does not necessarily commute for an arbitrary witness α, but we may obtain such α once we get the behavioural image.) Using this concept, we may rephrase the above theorem in the following way.

Corollary 5.12. *If the behavioural image of a Σ,B-structure has a witness $\Sigma\nabla 1 \xrightarrow{\hat{r}} \nabla 1$ that satisfies Assumption 5.5, then the image is a λ-bialgebra for the induced natural transformation λ.*

6 Conclusions and Future Works

By Theorems 2.3, 4.1, and 5.11, when we restrict endofunctors B and Σ to those derived from algebraic specification style signatures, given a pair $\Sigma X \xrightarrow{h} X \xrightarrow{k} BX$, h respects B-bisimilarity if the pair is a λ-bialgebra for some λ. Under some additional conditions, in particular when B contain no operation whose coarity is the sort in focus, the converse also holds.

The last condition has been paid attention to from other perspectives. For example, in [1], the so-called observability kernel is defined via the set of operations with coarity other than the sort in focus, and is used to make proofs short and easy. In [12], a candidate relation for coinductive proofs is defined via a set of similar operations, and an automatic proof is attempted to show that the relation is a bisimulation. The results of the paper may be invoked as an evidence to the fact that, for proof methods and proof systems, this restriction on B is very convenient. Moreover, as stated previously, if we restrict ourselves to functors defined by usual algebraic signatures, we can often replace B with a constant functor that sends every set to the carrier of the terminal B-coalgebra.

In establishing the results, the restriction to polynomial functors was technical: in the definitions and proofs, the constructive nature of final coalgebras was crucial. However, such a restriction is not inherent to Σ,B-structures. In defining a general notion of Σ,B-structures, [4] does not impose restrictions on the functors Σ or B (apart from the existence of final coalgebras and preservation of weak pullbacks). Thus it is theoretically possible, although as of now we do not know how, to extend the results to more general functors, such as those involving (finite) powersets.

We would like to give a couple of remarks on the differences between λ-bialgebras and Σ,B-structures. Firstly, the former relies on the monad/comonad pairs, instead of apparently simpler plain functors. This is for technical reasons, especially for using the results of [7]. In the case of Σ,B-structures, (co)monads are not used, simply because the definitions and results do not need them. This difference is superficial, because of the isomporphisms between Set^{Σ} and Set^{T}, and Set_{B} and Set_{∇}.

A more significant difference seems to be in the nature of algebraic operations. In the original motivation behind λ-bialgebras, typical algebraic operators are parallel compositions and choices, which are nondeterministic. In addition, the notion of bisilimarities usually requires the possibility, not necessity, of the actions. In contrast, in the observational logic, algebraic operators may be underspecified, but are considered deterministic functions. For such a function to respect bisimilarity, it is required to act uniformly: possibilities are not enough. In this sense, an algebraic structure in the original examples of λ-bialgebras has more freedom when it tries to respect bisimilarity, hence a tighter framework can be used more easily. We think this informal observation directs us to a deeper understanding of the relations between the different formulations adopted by [18] and [4].

In (the statement of) Theorems 4.1 and 5.11, you may find a possibility of partitioning the category of Σ,B-structures via witnesses, and of putting an indexed or fibred structure on it. This, however, is not that easy. One major obstacle is that, for a Σ,B-structure, there may be more than one witness. In fact, it is easy to construct a Σ,B-structure that has uncountably many witnesses. It is an interesting topic for the future research to find a tighter relation between a subcategory of Σ,B-structures and the category of associated λ-bialgebras.

For another future investigation, we would like to point to a recent paper [9] where distributive natural transformations are considered for weaker structures than monads and/or comonads. In particular, we are interested in the case where the comultiplication δ is absent, because that makes Assumption 5.5 partly redundant. The above paper established some of the results in [18] with the weaker structure, and it is worthwhile to see to what extent the further results can be obtained within their framework. On the other hand, even without δ, Assumption 5.5 cannot be disposed of entirely, since it was used also in the proof of Theorem 5.11. It is interesting to see if weaker assumptions may be used for the proof.

Acknowledgement

We enjoyed fruitful discussions on the subjects of the paper with many people. Special thanks should be given to Rolf Hennicker, Alexander Kurz, Daniele Turi, and Martin Wirsing, who all gave us valuable suggestions for improvements. We also thank anonymous referees for giving very useful comments on the earlier draft.

References

1. Bidoit, M. and Hennicker, R., "Proving Behavioural Theorems with Standard First-Order Logic", *Proc. Algebraic and Logic Programming '94*, LNCS 850, 1994, pp. 41–58 345

2. Bidoit, M. and Hennicker, R., "Observational Logic", *Proc. AMAST'98*, LNCS 1548, Springer, 1999, pp.263–277 329, 333
3. Diaconescu, R. and Futatsugi, K., *Behavioural Coherence in Object-Oriented Algebraic Specification*, Technical Report IS-RR-98-0017F, Japan Advanced Institute of Seance and Teleology, 1998 329
4. Hennicker, R. and Kurz, A., "(Ω, Ξ)-Logic: On the Algebraic Extension of Coalgebraic Specification", *Proc. Coalgebraic Methods in Computer Science '99*, Electronic Notes in Theoretical Computer Science volume 19 (on line), Elsevier, 1999 329, 332, 333, 338, 344, 345, 346
5. Goguen, J. and Malcolm, G., *A Hidden Agenda*, Technical Report CS97-538, University of California, San Diego, 1997 330
6. Jacobs, B. and Rutten, J., "A Tutorial on (Co)algebras and (Co)induction", *Bulletin of the EATCS*, vol.62, 1997, pp.222–259
7. Johnstone, P., "Adjoint Lifting Theorems for Categories of Algebras", *Bulletin of the London Mathematical Society* vol.7, 1975, pp.294–297 335, 345
8. Kurz, A. and Hennicker, R., "On Institutions for Modular Coalgebraic Specifications", to appear in *Theoretical Computer Science*, 2000 330
9. Lenisa, M., Power, J., and Watanabe, H., "Distributivity for Endofunctors, Pointed and Co-pointed Endofunctors, Monads and Comonads", *Proc. Coalgebraic Methods in Computer Science 2000*, Electronic Notes in Theoretical Computer Science volume 33 (on line), Elsevier, 2000 346
10. Mac Lane, S., *Categories for the Working Mathematician*, Springer, 1971; the second edition was published in 1998 329
11. Malcolm, G., "Behavioural Equivalence, Bisimulation, and Minimal Realisation", *Recent Trends in Data Type Specification, 11th WADT*, LNCS 1130, 1996, pp. 359–378 329
12. Nakagawa, A.T., Sawada, T., and Futatsugi, K., *CafeOBJ Manual*, SRA/JAIST, ftp.sra.co.jp/pub/lang/CafeOBJ/, 1997 345
13. Padawitz, P., "Swinging Data Types", *Recent Trends in Data Type Specifications*, Lecture Notes in Computer Science, 1996
14. Rosu, G., "Hidden Congruent Deduction", *Proc. First-Order Theorem Proving '98*, 1998 329
15. Rutten, J., *Universal Coalgebra: A Theory of Systems*, Technical Report CS-R9652, CWI, 1996; to appear in Theoretical Computer Science 329, 338
16. Rutten, J. and Turi, D., *Initial Algebra and Final Coalgebra Semantics for Concurrency*, CWI Technical Report; also in *Proc. of the TEX Workshop: A Decade of Concurrency — Reflections and Perspectives*, LNCS 803, Springer, pp.530–582, 1994 329
17. Turi, D, "Functorial Operational Semantics and its Denotational Dual", PhD thesis, Free University, Amsterdam, 1996 329
18. Turi, D. and Plotkin, G., "Toward a Mathematical Operational Semantics", *Proc. Logic in Computer Science '97*, IEEE, 1997 329, 334, 346

A Uniform Model Theory for the Specification of Data and Process Types

Horst Reichel

Institut Theoretical Computer Science, Dresden University of Technology
D–01062 Dresden, Germany
reichel@tcs.inf.tu-dresden.de

Abstract. Generalizing products in Lawvere's algebraic theories to projective and injective Kan extensions and their conjunctive combinations one gets a powerful categorical model theory. Based on this categorical model theory the foundations of a uniform axiomatic specification formalism for data and process types is developed.

1 Introduction

For the specification of processes, reactive systems or dynamic systems at present there is a confusing multitude of models available. None of them dominate clearly the other ones with respect to applicability, theoretical foundations ore dissemination.

Recently there has been designed the algebraic specifications language *CASL* for the specification of data types and software components [oLD98]. But, the specification of processes or reactive systems is not supported by *CASL*. There is an initiative to extend *CASL* or a sublanguage of it to a specification of data and process types. Let's call the intended language *Reactive CASL*. What kind of semantic foundations should be chosen for *Reactive CASL* in view of the present situation described above?

At the very beginning of research on data types one could observe a similar situation. Some researchers took one data structure as a universal one and developed a language based on that selection. *LISP* and *SETL* are outcomes of that positions. But, languages like *SML* and *CASL* do not distinguish some specific data types as universal ones, they offer the users the possibility to define constructively or axiomatically their own data types.

The aim of the present paper is to develop a semantic foundation for the development of *Reactive CASL* along the same intuition. We will present a semantic framework that offers the possibility to define both data types and process types axiomatically. It will be possible to iterate both kinds of specifications so that process types can be specified on top of data types, representing the result types of the defining observations of the process types. But it is also possible to specify process types on top of other process types. This leads to process types which can be seen as higher order process types. Specifying data types on top of process types leads to specifications of process systems, where the data type on top

D. Bert, C. Choppy, and P. Mosses (Eds.): WADT'99, LNCS 1827, pp. 348–365, 2000.

of the specification describes the structure of the state space of the specified system.

The uniform model theory is developed as a generalization of Lawveres categorical algebra [Law63]. In this approach categories with products represent the syntactic level, called a theory, which are interpreted by product preserving functors into a semantic range category, usually the category of sets. Products within the syntactic category can be generalized to finite limits which leads to equationally partial algebras, and products and finite limits can be weakened to sketches as presented in [BW96]. To represent classes of models which naturally appear by initial specifications of data types [AKKB99] and terminal specifications of process types [JR97] the finite limits will be generalized to projective Kan extensions, injective Kan extensions and their conditional and conjunctive combinations.

Formally, data types will be specified by the *injective universal property of the corresponding constructors* of the data type, and process types will be specified by the *projective universal property of the corresponding observations* of the process type. This intuition is formalized by means of *projective and injective Kan extensions* [ML71].

Injective and projective Kan extensions (also called left and right Kan extension) will be weakened to *injective and projective sketches* in the same way as injective and projective limits are weakened to limit or colimit sketches [BW96]. The essentially new concept is given by *Nested Sketches* [Rei98], since conjunctions of projective and injective sketches are not able to define those categories of models that arise naturally in the intended application areas. Nesting of sketches is used to constrain the domain of a universal property required for a specific sketch.

The paper is structured as follows. In Section 2 categorical basic notions are provided. Section 3 investigates nested sketches and there models. A basic result shows the existence of a generic model for each category constraint by a nested sketch. The construction of a generic model generalizes the notion of a term algebra, but it will be proved in Section 4 that the Hennessy–Milner logic can also be seen as an instance of a generic model, if one specifies the most abstract image finite transition system for any given set of actions. Therefore, the generic model can be seen as a minimal logic for the class of structures specified. By means of examples we show in which way essential properties of the semantic range category can be lifted on the theory level. An important example of that kind of properties is the distributivity between sums and products in the category of sets. Finally we exemplify a constructive specifications of dynamic properties of processes.

2 Basic Notions of Category Theory

The basic notions are that of projective (or right) and injective (or left) Kan extensions.

Definition 1. *Let*

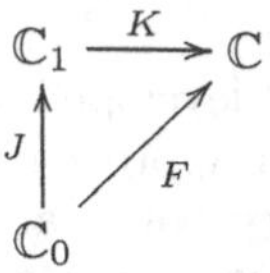

be given functors. The functor $K : \mathbb{C}_1 \to \mathbb{C}$ *together with the a natural transformation* $\pi : J; K \Rightarrow F$ *is called a* projective Kan extension *of* $F : \mathbb{C}_0 \to \mathbb{C}$ *along* $J : \mathbb{C}_0 \to \mathbb{C}_1$ *if for each functor* $H : \mathbb{C}_1 \to \mathbb{C}$ *and each natural transformation* $\alpha : J; H \Rightarrow F$ *there is a unique natural transformation* $\alpha^* : H \Rightarrow K$ *with* $\alpha = (J; \alpha^*) \circ \pi$.

Dually, $\langle K, \eta : F \Rightarrow J; K \rangle$ *is called an* injective Kan extension *if for each functor* $H : \mathbb{C}_1 \to \mathbb{C}$ *and each natural transformation* $\alpha : F \Rightarrow J; H$ *there is a unique natural transformation* $\alpha^* : K \Rightarrow H$ *with* $\alpha = \eta \circ (J; \alpha^*)$.

In the same way as limits are weakened to sketches in [BW96], Kan extensions will be weakened to more general sketches that could be called Kan-sketches, but we will call them again sketches.

It turns out that there is some kind of normal form of sketches, consisting basically of the embedding $J : \mathbb{C}_0 \hookrightarrow \mathbb{C}_1$ of a subcategory $\mathbb{C}_0$ into $\mathbb{C}_1$ and a functor $K : \mathbb{C}_1 \to \mathbb{C}$.

Definition 2. *A commutative diagram*

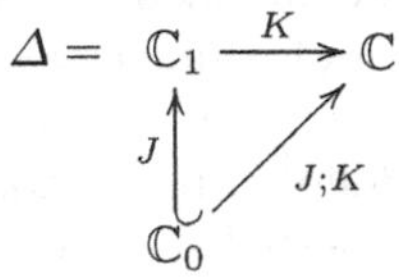

where $J : \mathbb{C}_0 \hookrightarrow \mathbb{C}_1$ *is the embedding of a subcategory defines both an* injective sketch

$$S_{free} = \mathbb{C}_1 \textit{ free over } \mathbb{C}_0 \textit{ with } K : \mathbb{C}_1 \to \mathbb{C}$$

and a projective sketch

$$S_{co-free} = \mathbb{C}_1 \textit{ co-free over } \mathbb{C}_0 \textit{ with } K : \mathbb{C}_1 \to \mathbb{C}$$

in the category $\mathbb{C}$.

A functor $M : \mathbb{C} \to Sem$ *is a* model of S_{free}*, denoted* $M \models S_{free}$*, if the functor* $K; M : \mathbb{C}_1 \to Sem$ *together with the identity as natural transformation is an injective Kan extension of* $K|_{\mathbb{C}_0}; M : \mathbb{C}_0 \to Sem$ *along* $J : \mathbb{C}_0 \to \mathbb{C}_1$*, where* $K|_{\mathbb{C}_0} : \mathbb{C}_0 \to \mathbb{C}$ *denotes the restriction of* $K : \mathbb{C}_1 \to \mathbb{C}$ *to* $\mathbb{C}_0$.

Dually, a functor $M : \mathbb{C} \to Sem$ *is called a model of* $S_{co-free}$*, denoted* $M \models S_{co-free}$*, if* $K; M : \mathbb{C}_1 \to Sem$ *together with the identity as natural transformation is a projective Kan extension of* $K_| \mathbb{C}_0; M : \mathbb{C}_0 \to Sem$ *along* $J : \mathbb{C}_0 \to \mathbb{C}_1$.

If one takes $\mathbb{C} = \mathbb{C}_1 = \mathbf{1}$, $\mathbb{C}_0 = \emptyset$ and $K = Id_{\mathbb{C}}$ the resulting injective and projective sketches describe as models the *initial resp. terminal objects* in a category.

The expressiveness of injective and projective sketches will be illustrated by some examples.

```
INITIAL  is
 free
   obj 0 .
 over
end
```

```
TERMINAL  is
 co-free
   obj  1 .
 over
end
```

In these examples the base category $\mathbb{C}_0$ is the empty category. In the following examples we present non–recursive data and process types.

```
SUM  is
 free
   obj  A+B .
   mor  inA : A -> A+B .
   mor  inB : B -> A+B .
 over
   objs   A B .
end
```

```
PRODUCT  is
 co-free
   obj  A*B .
   mor  prA : A*B -> A .
   mor  prB : A*B -> B .
 over
   objs   A B .
end
```

The next examples illustrate recursive data and process types.

```
NAT1  is
 free
   obj  Nat .
   mor  base : Base -> Nat .
   mor  suc : Nat -> Nat .
 over
   obj  Base .
end

STREAMS  is
 co-free
   obj  Str .
   mor  head : Str -> Base .
   mor  tail : Str -> Str .
 over
   obj  Base .
end
```

In the case of the recursive process type STREAMS the constraint category $\mathbb{C}_{STREAMS} = \mathbb{C}$ equals $\mathbb{C}_1$ and consists of two objects, named Str and Base and of infinitely many morphisms, freely generated by the morphisms $head : Str \rightarrow$

Base, $tail : Str \to Str$. One can easily check that a functor $M : \mathbb{C}_{STREAMS} \to Set$ is a model of the STREAMS–sketch iff $M(Str) = M(Base)^{\mathbb{N}}$, $(M(head))(f) = f(0)$ and $(M(tail))(f) = \lambda x.f(x+1)$ for each $f : \mathbb{N} \to M(Base) \in M(Str)$.

Examples of the conjunctive combination of sketches are given by

```
BOOLE  is
  free
    obj  Boole .
    mor  true : Base -> Boole .
    mor  false : Base -> Boole .
  over
    obj Base .
  and
  TERMINAL with [1 -> Base] .
 end
```

```
TRUE-NAT  is
  free
    obj  Nat .
    mor  base : Base -> Nat .
    mor  suc : Nat -> Nat .
  over
      obj  Base .
  and
  TERMINAL with [1 -> Base] .
 end
```

and

```
NAT-STREAMS  is
  co-free
    obj  Str .
    mor  head : Str -> Base .
    mor  tail : Str -> Str .
  over
    obj  Base .
  and
    TRUE-NAT with [Nat -> Base] .
end
```

3 Nested Sketches

However, the introduced notion of sketches and there conjunctive combinations are not expressive enough to define more complex data and process types, like the parametric data types of finite lists or finite subsets and the parametric process types of sequences (finite and infinite streams) and of image finite transition systems. In case of finite lists the universal property of finite list does not hold within the class of all functors but only within the class of those functors that respect the domain types of the defining constructors which are instances of finite products. Dually, the universal property of sequences does again not hold within the class of all functors, but only within the class of those functors respecting the types of the codomains of the defining observations , i.e., which respect a binary sum and the terminal object since the defining observations would be typed as follows $head : Seq \to Base$, $tail : Seq \to Seq + 1$.

The necessary relativization of the universal properties can be achieved be the concept of **nested sketches** defined in the following.

A nested sketch of nesting depth two in a category $\mathbb{C}$ is given by

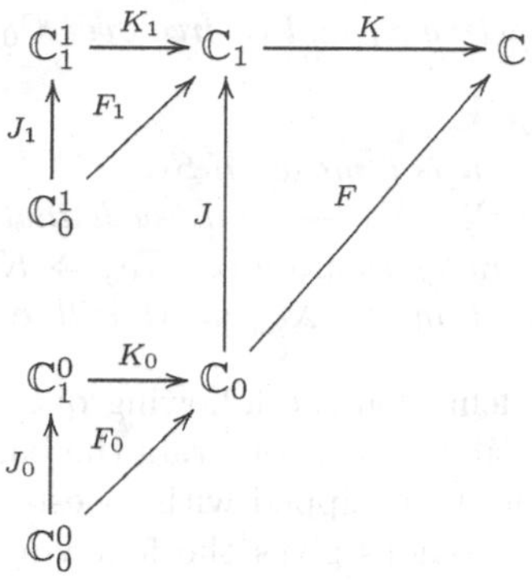

Definition 3. *1. Any finite set of nested sketches in a category* $\mathbb{C}$ *is again a nested sketch in* $\mathbb{C}$*, written*

$$S = \{S_1, \ldots, S_n\},$$

and called the conjunction *of* $S_1, \ldots, S_n$.

2. Let

$$S_{free} = \mathbb{C}_1 \textit{ free } \textit{ over } \mathbb{C}_0 \textit{ with } K : \mathbb{C}_1 \to \mathbb{C}$$

be an injective sketch in $\mathbb{C}$ *and let* S_1 *be a nested sketch in* $\mathbb{C}_1$*. Then*

$$S = \mathbb{C}_1 \textit{ protecting } S_1 \textit{ and free over } \mathbb{C}_0 \textit{ with } K : \mathbb{C}_1 \to \mathbb{C}$$

is an injective nested sketch *in* $\mathbb{C}$.

3. Let

$$S_{cofree} = \mathbb{C}_1 \textit{ co-free } \textit{ over } \mathbb{C}_0 \textit{ with } K : \mathbb{C}_1 \to \mathbb{C}$$

be a projective sketch in $\mathbb{C}$ *and let* S_1 *be a nested sketch in* $\mathbb{C}_1$*. Then*

$$S = \mathbb{C}_1 \textit{ protecting } S_1 \textit{ and co-free over } \mathbb{C}_0 \textit{ with } K : \mathbb{C}_1 \to \mathbb{C}$$

is a projective nested sketch *in* $\mathbb{C}$.

In the following we define under which conditions a functor $M : \mathbb{C} \to Sem$ *is a* model of a nested sketch *in* $\mathbb{C}$*:*

1. $M : \mathbb{C} \to Sem$ *is a model of* $S = \{S_1, \ldots, S_n\}$, $0 \leq n$, *if it is a model for each* S_i, $i = 1, \ldots, n$.
2. $M : \mathbb{C} \to Sem$ *is a model of an injective nested sketch*

$$S = \mathbb{C}_1 \textit{ protecting } S_1 \textit{ and free over } \mathbb{C}_0 \textit{ with } K : \mathbb{C}_1 \to \mathbb{C}$$

if

(a) $(K; M) : \mathbb{C}_1 \to Sem$ *is a model of* S_1.

(b) For each functor $X : \mathbb{C}_1 \to Sem$ *such that* X *is a model of* S_1 *and for each natural transformation* $\alpha : K_{\mathbb{C}_0}; M \Rightarrow X_{\mathbb{C}_0}$ *there is exactly one natural transformation* $\alpha^* : K; M \Rightarrow X$ *with* $\alpha = \alpha^*_{\mathbb{C}_0}$.

3. $M : \mathbb{C} \to Sem$ *is a model of a projective nested sketch*

$$S = \mathbb{C}_1 \text{ protecting } S_1 \text{ and co-free over } \mathbb{C}_0 \text{ with } K : \mathbb{C}_1 \to \mathbb{C}$$

if

(a) $(K; M) : \mathbb{C}_1 \to Sem$ *is a model of* S_1.

(b) For each functor $X : \mathbb{C}_1 \to Sem$ *such that* X *is a model of* S_1 *and for each natural transformation* $\alpha : X_{\mathbb{C}_0} \Rightarrow K_{\mathbb{C}_0}; M$ *there is exactly one natural transformation* $\alpha^* : X_{\mathbb{C}_0} \Rightarrow M$ *with* $\alpha = \alpha^*_{\mathbb{C}_0}$.

With respect to the definition the following question arises naturally: Why there are no sketches possible which constrain the base category $\mathbb{C}_0$ in a sketch, in the same way as $\mathbb{C}_1$ can be equipped with a nested sketch?

The answer to that questions gives the following proposition, which needs some denotational preparation. Let

$$S = \mathbb{C}_1 \text{ protecting } S_1 \text{ and (co-)free over } \mathbb{C}_0 \text{ with } K : \mathbb{C}_1 \to \mathbb{C}$$

be a sketch in $\mathbb{C}$ and let $F : \mathbb{C} \to \mathbb{D}$ be any functor. Then

$$S; F = \mathbb{C}_1 \text{ protecting } S_1 \text{ and (co-)free over } \mathbb{C}_0 \text{ with } (K; F) : \mathbb{C}_1 \to \mathbb{D}$$

denotes the *translation* of S along $F : \mathbb{C} \to \mathbb{D}$.

By induction on the nesting depth of sketches one obtains

Proposition 1. *If* S *is a nested sketch in* $\mathbb{C}$ *and* $F : \mathbb{C} \to \mathbb{D}, H : \mathbb{D} \to \mathbb{E}$ *are functors, then*

$$H \models S; F \;\text{ iff }\; F; H \models S.$$

Using this proposition each nested sketch in a base category $\mathbb{C}_0$ can be translated by means of the inclusion $J : \mathbb{C}_0 \to \mathbb{C}_1$ into a semantically equivalent nested sketch in $\mathbb{C}_1$

The proposition allows to consider nested sketches as an institution in the sense of Goguen and Burstall [GB92]. The category of signatures is the category of finitely presentable categories. In the context of institutions the proposition above just states that the satisfaction condition for the institution of nested sketches is satisfied.

A typical example for the use of nested sketches is the following specification of image finite CCS–processes (without considering the silent action):

```
CCS  is
 co-free
   objs States StateSets  ActionsXStates StatesXStates Boole .
   mor next : ActionsXStates -> StateSets .
   protecting PRODUCT with [A*B -> ActionsXStates,
       A -> Actions, B -> States, prA -> pr1, prB -> pr2] .
   protecting PRODUCT with [A*B -> StatesXStates,
       A -> States, B -> States, prA -> spr1, prB -> spr2] .
```

```
  protecting SETS with [Sets -> StateSets, Elem -> States] .
  protecting BOOLE
over
  obj Actions .
end
```

It it worth to mention, that this specification does not need any of the process composing operations that are used in the original definition given by Milner [Mil80]. Additionally, one has to take into account that this specification does not specify all image finite CCS–processes, but only the most abstract ones, represented as states in the unique terminal model within the class of all image finite CCS–processes.

Whereas image finite CCS–processes can be represented as coalgebras, the concept of coalgebras is not general enough to represent structured transition systems like Petri nets. The following incomplete specification shows in which way for instance P/T-nets can be specified:

```
P/T-NETS  is
  objs   Pl  Tr  PlBags  TrSets  1 .
  mor pre : Tr -> PlBags .
      post : Tr -> PlBags .
      pre* : TrSets -> PlBags .
      post* : TrSets -> PlBags .
      next : PlBagsxTrSets -> PlBags+1 .
  eq      . . .
          . . .
          . . .
  protecting TERMINAL
  protecting SETS with [Sets -> TrSets, ...]
  protecting BAGS with [Bags -> PlBags, ...]
  protecting PROD with [A*B -> PlagsxTrSets, ...]
  protecting SUM with [A+B -> PlBags+1, ...]
end
```

The incomplete specification is a direct translation of the algebraic view at Petri nets as suggested by Meseguer and Montanari [MM90]. The omitted equations define the extension from *pre* and *post* to sets of transitions by means of the union of bags, and they define that the next–operation gives the union of the post–bag of the given transition with the given bag of places if the pre–bag of the given transition is a sub–bag of the given bag of places, otherwise the result is the runtime error represented by 1.

4 Induction, Coinduction and the Generic Model

A basic result that can be proved for the presented categorical model theory is the existence of a generic model.

Definition 4. *Let S be any nested sketch in a category $\mathbb{C}$. A model $M_S : \mathbb{C} \to \mathbb{L}$ is called a generic model of S, if for each model $M : \mathbb{C} \to Sem$ there exists a unique functor $X : \mathbb{L} \to Sem$ with $M = L; X$.*

Theorem 1. *Fore each nested sketch S in a finitely representable category $\mathbb{C}$ there exists (up to isomorphisms) a unique generic model.*

For a proof we refer to [Rei98], where the generic model is constructed successively by adding new morphisms, if for some sketch the existence requirement is not yet satisfied, and by adding new defining equations, if the uniqueness requirement is not yet satisfied. In that way the generic model becomes the injective limit of an enumerable chain of approximating categories.

Intuitively, the generic model is the weakest completion of the category $\mathbb{C}$ such that the universal properties of the sketches in S are satisfied. The existence requirement of the universal property provides a definition principle, corresponding to induction in case of injective sketches and to coinduction in case of projective sketches. The uniqueness requirement of the universal property provides a proof principle which corresponds to inductive respectively to coinductive proofs.

In the classical case of algebraic structures the sketch consists of a conjunction of product sketches. For the generic model this implies the closure with respect to tupeling and sequential composition which leads to the term model, or to that fragment of the Lawvere theory in which the required equations can be formulated.

More interesting is the generic model for sketches containing recursive data types, recursive process types and the combination of recursive data and process types. In that cases the generic model reflects the possibilities of inductive and coinductive function definitions. From Charity, see [CS95,CF92], one knows that the combination of induction and coinduction leads behind primitive recursive functions, since the Ackermann function can be defined in that way.

To illustrate coinductive function definitions we use the following specification.

```
STREAMS-2  is
 co-free
   obj  Str .
   mor  head : Str -> Base .
   mor  tail : Str -> Str .
 over
   obj  Base  BaseXBase  Boole .
   mor  p1, p2 : BaseXBase -> Base .
   mor  op : BaseXBase -> Base   .
   mor  prop : Base -> Boole   .
   protecting PRODUCT with [A*B -> BaseXBase,
     A -> Base, B -> Base, prA -> p1, prB -> p2] .
   protecting BOOLE .
end
```

In order to improve readability we allow to constrain the base category, even if this possibility is not given by the definition, since this constraints can be lifted up. In the given specification `STREAMS-2` beside the unconstrained object *Base* there are two unconstrained morphisms $op : BaseXBase \to Base$ and $prop : Base \to Boole$, representing an arbitrary binary operation and an arbitrary property on the parametric base type.

Using the universal properties of the projective sketches one obtains in the generic model of STREAMS-2 infinitely many additional morphisms. Independently from the binary operation and the property on the base set there exists for each natural number $n \in \mathbb{N}$ a morphism $i_n : Str \to Str$ uniquely defined by the two equations

$$i_n; head = head,$$

$$i_n; tail = \underbrace{tail; \ldots; tail}_{n-times}; i_n.$$

If $M : \mathbb{C}_{STREAMS-2} \to Set$ is any model, then $M(i_n)$ maps any $\sigma \in M(Str)$ to $M(i_n)(\sigma) \in M(Str)(= M(Base)^{\mathbb{N}})$ with $[M(i_n)(\sigma)](x) = \sigma(n * x)$ for each $x \in \mathbb{N}$.

Another morphism $h : Str \to Str$ in the generic model of STREAMS-2 would be given by the following two equations:

$$h; head = \langle head, (tail; head)\rangle; op,$$

$$h; tail = (tail; tail); h,$$

where $\langle head, (tail; head)\rangle : Base \to BaseXBase$ denotes the morphism that is induced by the product sketch from the two morphisms $head : Str \to Base$, $tail; head : Str \to Base$. For any model $M : \mathbb{C}_{STREAMS-2} \to Set$ the meaning of $h : Str \to Str$ is now given by

$$[M(h)(\sigma)](x) = M(op)(\sigma(2 * x), \sigma(2 * x + 1)).$$

In the terminology of Charity and some other functional programming languages these two definitions of morphisms are examples of *unfold*–definitions, *fold*–definitions are related to the definition principles of injective sketches. With respect to the formal foundations of Charity the presented approach has a significant different. Charity relays essentially on the concept of strong categorical data types [CS95,CS92]. The approach of nested sketches doe not need the concept of strength of a functor. Instead of strength of a functor distributivity properties of injective and projective sketches are studied.

We will exemplify the problem by means of the simplest data type, namely `BOOLE`. In which way we have to specify the truth values such that all the usual binary operations on truth values are present in the associated generic model? What happens if we take the following specification?

```
BOOLE1 is
  free
    objs  Boole  BooleXBoole .
    mor  true : Base -> Boole .
    mor  false : Base -> Boole .
    mor  p1, p2 : BooleXBoole -> Boole .
    protecting PRODUCT with [A*B -> BooleXBoole,
       A -> Boole, B -> Boole, prA -> p1, prB -> p2] .
  over
    obj Base .
  and
  TERMINAL with [1 -> Base] .   end
```

What kind of morphisms $m : BooleXBoole \rightarrow Boole$ will be generated in the generic model of BOOLE1? It turns out that there are no other morphisms then the two declared projections, since the product sketch, defining *BooleXBoole*, allows only the definition of morphism with codomain *BooleXBoole*, and the sum sketch, defining *Boole*, allows only the definition of morphisms with domain *Boole*.

In the category of sets it holds $(1+1)\times(1+1) \simeq (1+1)+(1+1)$. This implies, that the in *Set* the product *BooleXBoole* can be represented by *Boole* + *Boole*. The relations between *Boole* + *Boole* and *BooleXBoole* in arbitrary categories can be analyzed by means of the generic model of the following specification:

```
BOOLE2 is
  free
    objs  Boole  BooleXBoole  Boole+Boole .
    mor  true1 : Base -> Boole .
    mor  false1 : Base -> Boole .
    mor  true2 : Boole -> Boole+Boole .
    mor  false2 : Boole -> Boole+Boole .
    mor  p1, p2 : BooleXBoole -> Boole .
    protecting PRODUCT with [A*B -> BooleXBoole,
     A -> Boole, B -> Boole, prA -> p1, prB -> p2] .
    protecting SUM with [A+B -> Boole+Boole,
     A -> Boole, B -> Boole, inA -> true2, inB -> false2] .
  over
    obj Base .
  and
  TERMINAL with [1 -> Base] .
end
```

Using the sum sketch defining *Boole*+*Boole* one obtains the existence of the two morphisms $q_1, q_2 : Boole + Boole \rightarrow Boole$ uniquely defined by the equations:

$$true2; q_1 = id_{Boole},\ \ false2; q_1 = id_{Boole},$$

$$true2; q_2 = !_{Boole}; true1,\ \ false2; q_2 = !_{Boole}; false1,$$

where $!_{Boole} : Boole \to 1$ denotes the unique morphism induced by the universal property of the TERMINAL–sketch. These two morphism in the generic model induce due to the product sketch a unique morphism $q : Boole + Boole \to BooleXBoole$, uniquely defined by the equations $q; p1 = q_1$, $q; p2 = q_2$.

It is not difficult to see that for each model $M : \mathbb{C}_{BOOLE2} \to Set$ the mapping $M'(q) : M(Bool + Boole) \to M(BooleXBoole$ becomes a bijection, where M' denotes the unique functor from the generic model associated to BOOLE2 to Set factorizing the given model M.

If we take the specification

```
D-BOOLE is
  free
    objs  Boole  BooleXBoole  Boole+Boole .
    mor  true1 : Base -> Boole .
    mor  false1 : Base -> Boole .
    mor  true2 :Boole -> Boole+Boole .
    mor  false2 : Boole -> Boole+Boole .
    mor  p1, p2 : BooleXBoole -> Boole .
    mor  q1, q2 : Boole+Boole -> Boole .
    mor  q : Boole+Boole -> BooleXBoole .
    mor  q' : BooleXBoole -> Boole+Boole .
    mor  t : Boole -> 1 .
    eq   q;q' = id(Boole+Boole) .
    eq   q';q = id(BooleXBoole) .
    eq   q;p1 = q1 .
    eq   q;p2 = q2 .
    eq   true2 ; q1 = id(Boole) .
    eq   false2 ; q1 = id(Boole) .
    eq   true2 ; q2 = t ; true1 .
    eq   false2 ; q2 = t ; false1.
    protecting PRODUCT with [A*B -> BooleXBoole,
     A -> Boole, B -> Boole, prA -> p1, prB -> p2] .
    protecting SUM with [A+B -> Boole+Boole,
     A -> Boole, B -> Boole, inA -> true2, inB -> false2] .
  over
    obj Base .
  and
  TERMINAL with [1 -> Base] .
end
```

then BOOLE2 and D-BOOLE have the same models in the category Set, but in a category which does not have the distributivity property only BOOLE2 models exist, since in those categories there is no fitting interpretation for the morphism $q' : BooleXBoole \to Boole + Boole$.

Let D-BOOL-CCS(Act) denote the specification that results from CCS where D-BOOLE is used instead of BOOLE and in which additionally $Action = \sum_{a \in Act} 1$ is assumed.

Proposition 2. *In the generic model of* D-BOOL-CCS(Act) *the set of morphisms from the object States to the object Boole, i.e., the set of truth valued observations of* CCS*–states, coincides with the set of expressions of the Hennessy–Milner logic.*

Proof. Since the specification of the data type of finite sets is not explicitly given we remind of the generators and there defining properties. We assume that the finite sets are generated by the generators $empty : 1 \to Sets$ and $add : BaseXSets \to Sets$ being commutative and idempotent. If $prop : Base \to Boole$ would be any property then the universal property of the nested, injective sketch, defining the data type of finite sets, induces the existence of two morphisms $\forall_{prop} : Sets \to Boole$, $\exists_{prop} : Sets \to Boole$, that are induced by the functor $H_\forall$ with $[Base \mapsto Boole, Sets \mapsto Boole, empty \mapsto true, add \mapsto and]$ and the natural transformation α with $\alpha_{Base} = prop$, respectively by $H_\exists$ with $[Base \mapsto Boole, Sets \mapsto Boole, empty \mapsto false, add \mapsto or]$ and the natural transformation β with $\beta_{Base} = prop$, where *and* respectively *or* denote the conjunction respectively the disjunction of truth values, whose existence in the generic model can be proved by induction on distributive truth values. It is easy to see that both conjunction and disjunction are commutative and idempotent. Therefore the SET–sketch induces the described morphisms. At the very beginning we have only the morphisms $!_{States}; true : States \to Boole$, $!_{States}; false \to Boole$ which imply by the construction above the morphisms

$$\forall_{!_{States};true},\ \exists_{!_{States};true},\ \forall_{!_{States};false},\ \exists_{!_{States};false} : StateSets \to Boole$$

. By induction one can prove that $\forall_{!_{States};true} = (!_{StateSets}); true$, $\exists_{!_{States};false} = (!_{StateSets}); false$ and

$$\exists_{!_{States};true} = (\forall_{!_{StateSets});false}); neg : StateSets \to Boole$$

represents the non-emptyness check for finite sets. For each $a \in Act$ there is the morphism $next(a, \_) : States \to StateSets$ which can be composed with $\exists_{!_{States};true}$ leading to the morphisms

$$next(a, \_); (\exists_{!_{States};true}) : States \to Boole.$$

Evidently, for each model in *Set* the meaning of that morphisme coincides with the formula $\langle a \rangle true$ of the Hennessy-Milner logic. Using the negation and iterating the construction, one gets all and only the formulae of the Hennessy-Milner logic . □

These examples motivate the following observation: *In the generic model of a nested sketch specification there are enough morphisms to generate the elements of data types and enough morphisms representing observations that are able to separate states in process types up to strong bisimulation.*

It is worth to mention, that in the presented approach neither a specific category is chosen as fixed range for semantic interpretations, as it is the case in Lawvere's categorical algebra, nor it is supposed that the category *Sem* has to be an algebraically complete category, [Fre90], which would imply that data types and process types coincide. In many papers on functional programming languages it is claimed, that only algebraically complete categories should be used as ranges for semantic interpretations. Contrary to the functional programming community we just try to exploit the differences between data and process types.

5 Constructive Specifications of Dynamic Properties

We observed above, that in the generic model of a specification enough observations are available to distinguish states with respect to strong bisimulation. What about liveness, safety and fairness properties? Can specifications be extended in such a way that these properties are also represented by truth valued observations?

A *safety property* describes a subset (of states) that is maintained by all operations (state changes). This shows immediately that safety properties are represented by the concept of *sub-structures.* From the point of view of algebraic foundations liveness and fairness properties are more interesting. We conjecture that each morphism in a generic model represents an *effectively computable mapping.* Therefore we do not expect that liveness and fairness properties can be represented by morphisms in the generic models from process type to the type of truth values.

Methodologically safety, liveness and fairness properties can be specified by means of *characterizing properties of the declared state changing operations and observations, and also by means of additional, characterizing observations and their properties.*

In the following we illustrate this methodology by typical examples.

Safety property of CCS processes:
Let us assume that there is given a morphisms $bad : Action \to Boole$, representing a property of actions. The safety property that a bad action can never be executed is formalized by the following conditional equation:

$$empty(next(a, s)) = true \quad \textbf{if} \quad bad(a) = true.$$

Fairness properties:
With respect to the example `STREAMS-2` of streams some fairness property would be given by the subset of all those streams that contain infinitely many elements satisfying some given basic property: *always sometimes* $prop(head(s)) = true$. For the given example one can effectively compute for each stream, satisfying the fairness property, a natural number which represents the length of the initial segment consisting only of elements having not the required property, and this function can only be computed for those streams satisfying the fairness property. This observation leads to the following specification:

```
p_FAIRSTREAMS  is  STREAMS-2  and
   co-free
   objs  FStreams  Nat  NatxFSteams .
```

```
  mor  head : FStreams -> Base .
       tail : FStreams -> FStreams .
          g : FStreams -> Nat .
       read : NatxFStreams -> FStreams .
  vars  x : Nat  s : FStreams .
  eq   read(zero,s) = s .
       read(succ(x),s) = tail(read(x,s)) .
       prop(head(read(g(s),s))) = true .
  ceq  prop(head(read(x,s))) = false  if  less(x,g(s)) = true .
  protecting NAT .
  protecting PROD with{A*B -> NatxFStreams, ...}
  over
  obj  Base  .
end
```

In the generic model there is now a morphisms $fair : FStreams \rightarrow Str$ which embeds the corresponding subtype of fair streams into the process type of all streams.

Terminating processes:
To illustrate this kind of dynamic properties we use the process type SEQUENCE of finite and infinite sequences of elements of the parametric base type *Base*:

```
SEQUENCES  is
  co-free
    obj   Seq  BasexSeq  BasexSeq+1 .
    mor   next : Seq -> BasexSeq+1 .
    protecting PROD with (A*B -> BasexSeq, A -> Base,
          B -> Seq, prA -> pr1, prB -> pr2}
    protecting SUM with{A+B -> BasexSeq+1,
          A -> BasexSeq, inA -> i, inB -> i1} .
    protecting TERMINAL with{1 -> B} .
  over
    obj   Base .
end
```

In the following specification of terminating sequences we give an explicit construction of the terminating processes.

```
SEQUENCES1 is  SEQUENCES and
  free
  obj  Lists  BasexLists  BasexLists+1  .
  mor cons : BasexLists+1 -> Lists  .
  mor decons : Lists -> BasexLists+1 .
  var  l : Lists  x : BasexLists+1  .
  eq   cons(decons(l)) = l .
  eq   decons(cons(x)) = x  .
  protecting PROD with {A*B -> BasexLists, A -> Base,
```

```
      B -> Lists, ...} .
  protecting SUM with {A+B -> BasexLists+1,
      A -> BasexLists,...}
  protecting TERMINAL with {1 -> B}
  over
  obj Base
end
```

We extend the specification **SEQUENCES** by the initial data type of finite lists over the common base type **Base** together with an additional operation of decomposing lists. The operation *decons* allows to see finite lists as processes of the process type *Seq*. Therefore, the universal property of the process type induces in the generic model of the specification **SEQUENCES1** a unique morphism

$$fin : Lists \rightarrow Seq$$

characterized by the equation

$$fin; next = decons; [id_{Base} \times fin, id_1],$$

where

$$[id_{Base} \times fin, id_1] : \mathtt{BasexLists} + 1 \rightarrow \mathtt{BasexSeq} + 1\,.$$

This three examples can only give a fist impression of the diversity of possibilities to specify dynamic properties in a constructive style. This section is far from a comprehensive investigation of *constructive specifications of dynamic properties of processes.* Even the concept of constructive specifications is still on the intuitive level. Whether the presented approach is a sufficient formalization has to be investigated in future. But, we argue that usual temporal logics like CTL* or the μ–calculus can not be used for constructive specifications of dynamic properties.

6 Concluding Remarks

The presented uniform model theory for data and process types is evidently in a rudimentary state. The presented approach needs both, a deeper mathematical foundation and applications to more demanding applications in systems specification. With respect to the mathematical foundations the author got the information from anonymous referees that in 1987 Christian Lair, [Lai87] has developed a more general categorical approach. So it remains for future work to use this more general mathematical foundation for the intended applications and to check if this approach offers additional possibilities.

The chosen formalization by nested sketches offers some possibilities for more general notions. One possibility would be to abstain from the existence requirement of the universal property of Kan extensions. In that case, the definition principle is lost, but still the proof principles of inductive and coinductive proofs are available. This would relate the presented approach to the most recent approach of Hidden Algebras with binary methods [GR99]. In that case the existence of terminal model is not guaranteed, but still coinductive proof techniques can be developed and applied.

Another topic that could be studied is given by *partial methods.* Partial methods make visible the difference in the external behavior of a divergent process, performing for ever internal action, and of a lazy process that is not able to perform any action. If an external user tries to activate the lazy process, he gets after a finite time the information that the lazy process is not able, or not willing, to interact with the user, with the exception to give the user exactly this information.

References

AKKB99. E. Astesiano, H.-J. Kreowski, and B. Krieg-Brücker, editors. *Algebraic Foundations of Systems Specification.* IFIP state-of-the-art reports. Springer, 1999. 349

BW96. M. Barr and C. Wells. *Category Theory for Computing Science (second edition).* International series in computer science. Prentice Hall, 1996. 349, 350

CF92. J. R. B. Cockett and T. Fukushima. About charity. Technical Report 92/480/18, Department of Computer Science, University of Calgary, 1992. 356

CS92. J. R. B. Cockett and D. Spencer. Strong categorical datatypes i. In R. A. G. Seely, editor, *Canadian Mathematical Society Proceedings.* Montreal, 1992. 357

CS95. J. R. B. Cockett and D. Spencer. Strong categorical datatypes ii: A term logic for categorical programming. *Theoretical Computer Science*, 139:69–113, 1995. 356, 357

Fre90. Peter Freyd. Algebraically complete categories. In A. Carboni et al, editor, *1990 Como Category Theory Conference*, volume 1488 of *Lecture Notes in Math.*, pages 95–104. Springer, Berlin, 1990. 361

GB92. J. A. Goguen and R. M. Burstall. Institutions: Abstract model theory for specification and programming. *Journal of the Association for Computing Machinery*, 39:95–146, 1992. 354

GR99. Joseph Goguen and Grigore Rosu. Hiding more of hidden algebra. In J. M. Wing, J. Woodcock, and J. Davies, editors, *FM'99 - Formal Methods, Volume II*, volume 1709 of *Lecture Notes in Math.*, pages 1704–1719. Springer, Berlin, 1999. 364

JR97. Bart Jacobs and Jan Rutten. A tutorial on (co)algebras and (co)induction. *Bulletin of the EATCS*, (62):222–259, June 1997. 349

Lai87. Christian Lair. Trames et semantiques categoriques des systems de trames. *Diagrammes*, 19, 1987. 363

Law63. F. W. Lawvere. Functorial semantics of algebraic theories. *Proc. Nat. Acad. Sci. U. S. A.*, 50:869–873, 1963. 349

Mil80. R. Milner. *A Calculus of Communicating Systems*, volume 92 of *Lecture Notes in Computer Science.* Springer–Verlag, 1980. 355

ML71. Saunders Mac Lane. *Categories for the Working Mathematician.* Springer Verlag, 1971. 349

MM90. Jose Meseguer and Ugo Montanari. Petri nets are monoids. *Information and Computation*, 88:105–155, 1990. 355

oLD98. CoFI Task Group on Langugage Design. Casl, the common algebraic specification language (summary). Technical report, CoFI: The Common Framework Initiative, 1998. 348

Rei98. Horst Reichel. Nested sketches. Technical Report ECS-LFCS-98-401, Edinburgh University, Laboratory for Foundations of Computer Science, December 1998. 349, 356

Relating Abstract Datatypes and Z-Schemata*

Hubert Baumeister

University of Munich, Institute of Computer Science,
Oettingenstr. 67, D-80358 Munich, Germany
baumeist@informatik.uni-muenchen.de

Abstract. In this paper we investigate formally the relationship between the notion of abstract datatypes in an arbitrary institution, found in algebraic specification languages like Clear, ASL, and CASL; and the notion of schemata from the model-oriented specification language Z. To this end the institution $\mathcal{S}$ of the logic underlying Z is defined, and a translation of Z-schemata to abstract datatypes over $\mathcal{S}$ is given. The notion of a schema is internal to the logic of Z, and thus specification techniques of Z relying on the notion of a schema can only be applied in the context of Z. By translating Z-schemata to abstract datatypes, these specification techniques can be transformed to specification techniques using abstract datatypes. Since the notion of abstract datatypes is institution independent, this results in a separation of these specification techniques from the specification language Z and allows them to be applied in the context of other, e.g. algebraic, specification languages.

1 Introduction

As already noted by Spivey [12], schema-types, as used in the model-oriented specification language Z, are closely related to many-sorted signatures, and schemata are related to the notion of abstract datatypes found in algebraic specification languages.

Z is a model-oriented specification language based on set-theory. In the model-oriented approach to the specification of software systems, specifications are explicit system models constructed out of either abstract or concrete primitives. This is in contrast to the approach used with algebraic or property-oriented specification languages like CASL [10], which identifies the interface of a software module, consisting of sorts and functions, and states the properties of the interface components using first-order formulas.

Specifications written in Z are structured using schemata and operations on schemata. A schema denotes a set of bindings of the form $\{(x_1, v_1), \ldots, (x_n, v_n)\}$. Operations on schemata include restriction of the elements of a schema to those satisfying a formula; logical operations like negation, conjunction, disjunction, and quantification; and renaming and hiding of the components of a schema. Schemata, and thus the structuring mechanism of Z, are elements of the logic

* This research has been partially supported by ESPRIT working group 29432 (CoFI WG).

D. Bert, C. Choppy, and P. Mosses (Eds.): WADT'99, LNCS 1827, pp. 366–382, 2000.

used by Z. This, on one hand, has the advantage of using Z again to reason about the structure of a specification, but, on the other hand, has the disadvantage that development methods and theoretical results referring to the structure of specifications cannot be easily transfered to other specification languages based on different logics.

In contrast, the structuring primitives of property-oriented specification languages can be formulated independent from the logic underlying the particular specification language. This is done by using the notion of an institution introduced by Goguen and Burstall [6] to formalize the informal notion of a logical system. The building blocks of specifications are abstract datatypes, which consist of an interface and a class of possible implementations of that interface. Operations on abstract datatypes are the restriction of the implementations to those satisfying a set of formulas; the union of abstract datatypes; and hiding, adding and renaming of interface components. What exactly constitutes the components of an interface and how they are interpreted in implementations depends on the institution underlying the specification language. For example, in the institution of equational logic the components of an interface are sorts and operations. The implementations interpret the sorts as sets and the operations as functions on these sets.

The goal of this paper is to formalize the relationship between schemata and abstract datatypes, and to show a correspondence between the operations on abstract datatypes and operations on schemata. This relationship can be used to transfer results and methods from Z to property-oriented specification languages and vice versa. For example, the Z-style for the specification of sequential systems can be transfered to property-oriented specification languages [2]. Further, the correspondence between operations on abstract datatypes and operations on schema suggests new operations on abstract datatypes like negation and disjunction.

However, we cannot compare schemata with abstract datatypes in an arbitrary institution; instead, we have to define first an institution $\mathcal{S}$ which formalizes the notion of the set-theory used in Z, and then compare schemata with abstract datatypes in this institution. The definition of the institution $\mathcal{S}$ has the further advantage that it can be used to define a variant of the specification language CASL, CASL-$\mathcal{S}$, based on set-theory instead of order-sorted partial first-order logic. This is possible because the semantics of most of CASL is largely independent from a particular institution (cf. Mossakowski [9]).

2 Institutions and Abstract Datatypes

The notion of institutions attempts to formalize the informal notion of a logical system, and was developed by Goguen and Burstall [6] as a means to define the semantics of the specification language Clear [4] independent from a particular logic.

Definition 1 (Institution). *An institution* $\mathcal{I} = \langle \text{SIGN}_{\mathcal{I}}, \mathsf{Str}_{\mathcal{I}}, \mathsf{Sen}_{\mathcal{I}}, \models^{\mathcal{I}} \rangle$ *consists of*

- *a category of* signatures $\text{SIGN}_{\mathcal{I}}$,
- *a functor* $\mathsf{Str}_{\mathcal{I}} : \text{SIGN}_{\mathcal{I}}^{op} \to \text{CAT}$ *assigning to each signature* Σ *the category of* Σ*-structures and to each signature morphism* $\sigma : \Sigma \to \Sigma'$ *the reduct functor* $\_|_{\sigma} : \mathsf{Str}_{\mathcal{I}}(\Sigma') \to \mathsf{Str}_{\mathcal{I}}(\Sigma)$,
- *a functor* $\mathsf{Sen}_{\mathcal{I}} : \text{SIGN}_{\mathcal{I}} \to \text{SET}$ *assigning to each signature* Σ *the set of* Σ-formulas *and to each signature morphism* $\sigma : \Sigma \to \Sigma'$ *a translation* $\overline{\sigma}$ *of* Σ*-formulas to* Σ'*-formulas, and*
- *a family of* satisfaction relations $\models^{\mathcal{I}}{}_{\Sigma} \subseteq \mathsf{Str}_{\mathcal{I}}(\Sigma) \times \mathsf{Sen}_{\mathcal{I}}(\Sigma)$ *for* $\Sigma \in \text{SIGN}_{\mathcal{I}}$ *indicating whether a* Σ*-formula* φ *is valid in a* Σ*-structure* m*, written* $m \models^{\mathcal{I}}{}_{\Sigma} \varphi$ *or for short* $m \models^{\mathcal{I}} \varphi$,

such that the satisfaction condition *holds: for all signature morphisms* $\sigma : \Sigma \to \Sigma'$*, formulas* $\varphi \in \mathsf{Sen}_{\mathcal{I}}(\Sigma)$*, and structures* $m' \in \mathsf{Str}_{\mathcal{I}}(\Sigma')$ *we have*

$$m'|_{\sigma} \models^{\mathcal{I}} \varphi \text{ if and only if } m' \models^{\mathcal{I}} \overline{\sigma}(\varphi)$$

We may write $M \models^{\mathcal{I}} \varphi$ for a class of Σ-structures M and a Σ-formula φ instead of $\forall m \in M\colon\ m \models^{\mathcal{I}} \varphi$, and similar for $m \models^{\mathcal{I}} \Phi$ and $M \models^{\mathcal{I}} \Phi$ for a set of Σ-formulas Φ and a Σ-structure m.

Traditionally, an abstract datatype (Σ, M) is a specification of a datatype in a software system. The signature Σ defines the external interface as a collection of sort and function symbols, and M is a class of Σ-algebras considered admissible implementations of that datatype. In the context of an arbitrary institution $\mathcal{I}$ an *abstract datatype* is a pair (Σ, M) where Σ is an element of $\text{SIGN}_{\mathcal{I}}$ and M is a full subcategory of $\mathsf{Str}_{\mathcal{I}}(\Sigma)$.

The basic operations on abstract datatypes are I_{Φ} (impose), D_{σ} (derive), T_{σ} (translate), and $+$ (union) (cf. Sannella and Wirsing [11]):

Impose allows to impose additional requirements on an abstract datatype. The semantics of an expression $I_{\Phi}(\Sigma, M)$ is the abstract datatype (Σ, M') where M' consists of all Σ-structures m in M satisfying all formulas in Φ, i.e.

$$I_{\Phi}(\Sigma, M) = (\Sigma, \{m \in M \mid m \models^{\mathcal{I}} \Phi\}).$$

The *translate* operation can be used to rename symbols in a signature, but also to add new symbols to a signature. If σ is a signature morphism from Σ to Σ' then the expression $T_{\sigma}(\Sigma, M)$ denotes an abstract datatype (Σ', M') where M' contains all Σ'-structures m which are extensions of some Σ-structure m in M, i.e.

$$T_{\sigma}(\Sigma, M) = (\Sigma', \{m' \in \mathsf{Str}_{\mathcal{I}}(\Sigma') \mid m'|_{\sigma} \in M\}).$$

The *derive* operation allows to hide parts of a signature. $D_{\sigma}(\Sigma', M')$ denotes the abstract datatype having as signature the domain of σ and as models the translations of the models of SP by $\_|_{\sigma}$, i.e.

$$D_{\sigma}(\Sigma', M') = (\Sigma, \{m'|_{\sigma} \mid m' \in M'\}).$$

At last, the *union* operation is used to combine two specifications. Since for arbitrary institutions the union of signatures is not defined, we have to require that both specifications have the same signature. To form the union of two specifications of different signatures Σ_1 and Σ_2, one has to provide a signature Σ and signature morphisms $\sigma_1 : \Sigma_1 \to \Sigma$ and $\sigma_2 : \Sigma_2 \to \Sigma$, and write $T_{\sigma_1}\mathrm{SP}_1 + T_{\sigma_2}\mathrm{SP}_2$. The semantics of $(\Sigma, M_1) + (\Sigma, M_2)$ is the abstract datatype (Σ, M') where M' is the intersection M_1 and M_2, i.e.

$$(\Sigma, M_1) + (\Sigma, M_2) = (\Sigma, M_1 \cap M_2).$$

3 The Institution $\mathcal{S}$

In this section we introduce the components of the institution $\mathcal{S}$ formalizing a reasonable large subset of the logic underlying the specification language Z from the Z standard [13]. What is missing, for example, are generic definitions. Other constructs, like the free type construct, can be easily added and their semantics defined by transformation as it is done in the Z standard. We also don't treat the types and operations defined in the prelude and the mathematical toolkit, e.g. natural numbers; these can be easily added if needed.

Note that this is not an attempt to give a semantics to the Z specification language. The relationship between $\mathcal{S}$ and Z is similar to the relationship between the institution of equational logic and the semantics of a specification language based on this institution.

3.1 Signatures

A signature Σ in $\mathrm{SIGN}_{\mathcal{S}}$ consists of a set of names for *given-types* G and a set of *global-variables* O. Each global-variable id in O is associated with a type $\tau(id)$ built from the names of given-types and the constructors cartesian product, power-set, and schema-type. Note that $\mathcal{S}$ has no type constructor for function types. Instead, a function from T_1 to T_2 is identified with its graph and is of type $\mathcal{P}(T_1 \times T_2)$. This allows functions to be treated as sets and admits higher-order functions, as functions may take as arguments the graph of a function and also return the graph of a function.

Definition 2 (Signatures). *Let F and V be two disjoint, recursive enumerable sets of names. A signature Σ in $\mathrm{SIGN}_{\mathcal{S}}$ is a tuple (G, O, τ) where G and O are finite disjoint subsets of F. The function τ assigns each name in O a type in $\mathcal{T}(G)$, where $\mathcal{T}(G)$ is inductively defined by:*

- $G \subseteq \mathcal{T}(G)$
- *(product-type)* $T_1 \times \cdots \times T_n \in \mathcal{T}(G)$ *for* $T_i \in \mathcal{T}(G)$, $1 \leq i \leq n$
- *(power-set-type)* $\mathcal{P}(T) \in \mathcal{T}(G)$ *for* $T \in \mathcal{T}(G)$
- *(schema-type)* $<x_1 : T_1, \ldots, x_n : T_n> \in \mathcal{T}(G)$ *for* $T_i \in \mathcal{T}(G)$ *and* $x_i \in V$ *and* $x_i \neq x_j$ *for* $1 \leq i, j \leq n$.

Note that the elements of $\mathcal{T}(G)$ are names of types and not sets; therefore the type constructors $\mathcal{P}(\_)$ and $\times$ should not be confused with the familiar operations on sets.

The function $\mathcal{T}$, mapping a set of given-type names G to $\mathcal{T}(G)$, is extended to a functor from SET to SET by extending the function $f : G \to G'$ to a function $\mathcal{T}(f) : \mathcal{T}(G) \to \mathcal{T}(G')$ as follows:

- $\mathcal{T}(f)(g) = f(g)$ for $g \in G$,
- $\mathcal{T}(f)(T_1 \times \ldots \times T_n) = \mathcal{T}(f)(T_1) \times \ldots \times \mathcal{T}(f)(T_n)$ for $T_1, \ldots, T_n \in \mathcal{T}(G)$,
- $\mathcal{T}(f)(\mathcal{P}(T)) = \mathcal{P}(\mathcal{T}(f)(T))$ for $T \in \mathcal{T}(G)$,
- $\mathcal{T}(f)(<x_1 : T_1, \ldots, x_n : T_n>) = <x_1 : \mathcal{T}(f)(T_1), \ldots, x_n : \mathcal{T}(f)(T_n)>$ for $T_1, \ldots, T_n \in \mathcal{T}(G)$.

A signature morphism $\sigma : (G, O, \tau) \to (G', O', \tau')$ is a pair of maps between the given-types and the set of global-variables.

Definition 3 (Signature-Morphisms). *A signature morphism σ from a signature (G, O, τ) to a signature (G', O', τ') is a pair of functions $\sigma_G : G \to G'$ and $\sigma_O : O \to O'$ such that σ_G and σ_O are compatible with τ and τ', that is $\tau; \mathcal{T}(\sigma_G) = \sigma_O; \tau'$.*

The category $\text{SIGN}_\mathcal{S}$ has as objects signatures $\Sigma = (G, O, \tau)$ and as morphisms signature morphisms $\sigma = (\sigma_G, \sigma_O)$ as defined above.

Example 1. As an example consider the following small Z specification of a bank account which defines a given-type *Integer*, a global-variable +, and a schema *ACCOUNT*:

[*Integer*]

| $+ : Integer \times Integer \to Integer$

ACCOUNT
---
bal : *Integer*

The signature of this specification is $\Sigma = (\{Integer\}, \{+, ACCOUNT\}, \tau)$ where τ maps + to the type $\mathcal{P}(Integer \times Integer \times Integer)$ and $ACCOUNT$ to the type $\mathcal{P}(<bal : Integer>)$. Note that the function type of + is translated to the type $\mathcal{P}(Integer \times Integer \times Integer)$ of its graph.

A property necessary for writing modular specifications is the cocompleteness of the category of signatures of an institution.

Theorem 1. *The category $\text{SIGN}_\mathcal{S}$ is finitely cocomplete.*

The colimit of a functor $F : J \to \text{SIGN}_\mathcal{S}$ is given by the colimits of the sets of given-type names and the sets of global-variables. Let $F(i) = (G_i, O_i, \tau_i)$. If the functor F_G from J to SET is defined by $F_G(i) = G_i$ and the functor F_O from J to SET by $F_O(i) = O_i$, then the colimit (G, O, τ) of F is given by the colimit G of F_G and the colimit O of F_O. The function τ is uniquely determined by the colimit property of G. Note that, because we have assumed that the set of given-type names and the set of global-variables are finite, $\text{SIGN}_\mathcal{S}$ is only finitely cocomplete

3.2 Structures

Given a signature $\Sigma = (G, O, \tau)$, a Σ-structure A interprets each given-type in G as a set from SET and each global-variable *id* in O as a value of the set corresponding to the type of *id*.

Definition 4 (Σ-structures). *For a given signature $\Sigma = (G, O, \tau)$ the category $\mathsf{Str}_S(\Sigma)$ of Σ-structures has as objects pairs (A_G, A_O) where A_G is a functor from the set G, viewed as a discrete category, to* SET, *and A_O is the set $\{(o_1, v_1), \ldots, (o_n, v_n)\}$ for $O = \{o_1, \ldots, o_n\}$ and $v_i \in \bar{A}_G(\tau(o_i))$. The functor $\bar{A}_G : \mathcal{T}(G) \to$ SET is given by:*

- $\bar{A}_G(T) = A_G(T)$ *for* $T = g$ *and* $g \in G$
- $\bar{A}_G(T_1 \times \cdots \times T_n) = (\bar{A}_G(T_1) \times \cdots \times \bar{A}_G(T_n))$ *for* $T_1 \times \cdots \times T_n \in \mathcal{T}(G)$
- $\bar{A}_G(\mathcal{P}(T)) = 2^{\bar{A}_G(T)}$ *for* $\mathcal{P}(T) \in \mathcal{T}(G)$
- $\bar{A}_G(<x_1 : T_1, \ldots, x_n : T_n>)$
$$= \{\{(x_1, v_1), \ldots, (x_n, v_n)\} \mid v_i \in \bar{A}_g(T_i),\ i \in 1 \ldots n\}$$
for $<x_1 : T_1, \ldots, x_n : T_n> \in \mathcal{T}(G)$.

Example 2. An example of a structure A over the signature defined in Ex. 1 consists of a function A_G mapping *Integer* to Z and the set

$$A_O = \{(ACCOUNT, \{\{(bal, n)\} \mid n \in \mathrm{Z}\}), (+, graph(\lambda(x, y).x + y))\}.$$

The notation *graph*(f) is used to denote the graph of a function $f : T \to T'$.

A morphism h from a Σ-structure A to a Σ-structure B is a family of functions between the interpretations of the given-types which is compatible with the interpretations of the global-variables in O.

Definition 5 (Σ-homomorphism). *A Σ-homomorphism h from a structure $A = (A_G, A_O)$ to a structure $B = (B_G, B_O)$ is a natural transformation $h : A_G \Rightarrow B_G$ for which $\bar{h}_{\tau(o)}(v_A) = v_B$ for all $o \in O$, $(o, v_A) \in A_O$ and $(o, v_B) \in B_O$ holds. $\bar{h}$ is the extension of $h : A_G \Rightarrow B_G$ to $h : \bar{A}_G \Rightarrow \bar{B}_G$ given by:*

- $\bar{h}_T(v) = h_T(v)$ *for* $T \in G$ *and* $v \in \bar{A}_G(T)$
- $\bar{h}_T((v_1, \ldots, v_n)) = (\bar{h}_{T_1}(v_1), \ldots, \bar{h}_{T_n}(v_n))$ *for* $T = T_1 \times \cdots \times T_n \in \mathcal{T}(G)$ *and* $(v_1, \ldots, v_n) \in \bar{A}_G(T)$
- $\bar{h}_T(S) = \{\bar{h}_{T'}(v) \mid v \in S\}$ *for* $T = \mathcal{P}(T') \in \mathcal{T}(G)$ *and* $S \in \bar{A}_G(T)$
- $\bar{h}_T(\{(x_1, v_1), \ldots, (x_n, v_n)\}) = \{(x_1, \bar{h}_{T_1}(v_1)), \ldots, (x_n, \bar{h}_{T_n}(v_n))\}$ *for* $T = <x_1 : T_1, \ldots, x_n : T_n> \in \mathcal{T}(G)$ *and* $\{(x_1, v_1), \ldots, (x_n, v_n)\} \in \bar{A}_G(T)$

Definition 6 (σ-reduct). *Given a signature morphism σ from $\Sigma = (G, O, \tau)$ to $\Sigma' = (G', O', \tau')$ in* SIGNS *and a Σ'-structure $A = (A_G, A_O)$, the σ-reduct of A, written $A|_\sigma$, is the Σ-structure $B = (B_G, B_O)$ given by:*

- $B_G = \sigma_G; A_G$
- $B_O = \{(o, v) \mid (\sigma_O(o), v) \in A_O,\ o \in O\}$

For a Σ'-homomorphism $h : A \to B$ the σ-reduct is defined as $h|_\sigma = \sigma_G; h$.

Definition 7 ($\mathsf{Str}_\mathcal{S}$). *The contravariant functor $\mathsf{Str}_\mathcal{S}$ from $\mathrm{SIGN}_\mathcal{S}$ to CAT assigns to each signature Σ the category having as objects Σ-structures and as morphisms Σ-homomorphisms, and to each $\mathrm{SIGN}_\mathcal{S}$-morphism σ from Σ to Σ' the functor from the category $\mathsf{Str}_\mathcal{S}(\Sigma')$ to the category $\mathsf{Str}_\mathcal{S}(\Sigma)$ mapping a Σ-structure A and a Σ-homomorphism to their σ-reduct.*

If an institution has amalgamation, two structures A and B over different signatures Σ_A and Σ_B can be always combined provided that the common components of both signatures are interpreted the same in A and B. This allows to build larger structures from smaller ones in a modular way. An institution has amalgamation if and only if its structure functor preserves pushouts, i.e. maps pushout diagrams in $\mathrm{SIGN}_\mathcal{I}$ to pullback diagrams in the category of categories. The functor $\mathsf{Str}_\mathcal{S}$ not only preserves pushouts but also arbitrary finite colimits.

Theorem 2. *The functor $\mathsf{Str}_\mathcal{S}$ preserves finite colimits.*

3.3 Expressions

The Σ-formulas are first-order formulas over expressions denoting sets and elements in sets. Expressions can be tested for equality and membership. An important category of expressions, called schema-expressions S, denote sets of elements of schema-type. Schema-expressions will be discussed later in this paper.

$$E ::= id \mid (E, \dots, E) \mid E.i \mid <x_1 := E, \dots, x_n := E> \mid E.x \mid E(E)$$
$$\mid \{E, \dots, E\} \mid \{S \bullet E\} \mid \mathcal{P}(E) \mid E \times \dots \times E \mid S$$

The function application $E_1(E_2)$ is well-formed if E_1 is of type $\mathcal{P}(T_1 \times T_2)$ and E_2 is of type T_1. The result is of type T_2. If E_1 represents the graph of a total function, then $E_1(E_2)$ yields the result of that function applied to E_2. Otherwise, if E_1 is the graph of a partial function or not functional at all, then the result of the function application where E_2 is not in the domain of that function or where several results are associated with E_2 in E_1 is not specified in the Z standard [13]. This leaves room for different treatments of undefinedness. A possible choice described in the standard and which we will adopt in this paper is to choose an arbitrary value from $\bar{A}_G(T_2)$ in these cases.

Well-formedness of expressions over a signature $\Sigma = (G, O, \tau)$ is defined wrt. an *environment* $\epsilon = (\Sigma, (X, \tau_X))$ which consists of the signature Σ, a set of variables $X \subset V$, and a function $\tau_X : X \to \mathcal{T}(G)$ mapping a variable to its type.

We use the notation $\epsilon[<x_1 : T_1, \dots, x_n : T_n>]$ to denote the environment $(\Sigma, (X', \tau'_X))$ given by $X' = X \cup \{x_1, \dots, x_n\}$ and

$$\tau'_X(id) = \begin{cases} T_i & \text{if } id = x_i \text{ for some } 1 \le i \le n \\ \tau_X(id) & \text{else} \end{cases}$$

An expression E is well-formed with respect to ϵ if

- $E = id$ and $id \in X \cup O \cup G$. The type of E wrt. ϵ is

$$\tau^{\epsilon}(E) = \begin{cases} \tau_X(id) & \text{if } id \text{ is in } X, \\ \tau(id) & \text{if } id \text{ is in } O, \\ \mathcal{P}(id) & \text{if } id \text{ is in } G. \end{cases}$$

- $E = (E_1, \dots, E_n)$ and each E_i is well-formed for all $1 \leq i \leq n$. Then $\tau^{\epsilon}(E) = \tau^{\epsilon}(E_1) \times \ldots \times \tau^{\epsilon}(E_n)$.
- $E = E_1.i$, $\tau^{\epsilon}(E_1) = T_1 \times \ldots \times T_n$ and $1 \leq i \leq n$. The type of E is T_i.
- $E = <x_1 := E_1, \dots, x_n := E_n>$, $x_i \in V$, $x_i \neq x_j$, and each E_i is well-formed. The type of E is $<x_1 : \tau^{\epsilon}(E_1), \dots, x_n : \tau^{\epsilon}(E_n)>$.
- $E = E_1.x$, $\tau^{\epsilon}(E_1) = <x_1 : T_1, \dots, x_n : T_n>$ and $x = x_i$ for some $1 \leq i \leq n$. The type of E is T_i.
- $E_1(E_2)$, $\tau^{\epsilon}(E_1) = \mathcal{P}(T_1 \times T_2)$ and $\tau^{\epsilon}(E_2) = T_1$. The type of E is T_2.
- $E = \{E_1, \dots, E_n\}$, each E_i is well-formed, and all E_i have the same type T for $1 \leq i \leq n$. The type of E is $\mathcal{P}(T)$.
- $E = \{S \bullet E_1\}$, S is well-formed and has type $\mathcal{P}(<x_1 : T_1, \dots, x_n : T_n>)$, and E_1 is well-formed with respect to $\epsilon[<x_1 : T_1, \dots, x_n : T_n>]$. The type of E is $\mathcal{P}(\tau^{\epsilon'}(E_1))$.
- $E = \mathcal{P}(E_1)$ and E_1 is well-formed. The type of E is $\mathcal{P}(\tau^{\epsilon}(E_1))$.
- $E = E_1 \times \ldots \times E_n$ and each E_i is well-formed. The type of E is $\mathcal{P}(\tau^{\epsilon}(E_i) \times \ldots \times \tau^{\epsilon}(E_n))$.
- $E = S$ and S is a well-formed schema-expression with respect to ϵ (well-formedness of schema-expressions is defined later in this paper.) The type of E is the type of S with respect to ϵ.

Let E be an expression well-formed with respect to an environment $\epsilon = (\Sigma, (X, \tau_X))$, and let $A = (A_G, A_O)$ be a Σ-structure. The semantics of an expression E is given with respect to a *variable binding* β compatible with the environment ϵ. Let $X = \{x_1, \dots, x_n\}$, a variable binding $\beta = (A, A_X)$ *compatible* with ϵ consists of a Σ-structure A and a set $A_X = \{(x_1, v_1) \ldots (x_n, v_n)\}$ with $v_i \in \bar{A}_G(\tau_X(x_i))$ for all $1 \leq i \leq n$.

If $v = \{(x_1, v_1), \dots, (x_n, v_n)\}$ is an element of type $T = <x_1 : T_1, \dots, x_n : T_n>$ then the notation $\beta[v]$ is used to describe the variable binding (A, A'_X) where (x_i, v_i) is in A'_x iff (x_i, v_i) is in v or (x_i, v_i) is in A_X but not in v.

Now the semantics of an expression E wrt. β is defined as follows:

- $[\![id]\!]^{\beta} = v$ if $(id, v) \in A_X$ and $id \in X$ or $(id, v) \in A_O$ and $id \in O$, or $[\![id]\!]^{\beta} = A_G(id)$ if id is in G.
- $[\![(E_1, \dots, E_n)]\!]^{\beta} = ([\![E_1]\!]^{\beta}, \dots, [\![E_n]\!]^{\beta})$.
- $[\![E.i]\!]^{\beta} = v_i$ if $[\![E]\!]^{\beta} = (v_1, \dots, v_n)$.
- $[\![<x_1 := E_1, \dots, x_n := E_n>]\!]^{\beta} = \{(x_1, [\![E_1]\!]^{\beta}), \dots, (x_n, [\![E_n]\!]^{\beta})\}$.
- $[\![E.x]\!]^{\beta} = v_i$ if $[\![E]\!]^{\beta} = \{(x_1, v_1), \dots, (x_n, v_n)\}$ and $x = x_i$.
- $[\![E_1(E_2)]\!]^{\beta} = v$ if v is unique with $([\![E_2]\!]^{\beta}, v)$ in $[\![E_1]\!]^{\beta}$. If another v' with $([\![E_2]\!]^{\beta}, v')$ in $[\![E_1]\!]^{\beta}$ exists, or if none exists, then v is an arbitrary element of $\bar{A}_G(T_2)$ where T_2 is the co-domain of the E_1, that is, $\tau^{\epsilon}(E_1) = \mathcal{P}(T_1 \times T_2)$.

- $[\![\{E_1, \ldots, E_n\}]\!]^\beta = \{[\![E_1]\!]^\beta, \ldots, [\![E_n]\!]^\beta\}$.
- $[\![\{S \bullet E\}]\!]^\beta = \{[\![E]\!]^{\beta[v]} \mid v \in [\![S]\!]^\beta\}$.
- $[\![\mathcal{P}(E)]\!]^\beta = 2^{[\![E]\!]^\beta}$.
- $[\![E_1 \times \ldots \times E_n]\!]^\beta = [\![E_1]\!]^\beta \times \ldots \times [\![E_n]\!]^\beta$.

Schema-expressions A schema denotes a set of elements of schema-type which have the form $\{(x_1, v_1), \ldots, (x_n, v_n)\}$ and are called *bindings*. Thus the *type of a schema* is $\mathcal{P}(<x_1 : T_1, \ldots, x_n : T_n>)$ if T_i is the type of v_i for $1 \leq i \leq n$.

A simple schema of the form $x_1 : E_1, \ldots, x_n : E_n$ defines the identifiers of a schema and a set of possible values for each identifier. Given a schema S, the schema $S|P$ has as elements all the elements of S satisfying the predicate P. Other operations on schemata include forming the negation, disjunction, conjunction and implication of schemata. Negation, disjunction and conjunction correspond to the complement, union, and intersection of the sets denoted by the arguments. For the disjunction, conjunction, and implication of schema-expressions, the type of the arguments have to be compatible, that is, if two components have the same name, they have to have the same type. The type of the result has as components the union of the components of the arguments with all duplicates removed.

Adjustments to the type of schemas can be made by using hiding and renaming. Hiding hides some components of a schema-type and renaming renames some components. A particular kind of renaming is decorating the identifiers with finite sequences of elements from $\{', !, ?\}$.

An existentially quantified schema $\exists S_1.S_2$ denotes the set of all bindings of the identifiers of S_2 without the ones in S_1 such that there exists a binding in S_1 and the union of the bindings is an element of S_2. An universally quantified schema $\forall S_1.S_2$ is an abbreviation for $\neg\exists S_1.\neg S_2$.

$$\begin{aligned} S ::= {} & x_1 : E, \ldots, x_n : E \mid (S|P) \mid \neg S \mid S \vee S \mid S \wedge S \mid S \Rightarrow S \\ & \mid \forall S.S \mid \exists S.S \mid S \setminus [x_1, \ldots, x_n] \mid S[x_1/y_1, \ldots, x_n/y_n] \\ & \mid S\ \mathit{Decor} \mid E \end{aligned}$$

Note that the schema operations ΔS and ΞS, used in Z for the specification of sequential systems, are only convenient abbreviations for schema expressions involving the schema operations defined above. For example, ΔS is the same as the conjunction of the schema S with S', and ΞS is the same as the schema $S \wedge S'|(x_1 = x'_1 \wedge \ldots \wedge x_n = x'_n)$ given that the type of S is $\mathcal{P}(<x_1 : T_1, \ldots, x_n : T_n>)$.

A schema-expression S is well-formed with respect to an environment $\epsilon = (\Sigma, (X, \tau_X))$ with $\Sigma = (G, O, \tau)$, if

- $S = x_1 : E_1, \ldots, x_n : E_n$, $x_i \in V$, and E_i is well-formed and has type $\mathcal{P}(T_i)$ for each $1 \leq i \leq n$. The type of S is $\mathcal{P}(<x_1 : T_1, \ldots, x_n : T_n>)$.
- $S = S_1|P$ and P is well-formed with respect to $\epsilon' = \epsilon[T]$, where the type of S_1 is $\mathcal{P}(T)$. The type of S is $\mathcal{P}(T)$.
- $S = \neg S_1$ and S_1 is well-formed. The type of S is $\tau^\epsilon(S_1)$.

- $S = S_1\ op\ S_2$, S_1 and S_2 have compatible types, S_1 and S_2 are well-formed, and $op \in \{\vee, \wedge, \Rightarrow\}$.
  Two types $\mathcal{P}(<x_1 : T_1, \ldots, x_n : T_n>)$ and $\mathcal{P}(<x'_1 : T'_1, \ldots, x'_m : T'_m>)$ are compatible if for all i and j such that $x_i = x'_j$ we have $T_i = T'_j$. The type of S has as components the union of the components of the type of S_1 and S_2 with the duplicates removed.
- $S = \exists S_1.S_2$, S_1 and S_2 are well-formed with respect to ϵ, and their types are compatible. The type of S is the type of S_2 with all the identifiers removed which occur in S_1.
- $S = S_1 \setminus [x_1, \ldots, x_n]$ and S is well-formed. Note that it is not required that the x_i have to be identifiers of the type of S_1. The type of S is the type of S_1 without the identifier x_i if x_i occurs in the type of S for all $1 \leq i \leq n$.
- $S = S_1[x_1/y_1, \ldots, x_n/y_n]$ and S is well-formed. Note that it is not required that the x_i have to be identifiers of the type of S_1. The type of S is the type of S_1 where x_i is replaced by y_i if x_i is an identifier of S_1. Note that the mapping from the identifiers of the type of S_1 to the identifiers of the type of S defined by this replacement has to be injective.
- $S = S_1\ Decor$ and S_1 is well-formed. *Decor* is a finite sequence of elements from $\{', !, ?\}$. The type of S is $\mathcal{P}(<\bar{x}_1 : T_1, \ldots, \bar{x}_n : T_n>)$ if S_1 is of type $\mathcal{P}(<x_1 : T_1, \ldots, x_n : T_n>)$. $\bar{x}_i$ is the decorated form of x_i, for example, if *Decor* is ! then $\bar{x}_i$ is $x_i!$.
- $S = E$ and E is well-formed with type $\mathcal{P}(<x_1 : T_1, \ldots, x_n : T_n>)$. The type of S is $\mathcal{P}(<x_1 : T_1, \ldots, x_n : T_n>)$.

Let v be the set $\{(x_1, v_1), \ldots, (x_n, v_n)\}$ and X be a set of variables, then $v|_X$ denotes the binding v restricted to the identifiers in the set X, i.e. the set $\{(x_i, v_i) \mid x_i \in X \wedge (x_i, v_i) \in v \wedge 1 \leq i \leq n\}$.

If a schema-expression S is well-formed with respect to ϵ, its semantics $[\![S]\!]^\beta$ with respect to a structure $A = (A_G, A_O)$ and a variable binding $\beta = (A, A_X)$ compatible with ϵ is defined as follows:

- $[\![x_1 : E_1, \ldots, x_n : E_n]\!]^\beta = \{\{(x_1, v_1), \ldots, (x_n, v_n)\} \mid v_i \in [\![E_i]\!]^\beta,\ 1 \leq i \leq n\}$.
- $[\![S|P]\!]^\beta = \{v \in [\![S]\!]^\beta \mid \beta[v] \models^S P\}$. The satisfaction relation $\models^S$ is defined in Sect. 3.4.
- $[\![\neg S]\!]^\beta = \{v \in \bar{A}_G(T) \mid v \notin [\![S]\!]^\beta\}$ and S has type T.
- $[\![S \setminus [y_1, \ldots, y_n]]\!]^\beta = \{v|_{\{x_1, \ldots, x_m\}} \mid v \in [\![S]\!]^\beta\}$, where $\{x_1, \ldots, x_m\}$ is the set of identifiers of the type of S without the identifiers $y_1, \ldots, y_n$.
- $[\![S_1\ op\ S_2]\!]^\beta = \{v \in \bar{A}_G(T) \mid v|_{X_1} \in [\![S_1]\!]^\beta\ op\ v|_{X_2} \in [\![S_2]\!]^\beta\}$ where *op* is in $\{\vee, \wedge, \Rightarrow\}$, $\mathcal{P}(T)$ is the type of $S_1\ op\ S_2$, and X_1 and X_2 are the set of components of schemata S_1 and S_2, respectively.
- $[\![\exists S_1.S_2]\!]^\beta = \{v \in \bar{A}_G(T) \mid \exists v_1 \in [\![S_1]\!]^\beta : (v_1 \cup v)|_{X_2} \in [\![S_2]\!]^\beta\}$ where $\mathcal{P}(()T)$ X_2 is the set of components of schema S_2 and $\mathcal{P}(T)$ is the type of $\exists S_1.S_2$.
- $[\![S[y_1/y'_1, \ldots, y_n/y'_n]]\!]^\beta = \{\bar{f}(v) \mid v \in [\![S]\!]^\beta\}$ where f is the function from the identifiers of type S to the identifiers of type S_1 defined by $[y_1/y'_1, \ldots, y_n/y'_n]$

as follows:

$$f(id) = \begin{cases} y'_i & \text{if } y_i = id \text{ for some } 1 \leq i \leq n \\ id & \text{else} \end{cases}$$

and $\bar{f}$ is the canonical extension of f to bindings.

- $[\![S_1\ Decor]\!]^\beta = \{\{(\bar{x}_1, v_1), \ldots, (\bar{x}_n, v_n)\} \mid \{(x_1, v_1), \ldots, (x_n, v_n)\} \in [\![S_1]\!]^\beta\}$. $\bar{x}_i$ is the identifier x_i decorated with *Decor*. For example, if *Decor* is $'$ then $\bar{x}_i$ is $x_i{}'$.

3.4 Formulas

The formulas in $\mathsf{Sen}_{\mathcal{S}}(\Sigma)$ are the usual first-order formulas built on the membership predicate and the equality between expressions.

$$\begin{aligned} P ::= &\ \text{true} \mid \text{false} \mid E \in E \mid E = E \mid \neg P \mid P \vee P \mid P \wedge P \\ &\mid P \Rightarrow P \mid \forall S.P \mid \exists S.P \end{aligned}$$

A formula P is well-formed in an environment $\epsilon = (\Sigma, (X, \tau_X))$ if

- $P = E_1 \in E_2$, $\tau^\epsilon(E_2) = \mathcal{P}(\tau^\epsilon(E_1))$, and E_1 and E_2 are well-formed.
- $P = (E_1 = E_2)$, $\tau^\epsilon(E_1) = \tau^\epsilon(E_2)$, and E_1 and E_2 are well-formed.
- $P = \neg P_1$ and P_1 is well-formed.
- $P = P_1\ op\ P_2$, P_1 and P_2 are well-formed, and $op \in \{\vee, \wedge, \Rightarrow\}$.
- $P = \forall S.P_1$, S is well-formed and has type $\mathcal{P}(T)$ where T is a schema-type and P_1 is well-formed with respect to $\epsilon[T]$.
- $P = \exists S.P_1$, S is well-formed and has type $\mathcal{P}(T)$ where T is a schema-type and P_1 is well-formed with respect to $\epsilon[T]$.

Given a signature-morphism $\sigma : \Sigma \to \Sigma'$ and a formula P well-formed with respect to $\epsilon = (\Sigma, (X, \tau_X))$, then the formula $\bar{\sigma}(P)$ is well-formed with respect to $(\Sigma', (X, \tau'_X))$ where $\tau'_X = \tau_X; T(\sigma_G)$ and $\bar{\sigma}(P)$ is given by:

- $\bar{\sigma}(id) = id$ if $id \in X$, $\bar{\sigma}(id) = \sigma_O(id)$ if $id \in O$, and $\bar{\sigma}(id) = \sigma_G(id)$ if $id \in G$.
- $\bar{\sigma}((E_1, \ldots, E_n)) = (\bar{\sigma}(E_1), \ldots, \bar{\sigma}(E_n))$.
- $\bar{\sigma}(E.i) = \bar{\sigma}(E).i$.
- $\bar{\sigma}(<x_1 := E_1, \ldots, x_n := E_n>) = <x_1 := \bar{\sigma}(E_1), \ldots, x_n := \bar{\sigma}(E_n)>$.
- $\bar{\sigma}(E.x) = \bar{\sigma}(E).x$.
- $\bar{\sigma}(E_1(E_2)) = \bar{\sigma}(E_1)(\bar{\sigma}(E_2))$.
- $\bar{\sigma}(\{E_1, \ldots, E_n\}) = \{\bar{\sigma}(E_1), \ldots, \bar{\sigma}(E_n)\}$.
- $\bar{\sigma}(\{S \bullet E\}) = \{\bar{\sigma}(S) \bullet \bar{\sigma}(E)\}$.
- $\bar{\sigma}(\mathcal{P}(E)) = \mathcal{P}(\bar{\sigma}(E))$.
- $\bar{\sigma}(E_1 \times \ldots \times E_n) = \bar{\sigma}(E_1) \times \ldots \times \bar{\sigma}(E_n)$.
- $\bar{\sigma}(x_1 : E_1, \ldots, x_n : E) = x_1 : \bar{\sigma}(E_1), \ldots, x_n : \bar{\sigma}(E_n)$.
- $\bar{\sigma}(S|P) = \bar{\sigma}(S)|\bar{\sigma}(P)$.
- $\bar{\sigma}(\neg S) = \neg\bar{\sigma}(S)$.
- $\bar{\sigma}(S_1\ op\ S_n) = \bar{\sigma}(S_1)\ op\ \bar{\sigma}(S_n)$ for $op \in \{\vee, \wedge, \Rightarrow\}$.
- $\bar{\sigma}(\exists S_1.S_2) = \exists\bar{\sigma}(S_1).\bar{\sigma}(S_2)$ and $\bar{\sigma}(\forall S_1.S_2) = \forall\bar{\sigma}(S_1).\bar{\sigma}(S_2)$.

- $\bar{\sigma}(S \setminus [x_1, \ldots, x_n]) = \bar{\sigma}(S) \setminus [x_1, \ldots, x_n]$.
- $\bar{\sigma}(S[x_1/y_1, \ldots, x_n/y_n]) = \bar{\sigma}(S)[x_1/y_1, \ldots, x_n/y_n]$.
- $\bar{\sigma}(E_1 \in E_2) = (\bar{\sigma}(E_1) \in \bar{\sigma}(E_2))$.
- $\bar{\sigma}(E_1 = E_2) = (\bar{\sigma}(E_1) = \bar{\sigma}(E_n))$.
- $\bar{\sigma}(\text{true}) = \text{true}$ and $\bar{\sigma}(\text{false}) = \text{false}$.
- $\bar{\sigma}(\neg P) = \neg\bar{\sigma}(P)$.
- $\bar{\sigma}(P_1 \; op \; P_2) = \bar{\sigma}(P_1) \; op \; \bar{\sigma}(P_2)$ for $op \in \{\vee, \wedge, \Rightarrow\}$.
- $\bar{\sigma}(\forall S.P) = \forall\bar{\sigma}(S).\bar{\sigma}(P)$ and $\bar{\sigma}(\exists S.P) = \exists\bar{\sigma}(S).\bar{\sigma}(P)$.

Definition 8 ($\mathsf{Sen}_{\mathcal{S}}$). *The functor $\mathsf{Sen}_{\mathcal{S}}$ from $\text{SIGN}_{\mathcal{S}}$ to SET maps each signature Σ to the set formulas well-formed wrt. $\epsilon = (\Sigma, (\{\}, \tau_X))$ and each signature morphism σ from Σ to Σ' to the translation of Σ-formulas to Σ'-formulas given by $\bar{\sigma}$.*

Validity of a well-formed formula P in $\beta = (A, A_X)$, $\beta \models^{\mathcal{S}} P$, is defined by:

- $\beta \models^{\mathcal{S}} \text{true}$.
- $\beta \models^{\mathcal{S}} E_1 \in E_2$ iff $[\![E_1]\!]^\beta \in [\![E_2]\!]^\beta$.
- $\beta \models^{\mathcal{S}} E_1 = E_2$ iff $[\![E_1]\!]^\beta = [\![E_2]\!]^\beta$.
- $\beta \models^{\mathcal{S}} \neg P$ iff not $\beta \models^{\mathcal{S}} P$.
- $\beta \models^{\mathcal{S}} P_1 \; op \; P_2$ iff $\beta \models^{\mathcal{S}} P_1 \; op \; \beta \models^{\mathcal{S}} P_2$ for $op \in \{\vee, \wedge, \Rightarrow\}$.
- $\beta \models^{\mathcal{S}} \forall S.P$ iff $\beta[v] \models^{\mathcal{S}} P$ for all $v \in [\![S]\!]^\beta$.
- $\beta \models^{\mathcal{S}} \exists S.P$ iff $\beta[v] \models^{\mathcal{S}} P$ for some $v \in [\![S]\!]^\beta$.

Definition 9 (Satisfaction). *Given a signature Σ, a formula P which is well-formed with respect to $(\Sigma, (\{\}, \tau_X))$, and a Σ-structure A, then $A \models^{\mathcal{S}}_{\Sigma} P$ if $(A, \{\}) \models^{\mathcal{S}} P$.*

Theorem 3 (The Institution $\mathcal{S}$). *The category $\text{SIGN}_{\mathcal{S}}$, the functor $\mathsf{Str}_{\mathcal{S}}$, the functor $\mathsf{Sen}_{\mathcal{S}}$ and the family of satisfaction relations given by $\models^{\mathcal{S}}_{\Sigma}$ define the institution $\mathcal{S} = \langle \text{SIGN}_{\mathcal{S}}, \mathsf{Str}_{\mathcal{S}}, \mathsf{Sen}_{\mathcal{S}}, \models^{\mathcal{S}} \rangle$.*

Example 3. To complete our small example of a bank account we define the schema $\Delta ACCOUNT$ and the operation $UPDATE$ adding n to the balance of the account:

$$\Delta ACCOUNT = ACCOUNT \wedge ACCOUNT'$$

$UPDATE$
$\Delta ACCOUNT$
$n : Integer$
$bal' = bal + n$

The abstract datatype in $\mathcal{S}$ corresponding to this specification consists of the signature:

$$\Sigma_{BA} = (\{Integer\}, \{+, ACCOUNT, \Delta ACCOUNT, UPDATE\}, \tau)$$

where τ is given by

$$\tau(id) = \begin{cases} \mathcal{P}(\mathit{Integer} \times \mathit{Integer} \times \mathit{Integer}) & \text{if } id = + \\ \mathcal{P}(<\mathit{bal} : \mathit{Integer}>) & \text{if } id = \mathit{ACCOUNT} \\ \mathcal{P}(<\mathit{bal} : \mathit{Integer},\ \mathit{bal}' : \mathit{Integer}>) & \text{if } id = \Delta\mathit{ACCOUNT} \\ \mathcal{P}(<\mathit{bal} : \mathit{Integer},\ \mathit{bal}' : \mathit{Integer},\ n : \mathit{Integer}>) & \text{if } id = \mathit{UPDATE} \end{cases}$$

The following set of formulas specifies the schemata $ACCOUNT$, $\Delta ACCOUNT$ and the $UPDATE$ operation:

$$\Phi = \begin{array}{l} \{ACCOUNT = (bal : Integer), \\ \Delta ACCOUNT = ACCOUNT \wedge ACCOUNT', \\ UPDATE = ((\Delta ACCOUNT \wedge (n : Integer)) \mid bal' = bal + n)\}. \end{array}$$

A Σ_{BA}-structure $A = (A_G, A_O)$ satisfying Φ is given by function A_G mapping *Integer* to Z and the set

$$A_O = \begin{array}{l} \{(+, graph(\lambda(x, y).x + y)), \\ (ACCOUNT, \{\{(bal, x)\} \mid x \in Z\}), \\ (\Delta ACCOUNT, \{\{(bal, x), (bal', y)\} \mid x, y \in Z\}), \\ (UPDATE, \{\{(bal, x), (bal', y), (n, z)\} \mid x, y, z \in Z \wedge y = x + z\})\}. \end{array}$$

Now the interpretation of $UPDATE$ in A, denoted by $A(UPDATE)$, defines an operation that given an integer n transforms a state, which is an element of the interpretation of $ACCOUNT$ in A, to another state:

$$(\{(bal, x)\}, z) \mapsto \{(bal, y)\} \text{ iff } \{(bal, x), (bal', y), (n, z)\} \text{ is in } A(UPDATE).$$

4 Relating Abstract Datatypes to Schemata

Let $\Sigma = (G, O, \tau)$ be a signature in $\mathcal{S}$. A schema-type

$$T = <x_1 : T_1, \ldots, x_n : T_n>$$

defines a signature $\Sigma' = (G, O \cup \{x_1, \ldots, x_n\}, \tau')$ where $\tau'(x_i) = T_i$ and $\tau'(id) = \tau(id)$ for $id \in O$.[1]

Given a Σ-structure $A = (A_G, A_O)$, an element $\{(x_1, v_1), \ldots, (x_n, v_n)\}$ of type T defines a Σ'-structure $A' = (A_G, A_O \cup \{(x_1, v_1), \ldots, (x_n, v_n)\})$.

Definition 10. *Given a signature $\Sigma = (G, O, \tau)$, a schema-expression S of type $\mathcal{P}(<x_1 : T_1, \ldots, x_n : T_n>)$ and a Σ-structure $A = (A_G, A_O)$. We define an abstract datatype (Σ_S, M_S^A) by*

[1] Note that Σ' is not a signature as defined in Def. 2 because $\{x_1, \ldots, x_n\}$ is not a subset of F since, for technical reasons, we had to require that the set of variable names and the set of identifier names are disjoint. However, we can assume that O' is the set $O \cup \{\bar{x}_1, \ldots, \bar{x}_n\}$ where the $\bar{x}_i$ are suitable renamings of x_i to symbols in F not occurring in O.

- $\Sigma_S = (G, O \cup \{x_1, \ldots, x_n\}, \tau_S)$ *where* $\tau_S(x_i) = T_i$ *for* $1 \leq i \leq n$ *and* $\tau_S(id) = \tau(id)$ *for* $id \in O$ *and*
- $M_S^A = \{(A_G, A_O \cup v_S) \mid v_S \in [\![S]\!]^{((A_G, A_O), \{\})}\}$.

This definition can be extended to abstract datatypes $\mathrm{SP} = (\Sigma, M)$ *in* ADT_S *by taking the union of all* M_S^A *for* $A \in M$*:*

$$\mathrm{SP}_S = (\Sigma_S, \bigcup_{A \in M} M_S^A).$$

Example 4. Given $\Sigma = (\{Integer\}, \{+\}, \tau)$, then the signatures corresponding to the schemata *ACCOUNT*, *ΔACCOUNT*, and *UPDATE* are:

$$\begin{aligned}
\Sigma_A &= (\{Integer\}, \{+, bal\}, \tau_A), \\
\Sigma_{\Delta A} &= (\{Integer\}, \{+, bal, bal'\}, \tau_{\Delta A}), \\
\Sigma_U &= (\{Integer\}, \{+, bal, bal', n\}, \tau_U).
\end{aligned}$$

The next theorem relates the operations on schemata with the operations on abstract datatypes:

Theorem 4. *Let* $\mathrm{SP} = (\Sigma, M)$ *be an abstract datatype in* $\mathcal{S}$*. If*

- $S = x_1 : E_1, \ldots, x_n : E_n$*, then* $\mathrm{SP}_S = I_{\{x_i \in E_i | 1 \leq i \leq n\}} T_\sigma \mathrm{SP}$ *where* σ *is the inclusion of* Σ *into* Σ_S*.*
- $S = S_1 | P$*, then* $\mathrm{SP}_S = I_{\{P\}} \mathrm{SP}_{S_1}$*.*
- $S = S_1 \wedge S_2$*, then* $\mathrm{SP}_S = T_{\sigma_1} \mathrm{SP}_{S_1} + T_{\sigma_2} \mathrm{SP}_{S_2}$*. The signature morphisms* σ_1 *and* σ_2 *are the inclusions of the signatures* Σ_{S_1} *and* Σ_{S_2} *into* $\Sigma_{S_1 \wedge S_2}$*. This is needed because, in contrast to the union of abstract datatypes, the types of* S_1 *and* S_2 *in the union of* S_1 *and* S_2 *are only required to be compatible.*
- $S = S_1 \setminus [x_1, .., x_n]$*, then* $\mathrm{SP}_S = D_\sigma \mathrm{SP}_{S_1}$ *where* σ *is the inclusion of* Σ_S *into* Σ_{S_1}*.*
- $S = S_1[x_1/y_1, .., x_n/y_n]$*, then* $\mathrm{SP}_S = T_\sigma \mathrm{SP}_{S_1}$ *where* σ_G *is the identity and* $\sigma_O(x) = y_i$ *if* $x = x_i$ *for some* i *and* $\sigma_O(x) = x$ *if* $x \neq x_i$ *for all* i*.*

Example 5. Given $\mathrm{SP} = (\Sigma, M)$ and $UPDATE = (\Delta ACCOUNT \wedge (n : Integer) \mid bal' = bal + n)$ we can write $\mathrm{SP}_U = (\Sigma_U, M_U)$ as:

$$\mathrm{SP}_U = I_{\{bal' = bal + n\}}(T_{\sigma_1} \mathrm{SP}_{\Delta A} + T_{\sigma_2} I_{\{n \in Integer\}} T_{\sigma_3} \mathrm{SP}).$$

Here, σ_1 is the inclusion of $\Sigma_{\Delta A}$ into Σ_U, σ_3 the inclusion of Σ into $\Sigma_{(n:Integer)}$, and σ_2 the inclusion of $\Sigma_{(n:Integer)}$ into Σ_U. $\Sigma_{(n:Integer)} = (\{Integer\}, \{+, n\}, \tau')$ is the signature corresponding to the schema $(n : Integer)$.

What about the other schema operations $\neg S$, $S_1 \vee S_2$, $S_1 \Rightarrow S_2$, and $\exists S_1 . S_2$? The existential quantifier is the same as hiding the schema variables of S_1 in the conjunction of S_1 and S_2. Let $x_1, \ldots, x_n$ be the schema variables of S_1, then $\exists S_1 . S_2$ and $(S_1 \wedge S_2) \setminus [x_1, .., x_n]$ have the same semantics. This yields the following theorem:

Theorem 5. *Let* $\text{SP} = (\Sigma, M)$ *be an abstract datatype in* $\mathcal{S}$*, and* $S = \exists S_1.S_2$ *a well-formed schema expression. Then*

$$\text{SP}_S = D_\sigma(T_{\sigma_1}\text{SP}_{S_1} \wedge T_{\sigma_2}\text{SP}_{S_2})$$

where σ_1 *and* σ_2 *are the inclusions of* Σ_{S_1} *and* Σ_{S_2} *into* $\Sigma_{S_1 \wedge S_2}$*, and* σ *is the inclusion of the signature of the whole expression into* $\Sigma_{S_1 \wedge S_2}$*.*

It is easy to define negation, disjunction and implication on abstract datatypes:

Definition 11. *Let* (Σ, M)*,* (Σ, M_1) *and* (Σ, M_2) *be abstract datatypes in an arbitrary institution* $\mathcal{I}$*, define:*

$$\neg(\Sigma, M) = (\Sigma, \{m \in \mathsf{Str}_{\mathcal{I}}(\Sigma) \mid m \notin M\})$$
$$(\Sigma, M_1) \vee (\Sigma, M_2) = (\Sigma, M_1 \cup M_2)$$
$$(\Sigma, M_1) \Rightarrow (\Sigma, M_2) = (\Sigma, \{m \in \mathsf{Str}_{\mathcal{I}}(\Sigma) \mid m \in M_1 \Rightarrow m \in M_2\})$$

What is the relationship of these operations to the corresponding schema operations? Disjunction can be treated similar to conjunction; however, while it seems natural to expect $\text{SP}_{\neg S} = \neg\text{SP}_S$, this does not hold. The reason is that in $\text{SP}_{\neg S}$ the negation of S is interpreted within a given abstract datatype SP while the negation of SP_S also permits the negation of SP itself. If $(A_G, A_O \cup v)$ is a model of $\text{SP}_{\neg S}$, then v is not in $[\![S]\!]^\beta$ and (A_G, A_O) is always a model of SP. On the other hand, if $(A_G, A_O \cup v)$ is a model of $\neg\text{SP}_S$, either v is not in $[\![S]\!]^\beta$ or (A_G, A_O) is not a model of SP. The solution is to add the requirement that (A_G, A_O) is a model of SP to $\neg\text{SP}_S$. Implication has a similar problem.

Theorem 6. *Let* $\text{SP} = (\Sigma, M)$ *be an abstract datatype in* $\mathcal{S}$*. If*

- $S = S_1 \vee S_2$*, then* $\text{SP}_S = T_{\sigma_1}\text{SP}_{S_1} \vee T_{\sigma_2}\text{SP}_{S_2}$*. The signature morphisms* σ_1 *and* σ_2 *are the inclusions of the signatures* Σ_{S_1} *and* Σ_{S_2} *into* $\Sigma_{S_1 \vee S_2}$*.*
- $S = \neg S_1$*, then* $\text{SP}_S = \neg\text{SP}_{S_1} + T_{\sigma_{S_1}}\text{SP}$ *where* σ_S *is the inclusion of the* Σ *into* Σ_S*.*
- $S = S_1 \Rightarrow S_2$*, then* $\text{SP}_S = (T_{\sigma_1}\text{SP}_{S_1} \Rightarrow T_{\sigma_2}\text{SP}_{S_2}) + T_{\sigma_S}\text{SP}$*. The signature morphisms* σ_1 *and* σ_2 *are the inclusions of the signatures* Σ_{S_1} *and* Σ_{S_2} *into* $\Sigma_{S_1 \Rightarrow S_2}$*.*

5 Conclusion

In this paper we have formalized the relationship between the structuring mechanism in Z and the structuring mechanism of property-oriented specification languages. Z specifications are structured using schemata and operations on schemata, which are based on the particular logic underlying Z. In contrast, property-oriented specifications are structured using abstract datatypes and operations on abstract datatypes, which can be formulated largely independent of the logic used for the specifications.

The advantage of having the structuring mechanism represented as part of the logic is that it is possible to reason within that logic about the structure of specifications. The disadvantage is that it is not easy to transfer results and methods to be used with a different logic and specification language. For example, the specification of sequential systems in Z consists of a schema for the state space and a schema for each operation. In the example of the bank account the schema *ACCOUNT* defines the state space of the bank account, and the schema *UPDATE* defines the update operation that changes the state of the account. Using the results of this paper we can use abstract datatypes instead of schemata for the specification of sequential systems and the bank account specification can be written without the use of schemata as a CASL-$\mathcal{S}$ specification as follows:

spec *BASE* =
  sort *Integer*
  op $+ : \mathcal{P}(Integer \times Integer \times Integer)$

spec *ACCOUNT* = *BASE* **then**
  op *bal*: *Integer*

spec $\Delta ACCOUNT$ = *ACCOUNT* **and** { *ACCOUNT* **with** $bal \mapsto bal'$ }

spec *UPDATE* = $\Delta ACCOUNT$ **then**
  op n : *Integer*
  axioms $bal' = bal + n$

Note that this specification does not make any reference to schemata anymore. Instead of schemata the structuring facilities of CASL-$\mathcal{S}$ are used. Since these structuring facilities are institution independent[2], this allows the use of the Z-style for the specification of sequential systems also with other specification languages. For example, this specification style can be used in the state as algebra approach (e.g. [1,2,5,7]).

In the process of relating schemata and their operations to abstract datatypes we have defined the operations negation, disjunction and implication on abstract datatypes, which were previously not defined. Further work needs to be done to study the relationship of these new operations with the other operations on abstract datatypes, and how to integrate the new operations into proof calculi, like that of Hennicker, Wirsing, and Bidoit [8]. Work in this direction has been done for the case of disjunction in Baumeister [3].

[2] To be precise, CASL is parameterized by the notion of an institution with symbols (cf. Mossakowski [9]). However, it is easy to show that $\mathcal{S}$ is an institution with symbols.

References

1. Hubert Baumeister. Relations as abstract datatypes: An institution to specify relations between algebras. In Peter D. Mosses, Mogens Nielsen, and Michael I. Schwartzbach, editors, *TAPSOFT 95, Proceedings of the Sixth Joint Conference on Theory and Practice of Software Development*, number 915 in LNCS, pages 756–771, Århus, Denmark, May 1995. Springer. 381
2. Hubert Baumeister. Using algebraic specification languages for model-oriented specifications. Technical Report MPI-I-96-2-003, Max-Planck-Institut für Informatik, Saarbrücken, Germany, February 1996. 367, 381
3. Hubert Baumeister. *Relations between Abstract Datatypes modeled as Abstract Datatypes.* PhD thesis, Universität des Saarlandes, Saarbrücken, May 1999. 381
4. R. M. Burstall and J. A. Goguen. The semantics of Clear, a specification language, February 1980. 367
5. Hartmut Ehrig and Fernando Orejas. Dynamic abstract data types, an informal proposal. *Bulletin of the EATCS*, 53:162–169, June 1994. 381
6. J. A. Goguen and R. Burstall. Institutions: Abstract model theory for specification and programming. *Journal of the Association for Computing Machinery*, 39(1):95–146, January 1992. 367
7. Yuri Gurevich. Evolving algebras: An attempt to discover semantics. *Bulletin of the EATCS*, 43:264–284, February 1991. 381
8. Rolf Hennicker, Martin Wirsing, and Michel Bidoit. Proof systems for structured specifications with observability operators. *Theoretical Computer Science*, 173(2):393–443, February 28 1996. 381
9. Till Mossakowski. Specifications in an arbitrary institution with symbols. In Didier Bert and Christine Choppy, editors, *Recent Trends in Algebraic Development Techniques, 14th International Workshop, WADT'99, Bonas, France, September 1999; Selected Papers;*, volume 1827 of *LNCS*. Springer, 2000. 367, 381
10. Peter D. Mosses. CoFI: The common framework initiative for algebraic specification and development. In Michel Bidoit and Max Dauchet, editors, *TAPSOFT '97: Proceedings of the Seventh Joint Conference on Theory and Practice of Software Development, 7th International Joint Conference CAAP/FASE*, number 1214 in LNCS, Lille, France, April 1997. Springer. 366
11. Donald Sannella and Martin Wirsing. A kernel language for algebraic specification and implementation. In M. Karpinski, editor, *Colloquium on Foundations of Computation Theory*, number 158 in LNCS, pages 413–427, Berlin, 1983. Springer. 368
12. J. M. Spivey. *Understanding Z: A Specification Language and its Formal Semantics*, volume 3 of *Cambridge tracts in theoretical computer science.* Cambridge Univ. Press, Cambridge, GB, repr. 1992 edition, 1988. 366
13. Z notation, final committee draft, cd 13568.2, August 24 1999. Available at `http://web.comlab.ox.ac.uk/oucl/research/groups/zstandards/index.html`. 369, 372

Algebraic Specification of Operator-Based Multimedia Scenarios

Didier Bert and Stéphane Lo Presti

Laboratoire Logiciels Systèmes Réseaux - LSR-IMAG - Grenoble, France
{Didier.Bert,Stephane.Lo-Presti}@imag.fr

Abstract. Multimedia presentations are complex compositions of monomedia objects. In this paper, we focus on the temporal model of multimedia presentations. After recalling existing approaches, we present a set of algebraic operators to create complex scenarios. Then, we define their semantics based on causal relations between temporal points. We finally present useful properties of multimedia terms derived from this semantics.

1 Introduction

Multimedia concerns several monomedia data that can be discrete (such as a text or a picture) or continuous (such as an audio stream or a video clip). New monomedia data such as streaming audio and digital video begin to appear in multimedia documents as seen in the context of the World Wide Web. Such multimedia documents bring more interactivity to the user making them more attractive. All these considerations strengthen the idea that temporal composition is more than ever a central issue in multimedia documents.

We call such documents *multimedia presentations* to stress upon the fact that they are composed in order to be presented to the end-user. We would like to point out that *multimedia applications* can be seen as presentations if there is an underlying execution engine attached to each presentation. Multimedia presentation management encompasses many different aspects that can be addressed at various levels between the system and the user. While presentation authoring is at the user level, storage problems of large data volumes are at the system level. Other aspects that should be taken into consideration are spatial positioning, temporal synchronization and data annotation.

The work presented here will only focus on the temporal composition of multimedia presentations. Section 2 recalls some existing works on temporal models. Section 3 introduces the set of operators defined in this framework to compose multimedia objects. Section 4 develops a non standard semantics based on causal relations between temporal end points of objects. Then, in Section 5, we sketch how to take advantage of the term structure to define properties on multimedia presentations and we explain the links with some other temporal frameworks. Finally, in Section 6, we consider other issues that should be adressed in future work.

D. Bert, C. Choppy, and P. Mosses (Eds.): WADT'99, LNCS 1827, pp. 383–401, 2000.

2 Related Work

As Wahl and Rothermel [21] have stated, multimedia time models can be classified depending on the elementary concepts that they manage. Historically, time information was first expressed as *points* on a timeline. The ISO language Hytime (Hypermedia Time-based Structuring Language) [8] uses various *Finite Coordinates Spaces* to position time points on interrelated temporal axes. Buchanan and Zellweger used temporal point nets [4] as a paradigm for authoring multimedia presentations. In the context of the World Wide Web, Rousseau [19] presented the concept of *hypertime link* derived from those temporal point nets. Indeed, all the temporal systems (which may be based on a language or a model) manage events at the lowest level.

In the field of artificial intelligence, Allen [1] noticed that this concept of time points was not sufficiently intuitive for modelling real cases. Following Hamblin [7], he considered the notion of an *interval* that is the time span going from a beginning to an ending time point. He presented thirteen relations between two intervals, describing all possible arrangements between those intervals. One of the major problems with the relations, pointed out in [12], is that inconsistent scenarios may be built. This makes mandatory to check for inconsistencies in every scenario. The declarative interval model has been used in many other contexts. For example Wahl and Rothermel [21] used Allen relations to compare synchronization frameworks and developed ten new relations by specifying the activation delay for intervals in the Allen relations. Allen relations are also used in authoring environments such as Madeus [9].

A second approach based on intervals was introduced by Weiss, Gifford and Duda [22]. We may put this approach along with the remark of Allen [1] stating that most of the useful applications using interval relations effectively build tree-like structures. This approach consists of operators to compose basic components and obtain more complex structures. It was called Video Algebra because operators build new video "segments" from existing ones. This work was later carried on and extended by Keramane and Duda [6] where a composition model was developed and the set of temporal operators was extended. Causal relations were introduced in [11] to express the exact meaning of the operators. Pazandak et al. [18] used at the same time a similar notion of *activation*. The W3C proposed the World Wide Web recommendation of SMIL (Synchronized Multimedia Integrated Language) [2]. This language has an hybrid temporal model. It uses three markups (<par>, <seq> and <excl>) to specify temporal composition between media objects. An author can additionally link begin and end time points to some events through *sync-arcs*. The ISO language MHEG (Multimedia and Hypermedia Information Coding Experts Group) [13] is also hybrid from the point of view of temporal composition. It features *object actions* which are ordered either as parallel, or as sequential, and, changing their duration, can lead to interval relations. Our work builds upon the *Menkalinan algebra* [10] of Keramane and Duda. We introduced the *link* and *delay* operators in [3].

3 Operator Description and Specification

In this section, we present the temporal multimedia operators. For each group of operators, we give the informal meaning, the signature and the properties or axioms in the CASL language [17,16]. We introduce first the types (called "sorts" in the algebraic formalism) of the multimedia objects and their basic attributes.

3.1 Multimedia Objects

Multimedia objects are either *primitive* objects, such as monomedia data (texts, images, video clips and audio streams), or *composed* ones. We consider programs as specific primitive multimedia objects. Each object is identified by a name. Primitive objects are made up from a reference to monomedia data, while composed ones are made up by expressions built with our multimedia operators. Primitive objects have attributes giving information about them, like the class, the application needed in order to be presented, the content and so on. Considering the temporal characteristics of multimedia objects, the following features are introduced:

- multimedia objects are considered as intervals or *segments* on the time line.
- for each segment, there exists two end points [21]: the *beginning*, the instant or time point when the segment starts, and the *end*, the time point when it is assumed to end.
- there is a predicate that indicates whether the segment duration is statically known or not.
- an attribute gives the value of the static duration if it is known. It is called the "length" (len) of a segment. In this paper, we consider that the length is constant and not a function depending on parameters (e.g. play rate) for the sake of simplicity.
- there is a way to know the value of the effective duration when a segment is presented. The dynamic duration is named "duration" (dur). In the framework presented here, if the static duration is known for a segment s, we have $\mathsf{dur}(s) \leq \mathsf{len}(s)$.
- multimedia objects can be combined by operators. Well-formed expressions are called *scenarios*. In a scenario, we assume that each segment is uniquely identified. For example, several occurrences of the same object constitute distinct segments.

Moreover, the multimedia objects can raise *events* when the scenarios are presented. For all the segments, the end points are events. Programs are specific segments in the sense that they may raise events that can occur during their presentation. The presentation of a program is its execution. The events are specified as time points. Such points are not considered as being absolute, but rather relative to the scenario where they appear.

In the algebraic specification below, the sort of the segments is denoted by "*seg*". The programs are specified by a subsort denoted by "*prog*". The duration data type "*Dur*" is not defined here, but it can be considered as a renaming of the data type of the positive (zero included) real numbers [15]. The sort *point* is the sort of the time points. For a segment s, $\mathsf{begin}(s)$ denotes the point of the beginning; $\mathsf{end}(s)$ denotes the point of the end. The operation $\varphi.tp$ returns the relative position on the time line of the point tp inside the term φ. The predicate *known* asserts if the length of a segment is known and the overloaded predicate $x \in \varphi$ is true if x is actually either a time point or a segment in the term φ.

spec *Multimedia_Objects* = *Duration*
then
  sorts *seg*, *prog* < *seg*, *point*
  ops $\mathsf{len} : seg \to ?\ Dur$
    $\mathsf{begin}, \mathsf{end} : seg \to point$
    $\_\_.\_\_ : seg \times point \to ?\ Dur$
  preds *known*, *unknown* : *seg*
    $\_\_ \in \_\_ : seg \times seg$
    $\_\_ \in \_\_ : point \times seg$
  vars $x, \varphi : seg$
  • $known(x) \Leftrightarrow \neg\ unknown(x)$
  • $x.\mathsf{begin}(x) = 0$
  • $x.\mathsf{end}(x) = \mathsf{len}(x)$ **if** $known(x)$
  • $\varphi.\mathsf{begin}(x) \leq \varphi.\mathsf{end}(x)$ **if** $x \in \varphi$ %% interval consistency property
end

When properties are stated in the same context (i.e. segment expression), this context can be factorized in front of the formula. For instance, the last axiom above can be written in short:

• $\varphi.\{\ \mathsf{begin}(x) \leq \mathsf{end}(x)\ \}$ **if** $x \in \varphi$

3.2 Sequential Operators and Constants

First of all, two segments A and B can be composed sequentially, denoted by $A \underset{-}{;} B$. This corresponds to the presentation of A followed by the one of B. We use here the notation " $\underset{-}{;}$ ", instead of the simpler ";" [3], so that this operator does not conflict with the ";" keyword of the CASL language. Any number of segments can be composed sequentially as follows: $A \underset{-}{;} B \underset{-}{;} C = (A \underset{-}{;} B) \underset{-}{;} C$. We then introduce repetition in the scenarios with the loop notation. The expression $\mathsf{loop}(A)$ repeats A infinitely and $\mathsf{loop}[n](A)$ repeats A n times. We add an operator defining a delay of known duration d, denoted by $\mathsf{delay}[d]$, when we would like to wait for a certain time without presenting anything. If the duration of the delay is not known, one can simply write delay.

The formal specification gives the syntax of each operator, the duration knowledge property and the length (if it exists).

spec *Sequential_Operators* = *Multimedia_Objects* **and** *Nat*
then
  ops $\_\_ \underset{-}{;} \_\_ : seg \times seg \to seg$
    $\mathsf{loop} : seg \to seg$
    $\mathsf{loop}[\_\_](\_\_) : Nat \times seg \to seg$
    $\mathsf{delay}[\_\_] : Dur \to seg$

delay : *seg*
vars $A, B : seg;\ n : Nat;\ d : Dur$
%% duration knowledge properties
- $known(A \,;\, B) \Leftrightarrow known(A) \wedge known(B)$
- $unknown(\mathsf{loop}(A))$
- $known(\mathsf{loop}[n](A)) \Leftrightarrow known(A)$
- $known(\mathsf{delay}[d])$
- $unknown(\mathsf{delay})$

%% length calculus if the duration is known
- $\mathsf{len}(A \,;\, B) = \mathsf{len}(A) + \mathsf{len}(B)$ **if** $known(A) \wedge known(B)$
- $\mathsf{len}(\mathsf{loop}[n](A)) = n * \mathsf{len}(A)$ **if** $known(A)$
- $\mathsf{len}(\mathsf{delay}[d]) = d$

end

3.3 Simple Parallel Composition

Parallel composition of segments is first defined for operators with a simple behaviour. In the master parallel operator, denoted by master[$A \parallel B$], the first segment controls the duration of the second one. That is, if B is longer than A, the end of A stops B and in any case, the end of the resulting segment occurs when A ends. The other simple parallel operators express meanings based on comparisons between durations of some arguments. For the min and max operators, either the shorter or the longer argument respectively determines the length of the resulting segment and stops the other interval for the min operator. These first three operators are defined for only two parameters. They can be naturally extended to any number of arguments by the following left-associative compositions:

$\mathsf{master}[\ A \parallel B_1 \parallel B_2\ ] = \mathsf{master}[\mathsf{master}[\ A \parallel B_1\ ] \parallel B_2\ ]$
$\mathsf{min}[\ A_1 \parallel A_2 \parallel A_3\ ] = \mathsf{min}[\mathsf{min}[\ A_1 \parallel A_2\ ] \parallel A_3\ ]$
$\mathsf{max}[\ A_1 \parallel A_2 \parallel A_3\ ] = \mathsf{max}[\mathsf{max}[\ A_1 \parallel A_2\ ] \parallel A_3\ ]$

The alternative operator, denoted by $\mathsf{alt}[\ A_1 \Rightarrow B_1 \parallel A_2 \Rightarrow B_2 \ldots \parallel A_n \Rightarrow B_n\ ]$, means that the A_k ($k \in 1..n$) start in parallel. Then, the first terminating A_i stops the other $A_j (j \neq i)$ and starts the associated B_i. In the specification below, we introduce the sort *Lalt* which denotes pairs of segment lists as $alt([A_1, \ldots, A_n], [B_1, \ldots, B_m])$. The selector $l1$ provides the first list of segments, while $l2$ provides the second list. The subsorting restriction of the sort *lalt* imposes that both lists have the same length (# returns the size of a list). The operator *minl* returns the index of the shorter segment in the first list, and the expression $L\ !\ i$ selects the segment indexed by i in the list L. The predicate $s\ in\ L$ is true if the segment s belongs to the list L (recall that segments are uniquely identified in an expression). The auxiliary operators are not completely axiomatized in this paper (clerical work on lists). For this specification, we use the *List* specification provided by the library of "Basic datatypes in CASL" [14].

spec *Simple_Parallel_Operators* = *Sequential_Operators*
and { *List*[*Multimedia_Objects* **fit** *Elem* ↦ *seg*] }
then

free type $Lalt ::= alt(l1 : List[seg]; l2 : List[seg]);$
sort $lalt = \{ll : Lalt \bullet \# l1(ll) = \# l2(ll)\}$
local
pred $\_\_in\_\_ : seg \times List[seg]$
ops $minl : List[seg] \to ?\ Pos$
$\_\_ \,!\, \_\_ : List[seg] \times Pos \to ?\ seg$
vars $lA : List[seg];\ i : Pos$
%% auxiliary definitions
• **def** $minl(lA) \Leftrightarrow \neg isEmpty(lA) \wedge \forall x : seg \cdot (x\ in\ lA \Rightarrow known(x))$
• **def** $lA \,!\, i \Leftrightarrow i \leq \# lA$
• … %% other axioms missing
within
ops $\mathsf{master}[\_\_ \parallel \_\_] : seg \times seg \to seg$
$\mathsf{min}[\_\_ \parallel \_\_] : seg \times seg \to seg$
$\mathsf{max}[\_\_ \parallel \_\_] : seg \times seg \to seg$
$\mathsf{alt}[\_\_] : lalt \to seg$
$\_\_ \Rightarrow \_\_ : seg \times seg \to lalt$
$\_\_ \parallel \_\_ : lalt \times lalt \to lalt$
vars $A, B : seg;\ llA, llB : lalt;\ i : Pos$
%% defined operations
• $A => B = alt(A :: nil, B :: nil)$
• $llA \parallel llB = alt(l1(llA) ++ l1(llB), l2(llA) ++ l2(llB))$
%% duration knowledge properties
• $known(\mathsf{master}[A \parallel B]) \Leftrightarrow known(A)$
• $known(\mathsf{min}[A \parallel B]) \Leftrightarrow known(A) \wedge known(B)$
• $known(\mathsf{max}[A \parallel B]) \Leftrightarrow known(A) \wedge known(B)$
• $known(\mathsf{alt}[llA]) \Leftrightarrow \forall x : seg \cdot (x\ in\ l1(llA) \Rightarrow known(x))$
$\wedge\, known(l2(llA) \,!\, minl(l1(llA)))$
%% length calculus if the duration is known
• $\mathsf{len}(\mathsf{master}[A \parallel B]) = \mathsf{len}(A)$ **if** $known(A)$
• $\mathsf{len}(\mathsf{min}[A \parallel B]) = min(\mathsf{len}(A), \mathsf{len}(B))$ **if** $known(A) \wedge known(B)$
• $\mathsf{len}(\mathsf{max}[A \parallel B]) = max(\mathsf{len}(A), \mathsf{len}(B))$ **if** $known(A) \wedge known(B)$
• $\mathsf{len}(\mathsf{alt}[llA]) = \mathsf{len}(l1(llA) \,!\, j \,\underline{;}\, l2(llA) \,!\, j)$ **if** $known(\mathsf{alt}[llA]) \wedge j = minl(l1(llA))$

3.4 General Parallel Composition and Link Operators

In this section, a general parallel operator par is introduced. The arguments of this operator are segments labelled by identifiers of sort *ref* defined in a specification *Reference* (not given). These identifiers are references to the segments that they label in the scope of a par operator. As for the $\underline{;}$ symbol in 3.3, we use the $\underline{:}$ symbol in the CASL lists of parallel expressions. An expression as $\mathsf{par}[\ a_1 \underline{:} A_1 \parallel a_2 \underline{:} A_2 \ldots \parallel a_n \underline{:} A_n\ ]$ means that the segments $A_k (k \in 1..n)$ start in parallel and when the last A_i ends, then the parallel expression ends too. A pair as $a_j \underline{:} A_j$ is called a *branch* of the parallel operator. The main difference with the max operator is that, in the branches of a par expression, *link operators* are allowed to control the behaviour of these branches. These operators, unlike other operators, do not build a simple tree structure but they add links between the child nodes of the par sub-tree. The expression $A \searrow_{\{b\}}$ in the branch a means that the end of the segment A stops the branch labelled by b if this branch is being presented. The expression $A \nwarrow_{\{p\}}$ means that the segment A is stopped by an event represented by the time point p. Such a time point may be the end of another parallel branch labeled by b, denoted by b.end, or an end point of a segment in the branch b. Also it may be an event e raised by P, denoted by $P.e$, where P is a program segment in the branch b.

spec *Parallel_Operators* = *Simple_Parallel_Operators*
  and *Reference* **and** { *List*[*Reference* **fit** *Elem* ↦ *ref*] }
then
  free type $Lpar ::= par(lr : List[ref];\ lbr : List[seg])$;
  sort $lpar = \{lb : Lpar \bullet \#lr(lb) = \#lbr(lb)\}$;
  ops $\mathsf{par}[\_\_] : lpar \to seg$
    $\_\_ \,\underline{:}\, \_\_ : ref \times seg \to lpar$
    $\_\_ \parallel \_\_ : lpar \times lpar \to lpar$
    $\_\_ \searrow_{\{\_\_\}} : seg \times ref \to seg$
    $\_\_ \nwarrow_{\{\_\_\}} : seg \times point \to seg$
  vars $a, b : ref;\ A : seg;\ lpA, lpb : lpar;\ p : point$
  %% defined operations $\underline{:}$ and $\parallel$
  ...   %% similar to the previous axiomatization of => and $\parallel$
  %% duration knowledge properties
  • $known(\mathsf{par}[\ lpA\ ]) \Leftrightarrow \forall x : seg \cdot (x\ in\ lbr(lpA) \Rightarrow known(x))$
  • $known(A \searrow_{\{b\}}) \Leftrightarrow known(A)$
  • $unknown(A \nwarrow_{\{p\}})$
  %% length calculus if the duration is known
  • $\mathsf{len}(\mathsf{par}[\ lpA\ ]) = max(\{x : seg \mid x\ in\ lbr(lpA)\})$ **if** $known(\mathsf{par}[\ lpA\ ])$
  • $\mathsf{len}(A \searrow_{\{b\}}) = \mathsf{len}(A)$ **if** $known(A)$
end

3.5 Examples of Scenarios

To illustrate this language of multimedia scenarios, here are short examples. The first one is the definition of a *Button* which is composed of a program *BC* to control the button and of two images *Bup* and *Bdn* respectively representing the button up and down. Considered as a multimedia object, the program can raise two events: *OnClick* when it receives the information that the mouse button has been clicked on a given region of the screen and *OnRelease* when it has been released. We assume that the button images are displayed in the exact region controlled by the program[1]. The resulting multimedia object is considered as a program because it exports the events raised by the program.

ops *Button* : *prog*
  Button.OnClick, *Button.OnRelease* : *point*
axioms
• $Button = \mathsf{par}\ [\ BControler \,\underline{:}\, BC$
    $\parallel BImage \,\underline{:}\ \ \mathsf{loop}(Bup \nwarrow_{\{BC.OnClick\}} \underline{:}\ Bdn \nwarrow_{\{BC.OnRelease\}})\ ]$
• $Button.\{OnClick = BC.OnClick\}$
• $Button.\{OnRelease = BC.OnRelease\}$

[1] The region coordinates could be parameters of the program and of the images, but we do not address the spatial attributes of the multimedia data in this paper.

Built on this object, one can define the scenario where a text T is presented during one minute, then it is followed by a video V, which can be stopped by the button *Button*. This can be expressed by:

ops $show\_Video : seg$
$OneMinute : Dur$

axiom

- $show\_Video = \mathsf{master}[\mathsf{delay}[OneMinute] \parallel T] \mathbin{\underline{;}} \mathsf{par}\ [vv \mathbin{\underline{:}} V \nwarrow_{\{Button.OnClick\}} \parallel cc \mathbin{\underline{:}} Button \nwarrow_{\{vv.\mathsf{end}\}}]$

4 Operator Semantics

4.1 Interpretation Models

The usual semantics of algebraic specifications as given in the previous section is the class of the models determined by the signature and axioms. We conjecture that all the executable scenarios, under a set of given constants (primitive monomedia objects), can be expressed by means of our operators. This semantics is intended to determine statically what are the values (in the model of real numbers) of end points of segments in a scenario, if the lengths of the arguments are known. For example, the property:

$$(A \mathbin{\underline{;}} B \mathbin{\underline{;}} C).\mathsf{begin}(C) = \mathsf{len}(A) + \mathsf{len}(B)$$

holds within the condition $known(A) \wedge known(B)$.

However, we want to define a more refined semantics which is based on *causal relations*. Following the Keramane and Duda approach [11], we define explicitly that some time points occur because other ones have just occurred. So, a scenario is a way to precisely indicate which points are related by the causal relations. In the models, causal relations between time points are denoted by:

$$p \mapsto q$$

which means that "the occurrence of q is caused by the occurrence of p". The point p is called the "cause" and q is the "consequence". It is important to distinguish between the *observation* of a point occurrence and the *generation* of end points for a multimedia object. The causes are the observed points. They are denoted by $\mathsf{begin}(A)$, $\mathsf{end}(A)$ or v (if v is produced by a program). The consequences are the generated occurrences and are denoted respectively by $\mathsf{start}(A)$ or $\mathsf{stop}(A)$. The notation $p \mapsto q, r$ stands for $p \mapsto q \;\&\; p \mapsto r$ and $p, q \mapsto r$ stands for $p \mapsto r \;\&\; q \mapsto r$, with obvious generalization to any number of points on both sides. The symbol & is the relation connector. A causal relation may be conditional. This is denoted by:

$$p \mapsto q \quad if \quad c$$

where c is a condition (predicate). The conditional form means that the causal relation $p \mapsto q$ holds if c is true. Conditions can express the way that time points are related using the relations: $<, \leq, =, \neq, \geq, >$ [21]. Notice that we do not need the "?" (unknown) relation. The notation $p \in q..r$ is a shortcut for $q \leq p \wedge p \leq r$. The following mathematical properties hold:

distributivity:	$(p \mapsto q \;\&\; r \mapsto s)\ \mathit{if}\ c \;\Leftrightarrow\; (p \mapsto q\ \mathit{if}\ c) \;\&\; (r \mapsto s\ \mathit{if}\ c)$
transitivity:	$(p \mapsto q\ \mathit{if}\ c_1) \;\&\; (q \mapsto r\ \mathit{if}\ c_2) \;\Rightarrow\; p \mapsto r\ \mathit{if}\ c_1 \wedge c_2$
triangularization:	$(p \mapsto q\ \mathit{if}\ c_1) \;\&\; (p \mapsto r\ \mathit{if}\ c_2) \;\Rightarrow\; q \mapsto r\ \mathit{if}\ (c_1 \Rightarrow c_2)$
simultaneity:	$p \mapsto q \Rightarrow p = q$
properties of the & connector:	associative, commutative and idempotent

4.2 Formal Definition of the Operators

The operators can be formally defined by causal relations imposed on the end points of the arguments. This semantics is presented under two forms below, a diagrammatic form and a textual one. In the first form, argument segments are rectangles, the segment resulting from the operator is a dash rectangle. The arrows connecting the end points of the arguments are the causal relations of the second form. In the loop construct, the occurrences of the argument are indexed (they must be distinguished by different names). In the description relative to a particular node t, the point begin without argument denotes the observation of the beginning of t. The causal relation with begin as origin must be unconditional. The generation of stop without argument represents a case for the termination of t. Each segment is uniquely identified in each node and there is only one start(A) for each segment A. A term (i.e. a scenario) is a tree where the node operators can be well identified, so each segment in a term is uniquely identified and may be started only once. Constant segments (delay, ...) do not contain causal relations because they do not have segment arguments.

Expression	Diagram	Causal Relations
$A \,\underline{;}\, B$	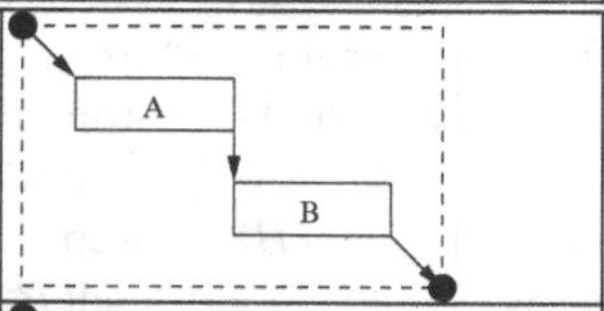	begin $\mapsto$ start(A) & end(A) $\mapsto$ start(B) & end(B) $\mapsto$ stop
loop(A)	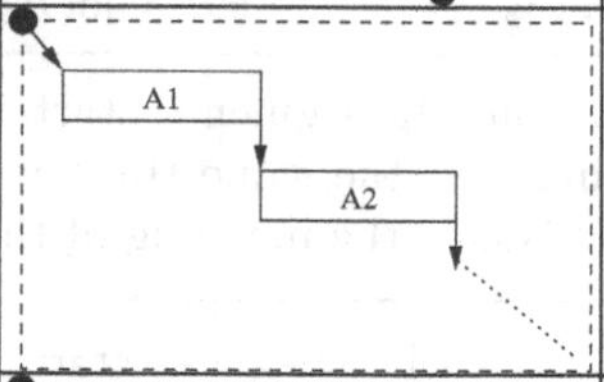	begin $\mapsto$ start(A_1) & end(A_1) $\mapsto$ start(A_2) & ...
loop[n](A)	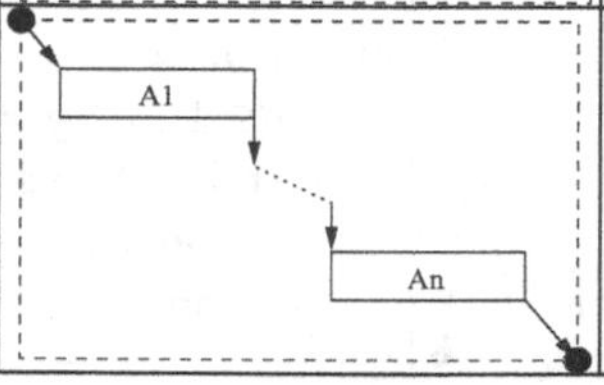	begin $\mapsto$ start(A_1) & end(A_1) $\mapsto$ start(A_2) & ... & end(A_n) $\mapsto$ stop

In the second formal definition set below, the arguments of the operators start in parallel. We use conditional causal relations to determine which are the causal relations which hold, depending on the respective duration of the segments. For these parallel operators, let us consider the end of an argument s caused by causal relations inside the segment: there may be several causes that stop the segment s from inside. For example, if the length of s is known, the fact that the end of the data presented has been reached (at the instant $s.\mathsf{begin}(s) + \mathsf{len}(s)$) implicitly generates a $s.\mathsf{stop}(s)$ point. The set of the stop points inside s is denoted by $s.\mathsf{stopSet}$. The points in this set are ordered by the time order relation. So the actual end of a segment s from inside is defined by the first point in $s.\mathsf{stopSet}$ which is denoted by $s.\mathsf{fstop}$. Then, in the current node, an argument s can be stopped "from outside". Indeed, there is no way to declare other causal relations elsewhere, because the segment s cannot be referenced from the other nodes. The causal relation is conditional with respect to the observation of $s.\mathsf{fstop}$. One can notice that the conditions of causal relations depend only on observed time points.

$\mathsf{master}[\ A \parallel B\ ]$	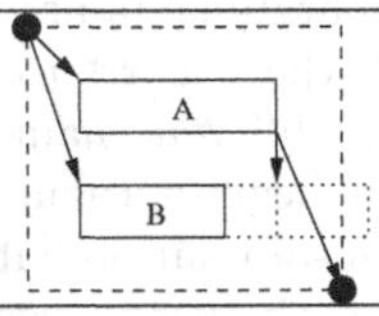	$\mathsf{begin} \mapsto \mathsf{start}(A), \mathsf{start}(B)$ $\&\ \mathsf{end}(A) \mapsto \mathsf{stop}(B)$ $\quad \mathit{if}\ \mathsf{end}(A) \leq B.\mathsf{fstop}$ $\&\ \mathsf{end}(A) \mapsto \mathsf{stop}$
$\mathsf{min}[\ A \parallel B\ ]$	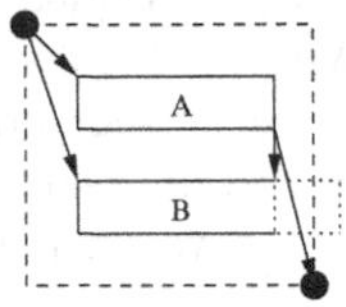	$\mathsf{begin} \mapsto \mathsf{start}(A), \mathsf{start}(B)$ $\&\ \mathsf{end}(A) \mapsto \mathsf{stop}(B), \mathsf{stop}$ $\quad \mathit{if}\ \mathsf{end}(A) < B.\mathsf{fstop}$ $\&\ \mathsf{end}(B) \mapsto \mathsf{stop}(A), \mathsf{stop}$ $\quad \mathit{if}\ \mathsf{end}(B) < A.\mathsf{fstop}$ $\&\ \mathsf{end}(A) \mapsto \mathsf{stop}$ $\quad \mathit{if}\ A.\mathsf{fstop} = B.\mathsf{fstop}$
$\mathsf{max}[\ A \parallel B\ ]$	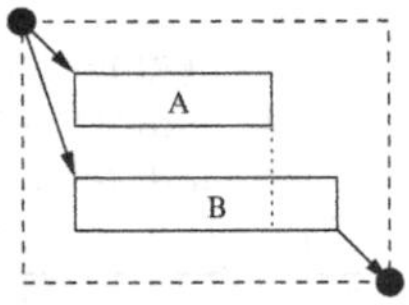	$\mathsf{begin} \mapsto \mathsf{start}(A), \mathsf{start}(B)$ $\&\ \mathsf{end}(A) \mapsto \mathsf{stop}$ $\quad \mathit{if}\ \mathsf{end}(A) \geq B.\mathsf{fstop}$ $\&\ \mathsf{end}(B) \mapsto \mathsf{stop}$ $\quad \mathit{if}\ \mathsf{end}(B) > A.\mathsf{fstop}$

In the "alternative" expression, all the A_k segments start in parallel. If two segments A_i and A_j $(j \neq i)$ terminate at the same time, we assume that the segment A_i such as $i < j$ is chosen. This is the meaning of the $<^+$ ordering.

$\mathsf{alt}[\ A_1 => B_1$ $\parallel A_2 => B_2$ $\dots$ $\parallel A_n => B_n$ $]$	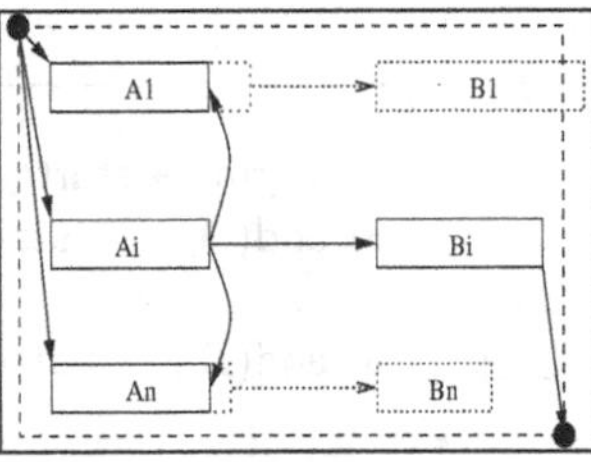	$\mathsf{begin} \mapsto \mathsf{start}(A_1), \dots, \mathsf{start}(A_n)$ $\forall i \in 1..n \Rightarrow$ $(\&\ \forall j \in 1..n \wedge j \neq i \Rightarrow$ $\quad ((\mathsf{end}(A_i) \mapsto \mathsf{stop}(A_j), \mathsf{start}(B_i)$ $\quad \&\ \mathsf{end}(B_i) \mapsto \mathsf{stop})$ $\quad \mathit{if}\ \mathsf{end}(A_i) <^+ A_j.\mathsf{fstop}))$

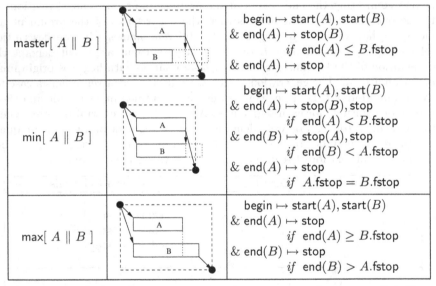

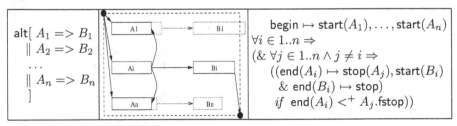

For the general parallel operator, the causal relations which are able to stop a branch labelled by a_i can be either inside the segment A_i ($A_i.\mathsf{stopSet}$) or in any branch a_j for $j \neq i$ by the way of link operators in the same par node. So the set of the observable points for the termination of a segment A_i in a par node is denoted by A_i.parstopSet. In such a node, the overloaded expression A_i.fstop is again the first point of the set. The expression *ref*(b) denotes the segment labelled by b.

par[$a_1 \,\underline{:}\, A_1$ $\parallel a_2 \,\underline{:}\, A_2$ ... $\parallel a_n \,\underline{:}\, A_n$]	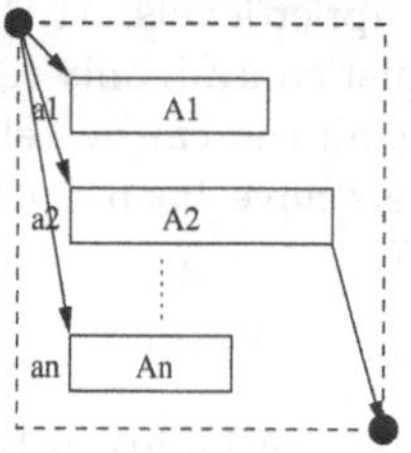	begin $\mapsto$ start(A_1), ..., start(A_n) $\forall i \in 1..n \Rightarrow$ (& $\forall j \in 1..n \wedge j \neq i \Rightarrow$ (end(A_i) $\mapsto$ stop *if* end(A_i) $>^+$ A_j.fstop))
$A \searrow \{b\}$	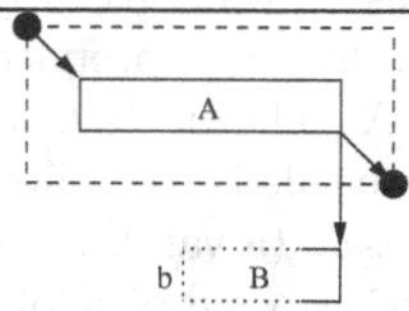	begin $\mapsto$ start(A) & end(A) $\mapsto$ stop(*ref*(b)) *if* end(A) $<$ *ref*(b).fstop & end(A) $\mapsto$ stop
$A \nwarrow \{v\}$	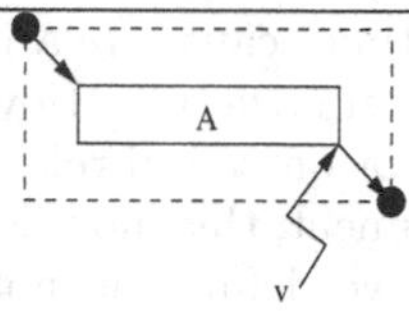	begin $\mapsto$ start(A) & $v \mapsto$ stop(A) *if* $v \in$ begin(A)..A.fstop & end(A) $\mapsto$ stop

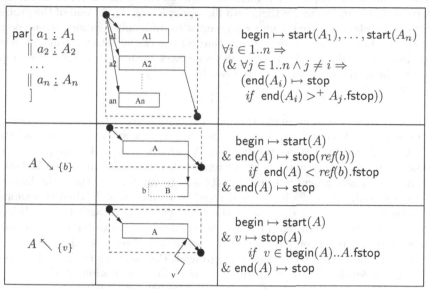

4.3 Causal Relations of Terms

In the previous section, we defined the set of causal relations attached to each operator. The aim of this section is to define how to compute such a set (denoted *CRel*) for any term. The *CRel* set of a term is the set of all the causal relations which hold between end points of the objects located at the leaves of the term tree. These objects are either constants (i.e. monomedia data) or variables on segments. If ψ is a term, then its *CRel* set can be computed by $Rel(\psi)$ defined below. Several auxiliary definitions are needed. A causal relation *level* is a pair $\psi.\rho$ where ψ is a term and ρ is a set of *CRel.* Obviously such a pair is valid iff ρ is the set of causal relations of ψ. The formal definitions of the operators in the previous section are semantic definitions of levels, parameterized by the variables that are arguments of the root operator: let $f(A_1, \ldots, A_n)$ be the left-hand side of a definition, then $sem[f](A_1, \ldots, A_n)$ is the *CRel* set of the textual form at the right-hand side. For example:

$$sem[\,\underline{;}\,](A, B) = \mathsf{begin} \mapsto \mathsf{start}(A)\ \&\ \mathsf{end}(A) \mapsto \mathsf{start}(B)\ \&\ \mathsf{end}(B) \mapsto \mathsf{stop}$$

Levels are hierarchically organized by the tree structure of the terms. The operator *Norm* normalizes structured levels and returns the flat set of relations associated with the whole term. The operator *rel* is used to generate inductively the sub-levels of a term. In the last rule below, *rel* is applied on the arguments, i.e. $\alpha_i.rel(\alpha_i)$ only if α_i is of sort *seg* and not *ref* (nor *point*, *Nat*, ...). The normalization is defined by:

$$
\begin{aligned}
Rel(\psi) &= Norm(\psi.rel(\psi)) \\
\psi.rel(A) &= \emptyset \qquad\qquad\qquad \text{if } A \text{ is a leaf object} \\
\psi.rel(f(\ldots,\alpha_i,\ldots)) &= \psi.sem[f](\ldots,\alpha_i,\ldots)\ldots \cup\ \alpha_i.rel(\alpha_i)\ \cup \ldots
\end{aligned}
$$

The normalization operator is intended to fetch the basic causal relations from the sub-levels and to merge them into the upper levels. At the end of the process, the causal relation set of the upper level must contain only relations on end points of constants or variables, that means that all the causal relations on end points of constants and variables of the sub-levels have been pushed up to the upper level. Then, this set is the expected result:

$$Norm(\psi.\{r_1\ \&\ldots\&\ r_k\}\ \cup\ \ldots) = r_1\ \&\ldots\&\ r_k$$

The definition of the normalization process can be given by cases. Each case is an inference rule containing a name, a condition P, premises α and a conclusion β. A rule generally depends on variables X. The parts α and β are pairs $\psi.\rho$ or union of pairs. The meaning of an inference rule is the following: in a *CRel* set T, if there is an assignment m to the variables X (a valuation of the variables) such that the predicate $m(P)$ is true and $m(\alpha)$ is a subpart of T, then this subpart can be replaced by $m(\beta)$. Most of the time, causal relations of the sub-levels can be propagated bottom-up in the term structure. However for some rules, propagation depends on level conditions or on causal relations on sub-levels. In fact, if an upper-level point stops an argument, this modifies the causal relations of the sub-levels of this argument. So, we define the notion of *independence* between the level of a term and the levels of its subterms. We denote by $\psi < \psi'$ the relation stating that ψ' is a strict subterm of ψ (and $\leq$ for $<$ or $=$). If the consequence $\mathsf{stop}(\psi')$ does not occur in the causal relation set of ψ, we say that ψ' is a subterm independent of the term ψ, what is written $\psi \lhd \psi'$. More precisely, we have:

$$\psi \lhd \psi' \ \Leftrightarrow\ \forall \psi'' \cdot (\psi < \psi'' \wedge \psi'' \leq \psi' \Rightarrow p \mapsto \mathsf{stop}(\psi'') \notin \psi.\rho)$$

where ρ is the semantics of the root operator of ψ.

We give here only five inference rules. The other ones are stated and will be given in a future publication. In those rules, the variables p, q stand for points different from begin and stop without parameters; ψ, α, β stand for terms and c, c' stand for conditions. The first three rules (lift, i-begin and i-end) are general rules under the independence hypothesis.

Name	Condition	Rule
lift	$(p \mapsto q\ \mathit{if}\ c) \in \psi' \wedge \psi \lhd \psi'$	$\dfrac{}{\psi.\{p \mapsto q\ \ \mathit{if}\ \ c\}}$
i-begin	$(\mathsf{begin} \mapsto q) \in \psi' \wedge \psi \lhd \psi'$	$\dfrac{\psi.\{p \mapsto \mathsf{start}(\psi')\ \mathit{if}\ c\}}{\psi.\{p \mapsto q\ \ \mathit{if}\ \ c\}}$
i-end	$(p \mapsto \mathsf{stop}\ \mathit{if}\ c') \in \psi' \wedge \psi \lhd \psi'$	$\dfrac{\psi.\{\mathsf{end}(\psi') \mapsto q\ \mathit{if}\ c\}}{\psi.\{p \mapsto q\ \ \mathit{if}\ \ c \wedge c'\}}$

The following rule, named "stop-seq", shows the effect of stopping a segment which is composed of a sequence of two segments. It holds under the condition $\psi < \alpha \,\underset{-}{;}\, \beta$.

$$\frac{\begin{array}{l}\psi.\{\ p \mapsto \mathsf{stop}(\alpha \,\underset{-}{;}\, \beta) \ \ \mathit{if}\ \ c\ \} \\ \cup\ \ (\alpha \,\underset{-}{;}\, \beta).\{\ \mathsf{begin} \mapsto \mathsf{start}(\alpha)\ \&\ \mathsf{end}(\alpha) \mapsto \mathsf{start}(\beta)\ \&\ \mathsf{end}(\beta) \mapsto \mathsf{stop}\ \}\end{array}}{\begin{array}{l}\psi.\{\ p \mapsto \mathsf{stop}(\alpha)\ \ \mathit{if}\ \ p \in \mathsf{begin}(\alpha)..\alpha.\mathsf{fstop} \wedge c \\ \quad \&\ (\mathsf{end}(\alpha) \mapsto \mathsf{start}(\beta)\ \&\ p \mapsto \mathsf{stop}(\beta))\ \ \mathit{if}\ \ p \in \mathsf{begin}(\beta)..\beta.\mathsf{fstop} \wedge c\ \} \\ \cup\ (\alpha \,\underset{-}{;}\, \beta).\{\ \mathsf{begin} \mapsto \mathsf{start}(\alpha) \\ \qquad \&\ (\mathsf{end}(\alpha) \mapsto \mathsf{start}(\beta)\ \&\ \mathsf{end}(\beta) \mapsto \mathsf{stop}) \\ \qquad\qquad\qquad\qquad \mathit{if}\ \ p < \mathsf{begin}(\alpha) \vee p > \mathsf{end}(\beta) \vee \neg c\ \}\end{array}}$$

The second example of a top-down stop rule is the replacement of a $\mathsf{stop}(\mathsf{max}[\alpha \parallel \beta])$ point. Under the condition $\psi < \mathsf{max}[\alpha \parallel \beta]$, the "stop-max" rule is:

$$\frac{\begin{array}{l}\psi.\{\ p \mapsto \mathsf{stop}(\mathsf{max}[\alpha \parallel \beta])\ \ \mathit{if}\ \ c\ \} \\ \cup\ \ \mathsf{max}[\alpha \parallel \beta].\{\ \mathsf{begin} \mapsto \mathsf{start}(\alpha), \mathsf{start}(\beta) \\ \qquad\qquad \&\ \mathsf{end}(\alpha) \mapsto \mathsf{stop}\ \ \mathit{if}\ \ \mathsf{end}(\alpha) \geq \beta.\mathsf{fstop} \\ \qquad\qquad \&\ \mathsf{end}(\beta) \mapsto \mathsf{stop}\ \ \mathit{if}\ \ \mathsf{end}(\beta) > \alpha.\mathsf{fstop}\ \}\end{array}}{\begin{array}{l}\psi.\{\ p \mapsto \mathsf{stop}(\alpha), \mathsf{stop}(\beta)\ \ \mathit{if}\ \ p \in \mathsf{begin}(\alpha)..\mathit{min}(\alpha.\mathsf{fstop}, \beta.\mathsf{fstop}) \wedge c \\ \quad \&\ p \mapsto \mathsf{stop}(\beta)\ \ \mathit{if}\ \ \alpha.\mathsf{fstop} < \beta.\mathsf{fstop} \wedge p \in \alpha.\mathsf{fstop}..\beta.\mathsf{fstop} \wedge c \\ \quad \&\ p \mapsto \mathsf{stop}(\alpha)\ \ \mathit{if}\ \ \beta.\mathsf{fstop} < \alpha.\mathsf{fstop} \wedge p \in \beta.\mathsf{fstop}..\alpha.\mathsf{fstop} \wedge c\ \} \\ \cup\ \ \mathsf{max}[\alpha \parallel \beta].\{\ \mathsf{begin} \mapsto \mathsf{start}(\alpha), \mathsf{start}(\beta) \\ \ \&\ \mathsf{end}(\alpha) \mapsto \mathsf{stop}\ \ \mathit{if}\ \ \mathsf{end}(\alpha) \geq \beta.\mathsf{fstop} \wedge (p < \mathsf{begin}(\alpha) \vee p > \mathsf{end}(\alpha) \vee \neg c) \\ \ \&\ \mathsf{end}(\beta) \mapsto \mathsf{stop}\ \ \mathit{if}\ \ \mathsf{end}(\beta) > \alpha.\mathsf{fstop} \wedge (p < \mathsf{begin}(\beta) \vee p > \mathsf{end}(\beta) \vee \neg c\ \}\end{array}}$$

5 Properties

5.1 Term Equivalences

There are three notions of equivalence that we can define on multimedia segments. The first one is the *observational equality* denoted by "$\simeq$". We say that $A \simeq B$ iff A and B have the same rendering in every context. By *rendering*, we mean the content effectively presented to a user when the presentation is executed. For example, if B has the same length as A, then:

$$\mathsf{par}[a \,\underset{-}{:}\, (A \,\underset{-}{;}\, C) \parallel b \,\underset{-}{:}\, B] \simeq \mathsf{par}[a \,\underset{-}{:}\, A \parallel b \,\underset{-}{:}\, (B \,\underset{-}{;}\, C)]$$

Causal relations between end points are different in both expressions. In the first one, the end of A starts C, while in the second one, the end of B starts C. However the rendering is the same, that is, A and B are presented in parallel until they stop together at the same time, then C is presented immediately after. Another equivalence could be the one induced by the axiomatization of Section 3.

As explained in Section 4.1, this semantics reflects the static properties on the lengths of the segments. It does not provide any property on the scenarios.

In this section, we investigate another equivalence, denoted by "$\sim$" which represents the equivalence of the causal relation sets of two terms. It is defined by:

$$A \sim B \Leftrightarrow Cl(Rel(A)) \approx Cl(Rel(B))$$

where Cl is the closure of a causal relation set by transitivity and triangularization and $\approx$ is the equality modulo commutativity, associativity, idempotence of & and semantic equivalence of the conditions. Our condition language contains expressions of the form $p < s.\mathsf{fstop}$, $p = s.\mathsf{fstop}$, $p > s.\mathsf{fstop}$, $p <^{+} s.\mathsf{fstop}$, $p >^{+} s.\mathsf{fstop}$. All these expressions are finite conjunctions or disjunctions of single comparisons between time points. So, we have to deal with litterals of the form: $x = y$, $x < y$ which are combined by negation and finite conjunctions and disjunctions. Such a logic formalism has been proven decidable on the field of reals [5]. It is then possible to determine a normal form for the conditions, making the closure operation decidable.

From this equivalence, some interesting axioms can be deduced, as the following ones:

$$\begin{array}{rcl} A_1 \underline{;} (A_2 \underline{;} A_3) & \sim & (A_1 \underline{;} A_2) \underline{;} A_3 \\ \mathsf{max}[A \parallel B] & \sim & \mathsf{par}[a \underline{:} A \parallel b \underline{:} B] \end{array}$$

Other term equivalences for $\sim$ can be found in [3].

5.2 Properties on Scenarios

Scenarios defined by operators are consistent by construction [22]. Besides this fundamental characteristic, another advantage of the algebraic approach is that properties can be inductively defined on the term structure of the scenarios. In this section, we consider the "controllability" property of a scenario. A scenario S is said *controlled*, either if it is terminating (its length is known) or if it can be stopped by an interaction with the user. Typically, a scenario such as *show_Video* (Section 3.5) is controlled because the user can click on the button and stop the presentation.

In the following axiomatization, for any term ψ we compute the value $\mathsf{nc}(\psi)$: a set of subterms that are not known to be controlled, while subterms outside this set are. We should then control the elements of this set to control the whole presentation. An example of non-controlled term is $\mathsf{loop}(A)$, because its presentation is not terminating by itself. On the contrary, $\mathsf{master}[B \parallel \mathsf{loop}(A)]$ is controlled iff B is also controlled. Notice that "controlled" does not mean "terminating" because, taking again the example of Section 3.5, the user can never click on the button. For a basic monomedia object A, the value of $\mathsf{nc}(A)$ is $\{A\}$ if the object is not controlled or $\emptyset$ if it is controlled. The inductive definition of nc is:

$$\begin{array}{ll} \mathsf{nc}(A \mathbin{;} B) = \mathsf{nc}(A) \cup \mathsf{nc}(B) & \mathsf{nc}(\mathsf{min}[A \parallel B]) = \mathsf{nc}(A) \cup \mathsf{nc}(B) \\ \mathsf{nc}(\mathsf{loop}(A)) = \{\mathsf{loop}(A)\} & \mathsf{nc}(\mathsf{max}[A \parallel B]) = \mathsf{nc}(A) \cup \mathsf{nc}(B) \\ \mathsf{nc}(\mathsf{loop}[n](A)) = \emptyset & \mathsf{nc}(\mathsf{alt}[\|_i A_i => B_i]) = \bigcup_i \mathsf{nc}(A_i) \cup \bigcup_i \mathsf{nc}(B_i) \\ \mathsf{nc}(\mathsf{delay}) = \{\mathsf{delay}\} & \mathsf{nc}(\mathsf{par}[\|_i a_i : A_i]) = \bigcup_i \mathsf{nc}(A_i) \\ \mathsf{nc}(\mathsf{delay}[d]) = \emptyset & \mathsf{nc}(A \searrow_{\{b\}}) = \mathsf{nc}(A) \\ \mathsf{nc}(\mathsf{master}[A \parallel B]) = \mathsf{nc}(A) & \mathsf{nc}(A \nwarrow_{\{v\}}) = \mathsf{nc}(A) \end{array}$$

The definition of nc that we give build an approximate greater set. It could be reduced using some conditions on time points that give more precise cases when a term is not controlled. For example, in the calculus of $\mathsf{nc}(A \nwarrow_{\{v\}})$, we could state that:

$$\begin{array}{l} \mathsf{nc}(A \nwarrow_{\{v\}}) = \emptyset \;\; \textit{if} \;\; \mathsf{begin}(A) \leq v \\ \mathsf{nc}(A \nwarrow_{\{v\}}) = \mathsf{nc}(A) \;\; \textit{if} \;\; \mathsf{begin}(A) > v \end{array}$$

5.3 Relations with other Frameworks

In the end of the paper, we would want to discuss the relationships between our model and interval-based and point-based models. First, because our model deals with segments, one can wonder if there exists a correspondence between the Allen interval-based model [1] and the algebraic one. Clearly, the models are not strictly comparable, because the first one does not consider that some intervals have an effect on the duration of other intervals. However, it is easy to see that for every consistent description using interval relations there exists a model (a term or more often a set of terms) in the algebraic framework, that satisfies the description. For example, the following relations at the left-hand side are satisfied by the terms at the right-hand side:

$$\begin{array}{ll} A \text{ meets } B & A \mathbin{;} B \\ A \text{ starts } B & \mathsf{par}[a : A \parallel b : B] \\ A \text{ during } B & \mathsf{par}[a : \mathsf{delay}[d] \mathbin{;} A \parallel b : B] \\ A \text{ equal } B & \mathsf{par}[a : A \parallel b : B] \;\; \textit{if} \quad \mathsf{len}(A) = \mathsf{len}(B) \end{array}$$

For the model of the during relation, the duration d must be tuned according to the respective lengths of A and B as in the the Wahl and Rothermel model [21]. We can see in the last example (equal) that there are many ways to achieve the rendering of the relation A equal B in the algebraic model. One could use $\mathsf{master}[A \parallel B]$ if $\mathsf{len}(B) > \mathsf{len}(A)$. In these cases, segments may have different durations considering them alone or as argument of an operator. At each level, segments get an "a priori" and an "a posteriori" duration. This is the originality of the algebraic approach with respect to the classic interval-based approach.

It is even more interesting to discuss the point-based model because one can use the properties on time points in an expression for the ordering and for the calculation of unspecified relations. For each segment, we have defined the beginning and the end, which are time points. By the simultaneity axiom (Section 4.1) and the interval consistency property (Section 3.1), one can translate automatically an algebraic scenario into a set of point relations. In this translation the generation $\mathsf{start}(s)$ is considered as the point $\mathsf{begin}(s)$. In the same way, the generation of $\mathsf{stop}(s)$ can be considered as $\mathsf{end}(s)$ if it is the first stop point of the segment s within the current conditions. In the sequel, $\mathsf{b}s$ and $\mathsf{e}s$ are put respectively for $\mathsf{begin}(s)$ and $\mathsf{end}(s)$. The point b denotes the beginning of the expression and e denotes its end. For example, the expression $B \,\underline{;}\, C$ can be translated into the set of relations between the end points of the arguments:

$$\mathsf{b} = \mathsf{b}B \wedge \mathsf{b}B \leq \mathsf{e}B \wedge \mathsf{e}B = \mathsf{b}C \wedge \mathsf{b}C \leq \mathsf{e}C \wedge \mathsf{e}C = \mathsf{e}$$

In particular cases, one can impose that some segments s are not empty, stating that $\mathsf{begin}(s) < \mathsf{end}(s)$. When a scenario is more complex, then it defines several cases depending on the relative positioning of points. For example, taking the simple scenario: $S = \mathsf{master}[A \parallel B \,\underline{;}\, C]$, the causal relation set $Rel(S)$ computed by applying the rules of Section 4.3 is as follows. In the conditions, we replace $X.\mathsf{fstop}$ by $\mathsf{e}X$, that is, in this case, the point reached at the normal end of the segment X (if it exists, otherwise the point is greater than any other point).

$$\begin{array}{l}
\mathsf{begin} \mapsto \mathsf{start}(A), \mathsf{start}(B) \\
\ \&\ \mathsf{end}(A) \mapsto \mathsf{stop}(B) \ \ \textit{if}\ \ \mathsf{b}B \leq \mathsf{e}A \wedge \mathsf{e}A \leq \mathsf{e}B \wedge \mathsf{e}A \leq \mathsf{e}C \\
\ \&\ (\mathsf{end}(B) \mapsto \mathsf{start}(C)\ \&\ \mathsf{end}(A) \mapsto \mathsf{stop}(C)) \ \ \textit{if}\ \ \mathsf{b}C < \mathsf{e}A \wedge \mathsf{e}A \leq \mathsf{e}C \\
\ \&\ \mathsf{end}(B) \mapsto \mathsf{start}(C) \ \ \textit{if}\ \ \mathsf{e}A < \mathsf{b}B \vee \mathsf{e}A > \mathsf{e}C \\
\ \&\ \mathsf{end}(A) \mapsto \mathsf{stop}
\end{array}$$

The conditions after *if* determine four disjoint regions, that correspond to the relative positioning of $\mathsf{e}A$ on the time line. These regions are, after simplifications using the point relations coming from lower levels: $\mathsf{e}A < \mathsf{b}B$, $\mathsf{b}B \leq \mathsf{e}A \wedge \mathsf{e}A \leq \mathsf{e}B$, $\mathsf{b}C < \mathsf{e}A \wedge \mathsf{e}A \leq \mathsf{e}C$ and $\mathsf{e}C < \mathsf{e}A$. They are "a priori conditions" on the segments. The causal relations introduced by the master operator modify some end points: the $\mathsf{stop}(X)$ point in the causal relations become a new point for the end of the segment X. For example, in the rule:

$$(\mathsf{end}(B) \mapsto \mathsf{start}(C)\ \&\ \mathsf{end}(A) \mapsto \mathsf{stop}(C)) \ \ \textit{if}\ \ \mathsf{b}C < \mathsf{e}A \wedge \mathsf{e}A \leq \mathsf{e}C$$

The old relation $\mathsf{e}A \leq \mathsf{e}C$ is overriden by the relation $\mathsf{e}A = \mathsf{e}C$ deduced from the simultaneity property. One can notice that a $\mathsf{start}(X)$ point allows the segment X to be presented. Some cases may become inconsistent and must be removed from the possible scenarios. For example, let us take the following case in our scenario:

$$\begin{array}{l}
(\mathsf{begin} \mapsto \mathsf{start}(A), \mathsf{start}(B)\ \&\ \mathsf{end}(B) \mapsto \mathsf{start}(C)\ \&\ \mathsf{end}(A) \mapsto \mathsf{stop}) \\
\quad \textit{if}\ \ \mathsf{e}A < \mathsf{b}B
\end{array}$$

There is no modification on the points of segment ends. Applying the simultaneity property provides: $\mathsf{b} = \mathsf{b}A \wedge \mathsf{b} = \mathsf{b}B \wedge \mathsf{e}B = \mathsf{b}C \wedge \mathsf{e}A = \mathsf{e}$. These relations are combined with the consistency properties of the segments $\mathsf{b}A \leq \mathsf{e}A \wedge \mathsf{b}B \leq \mathsf{e}B \wedge \mathsf{b}C \leq \mathsf{e}C$ which produce easily the relation $\mathsf{b}B \leq \mathsf{e}A$. We obtain a contradiction with the condition, so such a scenario is deleted. An algorithm for checking consistency of point relations in polynomial time can be found in [20]. At the end of the process of the point calculus of the scenario S, in all cases we have $\mathsf{b} = \mathsf{b}A \wedge \mathsf{b} = \mathsf{b}B$ for the beginning and $\mathsf{e}A = \mathsf{e}$ for the end. The other relations between end points of the segments characterize the three scenarios (in the first one, C is not even partially presented):

$$\begin{array}{l}
\ \ \ (\mathsf{b}A \leq \mathsf{e}A \wedge \mathsf{b}B \leq \mathsf{e}B \wedge \mathsf{e}A = \mathsf{e}B) \\
\vee\ (\mathsf{b}A \leq \mathsf{e}A \wedge \mathsf{b}B \leq \mathsf{e}B \wedge \mathsf{e}B = \mathsf{b}C \wedge \mathsf{b}C \leq \mathsf{e}C \wedge \mathsf{b}C < \mathsf{e}A \wedge \mathsf{e}A = \mathsf{e}C) \\
\vee\ (\mathsf{b}A \leq \mathsf{e}A \wedge \mathsf{b}B \leq \mathsf{e}B \wedge \mathsf{e}B = \mathsf{b}C \wedge \mathsf{b}C \leq \mathsf{e}C \wedge \mathsf{e}C < \mathsf{e}A)
\end{array}$$

6 Conclusion and Future Work

We presented in this paper an operator algebra to specify temporal scenarios of multimedia presentations. Beyond its standard semantics, our model has a specific semantics based on causal relations. This semantics stands apart from usual ones with taking into consideration dynamic behavior in operators, such as alt or link operators. The model is able to deal with non-determinism, either like unknown duration objects or user actions (corresponding to program events). The algebraic semantics and the term structure of scenarios provide an inductive way for reasoning about equivalences or properties of presentations, as shown in the paper. The translation of scenarios into the time point framework has been only sketched. Thanks to the algorithms developed on point networks, this can help to check if parts of the scenario will be effectively presented.

Another application of the consistency algorithms could be to answer to queries about scenarios. These queries should be related to temporal positioning of segments. In this way, it should be possible to check if a presentation represented by an expression actually satisfies given conditions such as for example some Allen relations.

The normalization presented here is a step in the process of compiling expressions aiming at the "execution" of scenarios. This topic addresses new issues tackled in [3]. We intend to investigate the automatic translation of our causal relation sets in an operational form that can be executed by a dedicated execution engine. Another important challenge is the integration of spatial information in our framework and the ability to compose the spatial characteristics of the objects as we did with the temporal ones. Moreover it should be interesting to consistently combine a spatial operator algebra with the temporal operator algebra presented here.

Acknowledgements

We are grateful to Andrzej Duda for his help to understand the algebraic video model and for fruitful discussions.

References

1. J. F. Allen. Maintaining knowledge about temporal intervals. *Communications of the ACM*, 26(11), November 1983. 384, 397
2. J. Ayars, A. Cohen, K. Day, and al. Synchronized multimedia integration langage(smil) boston specification. Technical report, W3C : World Wide Web Consortium, 1999. WD-smil-boston-19991115. 384
3. D. Bert and S. Lo Presti. Algebraic Operators and Causal Relations for Modeling Multimedia Presentations. November 1999. Presented at the Symposium on Modal and Temporal Logic-based Planning for Open Networked Multimedia Systems (Boston), To appear in AAAI Press. 384, 386, 396, 399

4. M. C. Buchanan and P. T. Zellweger. Automatic temporal layout mechanisms. In *Proc. First ACM International Conference on Multimedia.*, pages 341–350, Anaheim, CA, August 1993. 384
5. P. J. Cohen. Decision procedures for real and p-adic fields. *Comm. Pure Applied Math.*, (22):131–151, 1969. 396
6. A. Duda and C. Keramane. Structured Temporal Composition of Multimedia Data. In *Proc. International Workshop on Multi-media Database Management Systems*, Blue Mountain Lake, NY, August 1995. 384
7. C.L. Hamblin. Instants and intervals. In *Proc. of the 1st Conf. of the Int. Society for the Study of Time*, pages 324–331, New York, 1972. 384
8. ISO. Information technology hypermedia/time-based structuring language (HyTime). *ISO International Standard*, (ISO/IEC IS 10744), August 1992. 384
9. M. Jourdan, N. Layaïda, C. Roisin, L. Sabry-Ismaïl, and L. Tardif. Madeus, an authoring environment for interactive multimedia documents. In *ACM Multimedia'98*, pages 267–272, Bristol, UK, September 1998. ACM. 384
10. C. Keramane. *Spécification de présentations multimédia interactives.* PhD thesis, Institut National Polytechnique de Grenoble, Octobre 1997. 384
11. C. Keramane and A. Duda. Interval Expressions - a Functional Model for Interactive Dynamic Multimedia Presentations. In *Proc. IEEE Int. Conference on Multimedia Computing and Systems*, Hiroshima, June 1996. 384, 390
12. N. Layaida and C. Keramane. Maintaining temporal consistency of multimedia documents. In *Effective Abstractions in Multimedia Layout, Presentation and Interaction ACM 95 Workshop*, San Francisco, CA, November 1995. 384
13. T. Meyer-Boudnik and W. Effelsberg. MHEG explained. *IEEE Multimedia*, 2(1), 1995. 384
14. T. Mossakowski and M. Roggenbach. Basic Datatypes in CASL. Technical Report CoFI M-6, URL: http://www.brics.dk/Projects/CoFI/Notes/M-6/, March 1999. 387
15. T. Mossakowski and M. Roggenbach. The Datatypes REAL and COMPLEX in CASL. Technical Report CoFI Note M-7, URL: http://www.brics.dk/Projects/CoFI/Notes/M-7/, April 1999. 386
16. P. D. Mosses. CASL: A guided tour of its design. In J. L. Fiadeiro, editor, *Recent Trends in Algebraic Development Techniques, LNCS 1589, Springer-Verlag*, pages 216–240, 1999. 385
17. CoFI Task Group on Language Design. CASL: The Common Algebraic Specification Language, Summary. Technical Report CoFI Document, URL: http://www.brics.dk/Projects/CoFI/Documents/CASL/Summary/, October 1998. 385
18. P. Pazandak, J. Srivastava, and J. Carlis. The temporal component of damsel. In *Second Workshop on Protocols for Multimedia Systems(PROMS'95)*, Salzburg, Austria, 1995. 384
19. F. Rousseau and A. Duda. Synchronized Multimedia for the WWW. In *Proceedings of the Seventh International World Wide Web Conference(WWW7), Computer Networks and ISDN Systems*, pages 417–429, Brisbane, Australia, 1998. 384
20. M. Vilain and H. Kautz. Constraint Propagation Algorithms for Temporal Reasoning. In *Fifth National Conference on Artificial Intelligence*, pages 377–382, Philadelphia, 1986. 398
21. T. Wahl and K. Rothermel. Representing time in multimedia systems. In *Proc. IEEE International Conference on Multimedia Computing and Systems.*, Boston, MA, May 1994. 384, 385, 390, 397

22. R. Weiss, A. Duda, and D.K. Gifford. Composition and search with a Video Algebra. *IEEE Multimedia*, 2(1), 1995. 384, 396

Higher-Order Logic and Theorem Proving for Structured Specifications*

Tomasz Borzyszkowski

Institute of Mathematics, University of Gdańsk
T.Borzyszkowski@guests.ipipan.gda.pl

Abstract. In this paper we present the higher-order logic used in theorem-provers like the HOL system (see [GM 93]) or Isabelle HOL logic (see [Paul 94]) as an institution. Then we show that for maps of institutions into HOL that satisfy certain technical conditions we can reuse the proof system of the higher-order logic to reason about structured specifications built over the institutions mapped into HOL. We also show some maps of institutions underlying the CASL specification formalism (see [CASL 99]) into HOL that satisfy conditions needed for reusing proof systems.

1 Introduction

Following [MKB 97] we want to prepare a theoretical background for the tools support for CASL. We choose the higher-order logic (see [An 86]) as a logic which is a bridge from CASL to theorem-proving and transformation development, because on one hand it seems most appropriate to express the logic of the CASL language and on the other hand it has a quite effective and widely-used tools/machine support (e.g. the HOL system described in [GM 93] or the HOL logic of the Isabelle system described in [Paul 94]).

First we define the higher-order logic, presented in [An 86], as an institution (the technical details are based on [GM 93] and [Paul 94]). Next, we propose several maps of institutions from the logics underlying the CASL specification formalism to the HOL logic. We also show that those maps satisfy the conditions (essentially: β-expansion and weak-$\mathcal{D}$-amalgamation, see [Borz 98]) required for reusing the proof system of the HOL logic for the CASL logics. Finally we propose a methodology for reusing the proof system of the HOL logic for reasoning about structured specifications. This methodology allows us to translate the reasoning about structured specifications (e.g. about CASL specifications) to the HOL logic and consequently to some of the theorem provers for the HOL logic.

2 Language, Models and Satisfaction

In this section we present the language of the HOL logic. Most of the definitions and notions follow [GM 93].

* This research was partially supported by ESPRIT CRIT2 program, working group 29432 (CoFI WG) and KBN grant 8 T11C 037 16.

D. Bert, C. Choppy, and P. Mosses (Eds.): WADT'99, LNCS 1827, pp. 401–418, 2000.

Let *TyVars* be an infinite set of *type variables*, given with a fixed linear order. Greek letters $\alpha, \beta, \ldots$, possibly with subscripts or primes, are used to range over *TyVars*. We assume that an infinite set *TyNames* of the *names of type constants* is given. The Greek letter ν is used to range over arbitrary members of *TyNames*. We also assume that sets *TyVars* and *TyNames* are disjoint.

A *type structure* is a set Ω of type constants. A *type constant* is a pair (ν, n), where $\nu \in$ *TyNames* is the name of the type constant and the natural number n is its arity. We assume that no two distinct type constants have the same name, i.e. whenever $(\nu, n_1) \in \Omega$ and $(\nu, n_2) \in \Omega$, then $n_1 = n_2$. The set $Types_\Omega$ of *types* over the type structure Ω is defined as the smallest set such that:

- $TyVars \subseteq Types_\Omega$;
- if $(\nu, 0) \in \Omega$, then $()\nu \in Types_\Omega$;
- if $(\nu, n) \in \Omega$ and $\tau_i \in Types_\Omega$, for $i = 1, \ldots, n$, then $(\tau_1, \ldots, \tau_n)\nu \in Types_\Omega$;
- if $\tau_1, \tau_2 \in Types_\Omega$, then $\tau_1 \to \tau_2 \in Types_\Omega$.

The distinguished type operator $\to$ is assumed to associate to the right, so that $\tau_1 \to \tau_2 \to \ldots \to \tau_n \to \tau$ abbreviates $\tau_1 \to (\tau_2 \to \ldots \to (\tau_n \to \tau) \ldots)$. Following [GM 93] we introduce the notion of *type-in-context*.

Definition 1 (Type-in-context). *A* type context, $\boldsymbol{\alpha}$ *is a finite (possibly empty) list of distinct type variables* $\alpha_1, \alpha_2, \ldots, \alpha_n$. *A* type-in-context *is a pair, written* $\boldsymbol{\alpha}.\tau$, *where* $\boldsymbol{\alpha}$ *is a type context,* τ *is a type and all the type variables occurring in* τ *appear also in the list* $\boldsymbol{\alpha}$. *A* canonical context *of type* τ *is its minimal context, where all the variables are listed in order.* □

If the type structure Ω includes type constants: $(o, 0)$ and $(\iota, 0)$ then the set $Types_\Omega$ of types and the type structure Ω are called *standard.* When Ω includes type constant $(\times, 2)$ then we say that the set $Types_\Omega$ and the type structure Ω *have product.*

Definition 2 (Type instance). *If* $\tau, \tau_1, \ldots, \tau_n \in Types_\Omega$ *are types, then* $\tau[\tau_1, \ldots, \tau_n / \beta_1, \ldots, \beta_n]$ *is the type which is a result of the simultaneous substitution for each type variable* β_i *in* τ *the type* τ_i, *for* $i = 1, \ldots, n$. *The resulting type is called an* instance *of* τ. □

Lemma 1. *Suppose* τ *is a type containing distinct type variables* $\beta_1, \ldots, \beta_n$ *and* $\tau' = \tau[\tau_1, \ldots, \tau_n / \beta_1, \ldots, \beta_n]$ *is an instance of* τ, *where* $\beta_1, \ldots, \beta_n$ *are all type variables in* τ. *Then the types* $\tau_1, \ldots, \tau_n$ *are uniquely determined by* τ *and* τ'.

Proof. By induction on the structure of type τ. □

Let *VarNames* be an infinite set of *names of variables*, which is given together with a fixed linear order. For a given type structure Ω a denumerable set of *typed variables* is defined as follows: $\mathcal{V} = \{\mathcal{V}_\tau \subseteq VarNames \times \{\tau\} \mid \tau \in Types_\Omega\}$, where each set $\mathcal{V}_\tau$ is denumerable. We will write x^τ as an abbreviation for (x, τ), or just x if it is clear that x is a variable of a given type τ. We assume that all variables have distinct names, i.e. if $x^{\tau_1} \in \mathcal{V}_{\tau_1}$ and $x^{\tau_2} \in \mathcal{V}_{\tau_2}$, then $\tau_1 = \tau_2$.

Let *Names* be an infinite set of *names of constants*, disjoint from *VarNames*, and then for a given type structure Ω, a denumerable set of *typed constants* is defined as follows: $\mathcal{C} = \{\mathcal{C}_\tau \subseteq Names \times \{\tau\} \mid \tau \in Types_\Omega\}$, where each set $\mathcal{C}_\tau$ is denumerable. Similarly as for variables, we will write c_τ as an abbreviation for (c, τ) or c if the type follows from the context. For a given standard type structure Ω, the set $\mathcal{C}$ of constants is *standard* if it contains constants: $\mathbf{Q}_{\alpha\to\alpha\to o}$ and $\iota_{(\alpha\to o)\to\alpha}$, where α is a type variable.

A **HOL** signature is a pair $\Sigma = (\Omega, \mathcal{C})$, where Ω is a type structure and $\mathcal{C}$ is a set of constants typed by types from $Types_\Omega$. The signature Σ is called *standard*, if Ω and $\mathcal{C}$ are standard. We also say that Σ *has product*, if Ω has product and $\mathcal{C}$ contains constants: $pair_{\alpha\to\beta\to\alpha\times\beta}$, $fst_{\alpha\times\beta\to\alpha}$ and $snd_{\alpha\times\beta\to\beta}$, where α and β are type variables. For any signature $\Sigma = (\Omega, \mathcal{C})$, the set $\mathcal{V}$ of typed variables, defined for the type structure Ω, is called a Σ*-variable system*. The set $Terms_\Sigma$ of terms over signature Σ is the smallest set closed under the following rules:

- each variable x^τ from the Σ-variable system $\mathcal{V}_\tau$ is in $Terms_\Sigma$;
- if $c_\tau \in \mathcal{C}$ and $\tau' \in Types_\Omega$ is an instance of τ, then $c_{\tau'} \in Terms_\Sigma$;
- if $t_{\tau_1\to\tau} \in Terms_\Sigma$ and $t^1_{\tau_1} \in Terms_\Sigma$, then $(t_{\tau_1\to\tau}t^1_{\tau_1})_\tau \in Terms_\Sigma$;
- if $x^{\tau_1} \in Terms_\Sigma$ and $t_{\tau_2} \in Terms_\Sigma$, then $(\lambda x^{\tau_1}.t_{\tau_2})_{\tau_1\to\tau_2} \in Terms_\Sigma$.

Usually we will drop some type subscripts in terms, writing $(t_{\tau_1\to\tau}t^1_{\tau_1})$ or just $(t\,t^1)$ for $(t_{\tau_1\to\tau}t^1_{\tau_1})_\tau$, and $(\lambda x^{\tau_1}.t_{\tau_2})$ or $(\lambda x^{\tau_1}.t)$ for $(\lambda x^{\tau_1}.t_{\tau_2})_{\tau_1\to\tau_2}$. Function application is assumed to associate to the left, so that $t^1_{\tau_1}t^2_{\tau_2}t^3_{\tau_3}\dots t^n_{\tau_n}$ abbreviates $(\dots((t^1_{\tau_1}t^2_{\tau_2})t^3_{\tau_3})\dots t^n_{\tau_n})$. The notation $\lambda x^{\tau_1}x^{\tau_2}\cdots x^{\tau_n}.t_\tau$ abbreviates $\lambda x^{\tau_1}.(\lambda x^{\tau_2}.\cdots(\lambda x^{\tau_n}.t_\tau)\cdots)$. A *free* and *bound* occurrence of a variable in a term is defined as usually (see [Bar 98]). If $\mathcal{C}$ is standard then we can introduce following abbreviations (see also [An 86]):

We define	As an abbreviation for
$t_\tau = t'_\tau$	$\mathbf{Q}_{\tau\to\tau\to o}t_\tau t'_\tau$
T_o	$\mathbf{Q}_{o\to o\to o} = \mathbf{Q}_{o\to o\to o}$
F_o	$(\lambda x^o.T_o) = (\lambda x^o.x^o)$
$\forall x^\tau.t_o$	$(\mathbf{Q}_{(\tau\to o)\to(\tau\to o)\to o}(\lambda x^\tau.T_o))(\lambda x^\tau.t_o)$
$\wedge_{o\to o\to o}$	$\lambda x^o.\lambda y^o.(\lambda g^{o\to o\to o}.(gT_oT_o)) = (\lambda g^{o\to o\to o}.(gx^oy^o))$
$\Rightarrow_{o\to o\to o}$	$\lambda x^o.\lambda y^o.(x^o = (x^o \wedge y^o))$
$\neg_{o\to o}$	$\mathbf{Q}_{o\to o\to o}F_o$
$\exists x^\tau.t_o$	$\neg(\forall x^\tau.\neg t_o)$
$\mathbf{IF}_{o\to\tau\to\tau\to\tau\to o}$	$\lambda b^o.\lambda x^\tau.\lambda y^\tau.\lambda z^\tau.(b^o \Rightarrow z^\tau = x^\tau) \wedge (\neg b^o \Rightarrow z^\tau = y^\tau)$
$(\textbf{if } t_o \textbf{ then } t'_\tau \textbf{ else } t''_\tau)_\tau$	$\iota(\mathbf{IF}\ t_o\ t'_\tau\ t''_\tau)$

Σ-terms of type o, where Σ is standard, are called Σ*-formulas*; we use metavariables φ and ψ to range over them. Σ-formulas that do not contain free variables are called Σ*-sentences*. If Σ has product then we will write (a, b) for $((pair\ \ a)\ b)$. Similarly as for types we introduce *term context* and *term-in-context*.

Definition 3. *A* context $\boldsymbol{\alpha}, \boldsymbol{x}$ *consists of type context* $\boldsymbol{\alpha}$ *and a list* $\boldsymbol{x} = (x_1^{\tau_1}, \ldots, x_n^{\tau_n})$ *of distinct variables whose types only contain type variables from the list* $\boldsymbol{\alpha}$. *A* term-in-context $\boldsymbol{\alpha}, \boldsymbol{x}.t$ *consists of a context* $\boldsymbol{\alpha}, \boldsymbol{x}$ *and a term satisfying the following conditions: 1)* $\boldsymbol{\alpha}$ *contains all type variables that occur in* t*; 2)* $\boldsymbol{x}$ *contains all variables that occur freely in* t*; and 3)* $\boldsymbol{x}$ *does not contain any variable that occurs bound in* t*. The* canonical context *of a term* t *is its minimal context, such that both lists* $\boldsymbol{\alpha}$ *and* $\boldsymbol{x}$ *are listed in order.* □

The combination of the second and the third condition in the above definition implies that a variable cannot have both free and bound occurrences in t, but for any term t there always exists a term t', such that t and t' are equal up to renaming of bound variables, which satisfies the above conditions. In the rest of the paper we will work with terms which do not have both free and bound occurrences of a variable. Following [GM 93] we define a *universe* as a class $\mathcal{U}$ of sets satisfying the following conditions: 1) each element of $\mathcal{U}$ is a non-empty set; 2) if $X \in \mathcal{U}$ and $\emptyset \neq Y \subseteq X$ then $Y \in \mathcal{U}$; 3) if $X \in \mathcal{U}$ and $Y \in \mathcal{U}$ then $X \times Y \in \mathcal{U}$; 4) if $X \in \mathcal{U}$ then the powerset $\mathcal{P}(X) = \{Y \mid Y \subseteq X\} \in \mathcal{U}$; 5) $\mathcal{U}$ contains a distinguished infinite set I; and 6) there exists a distinguished element $ch \in \Pi_{X \in \mathcal{U}} X$, where the elements of the product $\Pi_{X \in \mathcal{U}} X$ are dependently typed functions and $ch(X) \in X$ witnesses property 1).

Consequences of the above properties are: 1) if $X \in \mathcal{U}$ and $Y \in \mathcal{U}$, then $X \to Y \in \mathcal{U}$, where $X \to Y$ is a set of all functions from X to Y; 2) $\mathcal{U}$ contains a distinguished one-element set $\mathbf{1}$; 3) $\mathcal{U}$ contains a distinguished two-element set $\mathbf{2}$ and one-element set $\mathbf{0}$, such that $\mathbf{1} \cup \mathbf{0} = \mathbf{2}$. In the rest of the paper we will work with an arbitrary but fixed universe $\mathcal{U}$.

Let $\Sigma = (\Omega, \mathcal{C})$ be a fixed signature. A *Σ-structure* is a pair $\mathcal{M} = (\mathfrak{T}, \mathfrak{I})$, where $\mathfrak{T}$ is an interpretation of type constants from Ω and $\mathfrak{I}$ is an interpretation of constants from $\mathcal{C}$. An interpretation of a type constant $(\nu, n) \in \Omega$ is an n-ary function $\mathfrak{T}(\nu, n) : \mathcal{U}^n \to \mathcal{U}$.

Definition 4 (Interpretation of types-in-context). *For each type-in-context* $\boldsymbol{\alpha}.\tau$ *and a given interpretation of type constants* $\mathfrak{T}$ *we define a function* $\mathfrak{T}[\![\boldsymbol{\alpha}.\tau]\!] : \mathcal{U}^n \to \mathcal{U}$*, where* $\boldsymbol{\alpha} = (\alpha_1, \ldots, \alpha_n)$*, by induction as follows:*

- $\mathfrak{T}[\![\boldsymbol{\alpha}.\alpha_i]\!](X_1, \ldots, X_n) = X_i$*, for* $X_i \in \mathcal{U}$ *and* $i \in \{1, \ldots, n\}$*;*
- $\mathfrak{T}[\![\boldsymbol{\alpha}.(\tau_1, \ldots, \tau_m)\nu]\!](\boldsymbol{X}) = \mathfrak{T}(\nu, m)(\mathfrak{T}[\![\boldsymbol{\alpha}.\tau_1]\!](\boldsymbol{X}), \ldots, \mathfrak{T}[\![\boldsymbol{\alpha}.\tau_m]\!](\boldsymbol{X}))$*;*
- $\mathfrak{T}[\![\boldsymbol{\alpha}.\tau_1 \to \tau_2]\!](\boldsymbol{X}) = \mathfrak{T}[\![\boldsymbol{\alpha}.\tau_1]\!](\boldsymbol{X}) \to \mathfrak{T}[\![\boldsymbol{\alpha}.\tau_2]\!](\boldsymbol{X})$*,*

where $\boldsymbol{X} \in \mathcal{U}^n$. □

Definition 5 (Interpretation of types). *For a given interpretation of type constants* $\mathfrak{T}$ *the interpretation of a type* $\tau \in Types_{\Omega}$*,* $\mathfrak{T}[\![\tau]\!] : \mathcal{U}^n \to \mathcal{U}$*, is given by* $\mathfrak{T}[\![\boldsymbol{\alpha}.\tau]\!]$*, where* $\boldsymbol{\alpha}$ *is the canonical context of* τ. □

Lemma 2. *Given types-in-context* $\boldsymbol{\beta}.\kappa$ *and* $\boldsymbol{\alpha}.\tau_i$*, where* $\boldsymbol{\beta} = \beta_1, \ldots, \beta_p$ *and* $i = 1, \ldots, p$*, if* $\kappa' = \kappa[\tau_1, \ldots, \tau_p/\beta_1, \ldots, \beta_p]$ *then* $\boldsymbol{\alpha}.\kappa'$ *is also type-in-context and for a given interpretation of type constants* $\mathfrak{T}$ *and for every* $\boldsymbol{X} \in \mathcal{U}^n$*, where* n *is the length of* $\boldsymbol{\alpha}$*,* $\mathfrak{T}[\![\boldsymbol{\alpha}.\kappa']\!](\boldsymbol{X}) = \mathfrak{T}[\![\boldsymbol{\beta}.\kappa]\!](\mathfrak{T}[\![\boldsymbol{\alpha}.\tau_1]\!](\boldsymbol{X}), \ldots, \mathfrak{T}[\![\boldsymbol{\alpha}.\tau_p]\!](\boldsymbol{X}))$

Proof. By induction on the structure of κ. □

Definition 6 (Interpretation of constants). *For a given interpretation of type constants $\mathfrak{T}$ an interpretation of a constant $c_\tau \in \mathcal{C}_\tau$ is an element $\mathfrak{I}(c_\tau) \in \Pi_{\boldsymbol{X} \in \mathcal{U}^n} \mathfrak{T}[\![\tau]\!](\boldsymbol{X})$, where n is the number of type variables occurring in τ.* □

Definition 7 (Interpretation of terms-in-context). *Let Σ be a signature, t_τ a Σ-term, $\boldsymbol{\alpha}, \boldsymbol{x}.t_\tau$ be a term-in-context, where $\boldsymbol{x} = (x_1^{\tau_1}, \ldots, x_m^{\tau_m})$ and $\boldsymbol{\alpha} = (\alpha_1, \ldots, \alpha_n)$, and $(\mathfrak{T}, \mathfrak{I})$ be a Σ-structure. The interpretation of the term-in-context $\boldsymbol{\alpha}, \boldsymbol{x}.t_\tau$ is given by an element*

$$\mathfrak{I}[\![\boldsymbol{\alpha}, \boldsymbol{x}.t_\tau]\!] \in \Pi_{\boldsymbol{X} \in \mathcal{U}^n} (\mathfrak{T}[\![\boldsymbol{\alpha}.\tau_1]\!](\boldsymbol{X}) \times \cdots \times \mathfrak{T}[\![\boldsymbol{\alpha}.\tau_m]\!](\boldsymbol{X})) \to \mathfrak{T}[\![\boldsymbol{\alpha}.\tau]\!](\boldsymbol{X}),$$

and for $\boldsymbol{X} = (X_1, \ldots, X_n) \in \mathcal{U}^n$ and $\boldsymbol{y} = (y_1, \ldots, y_m) \in \mathfrak{T}[\![\boldsymbol{\alpha}.\tau_1]\!](\boldsymbol{X}) \times \cdots \times \mathfrak{T}[\![\boldsymbol{\alpha}.\tau_m]\!](\boldsymbol{X})$ is defined by induction as follows:

- $\mathfrak{I}[\![\boldsymbol{\alpha}, \boldsymbol{x}.x_i^{\tau_i}]\!](\boldsymbol{X})(\boldsymbol{y}) = y_i$, *for* $i \in \{1, \ldots, m\}$;
- $\mathfrak{I}[\![\boldsymbol{\alpha}, \boldsymbol{x}.c_{\tau'}]\!](\boldsymbol{X})(\boldsymbol{y}) = \mathfrak{I}(c_\tau)(\mathfrak{T}[\![\boldsymbol{\alpha}.\tau_1']\!](\boldsymbol{X}), \ldots, \mathfrak{T}[\![\boldsymbol{\alpha}.\tau_p']\!](\boldsymbol{X}))$, *where* $c_\tau \in \mathcal{C}_\tau$, τ' *is an instance of* τ *and, by Lemma 1,* $\tau' = \tau[\tau_1', \ldots, \tau_p'/\beta_1, \ldots, \beta_p]$ *for uniquely determined types* $\tau_1', \ldots, \tau_p'$ *(by Lemma 2* $\mathfrak{I}[\![\boldsymbol{\alpha}, \boldsymbol{x}.c_{\tau'}]\!](\boldsymbol{X})(\boldsymbol{y})$ *is an element of* $\mathfrak{T}[\![\boldsymbol{\alpha}.\tau]\!](\boldsymbol{X})$*);*
- $\mathfrak{I}[\![\boldsymbol{\alpha}, \boldsymbol{x}.(t^1_{\tau_2 \to \tau} t^2_{\tau_2})]\!](\boldsymbol{X})(\boldsymbol{y}) = \big(\mathfrak{I}[\![\boldsymbol{\alpha}, \boldsymbol{x}.t^1_{\tau_2 \to \tau}]\!](\boldsymbol{X})(\boldsymbol{y})\big)\big(\mathfrak{I}[\![\boldsymbol{\alpha}, \boldsymbol{x}.t^2_{\tau_2}]\!](\boldsymbol{X})(\boldsymbol{y})\big)$;
- $\mathfrak{I}[\![\boldsymbol{\alpha}, \boldsymbol{x}.(\lambda x^{\tau_1}.t^2_{\tau_2})]\!](\boldsymbol{X})(\boldsymbol{y}) = \Lambda z : \mathfrak{T}[\![\boldsymbol{\alpha}.\tau_1]\!](\boldsymbol{X}).\mathfrak{I}[\![\boldsymbol{\alpha}, (\boldsymbol{x}, x).t^2_{\tau_2}]\!](\boldsymbol{X})(\boldsymbol{y}, z)$.

□

In the above definition the notation of the form $\Lambda x : X.y(x)$ denotes a function which for every element $v \in X$ yields the value $y(v)$.

Definition 8 (Interpretation of terms). *For a given Σ-structure $(\mathfrak{T}, \mathfrak{I})$ the interpretation of a term t_τ, $\mathfrak{I}[\![t_\tau]\!]$, is interpretation of t_τ in its canonical context.* □

Definition 9 (Standard interpretation). *Let Σ be a standard signature. A Σ-structure $\mathcal{M} = (\mathfrak{T}, \mathfrak{I})$ is called* standard, *if 1) $\mathfrak{T}(o, 0) = \mathbf{2}$ and $\mathfrak{T}(\iota, 0) = I$; 2) $\mathfrak{I}(\mathbf{Q}_{\alpha \to \alpha \to o}) \in \Pi_{X \in \mathcal{U}}.X \to X \to \mathbf{2}$ is the function assigning to each $X \in \mathcal{U}$ the equality test function; 3) $\mathfrak{I}(\boldsymbol{\iota}_{(\alpha \to o) \to \alpha}) \in \Pi_{X \in \mathcal{U}}.(X \to \mathbf{2}) \to X$ is the function assigning to each $X \in \mathcal{U}$ the function sending each function $f \in (X \to \mathbf{2})$ to*

$$(\mathfrak{I}(\boldsymbol{\iota}_{(\alpha \to o) \to \alpha}))f = \begin{cases} ch(f^{-1}\{\mathbf{1}\}) & \text{if } f^{-1}\{\mathbf{1}\} \neq \emptyset \\ ch(X) & \text{otherwise.} \end{cases}$$

If Σ has product then the Σ-structure $\mathcal{M} = (\mathfrak{T}, \mathfrak{I})$ is standard *if: $\mathfrak{T}(\times) = \Pi_{X,Y \in \mathcal{U}} X \times Y$, $\mathfrak{I}(pair_{\alpha \to \beta \to \alpha \times \beta}) \in \Pi_{X,Y \in \mathcal{U}} X \to Y \to X \times Y$ is a function sending each $x \in X$ and $y \in Y$ to $(x, y) \in X \times Y$, and $\mathfrak{I}(fst_{\alpha \times \beta \to \alpha}) \in \Pi_{X,Y \in \mathcal{U}} X \times Y \to X$ and $\mathfrak{I}(snd_{\alpha \times \beta \to \beta}) \in \Pi_{X,Y \in \mathcal{U}} X \times Y \to Y$ are the projection functions to the first and to the second element of the pair, respectively.* □

Definition 10 (Satisfaction). *A Σ-structure $\mathcal{M}$* satisfies *formula φ, written $\mathcal{M} \models_\Sigma \varphi$, iff for every $\boldsymbol{X} \in \mathcal{U}^n$ and $\boldsymbol{y} \in \mathfrak{T}[\![\boldsymbol{\alpha}.\tau_1]\!](\boldsymbol{X}) \times \cdots \times \mathfrak{T}[\![\boldsymbol{\alpha}.\tau_m]\!](\boldsymbol{X})$, $\mathfrak{I}[\![\varphi]\!](\boldsymbol{X})(\boldsymbol{y}) = \mathbf{1}$, where $(\alpha_1, \ldots, \alpha_n), (x_1^{\tau_1}, \ldots, x_m^{\tau_m})$ is the canonical context of φ and $\boldsymbol{\alpha} = (\alpha_1, \ldots, \alpha_n)$.* □

3 The Institution HOL

Definition 11 (Signature morphism). *Let $\Sigma = (\Omega, \mathcal{C})$ and $\Sigma' = (\Omega', \mathcal{C}')$ be signatures. A* signature morphism from Σ to Σ' *is a pair $\sigma = (\sigma_\Omega, \sigma_\mathcal{C})$, where $\sigma_\Omega : \Omega \to \Omega'$ and $\sigma_\mathcal{C} : \mathcal{C} \to \mathcal{C}'$ are functions satisfying the following conditions: 1) if $\sigma_\Omega(\nu, n) = (\nu', n')$, then $n = n'$; and 2) $\sigma_\mathcal{C}(c_\tau) \in \mathcal{C}'_{\sigma^\sharp_\Omega(\tau)}$, for $c_\tau \in \mathcal{C}_\tau$, where $\sigma^\sharp_\Omega$ is the homomorphic extension of σ_Ω to type expressions. We also extend $\sigma^\sharp_\Omega$ to types-in-context as follows: $\sigma^\sharp_\Omega(\boldsymbol{\alpha}.\tau) = \boldsymbol{\alpha}.\sigma^\sharp_\Omega(\tau)$. The composition of $\sigma : \Sigma \to \Sigma'$ and $\sigma' : \Sigma' \to \Sigma''$ is $\sigma; \sigma' = (\sigma_\Omega; \sigma'_\Omega, \sigma_\mathcal{C}; \sigma'_\mathcal{C})$. The identity morphism is $id = (id_\Omega, id_\mathcal{C})$.*
For standard signatures Σ and Σ', a signature morphism $\sigma : \Sigma \to \Sigma'$ is standard *if it preserves type constants $(o, 0)$ and $(\iota, 0)$, and constants $\mathbf{Q}_{\alpha\to\alpha\to o}$ and $\boldsymbol{\iota}_{(\alpha\to o)\to\alpha}$. When Σ and Σ' have product then σ is* standard *if it preserves the type constant $(\times, 2)$ and constants $pair_{\alpha\to\beta\to\alpha\times\beta}$, $fst_{\alpha\times\beta\to\alpha}$ and $snd_{\alpha\times\beta\to\beta}$.* □

Definition 12 (Translation of terms). *Let $\Sigma = (\Omega, \mathcal{C})$ and $\Sigma' = (\Omega', \mathcal{C}')$ be signatures, $\sigma : \Sigma \to \Sigma'$ be a signature morphism and $\mathcal{V}$ be a Σ-variable system, then the Σ'-variable system $\mathcal{V}'$ induced by $\mathcal{V}$ and σ is the set $\bigcup\{\mathcal{V}_\tau \mid \sigma^\sharp_\Omega(\tau) = \tau'\}$. The homomorphic extension of $\sigma_\mathcal{C}$ to Σ-terms is denoted by $\sigma^\sharp_\mathcal{C}$. Extension of $\sigma^\sharp_\mathcal{C}$ to terms-in-context is given as follows $\sigma^\sharp_\mathcal{C}(\boldsymbol{\alpha}, \boldsymbol{x}.t_\tau) = \boldsymbol{\alpha}, \sigma^\sharp_\mathcal{C}(\boldsymbol{x}).\sigma^\sharp_\mathcal{C}(t_\tau)$, where $\sigma^\sharp_\mathcal{C}(\boldsymbol{x}) = (\sigma^\sharp_\mathcal{C}(x_1^{\tau_1}), \ldots, \sigma^\sharp_\mathcal{C}(x_m^{\tau_m}))$, for $\boldsymbol{x} = (x_1^{\tau_1}, \ldots, x_m^{\tau_m})$.* □

We usually drop the sub- and superscripts when they are clear from the context, writing $\sigma(t)$ and $\sigma(\tau)$ for $\sigma^\sharp_\mathcal{C}(t_\tau)$ and $\sigma^\sharp_\Omega(\tau)$ respectively.

Definition 13. *Let $\sigma : \Sigma \to \Sigma'$ be a signature morphism and let $\mathcal{M}' = (\mathfrak{T}', \mathfrak{I}')$ be a Σ'-structure. The* σ-reduct *of $\mathcal{M}'$, $\mathcal{M}'|_\sigma$, is the Σ-structure $\mathcal{M} = (\mathfrak{T}, \mathfrak{I})$, where $\mathfrak{T}(\nu, n) = \mathfrak{T}'(\sigma(\nu, n))$, for $(\nu, n) \in \Omega$ and $\mathfrak{I}(c_\tau) = \mathfrak{I}'(\sigma(c_\tau))$, for $c_\tau \in \mathcal{C}_\tau$.* □

Lemma 3. *Let $\sigma : \Sigma \to \Sigma'$ be a signature morphism, $\mathcal{M}' = (\mathfrak{T}', \mathfrak{I}')$ be a Σ'-structure, and $\mathcal{M} = \mathcal{M}'|_\sigma$. Then for every Σ-type $\tau \in Types_\Sigma$ and $\boldsymbol{X} \in \mathcal{U}^n$, $\mathfrak{T}'[\![\boldsymbol{\alpha}.\sigma(\tau)]\!](\boldsymbol{X}) = \mathfrak{T}[\![\boldsymbol{\alpha}.\tau]\!](\boldsymbol{X})$, where $\boldsymbol{\alpha}.\tau$ is a type-in-context and $\boldsymbol{\alpha} = (\alpha_1, \ldots, \alpha_n)$.*

Proof. By induction on the structure of the Σ-type τ. □

Lemma 4. *Let $\sigma : \Sigma \to \Sigma'$ be a signature morphism, $\mathcal{M}' = (\mathfrak{T}', \mathfrak{I}')$ is a Σ'-structure, and $\mathcal{M} = \mathcal{M}'|_\sigma$. Then for every Σ-term t, $\boldsymbol{X} \in \mathcal{U}^n$ and $\boldsymbol{y} \in \mathfrak{T}[\![\boldsymbol{\alpha}.\tau_1]\!](\boldsymbol{X}) \times \cdots \times \mathfrak{T}[\![\boldsymbol{\alpha}.\tau_m]\!](\boldsymbol{X})$: $\mathfrak{I}[\![\boldsymbol{\alpha}, \boldsymbol{x}.t]\!](\boldsymbol{X})(\boldsymbol{y}) = \mathfrak{I}'[\![\sigma(\boldsymbol{\alpha}, \boldsymbol{x}.t)]\!](\boldsymbol{X})(\boldsymbol{y})$, where $(\alpha_1, \ldots, \alpha_n), (x_1^{\tau_1}, \ldots, x_m^{\tau_m})$ is the canonical context of t, $\boldsymbol{\alpha} = (\alpha_1, \ldots, \alpha_n)$ and $\boldsymbol{x} = (x_1^{\tau_1}, \ldots, x_m^{\tau_m})$.*

Proof. By induction on the structure of the Σ-term t. □

Lemma 5. *If $\sigma : \Sigma \to \Sigma'$ is a signature morphism, $\mathcal{M}' = (\mathfrak{T}', \mathfrak{I}')$ is a Σ'-structure then for every Σ-formula φ: $\mathcal{M}'|_\sigma \models_\Sigma \varphi$ iff $\mathcal{M}' \models_{\Sigma'} \sigma(\varphi)$.*

Proof. Immediately from Definition 10 and Lemma 4. □

In the next definition we define the **HOL** logic in terms of an *institution*, proposed by Goguen and Burstall in [GB 92].

Definition 14. *The institution* **HOL** *is defined as follows:*

- $\mathbf{Sign_{HOL}}$ *is the category of all standard signatures with product and standard signatures morphisms;*
- *For each signature $\Sigma \in |\mathbf{Sign_{HOL}}|$, $\mathbf{Sen_{HOL}}(\Sigma)$ is the set of all Σ-sentences, such that for each Σ-sentence φ there exists Σ-variable system $\mathcal{V}$ containing all the variables occurring in φ, and for each signature morphism $\sigma : \Sigma \to \Sigma'$ and a Σ-sentence φ, $\mathbf{Sen_{HOL}}(\sigma)(\varphi) = \sigma(\varphi)$.*
- *For each signature $\Sigma \in |\mathbf{Sign_{HOL}}|$, $\mathbf{Mod_{HOL}}(\Sigma)$ is the discrete category of all standard Σ-structures, and for each signature morphism $\sigma : \Sigma \to \Sigma'$ and a Σ'-model $\mathcal{M}'$, $\mathbf{Mod_{HOL}}(\sigma)(\mathcal{M}') = \mathcal{M}'|_\sigma$;*
- *For each signature $\Sigma \in |\mathbf{Sign_{HOL}}|$, the satisfaction relation is the relation $\models_\Sigma$ defined in Definition 10.*

□

By Lemma 5, the above definition really defines an institution.

4 CASL Logics in HOL

In this section we define maps of institutions (see [Mes 89]) underlying the CASL specification formalism into the **HOL** institution. We also prove the conditions under which the proof system of the **HOL** logic can be reused for reasoning about CASL specifications (see Section 5).

Definition 15. *The institution* **PFOL** *of* partial first-order logic *is defined as follows:*

- *the category $\mathbf{Sign_{PFOL}}$ is the category* **PFOSig** *of partial first-order signatures, where: objects are partial first-order signatures $\Sigma = \langle S, TF, PF, \Pi \rangle$, where S is a set of sort names, TF and PF are sets of total and partial operation names, respectively, such that $TF_{w,s} \cap PF_{w,s} = \emptyset$ for each $w \in S^*$ and $s \in S$, and Π is a set of predicate names; morphisms are first-order signature morphisms $\sigma = \langle \sigma_S, \sigma_{TF}, \sigma_{PF}, \sigma_\Pi \rangle : \Sigma \to \Sigma'$, where $\sigma_S : S \to S'$, σ_{TF} and σ_{PF} are families of functions respecting the arities and result sorts of operation names in Σ and their "totality", that is $\sigma_{TF} = \langle (\sigma_{TF})_{w,s} : TF_{w,s} \to TF'_{\sigma_S^*(w),\sigma_S(s)} \rangle_{w \in S^*, s \in S}$ and $\sigma_{PF} = \langle (\sigma_{PF})_{w,s} : PF_{w,s} \to PF'_{\sigma_S^*(w),\sigma_S(s)} \cup TF'_{\sigma_S^*(w),\sigma_S(s)} \rangle_{w \in S^*, s \in S}$, and $\sigma_\Pi = \langle (\sigma_\Pi)_w : \Pi_w \to \Pi_{\sigma_S^*(w)} \rangle_{w \in S^*}$;*

- *the functor* $\mathbf{Sen_{PFOL}} : \mathbf{PFOSig} \to \mathbf{Set}$ *for every signature* Σ *gives the set* $\mathbf{Sen_{PFOL}}(\Sigma)$ *of all partial first-order* Σ*-sentences built out of* atomic sentences *(i.e. existential equalities* $t_1 \stackrel{e}{=} t_2$*, where* t_1 *and* t_2 *are* Σ*-terms of the same sort; and predicate formulas of the form* $p(t_1, \ldots, t_n)$*, where* $p \in \Pi_{s_1,\ldots,s_n}$ *and* $t_1, \ldots, t_n$ *are* Σ*-terms of sorts* $s_1, \ldots, s_n$*, respectively) using the standard propositional connectives:* $\wedge$ *and* $\neg$*, and the universal quantifier* $\forall$*; additionally we assume that the sentence* $(\forall x : s)\varphi$ *is in* $\mathbf{Sen_{PFOL}}(\Sigma)$ *iff* $x : s$ *is not bound in* φ*, where the notion of bound (and free) variables in a formula is defined in the standard way (see [EFT 96]); for each signature morphism* $\sigma : \Sigma \to \Sigma'$*,* $\mathbf{Sen_{PFOL}}(\sigma)$ *is the* σ*-translation function taking* Σ*-sentence to* Σ'*-sentence;*
- *the functor* $\mathbf{Mod_{PFOL}} : \mathbf{PFOSig}^{op} \to \mathbf{Cat}$ *for each signature* Σ *gives the discrete category,* $\mathbf{Mod_{PFOL}}(\Sigma)$*, of partial first-order* Σ*-structures, where objects are partial first-order* Σ*-structures* $M = \langle \{|M|_s \in \mathcal{U}\}_{s\in S}, \{c_M : |M|_{s_1} \times \cdots \times |M|_{s_n} \to |M|_s\}_{c\in TF}, \{c_M : |M|_{s_1} \times \cdots \times |M|_{s_n} \rightharpoonup |M|_s\}_{c\in PF}, \{p_M \subseteq |M|_{s_1} \times \cdots \times |M|_{s_n}\}_{p\in\Pi}\rangle$*; for each signature morphism* $\sigma : \Sigma \to \Sigma'$*,* $\mathbf{Mod_{PFOL}}(\sigma)$ *is the reduct functor* $\_|_\sigma : \mathbf{Mod_{PFOL}}(\Sigma') \to \mathbf{Mod_{PFOL}}(\Sigma)$ *mapping partial first-order* Σ'*-structures to partial first-order* Σ*-structures;*
- *for each* $\Sigma \in |\mathbf{PFOSig}|$*, the satisfaction relation* $\models^{\mathbf{PFOL}}_\Sigma \subseteq |\mathbf{Mod_{PFOL}}(\Sigma)| \times \mathbf{Sen_{PFOL}}(\Sigma)$ *is defined as follows: let* φ *be a* Σ*-formula,* X *be the set containing all free variables of* φ*,* $M \in |\mathbf{Mod_{PFOL}}(\Sigma)|$ *and* $v : X \to |M|$ *be a valuation of* Σ*-variables from* X*. Then the satisfaction of the formula* φ *under valuation* v $M, v \models^{\mathbf{PFOL}}_\Sigma \varphi$ *is defined as follows:*
  - $M, v \models^{\mathbf{PFOL}}_\Sigma t_1 \stackrel{e}{=} t_2$ *iff* $v^\sharp(t_1)$ *and* $v^\sharp(t_2)$ *are defined and equal;*
  - $M, v \models^{\mathbf{PFOL}}_\Sigma p(t_1, \ldots, t_n)$ *iff all* $v^\sharp(t_i)$*, for* $i = 1, \ldots, n$*, are defined and* $(v^\sharp(t_1), \ldots, v^\sharp(t_n)) \in p_M$*;*
  - $M, v \models^{\mathbf{PFOL}}_\Sigma \varphi_1 \wedge \varphi_2$ *iff* $M, v \models^{\mathbf{PFOL}}_\Sigma \varphi_1$ *and* $M, v \models^{\mathbf{PFOL}}_\Sigma \varphi_2$*;*
  - $M, v \models^{\mathbf{PFOL}}_\Sigma \neg\varphi$ *iff it is not true that* $M, v \models^{\mathbf{PFOL}}_\Sigma \varphi$*; and*
  - $M, v \models^{\mathbf{PFOL}}_\Sigma \forall(x : s).\varphi$ *iff for every valuation* $v' : X \cup \{x : s\} \to |M|$*, such that* $v'(y) = v(y)$*, for* $y \in X$*,* $M, v' \models^{\mathbf{PFOL}}_\Sigma \varphi$*,*

  where $v^\sharp$ *is the maximal homomorphic extension of* v *to terms. A* Σ*-sentence* φ *is satisfied in a model* M*,* $M \models^{\mathbf{PFOL}}_\Sigma \varphi$*, iff* $M, v_\emptyset \models^{\mathbf{PFOL}}_\Sigma \varphi$*, where* $v_\emptyset : \emptyset \to |M|$ *is an empty valuation.* □

The **PFOL** institution presented in the above definition is the basic logic underlying the CASL formalism (see also [CASL 99]). In the next definition we use the notion of *institution representation* (see [Tar 95]) which is a special case of a *map of institutions* (see [Mes 89]), called also a *simple map of institutions*, for coding the **PFOL** institution into the **HOL** institution.

Definition 16. *The institution representation* $\rho : \mathbf{PFOL} \to \mathbf{HOL}$ *is defined as follows: the functor* $\rho^{\mathbf{Sign}} : \mathbf{PFOSig} \to \mathbf{Sign_{HOL}}$*:*

- *for each signature* $\Sigma = \langle S, TF, PF, \Pi\rangle \in |\mathbf{PFOSig}|$*,* $\rho^{\mathbf{Sign}}(\Sigma) = (\Omega, \mathcal{C})$*, where* $(\Omega, \mathcal{C}) \in |\mathbf{Sign_{HOL}}|$ *is the smallest* **HOL** *signature, such that: 1) for every* $s \in S$*,* $(s, 0) \in \Omega$*; 2) for every* $c : s_1 \times \cdots \times s_n \to s \in$

TF, $c_{s_1\times\cdots\times s_n\to s} \in \mathcal{C}$, *and we will write* $\rho^{\mathbf{Sign}}_{TF}(c : s_1 \times \cdots \times s_n \to s)$, *for* $c_{s_1\times\cdots\times s_n\to s}$*; 3) for every* $c : s_1 \times \cdots \times s_n \to s \in PF$, $c_{s_1\times\cdots\times s_n\to(o\times s)} \in \mathcal{C}$, *and we will write* $\rho^{\mathbf{Sign}}_{PF}(c : s_1 \times \cdots \times s_n \to s)$, *for* $c_{s_1\times\cdots\times s_n\to(o\times s)}$*; and 4) for every* $p : s_1 \times \cdots \times s_n \in \Pi$, $p_{s_1\times\cdots\times s_n\to o} \in \mathcal{C}$ *and we will write* $\rho^{\mathbf{Sign}}_{\Pi}(p : s_1 \times \cdots \times s_n)$, *for* $p_{s_1\times\cdots\times s_n\to o}$*;*
- *for each signature morphism* $(\sigma : \Sigma \to \Sigma') \in$ **PFOSig**, $\rho^{\mathbf{Sign}}(\sigma)$ *is a signature morphism in* **HOL** *such that:* $\rho^{\mathbf{Sign}}(\sigma)_{\Omega}(s,0) = (\sigma(s),0)$, *for* $s \in \Sigma$, $\rho^{\mathbf{Sign}}(\sigma)_{\mathcal{C}}(c_{s_1\times\cdots\times s_n\to s}) = \rho^{\mathbf{Sign}}_{TF}(\sigma(c : s_1 \times \cdots \times s_n \to s))$, *for* $c : s_1 \times \cdots \times s_n \to s \in TF$, $\rho^{\mathbf{Sign}}(\sigma)_{\mathcal{C}}(c_{s_1\times\cdots\times s_n\to(o\times s)}) = \rho^{\mathbf{Sign}}_{PF}(\sigma(c : s_1 \times \cdots \times s_n \to s))$, *for* $c : s_1 \times \cdots \times s_n \to s \in PF$, *and* $\rho^{\mathbf{Sign}}(\sigma)$ *preserves standard and product symbols;*

the natural transformation $\rho^{\mathbf{Sen}} : \mathbf{Sen}_{\mathbf{PFOL}} \to \rho^{\mathbf{Sign}}; \mathbf{Sen}_{\mathbf{HOL}}$ *is a family of functions* $\rho^{\mathbf{Sen}}_{\Sigma} : \mathbf{Sen}_{\mathbf{PFOL}}(\Sigma) \to \mathbf{Sen}_{\mathbf{HOL}}(\rho^{\mathbf{Sen}}(\Sigma))$, *given by the following extension to formulas (in the rest of the definition we write Def as an abbreviation for* $\rho^{\sharp}; fst$*):*

- $\rho^{\mathbf{Sen}}_{\Sigma}(p(\boldsymbol{t})) = Def(t_1) \wedge \ldots \wedge Def(t_n) \wedge \rho^{\mathbf{Sign}}_{\Pi}(p)\big(snd(\rho^{\sharp}(\boldsymbol{t}))\big)$, *where* $\boldsymbol{t} = (t_1, \ldots, t_n)$*;*
- $\rho^{\mathbf{Sen}}_{\Sigma}(t_1 \overset{e}{=} t_2) = Def(t_1) \wedge Def(t_1) \wedge snd(\rho^{\sharp}(t_1)) = snd(\rho^{\sharp}(t_2))$*;*
- $\rho^{\mathbf{Sen}}_{\Sigma}(\varphi_1 \wedge \varphi_2) = \rho^{\mathbf{Sen}}_{\Sigma}(\varphi_1) \wedge \rho^{\mathbf{Sen}}_{\Sigma}(\varphi_2)$*;*
- $\rho^{\mathbf{Sen}}_{\Sigma}(\neg\varphi) = \neg\rho^{\mathbf{Sen}}_{\Sigma}(\varphi)$ *and* $\rho^{\mathbf{Sen}}_{\Sigma}(\forall(x : s).\varphi) = \forall x^s.\rho^{\mathbf{Sen}}_{\Sigma}(\varphi)$,

where $\rho^{\sharp}$ *is the homomorphic extension of* $\rho^{\mathbf{Sign}}$ *to terms given as follows:*

- $\rho^{\sharp}(x : s) = (T_o, x^s)$*;*
- $\rho^{\sharp}(c(\boldsymbol{t})) = \begin{cases} \textbf{if } Def(t_1) \wedge \ldots \wedge Def(t_n) \textbf{ then } \rho^{\mathbf{Sign}}_{PF}(c)\Big(snd(\rho^{\sharp}(\boldsymbol{t}))\Big) \\ \textbf{else } \Big(F_o, \iota(\lambda x^s.T_o)\Big) \end{cases}$

  for $c \in PF_{(s_1,\ldots,s_n),s}$ *and* $\boldsymbol{t} = (t_1, \ldots, t_n)$*;*
- $\rho^{\sharp}(c(\boldsymbol{t})) = \begin{cases} \textbf{if } Def(t_1) \wedge \ldots \wedge Def(t_n) \textbf{ then } \Big(T_o, \rho^{\mathbf{Sign}}_{TF}(c)(snd(\rho^{\sharp}(\boldsymbol{t})))\Big) \\ \textbf{else } \Big(F_o, \iota(\lambda x^s.T_o)\Big) \end{cases}$

  for $c \in TF_{(s_1,\ldots,s_n),s}$ *and* $\boldsymbol{t} = (t_1, \ldots, t_n)$*;*

the natural transformation $\rho^{\mathbf{Mod}} : (\rho^{\mathbf{Sign}})^{op}; \mathbf{Mod}_{\mathbf{HOL}} \to \mathbf{Mod}_{\mathbf{PFOL}}$ *is a family of functions* $\rho^{\mathbf{Mod}}_{\Sigma} : \mathbf{Mod}_{\mathbf{HOL}}(\rho^{\mathbf{Sign}}(\Sigma)) \to \mathbf{Mod}_{\mathbf{PFOL}}(\Sigma)$ *given on* $\rho^{\mathbf{Sign}}(\Sigma)$*-structure* $\mathcal{M} = (\mathfrak{T}, \mathfrak{I})$ *as follows:*

$$\begin{aligned}
&\rho^{\mathbf{Mod}}_{\Sigma}(\mathcal{M}) = \langle \{\mathfrak{T}(\rho^{\mathbf{Sign}}_{S}(s))\}_{s\in S}, \{\mathfrak{I}(\rho^{\mathbf{Sign}}_{TF}(c))\}_{c\in TF},\\
&\{c_{\mathcal{M}} : \mathfrak{T}(s_1,0) \times \cdots \times \mathfrak{T}(s_n,0) \rightharpoonup \mathfrak{T}(s,0) \mid \forall \boldsymbol{a} \in \mathfrak{T}(s_1,0) \times \cdots \times \mathfrak{T}(s_n,0).\\
&\quad c_{\mathcal{M}}(\boldsymbol{a}) = snd_{\mathcal{M}}(\mathfrak{I}(\rho^{\mathbf{Sign}}(c))(\boldsymbol{a})) \textit{ if } fst_{\mathcal{M}}(\mathfrak{I}(\rho^{\mathbf{Sign}}(c))(\boldsymbol{a})) = \mathbf{1}\\
&\quad \textit{and } c_{\mathcal{M}}(\boldsymbol{a}) \textit{ is undefined otherwise}\}_{c\in PF}\\
&\{p_{\mathcal{M}} \subseteq \mathfrak{T}(s_1,0) \times \cdots \times \mathfrak{T}(s_n,0) \mid \forall \boldsymbol{a} \in \mathfrak{T}(s_1,0) \times \cdots \times \mathfrak{T}(s_n,0).\\
&\quad p_{\mathcal{M}}(\boldsymbol{a}) \quad \textit{iff} \quad (\mathfrak{I}(\rho^{\mathbf{Sign}}_{\Pi}(p)))(\boldsymbol{a}) = \mathbf{1}\}_{p\in\Pi}\rangle
\end{aligned}$$

□

Proposition 1. *Definition 16 defines an institution representation.*

Proof. Obviously $\rho^{\mathbf{Sign}}$ is a functor and $\rho^{\mathbf{Sen}} : \mathbf{Sen_{PFOL}} \rightarrow \rho^{\mathbf{Sign}}; \mathbf{Sen_{HOL}}$ and $\rho^{\mathbf{Mod}} : (\rho^{\mathbf{Sign}})^{op}; \mathbf{Mod_{HOL}} \rightarrow \mathbf{Mod_{PFOL}}$ are natural transformations. The representation condition

$$\rho_{\Sigma}^{\mathbf{Mod}}(\mathcal{M}) \models_{\Sigma} \varphi \quad \text{iff} \quad \mathcal{M} \models_{\rho^{\mathbf{Sign}}(\Sigma)} \rho_{\Sigma}^{\mathbf{Sen}}(\varphi),$$

where Σ is a **PFOL**-signature, φ is a Σ-sentence and $\mathcal{M}$ is a $\rho^{\mathbf{Sign}}(\Sigma)$-model, can be proved by induction on the structure of the sentence φ. □

Now, we recall properties of maps of institutions, mentioned also in [Borz 99], which are crucial for the results that will be presented in Section 5. Details concerning maps of institutions can be found in [Mes 89].

Definition 17 (β-expansion). *Let $(\Phi, \alpha, \beta) : I \rightarrow I'$ be a map of institutions and Th be a class of theories over the institution I. The map of institutions (Φ, α, β) has the* β-expansion for *Th, if for any theory $th \in Th$, any th-model M has a* β-expansion *to a $\Phi(th)$-model, that is, there exists a $\Phi(th)$-model M' such that $\beta_{th}(M') = M$. We say that the map (Φ, α, β) has the* β-expansion *property if it has β-expansion for the class $\{(\Sigma, \emptyset) \mid \Sigma \in |\mathbf{Sign}_I|\}$. If the map of institutions (Φ, α, β) is an institution representation ρ then we call this property* ρ-expansion. □

Definition 18 (Weak-$\mathcal{D}$-amalgamation). *Let $(\Phi, \alpha, \beta) : I \rightarrow I'$ be a map of institutions, Th be a class of theories over institution I and $\mathcal{D}$ be a class of morphisms of theories from Th. We say that the map of institutions (Φ, α, β) has the* weak-$\mathcal{D}$-amalgamation for *Th iff for every theories $th_1, th_2 \in Th$, $(d : th_2 \rightarrow th_1) \in \mathcal{D}$, $M_1 \in |\mathbf{Mod}(th_1)|$ and $M_2 \in |\mathbf{Mod}'(\Phi(th_2))|$, given as on the following diagram:*

$$\begin{array}{ccc}
\mathbf{Mod}(th_1) & \xleftarrow{\beta_{th_1}} & \mathbf{Mod}'(\Phi(th_1)) \\
\Big\downarrow{\scriptstyle -|_d} & & \Big\downarrow{\scriptstyle -|_{\Phi(d)}} \\
\mathbf{Mod}(th_2) & \xleftarrow[\beta_{th_2}]{} & \mathbf{Mod}'(\Phi(th_2))
\end{array}$$

if $\beta_{(th_2)}(M_2) = M_1|_d$ then there exists $M \in |\mathbf{Mod}'(\Phi(th_1))|$, such that $\beta_{(th_1)}(M) = M_1$ and $M|_{\Phi(d)} = M_2$. We say that the map (Φ, α, β) has weak-$\mathcal{D}$-amalgamation *property if it has weak-$\mathcal{D}$-amalgamation for the class $\{(\Sigma, \emptyset) \mid \Sigma \in |\mathbf{Sign}_I|\}$.* □

Observation 1 *The institution representation ρ :* **PFOL** $\rightarrow$ **HOL**, *defined by Definition 16, satisfies both ρ-expansion and weak-***PFOSig***-amalgamation properties for any class of theories over* **PFOL**. □

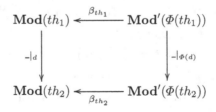

Now, we consider the extension of the **PFOL** institution to institution of partial first-order logic with subsorts **SubPFOL** (see also [CASL 99]).

Definition 19. *The institution* **SubPFOL** of subsorted partial first-order logic *is given as follows: signatures are subsorted partial first-order many-sorted signatures (with sort names S, disjoint sets TF of total and PF of partial operation names, predicate names P and a pre-order relation $\leq_S$ of subsort embedding on the sort names). The pre-order $\leq_S$ naturally extends to sequences of sorts. We also define overloading relations for operations as follows: $f_1 : w_1 \to s_1 \sim_F f_2 : w_2 \to s_2$ holds if there exist $w \in S^*$ and $s \in S$ such that $w \leq_S w_1, w_2$, $s_1, s_2 \leq_S s$ and $f_1 \equiv f_2$, similarly we define $\sim_P$ for predicates. Subsorted signature morphisms are usual signature morphisms (as in the institution* **PFOL**) *that preserve subsort relation and the overloading relations. Sentences are usual* **PFOL** *sentences, except that we can use implicit subsort embeddings. Models are usual* **PFOL** *models such that (see also [CASL 99]) for every sorts s_1 and s_2, if $s_1 \leq_S s_2$ then for the carrier sets $|M|_{s_1}$ and $|M|_{s_2}$ we have in model M an embedding $em^M_{s_1,s_2} : |M|_{s_1} \to |M|_{s_2}$, a partial projection $pr^M_{s_2,s_1} : |M|_{s_2} \rightharpoonup |M|_{s_1}$ and a membership predicate $in^M_{s_1,s_2} : |M|_{s_1}$ testing whether values in $|M|_{s_2}$ are embeddings of values in $|M|_{s_1}$, such that the obvious compatibility conditions hold (see [CASL 99] for details); the satisfaction relation is defined as in the* **PFOL** *institution.* □

Given an institution its category $\mathbf{Th}_0$ of *theories* has as objects pairs $T = (\Sigma, \Gamma)$, where Σ is a signature and Γ a set of sentences on Σ. Morphisms $\sigma : (\Sigma_1, \Gamma_1) \to (\Sigma_2, \Gamma_2)$ are the signature morphisms $\sigma : \Sigma_1 \to \Sigma_2$ such that $\mathbf{Sen}(\sigma)(\Gamma_1) \subseteq Cl(\Gamma_2)$, where $Cl(\Gamma_2)$ is the closure of Σ_2-sentences Γ_2 defined as follows (see [GB 92]): $Cl(\Gamma_2) = \{\varphi \in \mathbf{Sen}_I(\Sigma_2) \mid \Gamma_2 \models^I_{\Sigma_2} \varphi\}$.

Let us consider the following map of institutions:

Definition 20. *The map of institutions (Φ, α, β) :* **SubPFOL** $\to$ **PFOL** *is defined as follows:*

1. *$\Phi : \mathbf{Th}_0^{\mathbf{SubPFOL}} \to \mathbf{Th}_0^{\mathbf{PFOL}}$ is a functor such that: for every $\Sigma = \langle S, TF, PF, P, \leq_S \rangle \in |\mathbf{Sign}_{\mathbf{SubPFOL}}|$, $\Phi(\Sigma, \emptyset) = (\Sigma', \Gamma)$, where the signature Σ' is an extension of the signature $\langle S, TF, PF, P \rangle \in |\mathbf{Sign}_{\mathbf{PFOL}}|$ by a total embedding operation $em_{s_1,s_2} : s_1 \to s_2$, a partial projection operation $pr_{s_2,s_1} : s_2 \rightharpoonup s_1$, and a membership predicate $in_{s_1,s_2} : s_1$, for each pair of sorts $s_1, s_2 \in S$ such that $s_1 \leq_S s_2$; Γ is a set of axioms describing the obvious compatibility conditions between embeddings, projections and membership predicates (see also [CASL 99]); for every theory morphism $\sigma \in \mathbf{Th}_0^{\mathbf{SubPFOL}}$, $\Phi(\sigma)$ is the same as σ and additionally preserves the symbols used for embeddings, projections and membership relations;*
2. *for every $\Sigma \in |\mathbf{Sign}_{\mathbf{SubPFOL}}|$, $\alpha_\Sigma : \mathbf{Sen}_{\mathbf{SubPFOL}}(\Sigma) \to \mathbf{Sen}_{\mathbf{PFOL}}(\Phi(\Sigma, \emptyset))$ sends each Σ-sentence φ, with possibly implicit embeddings to a $\Phi(\Sigma, \emptyset)$-sentence ψ, where ψ is the same as φ, except that all implicit embeddings are made explicit;*

3. for every $\Sigma \in |\mathbf{Sign_{SubPFOL}}|$, $\beta_{(\Sigma,\emptyset)} : \mathbf{Mod_{PFOL}}(\Phi(\Sigma,\emptyset)) \to \mathbf{Mod_{SubPFOL}}(\Sigma)$ *just forgets about interpretations of embedding, projection and membership relation symbols axiomatized by* Γ, *where* $(\Sigma', \Gamma) = \Phi(\Sigma, \emptyset)$, *and translates them to the interpretation of the pre-order relation* $\leq_S$ *of subsort embedding on the sort names from* Σ *(see Definition 19).* □

Observation 2 *The map of institutions* $(\Phi, \alpha, \beta) : \mathbf{SubPFOL} \to \mathbf{PFOL}$ *defined in Definition 20 has* β*-expansion and weak-*$\mathbf{Sign_{SubPFOL}}$*-amalgamation properties.* □

Lemma 6. *Let* $(\Phi_1, \alpha_1, \beta_1) : I_1 \to I_2$ *and* $(\Phi_2, \alpha_2, \beta_2) : I_2 \to I_3$ *be maps of institutions satisfying* β_1*-expansion and* β_2*-expansion for the class of theories* $\{\Phi(\Sigma, \emptyset) \mid \Sigma \in |\mathbf{Sign}_I|\}$, *and weak-*$\mathcal{D}$*-amalgamation and weak-*$\Phi(\mathcal{D})$*-amalgamation for the class of theories* $\{\Phi(\Sigma, \emptyset) \mid \Sigma \in |\mathbf{Sign}_I|\}$, *respectively, where* $\mathcal{D}$ *is a class of morphisms of theory* $\{(\Sigma, \emptyset) \mid \Sigma \in |\mathbf{Sign}_I|\}$ *then the map of institutions* $(\Phi, \alpha, \beta) = (\Phi_1, \alpha_1, \beta_1); (\Phi_2, \alpha_2, \beta_2) : I_1 \to I_3$ *has* β*-expansion and weak-*$\mathcal{D}$*-amalgamation properties.*

Proof. Immediately from definitions. □

Corollary 1. *The map of institutions* $(\Phi_1, \alpha_1, \beta_1) = (\Phi, \alpha, \beta); \rho : \mathbf{SubPFOL} \to \mathbf{HOL}$, *where* $(\Phi, \alpha, \beta) : \mathbf{SubPFOL} \to \mathbf{PFOL}$ *is given by Definition 20 and* $\rho : \mathbf{PFOL} \to \mathbf{HOL}$ *by Definition 16, has* β_1*-expansion and weak-*$\mathbf{Sign_{SubPFOL}}$*-amalgamation properties.* □

Now, we define the institution **SubPCFOL** of partial first-order logic with subsorts and sort-generation which is the logic underlying the CASL specification formalism (see also [CASL 99]).

Definition 21. *The institution* **SubPCFOL** *of* partial first-order logic with subsorts and sort-generation *is the same as the institution* **SubPFOL** *defined in Definition 19 except that for every signature* $\langle S, TF, PF, P, \leq_S \rangle \in |\mathbf{Sign_{SubPCFOL}}|$ *the sentence functor* $\mathbf{Sen_{SubPCFOL}}$ *gives also* sort-generation sentences *of the form* (S', F'), *where* $S' \subseteq S$ *and* $F' \subseteq TF \cup PF$. *A sort-generation sentence* (S', F') *is satisfied in a* Σ*-model* M *if the carrier sets* $|M|_s$ *for* $s \in S'$, *are generated by the function symbols from* F' *(possibly using variables of sorts not in* S'*).* □

Corollary 2. *The map of institutions* $(\Phi', \alpha', \beta') : \mathbf{SubPCFOL} \to \mathbf{HOL}$, *which is the same as in Corollary 1 except that, for every signature* Σ *and a sort-generation sentence* (S', F'):

$$\alpha'_\Sigma(S', F') = \forall P_{s_1}^{s_1 \to o}. \cdots . \forall P_{s_n}^{s_n \to o}. \Big(\bigwedge_{s \in S', f^{s'_1 \times \cdots \times s'_m \to s} \in F'} \forall x_1^{s'_1}. \cdots . \forall x_m^{s'_m}. \\ P_{s'_{i_1}}(x_{i_1}^{s'_{i_1}}) \wedge \ldots \wedge P_{s'_{i_k}}(x_{i_k}^{s'_{i_k}}) \Rightarrow P_s(f(x_1^{s'_1}, \ldots, x_m^{s'_m})) \Big) \Rightarrow \bigwedge_{s \in S'} \forall x^s . P_s(x^s),$$

where $S' = \{s_1, \ldots, s_n\}$ *and* $\{i_1, \ldots, i_k\} \subseteq \{1, \ldots, m\}$ *has* β'*-expansion and weak-*$\mathbf{Sign_{SubPCFOL}}$*-amalgamation properties.* □

5 Specifications in HOL

In this section we will work with structured specifications presented also in [Borz 98] (based on the specifications presented in [SST 92]). The structured specifications presented below are also a part of structured specifications of the CASL formalism.

Definition 22 (Specifications). *Finite specifications over a* $(\mathcal{D}, \mathcal{T})$*-institution* I *(i.e., institution* I *with two distinguished classes of morphisms,* $\mathcal{D}_I$ *and* $\mathcal{T}_I$*, that are closed under composition, include all identities and for every* $d \in \mathcal{D}_I$ *and* $t \in \mathcal{T}_I$ *there exists* (d,t)*-pushout in* $\mathbf{Sign}_I$*, see [Borz 98] for details) and their semantics are defined inductively as follows:*

1. *Any pair* $\langle \Sigma, \Gamma \rangle$*, where* $\Sigma \in \mathbf{Sign}_I$ *and* $\Gamma \subseteq \mathbf{Sen}_I(\Sigma)$ *is a finite set of* Σ*-sentences, is a specification with the following semantics:*
   $\mathbf{Sig}[\langle \Sigma, \Gamma \rangle] = \Sigma$ *and* $\mathbf{Mod}[\langle \Sigma, \Gamma \rangle] = \{M \in |\mathbf{Mod}_I(\Sigma)| \mid M \models^I_\Sigma \Gamma\}$.
2. *For any signature* Σ *and* Σ*-specifications* SP_1 *and* SP_2*,* $SP_1 \cup SP_2$ *is a specification with the following semantics:*
   $\mathbf{Sig}[SP_1 \cup SP_2] = \Sigma$ *and* $\mathbf{Mod}[SP_1 \cup SP_2] = \mathbf{Mod}[SP_1] \cap \mathbf{Mod}[SP_2]$.
3. *For any morphism* $(t : \Sigma \to \Sigma') \in \mathcal{T}_I$ *and* Σ*-specification* SP*,*
   translate SP **by** t *is a specification with the following semantics:*
   $\mathbf{Sig}[\mathbf{translate}\ SP\ \mathbf{by}\ t] = \Sigma'$ *and* $\mathbf{Mod}[\mathbf{translate}\ SP\ \mathbf{by}\ t] = \{M' \in |\mathbf{Mod}_I(\Sigma')| \mid M'|_t \in \mathbf{Mod}[SP]\}$.
4. *For any morphism* $(d : \Sigma \to \Sigma') \in \mathcal{D}_I$ *and* Σ'*-specification* SP'*,*
   derive from SP' **by** d *is a specification with the following semantics:*
   $\mathbf{Sig}[\mathbf{derive\ from}\ SP'\ \mathbf{by}\ d] = \Sigma$ *and* $\mathbf{Mod}[\mathbf{derive\ from}\ SP'\ \mathbf{by}\ d] = \{M'|_d \mid M' \in \mathbf{Mod}[SP']\}$. □

Definition 23 (Specifications in HOL). *Let* SP *be a finite specification over a* $(\mathcal{D}, \mathcal{T})$*-institution* **HOL***, where* $\mathcal{D}_{\mathbf{HOL}}$ *is the class of signature morphisms which are identities on sort names, inclusions on operation names and such that for every* $(d : \Sigma \hookrightarrow \Sigma') \in \mathcal{D}_{\mathbf{HOL}}$ *there is only a finite number of operations in* Σ' *which are not in* Σ*. Then the* specification translation δ *is a family of functions* $\{\delta_\Sigma\}_{\Sigma \in |\mathbf{Sign}_{\mathbf{HOL}}|}$ *between specifications over a* $(\mathcal{D}, \mathcal{T})$*-institution* **HOL** *and* **HOL***-sentences defined inductively as follows:*

1. $\delta(\langle \Sigma, \{\varphi_1, \dots \varphi_n\} \rangle) = \varphi_1 \wedge \dots \wedge \varphi_n$*;*
2. $\delta(SP_1 \cup SP_2) = \delta(SP_1) \wedge \delta(SP_2)$*;*
3. $\delta(\mathbf{translate}\ SP_1\ \mathbf{by}\ t) = t(\delta(SP_1))$*, for* $t \in \mathcal{T}_{\mathbf{HOL}}$*;*
4. $\delta(\mathbf{derive\ from}\ SP_1\ \mathbf{by}\ (d : \Sigma \hookrightarrow \Sigma_1)) = \exists f_1. \cdots . \exists f_n. \delta(SP_1)$*, where* $f_1, \dots, f_n$ *are all the operations in* Σ_1 *which are not in* Σ*.* □

Lemma 7. *If* SP *is a* Σ*-specification over a* $(\mathcal{D}, \mathcal{T})$*-institution* **HOL***, where* $\mathcal{D}_{\mathbf{HOL}}$ *is the class of signature morphisms which are identities on sort names, inclusions on operation names and such that for every* $(d : \Sigma \hookrightarrow \Sigma') \in \mathcal{D}_{\mathbf{HOL}}$ *there is only a finite number of operations in* Σ' *which are not in* Σ *then* $\mathbf{Mod}[SP] = \mathbf{Mod}_{\mathbf{HOL}}(\delta(SP))$.

Proof. By induction on the structure of the specification SP. The **derive** case follows from the following fact in **HOL**: $\mathbf{Mod_{HOL}}((\Sigma', \{\varphi\}))|_d = \mathbf{Mod_{HOL}}((\Sigma, \{\exists_f.\varphi\}))$, where $(d : \Sigma \hookrightarrow \Sigma') \in \mathcal{D}_{\mathbf{HOL}}$, f is the only symbol that is in Σ' but is not in Σ and $\varphi \in \mathbf{Sen_{HOL}}(\Sigma')$. For this case we obtain: $\mathbf{Mod}[\mathbf{derive\ from}\ \langle\Sigma', \{\varphi\}\rangle\ \mathbf{by}\ d] = \mathbf{Mod_{HOL}}((\Sigma, \{\exists_f.\varphi\})) = \mathbf{Mod_{HOL}}(\delta(\mathbf{derive\ from}\ \langle\Sigma', \{\varphi\}\rangle\ \mathbf{by}\ d))$. □

In Definition 23 and in the above lemma we have restricted the class $\mathcal{D}_I$ to signature morphisms which are identities on sort names and inclusions on operation and predicate names. Similar result to Lemma 7 holds also for the class $\mathcal{D}_I$ of morphisms injective on operation and predicate names and bijective on sort names. Unfortunately we do not know how to obtain a similar result to those presented in this section for a class $\mathcal{D}_I$ of signature morphisms inclusive/injective on sort names (i.e. when sort names may be hidden by the **derive** specification).

Definition 24 (Specification representation [Borz 98]). *For any* $(\mathcal{D}, \mathcal{T})$-*institution representation* $\rho : I \to I'$, *the* specification representation $\hat{\rho}$ *is a family of functions* $\{\hat{\rho}_\Sigma\}_{\Sigma \in |\mathbf{Sign}|}$ *between classes of specifications over* $(\mathcal{D}, \mathcal{T})$-*institutions* I *and* I' *defined as follows:*

1. $\hat{\rho}_\Sigma(\langle\Sigma, \Gamma\rangle) = \langle\rho^{\mathbf{Sign}}(\Sigma), \rho^{\mathbf{Sen}}_\Sigma(\Gamma)\rangle$;
2. $\hat{\rho}_\Sigma(SP_1 \cup SP_2) = \hat{\rho}_\Sigma(SP_1) \cup \hat{\rho}_\Sigma(SP_2)$;
3. $\hat{\rho}_\Sigma(\mathbf{translate}\ SP_1\ \mathbf{by}\ t) = \mathbf{translate}\ \hat{\rho}_{\Sigma_1}(SP_1)\ \mathbf{by}\ \rho^{\mathbf{Sign}}(t)$;
4. $\hat{\rho}_\Sigma(\mathbf{derive\ from}\ SP_1\ \mathbf{by}\ d) = \mathbf{derive\ from}\ \hat{\rho}_{\Sigma_1}(SP_1)\ \mathbf{by}\ \rho^{\mathbf{Sign}}(d)$,

where $(t : \Sigma_1 \to \Sigma) \in \mathcal{T}_I$ *and* $(d : \Sigma \hookrightarrow \Sigma_1) \in \mathcal{D}_I$. □

Theorem 3. *Let* $\rho : I \to \mathbf{HOL}$ *be a* $(\mathcal{D}, \mathcal{T})$-*institution representation satisfying weak-*$\mathcal{D}_I$*-amalgamation, where* $\rho^{\mathbf{Sign}}(\mathcal{D}_I) \subseteq \mathcal{D}_{\mathbf{HOL}}$ *and* $\mathcal{D}_{\mathbf{HOL}}$ *satisfies assumptions of Lemma 7,* $\Sigma \in |\mathbf{Sign}_I|$ *and* SP *be a* Σ-*specification over* I. *Then, if every model* $M \in \mathbf{Mod}[SP]$ *has* ρ-*expansion to a* $\rho^{\mathbf{Sign}}(\Sigma)$-*model then for every* Σ-*sentence* φ: $\mathbf{Mod}[SP] \models^I_\Sigma \varphi$ *iff* $\delta(\hat{\rho}_\Sigma(SP)) \models^{\mathbf{HOL}}_{\rho^{\mathbf{Sign}}(\Sigma)} \rho^{\mathbf{Sen}}_\Sigma(\varphi)$.

Proof. Directly from Theorem 1 from Section 6 presented in [Borz 98] we have: $\mathbf{Mod}[SP] \models^I_\Sigma \varphi$ iff $\mathbf{Mod}[\hat{\rho}_\Sigma(SP)] \models^{\mathbf{HOL}}_{\rho^{\mathbf{Sign}}(\Sigma)} \rho^{\mathbf{Sen}}_\Sigma(\varphi)$. Next, by Lemma 7 $\mathbf{Mod}[\hat{\rho}_\Sigma(SP)] = \mathbf{Mod_{HOL}}(\delta(\hat{\rho}_\Sigma(SP)))$. □

An example of $(\mathcal{D}, \mathcal{T})$-institution representation satisfying assumptions of the above theorem is the $(\mathcal{D}, \mathcal{T})$-institution representation $\rho : \mathbf{PFOL} \to \mathbf{HOL}$ presented in Definition 16, with the class $\mathcal{D}_{\mathbf{PFOL}}$ satisfying assumptions of Lemma 7.

Similarly to [Borz 98] we obtain soundness of the following scheme of rules:

$$(\delta\text{-}\rho\text{-join}) \quad \frac{\delta(\hat{\rho}_\Sigma(SP)) \vdash^{\mathbf{HOL}}_{\rho^{\mathbf{Sign}}(\Sigma)} \rho^{\mathbf{Sen}}_\Sigma(\varphi)}{SP \vdash_\Sigma \varphi},$$

where ρ and SP satisfy assumptions of Theorem 3. A similar result we can obtain also for maps of $(\mathcal{D}, \mathcal{T})$-institutions.

Definition 25 (Map of specifications [Borz 99]). *For any map of $(\mathcal{D},\mathcal{T})$-institutions $(\Phi,\alpha,\beta): I \to I'$, the* map of specifications $\hat{\gamma}$ *is a family of functions $\{\hat{\gamma}_\Sigma\}_{\Sigma\in|\mathbf{Sign}|}$ between classes of specifications over $(\mathcal{D},\mathcal{T})$-institutions I and I' defined similarly as specification representation (see Definition 24), except:*

1. $\hat{\gamma}_\Sigma(\langle\Sigma,\Gamma\rangle) = \langle\Sigma',\Gamma'\cup\alpha_\Sigma(\Gamma)\rangle$;
2. $\hat{\gamma}_\Sigma(\textbf{translate } SP_1 \textbf{ by } t) = \textbf{translate } \hat{\gamma}_{\Sigma_1}(SP_1) \textbf{ by } \Phi(t)\cup\langle\Sigma',\Gamma'\rangle$,

where $(\Sigma',\Gamma') = \Phi(\Sigma,\emptyset)$, $(t:\Sigma_1\to\Sigma)\in\mathcal{T}_I$ and $\Phi(t)$ is considered as a signature morphism. □

Theorem 4. *Let $(\Phi,\alpha,\beta): I \to \mathbf{HOL}$ be a map of $(\mathcal{D},\mathcal{T})$-institutions satisfying weak-$\mathcal{D}_I$-amalgamation, where $\Phi(\mathcal{D}_I)\subseteq\mathcal{D}_{\mathbf{HOL}}$ and $\mathcal{D}_{\mathbf{HOL}}$ satisfies assumptions of Lemma 7, $\Sigma\in|\mathbf{Sign}_I|$ and SP be a Σ-specification over I. Then, if every model $M\in\mathbf{Mod}[SP]$ has β-expansion to a $\Phi(\Sigma,\emptyset)$-model then for every Σ-sentence φ: $\mathbf{Mod}[SP]\models^I_\Sigma\varphi$ iff $\delta(\hat{\gamma}_\Sigma(SP))\models^{\mathbf{HOL}}_{\mathbf{sign}'(\Phi(\Sigma,\emptyset))}\alpha_\Sigma(\varphi)$.*

Proof. Proof simillar to the proof of Theorem 3 (by Theorem 8.11 presented in [Borz 99] and Lemma 7). □

Examples of maps of institutions satisfying the theorem presented above are maps of $(\mathcal{D},\mathcal{T})$-institutions $(\Phi,\alpha,\beta): \mathbf{SubPFOL}\to\mathbf{HOL}$ (see Corollary 1) and $(\Phi',\alpha',\beta'): \mathbf{SubPCFOL}\to\mathbf{HOL}$ (see Corollary 2) with classes $\mathcal{D}_{\mathbf{SubPFOL}}$ and $\mathcal{D}_{\mathbf{SubPCFOL}}$ satisfying assumptions of Lemma 7 (see Appendix A for practical example). Results similar to those presented in Theorem 3 and Theorem 4 hold also for the refinement of specifications.

6 Conclusions and Future Work

In this paper we have defined the institution **HOL** of the higher-order logic, which best fits the ideas presented in [An 86] and also in [GM 93] and [Paul 94]. Then we have represented in the institution **HOL** institutions underlying the CASL specification formalism. Similar work was done in [MKB 97], but the maps of institutions presented there are different from the representations and maps presented in this paper. In [MKB 97] authors describe "partiality" by adding a new element $\perp$ to each carrier set, which represent the "undefined value", and many axioms described "undefinedness", whereas the maps of institutions presented in this paper *do not* produce any new sentences. We also have proved the conditions under which the proof system of the higher-order logic can be reused for the proof systems of represented (mapped) logics.

In the last section we have presented a methodology which allows us to reuse the proof system of the higher-order logic for reasoning about structured specifications over institutions which are presentable in **HOL**. This methodology allows us to translate the judgments about properties (and the refinement relation) of structured specifications directly to some of known machine supported tools, like the HOL system (see [GM 93]) or the Isabelle HOL logic (see [Paul 94]).

A task for the future is to extend presented work to the CASL language and to design a tool for automatic translation of the CASL specifications into one of the theorem-provers for HOL logic together with a set of tactics that will be well-suited for proving theorems translated by this tool.

References

An 86. P. B. Andrews. An introduction to mathematical logic and type theory: to truth through proof. Academic Press, INC., 1986. 401, 403, 415

Bar 98. H. P. Barendregt. The Lambda Calculus Its Syntax and Semantics. *Studies in Logic and The Foundations of Mathematics,* Elsevier 1998. 403

Borz 98. T. Borzyszkowski. Moving specification structures between logical systems. *Recent Trends in Algebraic Development Techniques, Selected Papers, 13th International Workshop WADT'98*, Lisboa, Portugal, April 1998, ed. José Luiz Fiadeiro, Springer LNCS 1589, pages 16-28, 1998. 401, 413, 414

Borz 99. T. Borzyszkowski. Logical systems for structured specifications. *Special issue of Theoretical Computer Science*, to appear[1]. 410, 415

CASL 99. CASL The Common Algebraic Specification Language - Summary, *by The CoFI Task Group on Language Design.* Version 1.0, 19 March 1999. Document is available on WWW[2] and FTP[3]. 401, 408, 411, 412

EFT 96. H. -D. Ebbinghaus, J. Flum, W. Thomas. Mathematical Logic. *Undergraduate Texts in Mathematics* Second Edition, Springer-Verlag, 1996. 408

GB 92. J. A. Goguen, R. M. Burstall. Institutions: abstract model theory for specifications and programming. *Journal of the Assoc. for Computing Machinery,* 39:95-146, 1992. 407, 411

GM 93. M. J. C. Gordon, T. F. Melham. Introduction to HOL. Cambridge University Press, 1993. 401, 402, 404, 415

Mes 89. J. Meseguer, General logic. *Logic Colloquium'87*, eds. H. D. Ebbinghaus et al., pages 279–329, North-Holland 1989. 407, 408, 410

MKB 97. T. Mossakowski, Kolyang, B. Krieg-Brückner. Static Semantic Analysis and Theorem Proving for CASL. *Recent Trends in Algebraic Development Techniques, Selected Papers,* 12th International Workshop WADT'97, Tarquinia, Italy, June 1997, ed. Francesco Parisi-Presicce, Springer LNCS 1376, pages 333-348, 1997. 401, 415

Paul 94. L. C. Paulson. Isabelle: A Generic Theorem Prover. Springer-Verlag LNCS 828, 1994. 401, 415

SST 92. D. Sannella, S. Sokołowski, A. Tarlecki. Towards formal development of programs from algebraic specification: parameterization revisited. *Acta Informatica,* volume 29, pages 689–736, 1992. 413

Tar 95. A. Tarlecki. Moving between logical systems. *Recent Trends in Data Type Specifications. Selected Papers. 11th Workshop on Specification of Abstract Data Types ADT'95,* Olso, September 1995, eds. M. Haveraaen, O. J. Dahl, O. Owe, Springer LNCS 1130, pages 478–502, 1996. 408

---

[1] See http://monika.univ.gda.pl/~mattb/papers.html

[2] http://www.brics.dk/Projects/CoFI/Notes/S-9/

[3] ftp://ftp.brics.dk/Projects/CoFI/Notes/S-9/

A Practical Example

In this appendix we define a specification of ordered lists over the institution **SubPCFOL** and then translate it to **HOL** to obtain an "input theory" for theorem provers for the HOL logic. First we define the specification of ordered lists *LOrd*.

$$\begin{array}{rll} \mathit{LOrd\text{-}Sig} = & \textbf{sorts} & \mathit{el, list;} \\ & \textbf{opns} & \mathit{nil} : \mathit{list};\ \mathit{cons} : \mathit{el} \times \mathit{list} \rightarrow \mathit{list}; \\ & \textbf{popns} & \mathit{hd} : \mathit{list} \rightarrow \mathit{el};\ \mathit{tl} : \mathit{list} \rightarrow \mathit{list}; \\ & \textbf{pred} & \mathit{le} : \mathit{el} \times \mathit{el}. \end{array}$$

$$\begin{array}{rl} \mathit{LOrd} = \langle & \mathit{LOrd\text{-}Sig},\ \{\forall_{l:list}.\neg(l \stackrel{e}{=} nil) \Rightarrow cons(hd(l), tl(l)) \stackrel{e}{=} l; \\ & \neg(hd(nil) \stackrel{e}{=} hd(nil));\ \neg(tl(nil) \stackrel{e}{=} tl(nil));\ \forall_{x:el}.le(x,x); \\ & \forall_{x,y,z:el}.le(x,y) \wedge le(y,z) \Rightarrow le(x,z); \\ & \forall_{x,y:el}.le(x,y) \wedge le(y,x) \Rightarrow x \stackrel{e}{=} y; \\ & (\{list\}, \{nil : list, cons : el \times list \rightarrow list\})\}\ \rangle \end{array}$$

Now, we extend the above specification by a new total operation $sort : list \rightarrow list$ and implement it in terms of a hidden operation $insert : el \times list \rightarrow list$. We define signatures:

$$\begin{array}{rll} \mathit{LSrt\text{-}Sig} = & \textbf{sorts} & \mathit{el, list;} \\ & \textbf{opns} & \mathit{nil} : \mathit{list}; \\ & & \mathit{sort} : \mathit{list} \rightarrow \mathit{list}; \\ & & \mathit{cons} : \mathit{el} \times \mathit{list} \rightarrow \mathit{list}; \\ & \textbf{popns} & \mathit{hd} : \mathit{list} \rightarrow \mathit{el};\ \mathit{tl} : \mathit{list} \rightarrow \mathit{list}; \\ & \textbf{pred} & \mathit{le} : \mathit{el} \times \mathit{el}. \end{array} \qquad \begin{array}{rll} \mathit{LSrtImp\text{-}Sig} = & \textbf{sorts} & \mathit{el, list;} \\ & \textbf{opns} & \mathit{nil} : \mathit{list}; \\ & & \mathit{sort} : \mathit{list} \rightarrow \mathit{list}; \\ & & \mathit{cons} : \mathit{el} \times \mathit{list} \rightarrow \mathit{list}; \\ & & \mathit{insert} : \mathit{el} \times \mathit{list} \rightarrow \mathit{list}; \\ & \textbf{popns} & \mathit{hd} : \mathit{list} \rightarrow \mathit{el}; \\ & & \mathit{tl} : \mathit{list} \rightarrow \mathit{list}; \\ & \textbf{pred} & \mathit{le} : \mathit{el} \times \mathit{el}. \end{array}$$

and specifications:

$$\begin{array}{rl} \mathit{LSrtImp} = & (\textbf{translate}\ \mathit{LOrd}\ \textbf{by}\ \imath_1) \cup \langle \mathit{LSrtImp\text{-}Sig},\ \{sort(nil) \stackrel{e}{=} nil; \\ & \forall_{a:el,l:list}.sort(cons(a,l)) \stackrel{e}{=} insert(a, sort(l)); \\ & \forall_{a:el}.insert(a, nil) \stackrel{e}{=} cons(a, nil) \\ & \forall_{a,b:el,l:list}.le(a,b) \Rightarrow insert(a, cons(b,l)) \stackrel{e}{=} cons(a, cons(b,l)) \\ & \forall_{a,b:el,l:list}.le(b,a) \Rightarrow insert(a, cons(b,l)) \stackrel{e}{=} cons(b, insert(a,l))\}\ \rangle \end{array}$$

$$\mathit{LSrt} = \textbf{derive from}\ \mathit{LSrtImp}\ \textbf{by}\ \imath_2,$$

where $\imath_1 : \mathit{LOrd\text{-}Sig} \hookrightarrow \mathit{LSrtImp\text{-}Sig}$ and $\imath_2 : \mathit{LSrt\text{-}Sig} \hookrightarrow \mathit{LSrtImp\text{-}Sig}$ are signature inclusions. By definitions and after removing tautologies we obtain:

$$\begin{aligned}
\delta(\hat{\gamma}(LSrt)) = \exists_{insert:(el,0)\times(list,0)\to(list,0)}.\Big(&\neg fst(hd(nil)) \wedge \neg fst(tl(nil))\wedge\\
&\forall_{l^{list}}.(\neg(l = nil) \wedge fst(hd(l)) \wedge fst(tl(l))) \Rightarrow\\
&\qquad\qquad cons(snd(hd(l)), snd(tl(l))) = l\wedge\\
&\forall_{x^{el}}.le(x,x) \wedge \big(\forall_{x^{el},y^{el},z^{el}}.le(x,y) \wedge le(y,z) \Rightarrow le(x,z)\big)\wedge\\
&\big(\forall_{x^{el},y^{el}}.le(x,y) \wedge le(y,x) \Rightarrow x = y\big)\wedge\\
&\big(\forall_{P:list\to o}.P(nil) \wedge (\forall_{a^{el},l^{list}}.P(l) \Rightarrow P(cons(a,l))) \Rightarrow \forall_{l^{list}}.P(l)\big)\wedge\\
&sort(nil) = nil \wedge \forall_{a^{el},l^{list}}.sort(cons(a,l)) = insert(a, sort(l))\wedge\\
&\forall_{a^{el}}.insert(a, nil) = cons(a, nil)\wedge\\
&\forall_{a^{el},b^{el},l^{list}}.le(a,b) \Rightarrow insert(a, cons(b,l)) = cons(a, cons(b,l))\wedge\\
&\forall_{a^{el},b^{el},l^{list}}.le(b,a) \Rightarrow insert(a, cons(b,l)) = cons(b, insert(a,l))\Big).
\end{aligned}$$

Now, to prove some of the properties of the specification *LSrt* e.g.:

$$LSrt \vdash^{\mathbf{SubPCFOL}} \forall_{a:el}.\forall_{l:list}.le(a, hd(l)) \Rightarrow sort(cons(a,l)) \overset{e}{=} cons(a, sort(l))$$

we can use one of theorem provers for the higher-order logic and prove:

$$\begin{aligned}
\delta(\hat{\gamma}(LSrt)) \vdash^{\mathbf{HOL}} \forall_{a^{el},l^{list}}.le(a, snd(hd(l))) \wedge fst(hd(l)) \Rightarrow&\\
sort(cons(a,l)) = cons(a, sort(l))&\,.
\end{aligned}$$

Extraction of Structured Programs from Specification Proofs

John N. Crossley[1], Iman Poernomo[1*], and Martin Wirsing[2]

[1] School of Computer Science and Software Engineering, Monash University
Clayton, Victoria, Australia 3168. {jnc,ihp}@csse.monash.edu.au
[2] Institut für Informatik, Ludwig-Maximilians-Universität
Oettingenstraße 67, 80538 München, Germany
wirsing@informatik.uni-muenchen.de

Abstract. We present a method using an extended logical system for obtaining programs from specifications written in a sublanguage of CASL. These programs are "correct" in the sense that they satisfy their specifications. The technique we use is to extract programs from proofs in formal logic by techniques due to Curry and Howard. The logical calculus, however, is novel because it adds structural rules corresponding to the standard ways of modifying specifications: translating (renaming), taking unions, and hiding signatures. Although programs extracted by the Curry-Howard process can be very cumbersome, we use a number of simplifications that ensure that the programs extracted are in a language close to a standard high-level programming language. We use this to produce an executable refinement of a given specification and we then provide a method for producing a program module that maximally respects the original structure of the specification. Throughout the paper we demonstrate the technique with a simple example.

1 Introduction

One of the most exciting applications of formal specifications is in the formal development of programs. By gradually refining a high-level specification one eventually obtains a low-level "program" or "executable specification" as in [17,18]. If each refinement step can be proved correct, then the resulting program is guaranteed to satisfy the original specification. In this paper instead of proving the correctness of a refinement step *a posteriori*, we show how we can construct refinements from proofs in a way similar to that in which programs are extracted from proofs in mathematical logic (see [4,7,2,13,1]). As our framework we use a subset of the algebraic specification language *CASL* [5] that supports structured algebraic specifications with first-order axioms and structuring mechanisms for translating, taking unions, and hiding symbols. As programs we consider executable specifications where function symbols are specified by means of terms from a simply typed lambda calculus: "lambda-terms" for brevity.

* Research partly supported by ARC grant A 49230989.

D. Bert, C. Choppy, and P. Mosses (Eds.): WADT'99, LNCS 1827, pp. 419–437, 2000.

We choose the simple notion of model inclusion for refinement. First, given a specification SP, we write sig(SP) for its signature. (Similarly, sig(A) denotes the smallest signature containing all the symbols in the formula A.) A specification SP_1 is then a *refinement* of a specification, SP, if all models of SP_1 (restricted to sig(SP)) are also models of SP. (Equality is interpreted as simply a congruence relation, see e.g. [20]). In the first step we derive a simply typed lambda-term e, for each function symbol f of a specification SP, by extracting lambda-terms from proofs of the axioms of SP over another data structure specification, say SP_0, to obtain SP_1 that is a correct refinement of SP_0 by definitions of the form $f = e$. If SP_0 is executable, then SP_1 is also executable and we are done. Otherwise we repeat the process. Only a finite number of steps will be necessary.

The new contributions of this paper to the development of specifications are as follows. As far as we know, ours is the first approach (building on our earlier [21]) using program-extraction from (formal) proofs in the area of structured algebraic specifications. Moreover it enhances the program extraction techniques already developed for first-order predicate calculus by methods for dealing with structural rules. A further advantage of our approach is that by the extraction techniques studied in [1,13] and [2], the programs that are automatically extracted are close to those of a human developer and the structure of the specification is mirrored in the dependencies of the module extracted. The only similar approach we know of is that of Smith's *SpecWare* system [19] but our technique differs from his both in the specification-building operations and in the program-extraction technique.

In Section 2, we introduce the specification language and introduce the example that is developed throughout the paper. Section 3 gives the background from mathematical logic, presenting a sound and complete proof-system for properties of structured specifications in constructive first-order logic. In Section 4 we present our method of program extraction from proofs (using well-known Curry-Howard reductions and strong normalization) and our map **extract** which maps the proofs to appropriate lambda terms. These techniques are then used in Section 4.3 to obtain successive executable refinements of a given specification. Finally, in Section 5, we show how to obtain program modules that mirror the structure of a partially executable specification.

2 Structured Specifications

In writing large specifications it is convenient to design specifications in a structural and modular fashion by combining and modifying smaller specifications. This helps us to master the complexity arising from a large number of function symbols and axioms.

We employ three specification-building operations from CASL [5]. A basic specification is of the form $\langle \Sigma, Ax \rangle$, where Σ is a signature consisting of a set of sorts, a set F of $(S^* \to S)$-sorted function symbols and a set P of $(S^* \times S)$-sorted predicate symbols. Ax is a set of Σ-formulae. Each such formula is a

spec NAT_0 =
sorts
Nat
ops $0 : Nat; s : Nat \to Nat; + : Nat \times Nat \to Nat$
preds
$\geq: Nat \times Nat$
axioms
$Nat\_0.1 : \forall x : Nat \bullet x + 0 = x$ $Nat\_0.2 : \forall x : Nat; \forall y : Nat \bullet x + s(y) = s(x + y)$
$Nat\_0.3 : \forall x : Nat \bullet x \geq 0$ $Nat\_0.4 : \forall x : Nat; \forall y : Nat \bullet x + y = y + x$
$Nat\_0.5 : \forall x : Nat \bullet s(x) \geq x$
$Nat\_0.6 : \forall x : Nat; \forall y : Nat; \forall v : Nat; \forall w : Nat \bullet x \geq v \wedge y \geq w \to x + y \geq v + w$
end

spec NAT_A =
NAT_0 **then**
ops $a : Nat$
axioms
$A : a \geq s(s(s(0)))$
end

spec NAT_B =
NAT_0 **then**
ops $b : Nat$
axioms
$B : b \geq s(0)$
end

spec NAT_C =
NAT_0 **then**
ops $c : Nat$
axioms
$C : c \geq s(s(s(s(0))))$
end

Fig. 1. The specifications NAT_A, NAT_B and NAT_C. Note that 1. the axioms are Harrop formula, see Remark 1, Section 2 and 2. we shall frequently write NAT_ALL for NAT_A **and** NAT_B **and** NAT_C

Harrop formula (see *Remark 1* below) sometimes of the form $f(x_1, \ldots, x_n) = e$ where e is a λ-expression. The specification-building operations for constructing specifications from basic ones are: *translation*, *union* and *hiding*. In *CASL translation* is written SP **with** ρ, where ρ is a symbol mapping, *union* is written SP_1 **and** SP_2 and *hiding* is written SP **hide** Σ, where Σ is a symbol list. Note that many of the other common specification operators (extension, revealing, and local specifications) used in *CASL* can be constructed from these three operators.[1] In particular, we use the expression SP **then** Σ Ax as a shorthand notation for SP **and** $\langle \Sigma, Ax \rangle$.

As the concrete syntax for our examples we use a subset of the specification language that admits all the above constructs together with the syntax of our simply typed lambda-calculus. We assume that all functions are total and all our specifications include the appropriate axioms for equality (see below, in Section 3). We restrict the other axioms to be Harrop formulae (see below, *Remark 1*).

[1] In [21] we used *SPECTRUM* instead of *CASL*, *building the sum* of two specifications instead of *union* and *export* instead of *hiding* and we wrote 1. $\rho \bullet$SP for the translation of SP by ρ, where ρ is a symbol mapping, 2. SP_1 + SP_2 for the sum of the two specifications and 3. $\text{SP}|_\Sigma$ for exporting the symbols in the symbol list Σ from the signature of SP.

Remark 1. A formula is a *Harrop formula* if it is 1. an atomic formula (including $\bot$), 2. of the form $(A \wedge B)$ where A, B are Harrop, 3. of the form $(Z \to A)$ where A (but not necessarily Z) is Harrop or 4. of the form $\forall x : s \bullet A$ where A is Harrop. Algebraic specifications will very often have only Harrop formulae for their axioms.

Example We use the following simple example throughout the paper to illustrate our method of program extraction from a structured specification.[2] Consider the four specifications NAT_0, NAT_A, NAT_B and NAT_C given in Fig 1.

We shall eventually show how we can obtain a program for c in NAT_C. First we unSkolemize (see Theorem 3, Section 4.3) the axiom for c obtaining:

$$\exists y : Nat \bullet y \geq s(s(s(s(0)))).$$

We prove this formula constructively, using the other two specifications (NAT_A and NAT_B), and then extract a program for y that computes c. From this, we can produce an executable specification, and also a program module corresponding to it, that is a refinement of NAT_C.

3 The Formal Calculus

We extend the logical calculus for structured algebraic specifications based on classical logic, introduced in [21], to one based on constructive logic because most proofs used in Computer Science to produce programs are either constructive or can easily be made so. There are two further reasons for doing this. First we can extract programs directly from the proofs, and secondly it allows us to make further extensions which we describe in Section 3.1.

We use the syntax of *CASL* with logical connectives $\bot$ (*falsum*), $\wedge$, $\vee$, $\to$, $\forall$ and $\exists$. (Negation, $\neg A$, is an abbreviation for $(A \to \bot)$.) The system uses sequents of the form $\Gamma \vdash_{\mathrm{SP}} d : A$ where Γ is a context, SP is a specification,[3] and d is a proof-term that gives a precise representation of the derivation of A from the assumptions from Γ in the environment of the specification SP. From a type-theoretic point of view A is the type of d. Recall that the axioms in SP may be used in addition to those from Γ to prove the formula A whose signature is (contained in) SP. We present the rules in natural deduction style (see [8] or [21]). The rules for the basic system are of two kinds, logical and structural, see Fig.2.

The logical rules are standard for a constructive system (see e.g. [16]). There are two kinds of logical rules: introduction rules and elimination rules. With the logical rules, the specification of the conclusion includes those of the premises while, for the structural rules, the change in the structure is reflected in the specification of the conclusion.

Remark 2. For the rules $(\vee_i I)$, B must be a $\mathtt{sig}(\mathrm{SP})$-formula in $(\vee_1 I)$ and A must be a $\mathtt{sig}(\mathrm{SP})$-formula in $(\vee_2 I)$.

[2] A more complicated example may be found in [15].

[3] As in [21], SP is considered as an equivalence class *modulo* a simple decidable equivalence relation on specifications.

Remark 3. $\perp$-introduction is a special case of $\rightarrow$-elimination: from $(A \rightarrow \perp)$ and A infer $\perp$. The restriction to Harrop formulae in ($\perp$ E) does not restrict the logical power, see e.g. [16].

Remark 4. The rule ($\vee E$) is most easily understood by its analogy to proof by cases. If we have a proof of C from A and also a proof of C from B then we get a proof of C from $A \vee B$. This motivates the reduction rule for **case** (see below Section 3.1). Likewise, if we have a proof of $\exists x : s \bullet A$ and a proof of C from a proof of A with free variable y, then we can get a proof of C and this is the motivation for the reduction rule for **select**. (See e.g. [8] or [7] for full details.)

Remark 5. $A[t/x]$ is the usual substitution of t for x in A.

Remark 6. As in [21] Section 3, we assume that there is a function sp(d) that takes the proof-term d in $\vdash_{\mathrm{SP}} d : A$ to the associated specification SP.

Remark 7. In (trans) Γ may contain symbols not in the domain of ρ. ρ' is an extension of ρ such that these are consistently translated (see e.g. [21]).

Theorem 1 (Soundness and completeness). *The above system of logical and structural rules is sound and complete.*

Proof. The proof of completeness proceeds as in Cengarle [6]. We use the flat (basic) normal form theorem as in [21], Section 2, the interpolation and compactness theorems for first-order constructive logic. □

In addition to logical axioms and the axioms in the specification, we also have some implicit axioms that must be made explicit in our logical system. First the usual axioms for equality are assumed (i.e. reflexivity, symmetry, transitivity and substitutivity in both functions and predicates). Secondly, if a specification predicate is decidable, then we have the (Harrop formula for the) law of double negation for such predicates (including equality) at the base level.

Example(*cont.*) We are now ready to prove the unSkolemized axiom for c

$$\vdash_{\mathrm{NAT\_C}} \exists y : Nat \bullet y \geq s(s(s(s(0)))) \tag{1}$$

using our calculus. We may use the axioms from NAT_C that do not involve c. We start with the NAT_A and NAT_B axioms A and B, see Fig. 1. Then, by ($\wedge$-I) on these, setting $q \equiv (ax(\mathrm{NAT\_A}, A), ax(\mathrm{NAT\_B}, B))$ we have:

$$\vdash_{\mathrm{NAT\_A}\ \textbf{and}\ \mathrm{NAT\_B}} q : a \geq s(s(s(0))) \wedge b \geq s(0)$$

Now, using axiom *Nat*_0.6 from NAT_0 (Fig. 1): and the fact that NAT_C is built from NAT_0 we obtain the proof-term

$$\vdash_{\mathrm{NAT\_C}} d : \forall x : Nat; \forall y : Nat;\ \forall v : Nat; \\ \forall w : Nat \bullet x \geq v \wedge y \geq w \rightarrow x + y \geq v + w \tag{2}$$

where $d = \mathrm{union}_2(ax(\mathrm{NAT\_0}, Nat\_0.6), \langle \mathbf{sig}(\mathrm{NAT\_0} \cup \{c\}), C : c \geq s(s(s(s(0)))) \rangle)$. If we perform the structural rule (union$_2$) twice on this axiom with respect to the specifications NAT_A and NAT_B, then, (writing NAT_ALL for NAT_A **and** NAT_B **and** NAT_C):

$$\vdash_{\mathrm{NAT\_ALL}} p : \forall x : Nat; \forall y : Nat; \forall v : Nat; \forall w{:}\ Nat \bullet x \geq v \wedge y \geq w \rightarrow x + y \geq v + w$$

Logical Rules

Initial Rules

$$\frac{}{\{x:A\} \vdash_{\langle \mathtt{sig}(A),\ \emptyset\rangle} ass(A,x):A}\ (\text{Ass I}) \qquad \frac{}{\emptyset \vdash_{\langle \Sigma, Ax\rangle} ax(\langle \Sigma, Ax\rangle, x):A}\ (\text{Ax I})$$

for $\{x:A\} \in Ax$

Introduction Rules

$$\frac{\Gamma \bar{\cup} \{x:A\} \vdash_{\mathrm{SP}} d:B}{\Gamma \vdash_{\mathrm{SP}} \lambda x:A.d:(A \to B)}\ (\to \text{I}) \qquad \frac{\Gamma_1 \vdash_{\mathrm{SP\_1}} d:A \quad \Gamma_2 \vdash_{\mathrm{SP\_2}} e:B}{\Gamma_1 \cup \Gamma_2 \vdash_{\mathrm{SP\_1}\ \mathbf{and}\ \mathrm{SP\_2}} \langle d,e\rangle:(A \wedge B)}\ (\wedge\ \text{I})$$

$$\frac{\Gamma \vdash_{\mathrm{SP}} d:A}{\Gamma \vdash_{\mathrm{SP}} \langle \pi_1, d\rangle:(A \vee B)}\ (\vee_1\ \text{I}) \qquad \frac{\Gamma \vdash_{\mathrm{SP}} e:B}{\Gamma \vdash_{\mathrm{SP}} \langle \pi_2, e\rangle:A \vee B}\ (\vee_2\ \text{I})$$

$$\frac{\Gamma \vdash_{\mathrm{SP}} d:A}{\Gamma \vdash_{\mathrm{SP}} \lambda x:s.d:\forall x:s \bullet A}\ (\forall\ \text{I}) \qquad \frac{\Gamma \vdash_{\mathrm{SP}} d:A[t/x]}{\Gamma \vdash_{\mathrm{SP}} (t,d):\exists x:s \bullet A}\ (\exists\ \text{I})$$

Elimination Rules

$$\frac{\Gamma_1 \vdash_{\mathrm{SP\_1}} d:(A \to B) \quad \Gamma_2 \vdash_{\mathrm{SP\_2}} r:A}{\Gamma_1 \cup \Gamma_2 \vdash_{\mathrm{SP\_1}\ \mathbf{and}\ \mathrm{SP\_2}} (dr):B}\ (\to \text{E}) \qquad \frac{\Gamma \vdash_{\mathrm{SP}} d:(A_1 \wedge A_2)}{\Gamma \vdash_{\mathrm{SP}} \pi_i(d):A_i}\ (\wedge\ \text{E})$$

$$\frac{\Gamma \vdash_{\mathrm{SP}} d:\forall x:s \bullet A}{\Gamma \vdash_{\mathrm{SP}} dt:A[t/x]}\ (\forall\ \text{E}) \qquad \frac{\Gamma \vdash_{\mathrm{SP}} d:\bot}{\Gamma \vdash_{\mathrm{SP}} dA:A}\ (\bot\ \text{E})$$

provided A is Harrop

$$\frac{\Gamma_1 \bar{\cup} \{x:A\} \vdash_{\mathrm{SP\_1}} d:C \quad \Gamma_2 \bar{\cup} \{y:B\} \vdash_{\mathrm{SP\_2}} e:C \quad \Gamma \vdash_{\mathrm{SP}} f:(A \vee B)}{\Gamma^* \vdash_{\mathrm{SP}^*} \mathbf{case}(x:A.d:C, y:B.e:C, f:(A \vee B)):C}\ (\vee\ \text{E})$$

where $\Gamma^* = (\Gamma_1 \cup \Gamma_2 \cup \Gamma) \bar{\cup} \{x:A\} \bar{\cup} \{y:B\}$ and $\mathrm{SP}^* = \mathrm{SP\_1}$ **and** $\mathrm{SP\_2}$ **and** SP

$$\frac{\Gamma_1 \vdash_{\mathrm{SP\_1}} d:\exists x:s \bullet A \quad \Gamma_2 \bar{\cup} \{y:A[z/x]\} \vdash_{\mathrm{SP\_2}} e:C}{(\Gamma_1 \cup \Gamma_2) \vdash_{\mathrm{SP\_1}\ \mathbf{and}\ \mathrm{SP\_2}} \mathbf{select}(z:s.y:A[z/x].e:C, d:\exists x:s \bullet A):C}\ (\exists\ \text{E})$$

Structural Rules

$$\frac{\Gamma \vdash_{\mathrm{SP}} d:A}{\rho'(\Gamma) \vdash_{\mathrm{SP}\ \mathbf{with}\ \rho} \rho \bullet d:\rho \bullet (A)}\ (\text{trans}) \qquad \frac{\Gamma \vdash_{\mathrm{SP}} d:A}{\Gamma \vdash_{\mathrm{SP}\ \mathbf{hide}\ \Sigma} d\ \mathbf{hide}\ \Sigma:A}\ (\text{hide})$$

if Γ is a $\mathtt{sig}(\mathrm{SP} - \Sigma)$-context
and A is a $\mathtt{sig}(\mathrm{SP} - \Sigma)$-formula

$$\frac{\Gamma \vdash_{\mathrm{SP\_1}} d:A \quad (\text{union}_1)}{\Gamma \vdash_{\mathrm{SP\_1}\ \mathbf{and}\ \mathrm{SP\_2}} union_1(d,\ \mathrm{SP\_2}):A} \qquad \frac{\Gamma \vdash_{\mathrm{SP\_2}} d:A \quad (\text{union}_2)}{\Gamma \vdash_{\mathrm{SP\_1}\ \mathbf{and}\ \mathrm{SP\_2}} union_2(d,\ \mathrm{SP\_1}):A}$$

Fig. 2. Logical and Structural Rules

where $p \equiv union_2(union_2(d, \text{NAT\_A}), \text{NAT\_B})$. We can then substitute a for x here, because a is in the current specification, i.e. applying $\forall$-E, with a for x, we obtain:

$$\vdash_{\text{NAT\_ALL}} pa : \forall y : Nat; \forall v : Nat; \forall w : Nat \bullet a \geq v \wedge y \geq w \rightarrow a + y \geq v + w$$

Next we apply $\forall$-E three more times, substituting b for y, $s(s(s(0)))$ for v and $s(0)$ for w. This gives:

$$\vdash_{\text{NAT\_ALL}} r : a \geq s(s(s(0))) \wedge b \geq s(0) \rightarrow a + b \geq s(s(s(0))) + s(0) \qquad (3)$$

with $r = (pab)s(s(s(0)))s(0)$.

Applying $(\rightarrow)$-E to (2) and (3), and setting $k \equiv rq$ gives:

$$\vdash_{\text{NAT\_ALL}} k : a + b \geq s(s(s(0))) + s(0) \qquad (4)$$

By the equality and the addition axioms in NAT_C and then applying $(\exists)$-I to (4) with $a + b$ as witness for y we obtain

$$\vdash_{\text{NAT\_ALL}} (a + b, k') : \exists y : Nat \bullet y \geq s(s(s(s(0)))) \qquad (5)$$

for some term k' which reduces greatly because of the Harrop formulae (see *Remark 1*).

Finally, since we wish to prove equation (1) $\exists y : Nat \bullet y \geq s(s(s(s(0))))$ for the specification NAT_C we hide the symbols a, b from the signatures of NAT_A and NAT_B. Setting NAT_C_1 = NAT_ALL **hide** a, b, we get

$$\vdash_{\text{NAT\_C\_1}} (a + b, k') \textbf{ hide } a, b : \exists y : Nat \bullet y \geq s(s(s(s(0)))) \qquad (6)$$

This is the derivation of the unSkolemized version of the axiom for c in NAT_C, as required. Later we shall show how to extract a program for c from the proof term.

3.1 Logical Reductions and Strong Normalization

In addition to the proof-term reductions to be found in [21] we have some additional ones: from the new logical reductions for the additional connectives $\vee$ and $\exists$, and from structural reductions. These are essentially the same as for ordinary intuitionistic logic but with the addition of specifications. (For fuller details see [8]). For example, if we have an $(\vee_1 I)$ introducing $(A \vee B)$ from A immediately followed by an $(\vee_1 E)$ eliminating B from $(A \vee B)$, assuming the same specifications, etc. Then **case**, which encodes this proof, reduces (written $\succ$) according to the following scheme

$$(\Gamma_1 \cup \Gamma) \vdash_{\text{SP\_1 and SP}} \textbf{case}(x : A.d : C, y : B.e : C, \langle \pi_1, g \rangle : (A \vee B)) : C$$

$$\succ (\Gamma_1 \cup \Gamma) \vdash_{\text{SP\_1 and SP}} d[g/x] : C$$

(Similarly for **select**.) Any sequence of such reductions always terminates, that is to say, we have *strong normalization*. The proof is like that in [21] using techniques from [8] and Girard [11].

$$\begin{aligned}(\lambda x : \tau_1.d)r &\longrightarrow d[r/x]\\ \text{case}(x_1 : \tau_1.d_1, x_2 : \tau_2.d_2, \langle \pi_i, f\rangle) &\longrightarrow d_i[f/x_i] \quad \text{for } i \in \{1,2\}\\ \text{select}(x : \tau_1.y : \tau_2.d, (a,b)) &\longrightarrow d[a/x][b/y]\\ \pi_i(t_1,t_2) &\longrightarrow t_i \quad \text{for } i \in \{1,2\}\end{aligned}$$

Fig. 3. Operational semantics for Λ

4 Extracting Programs from Proofs

There is a well-known map from constructive proof-terms to programs which are terms in a simply typed lambda calculus, Λ, with product types $(A \times B)$ and disjoint union types $(A|B)$. The operational semantics of Λ is given by the usual reduction rules for simply typed lambda calculus with product and union types as in Fig. 3.

In Section 4.1 we extend this technique to extracting programs from structured proofs in algebraic specifications. In Section 4.2 we describe how some of the complications that arise because of hiding can be overcome. Then in Section 4.3 we describe how to use these techniques to recursively obtain successive executable refinements of a given specification that contain programs for each declared function symbol of SP.

4.1 Extracting Programs form Modular Proofs

In a naïve method for program extraction (using the proof of strong normalization, see e.g. [21], for such a lambda calculus) one can consider a proof term as a program. Proof normalization, proof-term reduction and program evaluation may be considered as equivalent notions.

So, in this sense, the proof-term $(a+b, k')$ of

$$\vdash_{\text{NAT\_ALL}} (a+b, k') : \exists y : Nat \bullet y \geq s(s(s(s(0)))) \tag{5}$$

can be thought of as a program. But this, unfortunately, gives an awkward program since it contains too much unnecessary information: the whole subterm k' is unnecessary for constructing a witness for the constant c.

Modular Proof Terms In [1] or [4], for example, it is shown that, where the axioms are Harrop formulae, a large part of a proof term can be eliminated. In particular, k' in (5) can be reduced to the empty proof term () when it is also possible to eliminate the structural information. This is only possible if the proof term is modular according to the following:

Definition 1. *A proof-term d is said to be* critical *with respect to a symbol list Σ if 1. d is of the form e* **hide** *Σ and 2. if the term e depends on symbols that are in Σ: that is , if* $\mathbf{sig}(\text{sp}(e)) \cap \Sigma \neq \emptyset$. *A proof-term is said to* modular *if it contains no critical (sub-)proof-terms.*

$$\phi(A) = H \qquad \text{if } Harrop(A)$$

$$\phi(A \wedge B) = \begin{cases} \phi(A) & \text{if } Harrop(B) \\ \phi(B) & \text{if } Harrop(A) \\ \phi(A) \times \phi(B) & \text{otherwise} \end{cases}$$

$$\phi(A \vee B) = \phi(A)|\phi(B)$$

$$\phi(A \rightarrow B) = \begin{cases} \phi(B) & \text{if } Harrop(A) \\ \phi(A) \rightarrow \phi(B) & \text{otherwise} \end{cases}$$

$$\phi(\forall x : s \bullet A) = s \rightarrow \phi(A)$$

$$\phi(\exists x : s \bullet A) = \begin{cases} s & \text{if } Harrop(A) \\ s \times \phi(A) & \text{otherwise} \end{cases}$$

Fig. 4. The definition of the map ϕ used in defining **extract** in Fig. 5. (H is the unit type of (). $\perp$ is Harrop so comes under the first clause)

For instance, the proof-term in the formula (5)

$$\vdash_{\mathrm{NAT\_ALL}} (a+b, k') : \exists y : Nat \bullet y \geq s(s(s(s(0))))$$

is modular but the one in formula (6)

$$\vdash_{\mathrm{NAT\_C\_1}} (a+b, k') \ \textbf{hide} \ a, b : \exists y : Nat \bullet y \geq s(s(s(s(0))))$$

is not modular because it is obtained after applying (hide) to a and b.

The Extraction Map For modular proof terms we define a map **extract** to terms in Λ as follows: 1. Harrop subterms are reduced to (), 2. the structural information of taking unions can be ignored, 3. translations of symbols are carried out explicitly, and 4. hidings can be ignored since, in a modular proof, hidden symbols are not used "outside" their local environment. These are the first and last cases in the definition of **extract** which is then recursively extended as expected. First we have to define a map ϕ. We define a map ϕ over formulae of our logical system to types of Λ. Given a formula F, $\phi(F)$ will give us the (computational) type of the program extracted from the proof of F. ϕ is defined by cases.

The definition of ϕ is given in Fig. 4. The full definition of **extract** is given in Fig. 5. Thus **extract**(p) removes "non-computational" type information from p to extract a simple type.

Systematic treatment of Harrop formulae [12] enables us to extract more realistic programs. Harrop formulae have no "computational content" and it is well known that they can be "deleted" from the program (see e.g. [4,3] or [1]).

$$\mathfrak{E}(ass(A,x):A) = \begin{cases} () & \text{if } \mathfrak{H}(\mathrm{A}) \\ x & \text{otherwise} \end{cases}$$

$$\mathfrak{E}(ax(\langle \Sigma, Ax\rangle, x) : A) = ()$$

$$\mathfrak{E}((\lambda x : A.d) : A \to B) = \begin{cases} \mathfrak{E}(d) & \text{if } \mathfrak{H}(A) \\ () & \text{if } \mathfrak{H}(B) \\ \lambda x : \phi(A).\mathfrak{E}(d) & \text{otherwise} \end{cases}$$

$$\mathfrak{E}((a,b) : A \wedge B) = \begin{cases} \mathfrak{E}(a) & \text{if } \mathfrak{H}(A) \text{ and not } \mathfrak{H}(B) \\ \mathfrak{E}(b) & \text{if } \mathfrak{H}(B) \text{ and not } \mathfrak{H}(A) \\ () & \text{if } \mathfrak{H}(A \wedge B) \\ (\mathfrak{E}(a), \mathfrak{E}(b)) & \text{otherwise} \end{cases}$$

$$\mathfrak{E}((\lambda x : s.d) : \forall x : SB) = \begin{cases} () & \text{if } \mathfrak{H}(\forall x : S \bullet B) \\ \lambda x : s.\mathfrak{E}(d) & \text{otherwise} \end{cases}$$

$$\mathfrak{E}((t,d) : \exists x : s \bullet A) = \begin{cases} t & \text{if } \mathfrak{H}(A) \\ (t, \mathfrak{E}(d)) & \text{otherwise} \end{cases}$$

$$\mathfrak{E}(\langle \pi_1, d : A_1\rangle : A_1 \vee A_2) = \langle \pi_1, \mathfrak{E}(d)\rangle$$

$$\mathfrak{E}(\langle \pi_2, d : A_1\rangle : A_1 \vee A_2) = \langle \pi_2, \mathfrak{E}(d)\rangle$$

$$\mathfrak{E}((d : A \to B)(r : A) : B) = \begin{cases} \mathfrak{E}(d) & \text{if } \mathfrak{H}(A) \\ () & \text{if } \mathfrak{H}(B) \\ \mathfrak{E}(d)\mathfrak{E}(r) & \text{otherwise} \end{cases}$$

$$\begin{matrix} \mathfrak{E}((d : \forall x : s\bullet \\ B(x))(r : s) : B[r/x]) \end{matrix} = \begin{cases} () & \text{if } \mathfrak{H}(B[d/x]) \\ (\mathfrak{E}(d)r) & \text{otherwise} \end{cases}$$

$$\begin{matrix} \mathfrak{E}(\mathbf{case}(x : A.d : C, \\ y : B.e : C, f : (A \vee B)) : C) \end{matrix} = \begin{cases} () & \text{if } \mathfrak{H}(C) \\ \text{case}(x : \phi(A).\mathfrak{E}(d), \\ \quad y : \phi(B).\mathfrak{E}(e), \mathfrak{E}(f)) & \text{otherwise} \end{cases}$$

$$\begin{matrix} \mathfrak{E}(\mathbf{select}(z : s.y : A[z/x].e : C, \\ d : \exists x : s.A) : C) \end{matrix} = \begin{cases} () & \text{if } \mathfrak{H}(C) \\ (\lambda x : s.\mathfrak{E}(e))\mathfrak{E}(d) & \text{if } \mathfrak{H}(A) \\ \text{select}(z : s.y : \phi(A).\mathfrak{E}(e), \mathfrak{E}(d)) & \text{otherwise} \end{cases}$$

$$\begin{aligned} \mathfrak{E}(dA : A) &= () \\ \mathfrak{E}(union_i(d, SP)) &= \mathfrak{E}(d) \\ \mathfrak{E}(\rho \bullet d) &= \mathfrak{E}(\rho(d)) \\ \mathfrak{E}(d \textbf{ hide } l) &= \mathfrak{E}(d) \\ \mathfrak{E}(\mathbf{unextract}(d)) &= d \end{aligned}$$

Fig. 5. The definition of **extract** except we have written $\mathfrak{E}(d)$ for **extract**(d) and $\mathfrak{H}(A)$ for "A is Harrop". The definition of ϕ is given in Fig. 4

Lemma 1 (Extraction). *There is a "forgetful" map* **extract** *from proof-terms to terms in Λ, such that, given any proof $\vdash_{\text{SP}} d : A$, with the term d being modular, then* **extract**(d) *is in Λ, is of type $\phi(A)$ and is an extended realizer (see [4] and below) for A.*

The definition of **extract** is the same as in [2] or [4], *modulo* the hiding, translating and union operators and the algorithms we have given above in Section 1.

For the example above in (5) without **hide**, we have **extract**$(a + b, k') = a + b$.

Extended Skolemization and Constructing a Conservative Extension From the extracted program e for a function symbol f we can easily construct an executable definition of f by setting $f(x) = e$. This function f is then an extended realizer of the Skolem formula associated with the axioms A for f. We use both for constructing the desired conservative extension of SP.

Definition 2 (Extended Skolemization). *Given a closed formula A, we define the* extended Skolemization *of A to be the Harrop formula $Sk(A) = Sk'(A, \emptyset)$, where $Sk'(A, AV)$ is defined as follows. A unique function letter f_A is associated with each such formula A (see clause 6.). AV represents a list of application variables in A. (That is to say, those variables that will be the arguments of f_A.) If AV is $\{x_1 : s_1, \ldots, x_n : s_n\}$ then $f(AV)$ stands for the function application $f(x_1, \ldots, x_n)$.*

1. *If A is Harrop, then $Sk'(A, AV) \equiv A$*
2. *If $A \equiv B \vee C$, then*
$$Sk'(A, AV) \equiv \pi_1 f_A(AV) = \pi_1 \rightarrow (Sk'(B, AV)[\pi_2 f_A / f_B]) \wedge$$
$$\pi_1 f_A(AV) = \pi_2 \rightarrow (Sk'(C, AV)[\pi_2 f_A / f_C]).$$
3. *$Sk'(A \equiv B \wedge C, AV) \equiv Sk'(B, AV)[\pi_1 f_A / f_B] \wedge Sk'(C, AV)[\pi_2 f_A / f_C]$.*
4. *$Sk'(A \equiv B \rightarrow C, AV) \equiv Sk'(B, AV) \rightarrow Sk'(C, AV \cup \{f_B\})[f_A / f_C]$.*
5. *If $A \equiv \forall x : s \bullet B$, then $Sk'(A, AV) \equiv \forall x : s \bullet Sk'(B, AV \cup \{x : s\})[f_A / f_B]$.*
6. *If $A \equiv \exists y : s \bullet B$, then $Sk'(A, AV) \equiv Sk'(B, AV)[f_A(AV) / y : s]$.*

So, for example, $Sk(\exists y \bullet y \geq s(s(s(s(0)))))$ is $f_{\exists y \bullet y \geq s(s(s(s(0))))} \geq s(s(s(s(0))))$.

Definition 3 (Extended Realizer). *Given a formula A, f_A is an extended realizer of A if, and only if, $Sk(A)$ is provable.*

So for the example above, if we can prove $f_A \geq s(s(s(s(0))))$, then f_A is an extended realizer of A. When we extract a program for a proof of $\vdash_{\text{SP}} d : A$, we produce an extended realizer for A. In particular, if we define $f_A =$ **extract**$((a + b, k'))$ we obtain an extended realizer for our example. We also have

Lemma 2. *If $\vdash_{\text{SP}} A$ then there is an extended realizer f_A such that $\vdash_{\text{SP}} Sk(A)$ and conversely.*

Since e is an extended realizer of A, it follows that $Sk(A)$ is true when $f_A(x) = e(x)$. This yields the next theorem which shows how we refine a specification when we extract a Λ term from a proof.

Theorem 2.[4] *Given a proof* $\emptyset \vdash_{\mathrm{SP}} d : A$ *such that* d *is modular,* $e = \mathbf{extract}(d)$ *and* $\overrightarrow{x}$ *(of types* $T_1, \ldots, T_n$*, respectively) is the list of all free variables in* e*, let* f_A *be as given by definition 3 and define* $NewSpec(\mathrm{SP}, A, e) = \mathrm{NEW}$*, say, by*

spec NEW =
  SP **then**
 ops $f_A : T \rightarrow s$
 axioms $\forall \overrightarrow{x} \bullet f_A(\overrightarrow{x}) = e(\overrightarrow{x})$
  $Sk(A)$
end

where $T = T_1 \times \ldots \times T_n$*. Then* $NewSpec(\mathrm{SP}, A, e)$ *is a correct refinement of* SP.

We can also formally include the result of the extraction map into our calclculus by the following new proof rule which uses a proof term constructor called **unextract**.

Definition 4. *Assume* $\vdash d : A$*, then* $e = \mathbf{extract}(d)$ *is an extended realizer* e *of* A *in* SP*. We add a new constructor* **unextract** *for proof-terms and* $\vdash_{\mathrm{SP}}$ $\mathbf{unextract}(e, \mathrm{SP}) : A$ *to our calculus and define* $sp(\mathbf{unextract}(e, \mathrm{SP})) = \mathrm{SP}$*. (We set* $\mathbf{extract}(\mathbf{unextract}(d)) = d$*.)*

unextract is needed for eliminating critical subterms from proofs by extracting intermediate programs from subproofs. If the proof-term d is modular, then we can use Theorem 4 to give us the following rule as a conservative extension to our calculus.

$$\frac{\emptyset \vdash_{\mathrm{SP}} d : A}{\emptyset \vdash_{NewSpec(\mathrm{SP}, A, \mathbf{extract}(d))} \mathbf{unextract}(f_A, NewSpec(\mathrm{SP}, A, \mathbf{extract}(d))) : A} \text{(Sk)}$$

The resulting specification $NewSpec(\mathrm{SP}, A, \mathbf{extract}(d))$ is a conservative extension of SP because, if $NewSpec(\mathrm{SP}, A, \mathbf{extract}(d))$ is inconsistent, then, by Theorem 6.20 of [8], so too is SP.

In the same way, as well as functions from proof-terms, we can also consistently add functions given by explicit definitions but in the general case, proving consistency can be very difficult. The great advantage of the above process is that when we add a new function defined by a program obtained from a proof-term, then consistency is guaranteed.

Example (*cont.*). We extract a program from our proof of (5):

$$\frac{\vdash_{\mathrm{NAT\_ALL}} (a+b, k') : \exists y : Nat \bullet y \geq s(s(s(s(0))))}{\emptyset \vdash_{\mathrm{SP}} \mathbf{unextract}(f, \mathrm{SP}) : \exists y : Nat \bullet y \geq s(s(s(s(0))))}$$

where $\mathrm{SP} \equiv NewSpec(\mathrm{NAT\_ALL}, \exists y : Nat \bullet y \geq s(s(s(s(0)))), \mathbf{extract}((a+b, k')))$.

[4] Note that for *CASL* specifications this theorem will hold only if A is a Harrop formula or does not contain non-Harrop subformulae of the form $(B \rightarrow C)$. Otherwise, f_A will have a higher order type and other new operators f_B will be included in the signatures.

By Theorem 2, SP is a refinement of NAT_A **and** NAT_B **and** NAT_C which includes the function symbol f for the program extracted from $(a + b, t)$. Two axioms are given for f in SP: the equational (executable) definition and the Skolemized version of $\exists y : Nat \bullet y \geq s(s(s(s(0))))$ and in *CASL* syntax, SP is:

spec SP=
    NAT_A **and** NAT_B **and** NAT_C **then**
  ops $f : Nat$
  axioms $f = a + b$
    $f \geq s(s(s(s(0))))$
end

4.2 Eliminating Critical Sub-proofs

As has been noted, we are unable to use the rule (Sk) to extract a program directly from a term involving critical terms such as (6). If we *were* permitted to use (Sk) on (6), then the equational definition $f = a + b$ would be added as an axiom to the specification NAT_C. This axiom involves symbols that are not visible in the signature and here adding such an axiom to a specification would result in a specification that was not well formed. Critical terms occur often using program extraction because we use functions from other specifications. In order to achieve a refinement of a target specification, these functions are often hidden.

We eliminate critical terms by using the **extract** and **unextract** maps given above. In the process we sometimes acquire extra functions, definitions and axioms.[5] We first show how this may be done by traversing the proof tree in a depth-first manner and eliminating the corresponding occurrences of critical subterms.

Lemma 3. *Given any term* $\emptyset \vdash_{\mathrm{SP}} d : A$*, there is a term* $\emptyset \vdash_{\mathrm{SP}'} \psi(d) : A$ *such that* $\psi(d)$ *contains no critical subterms and* SP $\rightsquigarrow$ SP$'$.

Proof. We give a recursive definition of $\psi(d)$ using a depth-first traversal of the proof tree represented by d. Let $n(t)$ be the total number of critical subterms in the proof-term t. We define a terminating sequence of proof terms $d = d_0, \ldots, d_k = \psi(d)$. Given d_i, we determine d_{i+1} as follows.
Case 1. If d_i does not contain any critical subterm, then $d_{i+1} = \psi(d) = d_i$ (viz, the sequence terminates).
Case 2. Otherwise, normalize d_i to give a proof-term d'. As long as d_i has no assumptions, the normalized proof-term d' will contain no subterms of the form $(\lambda x : A.p)$ **hide** Σ.
1. Take the leftmost innermost critical subterm of the form $t = e$ **hide** $\Sigma : B$ in d'. That is, take the first critical subterm t in d' that does not contain any

[5] There is an alternative means of eliminating critical terms which involves replacing (hide) rules by (Ass-I) rules but it has the disadvantage that we lose information when we take the formula proved as a new assumption.

critical subterms. So, e itself contains no critical subterms.
2. Apply (Sk) to $e : B$ to yield a new program $f = \mathbf{extract}(e)$. Let $\text{SP} \equiv$ $NewSpec(sp(e), B, \mathbf{extract}(e))$. Then, in t, replace e by $\mathbf{unextract}(f, \text{SP})$, and replace all occurrences of Σ by $\Sigma \cup \{f\}$ to give t' (which we note is not a critical proof-term).
3. Replace all occurrences of t by t' in d', to give $d_{i+1} = d'[t'/t]$. Then d_{i+1} has at least one less critical subterm than d_i, and proves the same theorem as d_i.

Since $n(d_{i+1}) < n(d_i)$, this process yields a k such that $n(d_k) = 0$. Then we take $\psi(d) = d_k$, which is a proof-term with no critical subterms.

Note that $\text{SP}' = \text{sp}(d')$ and will be a conservative refinement of SP by the definition of **extract**. The final specification will be a refinement of sp(d). So, as a corollary of this lemma and our (Sk) rule, we can extract a program from any proof. First, we apply the procedure outlined in this lemma to remove critical subterms. Then we apply (Sk) to extract the program. □

Example (*cont.*). If we apply the procedure of Lemma 3 to (6), we obtain the proof-term

$\vdash_{\text{NAT\_C}'}$ **hide** $_{a,b}$ $(\mathbf{unextract}(f, \text{NAT\_C}'), k')$ **hide** $a, b \;:\; \exists y \;:\; Nat \bullet y \geq s(s(s(s(0))))$

where $\text{NAT\_C}'$ is $NewSpec(\text{NAT\_ALL}, \exists y : Nat \bullet y \geq s(s(s(s(0)))), \mathbf{extract}(a+b))$

As can be seen, this new term contains no critical subterms. If we now extract a program from this term using (Sk),we obtain the following executable specification:

spec NAT_C′ =
{ NAT_A **and** NAT_B **and** NAT_C **then**
ops $f : Nat$
axioms $f = a + b$
$f \geq s(s(s(s(0))))$
}
hide a, b
end

This is a conservative refinement of NAT_C (and of NAT_C_1) as required.

4.3 Executable Refinements

Now we show how we build executable refinements by systematically adding in new executable definitions for the functions in the signature of the specification that do not already have them. Given a specification SP we apply the following procedure to every declared function symbol f of SP: first we take the conjunction of all axioms for f and unSkolemize this obtaining a formula of the form $\forall x \exists y \bullet A$ and then we constructively prove this formula in a structured way using the calculus of Section 2, Fig. 2. In the third step we extract a program from the proof of $\forall x \exists y \bullet A$. This works in the usual way (see e.g. [4] or [8]), except that the structural information has to be taken into account. If the proof of $\forall x \exists y \bullet A$ is "modular", then this can easily be done as was shown in Section 4.1. As a result we obtain a program for f which we then use to construct a new specification that is a conservative extension of SP and contains the program for f.

If the proof of $\forall x \exists y A$ is not modular, then we transform the proof into a modular one using appropriate Skolemization and unSkolemization procedures. Then, in a finite number of steps, we refine a specification SP_*start* to an executable specification SP_*ex*. We can then say that this specification, SP_*ex*, is *executable* because every function in the signature has an equational definition in Ax(SP_*ex*) of the form $f = t$ (where t is a term in Λ). Recall (see *Remark 6*, above Section 3) that each valid proof-term t has an associated structured specification $sp(t)$. We use this property and our extraction rule (Sk) to produce the required executable refinement.

Theorem 3 (Executable refinements). *Given a specification* SP_*start. If every unSkolemized axiom in* Ax(SP_*start*) *is constructively provable in our calculus (possibly using other specifications), then there is an executable specification* SP_*ex that is a conservatively correct refinement of* SP_*start*.

Proof. We construct a finite series of refinements SP_*start* = SP_0 $\leadsto \ldots \leadsto$ SP_K = SP_*ex*. Given a specification SP_I, we obtain SP_I+1 as follows.

1. Take the first function symbol $g \in$ **sig**(SP_I) that is not a constructor for a sort and does *not* have an executable definition in Ax(SP_I).
2. Take the conjunction of all the axioms in Ax(SP) in which g occurs.
3. UnSkolemize this conjunction. This will produce a formula of the form $A \equiv \forall \overrightarrow{x}\ \exists y \bullet P(\overrightarrow{x}, y)$.
4. The proof of this conjunction (using any axioms from SP_*i* *except* those in which g occurs) gives a proof-term of the form $\vdash_{\mathrm{SP\_I}} d : A$ such that its structured specification sp(d) has exactly the same signature as SP_I.
   Now let SP_I+1 be SP′ **with** ρ where SP′ is as in Lemma 3 and ρ is the translation given by $f_A \mapsto g$. Then SP_I+1 is a refinement of SP′. SP_I+1 will contain an (executable) declaration of the form $\forall \overrightarrow{x} \bullet (g(\overrightarrow{x}) = p(\overrightarrow{x}))$ (where $\overrightarrow{x}$ is the list of variables in p). SP_I+1 has one less non-executable function in its signature than SP′.

Repeating the process yields a finite strict chain of refinements in which all functions of SP have executable definitions. □

Example (*cont.*) In NAT_C′ **with** ρ where ρ is the translation given by $f \mapsto c$, we have the required executable refinement of NAT_C.

5 Extracting Program Modules

In this section we show how to construct program modules from specifications that (as a result of the program extraction procedures of Section 4) contain executable definitions for each of its declared function symbols. In Section 5.1 we define our notion of program module, and in Section 5.2 we describe the procedure of extracting program modules from such "executable" specifications.

5.1 Program Modules

It would be desirable to take an executable specification and map it to a set of programs (a module) that has a structure that mirrors the structure of the executable specification. For the purposes of this paper we define a simple modular programming language with a clear semantics that supports translation, unions and hiding of modules. Formally, we take a basic program module to be defined by tuples of declarations. A declaration is an equality between a unique typed identifier $f : T$ and a program $p : T$ (where the types of f and p must coincide):

$$f = p$$

A *generic* module is a lambda abstraction from program modules to program modules. So a *non-generic* module is either a basic program module, or is formed from other non-generic modules via the operations of translating M **with** ρ, taking the union M **and** M' and hiding M **hide** Σ (where M, M' are non-generic modules, Σ is a symbol list and ρ is a symbol map). Here is the BNF notation for modules:

$$\begin{array}{lll}
Program & ::= & \Lambda\text{-term} \\
Name & ::= & \text{typed function variable} \\
Declaration & ::= & Name = Program \\
ModuleContents & ::= & Declaration \mid ModuleContents \times ModuleContents \\
Module & ::= & ModuleContents \mid Module \ \textbf{and} \ Module \mid \\
 & & Module \ \textbf{with} \ \rho \mid Module \ \textbf{hide} \ \Sigma \mid ModuleVar \\
GenericModule & ::= & \lambda ModuleVar.Module \mid \lambda ModuleVar.GenericModule \\
ModuleVar & ::= & Variable : Spec
\end{array}$$

where *Spec* ranges over structured specifications, Σ ranges over symbol lists, and ρ ranges over symbol maps.

Notes: 1. A program declared in a module may contain references to functions not declared within the same module. 2. The operator ρ can be thought of as a module *adapter*, which allows for modules to be reused with different names for functions.

We place the following restrictions on modules: 1. Semantically, generic modules are abstractions over basic (flat) program modules only. Higher order abstraction is not permitted. 2. The type of each name-program pair in any module must be first order. Higher order types are not permitted.

5.2 Extracting Modules from Specifications

We can extract a basic module from a basic executable specification SP simply by taking all function definitions as declarations in the module. We build a structured module from a structured specification by mapping the structure building operators of the specification to the corresponding operators of the module. One problem is that the declarations may contain references to functions of specifications that are not executable. We treat these specifications as module variables, and abstract over them at the end of the process to produce a generic module. This process gives us the following theorem.

Theorem 4 (Extracting Program Modules). *Given an executable specification* SP, *there exists a (possibly generic) module* $M \equiv \lambda X_1 : \mathrm{SP\_1}, \ldots, \lambda X_\mathrm{N} : \mathrm{SP\_N}.M'$ *such that* $M[U_1 : \mathrm{SP\_1}] \ldots [U_\mathrm{N} : \mathrm{SP\_N}]$ *is a realizer of* SP *if each* U_I *is a realizer of* SP_I *for* $\mathrm{I} = 1, \ldots, \mathrm{N}$.
If $\mathrm{N} = 0$, *then* $M \equiv M'$ *is a realizer of* SP.

Proof. M' is the result of the recursive procedure *GetModule* applied to SP. At the same time we define a list of variables $BV(\mathrm{SP}) \equiv \{X_1 : \mathrm{SP\_1}, \ldots, X_n : \mathrm{SP\_N}\}$.
1. If SP is basic and executable, then *GetModule*(SP) is the module obtained by taking all declarations in SP as declarations in the module. $BV(\mathrm{SP}) = \emptyset$. Clearly *GetModule*(SP) is a realizer of SP.
2. If SP is basic and not executable, then *GetModule*(SP) is a module variable $X : \mathrm{SP}$. $BV(\mathrm{SP}) = \{X : \mathrm{SP}\}$.
3. If SP is of the form SP_A **and** SP_*b* then *GetModule*(SP) = *GetModule*(SP_A) **and** *GetModule*(SP_B). $BV(\mathrm{SP}) = BV(\mathrm{SP\_A}) \cup BV(\mathrm{SP\_B})$.
4. If SP is of the form SP_A **hide** Σ, then *GetModule*(SP) = *GetModule*(SP_A) **hide** Σ. $BV(\mathrm{SP}) = BV(\mathrm{SP\_A})$.
5. If SP is of the form SP_A **with** ρ, then *GetModule*(SP) = *GetModule*(SP_A) **with** ρ. $BV(\mathrm{SP}) = BV(\mathrm{SP\_A})$.

Finally, let M be defined by $\lambda X_1 : \mathrm{SP\_1}, \ldots, \lambda X_n : \mathrm{SP\_N}.GetModule(\mathrm{SP})$ where $BV(\mathrm{SP}) = \{X_1 : \mathrm{SP\_1}, \ldots, X_n : \mathrm{SP\_N}\}$.
The rest of the proof follows from the definition of generic modules, and the fact that if SP is a basic executable specification, then *GetModule*(SP) is obviously a realizer for SP.
If SP and all its subspecifications are executable, then $BV(\mathrm{SP}) = \emptyset$, $\mathrm{N} = 0$ and M is a non-generic module. □

Example(*cont.*). The executable specification NAT_C′ is mapped to the following module using the algorithm of Theorem 4:

GetModule(NAT_C′) = $\lambda X_1 : \mathrm{NAT\_A}.\lambda X_2 : \mathrm{NAT\_B}.$
```
(
  ( X1 and X2 and
    f = a + b
    c = f
  ) hide a, b)
```

Because NAT_A and NAT_B are not executable specifications, they correspond to module variables X_1 and X_2 respectively. If we can find modules that realize these specifications, then we can instantiate this generic module, obtaining a working program that computes c. Although the programs for a and b are encapsulated in *GetModule*(NAT_C′), the function f is not encapsulated (although its definition is). So, $c = f$ is a correct definition of c that respects the encapsulation of the two submodules.

Design Considerations We have seen how specification building operations correspond to module building operations. The location of the (hide) rules breaks the proof up into sections that correspond to modules: once the location of the (hide) rule is fixed, a design decision has been made. The proof process corresponds to a module design process where fixed decisions are made with respect to the placement of the (hide) rules. The application of (hide) in a proof corresponds to a design decision about the encapsulation of the resulting modules.[6]

6 Conclusion

In this paper we have described a method that combines the techniques of structured specifications and program extraction in order to produce correct programs from structured specifications. As Sannella pointed out to us after seeing [21], it is not possible to separate the structural rules for building specifications from the logical rules in a proof completely. Nevertheless it *is* possible to provide a modified proof that gives rise to program modules. These modules are principally determined by the location of the applications of hiding (or export, as it was in [21]). We have shown how this can be done and illustrated the technique by a very simple example but see [15] for a more complicated one. The Curry-Howard technique we have used gives rise, in its simplest form, to very complicated programs. However, by the heavy use of techniques dependent on Harrop formulae we are able to reduce this dramatically. We have partially implemented our system and it produces readable programs, with a highly modular structure, in *ML*, directly from proofs. The techniques we use are readily extended to systems with induction (and therefore recursion in the programs). We have presented our work in the context of *CASL* and a logical system that is very standard so that it will be as easy as possible to read and use.

Acknowledgement

We thank the three referees who made us think hard about the structure of the paper and thereby led us, we hope, to a much clearer presentation of our intricate processes.

References

1. Albrecht, D. W. and J. N. Crossley, Program extraction, simplified proof-terms and realizability, Technical Report 271, Dept of Computer Science, Monash University, Australia, 1997. 419, 420, 426, 427
2. Anderson, P., Representing proof transformations for program optimization, in *Proceedings of the 12th International Conference on Automated Deduction*, Nancy, France, Springer LNAI 814, 1994, pp. 575–590. 419, 420, 429
3. Barbanera, F. and S. Berardi, A Symmetric Lambda-Calculus for "Classical" Program Extraction", *Information and Computation*, **125**, 1996, 103–117. 427
4. Berger, U. and H. Schwichtenberg, Program development by Proof Transformation, in *Proceedings of the NATO Advanced Study Institute on Proof and Computation*, Marktoberdorf, Germany, 1993, published in cooperation with the NATO Scientific Affairs Division, pp. 1–45. 419, 426, 427, 429, 432

[6] It is possible to move the other structural rules up and down proofs (see [21]). However, if a logical argument is reused for with changing specifications, then it will probably be convenient to leave all the translations to the end of the proof.

5. CoFI Language Design Task Group, *CASL – The CoFI Algebraic Specification Language – Summary, version 1.0*, 22 July 1999, available at `http://www.dcs.ed.ac.uk/home/dts/CoFI/Documents/CASL/Summary/index.html` 419, 420
6. Cengarle, M. V., *Formal Specifications with Higher-Order Parametrization*, PhD Thesis, Ludwig-Maximilians-Universität, München, 1994. 423
7. Constable, R. L., *Implementing Mathematics with the Nuprl Proof Development System*, Prentice Hall, 1986. 419, 423
8. Crossley, J. N. and J. C. Shepherdson, Extracting programs from proofs by an extension of the Curry-Howard process, in J. N. Crossley, J. B. Remmel, R. A. Shore, and M. E. Sweedler (eds),*Logical Methods*, Birkhäuser, Boston, 1993, pp. 222–288. 422, 423, 425, 430, 432
9. Crossley, J. N., I. H. Poernomo and M. Wirsing, Extracting Structured Programs from Specification Proofs (in preparation).
10. Gallier, J. Constructive Logics. A Tutorial on Proof-systems and Typed λ-Calculi, TCS, **110**, 1993, 249–339.
11. Girard, J.-Y., Y. Lafont and P. Taylor, *Proofs and types*, Cambridge University Press, 1989. 425
12. Harrop, R. Concerning formulas of the types $A \rightarrow B \vee C$, $A \rightarrow (Ex)B(x)$ in Intuitionistic Formal Systems, J. Symb. Logic, **25**, 1960, 27–32. 427
13. Hayashi, Susumu and Hiroshi Nakano. *PX, a computational logic.* MIT Press, Cambridge, MA., 1988. 419, 420
14. Hennicker, R., M. Wirsing and M. Bidoit, Proof systems for structured specifications with observability operators, TCS **173**, 1997, 393–443.
15. Jeavons, J., I. Poernomo, J. Crossley and B. Basit: Fred: an implementation of a layered approach to extracting programs from proofs. Part I: an application in graph theory, in J. W. Lloyd (ed.), *AWCL (Australian Workshop on Computational Logic), Proceedings*, Canberra, Australia, February 2000, pp. 57–66. 422, 436
16. Kleene, S. C. *Introduction to Metamathematics*, North-Holland, Amsterdam, 1952. 422, 423
17. Sannella, D. T. and A. Tarlecki, Toward formal development of programs from algebraic specifications: Implementations revisited. Acta Informatica, **25**, 1988, 233–281. 419
18. Santen, T, F. Kammüller, S. Jähnichen and M. Beyer, Formalization of Algebraic Specification in the Development language DEVA, in M. Broy and S. Jähnichen (eds.), *KORSO: Methods, Languages, and Tools for the Construction of Correct Software, Final Report*, LNCS 1009, Springer, 1995, pp. 223–238. 419
19. Smith, D. R. *Constructing Specification Morphisms*, J. Symbolic Computation, **15**, 1993, 571–606. 420
20. Wirsing, M. and M. Broy: A modular framework for algebraic specification and implementation, in J. Diaz and F. Orejas (eds), *TAPSOFT 89*, LNCS 351, vol. 1, Springer, 1989, pp. 42–73. 420
21. M. Wirsing, J. N. Crossley and H. Peterreins, Proof normalization of structured algebraic specifications is convergent, in J. Fiaderio (ed), *Proceedings of the Twelfth International Workshop on Recent Trends in Algebraic Development Techniques*, LNCS **1589**, Springer, 1999, pp. 322–337. 420, 421, 422, 423, 425, 426, 436

Towards a Verification Logic for Rewriting Logic

José Luis Fiadeiro[1], Tom Maibaum[2], Narciso Martí-Oliet[3], Jose Meseguer[4], and Isabel Pita[3]

[1] Faculdade de Ciências, Univ. de Lisboa, Portugal
[2] King's College London, UK
[3] Depto. Sistemas Informáticos, Univ. Complutense Madrid, Spain
[4] SRI International, Menlo Park, CA, USA

Abstract. This paper is an initial step in the development of a logic for verifying properties of programs in rewriting logic. Rewriting logic is primarily a logic of change, in which deduction corresponds directly to computation, and not a logic to talk about change in a more indirect and global manner, such as the different modal and temporal logics that can be found in the literature.
We start by defining a modal action logic (VLRL) in which rewrite rules are captured as actions. The main novelty of this logic is a topological modality associated with state constructors that allows us to reason about the structure of states, stating that the current state can be decomposed into regions satisfying certain properties. Then, on top of the modal logic, we define a temporal logic for reasoning about properties of the computations generated from rewrite theories, and demonstrate its potential by means of two simple examples.

1 Introduction

Rewriting logic was first proposed by Meseguer in 1990 as a unifying framework for concurrency [13,14]. Since then a large body of work by researchers around the world has contributed to the development of several aspects of the logic and its applications in different areas of computer science [16,8,17].

Rewriting logic is a logic for reasoning about the correctness of concurrent systems having states, and evolving by means of transitions. It is a logic of change in which the distributed states of a system are understood as algebraically axiomatized data structures, and the basic local changes that can concurrently occur in a system are axiomatized as rewrite rules that correspond to local patterns that, when present in the state of a system, can change into other patterns.

A rewrite theory consists of a signature (which is taken to be an equational theory) and a set of labelled (conditional) rewrite rules. The signature of a rewrite theory describes a particular structure for the states of a system—e.g., multiset, binary tree, etc.—so that its states can be distributed according to the laws of such a structure; for example, Petri nets use the notion of distributed state based on multisets [14,12]. The rewrite rules in the theory describe which

D. Bert, C. Choppy, and P. Mosses (Eds.): WADT'99, LNCS 1827, pp. 438–458, 2000.

elementary local transitions are possible in the distributed state by concurrent local transformations. The deduction rules of rewriting logic allow us to reason formally about which general concurrent transitions are possible in a system satisfying such a description. Thus, computationally, each rewriting step is a parallel local transition in a concurrent system. Alternatively, however, we can adopt a logical viewpoint instead, and regard each rewriting step as a logical entailment in a formal system.

Rewriting logic can be used directly as a wide spectrum language supporting specification, rapid prototyping, and programming of concurrent systems [10]. This is realized in the multiparadigm language Maude in which modules are theories in rewriting logic [2]. The examples developed in this paper are written using the Maude notation [3].

Note that rewriting logic is primarily a logic *of* change—in which the deduction directly corresponds to the change [12]—as opposed to a logic to talk *about* change in a more indirect and global manner, such as the different variants of modal and temporal logic. In our view these latter logics support a nonexecutable—as far as the system described is concerned—and more abstract level of specification above that of rewriting logic. Our approach envisions two different roles played by logics for concurrent systems: an *executable* role, played in our case by rewriting logic and making the programming itself declarative, and a *specification* role, played by an adequate logic for specification of concurrent systems.

Modal & Temporal Logic Specifications
↓
Executable Rewriting Logic Specifications
↓
Efficient Rewriting Logic Parallel Programs

1.1 Programs, Specifications, Verification, and All That

Central to the developments that we are about to describe is a notion of *program* (or software system). The modal formalisms that we are going to present are meant to support the specification and verification of such programs. Hence, we must make clear what we mean by programs, their specification and their verification.

Programs in rewriting logic manipulate equivalence classes of terms. These equivalence classes are determined by the rewrite signature $\langle \Sigma, E \rangle$. Therefore, a signature defines the universe of objects over which programs operate.

Programs introduce the notion of change into such a universe. In order to define the referent relative to which change is captured, programs have to fix which of the objects of that universe correspond to *states*. Hence, a program fixes a specific sort *State* in Σ. Furthermore, a program fixes the way in which state changes are performed. These are given by, possibly conditional, labelled rules $r(\overline{x}) : [t(\overline{x})]_E \rightarrow [t'(\overline{x})]_E$ where t and t' are Σ-terms and $\overline{x}$ denotes the set of variables occurring in either t or t'. Formally, we consider a program over a signature $\langle \Sigma, E \rangle$ to be a triple $\langle State, L, R \rangle$ where *State* is the designated sort of Σ, L is a ranked set, and R is a set of rules with labels in L. This is the notion of rewrite theory normally used in rewriting logic, except for the designation of the sort of states, which is necessary in order to define both the notions of computation and observation over which specifications will be written. In this way, the state is a visible sort and not a hidden one, since we will ask about its properties.

The rewrite rules that make up a program do not necessarily rewrite the state directly; that is to say, they do not denote, by themselves, state transitions. Instead, they provide the ingredients from which state transitions can be formed. State transitions apply one or several rewrite rules in the context of given states. We will be interested in the state transitions that can be considered to be atomic in the sense that, even if more than one rewrite takes place during such a transition, this happens because the structure of the state allows for such rewrites to be performed concurrently.

We consider a *specification* to be the expression of the properties intended for a certain system. In order to express such properties, we have to determine the means by which we are going to observe the behaviour of the system. We will take such observations to be determined by a family At of state attributes, each of which has an associated sort s. The observations in which we are interested may require an extension of the universe determined by the signature. So we consider that a specification requires both an extension $\langle \Sigma^+, E^+ \rangle$ of the signature $\langle \Sigma, E \rangle$ and the family At of state attributes. Notice that the observation attributes are not part of the signature extension. Furthermore, only conservative extensions of the original signature are admitted in order to protect the universe over which programs are developed (see example in Section 2.2).

The properties that constitute a specification are written in a logic different from that of the programs. We shall consider a temporal logic. The interesting problem, and the reason for this work, is precisely spelling out the relationship that needs to be established between programs and specifications, so that programs can be verified against specifications. For that purpose, we develop a logic, Verification Logic for Rewriting Logic (VLRL), that takes programs as models and allows observation properties to be derived through inference rules that relate the program and the specification logic (or logics). In this setting, given a program P and a specification S, verifying that P satisfies S consists in determining a set V of sentences in VLRL such that P is a model of V and V entails S. In this paper, we present VLRL and an interface inference system for temporal logic, that is, a set of rules allowing us to derive temporal logic properties from VLRL properties.

1.2 Logic Design Decisions

As already stated, our goal is to define logical mechanisms that support the development of software systems using rewriting logic. The idea is that such logical mechanisms should allow properties to be stated and proved about the computations generated by a rewrite theory. In choosing our logic we had two main options:

1. To choose a specific class of state configurations as given by the signature of a rewrite theory, and develop a logic for such configurations. For example, we could have chosen to restrict our logic to object-oriented state configurations consisting of multisets of objects and messages.
2. To try to remain as general as possible, i.e., making as few commitments to specific properties of the state configurations as possible.

A natural choice for the first option would have been object-oriented multiset configurations, for which Grit Denker has already considered a locally distributed modal logic based on the work of Thiagarajan and others [4]. There is also previous work by Ulrike Lechner on using the μ-calculus for Maude object-oriented specifications [9]. In both cases, existing logics are adapted to the object-oriented configurations of Maude, studying the refinement relationships between the specifications at both levels.

We have favoured the second option, motivated by the desire to investigate how much can be said at a specification level about the many different concurrency models embedded in rewrite theories. Having made this decision, we decided to develop and explore a new modal-action logic in which only the rewrite rules are captured as actions, and to define another logic for computations and corresponding interfaces to it. A similar situation arises in Stirling's account of temporal logic defined over the computations generated over a transition system [18], or the relationship between temporal logic and deontic action logic as developed by Fiadeiro and Maibaum [5].

The main benefit of our approach is that we do not restrict ourselves to a special type of state configuration as is done in [4,9]. Moreover, comparing with the locally distributed modal logic of Denker's work, we are interested in global properties of a system, object-oriented or not, instead of properties as seen by a local object; and comparing with Lechner's work, our formulas are more general than simple propositions asserting the presence of messages and/or objects. This is the main reason behind the introduction of observation attributes in order to express more interesting properties of the system.

2 Verification Logic

2.1 Signatures

Given a rewrite signature $\langle \Sigma, E\rangle$, a *verification signature* consists of

- a designated sort *State* of Σ;
- additional sorts and operations that define an extension Σ^+ of Σ, together with a set E^+ of equations that axiomatise the extension in a way that protects[1] the original signature, i.e., such that $T_{\Sigma^+,E^+}|_\Sigma \simeq T_{\Sigma,E}$;

[1] For $\langle \Sigma, E\rangle$ in membership equational logic, which is the version of equational logic used in Maude, the protecting extension $\langle \Sigma^+, E^+\rangle$ should be understood as yield-

- a family At of observation attributes, each of which has an associated sort s of Σ^+;
- a collection L (of labels) indexed over strings of sorts in Σ. The index corresponds to the sequence of sorts of the variables appearing in the rule that defines the action associated with the label (see Section 2.3).

The idea is to define a signature in the sense of other approaches to specification and program design such as CommUnity [6], i.e., we make available attributes for making observations of the state of a system and action symbols to account for its elementary state changes.

Two associated notions of signature will be useful. We denote by Σ_c^+ the extension of Σ^+ with attributes as constants, and by Σ_f^+ the extension of Σ^+ with attributes as function symbols of type $State \rightarrow s$, where s is the sort associated with the attribute.

We can consider sets of equations in Σ_f^+ that define or constrain the values taken by the attributes on the states, leading in this way to equational theories $\langle \Sigma_f^+, E_f^+ \rangle$ that extend, and protect, $\langle \Sigma^+, E^+ \rangle$.

2.2 A Vending Machine

We shall illustrate our approach using as an example a vending machine to buy cakes and apples [12]. A cake costs a dollar and an apple three quarters. The machine only accepts dollars and it returns a quarter when the user buys an apple. It also offers the possibility of changing four quarters into a dollar.

The rewrite theory (Σ, E, L, R) that specifies the vending machine is given by the following Maude system module:

```
mod VENDING-MACHINE is
  sort State .
  ops $ q a c : -> State .
  op __ : State State -> State [assoc comm] .
  rl [buy-c] : $ => c .
  rl [buy-a] : $ => a q .
  rl [change] : q q q q => $ .
endm
```

The possible states of the vending machine are represented by equivalence classes of terms of sort `State` in Σ, corresponding to nonempty multisets of resources built up from the four constants `$,q,a,c` by means of the binary associative and commutative operator `__`, written in mixfix empty juxtaposition notation. The three labelled rewrite rules define the possible actions of the vending machine, allowing several concurrent transitions to take place simultaneously.

ing a bijection at the level of sorts (see [1]). However, the examples in this paper only involve order-sorted equational theories $\langle \Sigma, E \rangle$ for which we have an actual isomorphism of the initial algebras.

To obtain Σ^+, we add to the rewrite signature the sort `Nat` of natural numbers, together with the operations and equations that axiomatise them. This is accomplished by means of the **protecting** module importation statement.

In Σ_c^+ the observation attributes that are of interest to us are $\#\$$, $\#q$, $\#c$, and $\#a$, representing the number of dollars, quarters, cakes, and apples in a state of the machine, and *wealth*, representing the total value of a state of the vending machine, measured in terms of quarters.

The following rewrite theory $(\Sigma_f^+, E_f^+, L, R)$ extends (Σ, E, L, R) by adding the natural numbers, by declaring the attributes as functions over the states, and by adding equations defining such functions by structural induction, with the exception of *wealth*, which is defined in terms of the other attributes by means of an arithmetic expression.

```
mod VENDING-MACHINE-OBSERVED is
  protecting VENDING-MACHINE .
  protecting NAT .
  ops #$ #q #c #a : State -> Nat .
  op wealth : State -> Nat .
  vars P1 P2 : State .
  eq #$($) = 1 .  eq #$(q) = 0 .  eq #$(c) = 0 .  eq #$(a) = 0 .
  eq #q(q) = 1 .  eq #q($) = 0 .  eq #q(c) = 0 .  eq #q(a) = 0 .
  eq #c(c) = 1 .  eq #c($) = 0 .  eq #c(q) = 0 .  eq #c(a) = 0 .
  eq #a(a) = 1 .  eq #a($) = 0 .  eq #a(q) = 0 .  eq #a(c) = 0 .
  eq #$(P1 P2) = #$(P1) + #$(P2) .
  eq #q(P1 P2) = #q(P1) + #q(P2) .
  eq #c(P1 P2) = #c(P1) + #c(P2) .
  eq #a(P1 P2) = #a(P1) + #a(P2) .
  eq wealth(P1) = 4*#$(P1)+#q(P1)+4*#c(P1)+3*#a(P1) .
endm
```

2.3 The Language of Action Terms

As already mentioned in the introduction, rewrite rules cannot always be regarded as actions *per se*. They may require the context in which they are being applied to be made explicit. This is achieved through the language of action terms defined below, which defines a (proper) subset of all concurrent one-step rewrites [14].

We start by defining *pre-action terms*, α. These correspond to the quotient of the set of proof terms obtained through the following rules of deduction:

– *Identities*: for each $[t] \in T_{\Sigma,E}(X)$, $\dfrac{}{[t] : [t] \to [t]}$,
– *Σ-structure*: for each $f \in \Sigma$,

$$\frac{\alpha_i : [t_i] \to [t'_i]}{f(\overline{\alpha}) : [f(\overline{t})] \to [f(\overline{t'})]},$$

– *Replacement*: for each labelled rewrite rule $r(\overline{x}) : [t(\overline{x})] \to [t'(\overline{x})]$ in R,

$$\frac{}{r(\overline{w}) : [t(\overline{w}/\overline{x})] \to [t'(\overline{w}/\overline{x})]},$$

modulo the following equations:

- Identity transitions: $f([t_1],\ldots,[t_n]) = [f(t_1,\ldots,t_n)]$,
- Axioms in $E : t(\overline{\alpha}) = t'(\overline{\alpha})$, for each equation $t = t'$ in E.

Action terms are the pre-action terms that rewrite terms of sort *State*.

With respect to the language of proof terms associated with rewriting logic [14, Section 3.1], we have omitted the rule of transitivity, and have restricted the replacement rule to identity transitions. Full replacement can be obtained as a sequential composition of an application of the replacement rule above and a Σ-structure rule to rewrite *inside*. Notice also that the above definition of action terms assumes that the rules in R are unconditional. The extension to conditional rules is straightforward; it mirrors the corresponding extension of the language of proof terms as defined in [14].

2.4 Models

Models for a verification signature $\langle \Sigma^+, E^+, \mathit{State}, \mathit{At}, L\rangle$ over a rewrite signature $\langle \Sigma, E\rangle$ are obtained from programs (rewrite theories) $\langle \Sigma, E, L, R\rangle$, i.e., from assignments of rewrite rules R to the labels L. Every such rewrite theory defines a Kripke frame as follows:

- the set of states (possible worlds) is the quotient set $T_{\Sigma,E,\mathit{State}}$ of equivalence classes of ground terms of sort *State* modulo the equations E;
- the family of state transitions is given by the ground action terms, that is, equivalence classes of suitable ground proof terms that rewrite states.

In order to obtain models for a verification signature, we still have to provide an interpretation for the observation attributes: for each sort s, an *attribute interpretation* I maps attributes of sort s to functions of type $T_{\Sigma,E,\mathit{State}} \rightarrow T_{\Sigma^+,E^+,s}$. Notice that, since the rewrite signature is protected by the extension to the verification signature, $T_{\Sigma,E,\mathit{State}}$ is the *same* set as $T_{\Sigma^+,E^+,\mathit{State}}$.

Each attribute interpretation I can be seen as an extension of T_{Σ^+,E^+} to a Σ_f^+-algebra. Hence, attribute interpretations may be defined axiomatically through sets of equations E_f^+ over the extended signature Σ_f^+, as we have already mentioned in Section 2.1. In fact, we may wish to reduce the set of attribute interpretations that we want to admit for verification purposes to those that satisfy given properties. Hence, we shall take *models* to be Kripke frames associated to the rewrite theories or programs over an extended signature $\langle \Sigma_f^+, E_f^+\rangle$. We call such programs *observed programs*, since they include together with the original program all the information about the observation attributes.

In our vending machine example, the rewrite theory associated to the system module `VENDING-MACHINE-OBSERVED` defines the observed program, and moreover it provides a uniquely determined interpretation for the observation attributes.

2.5 The Modal Language

The term language associated with a verification signature $\langle \Sigma^+, E^+, State, At, L\rangle$ is the term algebra $T_{\Sigma_c^+}(X)$, i.e., the extension of Σ^+ with attributes as constants, where X has an infinite set of variables for each sort in Σ_c^+.

The modal language associated with a verification signature is given by

$$\varphi ::= true \mid t_1 = t_2 \mid \neg\varphi \mid \varphi_1 \supset \varphi_2 \mid [\alpha]\varphi \mid f_{\overline{d}}[\varphi_1, \ldots, \varphi_n]$$

where $t_1, t_2 \in T_{\Sigma_c^+}(X)$ are two terms of the same sort, α is an action term, $f : s_1 \ldots s_m \to State \in \Sigma$, $\overline{d}$ is a sequence of data terms corresponding to the arguments of f that are not of sort *State*, and the φ_i are in one-to-one correspondence with the arguments of f that are of sort *State*.

We apply the same notational convention to action and state terms: given $f : s_1 \ldots s_m \to State \in \Sigma$, $\overline{d}$ a sequence of data terms corresponding to the arguments of f that are not of sort *State*, and action terms α_i in one-to-one correspondence with the arguments of f that are of sort *State*, we denote by $f_{\overline{d}}(\alpha_1, \ldots, \alpha_n)$ the action term that results from the application of f to the interleaving of $\overline{d}$ and $\overline{\alpha}$ prescribed by $s_1, \ldots, s_m$. Analogously, $f_{\overline{d}}(t_1, \ldots, t_n)$, where each t_i is a term of sort *State* and none of the d_i is of sort *State*, denotes the term obtained by applying f to the interleaving of $\overline{d}$ and $\overline{t}$ that conforms to the sort sequence $s_1, \ldots, s_m$.

Given an action term α, $[\alpha]$ is the usual modality that captures the state transitions performed by the action. In addition, the proposed language presents a new modality $f_{\overline{d}}[\text{-}]$ associated with state constructors. As formalised below, this topological modality allows us to reason about the *structure* of states, that is, about the fact that the current state of the system can be decomposed into components that satisfy certain properties (note that this decomposition may not be unique).

We will make use of the usual derived propositional connectives for conjuntion ($\wedge$), disjunction ($\vee$), and logical equivalence ($\equiv$).

2.6 The Satisfaction Relation

The satisfaction relation is defined for a given state, attribute interpretation, and substitution of ground Σ^+-terms for variables. For simplicity, we shall omit the reference to the set E^+ of equations over which states are formed as equivalence classes of terms. The term language $T_{\Sigma_c^+}(X)$ is interpreted in T_{Σ^+,E^+} as follows, where $[\![t']\!]^{I,\sigma}[t]$ is the value (an element of T_{Σ^+,E^+}) of t' at state $[t]$, for the attribute interpretation I and a ground substitution σ:

- $[\![x]\!]^{I,\sigma}[t] = \sigma(x)$,
- $[\![a]\!]^{I,\sigma}[t] = I(a)([t])$,
- $[\![f(t_1, \ldots, t_m)]\!]^{I,\sigma}[t] = f([\![t_1]\!]^{I,\sigma}[t], \ldots, [\![t_m]\!]^{I,\sigma}[t])$, for each operation $f : s_1 \ldots s_m \to s$ in Σ^+ .

The action terms are also subject to interpretation, because they may contain variables. We denote by $[\![\alpha]\!]^{I,\sigma}$ the transition that is given by the equivalence class of the ground term obtained by applying the ground substitutions to the action term α.

Satisfaction of formulae at a given state $[t]$ is defined as follows:

- $[t], I, \sigma \models t_1 = t_2$ iff $[\![t_1]\!]^{I,\sigma}[t] = [\![t_2]\!]^{I,\sigma}[t]$,
- $[t], I, \sigma \models \neg\varphi$ iff it is not the case that $[t], I, \sigma \models \varphi$,
- $[t], I, \sigma \models \varphi_1 \supset \varphi_2$ iff $[t], I, \sigma \models \varphi_1$ implies $[t], I, \sigma \models \varphi_2$,
- $[t], I, \sigma \models [\alpha]\varphi$ iff $[\![\alpha]\!]^{I,\sigma} : [t] \rightarrow [t']$ implies $[t'], I, \sigma \models \varphi$,
- $[t], I, \sigma \models f_{\overline{d}}[\varphi_1, \ldots, \varphi_n]$ iff for each $f_{\overline{w}}(t_1, \ldots, t_n) \in [t]$, where $\overline{w} = [\![\overline{d}]\!]^{I,\sigma}[t]$, there is some $i \in \{1, \ldots, n\}$ such that $[t_i], I, \sigma \models \varphi_i$.

As usual, the action modality captures properties that hold after the transition performed by the denotation of the term. Notice that, for a given attribute interpretation and substitution, actions are deterministic but partial, i.e., they do not apply to every state. In fact, once instantiated, an action term is only applicable to a single state.

The action modality has a dual with the following interpretation:

- $[t], I, \sigma \models \langle\alpha\rangle\varphi$ iff $[\![\alpha]\!]^{I,\sigma} : [t] \rightarrow [t']$ and $[t'], I, \sigma \models \varphi$.

Notice that this operator requires the action to denote an existing transition from the current state. The modality $[\alpha]$ does not impose the requirement that such a transition actually exists. Hence, $[\alpha]\varphi$ holds trivially if, for the given substitution, α cannot rewrite the current state.

The topological operator allows us to talk about the structure of states. Its dual is, perhaps, more intuitive:

- $[t], I, \sigma \models f_{\overline{d}}\langle\varphi_1, \ldots, \varphi_n\rangle$ iff there is a term $f_{\overline{w}}(t_1, \ldots, t_n) \in [t]$ with $\overline{w} = [\![\overline{d}]\!]^{I,\sigma}[t]$ such that $[t_i], I, \sigma \models \varphi_i$ for each $i = 1, \ldots, n$.

This formula allows us to say that the current state is decomposable according to the structure f into components that satisfy the formulae φ_i. The dual modality introduced above uses instead the subjunctive condition *if the state is decomposable in the specified way, then ....*

Finally, we say that a formula is valid in a model iff it is satisfied at every state for any attribute interpretation and any ground substitution for the variables.

We can give some examples of formula satisfaction for the program given in Section 2.2:

- In state `$qq`, the formulae $\_\_\langle \#\$ = 0, \#\$ = 1\rangle$, $\_\_\langle \#\$ = 1, \#q = 2\rangle$ and $\_\_\langle \#\$ = 1 \wedge \#q = 1, \#q = 1\rangle$ are all satisfied.
- In state `qqqq`, the formulae $[\texttt{change}](\#q = 0)$, $\langle\texttt{change}\rangle(\#q = 0)$ and $[\texttt{buy-c}](\#q = 0)$ are all satisfied, but $\langle\texttt{buy-c}\rangle(\#q = 0)$ is not, because the `buy-c` rule cannot be applied to this state.

2.7 Proof Theory

The Kripke models that we have adopted have standard properties as far as the action modality is concerned. The soundness of all of them is straightforward to prove.

The first rule is usually referred to as K [7]:

$$(\varphi \supset \psi) \vdash ([\alpha]\varphi \supset [\alpha]\psi) \ .$$

The property *it is possible to do α in the present state with the resulting state having property φ* is equivalent to the statement *after doing α the resulting state has property φ and it is possible to do α*:

$$\vdash \langle\alpha\rangle\varphi \equiv [\alpha]\varphi \wedge \langle\alpha\rangle \mathit{true} \ . \tag{1}$$

The topological operator also satisfies a version of K:

$$(\varphi_i \supset \psi_i) \vdash f_{\overline{d}}[\varphi_1, \ldots, \varphi_n] \supset f_{\overline{d}}[\varphi_1, \ldots, \varphi_{i-1}, \psi_i, \varphi_{i+1}, \ldots, \varphi_n] \ .$$

The more interesting properties concern the interaction between the two operators:

$$\{\varphi_i \supset [\alpha_i]\psi_i \mid i \in \{1, \ldots, n\}\}$$
$$\vdash f_{\overline{d}}\langle\varphi_1, \ldots, \varphi_n\rangle \supset [f_{\overline{d}}(\alpha_1, \ldots, \alpha_n)] f_{\overline{d}}\langle\psi_1, \ldots, \psi_n\rangle \tag{2}$$
$$\{\varphi_i \supset \langle\alpha_i\rangle \mathit{true} \mid i \in \{1, \ldots, n\}\} \vdash f_{\overline{d}}\langle\varphi_1, \ldots, \varphi_n\rangle \supset \langle f_{\overline{d}}(\alpha_1, \ldots, \alpha_n)\rangle \mathit{true} \tag{3}$$

The first rule relates the effects of a concurrent execution with the effects of the individual actions. The second rule reflects the fact that a concurrent rewrite can take place whenever its component actions can. Both rules are conditional on the state being decomposable in the prescribed way, requiring the application of the concurrent rewrite rules to be disjoint.

The following axiom schemas capture the behaviour of identity actions. Remember that $[t]$ denotes both a state $[t]$ and the identity transition on such a state, and note that $[[t]]$ is the modality $[\alpha]$ for $\alpha = [t]$.

$$\vdash \varphi \supset [[t]]\varphi$$
$$\vdash t = t' \supset [[t]]\varphi \equiv [[t']]\varphi \ .$$

The following axiom schema provides an interesting bridge between the dynamic and the topological operators, reflecting the double nature of the Σ-structure as acting on states and on actions:

$$\vdash \langle f_{\overline{d}}(\alpha_1, \ldots, \alpha_n)\rangle \mathit{true} \equiv f_{\overline{d}}\langle\langle\alpha_1\rangle \mathit{true}, \ldots, \langle\alpha_n\rangle \mathit{true}\rangle \ .$$

Concerning replacement, we have the following general inference rule for an arbitrary replacement $\overline{w}/\overline{x}$ of Σ^+-terms $\overline{w}$ for variables $\overline{x}$ (but not Σ_c^+-terms, because attributes are state-dependent):

$$\varphi \vdash \varphi(\overline{w}/\overline{x}) \ .$$

Note that substitutions also apply inside action modalities, i.e., substitutions apply to all occurrences of variables, even those inside action terms.

Necessitation also applies:

$$\varphi \vdash [\alpha]\varphi$$
$$\varphi_1, \ldots, \varphi_n \vdash f_{\overline{d}}\langle \overline{true} \rangle \supset f_{\overline{d}}\langle \varphi_1, \ldots, \varphi_n \rangle \ .$$

There are stronger forms of necessitation that apply to properties that do not involve state attributes. In the rules below, let t_1 and t_2 be terms in $T_{\Sigma^+}(X)$:

$$\vdash t_1 = t_2 \supset [\alpha](t_1 = t_2) \tag{4}$$
$$\vdash f_{\overline{d}}\langle \overline{true} \rangle \supset (t_1 = t'_1 \wedge \ldots \wedge t_n = t'_n \supset f_{\overline{d}}\langle t_1 = t'_1, \ldots, t_n = t'_n \rangle) \ .$$

3 Specifications

As explained in the introduction, we consider that specifications of concurrent rewrite systems may be given in a different logic in which properties can be stated about observations. At this level we only deal with abstract properties of behaviour that can be observed through the attributes without needing to prescribe the existence of specific states or of specific transitions (rewrite rules).

Different logics can be defined depending on the nature of the properties about which one wants to reason. For each logic, an interface needs to be given to support the verification of programs against specifications. This interface assumes the form of a collection of inference rules that allow properties stated in the specification logic to be inferred from properties of programs stated in VLRL. The correctness of the interface inference system for a given specification logic is based on a mapping that abstracts models (behaviours) of the specification logic from programs.

To verify that a program P (in fact, an observed program, in the sense that the program is taken over an extension of the original rewrite signature that defines how attributes can be interpreted, as explained in Section 2.4) satisfies a specification S, one has to find a set of properties V in VLRL that are satisfied by P and entail S. Ideally, we should be able to generate V in a systematic way from P, so that the verification can be reduced to the proof that V entails S.

3.1 Temporal Logic

To illustrate the ideas, we will use a branching time propositional temporal logic for writing specifications[2]. Three logical operators are provided with the following meaning:

- AXφ: the property φ holds at all possible successor states,
- A(φWψ): in every computation φ will hold until ψ holds (weak until),

[2] We refer the reader to [7,11,18], among others, for more information on temporal logic.

– EXφ: the property φ holds at some successor state.

Notice that AGφ (the property φ is valid at all possible future states) is equivalent to A(φW*false*).

We can interface VLRL with this temporal logic through the computation trees generated by the transition systems associated with the initial models of programs; that is, models of the program and the specification are built over the same semantic structures. The interface inference rules are:

$$\varphi \supset \psi,\ \{\varphi \supset [\alpha]\psi \mid \alpha \text{ action term}\} \vdash \varphi \supset \mathrm{AX}\psi$$

$$\{\varphi \wedge \neg\psi \supset [\alpha](\varphi \vee \psi) \mid \alpha \text{ action term}\} \vdash \varphi \supset \mathrm{A}(\varphi \mathrm{W} \psi) \qquad (5)$$

$$\varphi \supset \langle\alpha\rangle\psi \vdash \varphi \supset \mathrm{EX}\psi \quad \text{where } \alpha \text{ is an action term.} \qquad (6)$$

The first rule states that if φ implies ψ, and φ implies that, in the state resulting from doing α, ψ holds, then for any state where φ holds, the next state in *any* computation will satisfy ψ. The other rules are explained similarly. Note that the lefthand sides of these rules consist of formulae in the VLRL modal action logic, while the righthand sides are temporal formulae.

Correctness of the inference rules is derivable because, as pointed out above, we use the same Kripke structures as models for VLRL and the temporal logic.

How can we discharge the lefthand side in any of the first two interface inference rules above, when the set of action terms is infinite? Let $P(\alpha)$ be the property to be proved about α; $P(\alpha) = (\varphi \supset [\alpha]\psi)$ in the first case, and $P(\alpha) = (\varphi \wedge \neg\psi \supset [\alpha](\varphi \wedge \psi))$ in the second. We propose to use structural induction as follows:

- for each $f : s_1 \dots s_m \to \mathit{State}$ in Σ, with $\mathit{State} \notin \{s_1, \dots, s_m\}$, prove $f(x_1, \dots, x_n)\langle\rangle \supset P([f(x_1, \dots, x_n)])$,
- for each label r, prove $P(\alpha(r))$ for every *minimal* $\alpha(r)$ that puts r in context, as explained below,
- for each $f : s_1 \dots s_m \to \mathit{State}$ in Σ, with $\mathit{State} \in \{s_1, \dots, s_m\}$, prove

  $$\{P(\alpha_{i_j} \mid j \in \{1, \dots, k\}\} \vdash f_{\overline{x}}\langle \overline{\mathit{true}} \rangle \supset P(f_{\overline{x}}(\overline{\alpha})),$$

  where α_{i_j} are action terms in one-to-one correspondence with the arguments of f that are of sort *State*.

An action term puts a label r in context if it contains $r(\overline{x})$ as a subterm. The idea is that, when r does not rewrite states but rewrites inside states, we have to consider the possible contexts in which the rewrite rule can be applied. However, since there may be an infinite number of such contexts, we would like to restrict the proof to contexts that are minimal in the sense that the information that is put in the context is as little as possible. For example, if $f : s_1 s_2 s_3 \to \mathit{State}$ and r is a rule rewriting terms of sort s_2, a minimal $\alpha(r)$ is $f(x, r, y)$ where x and y are new variables of sort s_1 and s_3, respectively. In the examples that follow, all the rules rewrite states, and in this case a minimal $\alpha(r)$ for r is r itself. Indeed, because the rewrite rules apply to states, it is not necessary to consider wider contexts.

3.2 Properties of the Vending Machine

Let us illustrate the application of these inference rules to our example program.

First, we can easily obtain the following 12 formulae by systematically considering how each one of the 3 rewrite rules modifies the value of each one of the basic 4 attributes. These properties derive from the axiomatisation of the attribute interpretations that need to be provided together with the program to constitute an observed program. We are investigating the possibility of automatically deriving these properties from the program. In our example, the axiomatisation was given in Section 2.2.

$$(\#\$ = M) \supset [\texttt{buy-c}](\#\$ = M - 1)$$
$$(\#q = M) \supset [\texttt{buy-c}](\#q = M)$$
$$(\#c = M) \supset [\texttt{buy-c}](\#c = M + 1) \tag{7}$$
$$(\#a = M) \supset [\texttt{buy-c}](\#a = M) \tag{8}$$
$$(\#\$ = M) \supset [\texttt{buy-a}](\#\$ = M - 1)$$
$$(\#q = M) \supset [\texttt{buy-a}](\#q = M + 1)$$
$$(\#c = M) \supset [\texttt{buy-a}](\#c = M) \tag{9}$$
$$(\#a = M) \supset [\texttt{buy-a}](\#a = M + 1) \tag{10}$$
$$(\#\$ = M) \supset [\textbf{change}](\#\$ = M + 1)$$
$$(\#q = M) \supset [\textbf{change}](\#q = M - 4)$$
$$(\#c = M) \supset [\textbf{change}](\#c = M)$$
$$(\#a = M) \supset [\textbf{change}](\#a = M)$$

The following three formulae characterize the enabling conditions for the rewrite rules.

$$\langle \texttt{buy-c} \rangle \mathit{true} \equiv \#\$ \geq 1 \tag{11}$$
$$\langle \texttt{buy-a} \rangle \mathit{true} \equiv \#\$ \geq 1 \tag{12}$$
$$\langle \textbf{change} \rangle \mathit{true} \equiv \#q \geq 4$$

Now we prove some temporal properties about the vending machine.

1. The wealth of the machine is *invariant*:

$$\mathit{wealth} = N \supset \mathrm{AG}(\mathit{wealth} = N) \ .$$

First, by definition of the temporal connective G, $\mathrm{AG}\varphi \equiv \mathrm{A}(\varphi \mathrm{W} \mathit{false})$. Applying the interface inference rule (5) of temporal logic and VLRL, it is enough to prove

$$\{\mathit{wealth} = N \supset [\alpha](\mathit{wealth} = N) \mid \alpha \text{ action term}\} \ .$$

Using structural induction as introduced in Section 3.1, we have to prove:

- constants:
  1. $\$\langle\rangle \supset (wealth = N \supset [\$](wealth = N))$
  2. $q\langle\rangle \supset (wealth = N \supset [q](wealth = N))$
  3. $c\langle\rangle \supset (wealth = N \supset [c](wealth = N))$
  4. $a\langle\rangle \supset (wealth = N \supset [a](wealth = N))$
- rules:
  5. $wealth = N \supset [\text{buy-c}](wealth = N)$
  6. $wealth = N \supset [\text{buy-a}](wealth = N)$
  7. $wealth = N \supset [\text{change}](wealth = N)$
- state operations(in this case, only __):
  8. $(wealth = N_1 \supset [\alpha_1](wealth = N_1)), (wealth = N_2 \supset [\alpha_2](wealth = N_2)) \vdash \_\_\langle true, true\rangle \supset (wealth = N \supset [\alpha_1\alpha_2](wealth = N))$.

The proofs of the first seven properties are straightforward. We prove the last property as follows. Assume the hypotheses; using the inference rule (2) of VLRL, we derive

$$\_\_\langle wealth = N_1, wealth = N_2\rangle \supset [\alpha_1\alpha_2]\_\_\langle wealth = N_1, wealth = N_2\rangle \ .$$

From this and the following property of attributes

$$\_\_\langle true, true\rangle \supset (wealth = N \supset \exists N_1, N_2.\_\_\langle wealth = N_1, wealth = N_2\rangle \wedge N = N_1 + N_2) \ ,$$

we obtain

$$\_\_\langle true, true\rangle \supset (wealth = N \supset \exists N_1, N_2.[\alpha_1\alpha_2]\_\_\langle wealth = N_1, wealth = N_2\rangle \wedge N = N_1 + N_2) \ .$$

Since N, N_1, N_2 are not state variables, we can apply (4):

$$\_\langle true, true\rangle \supset (wealth = N \supset \exists N_1, N_2.[\alpha_1\alpha_2]\_\_\langle wealth = N_1, wealth = N_2\rangle \wedge [\alpha_1\alpha_2](N = N_1 + N_2)) \ .$$

Applying $[\alpha]\varphi \wedge [\alpha]\psi \equiv [\alpha](\varphi \wedge \psi)$ and $\exists X.[\alpha]\varphi \supset [\alpha]\exists X.\varphi$, we have

$$\_\_\langle true, true\rangle \supset (wealth = N \supset [\alpha_1\alpha_2]\exists N_1, N_2.\_\_\langle wealth = N_1, wealth = N_2\rangle \wedge (N = N_1 + N_2)) \ .$$

Finally, using the property of attributes

$$\_\_\langle wealth = N_1, wealth = N_2\rangle \wedge N = N_1 + N_2 \supset wealth = N \ ,$$

we arrive at the desired conclusion

$$\_\_\langle true, true\rangle \supset (wealth = N \supset [\alpha_1\alpha_2](wealth = N)) \ .$$

2. If the number of dollars is greater than 0, then it is possible to buy a cake:

$$(\#\$ > 0 \wedge \#c = N) \supset \mathrm{EX}(\#c = N + 1).$$

Using the interface inference rule (6), we need to prove

$$(\#\$ > 0 \wedge \#c = N) \supset \langle \alpha \rangle (\#c = N + 1)$$

for some action term α; we take $\alpha =$ `buy-c`. Putting together the formulae (7) and (11), we get

$$(\#c = N \wedge \#\$ > 0) \supset [\texttt{buy-c}](\#c = N + 1) \wedge \langle \texttt{buy-c} \rangle \mathit{true} \ .$$

Finally, it is enough to apply the equivalence (1) to the consequent above.

3. In a state that has at least two dollars, it is possible to buy both a cake and an apple:

$$(\#\$ \geq 2 \wedge \#c = M \wedge \#a = N) \supset \mathrm{EX}(\#c = M + 1 \wedge \#a = N + 1).$$

We use the interface inference rule (6), and prove

$$(\#\$ \geq 2 \wedge \#c = M \wedge \#a = N) \supset \langle \alpha \rangle (\#c = M + 1 \wedge \#a = N + 1)$$

for $\alpha =$ `buy-c buy-a`.

From the arithmetic property

$$\#\$ \geq 2 \supset \exists N_1, N_2 . \#\$ = N_1 + N_2 \wedge N_1 \geq 1 \wedge N_2 \geq 1 \ ,$$

we obtain

$$\begin{aligned} &(\#\$ \geq 2 \wedge \#c = M \wedge \#a = N) \supset \\ &(\exists N_1, N_2 . \#\$ = N_1 + N_2 \wedge N_1 \geq 1 \wedge N_2 \geq 1 \wedge \#c = M \wedge \#a = N) \ . \end{aligned}$$

Applying to this formula the structural property

$$\begin{aligned} &(\#\$ = N_1 + N_2 \wedge N_1 \geq 1 \wedge N_2 \geq 1 \wedge \#c = M \wedge \#a = N) \supset \\ &\qquad \_\_\langle \#\$ = N_1 \wedge \#c = M \wedge \#a = 0, \#\$ = N_2 \wedge \#c = 0 \wedge \#a = N \rangle \\ &\qquad \wedge N_1 \geq 1 \wedge N_2 \geq 1 \end{aligned}$$

asserting that a state with enough dollars can be decomposed in two nonempty substates with some dollars in each one, segregating cakes from apples at the same time, we get

$$\begin{aligned} &(\#\$ \geq 2 \wedge \#c = M \wedge \#a = N) \supset \\ &(\exists N_1, N_2 . \_\_\langle \#\$ = N_1 \wedge \#c = M \wedge \#a = 0, \#\$ = N_2 \wedge \#c = 0 \wedge \#a = N \rangle \\ &\qquad \wedge N_1 \geq 1 \wedge N_2 \geq 1) \ . \end{aligned} \tag{13}$$

The inference rule (2) of VLRL applied to the attribute properties (7), (8), (9), and (10) gives

$$\_\_\langle \#c = M \wedge \#a = 0, \#c = 0 \wedge \#a = N\rangle \supset$$
$$[\texttt{buy-c buy-a}]\_\_\langle \#c = M + 1 \wedge \#a = 0, \#c = 0 \wedge \#a = N + 1\rangle \ . \quad (14)$$

On the other hand, the inference rule (3) of VLRL applied to the attribute properties (11) and (12) gives

$$\_\_\langle \#\$ \geq 1, \#\$ \geq 1\rangle \supset \langle \texttt{buy-c buy-a}\rangle \mathit{true} \ . \quad (15)$$

Putting together the formulae (14) and (15), and using the equivalence (1), we get

$$\_\_\langle \#\$ \geq 1 \wedge \#c = M \wedge \#a = 0, \#\$ \geq 1 \wedge \#c = 0 \wedge \#a = N\rangle \supset$$
$$\langle \texttt{buy-c buy-a}\rangle \_\_\langle \#c = M + 1 \wedge \#a = 0, \#c = 0 \wedge \#a = N + 1\rangle \ . \quad (16)$$

Finally, chaining the formulae (13) and (16), and the following structural property of attributes

$$\_\_\langle \#c = M \wedge \#a = 0, \#c = 0 \wedge \#a = N\rangle \supset \#c = M \wedge \#a = N \ ,$$

we obtain the desired conclusion

$$(\#\$ \geq 2 \wedge \#c = M \wedge \#a = N) \supset$$
$$\langle \texttt{buy-c buy-a}\rangle (\#c = M + 1 \wedge \#a = N + 1) \ .$$

4 A Simple Mutual Exclusion Example

In this section, we develop another example based on a simple mutual exclusion protocol. In this case we assume object configurations [15,2]. Rewriting logic supports a logical theory of concurrent objects that can be reduced to a particular class of rewrite theories.

In Full Maude, concurrent object-oriented systems can be defined by means of *object-oriented modules* introduced by the keyword `omod`. An *object* in a given state is represented as a term `< O : C | a1 : v1,..., an : vn >`, where `O` is the object's name, belonging to a set `Oid` of object identifiers, `C` is its *class*, the `ai`'s are the names of the object's *attributes*, and the `vi`'s are their corresponding values. *Messages* are defined by the user for each application.

In a concurrent object-oriented system the concurrent state, which is called a *configuration*, has the structure of a multiset made up of objects and messages that evolves by concurrent rewriting using rules that describe the effects of *communication events* between some objects and messages.

The Maude module that specifies the system is:

```
omod MUTUAL-EXCLUSION-PROTOCOL is
  sort Status .
  op bcs : -> Status .   *** The object can enter critical section
  op ics : -> Status .   *** The object is in the critical section
  op acs : -> Status .   *** The object is not ready to enter c.s.
  class obj | status : Status .
  msg token : -> Msg .
  var X : Oid .
  rl [enter(X)] : token < X : obj | status : bcs > =>
                    < X : obj | status : ics > .
  rl [exit(X)] : < X : obj | status : ics > =>
                  < X : obj | status : acs > token .
  rl [ready(X)] : < X : obj | status : acs > =>
                    < X : obj | status : bcs > .
endom
```

The observation attributes that are of interest to us are $\#cs$, $\#tk$: `Nat` that return the number of objects in the critical section (that is, whose status is `ics`) and the number of tokens in the system, respectively.

The observed program is given by the following rewrite theory, where we have added the sort `Nat` and its operations to the system rewrite signature.

```
omod MEP-OBSERVED is
  protecting MUTUAL-EXCLUSION-PROTOCOL .
  protecting NAT .
  ops #cs #tk : Configuration -> Nat .
  vars C1 C2 : Configuration .
  var S : Status .
  eq #cs(< X : obj | status : ics >) = 1 .
  eq #cs(< X : obj | status : bcs >) = 0 .
  eq #cs(< X : obj | status : acs >) = 0 .
  eq #cs(token) = 0 .
  eq #cs(none) = 0 .
  eq #cs(C1 C2) = #cs(C1) + #cs(C2) .
  eq #tk(< X : obj | status : S >) = 0 .
  eq #tk(token) = 1 .
  eq #tk(none) = 0 .
  eq #tk(C1 C2) = #tk(C1) + #tk(C2) .
endom
```

Some formulae that model the actions of the system are

$$(\#cs = N \wedge \#tk = M) \supset [\mathtt{enter(X)}](\#cs = N + 1 \wedge \#tk = M - 1)$$
$$(\#cs = N \wedge \#tk = M) \supset [\mathtt{exit(X)}](\#cs = N - 1 \wedge \#tk = M + 1)$$
$$(\#cs = N \wedge \#tk = M) \supset [\mathtt{ready(X)}](\#cs = N \wedge \#tk = M)$$
$$\langle \mathtt{enter(X)} \rangle \mathit{true} \supset \#tk > 0$$

A structural property satisfied by the configurations of objects and messages is the following:

$$\#tk = N \equiv \exists N_1, N_2 . \_\_ \langle \#tk = N_1, \#tk = N_2 \rangle \wedge N = N_1 + N_2 \ .$$

1. We prove the following important property, stating that in a state with only one token, it is not possible for both objects to enter simultaneously in the critical section.

$$\#tk = 1 \supset [\texttt{enter(X) enter(Y)}]\mathit{false} \ .$$

Assume the antecedent $\#tk = 1$. By the structural property above,

$$\exists N_1, N_2 . \_\_\langle \#tk = N_1, \#tk = N_2 \rangle \wedge 1 = N_1 + N_2 \ ,$$

and by arithmetic

$$\_\_\langle \#tk = 1, \#tk = 0 \rangle \vee \_\_\langle \#tk = 0, \#tk = 1 \rangle \ .$$

In the first case, we can easily prove by means of the inference rule (2) of VRLR

$$\_\_\langle \#tk = 1, \#tk = 0 \rangle \supset [\texttt{enter(X) enter(Y)}]\_\_\langle \mathit{true}, \mathit{false} \rangle \ ,$$

and from this it follows

$$\_\_\langle \#tk = 1, \#tk = 0 \rangle \supset [\texttt{enter(X) enter(Y)}]\mathit{false} \ .$$

Analogously, in the second case, we can prove

$$\_\_\langle \#tk = 0, \#tk = 1 \rangle \supset [\texttt{enter(X) enter(Y)}]\mathit{false} \ .$$

2. Consider now the proof that the sum $\#cs + \#tk$ is *invariant*:

$$\#cs + \#tk = N \supset \mathrm{AG}(\#cs + \#tk = N)$$

Using the structural induction technique described in Section 3.1, it is enough to prove:

- constants (here we use also mixfix notation for objects):
  1. $\texttt{none}\langle\rangle \supset (\#cs + \#tk = N \supset [\texttt{none}](\#cs + \#tk = N))$
  2. $\texttt{token}\langle\rangle \supset (\#cs + \#tk = N \supset [\texttt{token}](\#cs + \#tk = N))$
  3. $\texttt{< X : obj | status : S >}\langle\rangle \supset (\#cs + \#tk = N \supset$
     $[\texttt{< X : obj | status : S >}](\#cs + \#tk = N))$
- rules:
  4. $\#cs + \#tk = N \supset [\texttt{enter(X)}](\#cs + \#tk = N)$
  5. $\#cs + \#tk = N \supset [\texttt{exit(X)}](\#cs + \#tk = N)$
  6. $\#cs + \#tk = N \supset [\texttt{ready(X)}](\#cs + \#tk = N)$
- state operations(in this case, only $\_\_$):
  7. $(\#cs + \#tk = N_1 \supset [\alpha_1](\#cs + \#tk = N_1)),$
     $(\#cs + \#tk = N_2 \supset [\alpha_2](\#cs + \#tk = N_2))$
     $\vdash \_\_\langle \mathit{true}, \mathit{true} \rangle \supset (\#cs + \#tk = N \supset [\alpha_1 \alpha_2](\#cs + \#tk = N)).$

The proofs of the first six properties are straightforward. Let us consider the proof of the induction step. Assume the hypotheses; using the inference rule (2) of VLRL we derive

$$\_\_\langle \#cs + \#tk = N_1, \#cs + \#tk = N_2\rangle \supset [\alpha_1\alpha_2]\_\_\langle \#cs + \#tk = N_1, \#cs + \#tk = N_2\rangle \tag{17}$$

Applying the following structural property of configurations

$$\#cs + \#tk = N \equiv \exists N_1, N_2 . \_\_\langle \#cs + \#tk = N_1, \#cs + \#tk = N_2\rangle \wedge N = N_1 + N_2 \ ,$$

to the antecedent $(\#cs + \#tk = N)$, and taking into account the formula (17), we obtain

$$[\alpha_1\alpha_2]\_\_\langle \#cs + \#tk = N_1, \#cs + \#tk = N_2\rangle \ ,$$

and it is enough to apply the same structural property in the other direction to conclude that $[\alpha_1\alpha_2](\#cs + \#tk = N)$.

5 Conclusions and Future Work

The verification logic for rewriting logic presented in the paper allows us to verify programs, that is software systems, against their specifications at a very high level. The main benefits of the use of VLRL are:

1. The properties that constitute the specification are given in a different logic independent of the programs;
2. It integrates well with rewriting logic, which is the logic used for concurrent execution;
3. It applies to rewrite theories in their full generality, thus accomodating many different kinds of concurrent systems;
4. It fits well in terms of expressive power and ease of proof with many practical programming applications, and supports reasoning about such applications at a very high level of abstraction;
5. It has nice modularity and parameterization properties, so that reasoning about large complex systems is substantially eased.

However, there is still a lot of work to be done, in particular: studying the completeness of VLRL; investigating more deeply the topological operator, especially in connection with the abstract properties that can be expressed with it; using a different specification logic, for example, one similar to the logic of UNITY; and developing practical applications that validate the potential of the logic to scale up to real systems using programming tools.

Acknowledgements

We are very grateful to Margarita Bradley and Alberto Verdejo for their comments to previous versions of this paper.

This work was partially developed while J. Fiadeiro and T. Maibaum were International Fellows at SRI International. J. Fiadeiro was partially supported by fellowships from Fundação para a Ciência e a Tecnologia (PRAXIS XXI BPD/16367/98) and Fundação Luso-Americana para o Desenvolvimento. T. Maibaum was partially supported by the Royal Academy of Engineering and Imperial College while on sabbatical. N. Martí-Oliet and I. Pita were partially supported by CICYT, TIC98–0445–C03–02. J. Meseguer was partially supported by DARPA and NASA through Contract NAS2-98073, and by Office of Naval Research Contract N00014-96-C-0114.

References

1. A. Bouhoula, J.-P. Jouannaud, and J. Meseguer. Specification and proof in membership equational logic. To appear in *Theoretical Computer Science*. Short version in M. Bidoit and M. Dauchet, editors, *Proceedings TAPSOFT'97*, LNCS 1214, pages 67–92. Springer, 1997. 442
2. M. Clavel, F. Duran, S. Eker, P. Lincoln, N. Martí-Oliet, J. Meseguer, and J. F. Quesada, *Maude: Specification and programming in rewriting logic*, Computer Science Laboratory, SRI International, January 1999, revised August 1999. `http://maude.csl.sri.com` 439, 453
3. M. Clavel, F. Duran, S. Eker, P. Lincoln, N. Martí-Oliet, J. Meseguer, and J. F. Quesada, *A Maude Tutorial*, Computer Science Laboratory, SRI International, March 2000. `http://maude.csl.sri.com` 439
4. G. Denker. From rewrite theories to temporal logic theories, in: [8]. 441
5. J. Fiadeiro and T. Maibaum, Temporal reasoning over deontic specifications, *Journal of Logic and Computation* 1(3), 1991, 357–395. 441
6. J. Fiadeiro and T. Maibaum, Categorical semantics of parallel program design, *Science of Computer Programming* 28(2–3), 1997, 111–138. 442
7. R. Goldblatt, *Logics of Time and Computation*, CSLI Lecture Notes 7, Center for the Study of Language and Information, Second edition, 1992. 447, 448
8. C. Kirchner and H. Kirchner, editors, *Proc. Second Int. Workshop on Rewriting Logic and its Applications, Pont-à-Mousson, France*, Electronic Notes in Theoretical Computer Science, Vol. 15, Elsevier Science, September 1998. 438, 457
9. U. Lechner, *Object-Oriented Specification of Distributed Systems*, Ph. D. Dissertation, Universitat Passau, June 23, 1997. 441
10. P. Lincoln, N. Martí-Oliet, and J. Meseguer, Specification, transformation, and programming of concurrent systems in rewriting logic, in: G. E. Blelloch *et al.* (eds.), *Specification of Parallel Algorithms, DIMACS Workshop, May 1994*, American Mathematical Society, 1994, 309–339. 439
11. Z. Manna and A. Pnueli, *The Temporal Logic of Reactive and Concurrent Systems: Specification*, Springer-Verlag, 1992. 448
12. N. Martí-Oliet and J. Meseguer, Action and change in rewriting logic, in: R. Pareschi and B. Fronhöfer (eds.), *Dynamic Worlds: From the Frame Problem to Knowledge Management*, Kluwer Academic Publishers, 1999, 1–53. 438, 439, 442

13. J. Meseguer, Rewriting as a unified model of concurrency, in: J. C. M. Baeten and J. W. Klop (eds.), *Proc. CONCUR'90*, LNCS 458, Springer-Verlag, 1990, 384–400. 438
14. J. Meseguer, Conditional rewriting logic as a unified model of concurrency, *Theoretical Computer Science* 96, 1992, 73–155. 438, 443, 444
15. J. Meseguer, A logical theory of concurrent objects and its realization in the Maude language, in: G. Agha, P. Wegner, and A. Yonezawa (eds.), *Research Directions in Concurrent Object-Oriented Programming*, The MIT Press, 1993, 314–390. 453
16. J. Meseguer, Research directions in rewriting logic, in: U. Berger and H. Schwichtenberg, editors, *Computational Logic, NATO Advanced Study Institute, Marktoberdorf, Germany, July 29 – August 6, 1997*, Springer–Verlag, 1999. 438
17. J. Meseguer, editor, *Proc. First Int. Workshop on Rewriting Logic and its Applications, Asilomar, California*, Electronic Notes in Theoretical Computer Science, Vol. 4, Elsevier Science, September 1996. 438
18. C. Stirling, Modal and temporal logics, in: S. Abramsky, D. Gabbay, and T. Maibaum (eds.), *Handbook of Logic in Computer Science*, Vol. II, Oxford University Press, 1992, 478–563. 441, 448

The Rôle of Normalisation in Testing from Structured Algebraic Specifications

Patricia D.L. Machado*

LFCS, Division of Informatics, University of Edinburgh, JMCB
King's Buildings, Edinburgh EH9 3JZ, UK
pdlm@dcs.ed.ac.uk

Abstract. This paper investigates the use of normalisation for testing from structured algebraic specifications. The intention is to compute a related, possibly simpler, specification, namely the *normal form*, and use it to test programs whenever testing from the original specification is too complex or undecidable in the sense that a procedure for interpreting the results cannot be given, the so-called oracle problem. We focus on specifications with testing interface, where test suites are defined at specification level, with axioms expressed in first-order logic. Three normal forms are presented for coping with some obstacles encountered when testing from structured specifications. Furthermore, it turns out that, under certain circumstances, tests based on normal forms can be more rigorous than tests based on the original specification.

1 Introduction

Normalisation of ordinary specifications as presented in [2], based on the laws of module algebra [1], aims at producing a flat version of a structured specification, the normal form, which is equivalent to the original w.r.t signature and model class. There, the intention is to use normalisation to define non-compositional proof systems for deriving theorems of a specification from a flat set of its axioms by using some standard proof system of the underlying institution. On the other hand, compositional proof systems perform derivations according to the modular structure of specifications, allowing proofs to be constructed in a structured way. The drawback of normalisation is the loss of structure which may be crucial for large specifications. Nevertheless, in practice, one may need to combine the two approaches so that normal forms are computed for some parts of the specification and compositional proof systems are considered for the overall specification.

Testing from structured algebraic specifications is presented in [7], where a framework for testing is given together with some problems which can arise and proposed solutions. There, the main issue investigated is the oracle problem, that is, whether a finite and executable procedure can be defined for interpreting the results of tests. For flat algebraic specifications expressed in first-order logic, a

* Supported by CNPq – Brazilian Research Council and on leave from DSC/CCT, Federal University of Paraíba, Campina Grande-PB, Brazil patricia@dsc.ufpb.br

D. Bert, C. Choppy, and P. Mosses (Eds.): WADT'99, LNCS 1827, pp. 459–476, 2000.

test consists in checking whether specification axioms are satisfied by a program w.r.t. a given test set. In this context, the oracle problem often reduces to the problem of comparing two values of a non-observable sort and also how to deal with quantifiers which may require test sets to be infinite [4,6]. However, this problem can be harder when structured specifications are considered, insofar as the structure of specifications has to be taken into account to make sense of axioms. In [7], testing from structured specifications can be done either in a pure compositional or non-compositional way, namely *structured testing* and *flat testing* respectively, where structured testing is more flexible than flat testing in the sense that oracles can be given under fewer assumptions. Again, structured and flat testing are two extreme ways of testing structured specifications and, in practice, many advantages can arise from combining them. Normalisation appears to be a way of making it possible to perform "semi-structured" testing, where programs are tested against specifications in a compositional way, but some parts of specifications are replaced by their corresponding normal forms. Also, normalisation gives rise to a non-compositional style of testing in which oracles can be given under fewer assumptions, and so, dealing more effectively with the oracle problem. Moreover, hidden axioms can be more appropriately handled as hidden definitions are grouped. Furthermore, under certain circumstances, normalisation can make testing experiments more rigorous in the sense of reducing the number of incorrect programs accepted and correct programs rejected.

In this paper, we present three normal forms and show the advantages of testing from them rather than from the original specification. Moreover, we provide the basis for effectively testing from specifications composed of structured specifications and normal forms. Structured specifications are defined from specification-building operations like *union*, *translate* and *hide* [9,8,5]. They also have a testing interface so that test suites can be uniformly planned and defined at specification level [7].

The paper is structured as follows. Section 2 gives some preliminary definitions of testing satisfaction and structured specifications and reviews previous results obtained in [7]. Section 3 presents the con normal form which increments test sets in the testing interface at each occurrence of the union operation. Section 4 describes an extended version of the normal form presented in [2], namely the nf normal form, for specifications with testing interface. Section 5 presents the strict normal form (snf) where each axiom is explicitly associated with a test set. Finally, Section 6 give some concluding remarks.

2 Preliminary Definitions

In this section, we introduce some preliminary definitions to make the paper self-contained. We assume the reader to be familiar with general concepts of algebraic specifications [9]. Let $\Sigma = (S, F)$ be a signature with $sorts(\Sigma) = S$ and $opns(\Sigma) = F$ and $T_\Sigma(X)$ be the Σ-term algebra, where X is a S-indexed set of countably infinite sets of variables. For any two Σ-terms t and t', $t = t'$ is a

Σ-equation and first-order Σ-formulas are built from Σ-equations, logical connectives ($\neg,\wedge,\vee,\Rightarrow,\Leftrightarrow$) and quantifiers ($\forall,\exists$). A Σ-formula without free variables is called a Σ-sentence. For any Σ-algebra A and valuation $\alpha : X \to |A|$, there exists a unique Σ-homomorphism $\alpha^{\#} : T_\Sigma(X) \to A$ which extends α. The value of $t \in |T_\Sigma(X)|_s$ in A under α is $\alpha^{\#}(t) \in |A|_s$, where $s \in S$. If $t \in T_\Sigma$, that is, t is a ground Σ-term, the value of t in A is $^{\#}(t)$, where $^{\#} : T_\Sigma \to A$ is the unique homomorphism. Let $\sigma : \Sigma' \to \Sigma$ be a signature morphism. Then, the Σ'-algebra $A|_\sigma$ is the reduct of A by σ. Also, σ extends to translate Σ'-terms to Σ-terms and Σ'-formulas to Σ-formulas.

2.1 Behavioural and Approximate Equality

The oracle problem for flat first-order logic specifications reduces to the problem of comparing two values of a non-observable sort and also how to deal with quantifiers. Values of a non-observable sort can be compared based on an indistinguishability relation, called *behavioural equality*, which is a partial Σ-congruence $\approx_A$, where $\approx_A$ is denoted by a family $\approx_A = (\approx_{A,s})_{s\in S}$ of partial equivalence relations which are symmetric and transitive relations such that $\forall f \in F : s_1 \ldots s_n \longrightarrow s$, $\forall a_i, b_i \in A_{s_i}$, if $a_i \approx_{A,s_i} b_i$, then $f^A(a_1,\ldots,a_n) \approx_{A,s} f^A(b_1,\ldots,b_n)$. Let $Obs \subseteq S$ be a distinguised set of observable sorts. The observational equality $\approx_{Obs,A} = (\approx_{Obs,A,s})_{s\in S}$ is a special case of the behavioural equality where related elements are those which cannot be distinguished by observable computations.[1] A Σ-congruence is *total* if all its relations are also reflexive. The definition domain of $\approx_A$ is given as $Dom(\approx_A) = \{a \mid a \approx_A a\}$. Let $\approx = (\approx_A)_{A\in Alg(\Sigma)}$ be a Σ-*behavioural equality*, a family of behavioural equalities, one for each Σ-algebra A [3]. Since the relations in $\approx$ are compatible with Σ, they are reflexive on values of ground terms, that is, $\forall v \in \#(T_\Sigma) \Rightarrow v \in Dom(\approx_A)$.

However, it is not always possible or it may be too hard to implement a behavioural equality. So, let a Σ-*approximate equality* $\sim = (\sim_A)_{A\in Alg(\Sigma)}$ be a family of approximate equalities, one for each Σ-algebra A, as defined in [6]. An *approximate equality* $\sim_A$ is a binary relation on A which is *sound* if and only if $\forall a, a' \in Dom(\approx_A) \cdot a \sim_A a' \Rightarrow a \approx_A a'$, and is *complete* if and only if $\forall a, a' \cdot a \approx_A a' \Rightarrow a \sim_A a'$. When two approximate equalities are applied together, one sound and one complete, they are enough to replace the behavioural equality under certain conditions [6].

2.2 Testing Satisfaction

The testing satisfaction relation of Σ-formulas given below is a generalisation of the standard notion of behavioural satisfaction [3] with equality interpreted by

[1] Values a and b of a non-observable sort s are observationally equal $a \approx_{Obs,A} b$ if and only if they cannot be distinguished by observable contexts, i.e., $\forall C \in C_{Obs}; \forall \alpha : X \to |A| \cdot \alpha_a^{\#}(C) = \alpha_b^{\#}(C)$, where $C_{Obs} \subseteq T_\Sigma(X \cup \{z_s\})$ is the set of all Σ-contexts of observable sorts with context variable of sort s and $\alpha_a, \alpha_b : X \cup \{z_s\} \to |A|$ are the unique extensions of α defined by $\alpha_a(z_s) = a$ and $\alpha_b(z_s) = b$.

approximate equalities and quantifiers ranging over values of Σ-test sets (sets of ground terms) rather than all values in the definition domain [7]. This relation models a test to check whether a Σ-algebra satisfies a Σ-formula w.r.t a given valuation, a pair of approximate equalities and a test set.

Definition 1 (Testing Satisfaction Relation). *Let Σ be a signature, T be a Σ-test set and $\sim, \triangleq$ be two Σ-approximate equalities. Let A be a Σ-algebra and $\alpha : X \to Dom(\approx_A)$ be a valuation. The testing satisfaction relation denoted by $\models^T_{\sim,\triangleq}$ is defined as follows.*

1. $A, \alpha \models^T_{\sim,\triangleq} t = t'$ *iff* $\alpha^\#(t) \sim_A \alpha^\#(t')$;
2. $A, \alpha \models^T_{\sim,\triangleq} \neg\psi$ *iff* $A, \alpha \models^T_{\triangleq,\sim} \psi$ *does not hold;*
3. $A, \alpha \models^T_{\sim,\triangleq} \psi_1 \wedge \psi_2$ *iff both* $A, \alpha \models^T_{\sim,\triangleq} \psi_1$ *and* $A, \alpha \models^T_{\sim,\triangleq} \psi_2$ *hold;*
4. $A, \alpha \models^T_{\sim,\triangleq} \forall x : s \cdot \psi$ *iff* $A, \alpha[x \mapsto v] \models^T_{\sim,\triangleq} \psi$ *holds for all* $v \in {}^\#(T)_s$.

where $\alpha[x \mapsto v]$ denotes the valuation α superseded at x by v. In this relation, $\sim$ is always applied in positive positions and $\triangleq$ is always applied in negative positions. Positive/negative positions are as usual. Note that equalities are reversed when negative positions are reached.

For the sake of simplicity, the connectives $\vee, \Rightarrow, \Leftrightarrow$ and the existential quantifier are omitted in definition 1. But they can always be defined in terms of the ones presented there. Also, if $A, \alpha \models^T_{\sim,\triangleq} \phi$ for all $\phi \in \Phi$, then $A, \alpha \models^T_{\sim,\triangleq} \Phi$, where Φ is a set of Σ-formulas. When ϕ is a Σ-sentence, $A, \alpha \models^T_{\sim,\triangleq} \phi$ coincides with $A, \beta \models^T_{\sim,\triangleq} \phi$, for any valuations α and β. Therefore, we write $A \models^T_{\sim,\triangleq} \phi$ without α.

When dealing with structured specifications, a number of different signatures must be taken into account. In the sequel, let $\approx = (\approx_\Sigma)_{\Sigma \in Sign}$ be a family of Σ-behavioural equalities, one for each signature Σ, where $Sign$ is the category of signatures. A Σ-behavioural equality is defined as before $\approx_\Sigma = (\approx_{\Sigma,A})_{A \in Alg(\Sigma)}$, one congruence relation for each algebra A. Whenever Σ is obvious, $\approx$ is used without subscript to denote $\approx_\Sigma$. When A is also obvious, $\approx$ is used to denote $\approx_{\Sigma,A}$. Likewise, let $\sim = (\sim_\Sigma)_{\Sigma \in Sign}$ and $\triangleq = (\triangleq_\Sigma)_{\Sigma \in Sign}$ denote families of Σ-approximate equalities. The *reduct* of $\sim_\Sigma$ by $\sigma : \Sigma' \to \Sigma$ is $(\sim_\Sigma)|_\sigma = ((\sim_{\Sigma,A})|_\sigma)_{A \in Alg(\Sigma)}$, where $(\sim_{\Sigma,A})|_\sigma = ((\sim_{\Sigma,A})_{\sigma(s)})_{s \in Sorts(\Sigma')}$.

Concerning signature morphisms, families can be compatible, reduction-compatible and translation-compatible [7]. The family $\sim$ is *compatible* with signature morphisms in $Sign$ if for all $\sigma : \Sigma' \to \Sigma$ and all Σ-algebras A, $\sim_{\Sigma',A|_\sigma} = (\sim_{\Sigma,A})|_\sigma$. The family $\sim$ is *reduction-compatible* if for all $\sigma : \Sigma' \to \Sigma$ and all Σ-algebras A, $\sim_{\Sigma',A|_\sigma} \supseteq (\sim_{\Sigma,A})|_\sigma$. The family $\sim$ is *translation-compatible* if for all $\sigma : \Sigma' \to \Sigma$ and all Σ-algebras A, $\sim_{\Sigma',A|_\sigma} \subseteq (\sim_{\Sigma,A})|_\sigma$. Clearly, the literal equality $=$ on values of an algebra is compatible, whereas the family $\approx = (\approx_{Obs,\Sigma})_{\Sigma \in Sign, Obs \subseteq sorts(\Sigma)}$ of Σ-observational equalities is reduction-compatible, but not translation-compatible.

Translations of Σ'-formulas and Σ'-test sets do only preserve the behavioural satisfaction and the testing satisfaction relation under certain conditions on the families of equalities being considered [7]. Let $\sigma : \Sigma' \to \Sigma$, $\alpha : X \to Dom(\approx_A)$ and $\alpha' : X' \to Dom(\approx_{A|_\sigma})$ such that $\forall s \in Sorts(\Sigma') \cdot \alpha'(x_s) = \alpha(\sigma(x_s))$. Let T' be a Σ'-test set and ϕ' be a Σ'-formula.

Proposition 1.

1. *If* $\approx$ *is compatible,* $A, \alpha \models^{\sigma(T')}_{\approx_\Sigma} \sigma(\phi')$ *iff* $A|_\sigma, \alpha' \models^{T'}_{\approx_{\Sigma'}} \phi'$.
2. *If* $\sim$ *is reduction-compatible and* $\simeq$ *is translation-compatible, then* $A, \alpha \models^{\sigma(T')}_{\sim_\Sigma, \simeq_\Sigma} \sigma(\phi')$ *implies* $A|_\sigma, \alpha' \models^{T'}_{\sim_{\Sigma'}, \simeq_{\Sigma'}} \phi'$.
3. *If* $\sim$ *is translation-compatible and* $\simeq$ *is reduction-compatible, then* $A|_\sigma, \alpha' \models^{T'}_{\sim_{\Sigma'}, \simeq_{\Sigma'}} \phi'$ *implies* $A, \alpha \models^{\sigma(T')}_{\sim_\Sigma, \simeq_\Sigma} \sigma(\phi')$.

2.3 Structured Specifications

Structured specifications with testing interface are introduced in [7]. The idea is that test sets are provided in the specification interface and specification-building operations are defined as usual.

Definition 2 (Structured Specifications). *The syntax and semantics of structured specifications are inductively defined as follows. The semantics is given in terms of signature, test set and classes of models.*

1. $SP = \langle \Sigma, \Phi, T \rangle$, *where* Σ *is a signature,* Φ *is a set of axioms and* T *is a* Σ*-test set*
   - $Sig(SP) \stackrel{def}{=} \Sigma$
   - $Test(SP) \stackrel{def}{=} T$
   - $Mod_\approx(SP) \stackrel{def}{=} \{A \in Alg(\Sigma) \mid A \models_{\approx_\Sigma} \Phi\}$
   - $ChMod_{\sim,\simeq}(SP) \stackrel{def}{=} \{A \in Alg(\Sigma) \mid A \models^T_{\sim_\Sigma, \simeq_\Sigma} \Phi\}$
2. $SP = SP_1 \cup SP_2$, *where* SP_1 *and* SP_2 *are structured specifications, with* $Sig(SP_1) = Sig(SP_2)$.
   - $Sig(SP) \stackrel{def}{=} Sig(SP_1) = Sig(SP_2)$
   - $Test(SP) \stackrel{def}{=} Test(SP_1) \cup Test(SP_2)$
   - $Mod_\approx(SP) \stackrel{def}{=} Mod_\approx(SP_1) \cap Mod_\approx(SP_2)$
   - $ChMod_{\sim,\simeq}(SP) \stackrel{def}{=} ChMod_{\sim,\simeq}(SP_1) \cap ChMod_{\sim,\simeq}(SP_2)$
3. $SP =$ translate SP' with σ, *where* $\sigma : \Sigma' \to \Sigma$ *and* $Sig(SP') = \Sigma'$.
   - $Sig(SP) \stackrel{def}{=} \Sigma$
   - $Test(SP) \stackrel{def}{=} \sigma(Test(SP'))$
   - $Mod_\approx(SP) \stackrel{def}{=} \{A \in Alg(\Sigma) \mid A|_\sigma \in Mod_\approx(SP')\}$
   - $ChMod_{\sim,\simeq}(SP) \stackrel{def}{=} \{A \in Alg(\Sigma) \mid A|_\sigma \in ChMod_{\sim,\simeq}(SP')\}$
4. $SP =$ hide sorts S' opns F' in SP', *where* S' *is a set of sorts,* F' *is a set of function declarations and* $\Sigma = Sig(SP)$ *is required to be a well-formed signature.*
   - $Sig(SP) \stackrel{def}{=} Sig(SP') - \langle S', F' \rangle$

- $Test(SP) \stackrel{def}{=} Test(SP') \cap T_\Sigma$
- $Mod_\approx(SP) \stackrel{def}{=} \{A'|_\Sigma \mid A' \in Mod_\approx(SP')\}$
- $ChMod_{\sim,\simeq}(SP) \stackrel{def}{=} \{A'|_\Sigma \mid A' \in ChMod_{\sim,\simeq}(SP')\}$

where $Mod_\approx(SP)$ *denotes the class of* "real" models *of* SP *w.r.t. the family of* Σ*-behavioural equalities* $\approx = (\approx_\Sigma)_{\Sigma \in Sign}$ *and* $ChMod_{\sim,\simeq}(SP)$ *denotes the class of* "checkable" models *of* SP *by testing w.r.t. the families of* Σ*-approximate equalities* $\sim = (\sim_\Sigma)_{\Sigma \in Sign}$ *and* $\simeq = (\simeq_\Sigma)_{\Sigma \in Sign}$.

Membership in the class of checkable models corresponds to a pure compositional approach to test, called *structured testing*, whereas testing satisfaction of *visible axioms*[2], called *flat testing*, is a pure non-compositional approach [7]. Structured testing may require different parts of the specification to be checked separately and also an implementation of hidden sorts and functions.

The following theorems present results obtained in [7] when comparing the class of real and checkable models. Theorem 1 shows a more prevalent situation where not all checkable models are real models, that is, incorrect programs can be accepted by testing, but correct programs cannot be rejected. On the other hand, Theorem 2 shows a situation where any checkable model is a real model but not the converse, that is, correct programs can be rejected by testing, but incorrect programs cannot be accepted. Let SP be a structured specification and A be a $Sig(SP)$-algebra.

Theorem 1. *If* $\sim$ *is complete,* $\simeq$ *is sound, and the axioms of* SP *have only positive occurrences of* $\forall$ *and negative occurrences of* $\exists$ *then* $A \in Mod_\approx(SP)$ *implies* $A \in ChMod_{\sim,\simeq}(SP)$.

Theorem 2. *If* $\sim$ *is sound,* $\simeq$ *is complete and the axioms of* SP *have only negative occurrences of* $\forall$ *and positive occurrences of* $\exists$ *then* $A \in ChMod_{\sim,\simeq}(SP)$ *implies* $A \in Mod_\approx(SP)$.

In the next sections, we present the normal forms, comparing testing from the original specification, pure structured testing, to testing from the normal forms and showing under which circumstances the conclusions of Theorems 1 and 2 can be met when taking the normal forms into account. Example 1 below is used to illustrate the normal forms.

Example 1. Let S_1 and S_2 be signatures defined as follows.

$$S_1 = \left(\begin{array}{ll} \mathsf{sorts} & \{list\} \\ \mathsf{opns} & \{nil : list \\ & \quad cons : int * list \to list \\ & \quad head : list \to int \\ & \quad tail : list \to list\} \end{array} \right)$$

[2] Axioms composed of visible/exported symbols only.

$$S_2 = \begin{pmatrix} \textsf{sorts}\ \{list\} \\ \textsf{opns}\ \{\dots\ S_1\ operations\ \dots \\ \quad is\_sorted : list \to bool \\ \quad sort : list \to list\} \end{pmatrix}$$

Let $\sigma : S_1 \hookrightarrow S_2$. The following are well-formed structured specifications.

$$List = \begin{bmatrix} \textsf{sig} & S_1 \\ \textsf{axioms} & \forall l : list; x : int \cdot cons(x, l) \neq l \\ & \forall l : list; x : int \cdot head(cons(x, l)) = x \\ & \forall l : list; x : int \cdot tail(cons(x, l)) = l \\ \textsf{test set}\ T_1 = (T_{1\,s})_{s \in \{int, bool, list\}} & \end{bmatrix}$$

$$SList1 = \textsf{translate}\ List\ \textsf{by}\ \sigma$$

$$SList2 = \begin{bmatrix} \textsf{sig} & S_2 \\ \textsf{axioms} & is\_sorted(nil) = true \\ & \dots \\ & \forall l \cdot is\_sorted(sort(l)) = true \\ \textsf{test set}\ T_2 = (T_{2\,s})_{s \in \{int, bool, list\}} & \end{bmatrix}$$

$$SList = SList1 \cup SList2$$

$$IntList = \textsf{hide sorts}\ \emptyset\ \textsf{opns}\ \{is\_sorted\}\ \textsf{in}\ SList$$

Let A be an $IntList$-algebra. Flat testing from $IntList$, i.e., testing from an unstructured set of visible axioms of this specification, corresponds to the test $A \models^{Test(IntList)}_{\sim_S, \simeq_S} \Phi$, where Φ is the set of visible axioms of $IntList$, $S = Sig(IntList)$ and $Test(IntList)$ is given according to Definition 2. On the other hand, structured testing ($A \in ChMod_{\sim,\simeq}(IntList)$), by Definition 2 and after some simplifications, corresponds to the following tests $A'|_{List} \models^{T_1}_{\sim_{S_1}, \simeq_{S_1}} \Phi_1$ and $A' \models^{T_2}_{\sim_{S_2}, \simeq_{S_2}} \Phi_2$, where Φ_1 and Φ_2 are the axioms of $List$ and $SList2$ respectively and A' is a $SList$-algebra with $A = A'|_{IntList}$. Advantages and drawbacks of structured testing and flat testing are discussed [7]. Here we focus on structured testing only and the use of normal forms. Notice that this example matches Theorem 1, since axioms are universal formulas, that is, they have only positive occurrences of $\forall$ and negative occurrences of $\exists$. □

3 The con Normal Form

When testing from a specification SP by structured testing, axioms are checked according to the test set defined in the subspecification where they belong to. On the other hand, flat testing considers only the resulting test set $Test(SP)$.

Clearly, axioms can be checked with different test sets in the former and in the second approach, mainly when SP has occurrences of *union* (see Example 1). Unless specifications are consistent w.r.t test sets[3] and *hide* is taken into account, an oracle in the second approach cannot be given [7].

The con normal form produces a new specification from SP which is consistent w.r.t. test sets by incrementing test sets of each sort in each occurrence of the union operation, while keeping the structure of the former specification. The intention is to allow non-compositional approaches like flat testing to be performed from the con normal form so that they can be appropriately interpreted according to the class of real models. Nevertheless, structured testing can also take advantage of incrementing test sets, since specifications with testing interface can always be incremented by additional test sets without compromising the final interpretation. Actually, adding test sets, makes the testing experiment be more rigorous. This might seem to be obvious if the specification axioms have only positive $\forall$ (and negative $\exists$). However, it is less obvious when the specification has only positive $\exists$ (and negative $\forall$), since, in this context, more programs are accepted when test sets are incremented. Specifications can be incremented by test sets as follows.

Definition 3 (Incremented Specifications). *Let SP be a structured specification and T' be a $Sig(SP)$-test set.*

1. *If $SP = \langle \Sigma, \Phi, T \rangle$, then $inc(SP, T') = \langle \Sigma, \Phi, T \cup T' \rangle$*
2. *If $SP = SP_1 \cup SP_2$, then $inc(SP, T') = inc(SP_1, T') \cup inc(SP_2, T')$*
3. *If $SP =$ translate SP' by σ, then $inc(SP, T') =$ translate $inc(SP', \{t \in T_{\Sigma'} \mid \sigma(t) \in T'\})$ by σ, where $\sigma : \Sigma' \to \Sigma$, $Sig(SP) = \Sigma$ and $Sig(SP') = \Sigma'$*
4. *If $SP =$ hide sorts S' opns F' in SP', then $inc(SP, T') =$ hide sorts S' opns F' in $inc(SP', T')$*

Lemmas 1 and 2 below relate testing with an incremented specification to testing with the original one. Let SP be a structured specification, T' be a $Sig(SP)$-test set and A be a $Sig(SP)$-algebra.

Lemma 1. *If the axioms of SP have only positive occurrences of $\forall$ and negative occurrences of $\exists$ then $A \in ChMod_{\sim,\doteq}(inc(SP, T'))$ implies $A \in ChMod_{\sim,\doteq}(SP)$.*

Proof. By induction on the structure of SP. The only interesting case to look at is when $SP = \langle \Sigma, \Phi, T \rangle$. Suppose $A \in ChMod_{\sim,\doteq}(inc(SP, T'))$. Then $A \models^{T \cup T'}_{\sim,\doteq} \Phi$. Because Φ does only have positive $\forall$ and negative $\exists$, then $A \models^{T}_{\sim,\doteq} \Phi$.

Lemma 2 is the dual of Lemma 1.

Lemma 2. *If the axioms of SP have only negative occurrences of $\forall$ and positive occurrences of $\exists$ then $A \in ChMod_{\sim,\doteq}(SP)$ implies $A \in ChMod_{\sim,\doteq}(inc(SP, T'))$.*

[3] If for every specification $SP_1 \cup SP_2$ which is part of SP, $Test(SP_1) \restriction_S = Test(SP_2) \restriction_S$, then SP is *consistent w.r.t. test sets*, where S is the sets of sorts of bound variables in the set of visible axioms of SP_1 and SP_2.

Proof. Follows the same pattern as the proof of Lemma 1.

The con normal form given below increments an specification with a test set at each occurrence of the *union* operation so that the resulting specification is consistent w.r.t. test sets.

Definition 4 (con Normal Form). *Let SP be a structured specification, the normal form $con(SP)$ is defined as follows.*

1. $con(\langle \Sigma, \Phi, T\rangle) \stackrel{def}{=} \langle \Sigma, \Phi, T\rangle$
2. $con(SP_1 \cup SP_2) \stackrel{def}{=} con(inc(SP_1, T)) \cup con(inc(SP_2, T))$, *where* $T = Test(SP_1 \cup SP_2)$
3. $con(\textsf{translate } SP' \textsf{ by } \sigma) \stackrel{def}{=} \textsf{translate } con(SP') \textsf{ by } \sigma$
4. $con(\textsf{hide sorts } S' \textsf{ opns } F' \textsf{ in } SP') \stackrel{def}{=} \textsf{hide sorts } S' \textsf{ opns } F' \textsf{ in } con(SP')$

Proposition 2. *$con(SP)$ is a well-formed specification.*

The reason why $con(SP)$ is a well-formed specification is that it has the same structure of SP and increments in test set occurs only when union is reached. At this point, only terms built from visible symbols relative to the corresponding argument specifications and not to the overall specification are added (see item 2 in Definition 4 and Definition 3). Thus, name clashes cannot occur and test sets in the outer structure can always be defined from test sets in the inner structure. Moreover, for any signature morphism $\sigma : \Sigma' \rightarrow \Sigma$, sorts $s \in sorts(\Sigma)$ which do not correspond to any sort in $sorts(\Sigma')$ do not have their test sets incremented.

Notice that con(con(SP)) = con(SP). Also, specifications which are consistent w.r.t to test sets are not necessarily in the con normal form, since this form standardises test sets of all visible sorts at each occurrence of *union*, including the ones which are not referred by visible axioms. Therefore, $\textsf{con}(SP) = SP$ holds, that is, SP is in the con normal form, if and only if, SP is *fully consistent w.r.t test sets*[4].

Obviously, the class of real models of a specification SP corresponds exactly to the class of real models of $con(SP)$, since $Mod_{\approx}$ does not take test sets into account. However, because SP and $con(SP)$ have different test sets, the classes of checkable models of SP and $con(SP)$ are not equivalent. The implication in both directions holds only under certain assumptions on quantifiers which are somehow contradictory (see Theorems 3 and 4 below) and can only be dropped if the test sets are either unbiased and valid or exhaustive [4,6].

Theorem 3. *If the axioms of SP have only positive occurrences of $\forall$ and negative occurrences of $\exists$, $A \in ChMod_{\sim,\doteq}(con(SP))$ implies $A \in ChMod_{\sim,\doteq}(SP)$.*

Proof. By induction on the structure of SP. The only interesting case to look at is when $SP = SP_1 \cup SP_2$. Suppose $A \in ChMod_{\sim,\doteq}(con(SP))$. Then, $A \in$

[4] If for every specification $SP_1 \cup SP_2$ which is part of SP, $Test(SP_1) = Test(SP_2)$, then SP is *fully consistent w.r.t. test sets.*

$ChMod_{\sim,\doteq}(con(inc(SP_1,T)))$ and $A \in ChMod_{\sim,\doteq}(con(inc(SP_2,T)))$, by Definitions 4 and 2, where $T = Test(SP)$. By induction hypothesis, $A \in ChMod_{\sim,\doteq}(inc(SP_1,T))$ and $A \in ChMod_{\sim,\doteq}(inc(SP_2,T))$. Thus, $A \in ChMod_{\sim,\doteq}(SP_1)$ and $A \in ChMod_{\sim,\doteq}(SP_2)$ by Lemma 1. Hence, $A \in ChMod_{\sim,\doteq}(SP)$.

Obviously, the converse holds if the assumptions of Lemma 2 are fulfilled.

Theorem 4. *If the axioms of SP have only negative occurrences of $\forall$ and positive occurrences of $\exists$, $A \in ChMod_{\sim,\doteq}(SP)$ implies $A \in ChMod_{\sim,\doteq}(con(SP))$.*

Proof. By definition 4 and Lemma 2.

The following corollaries relate the class of checkable models of the normalised specification to the class of real models of the original specification. Notice that if A is a real model of SP, then, by Corollary 1 below, it is a checkable model of $con(SP)$. By Theorem 3, A is a checkable model of SP. This means that under the assumptions of Corollary 1 and Theorem 3, it may be more interesting to test from the con normal form instead of the original specification.

Corollary 1. *If $\sim$ is complete, $\doteq$ is sound and the axioms of SP have only positive occurrences of $\forall$ and negative occurrences of $\exists$ then $A \in Mod_{\approx}(SP)$ implies $A \in ChMod_{\sim,\doteq}(con(SP))$.*

Proof. Suppose $A \in Mod_{\approx}(SP)$. Then, $A \in Mod_{\approx}(con(SP))$. Thus, by Theorem 1, $A \in ChMod_{\sim,\doteq}(con(SP))$.

Corollary 2. *If $\sim$ is sound, $\doteq$ is complete and the axioms of SP have only negative occurrences of $\forall$ and positive occurrences of $\exists$ then $A \in ChMod_{\sim,\doteq}(con(SP))$ implies $A \in Mod_{\approx}(SP)$.*

The normal form $con(SP)$ can be more efficient than SP in the sense that if the conditions of Theorem 3 and Corollary 1 are met, then testing from $con(SP)$ can accept fewer incorrect programs than testing from SP. Similarly, if the conditions of Theorem 4 and Corollary 2 are met, then testing from the former can reject fewer correct programs than testing from SP. Nevertheless, the class of checkable models of SP and $con(SP)$ may not be equivalent which implies that $con(SP)$ cannot always replace SP in the structure of another specification.

Example 2. Consider the $IntList$ specification given in example 1. From Definition 4, the normal form $con(IntList)$, is as follows.

hide sorts $\emptyset$ opns $\{is\_sorted\}$ in
  translate $\langle S_1, \Phi_1, T\rangle$ by $\sigma \cup$
  $\langle S_2, \Phi_2, T\rangle$

where $T = Test(SList1) \cup Test(SList2) = \sigma(Test(List)) \cup T_2 = T_1 \cup T_2$, Φ_1 is the set of axioms of $List$ and Φ_2 is the set of axioms of $SList2$. Let A be an $IntList$-algebra. From Definition 2, structured testing now corresponds to the following tests $A'|_{List} \models^T_{\sim_{S_1},\doteq_{S_1}} \Phi_1$ and $A' \models^T_{\sim_{S_2},\doteq_{S_2}} \Phi_2$ with $A = A'|_{Sig(IntList)}$. Obviously, from Corollary 1 and Theorem 3, if $\sim$ is complete and $\doteq$ is sound, structured testing from the con normal form can be more rigorous than from the original specification, since test sets are incremented in the former. □

4 The nf Normal Form

The nf normal form extends the normal form introduced in [2] for ordinary specifications to deal with structured specifications with testing interface. The intention is to handle the complexity of structured specifications by grouping axioms, taking hidden symbols into account so that the result is a flat specification which exports visible symbols. The symbols of a specification includes both visible and hidden symbols appropriately renamed to avoid name clashes.

Definition 5 (Symbols). *The symbols of a structured specification are as follows.*

1. $Symbols(\langle \Sigma, \Phi, T \rangle) \stackrel{def}{=} \Sigma$
2. $Symbols(SP_1 \cup SP_2) \stackrel{def}{=} Symbols(SP_1) +_{Sig(SP)} Symbols(SP_2)$ *(see Figure 1)*
3. $Symbols(\text{translate } SP' \text{ by } \sigma) \stackrel{def}{=} PO(Sig(SP') \hookrightarrow Symbols(SP'), \sigma)$, *where* $\sigma : Sig(SP') \rightarrow Sig(SP)$ *(see Figure 2)*
4. $Symbols(\text{hide sorts } S' \text{ opns } F' \text{ in } SP') \stackrel{def}{=} Symbols(SP')$

where diagrams in Figures 1 and 2 are pushout constructions which renames all hidden symbols so that $Sig(SP) \subseteq Symbols(SP)$.

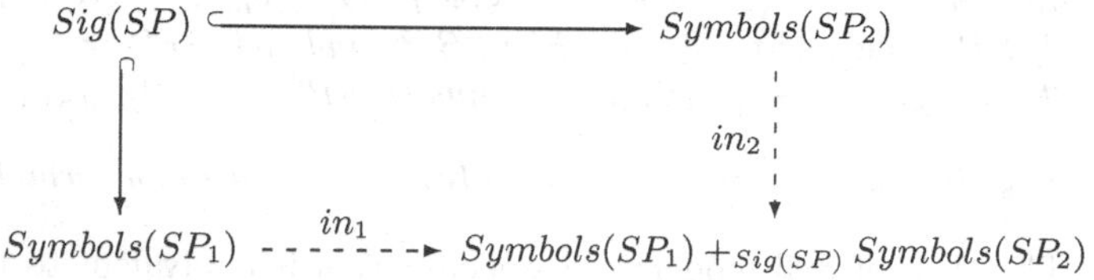

Fig. 1. $Symbols(SP_1 \cup SP_2)$

In the case of *union*, although the signatures of SP, SP_1 and SP_2 are the same (and this is the reason why the diagram in Figure 1 is simpler than the one presented in [2]), $Symbols(SP_1)$ may not coincide with $Symbols(SP_2)$, because the hidden symbols of SP_1 and SP_2 can be different.

The specification-building operation *export* is define in the sequel.

Definition 6 (Export). *Let* SP' *be a structured specification. Then* $SP = SP'|_\Sigma$ *is defined as follows, where* $\Sigma' = Sig(SP')$ *and* $\Sigma \subseteq \Sigma'$.

- $Sig(SP) \stackrel{def}{=} \Sigma$
- $Test(SP) \stackrel{def}{=} Test(SP') \cap T_\Sigma$
- $Mod_{\approx}(SP) \stackrel{def}{=} \{A'|_\Sigma \mid A' \in Mod_{\approx}(SP')\}$
- $ChMod_{\sim,\simeq}(SP) \stackrel{def}{=} \{A'|_\Sigma \mid A' \in ChMod_{\sim,\simeq}(SP')\}$

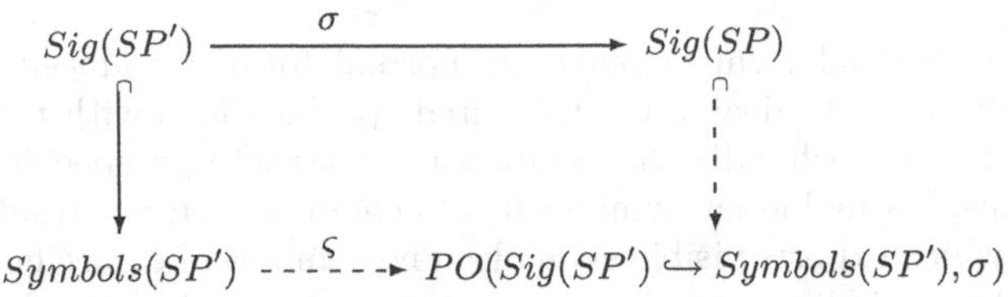

Fig. 2. $Symbols(\text{translate } SP' \text{ by } \sigma)$

The nf normal form is a basic specification restricted to a signature of exported symbols in the following sense.

Definition 7 (nf Normal Form). *Let SP be a structured specification, the normal form $nf(SP)$ is defined as follows.*

1. *If $SP = \langle \Sigma, \Phi, T \rangle$, then $nf(SP) \stackrel{def}{=} \langle \Sigma, \Phi, T \rangle|_{\Sigma}$*
2. *If $SP = SP_1 \cup SP_2$ and $nf(SP_i) = \langle Symbols(SP_i), \Phi_i, T_i \rangle|_{Sig(SP_i)}$ $i = 1, 2$, then $nf(SP) \stackrel{def}{=} \langle Symbols(SP), in_1(\Phi_1) \cup in_2(\Phi_2), in_1(T_1) \cup in_2(T_2) \rangle|_{Sig(SP)}$ (see Figure 1)*
3. *If $SP =$ translate SP' by σ and $nf(SP') = \langle Symbols(SP'), \Phi', T' \rangle|_{Sig(SP')}$, then $nf(SP) \stackrel{def}{=} \langle Symbols(SP), \varsigma(\Phi'), \varsigma(T') \rangle|_{Sig(SP)}$ (see Figure 2)*
4. *If $SP =$ hide sorts S' opns F' in SP' and $nf(SP') = \langle Symbols(SP'), \Phi', T' \rangle|_{Sig(SP')}$, then $nf(SP) = \langle Symbols(SP'), \Phi', T' \rangle|_{Sig(SP)}$*

where ς, in_1 and in_2 are extended to translate terms and formulas.

The class of real models of a specification is equivalent to the class of real models of its corresponding nf normal form, provided the family of behavioural equalities considered is compatible. In the sequel, let SP be a structured specification and A be a $Sig(SP)$-algebra

Theorem 5. *If $\approx$ is compatible, then $A \in Mod_{\approx}(SP)$ if and only if $A \in Mod_{\approx}(nf(SP))$.*

Proof. By induction on the structure of SP.

Testing from the nf normal form cannot always be interpreted, unless the original specification is consistent w.r.t. test sets. Under certain assumptions on the families of equalities, either any checkable model of SP is a checkable model of $nf(SP)$ or vice-versa.

Theorem 6. *Let SP be consistent w.r.t test sets. If $\sim$ is reduction-compatible and $\simeq$ is translation-compatible, then $A \in ChMod_{\sim,\simeq}(nf(SP))$ implies $A \in ChMod_{\sim,\simeq}(SP)$.*

Proof. By induction on the structure of SP, Proposition 1(2) and because SP is consistent w.r.t test sets.

Theorem 7. *Let SP be consistent w.r.t test sets. If $\sim$ is translation-compatible and $\doteq$ is reduction-compatible, then $A \in ChMod_{\sim,\doteq}(SP)$ implies $A \in ChMod_{\sim,\doteq}(nf(SP))$.*

Proof. Similar to the proof of Theorem 6.

Obviously, if the families of approximate equalities considered are compatible, then the classes of checkable models of SP and $nf(SP)$ are equivalent.

Corollary 3. *Let SP be consistent w.r.t test sets. If $\sim$ and $\doteq$ are compatible, then $A \in ChMod_{\sim,\doteq}(nf(SP))$ if and only if $A \in ChMod_{\sim,\doteq}(SP)$.*

Proof. Follows directly from Theorems 7 and 6.

If the assumptions of Theorem 5 are met then testing with the normal form can be interpreted according to the original specification. Again, any real model of SP is a checkable model of $nf(SP)$, provided the assumptions of Corollary 4 are met. Corollary 5 is the dual of 4.

Corollary 4. *If $\sim$ is complete, $\doteq$ is sound, $\approx$ is compatible and the axioms of SP have only positive occurrences of $\forall$ and negative occurrences of $\exists$, then $A \in Mod_{\approx}(SP)$ implies $A \in ChMod_{\sim,\doteq}(nf(SP))$.*

Proof. Suppose $A \in Mod_{\approx}(SP)$. By Theorem 5, $A \in Mod_{\approx}(nf(SP))$. By Theorem 1, $A \in ChMod_{\sim,\doteq}(nf(SP))$.

Corollary 5. *If $\sim$ is sound, $\doteq$ is complete, $\approx$ is compatible and the axioms of SP have only negative occurrences of $\forall$ and positive occurrences of $\exists$, then $A \in ChMod_{\sim,\doteq}(nf(SP))$ implies $A \in Mod_{\approx}(SP)$.*

Proof. Suppose $A \in ChMod_{\sim,\doteq}(nf(SP))$. Then $A \in Mod_{\approx}(nf(SP))$ by Theorem 2. By Theorem 5, $A \in Mod_{\approx}(SP)$.

Therefore, from Corollary 4 and Theorem 6 (Theorem 7 and Corollary 5), testing from the nf normal form can be more rigorous than from the original specification. The reason is that equality is interpreted in the normal form according to the resulting signature without *export*, whereas equality is interpreted in the original specification according to signature of the subspecification where the axiom being considered belong to. Also if $\sim$ is reduction-compatible, the reduct of $\sim_{\Sigma}$ is either equal to or finer than $\sim_{\Sigma}$ and if $\doteq$ is translation-compatible, then the reduct of $\doteq_{\Sigma}$ is either equal or coarser than $\doteq_{\Sigma}$.

If the nf normal form is applied to $con(SP)$, then the assumption that SP has to be consistent w.r.t. test sets can be dropped. Once more, in order to compare the class of checkable models of $nf(con(SP))$ and SP, it is necessary that the approximate equalities are either reduction-compatible or translation-compatible in the following sense.

Corollary 6. *If $\sim$ is reduction-compatible, $\doteq$ is translation-compatible and the axioms of SP have only positive occurrences of $\forall$ and negative occurrences of $\exists$, then $A \in ChMod_{\sim,\doteq}(nf(con(SP)))$ implies $A \in ChMod_{\sim,\doteq}(SP)$.*

Proof. Suppose $A \in ChMod_{\sim,\doteq}(nf(con(SP)))$. Then, by Theorem 6, $A \in ChMod_{\sim,\doteq}(con(SP))$. By Theorem 3, $A \in ChMod_{\sim,\doteq}(SP)$.

Corollary 7. *If $\sim$ is translation-compatible, $\doteq$ is reduction-compatible and the axioms of SP have only negative occurrences of $\forall$ and positive occurrences of $\exists$, then $A \in ChMod_{\sim,\doteq}(SP)$ implies $A \in ChMod_{\sim,\doteq}(nf(con(SP)))$.*

Proof. Suppose $A \in ChMod_{\sim,\doteq}(SP)$. Then, by Theorem 4, $A \in ChMod_{\sim,\doteq}(con(SP))$. By Theorem 7, $A \in ChMod_{\sim,\doteq}(nf(con(SP)))$.

Contrary to the con normal form, under certain conditions, the class of checkable models of SP and $nf(SP)$ are equivalent (see Corollary 3). However, the condition that SP has to be consistent w.r.t test sets can be restrictive if one wish to embed the nf normal into a compositional approach to testing.

Example 3. Consider again the *IntList* specification presented in example 1. From Definition 7, the normal form $nf(IntList)$ is as follows.

$$nf(IntList) = \langle S_2, \Phi_1 \cup \Phi_2, T_1 \cup T_2 \rangle|_{Sig(IntList)}$$

where Φ_1 is the set of axioms of *List*, Φ_2 is the set of axioms of *SList*2 and $Symbols(IntList) = Symbols(SList) = \sigma(S_1) +_{S_2} S_2 = S_2$, since no hidden symbols need to be renamed. Let A be an *IntList*-algebra. Structured testing from the normal form consists in a single test $A' \models^{T_1 \cup T_2}_{\sim_{S_2}, \doteq_{S_2}} \Phi_1 \cup \Phi_2$ with $A = A'|_{Sig(IntList)}$. Notice that this is similar to flat testing in Example 1, except from the fact that hidden symbols and axioms are also taken into account and the test set is not restricted to *IntList*. The *IntList* specification matches Corollary 4. So, in order to make it possible to test from the normal form instead of the original specification the following must be met. From Theorem 6, *IntList* must be consistent w.r.t test sets. This means that T_1 must coincide with T_2. From Corollary 4, $\approx$ must be compatible. Suppose $\approx$ is the family of observational equalities. This family is not compatible when focusing on *IntList*, since *is_sorted* which is a *list* observer is added in S_2 and not in S_1. Thus, S_1 must include *is_sorted* in order to make $\approx$ be compatible. Furthermore, $\sim$ need to be complete and reduction-compatible and $\doteq$ need to be sound and translation-compatible. It is easy to check that any $\sim$ defined from a finite subset of observable contexts is both complete and reduction-compatible. Also, the literal equality $=$ is both sound and translation-compatible. □

5 The snf Normal Form

The strict normal form (snf) is similar to the nf normal form, but aimed at achieving the main benefits of the con and nf normal form by assuring equivalence of model classes while eliminating the consistency w.r.t test sets condition of non-compositional approaches. In order to drop this consistency condition, it is necessary to make sure axioms are interpreted according to the test set defined in the signature where they belong to. Strict specifications are flat specifications where each axiom is associated with a test set.

Definition 8 (Strict Specification). *A* strict *specification $SP = \langle \Sigma, \Psi \rangle$ with $\Psi \subseteq \{(\psi, T) \mid \psi \in Sen(\Sigma)$ and $T \subseteq T_\Sigma\}$ is defined as follows.*

- $Sig(SP) = \Sigma$
- $Test(SP) = (\bigcup_{(\psi,T)\in\Psi} T)$
- $Mod_\approx(SP) = \{A \in Alg(\Sigma) \mid \bigwedge_{(\psi,T)\in\Psi} A \models_\approx \psi\}$
- $ChMod_{\sim,\simeq}(SP) = \{A \in Alg(\Sigma) \mid \bigwedge_{(\psi,T)\in\Psi} A \models^T_{\sim,\simeq} \psi\}$

The export operation on strict specifications is defined as usual.

Definition 9 (Strict Export). *Let $SP' = \langle \Sigma', \Psi' \rangle$ be a strict specification. Then $SP = SP'|_\Sigma$ is defined as follows, where $\Sigma \subseteq \Sigma'$.*

- $Sig(SP) \stackrel{def}{=} \Sigma$
- $Test(SP) \stackrel{def}{=} Test(SP') \cap T_\Sigma$
- $Mod_\approx(SP) \stackrel{def}{=} \{A'|_\Sigma \mid A' \in Mod_\approx(SP')\}$
- $ChMod_{\sim,\simeq}(SP) \stackrel{def}{=} \{A'|_\Sigma \mid A' \in ChMod_{\sim,\simeq}(SP')\}$

The strict normal form (snf) of a specification SP is a strict specification restricted by the export operator given in Definition 9.

Definition 10 (snf Normal Form). *Let SP be a structured specification, the strict normal form $snf(SP)$ is defined as follows.*

1. *If $SP = \langle \Sigma, \Phi, T \rangle$, then $snf(SP) \stackrel{def}{=} \langle \Sigma, \Psi \rangle|_\Sigma$, where $\Psi = \{(\phi, T) \mid \phi \in \Phi\}$*
2. *If $SP = SP_1 \cup SP_2$ and $snf(SP_i) = \langle Symbols(SP_i), \Psi_i \rangle|_{Sig(SP_i)}$ $i = 1, 2$, then $snf(SP) \stackrel{def}{=} \langle Symbols(SP), in_1(\Psi_1) \cup in_2(\Psi_2) \rangle|_{Sig(SP)}$ (see Figure 1)*
3. *If $SP =$ translate SP' by σ and $snf(SP') = \langle Symbols(SP'), \Psi' \rangle|_{Sig(SP')}$, then $snf(SP) \stackrel{def}{=} \langle Symbols(SP), \varsigma(\Psi') \rangle|_{Sig(SP)}$ (see Figure 2)*
4. *If $SP =$ hide sorts S' opns F' in SP' and $snf(SP') = \langle Symbols(SP'), \Psi' \rangle|_{Sig(SP')}$, then $snf(SP) = \langle Symbols(SP'), \Psi' \rangle|_{Sig(SP)}$*

where ς, in_1 and in_2 are extended to translate pairs of formulas and terms.

The classes of real models of SP and $snf(SP)$ are equivalent whenever the family of behavioural equalities considered is compatible. In the sequel, let SP be a structured specification and A be a $Sig(SP)$-algebra.

Theorem 8. *If $\approx$ is compatible, then $A \in Mod_\approx(SP)$ if and only if $A \in Mod_\approx(snf(SP))$.*

Proof. By induction on the structure of SP.

Correspondingly, the classes of checkable models of SP and $snf(SP)$ are equivalent if the families of approximate equalities are compatible. Yet this condition can be weakened if one is only interested in one or the other direction of the implication. Notice that, contrary to the nf normal form, conditions on test sets are not necessary.

Theorem 9. *If $\sim$ is reduction-compatible and $\doteq$ is translation-compatible, then $A \in ChMod_{\sim,\doteq}(snf(SP))$ implies $A \in ChMod_{\sim,\doteq}(SP)$.*

Proof. By induction of the structure of SP.

Theorem 10. *If $\sim$ is translation-compatible and $\doteq$ is reduction-compatible, then $A \in ChMod_{\sim,\doteq}(SP)$ implies $A \in ChMod_{\sim,\doteq}(snf(SP))$.*

Proof. By induction on the structure of SP.

The following corollary shows that we can always substitute the strict normal of SP for SP if the approximate equalities are compatible.

Corollary 8. *If $\sim$ and $\doteq$ are compatible, then $A \in ChMod_{\sim,\doteq}(snf(SP))$ if and only if $A \in ChMod_{\sim,\doteq}(SP)$.*

Proof. Follows from Theorems 10 and 9.

Similar to the nf normal form, testing from the snf normal form can be more rigorous than from the original specification if certain conditions are met (see Corollary 9 and Theorem 9).

Corollary 9. *If $\sim$ is complete, $\doteq$ is sound, $\approx$ is compatible and the axioms of SP have only positive occurrences of $\forall$ and negative occurrences of $\exists$, then $A \in Mod_{\approx}(SP)$ implies $A \in ChMod_{\sim,\doteq}(snf(SP))$.*

Proof. Suppose $A \in Mod_{\approx}(SP)$. By Theorem 8, $A \in Mod_{\approx}(snf(SP))$. By Theorem 1, $A \in ChMod_{\sim,\doteq}(snf(SP))$.

Corollary 10. *If $\sim$ is sound, $\doteq$ is complete, $\approx$ is compatible and the axioms of SP have only negative occurrences of $\forall$ and positive occurrences of $\exists$, then $A \in ChMod_{\sim,\doteq}(snf(SP))$ implies $A \in Mod_{\approx}(SP)$.*

Proof. Suppose $A \in ChMod_{\sim,\doteq}(snf(SP))$. Then $A \in Mod_{\approx}(snf(SP))$ by Theorem 2. Thus, by Theorem 8, $A \in Mod_{\approx}(SP)$.

Furthermore, as one might expect, snf normal forms can always be incremented by additional test sets (according to Definition 3), but equivalence of the classes of checkable models can be lost.

Example 4. Consider again the $IntList$ specification presented in Example 1. From Definition 10, the normal form $snf(IntList)$ is as follows.

$$snf(IntList) = \langle S_2, \Psi_1 \cup \Psi_2 \rangle|_{Sig(IntList)}$$

where $\Psi_i = \{(\phi_i, T_i) \mid \phi_i \in \Phi_i\}$ with $i = 1, 2$, Φ_1 is the set of axioms of *List*, Φ_2 is the set of axioms of *SList2* and $Symbols(IntList) = S_2$ as in Example 3. Let A be an *IntList*-algebra. Structured testing from the normal form corresponds to $\bigwedge_{(\psi,T)\in\Psi_1\cup\Psi_2} A' \models^T_{\sim_{S_2},\simeq_{S_2}} \psi$ with $A = A'|_{Sig(IntList)}$. Like structured testing, hidden symbols are taking into account and each axiom is checked with the original test set associated with it. On the other hand, like flat testing, axioms are grouped and equalities on a single signature, in this case S_2, are used. Notice that *IntList* matches Corollary 9. Unlike example 3, T_1 and T_2 need not coincide. However, the compatibility conditions are also necessary by Theorem 9 and Corollary 9. □

The main advantage of the snf normal form is to allow a combination of compositional and non-compositional testing, namely semi-structured testing, which is more likely to be adopted in practice. For instance, snf normal forms can be constructed for replacing some parts of a specification, specially when these parts are combined by *union*. Then, the resulting specification can be checked by structured testing. In order to do this, specification-building operations have to be defined in terms of specifications which are either structured or strict. One drawback of this combined approach is that compatibility of equalities which is not required by pure structured testing [7], has to be met for both behavioural and approximate equalities (see Theorem 8 and Corollary 8). How to weaken this condition still needs to be investigated. As we mentioned in Section 2, the family of observational equalities $\approx$ is not translation-compatible, unless the specification protects encapsulation.[5]

6 Concluding Remarks

Normalisation has been regarded as an approach for defining non-compositional proof systems for structured specifications such that theorems can be derived in the underlying institution. In this paper, we present normalisation as a way of simplifying testing from structured specification and handling the oracle problem. It is clear that pure compositional approaches can be inefficient in practice and non-compositional approaches are unstructured and limited by the oracle problem. Therefore, a combined approach in which parts of the specification are replaced by normal forms and the overall specification is checked by structured testing seems to be more promising. For instance, the number of experiments necessary can be reduced, mainly when the specification has several occurrences of *union*. Also, grouping hidden definitions can help to systematise an implementation of hidden sorts which can be a difficult task, but it is essential to test interesting properties expressed by hidden axioms when they cannot be replaced by their visible consequences. Moreover, tests from normal forms can be

[5] A specification SP protects encapsulation if for all $\sigma : \Sigma' \to \Sigma$ arising in SP, Σ does not introduce new observations for corresponding sorts in Σ'.

more rigorous than from the original specifications. This can be clearly achieved by applying the inc operation and, consequently, the con normal form. Regarding the nf and snf normal forms, if the complete (and the sound) equality for $Symbols(SP)$ whose family is required to be reduction-compatible (translation-compatible) is finer (coarser) than the ones for the signatures of the parts of SP, than testing from the normal forms can be more rigorous as well. Examples of such reduction-compatible (translation-compatible) families of approximate equalities which are complete (sound) w.r.t. a compatible family of behavioural equalities together with how this compatibility condition on approximate and behavioural equalities can be weakened are object of further investigation. Finally, the classes of real models of the normal forms and the original specification are equivalent (provided that the family of behavioural equalities considered is compatible, in the case of nf and snf). This, in principle, can make it possible to combine testing and proofs from specifications composed of structured specifications and normal forms.

Acknowledgements

The author wishes to thank Don Sannella for important discussions and also the referees for comments which helped to improve this paper. This research has been partially supported by EPSRC grant GR/K63795.

References

1. J. A. Bergstra, J. Heering, and P. Klint. Module algebra. *Journal of the Association for Computing Machinery*, 37(2):335–372, 1990. 459
2. M. Bidoit, M. V. Cengarle, and R. Hennicker. *Proof Systems for Structured Specifications and Their Refinements*, chapter 11. IFIP State-of-The-Art Reports. Springer, 1999. 459, 460, 469
3. M. Bidoit and R. Hennicker. Behavioural Theories and the Proof of Behavioural Properties. *Theoretical Computer Science*, 165(1):3–55, 1996. 461
4. M. Gaudel. Testing can be formal, too. In Peter D. Mosses, Mogens Nielsen, and Michael I. Schwartzbach, editors, *Proceedings of Theory and Practice of Software Development - TAPSOFT'95*, volume 915 of *LNCS*. Springer, 1995. 460, 467
5. R. Hennicker. *Structured Specifications with Behavioural Operators: Semantics, Proof Methods and Applications.* Habilitation thesis, Institut fur Informatik, Ludwig-Maximillians-Universitat Munchen, Munchen, Germany, june 1997. 460
6. P. D. L. Machado. On Oracles for Interpreting Test Results Against Algebraic Specifications. In A. M. Haeberer, editor, *Algebraic Methodology and Software Technology, AMAST'98*, volume 1548 of *LNCS*. Springer, 1999. 460, 461, 467
7. P. D. L. Machado. Testing from Structured Algebraic Specifications. In T. Rus, editor, *Algebraic Methodology and Software Technology, AMAST'00*, volume 1816 of *LNCS*. Springer, 2000. 459, 460, 462, 463, 464, 465, 466, 475
8. D. Sannella and A. Tarlecki. Essential concepts of algebraic specification and program development. *Formal Aspects of Computing*, 9:229–269, 1997. 460
9. M. Wirsing. Algebraic specification. In J. van Leeuwen, editor, *Handbook of Theoretical Computer Science*, volume B, chapter 13, pages 675–788. Elsevier Science Publishers, 1990. 460

Author Index

Ancona, Davide 53
Autexier, Serge 73

Baldan, Paolo 291
Baumeister, Hubert 366
Berg, Joachim van den 1
Bert, Didier 383
Borzyszkowski, Tomasz 401
Brand, Mark G. J. van den 89
Broy, Manfred 22

Cerioli, Maura 53
Choppy, Christine 106
Corradini, Andrea 291
Crossley, John N. 419

Fiadeiro, José Luis 438

Gilbert, David 311

Hannay, Jo Erskine 162
Haveraaen, Magne 182
Haxthausen, Anne 126
Huisman, Marieke 1
Hutter, Dieter 73

Jacobs, Bart 1

Krieg-Brückner, Bernd 126
Kinoshita, Yoshiki 201

Letichevsky, Alexander 311
Lo Presti, Stéphane 383
Lourenço, Hugo 219

Machado, Patricia D. L. 459
Maibaum, Tom 438
Mantel, Heiko 73
Martí-Oliet, Narciso 438
Mateus, Paulo 237
Meseguer, Jose 438
Montanari, Ugo 291
Mossakowski, Till 126, 146, 252

Nakagawa, Ataru T. 329

Orejas, Fernando 271
Owre, Sam 37

Pino, Elvira 271
Pita, Isabel 438
Poernomo, Iman 419
Poll, Erik 1
Power, John 201
Lo Presti, Stéphane 383

Reggio, Gianna 106
Reichel, Horst 348
Roggenbach, Markus 146

Schairer, Axel 73
Scheerder, Jeroen 89
Schröder, Lutz 146
Sernadas, Amílcar 219, 237
Sernadas, Cristina 237
Shankar, Natarajan 37

Wagner, Eric G. 182
Wirsing, Martin 419

Zucca, Elena 53

Lecture Notes in Computer Science

For information about Vols. 1–1795
please contact your bookseller or Springer-Verlag

Vol. 1796: B. Christianson, B. Crispo, J.A. Malcolm, M. Roe (Eds.), Security Protocols. Proceedings, 1999. XII, 229 pages. 2000.

Vol. 1797: B. Falsafi, M. Lauria (Eds.), Network-Based Parallel Computing. Proceedings, 2000. X, 179 pages. 2000.

Vol. 1798: F. Pichler, R. Moreno-Diaz, P. Kopacek (Eds.), Computer-Aided Systems Theory – EUROCAST'99. Proceedings, 1999. X, 602 pages. 2000.

Vol. 1800: J. Rolim et al. (Eds.), Parallel and Distributed Processing. Proceedings, 2000. XXIII, 1311 pages. 2000.

Vol. 1801: J. Miller, A. Thompson, P. Thomson, T.C. Fogarty (Eds.), Evolvable Systems: From Biology to Hardware. Proceedings, 2000. X, 286 pages. 2000.

Vol. 1802: R. Poli, W. Banzhaf, W.B. Langdon, J. Miller, P. Nordin, T.C. Fogarty (Eds.), Genetic Programming. Proceedings, 2000. X, 361 pages. 2000.

Vol. 1803: S. Cagnoni et al. (Eds.), Real-World Applications and Evolutionary Computing. Proceedings, 2000. XII, 396 pages. 2000.

Vol. 1804: B. Azvine, N. Azarmi, D.D. Nauck (Eds.), Intelligent Systems and Soft Computing. XVII, 359 pages. 2000. (Subseries LNAI).

Vol. 1805: T. Terano, H. Liu, A.L.P. Chen (Eds.), Knowledge Discovery and Data Mining. Proceedings, 2000. XIV, 460 pages. 2000. (Subseries LNAI).

Vol. 1806: W. van der Aalst, J. Desel, A. Oberweis (Eds.), Business Process Management. VIII, 391 pages. 2000.

Vol. 1807: B. Preneel (Ed.), Advances in Cryptology – EUROCRYPT 2000. Proceedings, 2000. XVIII, 608 pages. 2000.

Vol. 1809: S. Biundo, M. Fox (Eds.), Recent Advances in AI Planning. Proceedings, 1999. VIII, 373 pages. 2000. (Subseries LNAI).

Vol. 1810: R.López de Mántaras, E. Plaza (Eds.), Machine Learning: ECML 2000. Proceedings, 2000. XII, 460 pages. 2000. (Subseries LNAI).

Vol. 1811: S.W. Lee, H.. Bülthoff, T. Poggio (Eds.), Biologically Motivated Computer Vision. Proceedings, 2000. XIV, 656 pages. 2000.

Vol. 1813: P.L. Lanzi, W. Stolzmann, S.W. Wilson (Eds.), Learning Classifier Systems. X, 349 pages. 2000. (Subseries LNAI).

Vol. 1815: G. Pujolle, H. Perros, S. Fdida, U. Körner, I. Stavrakakis (Eds.), Networking 2000 – Broadband Communications, High Performance Networking, and Performance of Communication Networks. Proceedings, 2000. XX, 981 pages. 2000.

Vol. 1816: T. Rus (Ed.), Algebraic Methodology and Software Technology. Proceedings, 2000. XI, 545 pages. 2000.

Vol. 1817: A. Bossi (Ed.), Logic-Based Program Synthesis and Transformation. Proceedings, 1999. VIII, 313 pages. 2000.

Vol. 1818: C.G. Omidyar (Ed.), Mobile and Wireless Communications Networks. Proceedings, 2000. VIII, 187 pages. 2000.

Vol. 1819: W. Jonker (Ed.), Databases in Telecommunications. Proceedings, 1999. X, 208 pages. 2000.

Vol. 1821: R. Loganantharaj, G. Palm, M. Ali (Eds.), Intelligent Problem Solving. Proceedings, 2000. XVII, 751 pages. 2000. (Subseries LNAI).

Vol. 1822: H.H. Hamilton, Advances in Artificial Intelligence. Proceedings, 2000. XII, 450 pages. 2000. (Subseries LNAI).

Vol. 1823: M. Bubak, H. Afsarmanesh, R. Williams, B. Hertzberger (Eds.), High Performance Computing and Networking. Proceedings, 2000. XVIII, 719 pages. 2000.

Vol. 1824: J. Palsberg (Ed.), Static Analysis. Proceedings, 2000. VIII, 433 pages. 2000.

Vol. 1825: M. Nielsen, D. Simpson (Eds.), Application and Theory of Petri Nets 2000. Proceedings, 2000. XI, 485 pages. 2000.

Vol. 1826: W. Cazzola, R.J. Stroud, F. Tisato (Eds.), Reflection and Software Engineering. X, 229 pages. 2000.

Vol. 1827: D. Bert, C. Choppy, P. Mosses (Eds), Recent Trends in Algebraic Development Techniques. Proceedings, 1999. X, 477 pages. 2000.

Vol. 1829: C. Fonlupt, J.-K. Hao, E. Lutton, E. Ronald, M. Schoenauer (Eds.), Artificial Evolution. Proceedings, 1999. X, 293 pages. 2000.

Vol. 1830: P. Kropf, G. Babin, J. Plaice, H. Unger (Eds.), Distributed Communities on the Web. Proceedings, 2000. X, 203 pages. 2000.

Vol. 1831: D. McAllester (Ed.), Automated Deduction – CADE-17. Proceedings, 2000. XIII, 519 pages. 2000. (Subseries LNAI).

Vol. 1832: B. Lings, K. Jeffery (Eds.), Advances in Databases. Proceedings, 2000. X, 227 pages. 2000.

Vol. 1833: L. Bachmair (Ed.), Rewriting Techniques and Applications. Proceedings, 2000. X, 275 pages. 2000.

Vol. 1834: J.-C. Heudin (Ed.), Virtual Worlds. Proceedings, 2000. XI, 314 pages. 2000. (Subseries LNAI).

Vol. 1835: D. N. Christodoulakis (Ed.), Natural Language Processing – NLP 2000. Proceedings, 2000. XII, 438 pages. 2000. (Subseries LNAI).

Vol. 1836: B. Masand, M. Spiliopoulou (Eds.), Web Usage Analysis and User Profiling. Proceedings, 2000, V, 183 pages. 2000. (Subseries LNAI).

Vol. 1837: R. Backhouse, J. Nuno Oliveira (Eds.), Mathematics of Program Construction. Proceedings, 2000. IX, 257 pages. 2000.

Vol. 1838: W. Bosma (Ed.), Algorithmic Number Theory. Proceedings, 2000. IX, 615 pages. 2000.

Vol. 1839: G. Gauthier, C. Frasson, K. VanLehn (Eds.), Intelligent Tutoring Systems. Proceedings, 2000. XIX, 675 pages. 2000.

Vol. 1840: F. Bomarius, M. Oivo (Eds.), Product Focused Software Process Improvement. Proceedings, 2000. XI, 426 pages. 2000.

Vol. 1841: E. Dawson, A. Clark, C. Boyd (Eds.), Information Security and Privacy. Proceedings, 2000. XII, 488 pages. 2000.

Vol. 1842: D. Vernon (Ed.), Computer Vision – ECCV 2000. Part I. Proceedings, 2000. XVIII, 953 pages. 2000.

Vol. 1843: D. Vernon (Ed.), Computer Vision – ECCV 2000. Part II. Proceedings, 2000. XVIII, 881 pages. 2000.

Vol. 1844: W.B. Frakes (Ed.), Software Reuse: Advances in Software Reusability. Proceedings, 2000. XI, 450 pages. 2000.

Vol. 1845: H.B. Keller, E. Plöderer (Eds.), Reliable Software Technologies Ada-Europe 2000. Proceedings, 2000. XIII, 304 pages. 2000.

Vol. 1846: H. Lu, A. Zhou (Eds.), Web-Age Information Management. Proceedings, 2000. XIII, 462 pages. 2000.

Vol. 1847: R. Dyckhoff (Ed.), Automated Reasoning with Analytic Tableaux and Related Methods. Proceedings, 2000. X, 441 pages. 2000. (Subseries LNAI).

Vol. 1848: R. Giancarlo, D. Sankoff (Eds.), Combinatorial Pattern Matching. Proceedings, 2000. XI, 423 pages. 2000.

Vol. 1849: C. Freksa, W. Brauer, C. Habel, K.F. Wender (Eds.), Spatial Cognition II. XI, 420 pages. 2000. (Subseries LNAI).

Vol. 1850: E. Bertino (Ed.), ECOOP 2000 – Object-Oriented Programming. Proceedings, 2000. XIII, 493 pages. 2000.

Vol. 1851: M.M. Halldórsson (Ed.), Algorithm Theory – SWAT 2000. Proceedings, 2000. XI, 564 pages. 2000.

Vol. 1853: U. Montanari, J.D.P. Rolim, E. Welzl (Eds.), Automata, Languages and Programming. Proceedings, 2000. XVI, 941 pages. 2000.

Vol. 1854: G. Lacoste, B. Pfitzmann, M. Steiner, M. Waidner (Eds.), SEMPER — Secure Electronic Marketplace for Europe. XVIII, 350 pages. 2000.

Vol. 1855: E.A. Emerson, A.P. Sistla (Eds.), Computer Aided Verification. Proceedings, 2000. X, 582 pages. 2000.

Vol. 1857: J. Kittler, F. Roli (Eds.), Multiple Classifier Systems. Proceedings, 2000. XII, 404 pages. 2000.

Vol. 1858: D.-Z. Du, P. Eades, V. Estivill-Castro, X. Lin, A. Sharma (Eds.), Computing and Combinatorics. Proceedings, 2000. XII, 478 pages. 2000.

Vol. 1860: M. Klusch, L. Kerschberg (Eds.), Cooperative Information Agents IV. Proceedings, 2000. XI, 285 pages. 2000. (Subseries LNAI).

Vol. 1861: J. Lloyd, V. Dahl, U. Furbach, M. Kerber, K.-K. Lau, C. Palamidessi, L. Moniz Pereira, Y. Sagiv, P.J. Stuckey (Eds.), Computational Logic – CL 2000. Proceedings, 2000. XIX, 1379 pages. (Subseries LNAI).

Vol. 1862: P.G. Clote, H. Schwichtenberg (Eds.), Computer Science Logic. Proceedings, 2000. XIII, 543 pages. 2000.

Vol. 1863: L. Carter, J. Ferrante (Eds.), Languages and Compilers for Parallel Computing. Proceedings, 1999. XII, 500 pages. 2000.

Vol. 1864: B. Y. Choueiry, T. Walsh (Eds.), Abstraction, Reformulation, and Approximation. Proceedings, 2000. XI, 333 pages. 2000. (Subseries LNAI).

Vol. 1865: K.R. Apt, A.C. Kakas, E. Monfroy, F. Rossi (Eds.), New Trends Constraints. Proceedings, 1999. X, 339 pages. 2000. (Subseries LNAI).

Vol. 1866: J. Cussens, A. Frisch (Eds.), Inductive Logic Programming. Proceedings, 2000. X, 265 pages. 2000. (Subseries LNAI).

Vol. 1867: B. Ganter, G.W. Mineau (Eds.), Conceptual Structures: Logical, Linguistic, and Computational Issues. Proceedings, 2000. XI, 569 pages. 2000. (Subseries LNAI).

Vol. 1868: P. Koopman, C. Clack (Eds.), Implementation of Functional Languages. Proceedings, 1999. IX, 199 pages. 2000.

Vol. 1869: M. Aagaard, J. Harrison (Eds.), Theorem Proving in Higher Order Logics. Proceedings, 2000. IX, 535 pages. 2000.

Vol. 1872: J. van Leeuwen, O. Watanabe, M. Hagiya, P.D. Mosses, T. Ito (Eds.), Theoretical Computer Science. Proceedings, 2000. XV, 630 pages. 2000.

Vol. 1876: F. J. Ferri, J. Iñesta, A. Amin, P. Pudil (Eds.), Advances in Pattern Recognition. Proceedings, 2000. XVIII, 901 pages. 2000.

Vol. 1877: C. Palamidessi (Ed.), CONCUR 2000 – Concurrency Theory. Proceedings, 2000. XI, 612 pages. 2000.

Vol. 1880: M. Bellare (Ed.), Advances in Cryptology – CRYPTO 2000. Proceedings, 2000. XI, 545 pages. 2000.

Vol. 1881: C. Zhang, V.-W. Soo (Eds.), Design and Applications of Intelligent Agents. Proceedings, 2000. X, 183 pages. 2000. (Subseries LNAI).

Vol. 1889: M. Anderson, P. Cheng, V. Haarslev (Eds.), Theory and Application of Diagrams. Proceedings, 2000. XII, 504 pages. 2000. (Subseries LNAI).

Vol. 1892: P. Brusilovsky, O. Stock, C. Strapparava (Eds.), Adaptive Hypermedia and Adaptive Web-Based Systems. Proceedings, 2000. XIII, 422 pages. 2000.

Vol. 1893: M. Nielsen, B. Rovan (Eds.), Mathematical Foundations of Computer Science 2000. Proceedings, 2000. XIII, 710 pages. 2000.

Vol. 1896: R. W. Hartenstein, H. Grünbacher (Eds.), Field-Programmable Logic and Applications. Proceedings, 2000. XVII, 856 pages. 2000.

Vol. 1897: J. Gutknecht, W. Weck (Eds.), Modular Programming Languages. Proceedings, 2000. XII, 299 pages. 2000.

Vol. 1900: A. Bode, T. Ludwig, W. Karl, R. Wismüller (Eds.), Euro-Par 2000 Parallel Processing. Proceedings, 2000. XXXV, 1368 pages. 2000.